THE SOCIAL ORIGINS
OF CHRISTIAN ARCHITECTURE

THE SOCIAL ORIGINS OF CHRISTIAN ARCHITECTURE

▲ ▲ ▲

VOL. II

TEXTS AND MONUMENTS
FOR THE CHRISTIAN DOMUS ECCLESIAE
IN ITS ENVIRONMENT

L. Michael White

HARVARD
THEOLOGICAL
STUDIES

Trinity Press International
VALLEY FORGE, PENNSYLVANIA

Harvard Theological Studies 42

Trinity Press International is a division of the Morehouse Publishing Group.

Book design and typesetting: The HK Scriptorium, Inc.
Cover Art: Alinari/Art Resource, New York. Construction scene bas-relief. Museo Lateranese, Vatican Museums, Vatican State
Cover Design: Jim Gerhard

Library of Congress Cataloging-in-Publication Data

White, L. Michael.
The social origins of Christian architecture / L. Michael White.
p. cm. — (Harvard theological studies ; 42)
Vol. 1 originally published: Baltimore, Md. : Published for the American Schools of Oriental Research by Johns Hopkins University Press, ©1990. (ASOR library of biblical and Near Eastern archaeology).
Includes bibliographical references and indexes.
Contents: v. 1. Building God's house in the Roman world : architectural adaptation among pagans, Jews, and Christians — v. 2. Texts and monuments for the Christian domus ecclesiae in its environment.
ISBN 1-56338-180-X (v. 1 : alk. paper). — ISBN 1-56338-181-8 (v. 2 : alk. paper)
1. Architecture, Early Christian. 2. Basilicas. 3. Temples, Roman. 4. Mithraea. 5. Synagogues. 6. Buildings—Remodeling for other use—Rome. I. Title. II. Series: Harvard theological studies ; no. 42–43.
NA4817.W56 1996
726'.5'093709015--DC20 96-38709
CIP

The paper used in this publication meets the minimum requirements of American National Standard for Information Sciences—Permanence of paper for Printed Materials, ANSI Z329.48-1984.

Manufactured in the U.S.A
01 00 99 98 97 1 2 3 4 5 6 7 8 9 10

To Fitz, the truest of friends

Acknowledgments

The publisher gratefully thanks the following for permission to reprint illustrations in this volume.

Figure 1: Syria, Dura-Europos. Block M8 and the Christian building. Field plan (after H. Pearson). Based on plan in Dura-Europos Archive, Yale University Art Gallery, New Haven, Connecticut.

Figure 4: Syria, Qirqbize. Christian church, fourth-sixth centuries. Isometric reconstruction in stages (after Tchalenko). Librairie Orientaliste, Paris, France.

Figure 6: Syria, Umm el-Jimal. "Julianos's Church." Insula Plan. (After G. U. S. Corbett, PBSR, XXV, fig. 3). The British School at Rome, Rome, Italy.

Figure 9: Greece, Philippi. Octagonal Church complex and Episkopeion. Plan restoration of last phase. (Based on plan of S. Pelekanidis). Archaeological Society at Athens, Greece.

Figure 10: Greece, Philippi. Fourth-century Hall Church and Heroon, beneath the Octagonal-Church complex. Plan restoration. (Based on plan of S. Pelekanidis). Archaeological Society at Athens, Greece.

Figure 11b: Istria, Parentium. Villa and church beneath the Basilica Euphrasiana, third-fourth centuries. Plan restoration, composite. Arrangement of mosaic pavements beneath the basilica floor showing the North Site. After the plan of Piazzo, 1939 (from A. Terry, 1995). Soprintendenza Per I Beni Ambientali Architettonici, Archeologici, Italy.

Figure 12: Istria, Parentium. First basilica beneath the Euphrasiana, fourth century. Plan restoration, composite. Soprintendenza Per I Beni Ambientali Architettonici, Archeologici, Italy.

Figure 26a-b: Syria, Dura-Europos. Early and middle mithraeum, ca. 167-209 CE. Isometric reconstruction (after H. Pearson). Based on plan in Dura-Europos Archive, Yale University Art Gallery, New Haven, Connecticut.

Figure 27: Syria, Dura-Europos. Late mithraeum, ca. 256 CE. Isometric reconstruction (after H. Pearson). Based on plan in Dura-Europos Archive, Yale University Art Gallery, New Haven, Connecticut.

Figure 28: Syria, Dura-Europos. Block L7 and the synagogue, ca. 160-256 CE. Plan restoration in stages of construction (based on field plan of Andrews). Based on plan in Dura-Europos Archive, Yale University Art Gallery, New Haven, Connecticut.

Figure 29: Syria, Dura-Europos. Synagogue. Field plan (a) and plan restoration in stages (based on excavation field plan of Pearson). Based on plan in Dura-Europos Archive, Yale University Art Gallery, New Haven, Connecticut.

Figure 30: Syria, Dura-Europos. Late synagogue, ca. 256 CE. Diagram of west wall of Hall of Assembly (based on Kraeling). Based on plan in Dura-Europos Archive, Yale University Art Gallery, New Haven, Connecticut.

Figure 31: Lydia, Sardis. Municipal complex and synagogue. Plan restoration. (Seager, 1972). The Archaeological Exploration of Sardis, Harvard University, Cambridge, Massachusetts.

Figure 32: Lydia, Sardis. Synagogue. Plan restoration in stages. (Seager, 1972). The Archaeological Exploration of Sardis, Harvard University, Cambridge, Massachusetts.

Figure 36: Insulae Aegeae, Delos. Plan of Stadion Quarter and synagogue (after Bruneau and Ducat, *Guide de Délos,* pl. III). École Française d'Athènes (French Archaeological School), Athens, Greece.

Figure 45: Italia, Rome. Aventine mithraeum. Plan restoration, composite in stages of construction of the house (after Vermaseren and Van Essen). E. J. Brill Publishers, Leiden, Netherlands.

Contents

▲ ▲ ▲

Preface

▲ ▲ ▲

This collection of texts and monuments has been more than fifteen years in the making. It began in 1979 with an initial collection leading up to my Ph.D. dissertation at Yale (1982), which was entitled "Domus Ecclesiae — Domus Dei: Adaptation and Development in the Setting for Early Christian Assembly." In 1983 I began several years of fieldwork aimed at gathering new archaeological data as well as at rechecking a number of the sites that I had previously studied for the dissertation. During this period I was privileged to have the support of H. H. Powers Travel Grants from Oberlin College, which made much of this on-site research possible. In 1985 I also received an Andrew W. Mellon Fellowship in the Humanities for research on this project. The results of those years of research were published in the form of several articles on individual sites. This work also resulted in a partially revised and updated version of the collection, which was completed in 1988 and sent off for publication.

That collection was to be published as a separate volume, *The Christian Domus Ecclesiae in Its Environment.* The collection of materials contained therein was then used as the data base for my monograph *Building God's House in the Roman World: Architectural Adaptation among Pagans, Jews, and Christians* (Baltimore: Johns Hopkins University Press, 1990). More than a few friends and scholarly colleagues have wondered, however, what became of the "collection" that was supposed to have accompanied it. Delays caused by coordinating of efforts between different publishers overcame the best of intentions.

In the interim, I have continued to do fieldwork, including work at some of the same sites discussed in the collection. Finally, in 1993, thanks to the support of Prof. Helmut Koester at Harvard, there arose a new opportunity to publish the material. Unfortunately, by then it seemed that the collection was somewhat dated, and other editorial changes were needed. Since that time I have reworked the entire collection in order to update descriptions, plans, and bibliography and to incorporate some new entries. I have also included a new introductory chapter, more copious notes for discussion of individual sites, and several new appendices and tables. This process has included continued fieldwork and reports of current excavation work. Nonetheless, I have consciously attempted to retain the basic structure and order of material from the revised version of 1988, since that is the basis for the cross-referencing in my other study, *Building God's House in the Roman World.* Readers of that volume will discover that there are, of necessity, a few minor changes in numbering; however, in almost every case I was able to keep materials close to, if not at, the same number in the catalog. I regret any inconvenience or confusion that this may cause, but I trust that the inclusion of new materials will justify it.

Here I must add just a word regarding the relationship between these two volumes, since the present publication will finally allow them to appear together as a set under the new title *The Social Origins of Christian Architecture.* The first volume is a reprint of my 1990 book, *Building God's House in the Roman World: Architectural Adaptation among Pagans, Jews, and Christians.* All references in that work to the collection of texts and monuments (using the abbreviation *CDEE* [*The Christian Domus Ecclesiae in Its Environment*]) are to this second volume, which (as noted above) has been revised. This collection of texts, architectural sites, inscriptions, and papyri contains far more material and potential avenues of exploration or analysis than could be covered in a single monograph. My study of the social implications of architectural adaptation is but one such exploration. I hope that the publication of these materials will make it possible for others to explore on their own. On the other hand, the selection of materials there, whether Christian or non-Christian, is naturally determined by certain analytical considerations. This is not, after all, simply a catalog of all types of Christian archaeological evidence. The focus remains the development of Christian assembly prior to (and in some cases parallel with) the development of later, normative church architecture in the form of the basilica. Another obvious point at which this shows is in the decision to limit the comparative archaeological evidence to Mithraic and Diaspora Jewish materials. I have attempted to give some perspective on these issues in the introduction to this volume. I have not, however, changed the basic structure of this collection simply to conform to the conclusions reached in the first volume. As in any good archaeological work, I hope that by leaving some of my field unexcavated, it will allow others to reevaluate and explore further.

Finally, I must express my gratitude to a number of individuals who have made this study possible. Many people have provided me with information on their work at particular sites, and for this I am very grateful. I have typically indicated such indebtedness in the relevant entries in the text itself, usually following the listing of the literature on each site. The assistance of several others requires special mention. My interest in the archaeological evidence for early Christianity commenced under the tutelage of Dr. Everett Ferguson. Dr. John W. Cook, formerly of Yale Divinity School and now president of the Henry Luce Foundation, was really the first to introduce me to the Dura-Europos collection at Yale and to methods and issues in analyzing the material there. Professors Eric Meyers of Duke University and Tom Kraabel of Luther College have both contributed enormously to my awareness of archaeological sites and issues, especially concerning the development of the synagogue, while at the same time offering consistent support. My mentors at Yale, Profs. Wayne Meeks, Abe Malherbe, Bentley Layton, and Ramsay MacMullen have encouraged and sharpened this study from its inception and down to the present time. I am also grateful to Drs. Stephen Miller and William Coulson, directors of the American School of Classical Studies at Athens, where much of my field research has been based over the last twelve years. I add a special thanks to Dr. Bob Bridges, secretary of the American School, whose hospitality and organization have been especially instrumental. I am grateful to my former deans Robert Longsworth and Alfred MacKay and to Oberlin College for research and travel support to continue this work over several years. Dr. Charalambos Bakirtzis, ephor of Byzantine Antiquities for Eastern Macedonia and Thrace (Kavala, Greece), Fr. Paul Lawlor, S.J., docent in Archaeology at the Angelicum (Rome), Dr. Holland Hendrix, now president of Union Theological Seminary in New York, and Professors Susan Kane and Grover Zinn of Oberlin College have all given me special help and encouragement. Last, but by no means least, I thank Prof. Helmut Koester for his exemplary commitment to the study of archaeological resources and for his friendship throughout this endeavor. Without his efforts and encouragement the present volume would never have become a reality.

L.M.W.

Abbreviations

▲ ▲ ▲

AA	Lipsius-Bonnet, *Acta Apostolicorum Apocrypha*
AAES	*Syria: Publications of an American Archaeological Expedition to Syria in 1899–1900.*
AJA	*American Journal of Archaeology*
ANRW	*Aufstieg und Niedergang der römischen Welt* (ed. by H. Temporini and W. Haase)
Ariel	*Ariel, A Quarterly Review of Arts and Letters in Israel*
BA	*Biblical Archeologist*
BAC	*Bulletino di archeologia Cristiana*
BAR	*Biblical Archaeology Review*
BASOR	*Bulletin of the American Schools of Oriental Research*
BCH	*Bulletin correspondance hellenistique*
BJS	Brown Judaic Studies
Bull. epigr.	*Bulletin epigraphique*
CCCA	Corpus Cultorum Cybelis Attidisque (ed. M. Vermaseren)
CBCR	R. Krautheimer, *Corpus Basilicarum Christianarum Romae*, 5 vols.
CCSL	Corpus Christianorum, Series Latina (Turnholt)
CH	*Church History*
CIAC	*Atti del I* (–VIII) *Congresso Internazionale di archeologia cristiana.*
CIG	*Corpus inscriptionum graecarum*
CIJ	*Corpus inscriptionum iudaicarum*, 2 vols.
CIJ[2]	*Corpus of Jewish Inscriptions*, Vol. 1, 2nd ed. with Prolegomenon by B. Lifshitz.
CIL	*Corpus inscriptionum latinarum*

CIMRM	Vermaseren, *Corpus Inscriptionum et Monumentorum Religionis Mithriacae*, 2 vols.
Civ. Cat.	*La Civiltà Cattolica*
CPJ	*Corpus Papyrorum Iudaicarum*, 3 vols.
CRAI	*Comptes Rendus de l'Academie des Inscriptions et Belles-Lettres*
CSEL	Corpus scriptorum ecclesiasticorum latinarum
DACL	*Dictionaire d'archéologie chrétiene et de liturgie*
DEP	*Excavations at Dura-Europos, Preliminary Reports of the First through Ninth Seasons*
DOP	*Dumbarton Oaks Papers*
EAD	*Exploration Archéologique de Délos*
EPRO	*Études préliminaires aux religions orientales dans l'empire Romain*
GCS	Griechischen christliche Schriftsteller der ersten Jahrhunderte
GGA	*Göttingische Gelehrte Anzeigen*
GRBS	*Greek, Roman and Byzantine Studies*
H.E.	Eusebius, *Historia Eccesiastica*
HNT	Handbuch zum Neuen Testament
HTR	*Harvard Theological Review*
ID	Inscriptions de Délos
IEJ	*Israel Exploration Journal*
IG	*Inscriptiones graecae*
IGRR	*Inscriptiones graecae ad res Romanas pertinentes*
IL	E. Diehl, *Inscriptiones latinae christianae veteres*
JAAR	*Journal of the American Academy of Religion*
JAC	*Jahrbuch für Antike und Christentum*
JBL	*Journal of Biblical Literature*
JECS	*Journal of Early Christian Studies*
JFA	*Journal of Field Archaeoloay*
JJS	*Journal of Jewish Studies*
JQR	*Jewish Quarterly Review*
JRH	*Journal of Religious History*
JRS	*Journal of Roman Studies*
JTS	*Journal of Theological Studies*
LCL	Loeb Classical Library
LSJ	*A Greek-English Lexicon*, compiled by H. Liddel and R. Scott, revised by S. Jones

MAMA	*Monumenta Asiae Minoris Antiquae*
NBAC	*Nuovo Bullettino d'archeologia Cristiana*
NDIEC	*New Documents Illustrating Early Christianity*
NT	*Novum Testamentum*
NTS	*New Testament Studies*
OECT	Oxford Early Christian Texts
OGIS	Dittenberger, *Orientis Graeci Inscriptiones Selectae*
ΠΑΕ	Πρακτικά 'Αρχαιολογικῆς 'Εταιρείας (Practica Archaiologikes Etaireias)
PAES	*Syria: Publications of the Princeton Archaeological Expeditions to Syria in 1904–1905 and 1909.*
PBSR	*Papers of the British School at Rome*
PG	Patrologia Cursus Completus, Series Graece, ed. J.-P. Migne
PIR	*Prosopographia Imperii Romani*
PL	Patrologia Cursus Completus, Series Latina, ed. J.-P. Migne
PLRE	*Prosopography of the Later Roman Empire*
PW	*Paulys Realencyklopaedie der classischen Altertumswissenschaft*, ed. by G. Wissowa and H. Kroll
P. Oxy., etc.	for standard abbreviations of papyri see L-S-J
PSI	Pubblicazioni della Società Italiana per la ricerca dei Papiri: Papiri Greci e Latini
RAC	*Reallexikon für Antike und Christentum*
REG	*Revue des études grecques*
REJ	*Revue des études juives*
Rev. Phil.	*Revue philologique*
Rev. Rel.	*Review of Religion*
RGG	*Die Religion in Geschichte und Gegenwart*
RHR	*Revue de l'histoire des religions*
Riv. AC	*Rivista di archeologia cristiana*
RQ	*Römische Quartalschrift*
RSR	*Religious Studies Review*
SAB	Sitzungsbericht der preussischen/deutschen Akademie der Wissenschaften zu Berlin
SB	H. Rupprecht, *Sammelbuch griechischer Urkunden aus Ägypten*
SBL	Society of Biblical Literature
SBLDS	SBL Dissertation Series

SC	Sources chrétiennes
SEG	*Supplementum epigraphicum graecum*
SHA	Sitzungsbericht der Heidelbeger Akademie der Wissenschaften
SIG	Dittenberger, *Sylloge inscriptionum graecarum*
SKA	Sitzungsbericht der Kaiser - bayerischen Akademie der Wissenschaften phil.-historischen Klasse (Munich)
TLZ	*Theologische Literaturzeitung*
TMMM	F. Cumont, *Textes et monuments figures relatifs aux Mystères de Mithra*
TSC	*The Second Century: A Journal of Early Christian Studies*
TU	Texte und Untersuchungen zur Geschichte der altchristlichen Literatur
VC	*Vigiliae Christianae*
ZAW	*Zeitschrift für die alttestamentliche Wissenschaft*
ZKT	*Zeitschrift für katholische Theologie*
ZNW	*Zeitschrift für die neutestamentliche Wissenschaft*
ZPE	*Zeitschrift für Papyrologie und Epigraphik*
ZTK	*Zeitschrift für Theologie und Kirche*

Map, Tables, and Illustrations

▲ ▲ ▲

Map

Tables

Illustrations

INTRODUCTION

Layers of History and Paths of Discovery

A Stratigraphic Approach

▲ ▲ ▲

In Depths and Shadows

Standing virtually in the shadow of the Colosseum, the little brick church is dwarfed by the marble grandeur of imperial Rome. The majority of those who come to view the relics of ages past might even overlook this quaint building as they scurry along from the center of old Rome, the Forum and the Palatine, down the street to the seat of medieval Rome, the Cathedral of St. John Lateran. Yet there it stands, as it has for centuries, a monument, both in symbol and in fact, to the very history of church architecture and, indeed, to Christianity itself. To search its secret depths and to discover its course of growth and development are to rediscover the beginnings of church building.

To step down from the street-side entrance into the Basilica of San Clemente is to enter another age, actually several ages. One enters from the Via di San Giovanni in Laterano two blocks east of the Colosseum. The present church, built in the twelfth century, is a quaint but classic medieval basilica in red Italian brick. One feels a peace and a serenity upon entering the nave and strolling the portico of the cloister to the east. Yet one also senses the church's richness, not just in lavish decoration seen in the fifteenth-century painting or the baroque coffers of the nave ceiling. Here art and architecture are also a clue to its past; the apse mosaic comes from the rebuilt church of the twelfth century, while the marbles were preserved from the eighth century, before the church was sacked in 1084. The heaviness of the baroque ceiling hardly fits, but it is rich in its own way. It is a richness measured not in monetary or artistic terms alone but in the *depth* that comes from history and tradition.

San Clemente reflects the depth of ages when it comes to the history of Christian church building. Its layers run from the beginning to the present, as new renovations and archaeological excavations are conducted side by side. Its sense of layered depth is felt from the first step down into the building, when one discovers that the seemingly diminutive exterior looks much grander inside. The street is higher by several steps, but not because the church is sinking; the streets are rising. That's the way things go in Rome, as in most truly ancient cities where one builds up rather than out. It can be said with confidence that everything in Rome is built on top of something else, often something quite ancient and revealing. Of course, this is both a blessing and a curse to archaeologists; for while it ensures the preservation of earlier ages, it makes deciphering them more difficult. In the case of San Clemente it is another symbol of its *depth*.

From an anteroom off the north aisle of the present church nave one descends to another level (see fig. i). The lower church, as it is called, is the earlier basilica destroyed in the eleventh century. It was built at the end of the fourth century.[1] By looking carefully at the walls, one can make out the different types of brickwork that distinguish the earlier church from the buttressing and foundations of the superimposed medieval building. Here one discovers why the upper church has its apse on the west end, rather than the east as would most medieval churches. For the later building follows the pattern of its predecessor, where the curved brickwork line of the earlier apse can still be seen protruding below the narrower apse of the twelfth century church.[2] The spanners of the arches from the fourth century nave still show at the foot of the walls of the upper church, at least if you know where to look.

---

1. A comprehensive architectural history is given by Richard Krautheimer, *Corpus Basilicarum Christianarum Romae* (Vatican City: Pontifical Gregorian Institute, 1939–56) 1. 117–24. The archaeological analysis is presented in section II (No. 53) below. See also Krautheimer's *Early Christian and Byzantine Architecture* (3d ed.; New York: Penguin, 1979) 30; and Graydon F. Snyder, *Ante Pacem: Archaeological Evidence of Church Life before Constantine* (Macon, GA: Mercer University Press, 1985) 76–77. A good survey of different approaches has been done by Paul Corby Finney, "Early Christian Architecture: The Beginnings (A Review Article)," *HTR* 81 (1988) 319–39.

2. See below figs. 16 and 17.

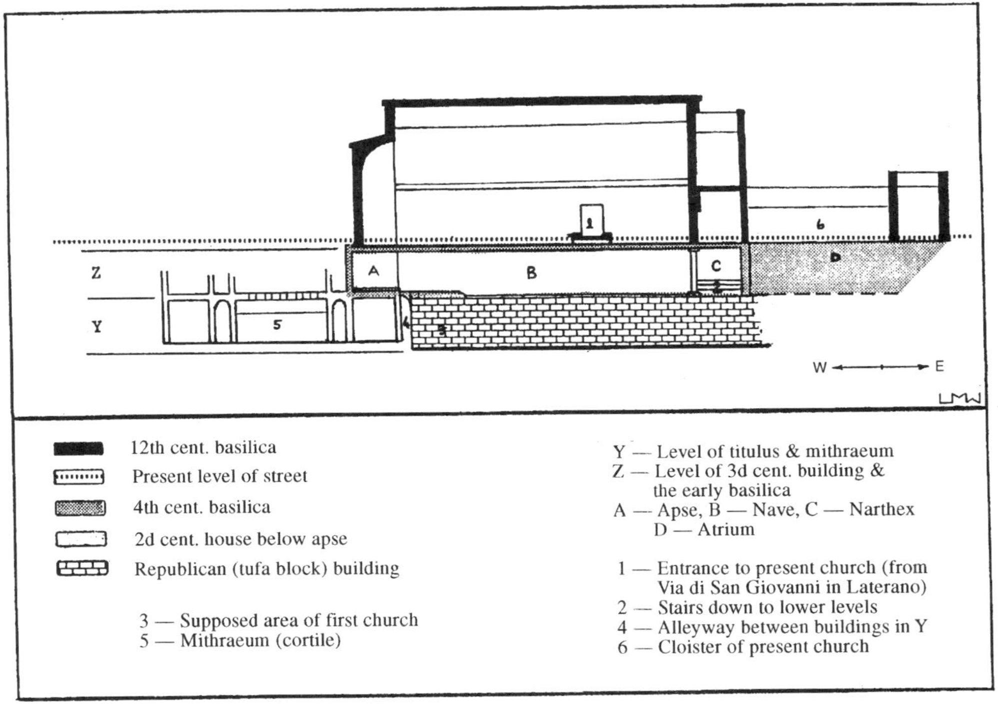

Fig. i
Italia, Rome. San Clemente. Schematic section, showing levels below present basilica

The fourth-century basilica of San Clemente takes one into yet another age in the history of Christianity. In many ways it is an oddity in Christian church architecture. As noted, the apse is on the wrong end of the building, the west; the atrium court, on the east. The side aisles, divided from the nave by rows of columns, are not symmetrical; the one on the north side of the building is narrower but with other flanking rooms. Such features in no way detract from the aesthetic of the building, but they signal the ways in which the building has grown and developed over the centuries. Each rebuilding and renovation carries forward the legacy of an earlier structure, an architectural continuity, yet transformations are introduced to fit the constraints of a new age.

In large measure the architectural peculiarities of the medieval basilica of San Clemente were dictated not only by the contours of the earlier basilica but also by the buildings that lie beneath its fourth-century layers. A narrow stair in the northeast corner descends to yet another lower level, which dates from as early as the first and second centuries. Now there is no basilica but a maze of rooms built in a noticeably different type of masonry. Great tufa blocks and travertine masonry outline a large rectangular building, probably some kind of warehouse from the first century CE. Although much of this layer cannot be excavated, the tunnels cut through in the nineteenth century have provided a substantial plan. Around the outer walls are squarish rooms with vaulted ceilings; the partition walls are in *opus reticulatum*. The floors are paved in the herringbone brickwork (*opus spicatum*) typical of commercial buildings. Across a narrow passageway, literally under the apse of the fourth-century basilica, stands a neighboring house, which was subsumed in later church construction. Its masonry is different yet, a fine *opus lateratium* typical of the beginning of the second century. In this adjoining house, one room contains a sanctuary of the Persian god Mithras, and other adjoining areas were also used for Mithraic cult functions.

At this level the buildings below the church nave no longer "look" like a church, but it may be that this was where one of the oldest Christian congregations in Rome assembled for worship. Tradition holds that this was the *titulus Clementis*, the "house church" of St. Clement of Rome (who was martyred in ca. 96 CE).[3] According to this tradition the "house church" was

---

3. J. M. Peterson, "House Churches in Rome," *VC* 23 (1969) 264–72. This same Clement of Rome is identified as the author of the letter to Corinth (usually dated to

later converted into a formal church building, a *domus ecclesiae*, and eventually into the basilica toward the end of the fourth century. Within its tradition San Clemente self-consciously embodies a continuous thread in the history of Christianity in the city of Rome.

In many ways the layers of San Clemente's architectural history typify the hazardous course of rediscovering the earliest Christian church buildings. At the beginning we follow a well-marked pathway down through neat layers of recognizable church forms. Here architecture and style are enough to point the way, for we quickly see the changes that have occurred over time. Style, planning, material, and iconography change; they constitute an architectural stratigraphy as clearly readable as ceramics or material culture. But then we reach a point in the stratigraphy where the path, seemingly unmistakable before, betrays us. It disappears in the depths and shadows of antiquity. Why? Because we come to that point in the history of Christianity where it is no longer a clearly identifiable institution apart from the environment in which it began.

Even though it is clear that San Clemente was a Christian church by the fourth century, the use of the building by Christians in the third century remains only a strong probability, not a certainty. There is no Christian art or inscriptions to prove the case. The archaeological evidence is weighted in that direction by the fact that a conscious plan of architectural adaptation was made to create a large hall, and that hall was similarly preserved in the basilical planning of the late fourth century. Thus, it is the continuity of usage as seen through architectural adaptation and renovation that is really unearthed in the archaeological work. But the farther down one goes, the less clear the evidence becomes. One cannot be sure that it was used by Christians in the first century; indeed, it is very unlikely. There are no clearly identifiable marks of Christian occupation and use, no altar or inscriptions. Nor is there unmistakably Christian iconography, no cross or martyr. Its pedigree is not etched in stone, just as the Christian movement itself had not fully established its own identity in the Roman world.

---

ca. 95 and called *First Clement*) and is also the namesake of a substantial pseudepigraphic literature. See Johannes Quasten, *Patrology* (3 vols.; Utrecht: Spectrum, 1950–62) 1. 53–54. He is also identified in tradition as the "third bishop of Rome," Flavius Clemens (husband of Flavia Domitilla), who was martyred under Domitian. See Cassius Dio, *History* 67.14; and Eusebius, *H.E.* 3.18.4.

There was no Christian *architecture*, in a formal sense, in the first centuries. How then shall we go about rediscovering the earliest Christian church buildings? How did they develop into a recognizable architecture? And what does this tell us about the development of Christian life and worship in that crucial period when the Christian church was being established in the Roman world? On the one hand, the primary task is archaeological, unearthing the ruins of ages past and deciphering the layers. On the other hand, it becomes a study of the religion and institution itself; for in observing its growth and development we are better able to understand its texture, life, and theology in historical context.

Paths of Discovery

The story of the earliest Christian church buildings must be told from several different sources and perspectives. One task is primarily archaeological and architectural. From this perspective the goal of discovery is to isolate layers of building and use. From an objectively archaeological standpoint, no single layer of San Clemente is any more significant than any other. Only when taken together, with a detailed analysis of each individual part, do the layers yield a comprehensive historical record. But a record of what? This purely archaeological or stratigraphic approach, the basis for all types of analysis, is concerned primarily with the occupation of one site. Thus, it looks at the cross-section of history in a vertical dimension through the stratigraphy. Indeed, one could easily spend several lifetimes just becoming knowledgeable about the details and idiosyncrasies of one such site.

Sorting out the layers in church buildings, as in any archaeological field, seems easier when one can recognize distinctive architectural styles. The style of the Gothic cathedral or baroque is visibly different from both earlier and later periods. Style, then, can be a useful comparative tool for understanding. Archaeology and architectural history are often symbiotic fields. But architectural "style" does not always provide the kind of refined historical analysis that the archaeologist seeks, for styles can often be fluid or anachronistic. A good example might be a modern church consciously built in Gothic style, perhaps even copied after existing church forms from the thirteenth century, as in the case of the Church of St. John the Divine in New York. Stylistic imitation or the inordinate combination of otherwise independent architectural forms can be confusing without other historical measures.

Even so, such examples can provide interesting insights in their own right. We must expect buildings to grow and change over time through renovation and remodeling, through destruction and rebuilding. One thinks instinctively of the massive architectural transformation undertaken in St. Peter's in Rome during the Renaissance in giving shape to the present Vatican complex.[4] It, too, like so many others, has its layers of construction and depths of tradition. Style is an indicator of historical changes, but style alone is not enough to tell the story. In archaeological analysis of buildings, the history of construction—the nature of structural development or evolution—is key to a larger picture.

From a slightly different perspective, archaeologists recognize the importance of a broader field of vision as the basis for analysis. The immediate context of a particular stratigraphic layer must be set into a broader context as well. At every level of discovery, one must ask how it compares with other sites from the same city or from roughly the same period. There are expanding circles of comparison that form concentric frames of reference. In the case of San Clemente, the very basis for dating and identifying the lowest levels comes from the type of masonry in the patchwork of wall construction. Though masonry types such as "tufa block" and *opus reticulatum* are visibly distinctive to even the first-time observer, any sense of their historical significance, or even the technical jargon, is lacking. Other historical and archaeological data must be supplied in order to make such findings intelligible. One needs to know from comparative study when certain types of masonry were common.

One of the perils of many buildings in a city such as Rome is that the stratigraphic layers are not always so neatly marked. At San Clemente the building of the fourth-century basilica required a shoring up of the lower levels to serve as an adequate foundation for the large edifice under construction. Thus, one finds that new wall construction (identifiable by virtue of its distinctive masonry type) was erected in and around earlier structural elements. In order to provide a more precise building history of the site, the archaeologist must distinguish the original wall construction of each phase of building. The broader field of vision takes in other historical and scientific disciplines as well, depending on the nature of the site being examined. This

4. See Krautheimer, *Early Christian and Byzantine Architecture*, 57; Spiro Kostof, *A History of Architecture* (New York: Oxford University Press, 1985) 500–509.

is where other archaeological finds, such as coins or artifacts, help in locating and dating a given layer. The historical picture is a complex archaeological puzzle.

The quest for the earliest Christian church buildings faces all these issues and more. The main problem is that prior to the fourth century there was no architectural "type" for the Christian place of assembly. The *basilica* was the first normative Christian architecture; that is, it was a building form that observed specific structural conventions and was immediately recognizable to a majority of people.[5] Arising only after the time of the emperor Constantine, the Christian basilica is characterized by its long central nave, columns separating side aisles, a curved *apse* on one end, and an entry vestibule (or *narthex*) on the other. Here the late-fourth-century layer at San Clemente is quite typical. Constantine, who legalized Christianity and began its cooptation as a state religion, is also known to have sponsored massive new building projects for churches. Archaeologists and architectural historians have now determined that the basilica had antecedents in Roman public architecture but was not used at all by Christians prior to the fourth century. Its introduction, then, marks a distinctly new era in church building.[6] Some would say that it marks an imperialization of Christian architecture, since the very name basilica comes from the Greek and means "royal house." But is it the "royal house" of the Roman emperor or of the Christian God? Some were not too sure even in the fourth century.[7]

One set of questions facing the historian concerns the effect on Christianity of the introduction of basilical church architecture. But with this the perspective shifts away from the purely archaeological task. How did it influence worship and theology? Indeed, it may be significant that we find Christian writers referring to their church buildings as "temples" after this period.[8] There is also an increased aesthetic dimension in the elaborate artic-

---

5. Krautheimer, *Early Christian and Byzantine Architecture*, 39–44; J. B. Ward-Perkins, "Constantine and the Origins of the Christian Basilica," *PBSR* 22 (1954) 69–90. Gregory T. Armstrong, "Constantine's Churches: Symbol and Structure," *Journal of the Society of Architectural Historians* 33 (1974) 5–16.

6. Krautheimer, *Early Christian and Byzantine Architecture*, 45–70.

7. Gregory T. Armstrong, "Imperial Church Building and Church-State Relations, A.D. 313–363," *CH* 37 (1967) 3–17. Paul Corby Finney, "TOPOS HIEROS und christlicher Sakralbau in vorkonstantinischer Überlieferung," *Boreas* 7 (1984) 193–226.

8. See Eusebius, *H.E.* 10.4.41 (text below, in section I, No. 23d).

ulation of a new public architectural style. Art and liturgy developed in certain directions as a result. With innovations such as cross-shaped buildings or orientation toward the east as a symbol of resurrection, one can even begin to speak of an iconography of architecture with theological dimensions. Also in a theological vein, the new architecture was viewed by some as the culmination of a divine plan. As it might be said, the development of the basilica became a concrete symbol of the triumph of the church. Indeed, archaeologists have found more than one instance in which the architectural design was not merely symbolic. In several cases, basilicas were built from or over existing pagan temples and Jewish synagogues. In other cases, we hear of riots in which temples and synagogues were destroyed by Christians who had too soon forgotten that they were once victims of similar intolerance.[9]

In many ways, then, the history of Christian architecture commences only in the fourth century with the introduction of the Constantinian basilica. A number of studies entitled "history of Christian architecture" rightly begin here, while giving little attention to anything that went before. Moreover, the architectural development was inextricably bound to the emergence of the Roman church as an official religion of the Roman state. So too, it is possible to follow the history through a convergence of architectural, artistic, liturgical, and theological developments down to modern times. One sees, then, in San Clemente a symbol of these same fortunes, since it still stands as a living church building. Its history and depth of tradition seen in archaeological layers are a symbol of its continuity with the past. Each rebuilding embodies elements of its own age in terms of planning and style. Yet basic features of orientation are fixed from the earliest levels. Down the street the Colosseum stands as a monument to the finitude of the Roman empire. Their roles and fortunes are reversed. The history of Christian church building afterward, like the later levels of San Clemente, is well documented. Remaining to be explored, however, is the time before the basilica was built, before there was a formal Christian architecture as such.

In the period before Constantine's introduction of the basilica, Christians did not have such well-defined notions of church building. In the beginning, from the days of Jesus and Paul, believers met in private homes of individual

9. R. P. C. Hanson, "Transformation of Pagan Temples into Churches in the Early Christian Centuries," *JSS* 23 (1978) 257–67.

members.[10] Here there were no specially designed rooms for assembly, no formal sense of liturgy or architecture. In many cases, as in the earliest levels at San Clemente, it may be impossible to determine with any high degree of certainty where the Christians met. As long as their meetings were restricted to buildings whose primary architectural form was for other purposes—that is, houses, storage rooms, or public halls—we shall not likely be able to distinguish them from their environment. For the early Christians there seems to have been little concern for church buildings. That fact in itself is worth some consideration. Yet over time church buildings as formal structures do emerge. For us the emergence of church building out of the depths of obscurity and out of the shadows of the environment is dependent on the gradual development of recognizable physical elements. Thus, the period between the inception of the Christian movement and the Constantinian revolution of the fourth century marks a crucial development not only in architecture but also in all aspects connected with worship and assembly. It is this period that the present study seeks to trace in greater detail.

Architectural Adaptation: Lessons from Dura-Europos

My own research has shown that the most detailed information comes from those archaeological sites where multiple stages of architectural renovation can be observed. Any decision on the part of a religious community to alter its place or manner of worship and assembly must reflect some recognizable changes within the group itself. Such changes can be readily observed in connection with the earliest known Christian building from Dura-Europos. It is significant, too, that, at Dura, a mithraeum and a synagogue were also discovered along the same street. The first task is to examine the *way* in which architectural definition of cultic space was achieved through renovation and adaptation in each of these cases at Dura. Then, on the basis of this analysis we shall begin to ask *why*.

---

10. Krautheimer, *Early Christian and Byzantine Architecture*, 23–26. Wayne A. Meeks, *The First Urban Christians: The Social World of the Apostle Paul* (New Haven: Yale University Press, 1983) 77–78; Abraham J. Malherbe, *Social Aspects of Early Christianity* (2d ed.; Philadelphia: Fortress, 1983) 68–75; Hans-Josef Klauck, *Hausgemeinde und Hauskirche im frühen Christentum* (Stuttgart: Katholisches Bibelwerk, 1981) passim.

By the third century, Dura-Europos was a Roman frontier outpost on the eastern *limes* of the empire. Originally founded by the Greeks, the city was occupied by the Parthians before the Romans took control in the campaign of Lucius Verus (165–168 CE). Sassanian incursions in the mid-third century finally wrested the city from the Romans in 256 after a devastating siege. The only area of the city that was not razed to the ground was the strip along the west city wall that had been buried in an earthen embankment as a defense measure. In this earthen fill along Wall Street were found the mithraeum (Block J5), the synagogue (L7), and the Christian house church (M8).[11]

The Mithraeum

The mithraeum was originally erected in one room of an older private house that dated from the Parthian period of the city's history (ca. 113 BCE to 165 CE).[12] The structure went through two more stages of renovation before the city was destroyed. The house (see figs. 24–27 below) was comprised of an outer court (D) that opened onto a central chamber (B) flanked by two anterooms (A and C). In order to create a Mithraic sanctuary, Room A was divided into three parts with two benches on either side of a central aisle. On the west wall of the chamber, a central altar table was erected. It consisted of a narrow platform reached by four steps; in front of this platform stood the main altar and, perhaps, two smaller ones. Above the altar table in a square recessed niche were set two gypsum reliefs of Mithras slaying the bull. According to dedicatory inscriptions from these reliefs the early mithraeum was constructed in ca. 168–171 CE.[13]

About 209 to 211 CE the mithraeum was rebuilt by a certain Antonius Valentinus, the *centurio princeps* of newly arrived *vexillationes* for the garrison.[14] The renovation corresponds to a massive reinforcement of the eastern

11. For the history of the city, see Mikhail I. Rostovtzeff, *Dura Europos and Its Art* (Oxford: Clarendon, 1943) passim. On the excavations and the discoveries, see the insightful account of Clark Hopkins, *The Discovery of Dura-Europos* (New Haven: Yale University Press, 1978) passim.

12. A more detailed archaeological description and full bibliography are given in section III (No. 58) below.

13. For the texts see *CIMRM* 1. 39, 41. For plans of the house, see figs. 24–27 below.

14. The dedication is No. 59 below.

legions in preparation for Caracalla's Persian campaign. The entire northern portion of the city was taken over and rebuilt by the military. Most of the older houses around the mithraeum were razed.

In the room of the mithraeum the walls were cut down to bench level; in the outer rooms on the south side of the house, to sill level. The size of the mithraeum proper was more than doubled. The main alterations consisted of annexing Room B by knocking out the partition wall and by extending the south wall of Room A almost the length of the building. Since the partition was a carrying wall, columns were installed on its foundations to support the new ceiling construction, a clerestory extending over the central aisle. The north podium was also extended at this time, but at a slightly lower level in the new section. The small Room E was created by partially rebuilding the earlier south wall of Room B. Finally, Room C was made the entrance to the building subdivided into a *pronaos* and an entry portico.

Some elaboration of the naos occurred at this same time. First, when the west wall was rebuilt, a brickwork arch was installed as an integral construction. It was faced on the interior with a plaster arcosoleum over the back of the altar and rising up into the clerestory. Second, an extensive decorative program was executed on the front and side walls. Perhaps even the ceiling of the clerestory was decorated to complete the effect of a *spelaeum* iconography.

The final stage of reconstruction in the mithraeum began in ca. 240 CE. The most striking feature of this renovation was the construction of a vaulted canopy above the altar and extending out to the first two columns of the clerestory. The construction probably would have entailed removing the entire roof. At this time the clerestory was extended the length of the sanctuary, and four more columns (nos. 5–8) were added. The narrow altar table was enlarged and embellished engulfing the main altar. The new naos was reached by a stair of seven symbolic steps. On the south the podium was extended by knocking down the walls of Room E.[15] Finally, a passageway was cut through the north podium between columns 6 and 8. It led to a door cut through the north wall to provide access to two newly annexed chambers (F and G). The decorations were embellished following the modification of the naos. Scenes from the zodiac and from the myth of Mithras appear

---

15. At this same time the north podium extension was filled in to the same level as the earlier podium (b).

around the central reliefs, and the ceiling of the vault was treated with stars on a field of blue.

These renovations suggest certain facts about the Mithraic community.

(1) There was substantial growth in numbers especially in the middle and late periods. This fact is indicated by the progressive expansion of the side benches, probably to accommodate more people at cultic meals. Such growth would seem to correspond to the reinforcement of the garrison first under Caracalla and later during the Sassanian incursions.

(2) Inscriptions and graffiti would suggest further that the composition of the cult had become more romanized as reinforcements were drawn from various parts of the empire. The earliest inscriptions (from the two central reliefs) are in Palmyrene and Greek, and in both the dedicants are *stratēgoi* with Semitic names.[16] Later graffiti are exclusively in Greek and Latin, and the names are more romanized.[17]

(3) There are clear indications of elaboration in the ritual activities, as evidenced in the progressive expansion and redecoration of the naos area. The placement of the altar steps and the presence of directions, e.g., *eisodos* ("enter") and *exodos* ("exit"), suggest processual movements.[18] Some of the art may symbolize aspects of cultic activity, e.g., in the arch vignette that shows a raven serving Sol and Mithras as they recline on the bull as a bolster.

(4) The members of the cult in the later stages, particularly high-ranking officers such as Valentinus, had the funds to finance extensive renovations and even the purchase of new property (Rooms F and G). In remodeling the shrine, they were apparently aware of a more formal iconography of Mithraic architecture. Under Valentinus a house shrine was transformed into an independent cultic sanctuary. Yet at the same time there would appear to be certain spatial features that are peculiar to the Durene cult. The orientation and the layout derive from the first mithraeum, even though the structure was transformed from its original domestic mode. Also, one may

---

16. *CIMRM* 1. 39, 41. The names are Ethpeni and Zenobios, but the latter is also called Eiaeibas. Both are Palymyrene. For further discussion see sec. III, n. 5, and the article by E. David Francis, "Mithraic Graffiti from Dura-Europos," in *Mithraic Studies*, ed. by J. Hinnels (Manchester: Manchester University Press, 1975) 424–45.

17. Cf. *CIMRM* 1. 46, 54, 55, 59–62. Also discussed by Francis, "Mithraic Graffiti," 432–40.

18. *CIMRM* 1. 66. Inscribed on column 3, and dating from the renovation of the middle mithraeum (ca. 209–211).

observe the place of ancillary chambers in each stage of renovation: Room B in the early period, Room E in the middle, and Rooms F and G in the late. Similarly, there are appurtenances that hold analogous functional positions in each period, e.g., the altar wells, floor pits, and small altars. Not the least of these holdover features are the two *tauroctonos* reliefs that in each stage are the focal point of the naos and the entire sanctuary. These facts suggest the preservation of an indigenous Mithraic tradition that influences subsequent developments in both ritual and architecture.

The Synagogue

The synagogue was constructed by renovating one of the private houses in the middle of a block (L7) of ten dwellings.[19] Adaptation for use as a synagogue occurred in the early Roman occupation of the city, ca. 165–200 CE. At the time of the first renovation, the entrance from Wall Street (Room 3) led to a central courtyard (Room 1) from which the other rooms of the house were accessible (see figs. 28–29).

In the remodeling, the open courtyard was embellished; it was paved with tiles and a low bench was set against its west side. On the north and east sides a colonnaded portico was constructed with a square basin in the northeast corner of the peristyle. The east portion of the earlier building was largely destroyed in the later period, but its plan can be restored from a few remaining wall fragments. There were three rooms (4, 5, and 6). Room 4 took the common form of a house *diwan* (i.e., a living/dining room) with plaster benches around the walls and, in the center of the room, a raised block for the brazier. Rooms 6 and 7, however, might have originally comprised one room, the *diwan* of the earlier private house. If that is the case, the conscious preservation of domestic quarters (Rooms 4 and 5) in the midst of extensive reconstruction elsewhere is worth noting.

The more significant renovation in the early synagogue occurred in Rooms 2 and 7. A massive formal entrance was added to Room 2 to indicate that this was the main room of the synagogue, the hall of assembly. Interior work on Room 2 included raising the floor level and installing benches around the walls. There was, in all likelihood, an *aedicula* set on columns constructed on the bench of the west wall at a point directly opposite the

19. For detailed discussion see section III (No. 60).

door.[20] At the south end of the room a second smaller door was cut through to Room 7. The latter also had benches around the walls, and the entrance from the courtyard had been widened and capped with an arch. Room 7, then, was a formal area like Room 2; despite E. R. Goodenough's solid objections, it is usually called the place for the women.[21] Both Room 2 and Room 7 show signs of decoration on the walls and ceilings; however, at this period there were only geometric designs and floral motifs.

Circumstances in Dura's Jewish community in the early third century made possible an extensive rebuilding project. Inscriptions in both Aramaic and Greek celebrate the event and set the date in the years 244/245 CE.[22] The building program consisted of three major projects: (a) the reconstruction and enlargement of formal rooms in the area of the early synagogue, (b) the annexation of House H to the east, and (c) the appointment and decoration of the new hall of assembly (in two successive stages).

The structural modifications undertaken in the area of the early synagogue were enormous. They consisted of knocking out all the interior walls of the house. The exterior walls were likewise destroyed down to foundation level (1.73 m), and the west wall was excavated down to bedrock. Thicker walls were erected on the west and east to carry greater height over a broader expanse. The new, monumental hall of assembly occupied the same basic space as that of the early synagogue, but it was expanded to the north and east. Moreover, the appointments of the room—a central niche, a massive formal entrance, and a smaller south entrance—held the same basic spatial orientation as in the early structure. Similarly, in the east compartment of the late synagogue an enlarged courtyard was embellished by a monumental colonnaded portico on three sides.

The entryway of the early synagogue was taken over in the expansion of the assembly hall to the north. At the same time, an entrance to the peristyle forecourt was cut through the party wall with House H in Room H4. House H is quite large, and the plan somewhat unusual for Durene domestic archi-

---

20. See the discussion in C. H. Kraeling, *The Synagogue* (The Excavations at Dura-Europos, Final Report VIII.1; New Haven: Yale University Press, 1956) 32–33; cf. E. R. Goodenough, *Jewish Symbols in the Graeco-Roman Period* (New York: Pantheon, 1956–64) 9. 30–31.

21. Compare Kraeling, *The Synagogue*, 31, with Goodenough, *Jewish Symbols*, 32.

22. See below No. 61a–f.

tecture. Both of these characteristics may be attributed to its annexation for use by the synagogue. From the entrance on Street A (Room 71) the exaggerated double vestibule (Rooms H1 and H2) led to two open courtyards (H3 and H9). While the two courtyards and Rooms H4 and H5 are interconnected, it is likely that House H was constituted as two suites of rooms. Rooms H1, H3, and H4, then, would have comprised a suite of entry rooms leading to the synagogue forecourt. The other rooms of the house (H2, H9, and H5–8) would have remained more private, domestic quarters, with H8 being the *diwan*. It should be remembered that the same provision for domestic quarters was made in Rooms 4, 5, and 6 of the early synagogue.

In the remodeling some elaborate, formal adornments were planned for the hall of assembly. A niched block of masonry was set roughly in the middle of the west wall but on the same spot as the *aedicula* of the early building.[23] It was embellished with steps, columns, and an ornamental facade. Flanking the aedicula steps and extending around the room were benches of two tiers. Along the west and north walls and on the north portion of the east wall these benches were provided with a wider bottom step and a footrest. At some time after the construction of the benches, the area immediately to the north of the Torah Shrine was overlaid with a construction of five steps rising almost one meter from the floor. The structure is usually cited as the seat of the elder or "Moses seat," but it is as likely a reader's stand.[24] In the central area of the floor molded holes mark the sites of various appurtenances, e.g., lampstands and, perhaps, a bema.

The decorations of the late synagogue are, of course, the most famous element. But they, too, were completed in two stages. The first wall decorations of the late synagogue were probably in the same vein as those of the early period, i.e., horizontal bands of dado design and a plinth painted to resemble

23. This point is the more striking when it is realized that the position of the Torah Shrine of the later synagogue is about half a meter off of center (toward the north) on the wall. The main door was directly opposite it. Thus, it gives further evidence of the continuity of usage from the earlier to the later stages.

24. I am not at all confident of the traditional interpretation of the physical evidence. The stepped structure beside the Torah Shrine could have served as the reader's stand or it might have served a dual purpose. It is quite striking that a reader standing on this top step would have stood just below and mirrored the posture of the painted figure (Moses reading the scroll) in the lower wing panel above the niche.

marble. Then, beginning in ca. 251 and continuing until the destruction of the building, the narrative frescoes were introduced.

There are again some conclusions to be drawn from the course of developments in the structure of the synagogue. We see here as in the mithraeum the practice of adapting domestic architecture for cultic use. The adaptation progresses through various stages. In the earlier period the synagogue remained very much a house in its structure, appearance, and, to a certain extent, in its use. Growth of the Jewish community in numbers, wealth, and status made possible the elaborate renovations of the late period.[25] The remodeling projects were not purely internal affairs. The destruction of the walls and the monumentalization of the dimensions created a structure that was no longer purely domestic in form. So massive was the construction activity that it had to have been a noticeable intrusion into the public life of this region of the city. At the same time, the houses immediately around the synagogue must have been greatly affected. The two houses next door (A/B) had already been converted into a commercial agency, called the "House of the Scribes" from frescoes found there. Some of the demolition in the synagogue project was directed at party walls (e.g., with Houses B and C). This fact has led some to think that much of the block, especially Houses C and D, had already passed into Jewish hands. Finally, the removal of the entrance from Wall Street around to the other side of the block was no simple result of expansion. It also reflects something of the new status and wealth of the Jewish community in the third century. It is significant to note, too, that a proselyte named Sila(s) was included among the community leaders and donors for the rebuilding.

While all of these social and economic factors were at work in the remodeling of the late synagogue, there are other determinative features. Despite its opulence and formality the structure still reflected some of the same spatial elements that were at work in the early period. The double entrance of the hall of assembly is peculiar, not at all in keeping with the tri-portal typical in later Galilean synagogue architecture. Likewise, the colonnaded portico would seem to hark back to formal elements at work in the very first renovation, while the decoration of the hall has some features drawn from pagan temples. It may well be that a cultural aesthetic for religious architec-

25. See Kraeling, *The Synagogue*, 329–31.

ture was influential, but the specific precedents and the spatial orientation were carried over from the early synagogue.

The provision for retaining domestic quarters in relation to the synagogue finds examples elsewhere, both in archeological and epigraphic data.[26] These quarters doubtless served both a resident caretaker *(ḥazzan)* and travelers needing hospitality. But, again, the spatial relation of the domestic quarters is quite significant; in both periods they were within the synagogue complex and contiguous to the formal areas of assemblage. Finally, there can be no doubt that cultic usage helped to define the layout of the hall of assembly. The centrality of the Torah in the life, the worship, and the self-consciousness of the community was an overriding factor in the architectural decisions of the Dura synagogue. Finally, there are certain elements in the artistic program that seem to reflect not only biblical narratives but also specific acts, implements, and themes from the synagogue worship.[27]

The Christian House Church

As we turn, finally, to the Christian building we should not be surprised to find that it too was a renovated private house.[28] Unlike the older mithraeum and synagogue complexes, however, this house was not erected until 231/2 CE. It was probably adapted for Christian use ca. 240/1. What we see here, then, is a process of adaptation cut short in its early stages.

For private dwellings at Dura this was a fairly large house, but the plan is

---

26. See the Ophel synagogue inscription (*CIJ* 2. 1404 = No. 62 below) and the dedication of Kl. Tiberios Polycharmos for the synagogue at Stobi (*CIJ* 1. 694 = No. 73 below).

27. See Goodenough, *Jewish Symbols,* 9. 35–50. The elements that most obviously reflect the perceptions of the local Jewish group are the idealized representation of the Temple and the depiction of the ark of the covenant (in panels WB4 and NB1). In both cases where the ark is shown, it takes the form of a box for the Torah scrolls and probably is the same as the item below a cover in the lower north wing panel, i.e., at the foot of Moses reading the scroll. In other words, to the worshiper in the Dura synagogue, the scroll of the law in their Torah ark was assimilated visually to the tradition of the ark of Moses. As for other thematic developments, especially in the central zone of the narrative scenes, see J. Gutmann, "Programmatic Painting in the Dura Synagogue," in *The Dura-Europos Synagogue: A Re-evaluation, 1932–1972,* ed. J. Gutmann (Missoula, MT: Scholars Press, 1973) 137–54.

28. See section II (No. 36) below.

quite usual—several rooms grouped around a central courtyard (see figs. 1–2). The three areas in which the main structural modifications occurred were (a) the courtyard, (b) the south suite (Rooms 3, 4A, and 4B), and (c) the west suite (Rooms 5 and 6). The main features in the remodeling of the courtyard included filling and paving the floor. Also, two L-shaped bench sections were installed in the northeast and southwest corners, and a number of finishing touches were added to embellish the court.

From the courtyard a formal door led to the row of chambers on the south side of the house. Originally, there were three rooms. Room 4A was the *diwan* of the house; around the walls were benches, and on the north wall a brazier box. Rooms 3 and 4B must have served as antechambers to the *diwan*, but the doorway to Room 5 would suggest that 4B served other functions as well. When the structure was remodeled, the partition between Rooms 4A and 4B was knocked out. The floor was filled in to the height of the benches, creating one large room. The enlarged area thus created served as the hall of assembly for the Christian community. There was a shuttered window set in the north wall facing onto the courtyard. At the east end of the room a small dais or platform was installed beside the entrance to Room 3. It must have served either as the place for the bishop's seat or as a reader's stand. Room 3, then, continued to serve as a storage area for portable equipment (e.g., an altar table) and utensils. Apparently there was no decoration on the walls of these rooms.

On the west side of the courtyard another formal doorway led to Room 5. In the original house plan, Rooms 5 and 6 must have comprised the *gynaikeion,* or women's quarters. Apart from finishing touches, only two significant changes were made in Room 5. First, a low, shuttered window (like that in Room 4) was made to communicate with the courtyard from the southeast corner of the room. Second, the doorway to Room 6 was embellished with an elaborate formal trim. Such trim is quite unusual for interior doors and, no doubt, was intended to give a more formal character to the entrance of Room 6.

Room 6 was originally only an ancillary chamber with modest appointments. In the Christian renovation of the house, Room 6 received a thorough transformation, more extensive than any other in the house. It was converted into the baptismal chamber of the church. A ceiling/floor structure was installed creating an upper and a lower chamber. A font was set in the west end of the room, and over the basin columns and pilasters carried a vaulted canopy. A low step was constructed beside the font, and another was set on the east end of the room. Finally, a small niche on the south wall (between the two doors) was dug out and arcuated. Following the structural modifications, the entire room was decorated. The canopy and the ceiling were treated with white stylized stars on a field of blue. The plaster columns were painted to resemble marble, and the canopy structure was given design motifs. The lunette of the arch and the other three walls of the room were painted with narrative compositions in fresco.

Since epigraphic data are minimal, we do not know the events that accompanied the acquisition and adaptation of the property by the Christians. But several facts are apparent. Compared to the Mithraic and Jewish communities, the Christian house/church was the product of a rather late-blooming cultic community. Prior to the renovation of the building, there is absolutely no evidence of a Christian presence at Dura. Yet in the acquisition and adaptation of the house some moderate social standing and economic capabilities are suggested. It may well be that a certain Proclus, who is memorialized in the primary inscription of the baptistry, was the patron who donated either the house itself or a large portion of the funds for its purchase and renovation.[29] More striking, however, are the spatial features of the building as adapted for Christian cultic use. Quite clearly there was a certain pragmatism involved in the architectural planning. No extensive restructuring of walls or foundations occurred apart from the removal of one partition wall (in Room 4) and the secondary creation of an upper chamber above Room 6. In this regard the adaptations are more along the lines of the early mithraeum, and a little less extensive than that of the early synagogue. But after renovation the Christian building no longer served as a residence.[30] So, although the changes in appearance and structure were relatively minor, the function and identity of the space were dramatically altered.

At this point the spatial arrangements again become significant. Rooms 4 and 6 were clearly adapted with definite rituals in mind. Apotropaic symbols (e.g., eyes, angels, stars, and *abecedaria*)[31] on the doorposts demark these as

---

29. See No. 37a.

30. This conclusion is supported by the fact that the renovation of the courtyard sealed up the cesspool, and the cesspool showed little sign of prior use. Hence, most typical aspects of domestic use ceased.

31. See C. H. Kraeling, *The Christian Building* (Excavations at Dura-Europos,

areas of special significance—or, if you will, "sacred spaces." Room 4 was an elongated space for assembly in which orientation and attention were focused toward the east end of the room. The formal doorways and the windows in both Room 4 and Room 6 provide access and communication. Presumably these provisions were for individuals to enter and leave the assembly and, at certain times, to wait in the courtyard. It is not hard to imagine the kinds of activities that would have governed such movements. The dismissal of catechumens, the summoning of initiates, or separated seating for men and women are distinct possibilities, and all three are attested in the roughly contemporary Syrian church order known as the *Didascalia Apostolorum*. On the contrary, it must be noticed that there is no apparent provision for communal dining in the final form of the building. If we assume that the Eucharist was observed in the context of this Christian assembly, it had become completely dissociated from the *agapē* meal.

In Room 6 the definition of space through ritual activity is even clearer. We can only guess at the developmental process that moved Christian initiation from streams and pools to an indoor setting. But the design of the Dura baptistry definitely shows some formalized ritual conceptions. Not the least of these is the architectural definition of the font itself. Of course, it may well be that professional workshops were contracted to do the actual construction. Still, the structure of the font and canopy indicates that the Christians were aware of formal notions of religious architecture similar to that found in the vaulted *spelaeum* of the mithraeum and the Torah *aedicula* of the synagogue. Moreover, it would seem that both a dominant symbolism and a processional form, based in the liturgy of baptism as practiced at Dura, were incorporated into the composition of the frescoes. The symbolism of death and life through water is quite in evidence in the scenes of the healing of the lame (John 5), Peter walking on the water, and the woman at the well (John 4). The scene that dominates the entire room is that of the women at the tomb. It stretches from the door in the southeast corner of the room around the east wall to the north wall and ends with the tomb of Christ portrayed beside the font. The processional posture of the women as they move from the back wall around the side must somehow reflect the movements of the initiate, who through baptism dies and rises with Christ.

Final Reports VIII.2; New Haven: Dura-Europos Publications, 1965) inscriptions nos. 1, 4, 5, 14.

Renovation and Architectural Adaptation

We may conclude this case study from the Dura Christian building with some more general observations that can be distilled from the cases at hand and may then be checked against the evidence of other archaeological sites. In the beginning I suggested that, once a detailed analysis of the architectural history of a site had been done, one could begin to ask why such adaptations were made. It seems to me that there are certain factors that interact in various combinations and are directly related to the architectural adaptations. These factors fall into five categories. At some point all of them will have played a part in our discussions.

(1) There are purely pragmatic considerations—numerical growth, property boundaries, the physical constraints of an existing structure, the destruction of an existing structure. These factors seem to play a part especially in the early stages of adaptation.
(2) There are cultural influences especially in the development of an aesthetic for religious architecture and precedents for adapting private structures. The Christians did not invent the practice of adapting private buildings for religious usage. There was an accepted climate for this kind of appropriation, and it appears that Jews and Mithraists were common practitioners.
(3) There are socioeconomic and political factors—patronage and endowment, change in social or legal status, group constituency and wealth. The adaptation of a physical space requires money not only for the construction work itself but also for the property. Thus, the increasing scale of renovation, adaptation, and eventually new construction marks some important economic and social indicators in the life of these local religious communities.
(4) There are attitudinal factors from within the community itself—attitudes toward the building, attitudes toward the community (i.e., self-concept or ethos), and attitudes toward outsiders.
(5) There are factors from within the cultic life of the community—group social structures and relationships within the context of assembly or worship, organization and administration, and (last but certainly not least) the central cultic rituals.

These factors, once they have been sorted out in this way, can be applied to any of the evidence from the Greco-Roman cults and, especially, to

Judaism and Christianity. What is sometimes most interesting is when one or another of these factors (e.g., ritual) can be seen to interact with, and occasionally override, the others.

I am not advocating that we naïvely try to take developments found in a third-century eastern garrison and push them back on earlier periods. Nor am I suggesting that the liturgical or architectural developments in one city were necessarily the same as in another. Local traditions as well as the socio-economic and legal circumstances of each religious group might have caused them to follow different courses or paces of development. What I am suggesting is that we can use these observations to develop a new perspective on some long-standing problems. In particular, we can observe the interrelation between social and economic circumstances, ritual patterns, and the place of religious assembly. This approach can also shed some new light on the literary sources, and three brief examples will show what I mean.

First, we may consider the separation of the Eucharist from the *agapē*, as already suggested in the Dura house/church. Here is one instance where ritual activities have a direct connection with an architectural setting. As long as the Eucharist and the *agapē* were held together in the context of assembly around a table (as is seen in the Pauline tradition), then a formal assembly hall did not develop. This observation also has a bearing on developments in the second and third centuries, e.g,. in church orders such as the *Didache* and the *Apostolic Tradition* of Hippolytus. There are also implications for the New Testament, especially texts such 1 Corinthians 11.

In our second example, we turn to Cyprian, bishop of Carthage in the mid-third century. In his letters Cyprian makes several references to ordination in relation to the *pulpitum* of his church building. Here, in an unselfconscious literary reference, we have an indication of some sort of formal development in the church building. The nature of this development needs to be checked further against contemporary archaeological and literary sources. The term seems to refer to a slightly raised dais or platform at one end of the assembly hall where the clergy sat. In one instance the honor of ordination is symbolized in ascending the *pulpitum* "in the loftiness of the higher place and conspicuous before the whole people" (*Ep.* 39.4).[32] The phrase "to come to the *pulpitum*" (*ad pulpitum venire*, *Ep.* 38.2) even becomes the technical term for the ordination of a reader in the church at Carthage.

---

32. Section I (No. 16a) p. 69 and n. 18 below.

The third example comes from the Johannine epistles. According to the reconstruction of Abraham Malherbe, Diotrephes (3 John 9) was the patron of a local house church somewhere in the vicinity of the writer of the letters.[33] Despite letters of recommendation from the writer of the letter (who is identified only as the "Elder") Diotrephes had refused to show hospitality to some traveling Christians from the other congregation and had barred them from the assembly (v. 10). In addition, in 2 John 10–11 there is the prohibition against admitting heretics to the house of assembly. The text suggests that admission to the house of assembly in this community, and especially for Diotrephes, had become a much more formalized concept. There is no indication here that the house had in any way been altered from a private dwelling where the Christians met. It was apparently still a private home owned by the individual who served as leader of the congregation. But the significant factor is the way they had come to think about their assembly and the place of assembly. The doors and walls of the house itself had begun to define the limits of the cultic community in assembly. Admission to the house was symbolic of admission to the fellowship of the church. This attitude is one step closer to the development of *domus ecclesiae* as an architectural definition of cultic space.

Continuity and Transformation

Because there was no formal church *architecture* in this early period, our study cannot claim to be an architectural history in the strict sense. Nor does it wish to be; that we shall leave to others. This study is constrained rather by three dimensions of the historical quest. First, it is concerned with the archaeological discoveries. Here we shall attempt to present the raw data currently available. The fact that we have no church buildings from the very earliest periods of the Christian movement is in itself a significant piece of evidence, albeit negative from the architectural perspective. Yet we know from other sources, primarily literary references from Christians and pagans alike, that the earliest Christians met in homes. So here the archaeological and historical field of reference is broadened to consider the nature and setting of earliest Christian assemblies. The popular view that Christians in the

33. A. J. Malherbe, "Hospitality and Inhospitality in the Church," in *Social Aspects of Early Christianity* (2d ed.; Philadelphia: Fortress, 1983) 90–120.

days before Constantine huddled for worship in the secrecy of the catacombs is misleading. There were early church buildings in Rome as elsewhere, though they may be hard to identify, as in the confusing subterranean mazes of San Clemente.

The early literature may give us a clue also to the process of development against which to check the archaeological evidence. By collecting together (section I, below) a number of the early literary sources regarding the nature and situation of early Christian assembly, this study will provide a base for analysis. From this literature two distinct stages begin to emerge: the first when Christians met in unrenovated homes of members, and the second when large buildings began to be built. Further refinement of these stages will require additional data and analysis.

It has become typical to use the term "house church" to designate the earliest stages of Christian assembly, as seen in Paul and elsewhere in the New Testament.[34] By definition, then, a "house church" did not entail alteration or architectural articulation of the space for specific religious functions. In the absence of a normative architectural definition or style, it remains indistinguishable from private or domestic buildings. Only with architectural adaptation or articulation of a space for religious functions, as seen at Dura-Europos does an edifice become archaeologically identifiable as a church building.

The earliest identifiable church building known from archaeological discoveries comes from the third century at Dura-Europos. It provides the most clearly datable case of a private house converted physically to serve as the Christian building, a church in the formal sense. Yet from the outside it still looked like a typical house. Only on the interior were significant changes made to create one large room for assembly and another separate area for baptism. For the archaeologist, the Dura church building is an invaluable discovery precisely because the city was destroyed in the year 256 CE, never again to be rebuilt or inhabited. Unlike San Clemente, where one must peel away the layers of later historical development, at Dura we have a pre-Constantinian church building frozen in time.

It is most significant that through renovation there was a conscious plan for adapting the existing space to specific liturgical functions. Clearly, then, these areas of the Dura house were transformed to an identifiably Christian

---

34. See the catalogue of New Testament passages below in section I (No. 1).

ecclesiastical usage—one for assembly, the other for baptism. Indeed, the archaeological evidence indicates further that normal domestic functions ceased with this stage of renovation, as its cistern was sealed over in the construction. As such, then, it is possible to say that the edifice had ceased functioning as a house, even though it retained its domestic architectural form on the exterior. Through interior articulation and adaptation, the edifice had become a church building instead. One cannot determine from the available archeological evidence whether the house was already in use by Christians prior to renovation. If it had we might well have termed it a "house church," since it contained no specific architectural articulation of its religious function. Whether in use previously or not, by virtue of the renovation the Dura house was transformed into what we may call a *domus ecclesiae*.[35]

The second part of this collection, then, entails a wider view of the historical environment of such construction and development. The question may be put this way: To what extent is the Dura Christian building typical of early Christian development in the move from house meetings to the beginnings of architectural definition?[36] This study assembles available architectural evidence (section II) for early Christian buildings prior to Constantinian transformation to basilical form. The archaeological data are presented in the form of archaeological reports of construction history in phases. Special attention is given to indications of phased renovation or adaptation for purposes of articulating space for specifically Christian functions. When we are able to examine all the relevant pieces of archaeological data from Dura and other Christian sites we can begin to chart out some of the lines of architectural development that occurred up to and including the period of transition in the fourth century. The following table summarizes this information, as distilled from the archaeological reports in section II, and shows the implications of using this kind of archaeological comparison.

35. The term is the Latin equivalent of the Greek οἶκος τῆς ἐκκλησίας, already in use as a designation for church buildings in the third century (see Eusebius, *H.E.* 7.30.19 [below No. 20b]). See also Krautheimer, *Early Christian and Byzantine Architecture*, 27; Willy Rordorf, "Was wissen wir über die christlichen Gottesdienstraum der vorkonstantinischen Zeit?" *ZNW* 55 (1964) 110–28.

36. Some parallels to Dura were suggested by C. H. Kraeling (*The Christian Building*, 144–45).

Table 1

Prebasilical Church Buildings
An Archaeological Survey of Adaptation and Renovation

SITE	**No. of PHASES**	**BLDG. TYPE**	**DATES**	**First Xn. PHASE/ DATE**
SYRIA (including Arabia)				
Dura-Europos	2	$^{1-2}$house/church	231–256	2/ca. 240
Qirqbize	5	$^{1-2}$house/hall $^{3-5}$basilical	330–VI	1/ca. 330
Umm el-Jimal	3	$^{1-2}$house, ^{3}basilica	IV–VI	2?–3/IV
PALESTINA				
Capernaum	3	^{1}house, ^{2}hall ^{3}octagonal church	IV–VI	2/IV
MACEDONIA				
Philippi	3	^{1}Heroon, ^{2}hall church, ^{3} octagon	IV–VI	2/c.334
ISTRIA				
Parentium	5	$^{1-2}$Roman edifice, ^{3}hall, ^{4}bas., ^{5}cathedr.	III–V	3/IV
Aquileia	4	^{1}house, ^{2}commerc. bldg. ^{3}hall cmplx., $^{4-5}$basilica	III–VI	3/IV
ITALIA				
Rome				
Ss.Giovanni e Paolo	6	$^{1-3}$insula, ^{4}hall $^{5-6}$basilica	II–V	3/III
S. Clemente	5	$^{1-2}$Mag./domus ^{3}hall?, $^{4-5}$bas.	I/III–V	3/III
S. Martino al Monti	4	$^{1-2}$commerc.bldg. $^{3-4}$hall/bas.	III–VI	4/IV
S. Crisogono	4	$^{1-2}$hall $^{3-4}$basilica	IV–VI	1/ca. 310
BRITANNIA				
Lullingstone	5	$^{1-4}$villa/chapel	IV–V	4/ca. 350

[All dates are CE]

As we have already noted, the fact that the earliest Christians saw no need to build special church buildings is significant in its own terms. Several factors may be at work here, such as the relationship of the Christian movement to Judaism, to the Temple, and to the synagogue. Many Christians arising out of this Jewish matrix apparently expected an imminent eschatological event. Further, the relationship of the emergent Christian movement to its Roman environment must be taken into account as we consider the growth of Christianity in the empire down to the time of Constantine. The term *ecclesia* (most often translated "church") originally meant "assembly." Only later did it come to mean the Christian assembly in a formal sense, and later still the *place* of assembly (the church building). The process of development seen here in a nutshell has direct bearing on the historical development both of church building and of the Christian church as a social and religious institution. Therefore, the study assembles other kinds of data as well. It includes comparative archaeological data (also presented in the form of construction history in phases) especially from Mithraism and Diaspora Judaism. Also included are relevant literary sources that give evidence of the intellectual climate in which such developments on the Christian side were taking place.

It is worth noting, then, that on the same street as the Dura Christian building (what the excavators designated "Wall Street") were two other small religious edifices. It has long been noted that these little sanctuaries do not conform to some typical elements in Durene temple style and planning. Instead it became readily apparent that their peculiar shape was determined by the fact that each was renovated in multiple stages from existing houses. In both cases, much as in the Christian building, the earliest stage involved only internal architectural adaptation of the exiting space to the particular needs of a religious group—one Jewish, the other Mithraic. At first the renovations were only partial and internal, but in the second stage the building was thoroughly transformed including exterior rebuilding and annexation of adjacent properties. This discovery remains one of the most significant in contemporary studies of synagogue development, since in its final form the hall of assembly contained both liturgical articulation for worship and elaborate artistic representations of biblical narratives.

In both the mithraeum and the synagogue at Dura, the architectural changes can be correlated with other indications of continuity as well as transformation. While it is usually assumed that there was uniform planning among mithraic sanctuaries, the case of Dura-Europos poses new questions based on considerations of adapting existing edifices to such a "typical" plan. In fact, a survey of all the excavated mithraea across the Roman empire reveals that the vast majority were not built *de novo* for explicitly mithraic use. The only ones that were built from the first as mithraea tend to come from the far western provinces (Gallia, Germania, Britannia). Those from Italy (including the well-known cases from Rome and Ostia) and the eastern Mediterranean were all created by renovating existing structures of various types, and many were not below ground. Thus, the patterns of adaptation seen at Dura-Europos need to be checked carefully against those from other Mithraic sites. A complete catalogue for the Mithraic sites is not possible here, but a sampling of the archaeological materials is collected in section III.

A comparative table for the Diaspora synagogues, distilled from the archaeological reports in section III, shows some of the basic similarities to the issues seen above for the Christian church building and now proposed for the mithraeum (see Table 2, p. 30). It is significant, then, that all of the synagogues from the Diaspora were renovated from existing buildings, and five of the six were houses or private insulae of some sort.

In turn, this leads us to the third dimension of the study, which deals more specifically with the social circumstances surrounding the architectural development. Such information is primarily derived from nonliterary archaeological sources, such as documentary papyri and inscriptions. Building inscriptions are an especially valuable source of information to be correlated with architectural developments, since they often provide us with prosopographic, dating, or context information either to supplement or to check data gained from archaeological analysis of building and construction. As in all three cases at Dura-Europos, the epigraphic remains give further information regarding the nature of the renovation projects and the circumstances of the religious groups. Such documentary data (from inscriptions, graffiti, and papyri) provide invaluable information alongside the physical elements of architectural renovation, and so are collected together in sections II and III.

The story of early church buildings is one of continuity and transformation through the layers of history. Christianity did not originate as a fully

Table 2:

The Diaspora Synagogue
An Archaeological Survey of Building History

SITE	**No. of PHASES**	**BLDG. TYPE**	**DATES**	**1st Synag. PHSE./DATE**
SYRIA				
Dura-Europos	3	^{1}house	Late I	2/ca. 150–200
		^{2}renov.synag.i	ca. 150–200	
		^{3}renov.synag.cmplx.	244/5	
		^{3a}paintings		
LYDIA				
Sardis	4	^{1}apodyterion	ca. 166	
		^{2}hall	late-II	
		^{3}synag.hall	beg.-III	3/III
		^{4}synag./court	IV	
		^{4a}refurb.		
Priene	3	$^{1-2}$house	I BCE	3/II
		^{3}renov.synag.		
INSULAE AEGEAE				
Delos	2	^{1}house	II BCE	
		^{2}synag.	I BCE	2/I BCE
		^{2a}refurb.?	I	
MACEDONIA				
Stobi	5	$^{1-2}$house	I–II	
		^{3}synag.i	III	3/III
		^{4}synag.ii	III–IV	
		^{5}Xn.basilica	IV–V	
ITALIA				
Ostia	4	^{1}insula?	I	
		^{2}synag.i	II–III	2/III
		^{3}synag.ii	III–IV	
		^{3b}aedicula	IV	
		^{4}synag.iib	IV–V	

[All dates are CE unless otherwise indicated.]

developed religious institution; it was not a separate religion at all but a sect of Judaism. Thus, in the beginning the forms of worship and assembly were thoroughly Jewish. In the development of Christianity, these Jewish backgrounds and components prove to be invaluable and influential. Eventually, however, institutionalized Judaism and Christianity would go their separate, and sometimes hostile, ways. With the parting of the ways came transformations for each. Yet for Judaism and Christianity at the core of religious experience stood the centrality of worship in the assembled community of faith.

Continuity and transformation can also be seen in the influence of the larger Roman world as the political and social stage for this historical drama. The synagogue, as a center of community life as well as a place of worship, entered this arena too. Sometimes, from the perspective of outsiders, it was difficult to discern a difference between these Jewish community buildings and the facilities of other social and religious groups, who also often met in the converted homes of members. Thus, despite the traditional polemic against idolatry, these Jewish communities in the Diaspora often bore striking similarities to their neighbors. Such was the kind of pathway that the earliest Christian missionaries would follow in taking their message from the mother soil of Palestine out into the Roman world. It is perhaps ironic, then, that a religious movement that began by challenging the very notion of the gods who resided in the pagan temples should over time come to adopt a form of pagan public architecture as its standard for church buildings. Yet the basilica was just such a form prior to the fourth century, when the emperor Constantine began to introduce it into Christian church planning.

By focusing on continuity and transformation commencing with the Jewish and pagan backgrounds, we will be able to follow some of the major lines of development in early Christian church building. Section I assembles a collection of literary sources with original text and English translation. Section II collects the archaeological and documentary evidence for the Christian architectural development according to a geographical order. Section III goes on to provide the same sort of collection of comparative evidence from Mithraism and Diaspora Judaism. Containing both construction history reports for archaeological sites and documentary sources, this collection is arranged geographically in same manner as Section II. Finally, Section IV assembles appendices and tables for analysis of the archaeological data, especially in regard to the architectural adaptation through incremental phases of renovation.[37]

37. This study is intended as a comprehensive collection of the primary sources (literary, architectural, and documentary) up through the Constantinian period. It is hoped that, as such, it can serve as a sourcebook for further study. The main feature of theoretical orientation that is represented here is based on the recognition of patterns of incremental adaptation both in Christian buildings and in comparable sources from Mithraism and Diaspora Judaism. For a very useful overview of different approaches to the issues, see Paul Corby Finney, "Early Christian Architecture: The Beginnings (A Review Article)," *HTR* 81 (1988) 319–39. I am grateful for the constructive criticism that my own 1982 dissertation received in this review, and I hope that this updated and expanded treatment of the archaeological evidence will help to advance the question.

SECTION I

Literary Sources for Early Christian Assembly

▲ ▲ ▲

In this section are assembled the major literary texts that reflect the nature and setting of early Christian assembly. The material has been divided into two parts. Part A contains the writings of the Christians themselves, an internal witness to assembly. Part B contains references to Christian assembly from non-Christian sources, though in some cases these texts are preserved within later Christian writings, chiefly Lactantius and Eusebius. The contents of each part are arranged chronologically. All texts are given according to the standard critical editions in the original languages. The critical editions are cited in the heading of each entry. A complete citation for each may be found in the bibliography at the end of the work. All translations are those of the author unless otherwise indicated.

Catalogue

Part A. Christian Sources

No. 1–4 New Testament Texts (not printed)
5 *Didache* 14.1–2
6 Ignatius of Antioch
a *Eph.* 5.2–3
b *Magn.* 6–7
c *Smyrn.* 8

b Imperial intervention and resolution
(Eusebius, *H.E.* 7.30.18–19)

21 *Acta Saturnini* 2, 8, 9

22 *Acta Phileae* (P. Bodmer XX)

23 Eusebius of Caesarea, *Historia Ecclesiastica*

a 7.15.3–4

b 8.1.5, 1.9–2.1

c 10.2.1, 3.1

d 10.4.43ff.

24 Lactantius, *De mortibus persecutorum* 12

Part B: Non-Christian Sources (some are preserved only in Christian sources)

No. 25 Pliny the Younger, *Epistles* 10.96

26 *The Edessene Chronicle* I (VIII), XII

27 Lampridius, *Historia Augusta*: *Severus Alexander* 49.6

28 The Emperor Gallienus, Edict of Toleration (257)
(Eusebius, *H.E.* 7.13)

29 Porphyry, *Adversus Christianos*, frag. 76
(Macarius Magnes, 4.21)

30 The Emperor Diocletian, The First Edict of Persecution (303)
(Eusebius, *H.E.* 8.2.4–5)

31 *Acta Munati Felicis*
(*Gestae apud Zenophilum*)

32 The Emperor Galerius

a Edict of Toleration (the Latin *Palinode*)
(Lactantius, *De mort.* 33.11–34.5)

b Greek *Palinode*
(Eusebius, *H.E.* 8.17.1)

33 The Emperors Licinius and Constantine, *Edict of Milan*
(Lactantius, *De mort.* 48; cf. Eusebius, *H.E.* 10.5.9–11)

34 The Emperor Maximinus, Edict of Toleration
(Eusebius, *H.E.* 9.9a.11–12; 9.10.10–11)

35 The Emperor Constantine, Letter to the Proconsul Anulinus
(Eusebius, *H.E.* 10.5.15–17)

Part A: Christian Sources

Nos. 1–4: New Testament Writings

[The text and translation of documents from the New Testament will not be reproduced here. The reader is referred for the Greek text to the twenty-seventh edition of Nestle's *Novum Testamentum Graece* (ed. K. Aland et al.).]

No. 1: Pauline Epistles

a. 1 Corinthians 11:17–22; 16:19
b. Philemon 1–2, 21–22
c. Romans 16:3–5, 14–15, 23
d. [Paul?] Colossians 4:15

No. 2: Luke-Acts

a. Luke 7:4–5; 24:28–35
b. Acts 1:12–13; 2:1
c. Acts 2:44–47; 4:23–31; 5:42
d. Acts 12:12–16
e. Acts 16:31–34
f. Acts 18:1–8; 19:8–10
g. Acts 20:7–20

No. 3: Epistle of James 2:1–7

No. 4: Johannine Epistles

a. 2 John 7–11
b. 3 John 9–10

No. 5: *Didache* 14.1–2 (early second century)

[ed. Funk-Bihlmeyer[3] (1970)]

14. Κατὰ κυριακὴν δὲ κυρίου συναχθέντες κλάσατε ἄρτον καὶ εὐχαριστήσατε, προεξομολογησάμενοι τὰ παραπτώματα ὑμῶν, ὅπως καθαρὰ ἡ θυσία ὑμῶν ᾖ. 2. πᾶς δὲ ἔχων τὴν ἀμφιβολίαν μετὰ τοῦ ἑταίρου αὐτοῦ μὴ συνελθέτω ὑμῖν, ἕως οὗ διαλλαγῶσιν, ἵνα μὴ κοινωθῇ ἡ θυσία ὑμῶν.

Translation. 1. On the Lord's Day of the Lord come together, break bread, and give thanks, having confessed your transgressions so that your sacrifice may be pure. 2. But if anyone has a quarrel with his fellow let him not participate until they be reconciled lest your sacrifice be defiled.

No. 6: Ignatius, Bishop of Antioch-on-the-Orontes (died ca. 110 CE at Rome)

[ed. Funk-Bihlmeyer^3 (1970)].

6a: *Epistle to the Ephesians* 5.2–3

5.2. μηδεὶς πλανάσθω· ἐὰν μή τις ᾖ ἐντὸς τοῦ θυσιαστηρίου, ὑστερεῖται τοῦ ἄρτου τοῦ θεοῦ. εἰ γὰρ ἑνὸς καὶ δευτέρου προσευχὴ τοσαύτην ἰσχὺν ἔχει, πόσῳ μᾶλλον ἥ τε τοῦ ἐπισκόπου καὶ πάσης τῆς ἐκκλησίας; 3. ὁ οὖν μὴ ἐρχόμενος ἐπὶ τὸ αὐτό, οὗτος ἤδη ὑπερηφανεῖ καὶ ἑαυτὸν διέκρινεν. . . .

Translation. 2. Let no one be deceived. Unless one is in the union of the altar, he is lacking the bread of God. For if the prayer of one or two has such power, how much more then has that of the bishop and the whole church? 3. Thus, the one who does not come together in assembly[1] is already behaving arrogantly and has separated himself. . . .

6b: *Epistle to the Magnesians* 6.1–7.2

6.1. Ἐπεὶ οὖν ἐν τοῖς προγεγραμμένοις προσώποις τὸ πᾶν πλῆθος ἐθεώρησα ἐν πίστει καὶ ἠγάπησα, παραινῶ, ἐν ὁμονοίᾳ θεοῦ σπουδάζετε πάντα πράσσειν, προκαθημένου τοῦ ἐπισκόπου εἰς τόπον θεοῦ καὶ τῶν πρεσβυτέρων εἰς τόπον συνεδρίου τῶν ἀποστόλων, καὶ τῶν διακόνων τῶν ἐμοὶ γλυκυτάτων πεπιστευμένων διακονίαν Ἰησοῦ Χριστοῦ, ὃς πρὸ αἰώνων παρὰ πατρὶ ἦν καὶ ἐν τέλει ἐφάνη. 2. πάντες οὖν ὁμοήθειαν θεοῦ λαβόντες ἐτρέπεσθε ἀλλήλους καὶ μηδεὶς κατὰ σάρκα βλεπέτω τὸν πλησίον, ἀλλ᾽ ἐν Ἰησοῦ Χριστῷ ἀλλήλους διὰ παντὸς ἀγαπᾶτε. μηδὲν ἔστω ἐν ὑμῖν, ὃ δυνήσεται ὑμᾶς μερίσαι, ἀλλ᾽ ἑνώθητε τῷ ἐπισκόπῳ καὶ τοῖς προκαθημένοις εἰς τύπον καὶ διδαχὴν ἀφθαρσίας.

---

1. For ἐπὶ τὸ αὐτό as Ignatius's designation for the eucharistic assembly see also *Eph*. 13.1 and *Mag*. 7.1 (No. 6b, below) and also compare the *Martyrdom of Justin* (No. 7b).

7.1. Ὥσπερ οὖν ὁ κύριος ἄνευ τοῦ πατρὸς οὐδὲν ἐποίησεν, ἡνωμένος ὤν, οὔτε δι᾽ ἑαυτοῦ οὔτε διὰ τῶν ἀποστόλων· οὕτως μηδὲ ὑμεῖς ἄνευ τοῦ ἐπισκόπου καὶ τῶν πρεσβυτέρων μηδὲν πράσσετε· μηδὲ πειράσητε εὔλογόν τι φαίνεσθαι ἰδίᾳ ὑμῖν, ἀλλ᾽ ἐπὶ τὸ αὐτὸ μία προσευχή, μία δέησις, εἷς νοῦς, μία ἐλπὶς ἐν ἀγάπῃ, ἐν τῇ χαρᾷ τῇ ἀμώμῳ, ὅ ἐστιν Ἰησοῦς Χριστός, οὗ ἄμεινον οὐδέν ἐστιν. 2. Πάντες ὡς εἰς ἕνα ναὸν συντρέχετε θεοῦ, ὡς ἐπὶ ἓν θυσιαστήριον, ἐπὶ ἕνα Ἰησοῦν Χριστόν, τὸν ἀφ᾽ ἑνὸς πατρὸς προελθόντα καὶ εἰς ἕνα ὄντα καὶ χωρήσαντα.

Translation. 6.1. Since in the persons mentioned above [*Mag*. 2] I have in faith seen and embraced the entire congregation I give (this) exhortation: Strive diligently to do everything in godly concord since the bishop presides in the position[2] of God and the presbyters in the position of the council of the apostles, and since the deacons—who are very dear to me—have been entrusted with the ministry of Jesus Christ, who was with the Father from eternity and appeared at the end of time. 2. All of you keeping the harmony of God, therefore, respect one another and let no one regard his neighbor according to the flesh, but in everything love one another in Jesus Christ. Let there be nothing among you that is able to divide you, but be united with the bishop and with those who preside as an example and lesson of immortality.

7.1. As the Lord, being united (with the Father), did nothing without the Father, either by himself or through the apostles, so you also do nothing without the bishop and the presbyters. Neither attempt to expound anything as appropriate on your own in private, but let there be in the assembly one prayer, one supplication, one mind, one hope in love, in the blameless joy, which is Jesus Christ, than whom nothing is greater. 2. Hasten all together as into the temple of God, as to one altar, to one Jesus Christ, who came forth from the one Father, is with, and returned to one.

6c: *Epistle to the Smyrneans* 8

8.1. Πάντες τῷ ἐπισκόπῳ ἀκολουθεῖτε, ὡς Ἰησοῦς Χριστὸς τῷ πατρί, καὶ τῷ πρεσβυτερίῳ ὡς τοῖς ἀποστόλοις· τοὺς δὲ διακόνους ἐντρέπεσθε

2. For τόπος as a designation of ecclesiastical or social rank/office, see *Smyrn*. 6.1. Lightfoot, however, read τύπος here based on the wording in 6.2, but this emendation does not seem to be warranted.

ὡς θεοῦ ἐντολήν. μηδεὶς χωρὶς ἐπισκόπου τι πρασσέτω τῶν ἀνηκόντων εἰς τὴν ἐκκλησίαν. ἐκείνη βεβαία εὐχαριστία ἡγείσθω, ἡ ὑπὸ τὸν ἐπίσκοπον οὖσα ἢ ᾧ ἂν αὐτὸς ἐπιτρέψῃ. 2. ὅπου ἂν φανῇ ὁ ἐπίσκοπος, ἐκεῖ τὸ πλῆθος ἔστω, ὥσπερ ὅπου ἂν ᾖ Ἰησοῦς Χριστός, ἐκεῖ ἡ καθολικὴ ἐκκλησία. οὐκ ἐξόν ἐστιν χωρὶς ἐπισκόπου οὔτε βαπτίζειν οὔτε ἀγάπην ποιεῖν· ἀλλ' ὃ ἂν ἐκεῖνος δοκιμάσῃ τοῦτο καὶ τῷ θεῷ ευάρεστον, ἵνα ἀσφαλὲς ᾖ καὶ βέβαιον πᾶν ὃ πράσσετε.

Translation. 1. Obey, all of you, the bishop just as Jesus Christ (obeyed) the Father, and obey the presbyters as the apostles. And respect the deacons as a command of God. Let no one do anything pertaining to the church without the bishop. Let that be considered a proper eucharist which is held by the bishop or by one whom he should appoint. 2. Wherever the bishop appears there let the congregation be present, just as wherever Jesus Christ is there is the catholic church. Without the bishop it is permitted neither to baptize nor to hold an *agape* (meal). But whatever he approves is also pleasing to God that everything you do be secure and safe.

No. 7: Justin Martyr (born Neo-Caesarea, Palestine; died ca. 164 at Rome)

7a: Justin, *Apology* 1.61.1–3; 65.1–5; 67.1–8 (Rome, ca. 155) [ed. Krüger (1896) as printed by A. W. F. Blunt, *The Apologies of Justin Martyr* (Cambridge, 1911)]

61. 1. Ὃν τρόπον δὲ καὶ ἀνεθήκαμεν ἑαυτοὺς τῷ θεῷ καινοποιηθέντες διὰ τοῦ Χριστοῦ, ἐξηγησόμεθα, ὅπως μὴ τοῦτο παραλιπόντες δόξωμεν πονηρεύειν τι ἐν τῇ ἐξηγήσει. 2. ὅσοι ἂν πεισθῶσι καὶ πιστεύωσιν ἀληθῆ ταῦτα τὰ ὑφ' ἡμῶν διδασκόμενα καὶ λεγόμενα εἶναι, καὶ βιοῦν οὕτως δύνασθαι ὑπισχνῶνται, εὔχεσθαί τε καὶ αἰτεῖν νηστεύοντες παρὰ τοῦ θεοῦ τῶν προημαρτημένων ἄφεσιν διδάσκονται, ἡμῶν συνευχομένων καὶ συννηστουόντων αὐτοῖς. 3. ἔπειτα ἄγονται ὑφ' ἡμῶν ἔνθα ὕδωρ ἐστί, καὶ τρόπον ἀναγεννήσεως, ὅν καὶ ἡμεῖς αὐτοὶ ἀνεγεννήθημεν, ἀναγεννῶνται· ἐπ' ὀνόματος γὰρ τοῦ πατρὸς τῶν ὅλων καὶ δεσπότου θεοῦ καὶ τοῦ σωτῆρος ἡμῶν Ἰησοῦ Χριστοῦ καὶ πνεύματος ἁγίου τὸ ἐν τῷ ὕδατι τότε λουτρὸν ποιοῦνται.

65. 1. Ἡμεῖς δὲ μετὰ τὸ οὕτως λοῦσαι τὸν πεπεισμένον καὶ συγκατατεθειμένον ἐπὶ τοὺς λεγομένους ἀδελφοὺς ἄγομεν ἔνθα συνηγμένοι εἰσί, κοινὰς εὐχὰς ποιησόμενοι ὑπέρ τε ἑαυτῶν καὶ τοῦ φωτισθέντος καὶ ἄλλων πανταχοῦ πάντων εὐτόνως, ὅπως καταξιωθῶμεν τὰ ἀληθῆ μαθόντες καὶ δι᾽ ἔργων ἀγαθοὶ πολιτευταὶ καὶ φύλακες τῶν ἐντεταλμένων εὑρεθῆναι, ὅπως τὴν αἰώνιον σωτηρίαν σωθῶμεν. 2. ἀλλήλους φιλήματι ἀσπαζόμεθα παυσάμενοι τῶν εὐχῶν. 3. ἔπειτα προσφέρεται τῷ προεστῶτι τῶν ἀδελφῶν ἄρτος καὶ ποτήριον ὕδατος καὶ κράματος, καὶ οὗτος λαβὼν αἶνον καὶ δόξαν τῷ πατρὶ τῶν ὅλων διὰ τοῦ ὀνόματος τοῦ υἱοῦ καὶ τοῦ πνεύματος τοῦ ἁγίου ἀναπέμπει καὶ εὐχαριστίαν ὑπὲρ τοῦ κατηξιῶσθαι τούτων παρ᾽ αὐτοῦ ἐπὶ πολὺ ποιεῖται· οὗ συντελέσαντος τὰς εὐχὰς καὶ τὴν εὐχαριστίαν πᾶς ὁ παρὼν λαὸς ἐπευφημεῖ λέγων· Ἀμήν. 4. τὸ δὲ ἀμὴν τῇ ἑβραΐδι φωνῇ τὸ γένοιτο σημαίνει. 5. εὐχαριστήσαντος δὲ τοῦ προεστῶτος καὶ ἐπευφημήσαντος παντὸς τοῦ λαοῦ οἱ καλούμενοι παρ᾽ ἡμῖν διάκονοι διδόασιν ἑκάστῳ τῶν παρόντων μεταλαβεῖν ἀπὸ τοῦ εὐχαριστηθέντος ἄρτου καὶ οἴνου καὶ ὕδατος καὶ τοῖς οὐ παροῦσιν ἀποφέρουσι.

. . .

67. 1. Ἡμεῖς δὲ μετὰ ταῦτα λοιπὸν ἀεὶ τούτων ἀλλήλους ἀναμιμνήσκομεν· καὶ οἱ ἔχοντες τοῖς λειπομένοις πᾶσιν ἐπικουροῦμεν, καὶ σύνεσμεν ἀλλήλοις ἀεί. 2. ἐπὶ πᾶσί τε οἷς προσφερόμεθα εὐλογοῦμεν τὸν ποιητὴν τῶν πάντων διὰ τοῦ υἱοῦ αὐτοῦ Ἰησοῦ Χριστοῦ καὶ διὰ πνεύματος τοῦ ἁγίου. 3. καὶ τῇ τοῦ ἡλίου λεγομένῃ ἡμέρᾳ πάντων κατὰ πόλεις ἢ ἀγροὺς μενόντων ἐπὶ τὸ αὐτὸ συνέλευσις γίνεται, καὶ τὰ ἀπομνημονεύματα τῶν ἀποστόλων ἢ τὰ συγγράμματα τῶν προφητῶν ἀναγινώσκεται, μέχρις ἐγχωρεῖ. 4. εἶτα παυσαμένου τοῦ ἀναγινώσκοντος ὁ προεστὼς διὰ λόγου τὴν νουθεσίαν καὶ πρόκλησιν τῆς τῶν καλῶν τούτων μιμήσεως ποιεῖται. 5. ἔπειτα ἀνιστάμεθα κοινῇ πάντες καὶ εὐχὰς πέμπομεν· καί, ὡς προέφημεν, παυσαμένων ἡμῶν τῆς εὐχῆς ἄρτος προσφέρεται καὶ οἶνος καὶ ὕδωρ, καὶ ὁ προεστὼς εὐχὰς ὁμοίως καὶ εὐχαριστίας, ὅση δύναμις αὐτῷ, ἀναπέμπει, καὶ ὁ λαὸς ἐπευφημεῖ λέγων τὸ Ἀμήν, καὶ ἡ διάδοσις καὶ ἡ μετάληψις ἀπὸ τῶν εὐχαριστηθέντων ἑκάστῳ γίνεται, καὶ τοῖς οὐ παροῦσι διὰ τῶν διακόνων πέμπεται. 6. οἱ εὐποροῦντες δὲ καὶ βουλόμενοι κατὰ προαίρεσιν ἕκαστος τὴν ἑαυτοῦ ὃ βούλεται δίδωσι, καὶ τὸ συλλεγόμενον παρὰ τῷ προεστῶτι ἀποτίθεται,

7. καὶ αὐτὸς ἐπικουρεῖ ὀρφανοῖς τε καὶ χήραις καὶ τοῖς διὰ νόσον ἢ δι᾿ ἄλλην αἰτίαν λειπομένοις, καὶ τοῖς ἐν δεσμοῖς οὖσι, καὶ τοῖς παρεπιδήμοις οὖσι ξένοις, καὶ ἁπλῶς πᾶσι τοῖς ἐν χρείᾳ οὖσι κηδεμὼν γίνεται. 8. τὴν δὲ τοῦ ἡλίου ἡμέραν κοινῇ πάντες τὴν συνέλευσιν ποιούμεθα, ἐπειδὴ πρώτη ἐστὶν ἡμέρα. . . .

Translation. 61. I will explain the manner in which we have dedicated ourselves to God, being renewed through Christ, so that we will not appear pernicious by leaving something out of the exposition. If any are persuaded and believe that what we teach and say is true and if they promise that they can live accordingly, they are instructed to pray and, while fasting, to beseech God for forgiveness of their past sins as we pray and fast along with them. Then they are led by us to where there is water, and they are reborn in the same manner of regeneration by which we ourselves have been reborn. For they are then given washing in the water in the name of God the Father and master of all, of our savior Jesus Christ, and of the Holy Spirit.

. . . . .

65. After thus washing the one who has been persuaded and who has assented, then we lead him to those who are called brothers, in the place where they regularly assemble. They earnestly offer common prayers for themselves, for the one who has been enlightened, and for all other (Christians) everywhere, that we may be made worthy, having learned the truth, that we may be found by (our) deeds to be good citizens and guardians of the commandments, to the end that we may be saved with eternal salvation. We finish the prayers and salute one another with a kiss. Then bread and a cup containing water and wine are brought to the president of the brethren. And taking them he offers praise and glory to the Father of all through the name of the Son and of the Holy Spirit, and he gives thanks at length for being judged worthy of these things by him. After he has completed the prayers and the thanksgiving the whole coterie present gives its assent by saying, "Amen." The word "Amen" in the Hebrew language means "so be it." When the president has given thanks and the whole congregation has assented, those who are called deacons by us give to each one present a portion of the bread and of the water mixed with wine for which the thanksgiving had been made. Then, they [the deacons] take it to those who were not present (at the assembly).

. . .

67. After these things [the baptismal services] we continually remind one another of them. Those who have means give aid to all those who are in need, and we constantly assemble together. For everything that we receive we bless the maker of everything through his son Jesus Christ and through the Holy Spirit. And on the day that is called the Day of the Sun there is a meeting together in one place of all those who dwell in cities or country; as long as time permits the memoirs of the apostles or the writings of the prophets are read. When the reader has finished the president in a discourse gives exhortation and invitation to imitate these good things. Then we all rise up in unison and offer prayers, and, as we said before [§ 65, above], when we have finished praying bread is brought and wine with water. The president, in the same manner, offers prayers and thanksgiving to the best of his ability, and the congregation assents by saying the Amen. The distribution and the sharing by each one of that for which thanks had been given takes place, and it is sent to those who were absent by the deacons. He who prospers and who so desires gives what he wishes of his own possessions, each according to his decision. What is collected is entrusted to the president. He gives aid to orphans and widows and to the sick or those who for other reasons are in need, and to those in prison, to strangers who sojourn (with him), and, in brief, he is the patron (guardian) of all those who are in need. We all hold this common assembly on the day of the sun since it is the first day. . . .

7b: *Passio sancti Justini et socii* 3.1–4 (ca. 165)
[ed. H. Musurillo, *Acts of the Christian Martyrs* (Oxford, 1972)]

3.1 Ῥούστικος ἔπαρχος εἶπεν· Ποῦ συνέρχεσθε; Ἰουστῖνος εἶπεν· Ἔνθα ἑκάστῳ προαίρεσις καὶ δύναμίς ἐστιν. πάντως γὰρ νομίζεις κατὰ αὐτὸ δυνατὸν συνέρχεσθαι ἡμᾶς πάντας; 2. Ῥούστικος ἔπαρχος εἶπεν· Εἰπέ, ποῦ συνέρχεσθε, ἢ εἰς τίνα τόπον; 3. Ἰουστῖνος εἶπεν· Ἐγὼ ἐπάνω μένω τοῦ Μυρτίνου βαλανείου παρὰ πάντα τὸν χρόνον ὃν ἐπεδήμησα τὸ δεύτερον τῇ Ῥωμαίων πόλει· οὐ γινώσκω δὲ ἄλλην τινὰ συνέλευσιν εἰ μὴ τὴν ἐκεῖ. καὶ εἴ τις ἐβούλετο ἀφικνεῖσθαι παρ᾽ ἐμοί, ἐκοινώνουν αὐτῷ τῶν τῆς ἀληθείας λόγων. 4. Ῥούστικος εἶπεν· Οὐκοῦν Χριστιανὸς εἶ; Ἰουστῖνος ἀπεκρίνατο· Ναί, Χριστιανός εἰμι.

Translation. 3.1. Rusticus[3] the prefect said, "Where do you (Christians) assemble?"

"Wherever is chosen and it is possible for each one," said Justin, "for do you think it possible for all of us to gather in the same place (of assembly)?"[4]

2. Rusticus the prefect said, "Tell me, where do you assemble, that is, in what place?"

3. Justin said, "I have been staying above the baths of Myrtinus[5] for the entire period I have resided in Rome for this the second time. And I know no other meeting place except the one there. If anyone wishes to come to me there, I am accustomed to share with him the words of truth."

4. Rusticus the prefect said, "You are a Christian then?"

Justin answered, "Yes, I am a Christian."

---

3. Rusticus here is Q. Junius Rusticus, urban prefect of the city of Rome between 163 and 168 CE (cf. *PW* 10 [1917] 1083).

4. The text provided here is that of *Cod. Parisinus. Gr.* 1470 (designated as Recension A), which Musurillo considers to be the most original of the three preserved recensions. (See the brief discussion and further bibliography in Musurillo, *Acts of the Christian Martyrs*, pp. xviiiff.). At this point in the longer version (Recension B, *Cod. Cantabrigiensis add.* 4489, still considered by a few scholars to be the earliest MS.), the reply of Justin continues with a more theological argument, as follows: πάντως γὰρ νομίζεις ἐπὶ τὸ αὐτὸ συνέρχεσθαι ἡμᾶς πάντας; Οὐχ οὕτως δέ, διότι ὁ θεὸς τῶν Χριστιανῶν τόπῳ οὐ περιγράφεται, ἀλλ᾽ ἀόρατος ὢν τὸν οὐρανὸν καὶ τὴν γῆν πληροῖ καὶ πανταχοῦ ὑπὸ τῶν πιστῶν προσκυνεῖται καὶ δοξάζεται. (*Translation*: for do you think it possible for all of us to gather in the same place of assembly? No, not at all, since the God of the Christians cannot be circumscribed by place. Rather, being invisible, he fills heaven and earth, and everywhere he is worshipped and glorified by those who believe.)

This theological retort is drawn from a well-known critique found in both philosophical and Jewish sources (see H. W. Attridge, "The Philosophical Critique of Religion under the Early Empire," *ANRW* 2.16.1 [1979] 45–68). Here, however, it takes the cross-examination of Justin in an entirely different direction from the rest of the text, which purports to be a court record. Hence, the reference to an actual place of assembly as reflected in Recension A appears to be authentic. Finally, Recension C, the most elaborate literary version, further emphasizes this theological retort and adds "evening" as the usual time of assembly.

5. τοῦ Μυρτίνου: Here Recension B reads τινὸς Μαρτίνου τοῦ Τιμιοτίνου, while Recension C omits all reference to the exact location. Franchi de Cavalieri has argued that the references of both Recensions A and B are hopelessly corrupt. See Cavalieri in "Note agiografiche 6°," *Studi e Testi* 33 (1920) 10–11.

No. 8: The Apocryphal Acts of Peter (composed before ca. 190; place of origin uncertain, but Asia Minor usually favored)

Acta petri cum Simoni (Acta Vercellenses) 6–8; 19–20
[ed. Lipsius-Bonnet, *AA* I:53–55; 66]

[Peter had sailed for Italy with the ship captain, Theon, arriving at Puteoli, where he stayed in the house of a certain Christian named Ariston. Upon hearing of the disturbances among the brethren at Rome caused by the charlatan Simon Magus, Peter decides to go to Rome.]

Theon autem . . . consecutus est Petrum Romae deducentem Aristonem in habitationem Narcissi praesbyteri.

7. Fama pervolavit in urbem ad dispersos fratres Petrum dicentem domi venisse Simonis causa, ut cum ostenderet seductorem et persecutorem bonorum esse. concurrit itaque multitudo omnis ut viderent domini apostolum fundari in Christum. prima autem sabbatorum multitudine conveniente Petrum videndi causa, coepit itaque voce maxima Petrus dicere: . . .

8. Paenitentes autem fratres rogabant Petrum, ut expugnaret Simonem, qui se dicebat dei virtutem esse, morantem in domo Marcelli senatoris persuasum carminibus eius, dicentes: Crede nobis, frater Petre: nemo fuit tam sapientior inter homines, quam hic Marcellus. viduae omnes sperantes in Christo ad hunc refugium habebant; omnes orfani ab eo pascebantur. quid plura, frater? Marcellum omnes pauperi patronum vocabant; cuius domus peregrinorum et pauperorum vocabulum habebat. . . .

Translation. So Theon . . . followed Peter to Rome, and Ariston escorted (them) to the house of Narcissus the presbyter.

7. The rumor spread throughout the city among the scattered brethren saying that Peter had come to the house on account of Simon, in order to show him to be a deceiver and persecutor of good men. Therefore, great multitudes came together [at the house of Narcissus] in order to see the Lord's apostle being established in Christ. So on the first day of the week, when the multitude came together to see Peter, he began to speak in a loud voice . . . [there follows the speech of Peter].

8. Then the brethren, repenting, began to call on Peter that he should refute Simon, who was saying that he was the power of God and who was staying in the house of Marcellus, a senator, who had been persuaded by his

wiles. They said, "Believe us, brother Peter, none among men was so wise as this Marcellus. All the widows who placed their hope in Christ found refuge with him; all the orphans were supported by him. What more, brother? All the poor called Marcellus their patron; his house had the reputation of being the house of travelers and the poor." . . .

[Peter confronts Simon in the house of Marcellus and is able to refute him, whereupon he returns to the house of Narcissus (chap. 13) and instructs the assembly there (which continues through chap. 18).]

19. Post haec autem a Petro dicta supervenit et Marcellum, qui dixit: Petre, ego tibi totam domum meam permundavi a vestigiis Simonis et scelesti pulveris ipsius perstirpavi. accepit enim aquam et invocans nomen Iesu Christi sanctum cum ceteris servis ipsius pertinentibus ad eum, adsparsi omnem domu meam et omnia triclinia et omnem porticationem usque foris ad ianuam et dixi: 'scio te, domine Iesu Christe, mundum et intactum esse ab omni immunditia,' ut exfugetur hostis et inimicus meus a conspectu tuo. et nunc, beatissime, iussi convenire in domum communem viduas et seniores ad te, ut orent nobiscum. accipient autem ministerii nomine singulos aureos, ut possint vocari vere Christi servi. cetera autem praeparata sunt omnia ad ministerium. rogo itaque, beatissime Petre, consignare praecibus eorum, ut et tu condecores orationes eorum pro me. eamus ergo, accipiamus et Narcissum ut[6] quicumque hic sunt fratres. adquiescens itaque Petrus simplicitati illius, ut et illi animum adimpleret, prodit cum eo et ceteris fratribus.

20. Petrus vero introivit et videns unam de senioribus viduam ab oculis, et filiam eius manum ei dantem et inducentem in domum Marcelli. et dixit ad eam Petrus: Accede, mater; tibi ex hodierno die Iesus dexteram suam dans, per quem 'lumen inaccessibilem' habemus quod 'non' operiunt 'tenebrae'; qui tibi per me dicit: 'Aperi oculos et vide et sola ambula'. et continuo vidit et viduam inponentem sibi Petrum manum introibit autem Petrus in triclinio et vidit evangelium legi. involues eum dixit: Viri, qui in Christo creditis et speratis, scitote, qualiter debeat sancta scribtura domini nostri pronuntiari. . . .

6. As suggested by Lipsius-Bonnet (*Acta Apostolicorum Apocrypha* [3 vols.; Leipzig: Mendelssohn, 1891–1903; reprinted Hildesheim/Zurich/New York: Georg Olms, 1990], hereafter abbreviated *AA*), this reading in the MS. should be corrected to *et*. So *AA* I. 66 (*ad not.* line 19).

Translation. 19. After these sayings of Peter were completed Marcellus arrived unexpectedly and said, "Peter, for you I have completely cleansed my entire house of the vestiges of Simon and thoroughly swept it of his accursed dust. For I took water, and with the aid of other servants of mine who had belonged to him, invoking the holy name of Jesus Christ, I sprinkled the entire house, all the dining rooms and all the porticoes right through to the entryway from the outside, and said, 'I know, Lord Jesus Christ, that you are pure and untouched by any impurity,' so that my enemy and opponent is driven from your sight. And now, most blessed one, I have directed the widows and the aged to meet in common with you in (my) house, in order that they may pray with us. And in accordance with (their) service they will (each) receive a single *aureus*, so that they may indeed be called the servants of Christ. Thus, everything else has been prepared for the service. I call on you, therefore, blessed Peter, to endorse their supplications so that you (may seal) their elaborate prayers for me. Let us go, therefore, and let us take both Narcissus and any of those here who are brothers." Thus, Peter assented to his extreme simplicity and went with him and the rest of the brethren so as to fulfill his desire.

20. Then, Peter went in and saw one of the elderly, a blind widow, with her daughter, who was leading her by the hand into the house of Marcellus. And Peter said to her, "Come, mother, for from this day forward Jesus gives you his right hand; through him we have 'inaccessible light' [1 Tim 6:16] which 'the darkness will not' hide [?Jn 1:5]. He says to you through me, 'Open your eyes and see, and walk on your own.'" And at once the widow saw Peter laying his hand on her. So Peter went into the dining room (*triclinium*) and saw the gospel being read. And rolling it up he said, "O men who believe and hope in Christ, you must know in what manner the holy scriptures of our Lord ought to be declared. . . ."

[Following Peter's speech he heals some elderly widows in the assembly and with the aid of Marcellus attends the needs of others. Then, on the following sabbath Peter, accompanied by Marcellus and in the presence of great crowds of believers, goes off to confront Simon publicly in the forum (chaps. 23–28). Finally, Peter continues to meet with the brethren in the house of Marcellus (chap. 29) until he is arrested and martyred (chaps. 30ff.), but there is a final miraculous epiphany to Marcellus (chaps. 40–41).]

No. 9: The Apocryphal Acts of Paul (composed before ca. 190, probably in Asia Minor)

9a: *Acta Pauli et Theclae* 5–7
[ed. Lipsius-Bonnet, *AA* I:238–40].

[On his arrival in Iconium, Paul goes to the house of Onesiphorus (cf. 1 Tim 1:16; 4:19).]

5. Καὶ εἰσελθόντος Παύλου εἰς τὸν τοῦ Ὀνησιφόρου οἶκον ἐγένετο χαρὰ μεγάλη, καὶ κλίσις γονάτων καὶ κλάσις ἄρτου καὶ λόγος θεοῦ περὶ ἐγκρατείας καὶ ἀναστάσεως, λέγοντος τοῦ Παύλου . . . [follows some 14 "beatitudes"].

7. Καὶ ταῦτα τοῦ Παύλου λέγοντος ἐν μέσῳ τῆς ἐκκλησίας ἐν τῷ Ὀνησιφόρου οἴκῳ, Θέκλα τις παρθένος Θεοκλείας μητρὸς μεμνηστευμένη ἀνδρὶ Θαμύριδι, καθεσθεῖσα ἐπὶ τῆς σύνεγγυς θυρίδος τοῦ οἴκου ἤκουεν νυκτὸς καὶ ἡμέρας τὸν περὶ ἁγνείας λόγον λεγόμενον ὑπὸ τοῦ Παύλου·

Translation. 5. And when Paul came into the house of Onesiphorus there was great joy — the bowing of knees, the breaking of bread, and (proclaiming) the word of God concerning self-control and the resurrection, as Paul said . . . [Paul's sermon follows].

7. And while Paul was speaking in the midst of the church in the house of Onesiphorus, a certain virgin (named) Thecla, whose mother was Theocleia and who was betrothed to a man (named) Thamyris, sat down on a nearby window of the house and listened night and day to the words being spoken by Paul concerning chastity. . . .

9b: *Passio Pauli* 1
[ed. Lipsius-Bonnet, *AA* I:104].

[Paul's arrival at Rome.]

Ἦσαν δὲ περιμένοντες τὸν Παῦλον ἐν τῇ Ῥώμῃ Λουκᾶς ἀπὸ Γαλλιῶν καὶ Τίτος ἀπὸ Δαλματίας. οὓς ἰδὼν ὁ Παῦλος ἐχάρη ὥστε ἔξω Ῥώμης ὅρριον μισθώσασθαι, ἐν ᾧ μετὰ τῶν ἀδελφῶν ἐδίδασκε τὸν λόγον τῆς ἀληθείας. διαβόητος δὲ ἐγένετο, καὶ πολλαὶ ψυχαὶ προσετίθεντο τῷ κυρίῳ, ὡς ἦχον κατὰ πᾶσαν τὴν Ῥώμην γενέσθαι καὶ προσεῖναι αὐτῷ πολὺ πλῆθος ἐκ τῆς Καίσαρος οἰκίας πιστεύοντας, καὶ εἶναι χαρὰν μεγάλην. . . .

Translation. Now Luke (having come) from Gaul and Titus from Dalmatia [cf. 2 Tim 4:10] had been waiting for Paul at Rome. When he saw them Paul rejoiced so that he hired a storehouse (*horreum*) outside the city, where with the brethren he taught the word of truth. It became famous and many souls were added to the Lord so that it became common knowledge throughout Rome, and there came to him a great number of believers from the household of Caesar, and there was great joy. . . .

No. 10: The Apocryphal Acts of Thomas (composed in the early third century, from Syria; originally in Syriac [now lost] but preserved in early Greek version[s] and in a later Syriac version)

Acta Thomae 131–33; 170
[ed. Lipsius-Bonnet, *AA* II.2:238–40; II.2:287]

[From part 10, concerning the conversion of Mygdonia, the wife of Charisius, a relative of King Misdaeus.]

131. Ὁ δὲ Ἰούδας ἐξελθὼν ἐκ τῆς Χαρισίου οἰκίας εἰς τὴν Σιφόρου οἰκίαν ἀπῄει· κἀκεῖ μετ᾽ αὐτοῦ ᾤκει. εἶπεν δὲ ὁ Σιφώρ· Εὐτρεπίσω τῷ Ἰούδᾳ τρίκλινον ἐν ᾧ διδάσκει. Καὶ ἐποίησεν οὕτως καὶ εἶπεν Σιφώρ· Ἐγώ τε καὶ ἡ ἐμὴ γυνὴ καὶ ἡ θυγάτηρ ἐν ἁγιωσύνῃ οἰκήσομεν λοιπόν, ἐν ἁγνείᾳ καὶ μιᾷ διαθέσει. δέομαί σου ἡμᾶς τὴν σφραγῖδα δέξασθαι παρὰ σοῦ, ἵνα γενώμεθα τῷ θεῷ τῷ ἀληθινῷ λάτραι καὶ ἐναρίθμιοι τοῖς αὐτοῦ ἀρνίοις καὶ ἀμνάσιν. Ὁ δὲ Ἰούδας λέγει· Φοβοῦμαι λέγειν ὅπερ ἐνθυμοῦμαι· οἶδα δέ τι, καὶ ὅπερ οἶδα ἐξαγορεύειν οὐχ οἷόν τέ μοι.

132. Καὶ ἤρξατο λέγειν περὶ τοῦ βαπτίσματος· Τὸ βάπτισμα τοῦτο ἁμαρτιῶν ἐστιν ἄφεσις· τοῦτο ἀναγεννᾷ φῶς περιεκχυνόμενον· *τοῦτο

ἀναγεννᾷ τὸν νέον ἄνθρωπον, τοὺς ἀνθρώπους μειγνύον πνεῦμα καινοῦν ψυχήν, ἀνιστῶν τρισσῶς καινὸν ἄνθρωπον, καὶ ἔστιν κοινωνὸν τῶν ἁμαρτιῶν ἀφέσεως. σοὶ δόξα τῷ ἀπορρήτῳ τῷ βαπτίσματι κοινωνούμενον· σοὶ δόξα ἡ ἐν τῷ βαπτίσματι ἀόρατος δύναμις· σοὶ δόξα ἀνακαινισμὸς δι᾽ οὗ ἀνακαινίζονται οἱ βαπτιζόμενοι οἱ μετὰ διαθέσεως σοῦ ἁπτόμενοι. *Καὶ ταῦτα εἰπὼν ἔλαιον κατὰ τῆς κεφαλῆς αὐτῶν κατέχεεν καὶ εἶπεν· Σοὶ δόξα ἡ τῶν σπλάγχνων ἀγάπη· σοὶ δόξα τὸ τοῦ Χριστοῦ ὄνομα· σοὶ δόξα ἡ ἐν Χριστῷ δύναμις ἱδρυμένη. Καὶ ἐκέλευσεν ἐνεχθῆναι σκάφην καὶ ἐβάπτισεν αὐτοὺς εἰς τὸ ὄνομα τοῦ πατρὸς καὶ τοῦ υἱοῦ καὶ τοῦ ἁγίου πνεύματος.

133. Βαπτισθέντων δὲ καὶ ἐνδυσαμένων ἄρτον καταθεὶς ἐπὶ τὴν τράπεζαν ηὐλόγησεν καὶ εἶπεν· Ἄρτον ζωῆς ὃν οἱ ἐσθίοντες ἄφθαρτοι διαμείνωσιν· ἄρτος ὁ κορεννὺς ψυχὰς πεινώσας τοῦ αὐτοῦ μακαρισμοῦ· σὺ εἶ ὁ καταξιώσας δέξασθαι δωρεὰν ἵνα γένῃ ἡμῖν ἄφεσις ἁμαρτιῶν καὶ οἱ ἐσθίοντες σε ἀθάνατοι γένωνται· ἐπιφημίζομέν σε τὸ τῆς μητρὸς ὄνομα, ἀπορρήτου μυστηρίου ἀρχῶν τε καὶ ἐξουσιῶν κεκρυμμένων· ἐπιφημίζομέν σου ὀνόματί σου Ἰησοῦ. Καὶ εἶπεν· Ἐλθάτω δύναμις εὐλογίας καὶ ἐνιδρύσθω ὁ ἄρτος, ἵνα πᾶσαι αἱ μεταλαμβάνουσαι ψυχαὶ ἀπὸ τῶν ἁμαρτιῶν ἀπολούσονται. Καὶ κλάσας ἐπέδωκεν τῷ τε Σιφόρῳ καὶ τῇ γυναικὶ αὐτοῦ καὶ τῇ θυγατρί.

Translation. 131. And Judas [Thomas] departed from the house of Charisius and went away to the house of Siphor [*the king's captain (cf. chaps. 62ff.), who had approached Thomas while they were meeting in the house of the deacon Xenophon (cf. chap. 67)*], and he stayed there with him. And Siphor said, "I will prepare for Judas (my) dining room (*triclinium*) in which he may teach."[7] And when he had done so, Siphor said, "Henceforth, I will

7. The Syriac version of this text provides some important variations that probably preserve early renderings. The critical edition of the Syriac is after W. Wright, *Apocryphal Acts of the Apostles* (2 vols.; London, 1871), hereafter abbreviated Wright, *AAA*. The Syriac version of the second sentence reads as follows [ed. Wright, *AAA* 1. 300 (ܫ)]: ܐܛܝܒ ܠܟ ܛܪܩܠܝܢܐ ܘܗܘܝ ܡܠܦ ܒܗ. Wright (*AAA* 2. 266) translated the phrase, "Prepare for thyself an apartment and be teaching in it"; however, the word translated "apartment" (*ṭrqlyn'*) is a transliteration of the Greek τρίκλινον, a loanword. On the church in Siphor's house, see also chap. 138 (Lipsius-Bonnet, *AA* II.2:248), where Thomas is pictured teaching the assembly seated on a θρόνον.

live, together with my wife and daughter, in holiness, chastity, and in a single disposition. I beseech you that we might receive the seal from you so that we may become servants of the true God and be numbered among his sheep and lambs." But Judas said, "I am afraid to say what is in my heart. But I know something, and what I know I am not able to explain to you."

132. And he began to speak concerning baptism: "This baptism is the forgiveness of sins. *It regenerates light which flows out all around. It regenerates the new man—mingling the spirit with men, renewing the soul, raising up the new man in threefold manner—and is a participant in the forgiveness of sins. Glory to you, the secret that is shared in baptism. Glory to you, the invisible power that is in baptism. Glory to you, the renewal through which those who are baptized, who take hold of you with (the proper) disposition, are renewed."*[8] And having said this he poured oil upon their heads and said, "Glory to you, the love of compassion. Glory to you, the name of Christ." He gave instructions that a basin (or tub) be brought in, and he baptized them in the name of the Father and the Son and the Holy Spirit.

133. And when they had been baptized and dressed, he placed bread upon the table and blessed it saying, "Bread of life, of which those who eat remain incorruptible, bread which fills hungry souls with its blessing, you are the one worthy to receive the gift so that you might become forgiveness of sins for us and so that the ones eating you might become immortal. We call upon you the name of the mother, the ineffable mystery of hidden archons and powers. We call upon you the name of Jesus." And he said, "Let the power of the blessing come, and let the bread be established (by it) so that all the souls who partake of it may be washed of their sins." And breaking it he gave it to Siphor and his wife and daughter.

[After Thomas converts the wife (chaps. 134ff.) and son (chaps. 139ff.) of the king, Misdaeus, he is arrested and dies a martyr's death (chaps. 159ff.). But when another son of the king becomes possessed by a demon, Misdaeus goes to the tomb of Thomas, and, finding that the remains had been removed, he uses the dust and invokes the name of Jesus, upon which the boy is cured (chap. 170). The story concludes with the following event.]

---

8. In the section marked [*-*] there is a substantial difference between two of the major Greek manuscript traditions of the text. We present here only the longer reading of the Vallicellanus Codex, as that of the Paris Codex is thought by the editors to be an interpolation. Cf. Lipsius-Bonnet, *AA* II.2:239.

170. . . . Ὑγιάνοντος δὲ τοῦ υἱοῦ αὐτοῦ τῷ τρόπῳ τούτῳ συνήγετο μετὰ τῶν λοιπῶν ἀδελφῶν ὑποκατακλινόμενος τῷ Σιφόρῳ· καὶ τοὺς ἀδελφοὺς πάντας παρεκάλει εὔξασθαι ὑπὲρ αὐτοῦ ἵνα ἐλέους τύχῃ παρὰ τοῦ κυρίου ἡμῶν Ἰησοῦ Χριστοῦ.

Translation. And when his son had been restored to health in this manner, he [Misdaeus] came together with the other brethren, submitting himself to Siphor. And he entreated all the brethren to pray for him so that he might find mercy from our Lord Jesus Christ.

No. 11: The Pseudo-Clementine Literature (from Syria, third century)

Recognitions 10.71.1–3 (apud Rufinus)

[ed. Rehm, GCS 51 (1965)]

71.1. tantam itaque sanctus spiritus in illa die gratiam suae virtutis ostendit, ut omnes a minimo usque ad maximum una voce confiterentur deum; 2. et ne multis inmorer, intra septem dies plus quam decem milia hominum credentes deo baptizati sunt sanctificatione consecrati, ita ut omni aviditatis desiderio Theofilus. qui erat cunctis potentibus in civitate sublimior, domus suae ingentem basilicam ecclesiae nomine consecraret, 3. in qua Petro apostolo constituta est ab omni populo cathedra, et omnis multitude cotidie ad audiendum verbum conveniens, credebant sanae doctrinae; quae sanitatum efficacitas adfirmabat.

Translation. How much, then, did the Holy Spirit demonstrate the grace of its power on that day, so that all, from the least to the greatest, with one voicc confessed God. And (lest I linger in many words) within seven days more than ten thousand men, coming to believe in God, were baptized and were consecrated in sanctification. Thus (it was) that Theophilus, who was exalted above all others in power in the city [Antioch], by the desire of all eagerness dedicated the great basilica of his house in the name of the (? or a) church, and in it a chair was established for the apostle Peter by all the people. And assembling daily to hear the word all the multitudes believed the sound doctrines, which were affirmed by the efficacy of healing.

No. 12: Clement of Alexandria (fl. ca. 180–203)

12a: *Stromata* 7.5 [29.3–4]
[ed. Stälin, GCS 15 (1909)]

29.3. εἰ δὲ τὸ ἱερὸν διχῶς ἐκλαμβάνεται, ὅ τε θεὸς αὐτὸς καὶ τὸ εἰς τιμὴν αὐτοῦ κατασκεύασμα, πῶς οὐ κυρίως τὴν εἰς τιμὴν τοῦ θεοῦ κατ' ἐπίγνωσιν ἁγίαν γενομένην ἐκκλησίαν ἱερὸν ἂν εἴποιμεν θεοῦ τὸ πολλοῦ ἄξιον καὶ οὐ βαναύσῳ κατεσκευασμένον τέχνῃ, ἀλλ' οὐδὲ ἀγύρτου χειρὶ δεδαιδαλμένον, βουλήσει δὲ τοῦ θεοῦ εἰς νεὼν πεποιημένον; 4. οὐ γὰρ νῦν τὸν τόπον, ἀλλὰ τὸ ἄθροισμα τῶν ἐκλεκτῶν ἐκκλησίαν καλῶ. ἀμείνων ὁ νεὼς οὗτος εἰς παραδοχὴν μεγέθους ἀξίας τοῦ θεοῦ.

Translation. But if "the sacred" is understood in two ways—both as God himself and as the structure built in his honor—how shall we not rightly call the church, made through knowledge for the honor of God, sacred to God—of great value, neither constructed by mechanical skill nor embellished by the hand of a vagabond priest, but by the will of God made into a temple? For I call not the place but the assembly of the elect the church. This is the better temple for receiving the great dignities of God.

12b: *Paedagogus* 3.ll [79.3–4, 80.1–4]
[ed. Stählin, GCS 12 (1936)]

79.3. Ἐπὶ δὲ τὴν ἐκκλησίαν ἀκτέον τὴν γυναῖκα καὶ τὸν ἄνδρα ἐστολισμένους κοσμίως, ἀπλάστῳ βαδίσματι, ἐχεμυθίαν ἀσπαζομένους, "ἀγάπην ἀνυπόκριτον" κεκτημένους, ἁγνοὺς τὰ σώματα, ἁγνοὺς τὰς καρδίας, ἐπιτηδείους προσεύξασθαι τῷ θεῷ. 4. Πλεῖον τοῦτο ἐχέτω ἡ γυνή· κεκαλύφθω τὰ πάντα, πλὴν εἰ μὴ οἴκοι τύχοι· σεμνὸν γὰρ τὸ σχῆμα καὶ ἀκατάσκοπον· καὶ οὔποτε αὐτὴ σφαλήσεται πρὸ τῶν ὀμμάτων τὴν αἰδῶ καὶ τὴν ἀμπεχόνην θεμένη οὐδὲ ἄλλον εἰς ὄλισθον ἁμαρτίας ἐκκαλέσεται τὸ πρόσωπον ἀπογυμνουμένη. Τοῦτο γὰρ ὁ λόγος βούλεται, ἐπεὶ πρέπον αὐτῇ ἐγκεκαλυμμένῃ προσεύχεσθαι. . . .

80.1. Τοιούτους δὲ ἐχρῆν παρ' ὅλον τὸν βίον φαίνεσθαι καὶ διαπλάττεσθαι τοὺς Χριστῷ τελουμένους οἵους σφᾶς ἐν ἐκκλησίαις ἐπὶ τὸ σεμνότερον σχηματίζουσιν, καὶ εἶναι, μὴ δοκεῖν εἶναι, τοιούτους, οὕτως πραεῖς, οὕτως εὐλαβεῖς, ἀγαπητικοὺς οὕτως· 2. νυνὶ δὲ οὐκ οἶδ' ὅπως συμμεταβάλλονται τοῖς τόποις καὶ τὰ σχήματα καὶ τοὺς τρόπους, καθάπερ καὶ τοὺς πολύποδας ταῖς πέτραις φασὶν ἐξομοιουμένους, αἷς ἂν προσομιλῶσιν, τοιούτους φαίνεσθαι καὶ τὴν χροιάν. 3. Τὸ γοῦν τῆς συναγωγῆς ἔνθεον μετὰ τὴν ἐνθένδε ἀπαλλαγὴν ἀποθέμενοι τοῖς πολλοῖς ἐξομοιοῦνται, μεθ' ὧν καὶ διαιτῶνται· μᾶλλον δὲ ἐλέγχονται, τὴν ἐπίπλαστον ἀποθέμενοι τῆς σεμνότητος ὑπόκρισιν, οἷοι ὄντες ἐλελήθεσαν· 4. καὶ τὸν περὶ θεοῦ λόγον σεβασάμενοι καταλελοίπασιν ἔνδον οὗ ἤκουσαν, ἔξωθεν δὲ ἄρα μετὰ τῶν ἀθέων ἀλύουσι, κρουμάτων καὶ τερετισμάτων ἐρωτικῶν αὐλῳδίας τε καὶ κρότου καὶ μέθης καὶ παντὸς ἀναπιμπλάμενοι συρφετοῦ· τοῦτο δὴ ᾄδοντες καὶ ἀντᾴδοντες αὐτοὶ οἱ πρόσθεν ἐξυμνοῦντες ἀθανασίαν. . . .

Translation. Women and men should go to church[9] decently attired, with natural step, clinging to silence [cf. 1 Cor 14:33f.], possessing "genuine love" [2 Cor 6:6], being pure in body and pure in heart, and fit to offer prayers to God. All the more, let the woman observe this: let her be completely veiled unless she happens to be at home. For this manner of dress is solemn and inaccessible to view. Never will she err who holds before her eyes modesty and a shawl; nor will she entice another to fall into sin by uncovering her face. For the Logos wishes this, seeing that it is "fitting" for her to pray veiled [cf. 1 Cor 11:13]. . . .

Those dedicated to Christ ought to present and shape themselves throughout life in the same manner as they fashion themselves with propriety in the churches. Thus ought they to be—not just seem to be—meek, pious, and loving. And yet I know not how they change their dress and manners with the place like octopi which, so they say, cling to rocks to which they assimilate themselves appearing the same in color. Indeed, after their departure thence [from the church] laying aside the inspiration of the assembly, these people become like the masses with whom they associate. But rather, in laying aside the artificial guise of solemnity, they prove what they were secretly. Having paid reverence to the word concerning God they leave inside [the church] what they have heard. But outside they foolishly amuse themselves with the atheists, infected with chords and erotic ditties, with flute playing, dancing, drunkenness, and every vulgarity. The very ones who sing thus

9. This is the earliest clear usage of the phrase so as to indicate a recognized place of assembly. The passage continues, moreover, with implicit reflections of going to the building, behavior in the worship setting, and departure from the building.

and respond in song are those who (just) before offered hymns of immortality. . . .

No. 13: Tertullian (fl. ca. 193–ca. 220, Carthage)

13a: *De idololatria* 7.1 (from ca. 196/7)
[ed. Reifferscheid, CCSL 2. 1106 (= CSEL 20)]

[Concerning Christians who work at the craft of sculpting idols.]

7.1. Ad hanc partem zelus fidei perorabit ingemens: Christianum ab idolis in ecclesiam venire, de adversaria officina in domum dei venire, attollere ad deum patrem manus matres idolorum, his manibus adorare, quae foris adversus deum adorantur, eas manus admovere corpori domini, quae daemoniis corpora conferunt?

Translation. On this account the zeal of faith will deliver its laments, crying out, "Does a Christian come from idols into the church, from the workshops of the adversary into the house of God; does he raise to God the Father hands that are the mothers of idols, to worship with those very hands which outside are worshiped in opposition to God; does he lay on the body of the Lord those very hands that confer bodies on demons?"

13b: *Apologeticum* 39 (from ca. 197/8)
[ed. Dekkers, CCSL 1. 150–52].

1. Edam iam nunc ego ipse negotia Christianae factionis, quo minus mala refutaverim, bona ostendam, si etiam veritatem revelaverim.

Corpus sumus de conscientia religionis et disciplinae unitate et spei, foedere. 2. Coimus in coetum et congregationem facimus, ut ad Deum quasi manu facta precationibus ambiamus. Haec vis Deo grata est. Oramus etiam pro imperatoribus, pro ministeriis eorum ac potestatibus, pro statu saeculi, pro rerum quiete, pro mora finis. 3. Coimus ad litterarum divinarum commemorationem, si quid praesentium temporum qualitas aut praemonere cogit aut recognoscere. Certe fidem sanctis vocibus pascimus, spem erigimus, fiduciam figimus, disciplinam praeceptorum nihilominus inculcationibus densamus. 4. Ibidem etiam exhortationes, castigationes et censura divina. Nam et iudicatur magno cum pondere, ut apud certos de Dei conspectu, summumque futuri iudicii praeiudicium est, si quis ita deliquerit, ut a communicatione orationis et conventus et omnis sancti commercii relegetur.

5. Praesident probati quique seniores, honorem istum non pretio, sed testimonio adepti, neque enim pretio ulla res Dei constat. Etiam, si quod arcae genus est, non de honoraria summa quasi redemptae religionis congregatur. Modicam unusquisque stipem menstrua die vel cum velit, et si modo velit et si modo possit, apponit. Nam nemo compellitur, sed sponte confert. 6. Haec quasi deposita pietatis sunt. Quippe non epulis inde nec potaculis nec ingratis voratrinis dispensatur, sed egenis alendis humandisque et pueris ac puellis re ac parentibus destitutis, [iamque] domesticis senibus iam otiosis, item naufragis, et si qui in metallis et si qui in insulis vel in custodiis, dumtaxat ex causa Dei sectae, alumni confessionis suae fiunt.

7. Sed eiusmodi vel maxime dilectionis operatio notam nobis inurit penes quosdam. "Vide, inquiunt, ut invicem se diligant," ipsi enim invicem oderunt, "et ut pro alterutro mori sint parati," ipsi enim ad occidendum alterutrum paratiores. 8. Sed et quod fratrum appellatione censemur, non alias, opinor, insaniunt, quam quod apud ipsos omne sanguinis nomen de affectione simulatum est. Fratres autem etiam vestri sumus iure naturae matris unius, etsi vos parum homines, quia mali fratres. 9. Quanto nunc dignius fratres et dicuntur et habentur, qui unum patrem Deum agnoverunt, qui unum spiritum biberunt sanctitatis, qui de uno utero ignorantiae eiusdem ad unam lucem expaverunt veritatis? 10. Sed eo fortasse minus legitimi existimamur, quia nulla de nostra fraternitate tragoedia exclamat, vel quia ex substantia familiari fratres sumus, quae penes vos fere dirimit fraternitatem. 11. Itaque qui animo animaque miscemur, nihil de rei communicatione dubitamus. Omnia indiscreta sunt apud nos praeter uxores. 12. In isto loco consortium solvimus, in quo solo ceteri homines consortium exercent . . . .

14. Quid ergo mirum, si tanta caritas convivatur? Nam et cenulas nostras, praeterquam sceleris infames, ut prodigas quoque suggillatis. De nobis scilicet Diogenis dictum est: "Megarenses obsonant quasi crastina die morituri, aedificant vero quasi numquam morituri." 15. Sed stipulam quis in alieno oculo facilius perspicit et quam in suo trabem. Tot tribubus et curiis et decuriis ructuantibus acescit aer; Saliis cenaturis creditor erit necessarius; Herculanarum decimarum et polluctorum sumptus tabularii supputabunt; Apaturiis, Dionysiis, mysteriis Atticis cocorum dilectus indicitur; ad fumum

cenae Serapiacae sparteoli excitabuntur. De solo triclinio Christianorum retractatur!

16. Cena nostra de nomine rationem sui ostendit: id vocatur quod dilectio penes Graecos. Quantiscumque sumptibus constet, lucrum est, pietatis nomine facere sumptum, siquidem inopes quosque refrigerio isto iuvamus, non qua penes vos parasiti affectant ad gloriam famulandae libertatis sub auctoramento ventris inter contumelias saginandi, sed qua penes Deum maior est contemplatio mediocrium. 17. Si honesta causa convivii est, reliquum ordinem disciplinae de causa aestimate. Quod sit de religionis officio, nihil vilitatis, nihil immodestiae admittit. Non prius discumbitur quam oratio ad Deum praegustetur; editur quantum esurientes capiunt; bibitur quantum pudicis utile est. 18. Ita saturantur, ut qui meminerint etiam per noctem adorandum Deum sibi esse; ita fabulantur, ut qui sciant Deum audire. Post aquam manualem et lumina, ut quisque de scripturis divinis vel de proprio ingenio potest, provocatur in medium Deo canere: hinc probatur quomodo biberit. Aeque oratio convivium dirimit. 19. Inde disceditur non in catervas caesionum nec in classes discursationum nec in inceptiones lasciviarum, sed ad eandem curam modestiae et pudicitiae, ut qui non tam cenam cenaverint quam disciplinam.

20. Haec coitio Christianorum merito sane illicita, si illicitis par, merito sane damnanda, si non dissimilis damnandis, si quis de ea queritur eo titulo, quo de factionibus querela est. 21. In cuius perniciem aliquando convenimus? Hoc sumus congregati quod et dispersi, hoc universi quod et singuli, neminem laedentes, neminem contristantes. Cum probi, cum boni coeunt, cum pii, cum casti congregantur, non est factio dicenda, sed curia.

Translation. Now I will show you the proceedings with which the Christian association occupies itself so that, while I refute the charge that they are evil, I may show that they are good if indeed I should reveal the truth. We are a society with a common religious feeling, a unity of discipline, and a bond of hope. We unite in (private) company and form a congregation to entreat God in prayer, massing our forces as if to surround him. This show of force is pleasing to God. We pray also for the emperors, for their ministers, and for those in authority, for the security of the world, for peace on earth, and for delay of the end. We meet to read the books of God to see if from anything in the nature of the times it draws together either prediction of the future or recognition (of the present). In any case, with these holy words we feed our faith, we lift up our hope, we confirm our confidence, and if nothing else we reinforce our discipline by inculcation of precepts; from the same source besides there are exhortations, rebukes, and divine censures. For judgment is made with great deliberation, as with the certainty that God sees them, and it is a preview of all future judgment if anyone has so sinned as to be expelled from our communication in prayer, from our assembly, and from our holy fellowship.

The president is one who has been proved from among the older men, an honor reached not for a price, but by testimony (as to his character). For nothing of God is established for a price. Even if there is a kind of treasury, it is not filled by levying entry fees, as if such were a purchase price for religion. For once a month, or whenever he wishes, each person brings a modest coin, if he wishes and is able to do so. Yet no one is compelled; it is offered voluntarily. These funds are, as it were, a deposit of piety. For they are spent neither on banquets nor drinking parties nor on thankless eating houses, but to feed and bury the poor—for boys, and girls as well, who are destitute of possessions or parents, for servants who are old and unemployed, and for those who have suffered shipwreck, and if any are in the mines or in exile or in prison, provided it is for the sake of God's guild, they become pensioners (on account) of their confession.

But such works of love brand us in the eyes of some. They say, "See how they love one another"—for these people hate one another—"and how each is ready to die for the other"—while each of them is readier to kill the other. And because we use the name brothers among ourselves they are indignant for no other reason, I think, than because among them all names of kinship are merely simulations of affection. But we are your brothers as well by virtue of nature (as having) one mother, even though you fall short as men since you are bad as brothers. But how much more fitting is it for those to be both called and treated as brothers who have come to know one father, God, who drink one spirit of holiness, who from the same womb of ignorance have been brought forth to the one light of truth? But perhaps we are thought to be less than legitimate (children) because no tragedy proclaims our fraternity or because we are brothers in the property of the family, whereas among you (property) usually ruins brotherliness. We, therefore, who are joined in mind and in spirit have no reservations concerning the sharing of property.

Among us everything is common property with the exception of our wives. In this point we dissolve the consortium while it is the only point at which other men enter into one. . . .

Why is it so extraordinary then that such loved ones should dine together? Yet you revile our modest dinners, leaving aside (for the moment) the infamous crimes, on account of their extravagance. Obviously, Diogenes must have been speaking of us (when he said), "Megarians feast as if they will die tomorrow and build as if they will never die." But any man sees the mote in another's eye more readily than the beam in his own. With all the belching by tribes and curiae and decurions the air turns sour. When the Salii dine, money lenders are needed; accountants will have to reckon the costs of Herculanean tithes and banquets; at the mysteries of Apaturis, Dionysus, and Attis they have to conscript cooks; at the smoke of Serapis's dinners the firemen must be called out. Only when it concerns the dining room of the Christians is an investigation called for!

Our dinner indicates its nature by means of its name; it is called by the Greek word for love [i.e., *agape*]. Whatever it costs it is profitable to spend in the name of piety if, indeed, by this *refrigerium* we give aid to those in need. In contrast, among you parasites strive passionately for the glory of selling their freedom as slaves in service to the belly to fatten it amid insults, whereas with God there is greater consideration for those of lower estate. If the reason for our common meals is respectable, then evaluate the other practices ordained by our teaching in the light of it. Since it is concerned with the duty of religion, it admits nothing vile, nothing immodest. No one reclines at the table until he has first dined in prayer to God. He eats just enough to satisfy hunger; drinks only so much as is suitable for modesty. Thus, they eat to their fill only insofar as they keep in mind that they must worship God even through the night: they talk as ones who know that God hears. After water for the hands and lights (are brought in) then each one, as he is able, is called forth to the middle to sing to God from the divine scriptures or from his own talents. This proves how much is drunk. Similarly, prayer concludes the banquet. Then, the assembly breaks up, but not in bands for killing, or gangs for disorder, or as instigators of lasciviousness. Rather, (they disperse) for each to pursue self-control and modesty as if they had dined not at table but in instruction.

This assembly of the Christians may properly be called illegal, if indeed it is like the illegal gatherings; it may properly be condemned, if indeed it is not dissimilar to outlawed association, (that is to say) if anyone brings charges against it on the same grounds by which complaints are leveled against the factious clubs. To whose injury have we ever come together? This is how we are when assembled and when apart, all together and singly; we harm no one, afflict no one. When decent and good people assemble together, when the pious and the chaste congregate, it should not be called a faction, but a *curia.*

13c: *De baptismo* 20.5 (from ca. 198–203)
[ed. E. Evans (London, 1964)]

20.5. igitur benedicti, quos gratia dei expectat, cum de illo sanctissimo lavacro novi natalis ascenditis et primas manus apud matrem cum fratribus aperitis, petite de patre, petite de domino, peculia gratiae, distributiones charismatum subiacere.

Translation. You, therefore, O blessed ones, upon whom the grace of God waits, when you ascend from the most holy washing of the new birth and for the first time in your mother's (house) spread out your hands together with your brothers, petition the Father, petition the Lord to give personal deposits of grace, grants of spiritual power.

13d: *De fuga in persecutione* 3.2; 14.1 (from ca. 208/9)
[ed. Thierry, CCSL 2. 1139, 1155]

3.2. Haec erunt ignea iacula diaboli, per quae fidei ustio et conflatio administratur, ex Dei tamen voluntate. De isto quis dubitare possit ignoro, nisi plane frivola et frigida fides, deprehendens eos, qui timide conveniunt in ecclesiam. Dicitis enim: [inquit] "quoniam incondite convenimus et simul convenimus et complures concurrimus in ecclesiam, quaerimur a nationibus et timemus, ne turbentur nationes."

. . .

14.1. "Sed quomodo colligemus," inquis, "quomodo dominica sollemnia celebrabimus?" Utique quomodo et apostoli, fide, non pecunia tuti, quae fides si montem transferre potest, multo magis militem. Esto sapientia, non praemio cautus. Neque enim statim et a populo eris tutus, si officia militaria redemeris. Una ergo tibi et fides et sapientia ad tutelam opus est, quibus non adhibitis et redemptionem tuam potes perdere, adhibitis autem redemptionem desiderare.

Postremo si colligere interdiu non potes, habes noctem, luce Christi luminosa adversus eam. Non potes discurrere per singulos, si tibi est in tribus ecclesia? Melius est turbas tuas aliquando non videas, quam addicas. . . .

Translation. 3.2. These [persecutions] will be the fiery darts of the devil, by which branding and burning are administered to the faith; however, (they are) by the will of God. Concerning these matters I do not know who could have doubts, except, of course, those of whom a trivial and frigid faith takes hold, who with fear assemble in the church. For you say, "Since we assemble without order and do so at the same time and in large number we rush together into the church, we will arouse investigation from the heathen and we are afraid, lest they should be disturbed."

. . .

14.1. "But how shall we assemble together," you say, "and how shall we celebrate the solemn feast of the Lord?" Well, to be sure, just as the apostles did, being protected not by a bribe [cf. chap. 13], but by faith, which, if it can remove a mountain, how much more (will it remove) a soldier. Let wisdom be your security, not a bribe. For you will not have complete protection from the people, even if you buy off the military's allegiance. For your guardianship, therefore, the only thing necessary is faith and wisdom; if you do not make use of these things, then the deliverance that you purchased will be wasted. If you make (the proper) use of them, however, you will not need such deliverance.

Finally, then, if you cannot assemble by day, you have the night illumined against its darkness by the light of Christ. If you are not able to come and go (to church) one at a time, then be a church among yourselves in groups of three. It is better for you at times not to see your crowds, than to sell yourself (into bondage of tribute).

13e: *De pudicitia* 3.4–5; 4.5; 13.7 (from ca. 210/11)
[ed. Dekkers, CCSL 2. 1286, 1287, 1304]

3.4. Ad dominum enim remissa et illi exinde prostrata, hoc ipso magis operabitur veniam, quod eam a solo Deo exorat, quod delicto sua humanam pacem sufficere non credit, quod ecclesiae mavult erubescere quam communicare. 5. Adsistit enim pro foribus eius et de notae suae exemplo ceteros admonet et lacrimas fratrum sibi quoque advocat et redit plus utique negotiata, compassionem scilicet quam communicationem.

. . .

4.5. Reliquas autem libidinum furias impias et in corpora et in sexus ultra iura naturae non modo limine, verum omni ecclesiae tecto submovemus, quia non sunt delicta, sed monstra.

. . .

13.7. Et tu quidem paenitentiam moechi ad exorandam fraternitatem in ecclesiam inducens conciliciatum et concineratum cum dedecore et horrore compositum prosternis in medium ante viduas, ante presbyteros, omnium lacrimas suadentem, omnium vestigia lambentem, omnium genua detinentem, inque eum hominis exitum quantis potes misericordiae inlecebris bonus pastor et benedictus papa contionaris et in parabola ovis capras tuas quaeris?

Translation. 3.4–5. [Concerning the necessity of repentance and the fact that the Lord alone pardons sins.] For (repentance), having been remitted to the Lord and consequently lying prostrate before him, will by this very fact be all the more effectual in acquiring pardon, because it obtains the pardon by entreaty from God alone, because it knows that human peace is not sufficient for its guilt, and because it prefers to blush in shame before the church rather than to communicate with it. For before the doors of the church it stands and admonishes others by example of its mark of disgrace; at the same time it calls forth the tears of the brothers and returns with a yet more profitable transaction than their communion, that is their compassion. . . .

4.5. [Concerning sexual immorality, one of the mortal sins.] But in matters concerning the other passions of lust, which are impieties both to the bodies and to the sexes and which are utterly beyond the laws of nature, we drive (the offenders) away not only from the threshold (of the assembly) but in fact from the shelter of the entire church building,[10] since these are not only sins but also monstrosities. . . .

10. For *non modo limine . . . submovemus*, compare *De pud.* 13.21: *extra ecclesiam proiectis*.

13.7. [Concerning "moderate indulgence" exercised by the bishop in the granting of peace.] Why do you [the bishop] in reconciling the penitent adulterer lead him into the church to entreat the brethren and covered with ashes, a combination of disgrace and horror, prostrate him in the midst (of the church)[11] before the widows, before the presbyters suing for the tears of all, wetting the feet of all with his tears, clasping the knees of all? And do you, good shepherd and blessed father, in bringing to its conclusion the case of this man address the assembly with all the allurements you are able, and do you, after the parable of the (lost) ewe, go in search of your goats? . . .

No. 14: Hippolytus, Presbyter and Schismatic Bishop at Rome (fl. ca. 217–235)

14a: *Commentary on Daniel* 1.20 [ed. G. Bardy and M. Lefèvre, SC 14]
[An excursus on the story of Susannah]

20.1 Τούτων οὖν τῶν ῥημάτων ἀκούσασα ἡ μακαρία Σωσάννα κατενύγη τὴν καρδίαν καὶ ἔφραξε τὸ στόμα, μὴ βουλομένη μιανθῆναι ὑπὸ ἀνόμων πρεσβυτέρων. 2. Ἔστι δὲ καὶ καταλαβέσθαι ἀληθῶς τὸ συμβὰν ἐπὶ τῇ Σωσάννῃ. Τοῦτο γὰρ νῦν καὶ ἐπὶ τῇ ἐκκλησίᾳ εὕροις πληρούμενον. 3. Ἡνίκα γὰρ οἱ δύο λαοὶ συμφωνήσουσι διαφθεῖραί τινας τῶν ἁγίων, "παρατηροῦνται ἡμέραν εὐθῆ" καὶ ἐπεισελθόντες εἰς τὸν οἶκον τοῦ θεοῦ προσευχομένων ἐκεῖ πάντων καὶ τὸν θεὸν ὑμνούντων, ἐπιλαβόμενοι ἕλκουσί τινας καὶ κρατοῦσι λέγοντες· δεῦτε, συγκατάθεσθε ἡμῖν καὶ τοὺς θεοὺς θρησκεύσατε, "εἰ δὲ μή, καταμαρτυρήσομεν" καθ' ὑμῶν. Τούτων δὲ μὴ βουλομένων προσάγουσιν αὐτοὺς πρὸς τὸ βῆμα καὶ κατηγοροῦσιν ὡς ἐναντία τοῦ δόγματος Καίσαρος πράσσοντας καὶ θανάτῳ κατακρίνονται.

Translation. Thus, having heard these words, the blessed Susanna was cut to the heart and she clenched her mouth, refusing to be defiled by the impious elders. And it is possible (for us) also to understand truly the situation that befell Susanna; for you may find this also coming to fulfillment now in

11. Concerning the acts of self-abasement in the congregational setting connected with the practice of *exomologesis* (Gk: ἐξομολόγησις) or public penitential discipline, see also *De poenitentiam* 9.

the church. For when the two peoples [i.e., the pagans and the Jews; cf. 1.21.2] make an agreement to destroy any of the saints they customarily "watch for a convenient day" [*Sus.* 15].[12] They come into the house of God while all those there are praying and singing hymns to God, and overwhelming them they drag some away and hold them saying, "Come now, give in to us and worship the gods! 'And if you do not we will testify against you' [*Sus.* 21]." And when they do not consent they bring them to the tribunal and charge that they have acted contrary to the decrees of Caesar, and they are condemned to death.

14b: *The Apostolic Tradition* 16.1–2; 18; 21.18–20; 35.3

[Because proposed reconstructions of the original Greek text remain hypothetical, we will print here only the Latin text of the Verona MS. as edited by B. Botte, SC 11, 2nd edition (1968). The English translation will be that of Gregory Dix, *The Treatise on the Apostolic Tradition of St. Hippolytus of Rome* (London, 1968). It will incorporate his notations and conventions for indicating the lines of the textual tradition from the Greek, Sahidic, Syriac, Arabic, and Ethiopic sources.[13] Numbering is also according to Dix.]

---

12. Verse references are to the text of *Susannah*, which was included as part of the Greek text of Daniel as chap. 13. The citations are from the Greek version of Theodotion, which is closest to the text used by Hippolytus. The Theodotion text is that printed by in Rahlfs's ed. of the *Septuagint* along with the shorter Septuagint text.

13. The following symbols are used by Dix in the English text. I have indicated the position of these relative to the Latin text using the same symbols, where appropriate. In some cases it will be necessary to print two versions of the text in order to indicate the differences.

< > = Words or phrases having no authority from any version but introduced into the English translation to assist the sense.

[ ] = Words or phrases having authority from one or more versions but probably forming no part of the original Greek.

⌜ ⌝ = Words or phrases having authority from one or more versions, but not all, yet probably forming part of the original Greek.

( ) = Greek words in ( ) within the English text are found transliterated in the Sahidic and/or Bohairic versions. They usually, but not invariably, come from Hippolytus's own Greek text.

Italics = Italicized words are less certain.

16 (=15, SC). 1. Qui autem adducuntur noviter ad audiendum verbum, adducantur primum coram doctores ⸢ ⸣ priusquam omnis populus intret, 2. et interrogentur de causa (αἰτία) propter quam accedunt ad fidem. Et dent testimonium super eos illi qui adduxerunt eos an sit eis virtus ad audiendum verbum.

Translation. 1. Those who come forward for the first time to hear the word shall first be brought to the teachers ⸢at the house⸣[14] before all the people (λαός) come in. 2. And let them be examined as to the reason (αἰτία) why they have come forward ⸢to the faith⸣ (πίστις). And (δέ) those who bring them shall bear witness for them whether they are able to hear.

18. Quando (ὅταν) doctor cessavit instructionem dare (κατηχεῖσθαι), catechumeni orent seorsum, separati a fidelibus, et mulieres stent orantes in aliquo loco in ecclesia seorsum, sive mulieres fideles sive mulieres catechumenae. Cum autem desierint orare, non dabunt pacem (εἰρήνη); nondum enim osculum eorum sanctum est. Fideles vero salutent (ἀσπάζεσθαι) invicem, viri cum viris et mulieres cum mulieribus; viri autem non salutabunt (ἀσπάζεσθαι) mulieres. Mulieres autem omnes operiant capita sua pallio (πάλλιον): sed non tantum per genus (εἶδος) lini, non enim est velum (κάλυμμα).

Translation. 1. Each time (ὅταν) the teacher finishes his instruction (καθηγεῖσθαι, *sic*) let the catechumens (κατ.) pray by themselves apart from the faithful (πιστός).

2. And let the women stand in the assembly (ἐκκλησία) by themselves [*apart from the men*], both (εἴτε) the baptized women (πιστός) and (εἴτε) the women catechumens (κατ.).

3. But (δέ) after the prayer is finished the catechumens (κατ.) shall not give the kiss of peace (εἰρήνη), for (γάρ) their kiss is not yet pure.

4. But (δέ) the baptized (πιστός) shall embrace (ἀσπάζεσθαι) one another, men with men and women with women. But (δέ) let not men embrace (ἀσπ.) women.

5. Moreover (δέ) let all the women have their heads veiled with a scarf

14. The phrase "at the house" is attested only in the Syriac text of the *Testamentum domini* (ca. fifth century), but Dix thinks it is from the Greek original of Hippolytus.

(πάλλιον) but (ἀλλά) not with the type <of veil> (εἶδος) of linen only, for that is not a <*sufficient*> covering (κάλυμμα).

21.18–20[15]

a.	b.
Dicat ergo qui bap-	Et iterum (πάλιν)
tizatur: Credo.	dicat: Credo.
Et sic tertia vice	
baptizetur.	
Et postea cum ascend-	Et ascendat ex aqua
erit, ungueatur a	et ungat eum pres-
praesbytero de illo	byter oleo gratiarum
oleo quod sanctifi-	actionis (εὐχαριστία)
catum est dicente:	dicens: Ungo te oleo
Ungueo te oleo sancto	sancto, in nomine Iesu
in nomine Ie(s)u	Christi. Hoc modo
Chr(ist)i. Et ita	ceteros per unuṃ ungat
singuli detergentes	et vestiat hoc modo
se induantur et	ceteros, et ingredian-
postea in ecclesia	tur ecclesiam
ingrediantur.	(ἐκκλησία).

Translation

18. And he who is being baptized shall say: I believe. And so let him ⌜baptize him⌝ the third time.

19. And afterwards when he comes up [*from the water*] he shall be anointed by the presbyter with the Oil of Thanksgiving (εὐχ.) saying: "I anoint thee with holy oil in the Name of Jesus Christ."

20. And ⌜so⌝ each one drying himself [*with a towel*] they shall ⌜now⌝ put on their clothes, ⌜and after this let them be together in the assembly⌝ (ἐκκλησία).[16]

---

15. Column *a* represents the Latin text of the Verona fragments: Column *b*, a composite from the Bohairic, Arabic, and Ethiopic versions, with the Bohairic taking precedence.

16. For the final phrase, as reflected in the translation above, Dix takes the unique reading of the Syriac *Testamentum domini* as the more original. However, the reading of the Bohairic: "Let them go into the church" (ⲟⲩⲟϩ ⲙⲁⲣⲟⲩϣⲉ ⲉϧⲟⲩⲛ ⲉϯⲉⲕⲕⲗⲏ-

35.3[17]

a.	b.
Si qua autem per verbum catecizatio fit, praeponat hoc ut pergat et audiat verbum d(e)i ad confortationem animae suae. Festinet autem et ad ecclesiam, ubi floret sp(iritu)s.	*Si autem verbum instructionis (κατήχησις) fit, praeponant pergere et audire verbum dei, ut confortent animam (ψυχή) suam.* Solliciti sint (σπουδάζειν) autem ire ad ecclesiam, ubi floret spiritus.

Translation. 3. *If there is a teacher there, let none of you be late in arriving at the assembly (ἐκκλησία) ⸢at the place⸣ where they give instruction (καθηγεῖσθαι). Then (τότε) ⸢indeed⸣ it shall be given to him who speaks to utter things which thou thinkest not <*to hear*> and thou shalt be profited (ὠφελεῖσθαι) by the things that the Holy Spirit (πνεῦμα) will give to thee by him who instructs (καθηγεῖσθαι) and so thy faith (πίστις) will be established by what thou hearest. And (δέ) further he shall tell thee there what thou oughtest to do in thine own house.* And therefore let each one be careful (σπουδάζειν, lit., *hasten, be zealous*) to go to the assembly (ἐκκλησία), to the place where the Holy Spirit abounds.

ⲥⲓⲁ) ought to be given more attention since it reflects a situation of spatial differentiation of baptism apart from the assembly areas. On the authority of the Bohairic, see also n. 17 below.

17. Column *a* again represents the Latin text of the Verona fragments; Column *b*, a composite from the Sahidic, Arabic, and Ethiopic, with the Sahidic taking precedence. Dix's translation gives more credence to the Bohairic version in establishing a longer text (*-*) for the original. According to Dix (p. 85), the Latin Version of §35 is actually a truncated text, which he places at the beginning of §32.

No. 15: Origen, (fl. Alexandria, ca. 203–254)
De oratione 31.5–6 (from ca. 233/34)
[ed. Koetschau, GCS 3 (1899)]

5. ἔχει δέ τι ἐπίχαρι εἰς ὠφέλειαν τόπος εὐχῆς, τὸ χωρίον τῆς ἐπὶ τὸ αὐτὸ τῶν πιστευόντων συνελεύσεως, ὡς εἰκὸς, καὶ ἀγγελικῶν δυνάμεων ἐφισταμένων τοῖς ἀθροίσμασι τῶν πιστευόντων καὶ αὐτοῦ τοῦ κυρίου καὶ σωτῆρος ἡμῶν δυνάμεως ἤδη δὲ καὶ πνευμάτων ἁγίων, οἶμαι δὲ ὅτι καὶ προκεκοιμημένων, σαφὲς δὲ ὅτι καὶ ἐν τῷ βίῳ περιόντων, εἰ καὶ τὸ πῶς οὐκ εὐχερὲς εἰπεῖν. καὶ περὶ μὲν ἀγγέλων . . . εἰκός ἐστι, πλειόνων συνεληλυθότων γνησίως εἰς δόξαν Χριστοῦ, "παρεμβαλεῖν" τὸν ἑκάστου "ἄγγελον" τὸν "κύκλῳ" ἑκάστου "τῶν φοβουμένων" μετὰ τούτου τοῦ ἀνδρὸς. ὃν φρουρεῖν καὶ οἰκονομεῖν πεπίστευται· ὥστ᾽ ἆιναι ἐπὶ τῶν ἁγίων συναθροιζομένων διπλῆν ἐκκλησίαν, τὴν μὲν ἀνθρώπων τὴν δὲ ἀγγέλων. . . . περὶ δὲ τῆς δυνάμεως τοῦ κυρίου συμπαρούσης τῇ ἐκκλησίᾳ . . . εἰ ὁ ἔτι τὸ σῶμα περικείμενος Παῦλος συνάρασθαι νενόμικε τῷ ἑαυτοῦ πνεύματι ἐν τῇ Κορίνθῳ, οὐκ ἀπογνωστέον οὕτω καὶ τοὺς ἐξεληλυθότας μακαρίους φθάνειν τῷ πνεύματι τάχα μᾶλλον τοῦ ὄντος ἐν τῷ σώματι ἐπὶ τὰς ἐκκλησίας· διόπερ οὐ καταφρονητέον τῶν ἐν αὐταῖς εὐχῶν, ὡς ἐξαίρετόν τι ἐχουσῶν τῷ γνησίως συνερχομένῳ αὐτῶν.

6. ὥσπερ δὲ δύναμις Ἰησοῦ καὶ τὸ πνεῦμα Παύλου καὶ τῶν ὁμοίων καὶ οἱ παρεμβάλλοντες ἑκάστου τῶν ἁγίων "κύκλῳ" ἄγγελοι κυρίου συνοδεύουσι καὶ συνέρχονται τοῖς γνησίως συναθροιζομένοις, οὕτω στοχαστέον μή ποτε, ἐὰν ἁγίου ἀγγέλου ἀνάξιός τις . . . ὅτι ὁ τοιοῦτος, σπανίων μὲν τῶν ὁμοίων αὐτῷ τυγχανόντων, οὐκ ἐπὶ πολὺ λήσεται τῆς τῶν ἀγγέλων προνοίας, ὑπηρεσίᾳ τοῦ θείου βουλήματος, ἐπισκοποῦντος τὴν ἐκκλησίαν, φερούσης εἰς γνῶσιν τῶν πολλῶν τοῦ τοιούτου τὰ πταίσματα· ἐὰν δὲ πλῆθος γενόμενοι οἱ τοιοῦτοι καθ᾽ ἑταιρείας ἀνθρωπικὰς καὶ σωματικώτερόν τι πραγματευόμενοι συνέρχωνται, οὐκ ἐπισκοπηθήσονται. . . .

Translation. [After asserting that every place is suitable for prayer (31.4), he continues:] But the place of prayer, which has a certain special charm for (our) benefit, is the spot where believers come together in one place, since it is likely that there stand near the assembly of the believers both the powers of the angels of our Lord and savior himself along with that of the spirits of the saints—as I think both of those who have already fallen asleep and, of course, of those who are still alive, even though it is not easy to say how. Now, concerning the angels . . . it is likely that, when a great number of people come together genuinely for the glory of Christ, each one's "angel," which "encircles" each of "those who fear (the Lord), encamps" [Ps 33:8, LXX (=34:7)] with this man, whom he is believed to guard and order. As a result, when the saints are gathered together there is a double church, one of men and the other of angels. . . . But concerning the powers of the Lord which are present in the church . . . if Paul, while yet clothed in the body, thought that he had joined in prayer with the Corinthians by means of his spirit, then we must not reject the opinion that the blessed ones who have departed thus come to the churches in the spirit more quickly than someone who is still in the body. Therefore, let no one disdain the prayers in the churches, since they possess a certain special quality for the one who assembles there genuinely.

6. But just as the power of Jesus, the spirit of Paul and the like, and the angels of the Lord, who encamp around each of the saints whom they "encircle," accompany and keep fellowship with those who assemble together genuinely, we must also maintain that, if someone is not worthy of (his) holy angel . . . , then such a person, even if there are not many like him, will not long escape the providential care of the angels, which care, in service to the divine will, oversees the church and brings their transgressions to the knowledge of the many. But if such people become the majority, assembling as human associations (ἑταιρεία) for conducting more corporeal matters, then they are not watched over (by the angels). . . .

No. 16: Cyprian, Bishop of Carthage (ca. 249–258)

16a: *Epistle* 39.4.1, 5.2 (from 250)
[ed. Hartel, CSEL 3; following the text of Bayard, SC (= *Ep.* 34 in *PL* 4)]

[To the church of Carthage concerning the ordination of the confessor Celerinus to the office of reader.]

4.1. Hunc ad nos, fratres dilectissimi, cum tanta Domini dignatione venientem, testimonio et miraculo eius ipsius qui se persecutus fuerat inlustrem, quid aliud quam super pulpitum id est super tribunal ecclesiae oportebat inponi, ut, loci altioris celsitate subnixus et plebi universae pro honoris sui claritate conspicuus, legat praecepta et evangelium Domini quae fortiter ac fideliter sequitur? Vox Dominum confessa in his cottidie quae Dominus locutus est audiatur. . . .

. . .

5.2. Hos tamen lectores interim constitutos sciatis, quia oportebat lucernam super candelabrum poni unde omnibus luceat, et gloriosos vultus in loco altiore constitui, ubi ab omni circumstante conspecti incitamentum gloriae videntibus praebeant. Ceterum presbyterii honorem designasse nos illis iam sciatis, ut et sportulis idem cum presbyteris honorentur et divisiones mensurnas aequatis quantitatibus partiantur, sessuri nobiscum provectis et corroboratis annis suis. . . .

Translation. 4.1. When this man [Celerinus] came to us, beloved brethren, with such honor of the Lord [i.e., his status as confessor], being honored even with the testimony and amazement of the very men by whom he had been persecuted, what else was there to do than to place him upon the pulpit,[18] that is, upon the tribunal of the church, so that, propped up in the place of highest elevation and conspicuous to the entire congregation for the fame of his honor, he may read the precepts and gospels of the Lord which he follows with such courage and faith? Let the voice that has confessed the Lord be heard daily concerning those things which the Lord spoke. . . .

5.2. Know, therefore, that these men [Celerinus and Aurelius][19] have for the present been ordained as readers; since it would be fitting for the lamp to

18. *pulpitum*. Compare the wording of *Ep*. 38.2 (in *PL* 4 = *Ep*. 32), where the phrase *ad pulpitum venire* ("to advance or ascend to the pulpit") is used as a technical term for the act of ordination. It undoubtedly derives from liturgical and ordination practices in the particular physical circumstances of the church building at Carthage; it assumes an elevated platform or dais construction (Latin *tribunal*). Consistent with the usage here, the Latin terms *pulpitum* and *tribunal* were virtually synonymous, with the latter simply denoting the formal platform (and hence the administrative office) of a public magistrate. Compare the attitude toward such edifices in the assembly in No. 20a below (the case of Paul of Samosata in the church at Antioch).

19. For Celerinus and Aurelius, see *Ep*. 27 and 38, cf. *Epp*. 21-22.

be placed upon the lampstand where it may give light to all [cf. Matt 5:15, Vulgate], I have established their glorious faces in the higher place where, being observed by all those who stand around them, they may give an incitement of glory to all who see. Moreover, know that we have already designated the honor of the presbytery for them, that they may be honored with the same gifts as the presbyters and be recipients of the monthly divisions in equal proportion, to sit with us[20] regularly in their advanced and strengthened years. . . .

16b: *De lapsis* 2 (from 251)
[ed. Bevenot, OECT]

Adest militum Christi cohors candida, qui persecutionis urgentis ferociam turbulentam stabili congressione fregerunt, parati ad patientiam carceris, armati ad tolerantiam mortis. Repugnastis fortiter saeculo, spectaculum gloriosum praebuistis Deo, secuturis fratribus fuistis exemplo. . . . Quam vos laeto sinu excipit mater ecclesia de proelio revertentes. Quam beata, quam gaudens portas suas aperit, ut adunatis agminibus intretis de hoste prostrato tropaea referentes. . . .

Translation. They [the confessors, upon returning from prison] are the shining cohort of the army of Christ, who by stable association beat back the turbulent ferocity of the pressing persecutions, prepared to be patient in prison and armed to endure death. Bravely you repulsed the attack of the world, offering to God a glorious spectacle and bidding the brethren to follow by example. . . . With what joy in (her) heart does mother church welcome you returning from the fray. With what happiness, what rejoicing does she open (her) doors for you to enter, marching in close order bearing the trophies of the vanquished enemy. . . .

---

20. In addition to the elevated platform, there are two further implicit reflections within this text as to the physical layout of Cyprian's church building at Carthage. The *pulpitum* apparently stood somewhere in the midst of the assembly area, where the people would have stood around it, while the presbytery or clergy would have been seated in a separate area, presumably at the front or side of the hall. This is the earliest clear reference to such a segregated area for the clergy. See also *Ep*. 59.18.1 (No. 16d), n. 24, below, and the Syriac *Didascalia* 12 (No. 18) below.

16c: *De ecclesiae catholicae unitate* 6, 8, 12 (from 251)
[ed. Hartel, CSEL 3 (after text of Bevenot, OECT)]

6. Adulterari non potest sponsa Christi, incorrupta est et pudica: unam domum novit, unius cubiculi sanctitatem casto pudore custodit. Haec nos Deo servat, haec filios regno quos generavit adsignat. Quisque ab ecclesia segregatus adulterae iungitur, a promissis ecclesiae separatur, nec perveniet ad Christi praemia qui relinquit ecclesiam Christi: alienus est, profanus est, hostis est. Habere iam non potest Deum patrem qui ecclesiam non habet matrem. Si potuit evadere quisque extra arcam Noe fuit, et qui extra ecclesiam foris fuerit evadet. Monet Dominus et dicit: "Qui non est mecum adversus me est, et qui non mecum colligit spargit." Qui pacem Christi et concordiam rumpit, adversus Christum facit; qui alibi praeter ecclesiam colligit, Christi ecclesiam spargit. . . .

Translation. The bride of Christ cannot be defiled. She is unspoiled and modest; she knows one home and in the sanctity of one bedroom she remains in complete chastity. She is the one who preserves us for God; she is the one who seals for the kingdom the children whom she has borne. Whoever separates (himself) from the church joins (himself) to an adulteress and cuts (himself) off from the promises of the church; he who relinquishes the church of Christ will not attain to the rewards of Christ: he is an alien, profane, an enemy. He can no longer have God for his father who does not have the church for his mother. If it was possible for anyone outside the ark of Noah to escape, then will he escape who is outside the church. For the Lord warns saying, "He who is not with me is against me, and he that does not assemble with me scatters" [Matt 12:30]. He who breaks the peace and harmony of Christ is against Christ; he who assembles a church anywhere else scatters the church of Christ. . . .

. . .

8. . . . Stare tu et vivere putas posse de ecclesia recedentem, sedes sibi alias et diversa domicilia condentem, cum dictum sit ei [*var. leg.,* Raab] in qua praeformabatur ecclesia: "Patrem tuum et matrem tuam et fratres tuos et totam domum patris tui colliges ad te ipsam in domum tuam: et erit, omnis qui exierit ostium domus tuae foras, reus sibi erit"; item sacramentum Paschae nihil aliud in Exodi lege contineat quam ut agnus, qui in figura

Christi occiditur, in domo una edatur? Loquitur Deus dicens: "In domo una comedetur: non eicietis de domo carnem foras." Caro Christi et sanctum Domini eici foras non potest, nec alia ulla credentibus praeter unam ecclesiam domus est. Hanc domum, hoc unianimitatis hospitium designat et nuntiat Spiritus sanctus in Psalmis, dicens: "Deus qui inhabitare facit unianimes in domo." In domo Dei, in ecclesia Christi unianimes habitant, concordes et simplices perseverant.

Translation. Do you think that a person can stand and live who has withdrawn from the church, who has established for himself a new place and a different home, when it was said to her [Rahab][21] in whom the church was prefigured: "Gather to yourself in your house your father and your mother and your brothers and all your father's house, and whoever shall pass outside through the door of your house, his blood shall be on his own head" [Josh 2:18f]? In the same way the sacrament of the Pascha, as set out in Exodus, comprises nothing else than that the lamb, which is slain as a figure of Christ, be eaten in one house. God speaks, saying, "In one house shall it be eaten; you shall not cast its flesh outside the house" [Exod 12:46]. The flesh of Christ, the holy (body) of the Lord, cannot be cast outside, nor is there any other house for the believers except the one church. This house, this chamber of harmony, the Holy Spirit designated and announced in the Psalms saying, "God who makes those who are of one mind to dwell in the house" [Ps 68(67):6]. In the house of God, in the church of Christ where those of one mind dwell, the harmonious and the simple continue.

12. Nec se quidam vana interpretatione decipiant quod dixerit Dominus: "Ubicumque fuerint duo aut tres collecti in nomine meo, ego cum eis sum." Corruptores evangelii adque interpretes falsi extrema ponunt et superiora praetereunt, partis memores et partem subdole conprimentes; ut ipsi ab ecclesia scissi sunt, ita capituli unius sententiam scindunt. Dominus enim, cum discipulis suis unianimitatem suaderet et pacem, . . . unianimitatem prius posuit, concordiam pacis ante praemisit, ut conveniat nobis fideliter et firmiter docuit. Quomodo autem potest ei cum aliquo convenire, cui cum corpore ipsius ecclesiae et cum universa fraternitate non convenit? Quo-

21. Based on the reference to the text of Josh 2:18, some of the manuscripts insert the name of Rahab here.

modo possunt duo aut tres in nomine Christi colligi, quos constet a Christo et ab eius evangelio separari? Non enim nos ab illis, sed illi a nobis recesserunt et, cum haeresis et schismata postmodum nata sint dum conventicula sibi diversa constituunt, veritatis caput adque originem reliquerunt.

Translation. Nor should certain ones deceive themselves with vain interpretations of what the Lord said: "Wherever two or three are gathered together in my name, I am with them" [Matt 18:20]. Corruptors and false interpreters of the Gospel cite the end and omit the beginning, remembering part and slyly suppressing the rest; just as they have cut themselves off from the church, they cut up the meaning of this one passage. For the Lord was urging harmony and peace among his disciples . . . ; he put harmony first and set the concord of peace at the head so that we should agree together, as he taught, with fidelity and steadfastness. But how is it possible for this one to agree with anyone when he does not even meet with the body of the church itself and with the universal fraternity? How can two or three gather together in Christ's name, when it is well known that they have been separated from Christ and his gospel? For it is not we who have withdrawn from them, but they from us, since by establishing for themselves different conventicles they have already given birth to heresies and schisms, and they have relinquished the source and origin of the realities.[22] . . .

16d: *Epistle* 59.14.1; 16; 18.1 (from 252)
[ed. Hartel, CSEL (after text of Bayard, SC [= *Ep*. 54 in *PL* 4])]

[To Cornelius, bishop of Rome, concerning the schismatics Fortunatus and Felicissimus.]

14.1. Quibus etiam satis non fuit ab evangelio recessisse, spem lapsis satisfactionis et paenitentiae sustulisse, fraudibus involutos vel adulteriis commaculatos vel sacrificiorum funesta contagione pollutos, ne Deum rogarent, ne in ecclesia exomologesin criminum facerent, ab omni et sensu et

22. On the "realities" (Latin *veritates*), see *De unitate* 3–4, where the term is discussed in relation to the *una ecclesia et una cathedra* ("one church and one throne") of Peter as established in the episcopal church of Carthage, Cyprian's church. On the schismatic "conventicles," compare *De unitate* 17, which refers to the establishment of a "different altar" and celebration of a "profane" Eucharist.

fructu paenitentiae removisse, foris sibi extra ecclesiam et contra ecclesiam constituisse conventiculum perditae factionis, quo male sibi consciorum et Deum rogare ac satisfacere nolentium caterva conflueret.

Translation. For them [the schismatics] it was not enough to withdraw from the gospel, to remove the hope of satisfaction and penance from the lapsed, to have removed both the sense and fruit of repentance from all those who have been involved in fraud or stained with adultery or polluted with the deadly contagion of sacrifice so that these neither call on God nor perform *exomologesis*[23] for their crimes before the church, and to have established for themselves elsewhere (lit., outside), outside the church and against it, conventicles of a perditious faction, to which has flocked a band of those who have consented in the evil with them and who are unwilling to call on God and make satisfaction (to the church). . . .

. . .

16.1. De istis vero quid dicam qui nunc ad te cum Felicissimo omnium criminum reo navigaverunt legati a Fortunato pseudoepiscopo missi, tam falsas ad te litteras adferentes quam est et ipse cuius litteras ferunt falsus, quam est eis peccatorum multiplex conscientia, quam execrabilis vita, quam turpis, ut etsi in ecclesia essent, eici tales de ecclesia debuissent? 2. Denique quia conscientiam suam norunt, nec audent venire aut ad ecclesiae limen accedere, sed foris per provinciam circumveniendis fratribus et spoliandis pererrant, et omnibus iam satis noti adque undique pro suis facinoribus exclusi, illuc etiam ad vos navigant. Neque enim potest illis frons esse ad nos accedendi aut apud nos consistendi, cum sint acerbissima et gravissima crimina quae eis a fratribus ingerantur. 3. Si iudicium nostrum voluerint experiri veniant. Denique si qua illis excusatio et defensio potest esse, videamus quem habeant satisfactionis suae sensum, quem adferant paenitentiae fructum. Nec ecclesia istic cuiquam cluditur nec episcopus alicui denegatur. Patientia et facilitas et humanitas nostra venientibus praesto est. Opto omnes in ecclesiam regredi, opto universos conmilitones nostros intra Christi castra et Dei patris domicilia concludi. Remitto omnia, multa dissimulo studio et voto colligendae fraternitatis. Etiam quae in Deum commissa sunt non pleno iudicio religionis examino. Delictis plus quam quod oportet remittendis

23. For this term, denoting the public penitential acts, see n. 11 above.

paene ipse delinquo. Amplector prompta et plena dilectione cum paenitentia revertentes, peccatum suum satisfactione humili et simplici confitentes.

Translation. But what should I say concerning these schismatics, who have sailed to you with Felicissimus, a man guilty of all crimes, as legates sent by the false bishop Fortunatus, and who bring you false letters—letters that are false inasmuch as he whose letters they bear is false, that are as multitudinous with sins as their consciences, that are as execrable as their lives, that are as base (as their bearers), so that, while these (schismatics) were in the church they should have been cast out of the church. 2. Furthermore, since they know their own conscience, they do not dare to come to or enter upon the threshold of the church. Outside, instead, they wander through the province defrauding and despoiling the brethren, but now sufficiently known to all and everywhere excluded on account of their criminal acts they have even sailed there to you. For they cannot be so impudent as to approach or take their stand with us, since the crimes that are alleged against them by the brethren are so bitter and serious. 3. If they wish to submit to our judgment let them come. Finally, if any excuse or defense is possible for them, let us see the sense of satisfaction they have, what fruit of repentance they bring. For the church here is not locked to anyone; the bishop is denied to no one. Our patience and willingness and humanity are available for those who come. I wish for all to return to the church; I wish for all our fellow soldiers to be enclosed within the camp of Christ, the home of God the Father. I pardon all things; I ignore much out of zeal and desire to assemble the brotherhood. Even things which have been committed against God I do not examine with the full judgment of scrupulous piety. I myself am delinquent in choosing to remit sins more often than I ought. I embrace with full and visible affection those who return penitently, who confess their sins with humble and simple satisfaction.

. . .

18.1. An ad hoc, frater carissime, deponenda est catholicae ecclesiae dignitas et plebis intus positae fidelis adque incorrupta maiestas et sacerdotalis quoque auctoritas ac potestas, ut iudicare velle se dicant de ecclesiae praeposito extra ecclesiam constituti haeretici . . .? Quid superest quam ut ecclesia Capitolio cedat, et recedentibus sacerdotibus ac Domini altare removentibus, in cleri nostri sacrum venerandumque congestum simulacra adque idola cum aris suis transeant . . . ?

Translation. For this reason, then, dearest Brother [Cornelius], is the dignity of the catholic church to be set aside and is the faithful and inviolate majesty of the congregation along with the authority and power of the priest to be restricted so that heretics, ordained outside the church, should say that they wish to pass judgment on the one who has been set over the church . . . ? What else is left but for the church to yield to the Capitolium, for the priests to withdraw and remove the altar of the Lord, and for statues and idols with their altars to cross over into the sacred and venerated gathering area (*congestum*)[24] of our clergy . . . ?

No. 17: Dionysius, Bishop of Alexandria (fl. 248–265)

Acta S. Dionysii (written after ca. 303)
(apud Eusebius *H.E.* 7.11.10–12)
[ed. Schwartz, GCS 9 (1903)]

[The record of Dionysius's trial before the deputy prefect Aemilianus under the edicts of arrest issued by the emperor Valerian in 257.]

10. Αἰμιλιανὸς διέπων τὴν ἡγεμονίαν αὐτοῖς εἶπεν· ὁρῶ ὑμᾶς ὁμοῦ καὶ ἀχαρίστους ὄντας καὶ ἀναισθήτους τῆς πραότητος τῶν Σεβαστῶν ἡμῶν· δι᾽ ὅπερ οὐκ ἔσεσθε ἐν τῇ πόλει ταύτῃ, ἀλλὰ ἀποσταλήσεσθε εἰς τὰ μέρη τῆς Λιβύης καὶ ἐν τόπῳ λεγομένῳ Κεφρώ· τοῦτον γὰρ τὸν τόπον ἐξελεξάμην ἐκ τῆς κελεύσεως τῶν Σεβαστῶν ἡμῶν. οὐδαμῶς δὲ ἐξέσται οὔτε ὑμῖν οὔτε ἄλλοις τισὶν ἢ συνόδους ποιεῖσθαι ἢ εἰς τὰ καλούμενα κοιμητήρια εἰσιέναι. 11. εἰ δέ τις φανείη ἢ μὴ γενόμενος εἰς τὸν τόπον τοῦτον ὃν ἐκέλευσα, ἢ ἐν συναγωγῇ τινι εὑρεθείη, ἑαυτῷ τὸν κίνδυνον ἐπαρτήσει· οὐ γὰρ ἐπιλείψει ἡ δέουσα ἐπιστρέφεια. ἀπόστητε οὖν ὅπου ἐκελεύσθητε.

καὶ νοσοῦντα δέ με κατήπειξεν. οὐδὲ μιᾶς ὑπέρθεσιν δοὺς ἡμέρας. ποίαν οὖν ἔτι τοῦ συνάγειν ἢ μὴ συνάγειν εἶχον σχολήν;

24. The term *congestum* (lit., "a collection, gathering, or heap") is clearly meant to indicate a segregated area in the hall of assembly set aside for the clergy. This is the first known reference to give such an area a technical term and probably designates what would later become the chancel and/or sacristy. Whether it was a raised platform cannot be determined with clarity, but it is possible. See also n. 20 above and No. 18 (the Syriac *Didascalia*) below.

Translation. 10. Aemilianos, the deputy prefect said to them, "I see that you are at once ungrateful and insensitive regarding the clemency of our Augusti. Therefore, you shall not be in this city; instead you will be dispatched to a part of Libya, in a place called Cephro. For I have selected this place in accordance with the commands of our Augusti. And it will under no circumstances be permitted for you or any others either to hold meetings or to enter what are termed "cemeteries."[25] 11. If it be shown that anyone is not

25. This text, if it is an authentic record of the judicial proceedings, is one of the earliest to mention the term "cemetery" as a specifically Christian place, presumably for burial. If so, it indicates a knowledge of church property on the part of a government official. Even so, it could be taken as an individual grave or tomb (with monument or enclosure) or associated group of burials (e.g., a family burial chamber), rather than an entire plot set aside for disposition of the Christian dead. The phrasing of this passage suggests that the term was not commonly recognized to mean "place of burial" outside of Christian circles. It would also seem that the prefect, Aemilianus, was unable to distinguish between regular church gatherings for worship and special funerary gatherings, either for burial proper or for the emergent cult of the dead.

On the other hand, the term as used here may come from Eusebius himself, who uses it extensively in his description of the Diocletianic persecutions. In Christian documentary sources, the term does not generally find public usage until the fourth century (cf. No. 41 below and *CIG* 4. 9439, from Thessalonica). The term may derive, however, from a parallel Jewish usage (cf. *CIJ* 1. 712 [=*CIG* 4. 9313], 713, both from Greece) where the term refers to the actual burial chamber.

An official recognition of church properties (including places of burial) may have been part of the imperial action under Valerian, as is indicated in the similar wording of the Latin *acta proconsularia* of Cyprian's martyrdom (in 258). The relevant portion of the text reads as follows: . . . *et adiecit: Praeceperunt etiam ne in aliquibus locis conciliabula faciant nec coemeteria ingrediantur. si quis itaque hoc tam salubre praeceptum non observaverit, capite plectetur* (*Acta Proconsulari sancti Cypriani* 1.7). (*Translation.* He [the proconsul Paternus] added: They [i.e., the emperors by published edict] have also given orders that they [the Christians] shall hold no meetings [or build no meeting places] in any place, nor shall they enter the cemeteries. Henceforth, if anyone does not observe this very sound order, he will receive the death penalty.)

The text of Cyprian above is that edited by Reitzenstein as used by H. Musurillo, *Acts of the Christian Martyrs*, 170. On the suggestion that it and the *Acta Dionysii* (from Eusebius) reflect an authentic witness of the Valerian edicts, see H. J. Lawlor and J. E. Oulton, *Eusebius: The Ecclesiastical History and the Martyrs of Palestine* (London: SPCK, 1954) 2:246. For more on the official recognition of church properties, and thus the implication that property ownership was possible before Constantine, see also No. 28 and n. 38 below.

in this place that I have ordered, or if he is found in any assembly, he will bring the peril upon himself. For the necessary observation will not be lacking. So, then, depart where you were commanded."

[Dionysius's comment on the incident:] "Even though I was sick, he sent me away; nor did he give a rest of one day. What sort of time did I have, then, for convening or not convening an assembly?"

[The account of Eusebius continues.]

εἶτα μεθ' ἕτερά φησιν

12. ἀλλ' οὐδὲ τῆς αἰσθητῆς ἡμεῖς μετὰ τοῦ κυρίου συναγωγῆς ἀπέστημεν, ἀλλὰ τοὺς μὲν ἐν τῇ πόλει στουδαιότερον συνεκρότουν ὡς συνών, ἀπὼν μὲν τῷ σώματι, ὡς εἶπεν, παρὼν δὲ τῷ πνεύματι. ἐν δὲ τῇ Κεφροῖ καὶ πολλὴ συνεπεδήμησεν ἡμῖν ἐκκλησία, τῶν μὲν ἀπὸ τῆς πόλεως ἀδελφῶν ἑπομένων, τῶν δὲ συνιόντων ἀπ' Αἰγύπτου. κἀκεῖ θύραν ἡμῖν ὁ θεὸς ἀνέῳξεν τοῦ λόγου.

Translation. 12. Then after other remarks, he [Dionysius] says, 12. "But we did not forgo the public assembly with the Lord. Instead I was banding together ever more earnestly those in the city as if I were together (with them), 'though being absent in body,' as he [Paul] said, 'being present in the spirit' [1 Cor 5:3]. But at Cephro also a large church banded together with us.[26] While some brothers followed from the city, others came together from Egypt. God opened for us there a door for the word. . . ."

No. 18: *Didascalia Apostolorum* (Syria, late third century)

[Syriac text edited by M. Gibson, Horae Semiticae I (1903); Latin version (Verona MS.) edited by R. H. Connolly (1956)]

12. (44b–46b)

ܘܐܠܦܘܢ ܕܢܬܟܢܫܘܢ. ܡܟܡܢ ܠܐܦܝܣܩܘܦܐ ܕܢܗܘܘܢ ܠܚܫܝܢ

ܘܡܬܡܢܝܢ. ܘܕܝܫܝܢ ܒܗ ܟܠܗ ܥܕܬܐ ܘܡܬܟܢܫܘܬܐ. ܘܡܠܦ

ܠܗܘܢ ܡܛܠ ܡܬܟܢܫܘܬܐ ܕܒܥܕܬܐ ܕܐܠܗܐ. ܘܕܐܢܫܐ ܢܦܩܝܢ

---

26. For the phenomenon of Christian assemblies among exiles during the great persecution, as reported by Eusebius, see his *Martyrs of Palestine* 12.1.

ܒܗ ܕܩܘܡܬܐ ܠܡܘܬܒܐ ܘܠܡܬܘܬܒܘ. ܠܟܠ ܚܕ ܡܢ ܛܟ̈ܣܐ ܐܝܟ
ܙܕܩܗ. ܘܕܐܢܫܐ ܕܐܬܐ ܐܢܫ ܡܢ ܥܕܬܐ ܐܚܪܬܐ. ܢܩܒܠܘܢ ܠܗ
ܐܝܩܪܐ ܐܝܟ ܙܕܩܗ. ܘܢܬܩܪܐ ܒܕܘܟܬܐ ܕܠܝܩܐ ܠܗ. ܘܠܐ
ܢܬܬܥܝܩ ܒܗ. ܡܫܒܚܢܐ ܬܒܥ ܐܦܣܩܘܦܐ ܐܢܬܘܢ ܕܝܢ ܐܘ̄
ܐܦܝܣܩܘܦܐ ܠܐ ܬܗܘܘܢ ܦܥܝܢ ܘܠܐ ܬܪܘܨܝܢ ܘܠܐ ܣܓܘܠܝܢ.
ܘܠܐ ܬܗܘܘܢ ܐܚܝܕܝܢ ܥܠ ܡܢܬܐ ܕܐܠܗܐ ܕܡܫܠܡ ܒܐܝ̈ܕܝܟܘܢ.
ܘܠܐ ܬܒܪܘܢ ܒܗܬܗ ܕܡܪܝܐ ܘܠܐ ܬܥܕܪܘܢ ܒܗܘܢ. ܐܠܐ ܐܒܘܢ
ܗܘܝܬܘܢ ܡܫܠܡܝܢ ܠܟܠܗܘܢ. ܕܬܗܘܘܢ ܡܕܒܪ̈ܢܐ ܒܗ ܐܠܗܐ
ܘܗܘܘ ܡܕܒܪܝܢ ܠܡܣܟ̈ܢܐ ܒܡܟܝܟܘܬܐ ܫܠܝܢܬܐ ܘܡܠܒܪܘܬ
ܪܘܚܐ ܘܡܡܫܡܫܢܘܬܐ ܕܠܐ ܪܘܓܙܐ. ܘܡܦܠܚܢܐ ܘܒܡܟܟܘܬܐ
ܐܝܟ ܡܫܡ̄ܫܢ ܕܡܠܟܘܬܐ ܕܐܠܗܐ. ܒܡܢܝܢܘܬܐ ܒܒܪ̈ܬܐ ܘܒܢ̈ܫܐ.
ܒܟܠ ܐܣܟܡ̈ܐ ܫܦܝ̈ܪܐ ܗܘܝܬܘܢ ܥܒܕܝܢ ܟܢܘܫ̈ܬܟܘܢ. ܘܗܘܘ
ܡܬܩܢܝܢ ܕܘܟܬܐ ܠܐܚ̈ܐ ܒܚܦܝܛܘܬ ܒܢܟܦܘܬܐ. ܠܩܫܝ̈ܫܐ ܕܝܢ
ܬܬܦܪܫ ܕܘܟܬܐ ܒܓܒܗ ܡܕܢܚܝܐ ܕܒܝܬܐ. ܘܢܗܘܐ ܣܝܡ
ܬܪܘܢܘܣ ܕܐܦܝܣܩܘܦܐ ܒܡܨܥܬܗܘܢ. ܘܢܬܒܘܢ ܥܡܗ ܩܫܝ̈ܫܐ.
ܘܬܘܒ ܕܝܢ ܒܓܒܗ ܐܚܪܢܐ ܕܒܝܬܐ. ܢܬܒܘܢ ܓܒܪ̈ܐ
ܒܢ̈ܝ ܥܠܡܐ. ܗܟܢܐ ܓܝܪ ܘܠܐ. ܕܒܓܒܐ ܡܕܢܚܝܐ ܕܒܝܬܐ
ܢܗܘܘܢ ܝܬܒܝܢ ܩܫܝ̈ܫܐ ܥܡ ܐܦܝܣܩܘܦܐ. ܘܡܢ ܒܬܪܗܘܢ ܓܒܪ̈ܐ
ܒܢ̈ܝ ܥܠܡܐ. ܘܗܝܕܝܢ ܢܫ̈ܐ. ܕܡܐ ܕܩܝܡܝܬܘܢ ܠܡܨܠܝܘ ܢܩܘܡܘܢ
ܡܕܒܪ̈ܢܐ ܩܕܡܝܐ. ܘܒܬܪܗܘܢ ܓܒܪ̈ܐ ܒܢ̈ܝ ܥܠܡܐ. ܘܗܝܕܝܢ
ܬܘܒ ܢܫ̈ܐ. ܠܡܕܢܚܐ ܓܝܪ ܘܠܐ ܠܟܘܢ ܕܬܗܘܘܢ
ܡܨܠܝܢ. ܐܝܟ ܕܝܕܥܝܢ ܐܢܬܘܢ ܕܟܬܝܒ ܕܗܒܘ ܬܫܒܘܚܬܐ
ܠܐܠܗܐ. ܕܪܟܝܒ ܒܫܡ̈ܝ ܫܡܝܐ ܥܠ ܡܕܢܚܐ. ܡܫܡ̈ܫܢܐ ܕܝܢ.
ܢܗܘܐ ܐܚܝܢ. ܘܩܐܡ ܚܕ ܡܢܗܘܢ ܥܠ ܩܘܪ̈ܒܢܐ ܕܐܘܟܪܣܛܝܐ.
ܘܐܚܪܢܐ ܕܝܢ. ܢܗܘܐ ܩܐܡ ܠܒܪ ܡܢ ܬܪܥܐ. ܘܢܗܘܐ ܚܙܐ
ܠܐܝܠܝܢ ܕܥܐܠܝܢ. ܘܡܢ ܒܬܪ ܗܢܐ ܕܡܩܪܒܝܢ ܐܢܬܘܢ ܢܗܘܘܢ
ܡܫܡܫܝܢ ܐܟܚܕܐ ܒܥܕܬܐ. ܘܐܢ ܗܘ ܕܢܫܬܟܚ ܐܢܫ ܕܝܬܒ
ܕܠܐ ܒܕܘܟܬܗ ܢܟܐܐ ܒܗ ܡܫܡܫܢܐ ܗܘ ܕܐܝܬ ܠܓܘ.
ܘܢܩܝܡܝܘܗܝ ܘܢܘܬܒܝܘܗܝ ܒܕܘܟܬܐ ܐܝܕܐ ܕܙܕܩܐ ܠܗ. ܠܛܝܪܐ ܓܝܪ
ܕܡܬܠ ܡܪܢ ܠܥܕܬܐ. ܐܝܟܢܐ ܓܝܪ ܕܚܙܝܢ ܠܚܝ̈ܘܬܐ ܕܠܐ ܡܡܠܠܢ.
ܐܠܦܝܢ ܬܘܪܐ ܘܥܢܐ ܘܥܙ̈ܐ ܕܪ̈ܒܥܝܢ ܥܠ̈ܝܢ ܪ̈ܥܝܢ. ܘܩ̈ܝܡܝܢ
ܘܡܬܟܢ̈ܫܢ. ܘܚܕܐ ܡܢܗܝܢ ܡܢ ܒܢܬ ܓܢܣܗ ܠܐ ܦܪܫܐ. ܘܬܘܒ
ܕܝܢ ܚܝܘܬܐ ܕܒܪܐ ܟܠ ܚܕܐ ܡܢܗܝܢ ܥܡ ܐܝܠܝܢ ܕܕܡ̈ܝܢ ܠܗܝܢ
ܡܬܗܠܟܢ ܒܛܘܪ̈ܐ. ܗܟܢܐ ܡܬܒܥܐ ܐܦ ܒܥܕܬܐ. ܕܐܝܠܝܢ
ܕܛܠܝܢ ܡܢܗܘܢ ܠܚܘܕܝܗܘܢ ܢܬܒܘܢ. ܐܢܫ ܕܐܝܬ ܕܘܟܬܐ. ܐܢ
ܠܐ ܢܩܘܡܘܢ ܥܠ ܪ̈ܓܠܝܗܘܢ. ܘܐܝܠܝܢ ܕܩܫܝܫܝܢ ܒܫ̈ܢܝܐ ܢܬܒܘܢ
ܡܢܗܘܢ ܘܠܗܘܢ. ܛܠܝ̈ܐ ܕܝܢ ܢܩܘܡܘܢ ܠܚܕ ܓܒܐ. ܐܘ

ܢܦܪܫܘܢ ܐܝܟ ܠܘܬܗܘܢ ܐܒܗܝܗܘܢ ܘܐܡܗܬܗܘܢ.
ܘܢܩܘܡܘܢ ܥܠ ܪ̈ܓܠܝܗܘܢ. ܘܬܩܘܒ. ܐܦ ܐܝܠܝܢ ܕܛܠ̈ܝܢ ܢܬܒ̈ܢ
ܡܢܗܝܢ ܘܠܗܝܢ. ܘܐܢ ܠܝܬ ܠܗ ܐܬܪܐ ܢܩܘ̈ܡܢ ܥܠ ܪ̈ܓܠܝܗܝܢ ܒܣܬܪ
ܢܫ̈ܐ. ܘܐܝܠܝܢ ܕܗܘ̈ܝ ܠܓܒ̈ܪܐ ܘܛܠ̈ܝܢ ܐܢ̈ܝܢ ܘܐܝܬ ܠܗܝܢ ܒܢ̈ܝܐ
ܢܩܘ̈ܡܢ ܡܢܗܝܢ ܘܠܗܝܢ. ܘܣܒ̈ܬܐ ܕܝܢ ܘܐܪ̈ܡܠܬܐ ܡܢܗܝܢ ܘܠܗܝܢ
ܢܬ̈ܒܢ. ܒܪ ܢܗܘܐ ܡܫܡܫܢܐ ܚܙܐ. ܘܟܠܢܫ ܡܢܗܘܢ̈ ܡܢ ܕܥܐܠ
ܢܐܙܠ ܠܕܘܟܬܗ. ܕܠܡܐ ܢܬܒ ܐܢܫ ܡܢܗܘܢ̈ ܕܠܐ ܒܕܘܟܬܗ.
ܘܡܚܒ ܕܝܢ ܚܙܐ ܡܫܡ̄ܫ. ܕܕܠܡܐ ܐܢܫ ܢܠܚܫ ܐܘ ܢܢܘܡ ܐܘ ܢܓܚܟ
ܐܘ ܢܪܡܙ. ܗ̇ܟܢܐ ܓܝܪ ܡܬܒܥܐ ܕܒܗܕܪܘܬܐ *ܘܒܐܣܟܡܐ
ܫܦܝܪܐ. ܢܗܘܘܢ̈ ܥܝܪ̈ܝܢ ܒܒܥܘܬܐ. ܘܦܬܝܚܐ ܡܫܡܥܬܗܘܢ̈
ܠܡܠܬܗ ܕܡܪܝܐ.. ܐܢܕܝܢ ܢܐܬܐ ܐܢܫ ܡܢ ܟܢܘܫܬܐ ܐܚܪܬܐ.
ܐܚܐ ܐܘ ܚܬܐ ܢܐܬܐ ܡܫܡ̄ܫ ܘܢܐܙܠ.. ܕܐܢ ܐܚܝܬ ܠܒܪܐ
ܗ̇ܝ، ܐܘ ܕܠܡܐ ܬܩܘܒ ܐܪ̈ܡܠܬܐ ܗ̇ܝ، ܡܫܡܫܢܝܬܐ. ܘܐܢ ܒܪܬ
ܥܕܬܐ ܗ̇ܝ، ܐܘ ܕܠܡܐ ܚܕܐ ܡܢ ܐܪ̈ܐܣܝܣ ܐܝܬܝܗ̇. ܘܗ̇ܝܕܝܢ
ܢܬܠ ܬܘܩܝܡܗ̇ ܒܕܘܟܬܐ ܕܙܕܩܐ ܠܗ̇. ܘܐܢܕܝܢ ܢܐܬܐ ܡܣܟܢܐ
ܡܢ ܟܢܘܫܬܐ ܐܚܪܬܐ. ܡܩܒܠܝܢܗ، ܐܢܬܘܢ̈ ܡܫܒ̈ܚܐ ܒܫܘܬܦܘܬܐ
ܒܕܘܟܬܗܘܢ̈. ܘܐܢ ܐܦܣܩܘܦܐ ܗ̣ܘ ܢܬܒ ܥܡ ܐܦܣܩܘܦܐ.
ܘܢܩܒܠܗܝ، ܠܐܝܩܪܐ ܕܕܘܟܬܗ ܐܝܟ ܢܦܫܗ. ܘܐܢܬ ܐܦܝܣ ܠܗ
ܐܦܣܩܘܦܐ ܕܢܬܪܓܡ ܠܥܡܟ. ܟܠܦܢܝܬܐ ܘܡܪܬܝܢܘܬܐ ܚܕܐ
ܕܐܟܣܢܝܐ ܗܟܢ ܡܚܕܪܐ. ܡܬܝܪܐ ܡܛܠ ܕܟܬܝܒ ܕܠܡܬ ܢܦܫܐ
ܕܡܬܩܒܠ ܒܐܬܪܗ. ܘܡܢܐ ܕܡܬܦܪܥܝܢ ܐܢܬܘܢ̈ ܡܩܪܒܢܐ ܗ̣ܘ
ܢܡܠܠ. ܐܢܕܝܢ ܣܒܝܪ ܗ̣ܘ ܘܠܝܬ ܩܕܡ ܐܬܪܐ ܘܠܐ ܓܘܐ ܕܢܬܒ.
ܐܦ ܥܠ ܟܘܪܣܐ ܢܡܠܠ. ܐܢܕܝܢ ܗ̣ܘ ܢܬܩܒܠ ܐܢܬܘܢ̈ ܢܬܒܐ ܐܢܫ
ܐܚܪܢܝ. ܐܘ ܓܒܪܐ ܐܘ ܐܢܬܬܐ ܕܐܝܬ ܠܗܘܢ ܐܝܩܪܐ ܒܥܠܡܐ.
ܐܘ ܡܢܗ̇ ܡܢ ܕܦܚܠܬܐ. ܐܘ ܡܢ ܟܢܘܫܬܐ ܐܚܪܬܐ. ܐܢܬ ܗ̇ܘܟܠ
ܐܦܣܩ̄ܐ ܕܡܬܓܠܠ ܐܢܬ ܡܠܬܐ ܕܐܠܗܐ. ܐܘ ܥܒܕ ܐܢܬ ܐܘ
ܚܐܪܐ ܐܢܬ. ܠܐ ܬܩܘܡ ܒܐܦܐ ܘܬܫܒܘܩ ܕܬܫܡܫܬܐ ܕܡܠܟܝܢ
ܘܬܬܦܢ ܠܗܘܢ ܕܘܟܬܐ. ܐܠܐ ܐܢܬ ܐܝܟ ܕܐܝܬܝܟ ܗܘܝ
ܒܥܠܡܐ. ܘܠܐ ܬܦܣܘܩ ܡܠܬܟ ܘܐܚܪ̈ܢܐ ܗ̇ܢܘܢ ܢܡܠܠܘܢ
ܐܢܘܢ. ܘܐܢܗܘ ܕܠܝܬ ܕܘܟܬܐ. ܐܢܫܐ ܡܢ ܕܡܠܐ ܣܘܟܐ.
ܘܢܣܡ ܐܚܘܗܝ، ܘܐܚܝܬܗܘܢ، ܡܩܪܒܢܐ. ܢܩܘܡ ܘܢܬܠ ܠܗܘܢ ܕܘܟܬܐ.
ܗ̣ܘ ܕܝܢ ܢܩܘܡ ܥܠ ܪ̈ܓܠܘܗܝ، ܘܐܢܕܝܢ ܗ̣ܘ ܦܠܚܝܢ ܐܝܠܝܢ ܕܛܠܝܢ
ܐܘ ܐܝܠܝܢ ܕܛܠ̈ܝܢ. ܢܩܘܡ ܐܢܫܐ ܕܣܐܒ ܐܘ ܐܢܬܬܐ ܕܣܐܒܐ.
ܘܢܬܠ ܕܘܟܬܗ. ܚܙܝ ܐܢܬ ܐܘ ܡܫܡ̄ܫ ܒܐܝܠܝܢ ܕܢܬܒܘܢ. ܕܐܢܫܐ
ܢܗܘܘܢ ܠܛܠܐ ܡܢ ܣܒ̈ܘܗܝ، ܐܘ ܐܢ̈ܫܐ ܕܛܠܝܐ. ܐܘܣܡ ܐܢܫ.
ܘܐܬܘܒ ܠܗ̇ܘ ܐܢܫܐ ܕܩܡ ܐܦ ܡܟܒ ܕܘܟܬܗ. ܘܠܗ̇ܘ ܕܐܩܝܡܬ
ܐܘܒܠ ܐܩܝܡܝܗܘܢ، ܒܩܦܬ ܣܒܝܪܘܗܝ، ܕܢܬܪܕܘܢ ܘܢܐܠܦܘܢ ܐܦ
ܐܚܪܢܐ. ܕܢܗܘܘܢ ܢܬܟܝܢ ܕܘܟܬܐ ܠܐܝܠܝܢ ܕܡܝܩܪܝܢ ܡܢܗܘܢ.

ܘܐܢܕܝܢ ܡܣܟܢܐ ܐܘ ܡܣܟܢܬܐ ܢܐܬܘܢ܆ ܐܘ ܡܢ ܒܢ̈ܝ ܟܢܘܫܬܐ
ܕܝܠܟ. ܐܘ ܡܢ ܟܢܘܫܬܐ ܐܚܪܬܐ. ܘܡܬܝܬܪܐܝܬ ܐܢܗܘ ܕܣܐܒܝܢ
ܐܢܘܢ܆ ܒܫܢ̈ܝܐ. ܘܠܝܬ ܐܬܪܐ ܠܐܝܠܝܢ ܕܗ̇ܟܢܐ ܐܢܬܗܘ܆ ܐܬܩܢ
ܠܗܘܢ܆ ܕܘܟܬܐ ܡܢ ܟܠܗ ܠܒܟ ܐܘ̄ ܐܦܝܣܩܘܦܐ. ܐܢ ܗܘܐ
ܠܟ ܠܡܬܒ ܥܠ ܐܪܥܐ. ܕܠܐ ܬܗܘܐ ܠܟ ܐܝܟ ܗܘ ܕܒܐ̈ܦ
ܒܢܝ̈ܢܫܐ ܢܣܒ ܐܢܬ. ܐܠܐ ܠܘܬ ܐܠܗܐ ܡܫܡܫܢܘܬܟ ܬܫܬܦܪܝܢ܀*

Verona Latin ms. (XXIX–XXX in the edition of Hauler) preserves a portion of this chapter (as marked *-*). The Latin version reads as follows:

[XXIX] . . . cum disciplina et sobrietate vigilare et intentam aurem habere ad verbum domini.

Si quis autem de parrocia frater aut soro venerit, diaconus requirat ab ea si adhuc virum habet, si vidua est aut fidelis, et si de ecclesia est et non de heresi. Et sic iam perducens eam faciat in decreto loco sedere. Si autem praesbyter de ecclesia parrociae venerit, suscipite eum, praesbyteri, communiter in loco vestro. Et si episcopus advenerit, cum episcopo sedeat, eundem honorem ab eo recipiens. Et petes eum tu, episcope, ut adloquatur plebem tuam, quoniam peregrinus, cum adloquium dat, deiubat populum; scriptum est enim: "Nullus profeta susceptus est in patria sua." Et in gratia agenda ipse dicat. Si autem, cum sit prudens et honorem tibi reservans, non velit, super calicem dicat.

Si autem, cum sedis, alius quis aut alia supervenerit honorabilior secundum saeculum, aut (peregrinus aut) de ipso loco, tu, o episcope, cum dicis verbum Dei aut audis aut legis, noli propter personarum acceptionem relinquere ministerium verbi tui et disponere eis sessoria, sed permane [in]quietus et noli mediare verbum: fratres autem eos suscipient. Sin vero locus non fuerit, qui dilectionem fraternam habet et caritatem et honorabilis est, surgens concedet ei(s) locum, et ipse stabit. Si autem, iuvenioribus sedentibus, senior aut anicula surgens concesserint locum, tu, diaconus, circuminspice de iuvenioribus [XXX] qui magis iunior est aut iuvencula, et exsurgere facies eam, et sedere eam quae locum concessit: eam vero, quae non cessit exsurgens, facies posteriorem omnibus stare, ut discant et ceteri concedere maioribus aetate. Si autem egenus aut egena, sive de loco sive peregrinus, supervenerit, et praeterea senior aetate, et locus non fuerit, tu, episcope, talibus locum ex toto corde fac, etiamsi tu ipse super humum sederis, ut non fiat aput homines a te personarum acceptio, sed aput Deum ministerium tuum placeat.

Translation. And you the bishops, be not hard, nor tyrannical, nor wrathful, and be not rough with the people of God which is delivered into your hands. And destroy not the Lord's house nor scatter his people; but convert all, that you may be helpers with God; and gather the faithful with much meekness and long-suffering and patience, and without anger, and with doctrine and exhortation, as ministers of the kingdom everlasting.

And in your congregations in the holy churches hold your assemblies with all decent order, and appoint the places for the brethren with care and gravity. And for the presbyters let there be assigned a place in the eastern part of the house; and let the bishop's throne be set in their midst, and let the presbyters sit with him. And again, let the laymen sit in another part of the house toward the east. For so it should be, that in the eastern part of the house the presbyters sit with the bishops, and next the laymen, and then the women; that when you stand up to pray, the rulers may stand first, and after them the laymen, and then the women also. For it is required that you pray toward the east, as knowing that which is written: "Give ye glory to God, who rideth upon the heaven of heavens toward the east" [Ps 67(68):34].

But of the deacons let one stand always by the oblations of the Eucharist; and let another stand without by the door and observe them that come in; and afterwards, when you offer, let them minister together in the church. And if any one be found sitting out of his place, let the deacon who is within reprove him and make him to rise up and sit in a place that is meet for him. For our Lord likened the church to a fold; for as we see the dumb animals, oxen and sheep and goats, lie down and rise up, and feed and chew the cud, according to their families, and none of them separate itself from its kind; and (see) the wild beasts also severally range with their like upon the mountains: so likewise in the church ought those who are young to sit apart, if there be room, and if not to stand up; and those who are advanced in years to sit apart. And let the children stand on one side, or let their fathers and mothers take them to them; and let them stand up. And let the young girls also sit apart; but if there be no room, let them stand up behind the women. And let the young women who are married and have children stand apart, and the aged women and widows sit apart. And let the deacon see that each of them on entering goes to his place, that no one may sit out of his place. And let the deacon also see that no one whispers, or falls asleep, or laughs, or makes signs. For so it should be, that* with decency and decorum they watch in the church, with ears attentive to the word of the Lord.

But if any brother or sister come from another congregation, let the deacon question her and learn whether she is married, or again whether she is a widow (who is) a believer; and whether she is a daughter of the church, or belongs perchance to one of the heresies; and then let him conduct her and set her in a place that is suitable for her. But if a presbyter should come from another congregation, do you the presbyters receive him with fellowship into your place. And if it be a bishop, let him sit with the bishop; and let him accord him the honor of his rank, even as himself. And do thou, O bishop, invite him to discourse to thy people; for the exhortation and admonition of strangers is very profitable, especially as it is written: "There is no prophet that is acceptable in his own place" [Luke 4:24]. And when you offer the oblation, let him speak. But if he is wise and gives the honor to thee, and is unwilling to offer, at least let him speak over the cup.

But if, as you are sitting, some one else should come, whether a man or a woman, who has some worldly honor, either of the same district or of another congregation: thou, O bishop, if thou art speaking the word of God, or hearing, or reading, shalt not respect persons and leave the ministry of thy word and appoint them a place; but do thou remain still as thou art and not interrupt thy word, and let the brethren themselves receive them. And if there be no place, let one of the brethren who is full of charity and loves his brethren, and is one fitted to do an honor, rise and give them place, and himself stand up. But if, while younger men or women sit, an older man or woman should rise and give up their place, do thou, O deacon, scan those who sit, and see which man or woman of them is younger than the rest, and make them stand up, and cause him to sit who had risen and given up his place; and him whom thou hast caused to stand up, lead away and make him to stand behind his neighbors: that others also may be trained and learn to give place to those more honorable than themselves. But if a poor man or woman should come, (whether of the same district) or of another congregation, and especially if they are stricken in years, and there be no place for such, do thou, O bishop, with all thy heart provide a place for them, even if thou have to sit upon the ground; that thou be not as one who respects the persons of men, but that thy ministry may be acceptable with God.* [Connolly's translation]

No. 19: Gregory Thaumaturgus, Bishop of Neocaesarea, Pontus (ca. 240–ca. 270)

Epistula Canonica, Canon 11 (dated ca. 265 ?)[27] [*PG* 10. 1048]

Ἡ πρόσκλαυσις ἔξω τῆς πύλης τοῦ εὐχτηρίου ἐστίν· ἔνθα ἑστῶτα τὸν ἁμαρτάνοντα χρὴ τῶν εἰσιόντων δεῖσθαι πιστῶν, ὑπὲρ αὐτοῦ εὔχεσθαι. Ἡ ἀκρόασις ἔνδοθι τῆς πύλης ἐν τῷ νάρθηκι, ἔνθα ἑστάναι χρὴ τὸν ἡμαρτηκότα ἕως τῶν κατηχουμένων, καὶ ἐντεῦθεν ἐξέρχεσθαι. Ἀκούων γὰρ, φησὶ, τῶν γραφῶν καὶ τῆς διδασκαλίας, ἐκβαλλέσθω, καὶ μὴ ἀξιούσθω προσευχῆς. Ἡ δὲ ὑπόπτωσις, ἵνα, ἔσωθεν τῆς πύλης τοῦ ναοῦ ἱστάμενος, μετὰ τῶν κατηχουμένων ἐξέρχηται. Ἡ σύστασις, ἵνα συνιστᾶται τοῖς πιστοῖς, καὶ μὴ ἐξέρχηται μετὰ τῶν κατηχουμένων· τελευταῖον ἡ μέθεξις τῶν ἁγιασμάτων.

Translation. *Weeping* takes place outside the gate of the house of prayer (Lat. *oratorium*),[28] and the (penitent) sinner stationed there ought to beseech the faithful as they enter to pray on his behalf. *Auditing*, then, takes place inside the gate (of the house of prayer) in the narthex (Lat. *porticus*), wherein the sinner must stay until the catechumens (depart), whereupon he too shall depart. For having heard the scriptures and the teaching, they say, let him be cast out and let him not be deemed worthy of prayer (of the mass). *Submitting* (takes place) when (the sinner) is stationed inside the door of the sanctuary (Lat. *templum*) and departs along with the catechumens. *Restoration* (takes place) when (the sinner) is united with the faithful and does not depart with the catechumens. Finally, (comes) *Participation in the holy rites*.

---

27. Despite the attribution, this portion of the text is usually thought to be a later interpolation from no earlier than the late fourth century because of the highly developed penitential system. The use of technical building terms from later basilical architecture (e.g., narthex) supports this view. On the other hand, there is evidence since the early third century of defining penitential exclusion in physical terms of the church building, notably the threshold or door of the place of assembly. So see Nos. 13e, 16b, 16d. Hence this text may show some of the later development of that same practice.

28. The technical terms for the penitential grades have been placed in italics for emphasis. Latin equivalents are from the parallel text in *PG* 10. 1047.

No. 20: Paul of Samosata and the Church at Antioch

20a: *Synodal Letter* of Malchion of Antioch (269–70)
[on the decision to excommunicate the bishop, Paul]
(apud Eusebius, *H.E.* 7.30.9–11)
[ed. Schwartz, GCS 9 (1903)]

[After an unflattering portrayal of Paul's wealth (allegedly gained from the exercise of his office as bishop) and of his conceit in matters of dress and bearing (both things that the synod claimed were not the source of their judgment against Paul, but clearly have a rhetorical function here), the letter continues with a description of the bishop's conduct in the assembly.]

9. οὔτε τὴν ἐν ταῖς ἐκκλησιαστικαῖς συνόδοις τερατείαν, ἣν μηχανᾶται, δοξοκοπῶν καὶ φαντασιοκοπῶν καὶ τὰς τῶν ἀκεραιοτέρων ψυχὰς τοῖς τοιούτοις ἐκπλήττων, βῆμα μὲν καὶ θρόνον ὑψηλὸν ἑαυτῷ κατασκευασάμενος, οὐχ ὡς Χριστοῦ μαθητής, σήκρητόν τε, ὥσπερ οἱ τοῦ κόσμου ἄρχοντες, ἔχων τε καὶ ὀνομάζων, παίων τε τῇ χειρὶ τὸν μηρὸν καὶ τὸ βῆμα ἀράττων τοῖς ποσὶν καὶ τοῖς μὴ ἐπαινοῦσιν μηδὲ ὥσπερ ἐν τοῖς θεάτροις κατασείουσιν ταῖς ὀθόναις μηδ' ἐκβοῶσίν τε καὶ ἀναπηδῶσιν κατὰ τὰ αὐτὰ τοῖς ἀμφ' αὐτὸν στασιώταις, ἀνδράσιν τε καὶ γυναίοις, ἀκόσμως οὕτως ἀκροωμένοις, τοῖς δ' οὖν ὡς ἐν οἴκῳ θεοῦ σεμνοπρεπῶς καὶ εὐτάκτως ἀκούουσιν ἐπιτιμῶν καὶ ἐνυβρίζων καὶ εἰς τοὺς ἀπελθόντας ἐκ τοῦ βίου τούτου παροινῶν ἐξηγητὰς τοῦ λόγου φορτικῶς ἐν τῷ κοινῷ καὶ μεγαλορημονῶν περὶ ἑαυτοῦ, καθάπερ οὐκ ἐπίσκοπος ἀλλὰ σοφιστὴς καὶ γόης· 10. ψαλμοὺς δὲ τοὺς μὲν εἰς τὸν κύριον ἡμῶν Ἰησοῦν Χριστὸν παύσας ὡς δὴ νεωτέρους καὶ νεωτέρων ἀνδρῶν συγγράμματα, εἰς ἑαυτὸν δὲ ἐν μέσῃ τῇ ἐκκλησίᾳ τῇ μεγάλῃ τοῦ πάσχα ἡμέρα ψαλμῳδεῖν γυναῖκας παρασκευάζων, ὧν καὶ ἀκούσας ἄν τις φρίξειεν· οἷα καὶ τοὺς θωπεύοντας αὐτὸν ἐπισκόπους τῶν ὁμόρων ἀγρῶν τε καὶ πόλεων καὶ πρεσβυτέρους ἐν ταῖς πρὸς τὸν λαὸν ὁμιλίαις καθίησιν διαλέγεσθαι· 11. τὸν μὲν γὰρ υἱὸν τοῦ θεοῦ οὐ βούλεται συνομολογεῖν ἐξ οὐρανοῦ κατεληλυθέναι (ἵνα τι προλαβόντες τῶν μελλόντων γραφήσεσθαι θῶμεν. καὶ τοῦτο οὐ λόγῳ ψιλῷ ῥηθήσεται, ἀλλ' ἐξ ὧν ἐπέμψαμεν ὑπομνημάτων δείκνυται πολλαχόθεν, οὐχ ἥκιστα δὲ ὅπου λέγει Ἰησοῦν Χριστὸν κάτωθεν), οἱ δὲ εἰς αὐτὸν ψάλλοντες καὶ ἐγκωμιάζοντες ἐν τῷ λαῷ ἄγγελον τὸν ἀσεβῆ διδάσκαλον ἑαυτῶν ἐξ

οὐρανοῦ κατεληλυθέναι λέγουσιν, καὶ ταῦτα οὐ κωλύει, ἀλλὰ καὶ λεγομένοις πάρεστιν ὁ ὑπερήφανος· . . .

Translation. Nor [did we base our decision] on the trickery in the ecclesiastical assemblies which he devised, courting popular opinion and personal appearance and astonishing the minds of the simpler people by means of the *bema* and the lofty throne which he had built for himself, not as a disciple of Christ but like the ruler of the world, and with a *secretum* [i.e., a magistrate's chamber in the tribunal] which he has and even calls it. In addition, he slaps his thigh with his hand and stamps the *bema* with his feet. And to those who do not applaud or wave handkerchiefs, as if they were in the theater, or who do not shout and jump after the fashion of those wretches, both men and women, who take sides on account of him, and listen in such an unseemly way—no, to those who listen with reverence and decency as in the house of God he gives insult and rebuke. And concerning the interpreters of the word who have passed from this life he delivers vulgar perorations in the common assembly, not as befits a bishop but rather as a sophist and charlatan. In the matter of psalms, whereas he stopped the practice of singing those addressed to our Lord Jesus Christ on the grounds that they were novelties and the compositions of modern men, he trains women to sing psalms to himself in the middle of the church on the great day of the Pascha, which would cause anyone who hears them to shudder. Such also are the discourses he sends down for the bishops of the neighboring country and towns who flatter him and for the presbyters as well, to deliver in their homilies to the congregation. For he is not willing to make the statement in harmony (with us) that the Son of God has descended from heaven (we say this in order to anticipate what we are about to write, and this will not merely be asserted but will be amply proved by notes which we have sent with this letter, not the least of which is the one where he says that Jesus Christ is from below). Yet those who sing psalms to him and deliver panegyrics to him in the congregation say that their impious teacher is an angel who came down from heaven. And he does not stop these practices; instead the arrogant fellow is present when they are said. . . .

20b: Eusebius's report of the resolution of the case
(apud *H.E.* 7.30.18–19) [ed. Schwartz, GCS 9 (1903)]

[Eusebius presents the conclusion of the letter in which the synod announces its decision to excommunicate Paul and to appoint as bishop in his stead Domnus, the son of the former bishop. Then Eusebius reports Paul's reaction to the decision and the final resolution of the case.]

18. τοῦ δὴ οὖν Παύλου σὺν καὶ τῇ τῆς πίστεως ὀρθοδοξίᾳ τῆς ἐπισκοπῆς ἀποπεπτωκότος, Δόμνος, ὡς εἴρηται, τὴν λειτουργίαν τῆς κατὰ Ἀντιόχειαν ἐκκλησίας διεδέξατο· 19. ἀλλὰ γὰρ μηδαμῶς ἐκστῆναι τοῦ Παύλου τοῦ τῆς ἐκκλησίας οἴκου θέλοντος, βασιλεὺς ἐντευχθεὶς Αὐρηλιανὸς αἰσιώτατα περὶ τοῦ πρακτέου διείληφεν, τούτοις νεῖμαι προστάττων τὸν οἶκον, οἷς ἂν οἱ κατὰ τὴν Ἰταλίαν καὶ τὴν Ῥωμαίων πόλιν ἐπίσκοποι τοῦ δόγματος ἐπιστέλλοιεν. οὕτω δῆτα ὁ προδηλωθεὶς ἀνὴρ μετὰ τῆς ἐσχάτης αἰσχύνης ὑπὸ τῆς κοσμικῆς ἀρχῆς ἐξελαύνεται τῆς ἐκκλησίας.

Translation. Then when Paul had fallen away from the episcopal office and even from orthodoxy in the faith, Domnus, as has been said, was appointed to the ministry of the church at Antioch. But whereas Paul would in no way relinquish the house of the church (the church-building), after an appeal the emperor Aurelian made a very just decision concerning the matter. He ordered that the building be made the property of those with whom the bishops of the (Christian) doctrine in Italy and Rome would communicate in writing. Thus was the aforesaid man expelled from the church with the utmost indignity by the ruler of the world.[29]

No. 21: The Martyrdom of Saturninus and Company (304)

Acta Saturnini presbyteri, Felicis, Dativi et al. 2,8,9
(at Abitina, Numidia, 12 February, 304) [*PL* 8. 689ff.]

2. Temporibus namque Diocletiani et Maximiani bellum diabolus Christianis indixit isto modo ut sacrosancta Domini testamenta Scripturasque divinas ad exurendum peteret, basilicas dominicas subverteret, et ritus sacros coetusque sanctissimos celebrari Domino prohiberet. Sed non tulit exercitus Domini Dei immane praeceptum, sacrilegamque jussionem perhorruit; et

29. On imperial intervention in a similar matter relating to disposition of a church building, compare No. 27 below.

mox fidei arma corripuit, descendit in praelium, non tam contra homines quam contra diabolum pugnaturus. . . . Advolabant igitur undique versum ad certaminis campum immensa agmina confessorum: et ubi quisque hostem repererat, castra illic dominica collocabat. Namque in civitate Alutinensi [var. leg. Abitinensi] in domo Occani [var. leg Octavi] Felicis, cum bellica caneret tuba, dominica signa gloriosi martyres erexerunt; ubique celebrantes ex more dominica sacramenta, a coloniae magistratibus atque ab ipso stationario milite apprehenduntur, Saturninus presbyter cum filiis quatuor, id est, Saturnino juniore et Felice lectoribus, Maria sanctimoniali, Hilarione infante, itemque Dativus, qui et senator, Felix, alius Felix, Emeritus, . . . [follows 39 more names].

8. . . . Hic cum interrogaretur utrum auctor ipse esset et omnes ipse adunasset, et diceret: Etiam, ego praesens in collecta fui, Emeritus lector ad certamen exiliens, congrediente presbytero: Ego sum auctor, inquit, in cuius domo collecta facta fuit. . . .

9. At vero Emerito applicito, in tua, inquit proconsul, domo collectae factae sunt contra praecepta imperatorum? Cui Emeritus sancto Spiritu inundatus: in domo mea, inquit, egimus dominicum. At ille: Quare permittebas, ait, illos ingredi? Respondit: Quoniam fratres mei sunt, et non poteram illos prohibere. Sed prohibere, inquit, illos debuisti. At ille: Non potui, ait, quoniam sine dominico non possumus. . . .

Translation. 2. In the times of Diocletian and Maximian, the devil declared war on the Christians in this way: by searching for the holy testaments of the Lord and the divine Scriptures for the purpose of having them burned, by destroying the dominical basilicas, and by prohibiting the celebration of sacred rites and most holy assemblies to the Lord. But the army of the Lord God could not tolerate so monstrous a command and shrank in horror from an order so sacrilegious. They seized the arms of faith and descended to the fray to fight, not against men, but against the devil. . . . Great hosts of confessors, therefore, hastened from all sides toward the field of battle, and wherever they found the enemy there they established the camp of the Lord. Thus, in the city of Abitina, in the house of Octavius Felix, the trumpet of war was sounded, and the glorious martyrs erected the standards of the Lord. There, as they were celebrating the sacrament according to custom, were arrested by the magistrates of the colony and its district troops Saturninus, the presbyter, and his four children—that is, Saturninus the younger and Felix, the readers, Maria, a holy virgin, and a lad, Hilarion

— along with Dativus, who was also a senator, [Octavius] Felix, the other Felix, Emeritus, etc. [48 names in all].

[After their arrest and an initial hearing in Abitina (chap. 3) the confessors were sent to Carthage to be tried before the proconsul Anulinus.]

8. . . . Then when he [Saturninus, the presbyter] was asked [by the proconsul] whether he himself was the leader and had brought together all the rest with him, and when he was about to answer, "Yes, I was the one presiding in the assembly," Emeritus, the lector, leaping into the fray with the presbyter said, "I am the guardian in whose house the congregation was assembled." . . .[30]

9. Then turning his attention to Emeritus [after sentencing Saturninus], the proconsul said, "In your house the congregation had been gathered contrary to the order of the emperors?" Since Emeritus was filled with the Holy Spirit, he said, "In my house we conducted the Lord's Supper." The proconsul asked, "Why did you permit them to enter?" Emeritus answered, "Because they are my brothers, and I cannot prohibit them." "But you should have stopped them," (said Anulinus). "Certainly not," said Emeritus, "for it is not possible for us to exist without the Lord's Supper. . . ."

No. 22: Phileas, Bishop of Thmuis (ca. 303–306)

Acta Phileae, P. Bodmer XX, columns IV.12–16, XI.9–XII.1[31]
(from Alexandria, ca. spring, 304–winter, 306/7)
[ed. H. Musurillo, *Acts of the Christian Martyrs* (Oxford, 1972)]

---

30. For the proconsul Anulinus and his role in this period, see No. 35 below. There seems to be some discrepancy in this literary version regarding in whose house they were assembled—that of Octavius Felix or Emeritus the lector. However, it should be noticed that the names suggest numerous familial ties among the church leaders. It is possible that the second Felix and Emeritus were sons of Octavius Felix, a local decurion. For an epigraphic parallel to this situation, also from North Africa, see No. 56 below.

31. As a papyrus record of the court proceedings, this text might be included among the documentary evidence, hence in section II below. Like other accounts of the persecutions, however, it has indications of literary activity by Christian redactors. (So compare the No. 21 above.) The *Acta Phileae* is part of a larger codex containing a number of Christian writings; hence its inclusion here as a literary text. On the basis of the hand, Musurillo dates the present text to ca. 310–325. See Musurillo,

col. IV

. . . . . .

. . . . Κ[ο]υλκ̣[ιαν]ὸς ε̣ἶπεν· Φεῖσαι [σε-]
αυτοῦ καὶ πάν̣[των τ]ῶν σου. θ[ῦσον.]
Φιλέας εἶπεν· Φ[ειδό]μενος ἐ[μαυ-]
τοῦ καὶ πάντων τῶν ἀνηκόντων μ̣ο̣ι, οὐ θύω. . . .

. . . . . .

col. XI

. . . . . .

Κουλκιανὸς εἶπεν· Εἰ μέν τις ἦς
κατὰ τοὺς ἀγροίκους ⟦τ̣ο̣υ̣⟧ τοὺς
δι᾽ ἔνδειαν ἐπιδεδωκότας ἑαυτούς, ‹οὐκ› ἠνειχόμην ἄν σου. ἐπειδὴ δὲ καὶ περιουσίαν ἱκανὴν
κέκτησαι ὡς μὴ μόνον σεαυ-
τὸν ἀλλὰ καὶ πόλιν ὅλην θρέ-
ψαι ‹καὶ› διόκησαι, διὰ τοῦτο φεισά-

col. XII

. . . . . .

μενος σεαυτοῦ θῦσον. . . .

Translation. (Col. IV) . . . Culcianus [the praefect][32] said, “Spare yourself and all your people. Offer the sacrifice.”

Phileas said, “It is to spare myself and all those who belong to me that I do not sacrifice.” . . .

(Col. XI) . . . Culcianus said, “If you were one of the uncultured who turned themselves in out of poverty I would not spare you. But you possess

---

Acts of the Christian Martyrs, xlvii and 331, n. 2. Cf. A. M. Emmet and S. R. Pickering, “The Importance of P. Bodmer XX, *The Apology of Phileas*, and its Problems,” *Prudentia* 7 (1975) 95–103. It should be remembered that Thmuis was the site of the literary activity of the bishop Serapion not much later (ca. 339–362).

32. According to other documents Clodius Culcianus was prefect of Egypt from Feb. 303 to at least May 306. So compare *P. Oxy.* 33.2673, dated 5 Feb. 304 (section II, No. 46 below).

sufficient wealth to nourish and sustain not only yourself but also an entire city.[33] Therefore, spare (Col. XII) yourself and offer sacrifice."

No. 23: Eusebius, Bishop of Caesarea (fl. 300 – ca. 338)
Historia ecclesiastica (written and revised ca. 303–324)
[ed. Schwartz, GCS 9 (1903)]

23a: *Passio S. Marini* (ca. 260–270)
(apud *H.E.* 7.15.3–4 [ca. 303])

[Concerning Marinus, a Christian soldier, upon being ordered to renounce his faith, ca. 265–270.]

15.3 . . . ὡς δ' ὁμολογοῦντα Χριστιανὸν ἐπιμόνως ἑώρα, τριῶν ὡρῶν ἐπιδοῦναι αὐτῷ εἰς ἐπίσκεψιν διάστημα. 4. ἐκτὸς δῆτα γενόμενον αὐτὸν τοῦ δικαστηρίου Θεότεκνος ὁ τῇδε ἐπίσκοπος ἀφέλκει, προσελθὼν δι' ὁμιλίας, καὶ τῆς χειρὸς λαβὼν ἐπὶ τὴν ἐκκλησίαν προάγει. εἴσω τε πρὸς αὐτῷ στήσας τῷ ἁγιάσματι, μικρόν τι παραναστείλας αὐτοῦ τῆς χλαμύδος καὶ τὸ προσηρτημένον αὐτῷ ξίφος ἐπιδείξας ἅμα τε ἀντιπαρατίθησιν προσαγαγὼν αὐτῷ τὴν τῶν θείων εὐαγγελίων γραφήν, κελεύσας τῶν δυεῖν ἑλέσθαι τὸ κατὰ γνώμην. ὡς δ' ἀμελλητὶ τὴν δεξιὰν προτείνας ἐδέξατο τὴν θείαν γραφήν.

Translation. 3. . . . When he [the judge, Achaeus] saw how persistently he [Marinus] confessed himself a Christian, he gave him a space of three hours to reconsider. 4. Then, when he came outside Theoteknos, the bishop there, approached, and drawing him aside in conversation, he took him by the hand and led him into the church building. Inside, standing beside the sanctuary[34] itself, he raised his cloak a little and pointed to the sword fas-

33. Compare the wording of the later Latin version, the *Passio beati Phileae* 5.4 (= Recension B in Musurillo, *Acts of the Christian Martyrs*, 345–53): *Culcianus dixit: Si scirem te indigere et sic in hanc amentiam venisse, non tibi parcerem, sed quia substantiam multam habes, ita ut non te solum sed prope cunctam provinciam alere possis, ideo parco tibi et sudeo te immolere.*

34. The text clearly presupposes a formal layout to the church building, since the "sanctuary," or "holy place" (τῷ ἁγιάσματι), is an articulated space *within* the edifice. K. Lake (in his LCL edition of Eusebius) translates the term as a reference to the "altar" of the church, a plausible suggestion. The term was more regularly used, however, as a synonym for θυσιαστήριον, rather than ἁγιαστήριον, so compare Amos

tened to him. At the same time he brought and placed before him the book of the divine gospels commanding him to take his choice of the two. Without delay he stretched forth his right hand and took the divine book.

23b: Eusebius. *H.E.* 8.1.5; 1.9–2.1 (ca. 285–303)
(from an early redaction of the work, ca. 303)[35]

[Concerning the great growth of the church in the period just prior to the persecution under Diocletian, Eusebius adduces proof from favors shown to the Christians by public officials and from the number of converts among the imperial families (8.1.1–4). He then continues.]

(1.5) οἵας τε καὶ τοὺς καθ' ἑκάστην ἐκκλησίαν ἄρχοντας παρὰ πᾶσιν ἐπιτρόποις καὶ ἡγεμόσιν ἀποδοχῆς ἦν ὁρᾶν ἀξιουμένους. πῶς δ' ἄν τις διαγράψειεν τὰς μυριάνδρους ἐκείνας ἐπισυναγωγὰς καὶ τὰ πλήθη τῶν κατὰ πᾶσαν πόλιν ἀθροισμάτων τάς τε ἐπισήμους ἐν τοῖς προσευκτηρίοις συνδρομάς; ὧν δὴ ἕνεκα μηδαμῶς ἔτι τοῖς πάλαι οἰκοδομήμασιν ἀρκούμενοι, εὐρείας εἰς πλάτος ἀνὰ πάσας τὰς πόλεις ἐκ θεμελίων ἀνίστων ἐκκλησίας. . . .

Translation. . . . With what favor one may observe the rulers in every church being honored by all procurators and governors. Or how could anyone describe those assemblies with numberless crowds and the great throngs gathered together in every city as well as the remarkable concourses in the houses of prayer? On account of these things, no longer being satisfied with their old buildings, they erected from the foundations churches of spacious dimensions in every city. . . .

7:13 and Lev 12:4 in the LXX and Eusebius, *H.E.* 10.4.33; 68. Hence, a "sacristy" or segregated space for the clergy and altar, of the sort suggested by the wording in Cyprian, *Ep.* 59.18.1 (*sacrum venerandumque congestum*, see no. 16d and n. 24 above) is also possible. On the other hand, in the proximate passage from *H.E.* 8.1.9 (No. 23b below) Eusebius uses the same term to refer to the building itself, based on the wording of Ps 88 (89), LXX.

35. On the stages of composition of the work, see Lawlor and Oulton, *Eusebius: The Ecclesiastical History and the Martyrs of Palestine*, 2. 5–6; H. J. Lawlor, *Eusebiana: Essays on the Ecclesiastical History of Eusebius* (Oxford: Clarendon, 1912) 211–35; R. M. Grant, "Eusebius H.E. VIII: Another Suggestion," *VC* 22 (1968) 16–18.

[After showing the growth and favor of the churches, Eusebius argues that the advent of the persecutions was an exercise of divine judgment as a result of the pride, sloth, and divisiveness that came with the growth.]

(1.9) κατά τε τὰ ἐν Ψαλμοῖς προθεσπισθέντα "κατέστρεψεν τὴν διαθήκην τοῦ δούλου αὐτοῦ" καὶ "ἐβεβήλωσεν εἰς γῆν" διὰ τῆς τῶν ἐκκλησιῶν καθαιρέσεως "τὸ ἁγίασμα αὐτοῦ" καὶ "καθεῖλεν πάντας τοὺς φραγμοὺς αὐτοῦ, ἔθετο τὰ ὀχυρώματα αὐτοῦ δειλίαν· διήρπασάν" τε τὰ πλήθη τοῦ λαοῦ πάντες οἱ διοδεύοντες ὁδόν, καὶ δὴ ἐπὶ τούτοις "ὄνειδος ἐγενήθη τοῖς γείτοσιν αὐτοῦ. ὕψωσεν γὰρ τὴν δεξιὰν τῶν ἐχθρῶν αὐτοῦ" καὶ "ἀπέστρεψεν τὴν βοήθειαν τῆς ῥομφαίας αὐτοῦ καὶ οὐκ ἀντελάβετο αὐτοῦ ἐν τῷ πολέμῳ·" ἀλλὰ καὶ "κατέλυσεν ἀπὸ καθαρισμοῦ αὐτὸν" καὶ "τὸν θρόνον αὐτοῦ εἰς τὴν γῆν κατέρραξεν ἐσμίκρυνέν" τε "τὰς ἡμέρας τοῦ χρόνου αὐτοῦ," καὶ ἐπὶ πᾶσιν "κατέχεεν αὐτοῦ αἰσχύνην." 2.1. συντετέλεσται δῆτα καθ' ἡμᾶς ἅπαντα, ὁπηνίκα τῶν μὲν προσευκτηρίων τοὺς οἴκους ἐξ ὕψους εἰς ἔδαφος αὐτοῖς θεμελίοις καταρριπτουμένους, τὰς δ' ἐνθέους καὶ ἱερὰς γραφὰς κατὰ μέσας ἀγορὰς πυρὶ παραδιδομένας αὐτοῖς ἐπείδομεν ὀφθαλμοῖς τούς τε τῶν ἐκκλησιῶν ποιμένας αἰσχρῶς ὧδε κἀκεῖσε κρυπταζομένους, τοὺς δὲ ἀσχημόνως ἁλισκομένους καὶ πρὸς τῶν ἐχθρῶν καταπαιζομένους. . . .

Translation. According to what was foretold in the Psalms [Ps 88 (89):40–46, LXX], "He [God] has overturned the covenant of his servant" and, through the destruction of the churches, "has profaned to the ground his sanctuary" and "has broken down all his hedges; he has made his strongholds cowardice. All those who pass by the way despoil" the multitudes of the people, and what is more, "he has become a reproach to his neighbors. For He has raised high the right hand of his adversaries" and has averted "the aid of his sword and" has "not" taken "his part in the battle." But He [God] has "ceased his purification," has cast "his throne to the ground," has shortened "the days of his time," and, above all, "has covered him with shame."

All these things were accomplished in our time, when we saw the houses of prayer cast down from top to bottom, to their very foundations. With our own eyes we saw the inspired sacred scriptures delivered to the fire in the midst of the market-places, and [we saw] the pastors of the churches: some hiding shamefully here and there; others captured indecently and mocked by their enemies. . . .

23c: Eusebius, *H.E.* 10.2.1; 3.1 (final redaction, ca. 324)

[Concerning the rebuilding of churches after the persecutions.]

2.1 . . . μάλιστα δ' ἡμῖν τοῖς ἐπὶ τὸν Χριστὸν τοῦ θεοῦ τὰς ἐλπίδας ἀνηρτημένοις ἄλεκτος παρῆν εὐφροσύνη καί τις ἔνθεος ἅπασιν ἐπήνθει χαρὰ πάντα τόπον τὸν πρὸ μικροῦ ταῖς τῶν τυράννων δυσσεβείαις ἠριπωμένον ὥσπερ ἐκ μακρᾶς καὶ θανατηφόρου λύμης ἀναβιώσκοντα θεωμένοις νεώς τε αὖθις ἐκ βάθρων εἰς ὕψος ἄπειρον ἐγειρομένους καὶ πολὺ κρείττονα τὴν ἀγλαΐαν τῶν πάλαι πεπολιορκημένων ἀπολαμβάνοντας. . . .

3.1. Ἐπὶ δὴ τούτοις τὸ πᾶσιν εὐκταῖον ἡμῖν καὶ ποθούμενον συνεκροτεῖτο θέαμα, ἐγκαινίων ἑορταὶ κατὰ πόλεις καὶ τῶν ἄρτι νεοπαγῶν προσευκτηρίων ἀφιερώσεις, ἐπισκόπων ἐπὶ ταὐτὸν συνηλύσεις, τῶν πόρρωθεν ἐξ ἀλλοδαπῆς συνδρομαί, λαῶν εἰς λαοὺς φιλοφρονήσεις, τῶν Χριστοῦ σώματος μελῶν εἰς μίαν συνιόντων ἁρμοίαν ἕνωσις. . . .

Translation. 2.1. And especially for us who had fixed our hopes on the Christ of God did unutterable happiness come to pass, and a divine joy blossomed in all as we beheld every place which, a short time before, had been torn down by the impious deeds of the tyrants. Reviving as from long and deadly mistreatment the temples were raised once again from the foundation to a lofty height and received in far greater measure the magnificence of those that had formerly been destroyed. . . .

3.1. And after these things there came to pass that spectacle for which we had all prayed and longed, namely festivals of dedication in every city and consecration of the newly-built houses of prayer,[36] convening of the bishops, assembling together of those from far-off lands, acts of kindness of congregations upon congregations, and union in the members of Christ's body as they came together in complete harmony. . . .

23d: Eusebius, *H.E.* 10.4.36–46 (final redaction, ca. 324)

[Eusebius's description of the newly built church at Tyre from his pane-

36. In *H.E.* 10.4 Eusebius records the panegyric that he himself delivered at just such an occasion, the rededication of the "temple" at Tyre, which had been rebuilt magnificently as a church under the patronage and direction of the bishop. For a description of this church, see 10.4.37–45 (No. 23d below).

gyric to the bishop of Tyre, Paulinus, on the occasion of the dedication, probably ca. 317; cf. *H.E.* 10.3.1; 4.1 (No. 23c, above).]

36. Τούτων δεῖν ἀπολαῦσαι τὴν διὰ θεὸν γενομένην ἔρημον τοῦ λόγου προαγορεύοντος, ἐπακούσας ὀξείᾳ διανοίας ἀκοῇ οὗτος ὁ νέος ἡμῶν καὶ καλὸς Ζοροβαβελ μετὰ τὴν πικρὰν ἐκείνην αἰχμαλωσίαν καὶ "τὸ βδέλυγμα τῆς ἐρημώσεως," οὐ παριδὼν τὸ πτῶμα νεκρόν, πρώτιστα πάντων παρακλήσεσιν καὶ λιταῖς ἵλεω τὸν πατέρα μετὰ τῆς κοινῆς ὑμῶν ἁπάντων ὁμοφροσύνης καταστησάμενος καὶ τὸν μόνον νεκρῶν ζῳοποιὸν σύμμαχον παραλαβὼν καὶ συνεργόν, τὴν πεσοῦσαν ἐξήγειρεν προαποκαθάρας καὶ προθεραπεύσας τῶν κακῶν, καὶ στολὴν οὐ τὴν ἐξ ἀρχαίου παλαιὰν αὐτῇ περιτέθεικεν, ἀλλ᾽ ὁποίαν αὖθις παρὰ τῶν θείων χρησμῶν ἐξεπαιδεύετο, σαφῶς ὧδε λεγόντων "καὶ ἔσται ἡ δόξα τοῦ οἴκου τούτου ἡ ἐσχάτη ὑπὲρ τὴν προτέραν."

37. Ταύτῃ δ᾽ οὖν πολὺ μείζονα τὸν χῶρον ἅπαντα περιλαβών, τὸν μὲν ἔξωθεν ὠχυροῦτο περίβολον τῷ τοῦ παντὸς περιτειχίσματι, ὡς ἂν ἀσφαλέστατον εἴη τοῦ παντὸς ἕρκος· 38. πρόπυλον δὲ μέγα καὶ εἰς ὕψος ἐπηρμένον πρὸς αὐτὰς ἀνίσχοντος ἡλίου ἀκτῖνας ἀναπετάσας, ἤδη καὶ τοῖς μακρὰν περιβόλων ἔξω ἱερῶν ἑστῶσιν τῆς τῶν ἔνδον παρέσχεν ἀφθονίαν θέας, μόνον οὐχὶ καὶ τῶν ἀλλοτρίων τῆς πίστεως ἐπὶ τὰς πρώτας εἰσόδους ἐπιστρέφων τὰς ὄψεις, ὡς ἂν μὴ παρατρέχοι τις ὅτι μὴ τὴν ψυχὴν κατανυγεὶς πρότερον μνήμῃ τῆς τε πρὶν ἐρημίας καὶ τῆς νῦν παραδόξου θαυματουργίας, ὑφ᾽ ἧς τάχα καὶ ἑλκυσθήσεσθαι κατανυγέντα καὶ πρὸς αὐτῆς τῆς ὄψεως ἐπὶ τὴν εἴσοδον προτραπήσεσθαι ἤλπισεν. 39. εἴσω δὲ παρελθόντι πυλῶν οὐκ εὐθὺς ἔφηκεν ἀνάγνοις καὶ ἀνίπτοις ποσὶν τῶν ἔνδον ἐπιβαίνειν ἁγίων, διαλαβὼν δὲ πλεῖστον ὅσον τὸ μεταξὺ τοῦ τε νεὼ καὶ τῶν πρώτων εἰσόδων, τέτταρσι μὲν πέριξ ἐγκαρσίοις κατεκόσμησεν στοαῖς, εἰς τετράγωνόν τι σχῆμα περιφράξας τὸν τόπον, κίοσι πανταχόθεν ἐπαιρομέναις· ὧν τὰ μέσα διαφράγμασι τοῖς ἀπὸ ξύλου δικτυωτοῖς ε(ἰ)ς τὸ σύμμετρον ἥκουσι μήκους περκλείσας, μέσον αἴθριον ἠφίει εἰς τὴν τοῦ οὐρανοῦ κάτοψιν, λαμπρὸν καὶ ταῖς τοῦ φωτὸς ἀκτῖσιν ἀνειμένον ἀέρα παρέχων. 40. ἱερῶν δ᾽ ἐνταῦθα καθαρσίων ἐτίθει σύμβολα, κρήνας ἄντικρυς εἰς πρόσωπον ἐπισκευάζων τοῦ νεὼ πολλῷ τῷ χεύματι τοῦ νάματος τοῖς περιβόλων ἱερῶν ἐπὶ τὰ ἔσω προϊοῦσιν τὴν ἀπόρυψιν παρεχομένας. καὶ πρώτη μὲν εἰσιόντων αὕτη διατριβή, κόσμον ὁμοῦ καὶ ἀγλαΐαν τῷ παντὶ τοῖς τε τῶν πρώτων εἰσαγωγῶν ἔτι δεομένοις κατάλληλον τὴν μονὴν παρεχομένη.

41. Ἀλλὰ γὰρ καὶ τὴν τούτων θέαν παραμειψάμενος, πλείοσιν ἔτι μαλ-

λον τοῖς ἐνδοτάτω προπύλοις τὰς ἐπὶ τὸν νεὼν παρόδους ἀναπεπταμένας ἐποίει, ὑπὸ μὲν ταῖς ἡλίου βολαῖς αὖθις τρεῖς πύλας ὑφ᾽ ἓν καταθεὶς πλευρόν, ὧν πολὺ τὰς παρ᾽ ἑκάτερα μεγέθει τε καὶ πλάτει πλεονεκτεῖν τῇ μέσῃ χαρισάμενος παραπήγμασί τε χαλκοῦ σιδηροδέτοις καὶ ποικίλμασιν ἀναγλύφοις διαφερόντως αὐτὴν φαιδρύνας, ὡς ἂν βασιλίδι ταύτῃ τοὺς δορυφόρους ὑπέζευξεν· 42. τὸν αὐτὸν δὲ τρόπον καὶ ταῖς παρ᾽ ἑκάτερα τοῦ παντὸς νεὼ στοαῖς τὸν τῶν προπύλων ἀριθμὸν διατάξας, ἄνωθεν ἐπὶ ταύταις ἄλλῳ πλείονι φωτὶ διαφόρους τὰς ἐπὶ τὸν οἶκον εἰσβολὰς ἐπενόει, ταῖς ἀπὸ ξύλου λεπτουργίαις καὶ τὸν περὶ αὐτὰς κόσμον καταποικίλλων.

Τὸν δὲ βασίλειον οἶκον πλουσιωτέραις ἤδη καὶ δαψιλέσι ταῖς ὕλαις ὠχύρου ἀφθόνῳ φιλοτιμίᾳ τῶν ἀναλωμάτων χρώμενος. 43. ἔνθα μοι δοκῶ περιττὸν εἶναι τοῦ δομήματος μήκη τε καὶ πλάτη καταγράφειν, τὰ φαιδρὰ ταῦτα κάλλη καὶ τὰ λόγου κρείττονα μεγέθη τήν τε τῶν ἔργων ἀποστίλβουσαν ὄψιν τῷ λόγῳ διεξιόντι ὕψη τε τὰ οὐρανομήκη καὶ τὰς τούτων ὑπερκειμένας πολυτελεῖς τοῦ Λιβάνου κέδρους, ὧν οὐδὲ τὸ θεῖον λόγιον τὴν μνήμην ἀπεσιώπησεν "εὐφρανθήσεται" φάσκον "τὰ ξύλα τοῦ κυρίου, καὶ αἱ κέδροι τοῦ Λιβάνου ἃς ἐφύτευσεν."

44. Τί με δεῖ νῦν τῆς πανσόφου καὶ ἀρχιτεκτονικῆς διατάξεως καὶ τοῦ κάλλους τῆς ἐφ᾽ ἑκάστου μέρους ὑπερβολῆς ἀκριβολογεῖσθαι τὴν ὑφήγησιν, ὅτε τῆς ὄψεως τὴν διὰ τῶν ὤτων ἀποκλείει μάθησιν ἡ μαρτυρία; ἀλλὰ γὰρ ὧδε καὶ τὸν νεὼν ἐπιτελέσας θρόνοις τε τοῖς ἀνωτάτω εἰς τὴν τῶν προέδρων τιμὴν καὶ προσέτι βάθροις ἐν τάξει τοῖς καθ᾽ ὅλου κατὰ τὸ πρέπον κοσμήσας ἐφ᾽ ἅπασίν τε τὸ τῶν ἁγίων ἅγιον θυσιαστήριον ἐν μέσῳ θείς, αὖθις καὶ τάδε, ὡς ἂν εἴη τοῖς πολλοῖς ἄβατα, τοῖς ἀπὸ ξύλου περιέφραττε δικτύοις εἰς ἄκρον ἐντέχνου λεπτουργίας ἐξησκημένοις, ὡς θαυμάσιον τοῖς ὁρῶσιν παρέχειν τὴν θέαν.

45. Ἀλλ᾽ οὐδὲ τοὔδαφος ἄρα εἰς ἀμελὲς ἔκειτο αὐτῷ· καὶ τόδε γοῦν λίθῳ μαρμάρῳ εὖ μάλα κόσμῳ παντὶ λαμπρύνας, ἤδη λοιπὸν καὶ ἐπὶ τὰ ἐκτὸς τοῦ νεὼ μετῄει, ἐξέδρας καὶ οἴκους τοὺς παρ᾽ ἑκάτερα μεγίστους ἐπισκευάζων ἐντέχνως ἐπὶ ταὐτὸν εἰς πλευρὰ τῷ βασιλείῳ συνεζευγμένους καὶ ταῖς ἐπὶ τὸν μέσον οἶκον εἰσβολαῖς ἡνωμένους· ἃ καὶ αὐτὰ τοῖς ἔτι καθάρσεως καὶ περιρραντηρίων τῶν διὰ ὕδατος καὶ ἁγίου πνεύματος ἐγχρῄζουσιν ὁ εἰρηνικώτατος ἡμῶν Σολομὼν ὁ τὸν νεὼν τοῦ θεοῦ δειμάμενος ἀπειργάζετο, ὡς μηκέτι λόγον, ἀλλ᾽ ἔργον γεγονέναι τὴν ἄνω λεχθεῖσαν προφητείαν. 46. γέγονεν γὰρ καὶ νῦν ὡς ἀληθῶς ἐστιν "ἡ δόξα τοῦ οἴκου τούτου ἡ ἐσχάτη ὑπὲρ τὴν προτέραν."

Translation. 36. Those things which the word foretold, namely that she (i.e., the church) who had been made desolate by God must be profited, this our youthful and nobel Zerubbabel [i.e., the bishop Paulinus, cf. Hag 2:2–9)[37] attended to with the sharp hearing of his mind following on that severe captivity and "the abomination of desolation" (Matt 24:15//Mark 13:14, cf. Dan 12:11, LXX). Not disregarding the corpse as dead he first of all propitiated the Father with entreaties and supplications by the common consent of you all. Then, taking as (his) ally and fellow-worker him alone who makes the dead alive, he raised up the fallen and cleansed and healed her of her ills. Nor did he clothe her with the old robe with which she had been wrapped from the beginning, but with such as he was instructed again by the divine oracles, which clearly say, "The latter glory of this house shall be greater than the former" (Hag 2:9, LXX with variants).

37. Thus, then, the whole area that he enclosed was much larger (than previously). The outer enclosure he fortified with a wall surrounding the whole, so that it might be a secure courtyard for the whole. 38. He spread out a gateway, great and raised on high toward the very rays of the rising sun. Even to those who stand far off outside the sacred enclosures, it provides an abundant view of what is within, well-nigh turning the gaze of even strangers to the faith toward the first entrances so that none might rush by without first having his soul "pricked" (cf. Acts 2:37) by the memory of the desolation of before and the marvelous miracle of today. He hoped that such a one, being struck by it, might be drawn to the sight and turned toward the entrance. 39. But he did not permit the one passing inside the gates to come immediately with unholy and unwashed feet upon the holy places within. Marking off a great expanse between the temple and the first gates he

37. Cf. 10.4.3. Eusebius will carry forward the thematic device of portraying Paulinus as the "new Zerubbabel," the one who rebuilt Solomon's Temple after the exile, for the sake of the panegyric. In this vein, he consistently refers to the church building as both "house of God" and "temple," and he lavishes praise on the new edifice, using Hag 2:9 as his catchphrase: "the latter glory of this house shall be greater than the former." (So note 10.4.45, at the end of this passage.) In 10.4.63–68 there follows an elaborate, layered allegory on the "spiritual temple" (i.e., the universal church) drawn point for point from this same description, in a manner similar to the Visions and Similitudes of the tower in *The Shepherd of Hermas*. Note, for example, *H.E.* 10.4.44 and 68, where the altar in the church is not only the "holy of holies" of the earthly temple but is also the very "soul" of Jesus himself.

adorned all around it with four transverse *stoai*, which enclosed the area in a kind of quadrangular figure with columns raised on all sides. He enclosed their intermittent spaces with wooden lattice-work partitions which reached an appropriate height, and he left an atrium in the middle for beholding the sky, providing it with airy brightness, open to the rays of light. 40. Herein he placed symbols of holy purification; he erected opposite the front (façade) of the temple fountains whose plenteous streams of flowing water provide cleansing for those who will proceed into the interior of the sacred enclosure. This is the first station for those who enter, providing at once adornment and splendor to everything for those who are yet in need of their first introductory instructions.

41. And verily, passing on from this spectacle, he made the entry passages to the temple wide openings by means of still more innermost gateways. Once again under the rays of the sun he placed on one side three gates, of which he favored the middle one in height and breadth to surpass far beyond those on either side. He distinguished it in brilliance with registers, fasteners of bronze, and varied relief-carvings, and he subjected (the others) as body guards to their queen. 42. In the same way also he arranged the number of gateways for the *stoai* on either flank of the whole temple, and in addition to these he designed up above different openings to the building for still more light, varying the adornment pertaining to them in finely worked wood-carving.

Now the Royal House (Gk. *Basileion oikon*) he fortified with richer and even more lavish materials, being endowed with an ungrudging liberality as to the cost. 43. I consider it superfluous for me to describe here the length and breadth of the edifice, its brilliant beauty, its magnitude too great for words, its loftiness reaching heaven, and stretching above, its costly "cedars of Lebanon," concerning which even the divine word does not refrain to mention, saying, "The trees of the Lord shall rejoice, even the cedars of Lebanon which he planted" (Ps 104[103]:16, LXX with variants).

44. Why need I now describe in detail (his) guidance of the wise and skillful architectural arrangements and the surpassing beauty of each part, since the testimony of the eyes leaves no room for instruction through the ears? But verily, having thus completed the temple he also adorned it with very lofty thrones in honor of the presidents and, moreover, with benches arranged throughout in accord with propriety, and, finally, he set in (their) midst the altar, the holy of holies. Once again, then, so that they might be inaccessible to the masses, he fenced around them with wooden lattice-

work, adorned with the craftsman's utmost artistry so as to present a wonderful scene to the beholder.

45. Nor did even the pavement escape his care. Indeed this, too, he made brilliant with all kinds of ornate marble. And even for the rest, passing on to the outside of the temple, he constructed *exedrai* (covered arcades or halls) and large buildings on either side; they were skillfully joined to the flanks of the Royal House, and they communicated with the openings into the central building. These also our most peaceful Solomon, who built the temple of God, completed for those who are in need of purification and sprinkling of water and the Holy Spirit, so that the prophecy mentioned before has become no longer only a word but is instead a deed. For, it has come to pass and now in truth *is* "the latter glory of this house greater than the former."

No. 24: Lactantius (fl. ca. 290–ca. 320; born in Africa but served in imperial courts at Nicomedia and Treves)

De mortibus persecutorum 12 (ca. 319)
[ed. Brandt, CSEL 27]

[A description of the destruction of the church building at Nicomedia on 23 February 303, at the outbreak of the Great Persecution.]

Quaeritur peragendae rei dies aptus et felix ac potissimum Terminalia deliguntur, quae sunt a. d. septimum Kalendas Martias, ut quasi terminus imponeretur huic religioni.

> Ille dies primus leti primusque malorum
> Causa fuit

quae et ipsis et orbi terrarum acciderunt. 2. Qui dies cum illuxisset, agentibus consulatum senibus ambobus octavum et septimum, repente adhuc dubia luce ad ecclesiam praefectus cum ducibus et tribunis et rationalibus venit: et revulsis foribus simulacrum dei quaeritur, scripturae repertae incenduntur, datur omnibus praeda, rapitur, trepidatur, discurritur. 3. Ipsi vero in speculis—in alto enim constituta ecclesia ex palatio videbatur—diu inter se concertabant utrum ignem potius supponi oporteret. 4. Vicit sententiam Diocletianus cavens, ne magno incendio facto pars aliqua civitatis arderet. Nam multae ac magnae domus ab omni parte cingebant. 5. Veniebant igitur praetoriani acie structa cum securibus et aliis ferramentis et immissi undique fanum illud editissimum paucis horis solo adaequarunt.

Translation. In the accomplishment of this matter a fitting and happy day was sought, and above all the Terminalia [the festival of the god Terminus], which were conducted on the seventh of the kalends of March [23 February], were selected so that a "termination," as it were, might be brought to this religion.

> *That day the harbinger of death arose,*
> *First cause of ill, and long-enduring woes*
> [*Aeneid* 4. 169f]

which befell both these very Christians [at Nicomedia] and the whole earth. When that day dawned, in the eighth and seventh consulship of the two emperors [Diocletian and Maximian], suddenly while it was hardly light the prefect with commanders, tribunes, and officers of the treasury came to the church. When its doors had been pulled away it was searched for an image of the god. When the scriptures were found they were burned. It [the building] was opened to all for desecration; it was looted, tossed, and trampled. Since the church was situated on a high spot it was visible from the palace; indeed, the two (emperors) disputed from a watchtower whether it ought to be set on fire. Diocletian prevailed in his opinion; he cautioned against causing such a great fire lest other parts of the city be set ablaze. For many larger houses surrounded (the building) on all sides. Thus, the praetorian guard came in battle array with axes and other tools. They attacked everywhere, and in a few hours they levelled to the ground that very lofty temple.

Part B: Non-Christian Sources

(some preserved by Christian writers)

No. 25: Pliny the Younger [Gaius Plinius Caecilius Secundus], *Legatur Augusti* of Bithynia-Pontus (ca. 110)

Letter to the emperor Trajan concerning the investigation of Christians [Pliny, *Ep.* 10.96.7–9 [ed. R. Mynors, *Plinius Minor* (Oxford Classical Texts; Oxford: Clarendon, 1963), as printed in A. N. Sherwin-White, *Fifty Letters of Pliny.*

7. Adfirmabant autem hanc fuisse summum vel culpae suae vel erroris, quod essent soliti stato die ante lucem convenire, carmenque Christo quasi

deo dicere secum invicem seque sacramento non in scelus aliquod obstringere, sed ne furta ne latrocinia ne adulteria committerent, ne fidem fallerent ne depositum adpellati abnegarent. Quibus peractis morem sibi discedendi fuisse rursusque coeundi ad capiendum cibum, promiscuum tamen et innoxium; quod ipsum facere desisse post edictum meum, quo secundum mandata tua hetaerias esse vetueram. 8. Quo magis necessarium credidi ex duabus ancillis, quae ministrae dicebantur, quid esset veri, et per tormenta quaerere. Nihil aliud inveni quam superstitionem pravam et immodicam.

9. Ideo dilata cognitione ad consulendum te decucurri. Visa est enim mihi res digna consultatione, maxime propter periclitantium numerum. Multi enim omnis aetatis, omnis ordinis, utriusque sexus etiam vocantur in periculum et vacabantur. Neque civitates tantum, sed vicos etiam atque agros superstitionis istius contagio pervagata est; quae videtur sisti et corrigi posse. . . .

Translation. They [those who were examined by Pliny] insisted that the sum of their guilt or error was this, that it was their customary practice to assemble before daylight on a fixed day and with one another sing hymns to Christ as god, and that they bound themselves with an oath not for any crime but that they should commit neither theft nor robbery nor adultery nor break a trust nor deny a deposit upon demand. After this was done, it was their custom to depart and to assemble again to partake of food, but food of an ordinary kind and harmless; but even this practice (they declared that) they had ceased after my edict, following your mandate, in which I had prohibited the existence of such clubs. In this matter I felt it necessary to examine under torture whether this were true from two (female) slaves who are called deaconesses. I discovered nothing more than a perverse and excessive superstition.

For this reason I took recourse of putting off the trial in order to consult you [the emperor]. It appears to me to be a matter worthy of (imperial) consultation, especially because of the number of those in (legal) danger. For many people, of all ages, of all ranks, and of both sexes, are summoned and will be summoned to trial. And not only in the cities but even to villages and the countryside has spread the contagion of this superstition. Even so it seems possible to arrest and correct the situation.

No. 26: *The Edessene Chronicle* (Codex Vaticanus Syr. 163; Syria, late seventh century CE)
[ed. L. Hallier, TU 9.1 (1892)]

I (VIII) [page 1 recto, column a].

ܒܫܢܬ ܚܡܫܡܐܐ ܘܬܠܬܥܣܪܐ ܒܡܠܟܘܬܗ ܕܣܘܪܘܣ.
ܘܒܡܠܟܘܬܗ ܕܐܒܓܪ ܡܠܟܐ ܒܪ ܡܥܢܘ ܡܠܟܐ. ܒܝܪܚ
ܬܫܪܝ ܐܚܪܝ. ܥܒܪ ܗܘܐ ܡܥܝܢܐ ܕܡ̈ܝܐ ܕܢܦܩ ܡܢ ܐܦܕܢܐ
ܪܒܐ· ܕܐܒܓܪ ܡܠܟܐ ܪܒܐ. ܘܥܒܪ ܘܣܠܩ ܐܝܟ ܥܝܕܗ ܡܥܝܕܐ.
ܘܡܠܐ ܗܘܐ ܘܫܦܥ ܠܟܘܠ ܓܒܝܢ. ܘܫܪܝ ܗܘܘ ܕܪ̈ܬܐ
ܘܐܣܛܘ̈ܐ ܘܒ̈ܬܐ ܕܡܠܟܘܬܐ ܕܢܬܡܠܘܢ. ܡ̈ܝܐ

[page 2 recto, column b].

ܠܬ̈ܚܘܡܝܗܘܢ ܗܘܘ ܩܕܡ ܠܡܘܪܐ ܡܒܕܪܐ
ܕܡܕܝܢܬܐ. ܘܚܒܠܘ ܠܗܝܟܠܐ ܡܕܝܢܬܐ. ܘܚܪܒܘ ܠܐܦܕܢܐ ܪܒܐ ܘܫܦܝܪܐ
ܕܡܪܢ ܡܠܟܐ. ܘܥܩܪܘ ܗܘܘ ܟܠ ܡܕܡ ܕܐܫܟܚܘ ܗܘܐ
ܡܛܝܒܝܢ. ܒ̈ܢܝܢܐ ܒܣ̈ܝܡܐ ܘܫܦܝܪܐ ܕܡܕܝܢܬܐ. ܟܠ ܡܕܡ ܕܩܪܝܒ
ܗܘܐ ܠܢܗܪܐ ܡܢ ܓܪܒܝܐ ܘܬܝܡܢܐ. ܘܚܪܒܘ ܗܘܘ ܐܦ
ܗܝܟܠܐ ܕܥܕܬܐ ܕܟܪ̈ܣܛܝܢܐ.

Translation. In the month of Tisri in the year 513 [Nov., 201 CE] in the reign of (the Caesar) Severus and in the reign of King Abgar (IX), son of King Ma'nu, the spring of water that rose in the great palace of Abgar (V) the Great flowed more strongly than ever, increased in a customary manner, and became full and overflowed on all sides, so that the royal halls, the stoai, and apartments began to stand with water. . . . The flood waters at the very same moment broke through the west wall of the city; they destroyed the great and magnificent palace of our Lord the King and tearing away everything that lay in their path and all the beautiful and splendid buildings that stood near the river on the north and the south. They even destroyed the temple (or holy place) of the church of the Christians. . . . [partially adapted from the German translation of Hallier, *TU* 9.1, 84f.]

XII [page 2 recto, column b].

ܒܫܢܬ ܫܬܡܐܐ ܘܥܣܪ̈ܝܢ ܘܐܪܒܥ. ܩܘܢܐ ܐܦܣܩܘܦܐ
ܫܬܐܣܬܗ ܕܥܕܬܐ ܕܐܘܪܗܝ. ܘܒܢܐ ܘܫܡܠܝܗ ܠܒܢܝܢܐ. ܣܥܕ
ܐܦܣܩܘܦܐ ܕܗܘܐ ܡܢ ܒܬܪܗ

Translation. In the year 624 [313 CE] bishop Ḳûnê (Ḳona') laid the foundation for the church of ʻOrhai [Edessa]; bishop Saʻad built and completed it after him.

No. 27: Severus Alexander (Emperor 222–235)
(apud Lampridius, *Historia Augusta, Severus Alexander* 49.6)
[ed. H. Peter, as printed in LCL edition of D. Magie, *Scriptores Historiae Augustae* (London, 1921)]

Cum Christiani quendam locum, qui publicus fuerat, occupassent, contra popinarii dicerent sibi eum deberi, rescripsit melius esse, ut quemadmodumcumque illic deus colatur, quam popinariis dedatur.

Translation. When Christians took possession of a certain place, which had been public (property), whereas the *popinarii* (cooks or keepers of an eating house) maintained that it should belong to them, he [Alexander] rendered the decision that it was better for any god whatsoever to be worshiped in that place than for it to be given over to *popinarii*.

No. 28: The Emperor Gallienus (260–268), Edict of Toleration, from a Letter Sent to the Christian Bishops Clarifying the Edict (261)
(apud Eusebius, *H.E.* 7.13 [ca. 303])
[ed. Schwartz, GCS 9 (1903)]

Αὐτοκράτωρ Καῖσαρ Πούπλιος Λικίνιος Γαλλιῆνος Εὐσεβὴς Εὐτυχὴς Σεβαστὸς Διόυσίῳ καὶ Πίννᾳ καὶ Δημητρίῳ καὶ τοῖς λοιποῖς ἐπισκόποις. τὴν εὐεργεσίαν τῆς ἐμῆς δωρεᾶς διὰ παντὸς τοῦ κόσμου ἐκβιβασθῆναι προσέταξα, ὅπως ἀπὸ τῶν τόπων τῶν θρῃσκευσίμων ἀποχωρήσωσιν, καὶ διὰ τοῦτο καὶ ὑμεῖς τῆς ἀντιγραφῆς τῆς ἐμῆς τῷ τύπῳ χρῆσθαι δύνασθε, ὥστε μηδένα ὑμῖν ἐνοχλεῖν. καὶ τοῦτο, ὅπερ κατὰ τὸ ἐξὸν δύναται ὑφ᾽ ὑμῶν ἀναπληροῦσθαι, ἤδη πρὸ πολλοῦ ὑπ᾽ ἐμοῦ συγκεχώρηται, καὶ διὰ τοῦτο Αὐρήλιος Κυρίνιος, ὁ τοῦ μεγίστου πράγματος προστατεύων, τὸν τύπον τὸν ὑπ᾽ ἐμοῦ δοθέντα διαφυλάξει.

Translation. The Emperor Caesar Publius Licinius Gallienus Pius Felix Augustus to Dionysius, Pinnas, Demetrius, and the rest of the bishops. I have ordered that the benefaction of my gift be published throughout the whole world, so that the places of worship should be given up (to you).[38] On account of which also you may use the seal on my rescript so that no one may trouble you. And this thing which is within your power to accomplish for yourself has for a long time now been conceded by me. Wherefore, also Aurelius Quirinius, who presides over the matters of conseuqence, will maintain the seal given by me.

No. 29: Porphyry (ca. 268–70)
Adversus Christianos, frag. 76
(apud Macarius Magnes 4.21)
[ed. A. Harnack, *Porphyrius: Gegen die Christen* (Berlin, 1916)]

ἀλλὰ καὶ οἱ Χριστιανοὶ μιμούμενοι τὰς κατασκευὰς τῶν ναῶν μεγίστους οἴκους οἰκοδομοῦσιν, εἰς οὓς συνιόντες εὔχονται, καίτοι μηδενὸς κωλύοντος ἐν ταῖς οἰκίαις τοῦτο πράττειν, τοῦ κυρίου δηλονότι πανταχόθεν ἀκούοντος . . .

Translation. But the Christians, imitating the construction of temples, erect great buildings in which they meet to pray, though there is nothing to prevent them from doing this in their own homes since, of course, their Lord hears them everywhere. . . .

No. 30: The Emperor Diocletian (284–305)
The First Edict of Persecution (March 303)
(apud Eusebius, *H.E.* 8.2.4–5 [ca. 303])
[ed. Schwartz, GCS 9 (1903)]

2.4. ἔτος τοῦτο ἦν ἐννεακαιδέκατον τῆς Διοκλητιανοῦ βασιλείας, Δύστρος μήν, λέγοιτο δ' ἂν οὗτος Μάρτιος κατὰ Ῥωμαίους, ἐν ᾧ τῆς τοῦ

38. Eusebius reports the existence of another edict that gave the Christians the right to recover their cemetery sites. The rescript came after Valerian had issued an edict against the Christian leaders in 257/258 (cf. Cyprian, *Ep.* 80 [=*Ep.* 81 *PL* 4]), during which time Fabian of Rome, Cyprian of Carthage, and Dionysius of Alexandria (cf. No. 20) were arrested.

σωτηρίου πάθους ἑορτῆς ἐπελαυνούσης ἥπλωτο πανταχόσε βασιλικὰ γράμματα, τὰς μὲν ἐκκλησίας εἰς ἔδαφος φέρειν, τὰς δὲ γραφὰς ἀφανεῖς πυρὶ γενέσθαι προστάττοντα, καὶ τοὺς μὲν τιμῆς ἐπειλημμένους ἀτίμους, τοὺς δ' ἐν οἰκετίαις, εἰ ἐπιμένοιεν τῇ τοῦ Χριστιανισμοῦ προθέσει. ἐλευθερίας στερεῖσθαι προαγορεύοντα. 5. καὶ ἡ μὲν πρώτη καθ' ἡμῶν γραφὴ τοιαύτη τις ἦν· μετ' οὐ πολὺ δὲ ἑτέρων ἐπιφοιτησάντων γραμμάτων. προσετάττετο τοὺς τῶν ἐκκλησιῶν προέδρους πάντας τοὺς κατὰ πάντα τόπον πρῶτα μὲν δεσμοῖς παραδίδοσθαι, εἶθ' ὕστερον πάσῃ μηχανῇ θύειν ἐξαναγκάζεσθαι.

Translation. It was the nineteenth year of the reign of Diocletian, in the month of Dystus, which is called March by the Romans, as the feast of the savior's passion was approaching, an imperial letter was spread abroad everywhere ordering the churches to be razed to the ground and the scriptures to be destroyed by fire. Moreover, those (Christians) in high places were to be stripped of their honors and those in the household (i.e., "imperial") service[39] were to be deprived of their freedom if they persisted in their profession of Christianity. Such was the first document against us, but not much later other letters came constantly. It was ordered that all the presidents of the churches in every place first be delivered to prison and then be compelled to sacrifice by all kinds of device.

No. 31: Records of Munatius Felix, Curator of the Colony of Cirta, Numidia (19 May 303)

Acta Munati Felicis (apud *Gestae apud Zenophilum*)
[ed. Ziwsa, CSEL 26. 186–88, paragraph divisions and numbers added]

1. Diocletiano VIII et Maximiano VII consulibus XIIII Kal. Iunias ex actis Munati Felicis flaminis perpetui, curatoris coloniae Cirtensium. cum ventum esset ad domum, in qua christiani conveniebant, Felix flamen perpetuus curator Paulo episcopo dixit: proferte scripturas legis et, si quid aliud

39. Since the term would normally refer to household slaves, this usage may be taken as a shortened form *familia Caesaris*, or those in the imperial service. On the term οἰκετίαις see the note by Norman Baynes in *Cambridge Ancient History,* 12. 665f.

hic habetis, ut praeceptum est, ut iussioni parere possitis. Paulus episcopus dixit: scripturas lectores habent. sed nos, quod hic habemus, damus. Felix flamen perpetuus curator Paulo episcope dixit: ostende lectores aut mitte ad illos. Paulus episcopus dixit: omnes cognoscitis. Felix flamen perpetuus curator reipublicae dixit: non eos novimus. Paulus episcopus dixit: novit eos officium publicum, id est Edusius et Iunius exceptores. Felix flamen perpetuus curator reipublicae dixit: manente ratione de lectoribus, quos demonstrabit officium, nos quod habetis, date.

2. sedente Paulo episcopo, Montano et Victore Deusatelio et Memorio presbyteris, adstante Marte cum Helio diaconis, Marcuclio Catullino Silvano et Caroso subdiaconis, Ianuario Meraclo Fructuoso Miggine Saturnino Victore et ceteris fossoribus, contra scribente Victore Aufidi in brevi sic: calices duo aurei, item calices sex argentei, urceola sex argentea, cucumellum argenteum, lucernas argenteas septem, cereofala duo, candelas breves aeneas cum lucernis suis septem, item lucernas aeneas undecim cum catenis suis, tunicas muliebres LXXXII, mafortea XXXVIII, tunicas viriles XVI, caligas viriles paria XIII, caligas muliebres paria XLVII, coplas rusticanas XVIIII. Felix flamen perpetuus curator reipublicae Marcuclio Silvano et Caroso fossoribus dixit: proferte hoc, quod habetis. Silvanus et Carosus dixerunt: quod hic fuit, totum hoc eiecimus. Felix flamen perpetuus curator reipublicae Marcuclio Silvano et Caroso dixit: responsio vestra actis haeret.

3. postea quam in bibliothecis inventa sunt [ibi] armaria inania, ibi protulit Silvanus capitulatam argenteam et lucernam argenteam, quod diceret se post orcam eas invenisse. Victor Aufidi Silvano dixit: mortuus fueras, si non illas invenisses. Felix flamen perpetuus curator reipublicae Silvano dixit: quaere diligentius, ne quid hic remanserit. Silvanus dixit: nihil remansit, totum hoc eiecimus.

4. et cum apertum esset triclinium, inventa sunt ibi dolia IIII et orcae VI. Felix flamen perpetuus curator reipublicae dixit: proferte scripturas, quas habetis, ut praeceptis imperatorum et iussioni parere possimus. Catullinus protulit codicem unum pernimium maiorem. Felix flamen perpetuus curator reipublicae Marcuclio et Silvano dixit: quare unum tantummodo codicem dedistis? proferte scripturas, quas habetis. Catullinus et Marcuclius dixerunt: plus non habemus, quia subdiacones sumus; sed lectores habent codices. Felix flamen perpetuus curator reipublicae Marcuclio et Catullino dixit: demonstrate lectores! Marcuclius et Catullinus dixerunt: non scimus, ubi maneant. Felix flamen perpetuus curator reipublicae Catullino et Marcuclio

dixit: si, ubi manent, non nostis, nomina eorum dicite. Catullinus et Marcuclius dixerunt: nos non sumus proditores. ecce sumus, iube nos occidi. Felix flamen perpetuus curator reipublicae dixit: recipiantur.

5. et cum ventum esset ad domum Eugeni, Felix flamen perpetuus curator reipublicae Eugenio dixit: profer scripturas, quas habes, ut praecepto parere possis. et protulit codices quattuor. Felix flamen perpetuus curator reipublicae Silvano et Caroso dixit: demonstrate ceteros lectores. Silvanus et Carosus dixerunt: iam dixit episcopus, quia Edusius et Iunius exceptores omnes noverunt; ipsi tibi demonstrent ad domus eorum. Edusius et Iunius exceptores dixerunt: nos eos demonstramus, domine.

6. et cum ventum fuisset ad domum Felicis sarsoris, protulit codices quinque; et cum ventum esset ad domum Victorini, protulit codices octo; et cum ventum fuisset ad domum Proiecti, protulit codices V maiores et minores II; et cum ad grammatici domum ventum fuisset, Felix flamen perpetuus curator Victori grammatico dixit: profer scripturas, quas habes, ut praecepto parere possis. Victor grammaticus optulit codices II et quiniones quattuor. Felix flamen perpetuus curator reipublicae Victori dixit: profer scripturas; plus habes. Victor grammaticus dixit: si plus habuissem, dedissem. et cum ventum fuisset ad domum Eutici Caesariensis, Felix flamen perpetuus curator reipublicae Euticio dixit: profer scripturas, quas habes, ut praecepto parere possis. Euticius dixit: non habeo. Felix flamen perpetuus curator reipublicae Euticio dixit: professio tua actis haeret.

7. et cum ventum fuisset ad domum Coddeonis, protulit uxor eius codices sex. Felix flamen perpetuus curator reipublicae dixit: quaere, ne plus habeatis, profer. mulier respondit: non habeo. Felix flamen perpetuus curator reipublicae Bovi servo publico dixit: intra et quaere, ne plus habeat. servus publicus dixit: quaesivi et non inveni. Felix flamen perpetuus curator reipublicae Victorino Silvano et Caroso dixit: si quid minus factum fuerit, vos contingit periculum.

Translation. 1. In the consulship of Diocletian for the eighth time and of Maximian for the seventh time, on the 14th day of the kalends of June [19 May 303], from the records of Munatius Felix, high priest in perpetuity and *curator* (mayor) of the colony of Cirta.

When (they) arrived at the house in which the Christians would assemble, Felix, the priest for life and mayor, said to Paul, the bishop, "Bring out the writings of the law and anything else you have here, as was ordered, so that you may obey the law."

Paul, the bishop, said, "The readers have the scriptures, but we will give you what we have here."

Felix, the mayor, said, "Point out the readers or send for them."

Paul, the bishop, said, "You all know them."

Felix, the mayor, said, "We do not know them."

Paul, the bishop, said, "The public office, that is the clerks Edusius and Junius, knows them."

Felix, the mayor, said, "Holding over the matter of the readers, whom the office will point out, hand over whatever you have."

2. In the presence of the bishop Paul, seated, with Montanus and Victor Deusatelius and Memorius, the presbyters, and standing by Martis and Helios, the deacons, with Marculius, Catullinus, Silvanus, and Carosus, the subdeacons, and with Januarius, Meraclus, Fructuosus, Migginis, Saturninus, Victor, and the rest, the (grave-?)diggers, (they brought out) before the scribe Victor of Aufidus, who wrote in brief as follows: 2 gold cups, 6 silver cups, 6 silver pitchers, a small silver kettle, 7 silver lamps, 2 wax candles, 7 small bronze lamps with their wicks, 11 bronze lamps with chains, 82 women's tunics, 38 *mafortea* [from Gk. μαφόρτης = a woman's head-dress or veil], 16 men's tunics, 13 pairs of men's shoes, 47 pairs of women's shoes, and 19 crude thongs.

Felix, the mayor, said to Marculius, Silvanus, and Carosus, the diggers,[40] "Bring forth what you have."

Silvanus and Carosus said, "We have brought out everything that was here."

Felix, the mayor, said to Marculius, Silvanus, and Carosus, "Your response is entered in the record."

3. After some empty cupboards had been found in the library, Silvanus then produced a silver (coin?) box and a silver lamp, which he said he had found behind a barrel.

Victor of Aufidus said to Silvanus, "You were dead, if you had not discovered these things."

40. Above Marculius, Catullinus, and Silvanus are called "subdeacons," while the title "diggers" is used for others. See also sec. 4 below.

Felix, the mayor, said to Silvanus, "Search again, in case you left something behind."

Silvanus said, "There is nothing left, we have brought out everything."

4. When the dining room was opened, 4 large jars and 6 barrels were found there.

Felix, the mayor, said, "Bring forth your scriptures so that we can obey the imperial order and the law."

Catullinus produced one exceedingly large volume.

Felix, the mayor, said to Marculius and Silvanus, "Why have you given only this one volume? Produce all the scriptures that you have."

Catullinus and Marculius said, "We have no more because we are subdeacons; the readers have the books."

Felix, the mayor, said to Marculius and Catullinus, "Point out the readers!"

Marculius and Catullinus said, "We know not where they live."

Felix, the mayor, said to them, "If you do not know where they live, then tell their names."

Catullinus and Marculius said, "We are not betrayers. Here we are; give the order for us to be killed."

Felix, the mayor, said, "They are under arrest."

5. When they came to the house of Eugenius, Felix, the mayor, said to Eugenius, "Bring out the scriptures that you have so that you may comply with the order."

He produced four volumes.

Felix, the mayor, said to Silvanus and Carosus, "Point out the rest of the readers." [Apparently they had informed on Eugenius after the threat of arrest.]

Silvanus and Carosus answered, "The bishop has already told you that the clerks Edusius and Junius know them all; they will show you to their houses."

Edusius and Junius, the clerks, said, "We will point them out, sir."

6. When they came to the house of Felix the tailor, he produced five volumes. When they came to the house of Victorinus, he produced eight volumes. When they came to the house of Projectus, he produced five large volumes and two small ones.

When they came to the house of the grammarian (or teacher), Felix, the mayor, said to Victor, the grammarian, "Bring forth the scriptures that you have so that you may comply with the order."

Victor, the grammarian, offered two volumes and four *quinions* (=parts of volumes, i.e., fascicles).

Felix, the mayor, said to Victor, "Bring out your scriptures; you have more."

Victor, the grammarian, said, "If I had more, I would give them to you."

When they came to the house of Eutychus of Caesarea, Felix, the mayor, said to Eutychus, "Bring out the scriptures that you have so that you may comply with the order."

Eutychus answered, "I have none."

Felix, the mayor said to him, "Your statement is entered in the record."

7. When they came to the house of Coddeon, his wife handed over six volumes.

Felix, the mayor, said, "Search (again) in case you have more; hand them over."

Coddeon's wife answered, "I have no more."

Felix, the mayor, said to Bovus, a public slave, "Go inside and look in case there are more."

The slave said, "I have searched and found nothing."

Felix, the mayor, said to Victorinus [a reader], Silvanus, and Carosus, "If anything has been left out, the responsibility is yours."

No. 32: The Emperor Galerius, Rescript Concerning the Christians, Issued at Nicomedia (30 April 311)

32a: The Greek *Palinode*
(apud Eusebius, *H.E.* 8.17; 8.17.1, 9 [ca. 313])
[ed. Schwartz, GCS 9 (1903)]

1. . . . εἶτα τοὺς ἀμφ' αὐτὸν ἀνακαλέσας, μηδὲν ὑπερθεμένους τὸν κατὰ Χριστιανῶν ἀποπαῦσαι διωγμὸν νόμῳ τε καὶ δόγματι βασιλικῷ τὰς ἐκκλησίας αὐτῶν οἰκοδομεῖν ἐπισπέρχειν καὶ τὰ συνήθη διαπράττεσθαι, εὐχὰς ὑπὲρ τοῦ βασιλείου ποιουμένους, προστάττει. . . .

9. "και ἐπειδὴ τῶν πολλῶν τῇ αὐτῇ ἀπονοίᾳ διαμενόντων ἑωρῶμεν μήτε τοῖς θεοῖς τοῖς ἐπουρανίοις τὴν ὀφειλομένην θρησκείαν προσάγειν

αὐτοὺς μήτε τῷ τῶν Χριστιανῶν προσέχειν, ἀφορῶντες εἰς τὴν ἡμετέραν φιλανθρωπίαν καὶ τὴν διηνεκῆ συνήθειαν δι᾽ ἧς εἰώθαμεν ἅπασιν ἀνθρώποις συγγνώμην ἀπονέμειν, προθυμότατα καὶ ἐν τούτῳ τὴν συγχώρησιν τὴν ἡμετέραν ἐπεκτεῖναι δεῖν ἐνομίσαμεν, ἵνα αὖθις ὦσιν Χριστιανοὶ καὶ τοὺς οἴκους ἐν οἷς συνήγοντο, συνθῶσιν οὕτως ὥστε μηδὲν ὑπεναντίον τῆς ἐπιστήμης αὐτοὺς πράττειν. δι᾽ ἑτέρας δὲ ἐπιστολῆς τοῖς δικασταῖς δηλώσομεν τί αὐτοὺς παραφυλάξασθαι δεήσει. . . ."

Translation. 1. . . . Then he [Galerius] recalled those around him without delay and gave them the order to stop the persecution against the Christians by law, and by imperial decree to urge them to rebuild their churches and to practice their customary rites offering prayers on the king's behalf. [The decree said:]

"9. Since the majority [of Christians] persisted in the same madness we saw that they neither offered the worship due to the heavenly gods nor devoted themselves to the God of the Christians. We looked to our own philanthropy and our unbroken custom by which we are in the habit of assigning pardon to all men, and we most earnestly thought it necessary to extend our indulgence in this matter, so that the Christians might once again exist and have their houses in which they used to assemble if they agree to the following: that they will do nothing contrary to understanding. In another letter we shall make known to the judges what will be necessary for them to watch over. . . ."

32b: The Latin Edict
(apud Lactantius, *De mortibus persecutorum* 33.11–34.5 [ca. 319])
[ed. Brandt, CSEL 27]

(33) . . . 11. Et haec facta sunt per annum perpetem, cum tandem malis domitus deum coactus est confiteri. Novi doloris urgentis per intervalla exclamat se restituturum dei templum satisque pro scelere facturum. Et iam deficiens edictum misit huiuscemodi:

34.1. "Inter cetera quae pro rei publicae semper commodis atque utilitate disponimus, nos quidem volueramus antehac iuxta leges veteres et publicam disciplinam Romanorum cuncta corrigere atque id providere, ut etiam christiani, qui parentum suorum reliquerant sectam, ad bonas mentes redirent, 2. siquidem quadam ratione tanta cosdem christianos voluntas invasisset et tanta stultitia occupasset, ut non illa veterum instituta sequerentur, quae forsitan primum parentes eorundem constituerant, sed pro arbitrio suo atque ut isdem erat libitum. ita sibimet leges facerent quas observarent, et per diversa varios populos congregarent. 3. Denique cum eiusmodi nostra iussio extitisset, ut ad veterum se instituta conferrent, multi periculo subiugati, multi etiam deturbati sunt. 4. Atque cum plurimi in proposito perseverarent ac videremus nec diis cosdem cultum ac religionem debitam exhibere nec christianorum deum observare, contemplatione mitissimae nostrae clementiae intuentes et consuetudinem sempiternam, qua solemus cunctis hominibus veniam indulgere, promptissimam in his quoque indulgentiam nostram credidimus porrigendam, ut denuo sint christiani et conventicula sua componant, ita ut ne quid contra disciplinam agant. 5. <Per> aliam autem epistolam iudicibus significaturi sumus quid debeant observare. Unde iuxta hanc indulgentiam nostram debebunt deum suum orare pro salute nostra et rei publicae ac sua, ut undique versum res publica perstet incolumis et securi vivere in sedibus suis possint."

Translation. . . . These things happened [to Galerius] in the space of a single year until finally, having been overcome by evils, he was compelled to confess God. He cried out through the intervals of pressing pain that he would restore the temple of God and make amends for his crimes. And when he was failing he issued the following edict:

"Among the other things that we have ordered for the constant interest and benefit of the state we have formerly purposed to bring all things into order with the ancient laws and public customs of the Romans. And we sought to make provision for this now even more so that the Christians, who have departed the mode of life of their ancestors, should return to a better mind, seeing as how for some reason such willfulness had seized and folly possessed these very Christians that they were not following these ancient precepts, which perchance their very own ancestors had instituted, but were rather making laws of their own which they observed for their own arbitrary reasons and were assembling a variety of peoples in diverse places (or ways?).

"In short, then, when our order had been set forth that they should devote themselves to the precepts of the ancients, many were subdued by the danger and many were also dispossessed. And when many persisted in their intention we saw that these neither offered worship and due observance to the gods nor respected the god of the Christians; therefore, in consideration of our mildest clemency and our eternal custom whereby we are used to grant indulgence to all men, we have thought it proper in this case to grant indulgence promptly, so that the Christians may exist again and construct their conventicles[41] provided that they do nothing contrary to order. In another letter we shall signify to the judges what they are to do. Hence in return for our indulgence they ought to pray to their god for our well-being and that of the state as well as for their own, that the state may continue safe and secure from all sides, and that they may live secure in their own homes."

No. 33: The Emperors Licinius and Constantine

The "Edict of Milan," issued at Milan (13 June 313)
(apud Lactantius, *De mortibus persecutorum* 48)
[ed. Brandt, CSEL 27]

1. Licinius . . . retulit ac die Iduum Iuniarum Constantino atque ipso ter consulibus de restituenda ecclesia huius modi litteras ad praesidem datas proponi ius it:

2. "Cum feliciter tam ego [quam] Constantinus Augustus quam etiam ego Licinius Augustus apud Mediolanum convenissemus atque universa quae ad commoda et securitatem publicam pertinerent, in tractatu haberemus, haec inter cetera quae videbamus pluribus hominibus profutura, vel in primis ordinanda esse credidimus, quibus divinitatis reverentia continebatur, ut daremus et christianis et omnibus liberam potestatem sequendi religionem quam quisque voluisset, quo quicquid <est> divinitatis in sede caelesti, nobis atque omnibus qui sub potestate nostra sunt constituti, placatum ac propitium possit existere. 3. Itaque hoc consilium salubri ac rectissima ratione ineundum esse credidimus, ut nulli omnino facultatem abnegandam putaremus, qui vel observationi christianorum vel ei religoni mentem suam

41. *Conventicula* is used consistently by Lactantius to refer to meeting places or church buildings; cf. *De. mort.* 34.4, 36.3, and 48.9 (No. 33 below). See also the comment of J. Vogt, "Pagans and Christians in the Family of Constantine the Great," in *The Conflict between Paganism and Christianity in the Fourth Century,* ed. A. Momigliano (Oxford: Clarendon, 1963) 44. The corresponding term in the Greek version of Eusebius changes from οἶκος here to σύνοδος, *De mort.* 48.9 (in *H.E.* 10.5.11).

dederet quam ipse sibi aptissimam esse sentiret, ut possit nobis summa divinitas, cuius religioni liberis mentibus obsequimur, in omnibus solitum favorem suum benivolentiamque praestare. 4. Quare scire dicationem tuam convenit placuisse nobis, ut amotis omnibus omnino condicionibus quae prius scriptis ad officium tuum datis super christianorum nomine <continebantur, et quae prorsus sinistra et a nostra clementia aliena esse> videbantur, <ea removeantur, et> nunc libere ac simpliciter unus quisque eorum, qui eandem observandae religionis christianorum gerunt voluntatem, citra ullam inquietudinem ac molestiam sui id ipsum observare contendant. 5. Quae sollicitudini tuae plenissime significanda esse credidimus, quo scires nos liberam atque absolutam colendae religionis suae facultatem isdem christianis dedisse. . . . 7. Atque hoc insuper in persona christianorum statuendum esse censuimus, quod, si eadem loca, ad quae antea convenire consuerant, de quibus etiam datis ad officium tuum litteris certa antehac forma fuerat comprehensa, priore tempore aliqui vel a fisco nostro vel ab alio quocumque videntur esse mercati, eadem christianis sine pecunia et sine ulla pretii petitione, postposita omni frustratione atque ambiguitate, restituant, 8. qui etiam dono fuerunt consecuti, eadem similiter isdem christianis quantocius reddant, etiam vel hi qui emerunt vel qui dono fuerunt consecuti, si petiverint de nostra benivolentia aliquid, vicarium postulent, quo et ipsis per nostram clementiam consulatur. Quae omnia corpori christianorum protinus per intercessionent tuam ac sine mora tradi oportebit. 9. Et quoniam idem christiani non [in] ea loca tantum ad quae convenire consuerunt, sed alia etiam habuisse noscuntur ad ius corporis eorum id est ecclesiarum, non hominum singulorum, pertinentia, ea omnia lege quam superius comprehendimus, citra ullam prorsus ambiguitatem vel controversiam isdem christianis, id est corpori et conventiculis eorum reddi iubebis, supra dicta scilicet ratione servata, ut ii qui eadem sine pretio sicut diximus restituant, indemnitatem de nostra benivolentia sperent. 10. In quibus omnibus supra dicto corpori christianorum intercessionem tuam efficacissimam exhibere debebis, ut praeceptum nostrum quantocius conpleatur, quo etiam in hoc per clementiam nostram quieti publicae consulatur. . . ."

13. His litteris propositis etiam verbo hortatus est, ut conventicula <in> statum pristinum redderentur. Sic ab eversa ecclesia usque ad restitutam fuerunt anni decem, menses plus minus quattuor.

Translation. 1. Licinius . . . on the ides of June, in behalf of Constantine and himself, consuls for the third time, issued the following edict concerning the restoration of the church for the president (of the province) to be promulgated by law:

2. "When I, Constantine Augustus, and I, Licinius Augustus, met happily at Milan and discussed all things pertaining to the benefit and security of the state, among other things which we viewed as profitable for the general populace we deemed to be ordained in the first place the reverence of the Divinity held by anyone. Thus we grant to Christians and all others free authority to follow whatever religion anyone chooses, by which whatever god is in the heavenly domain may be appeased and be propitious to us and to all who are under our authority. Therefore, we deemed it useful and completely proper for this resolution to be enacted as we think no one should be refused toleration in all matters — neither he who has given his mind to the devotion of the Christians nor he to that religion which he feels most appropriate to himself — so that the supreme Deity, whose religion we accept with a free mind, may grant us his accustomed favor and beneficence in all things. Let it be known, therefore, your dignity, that it pleases us that all conditions whatsoever concerning the name of the Christians (*nomen Christianorum*), which were formerly sent by rescript to your office, be abolished and what appears utterly adverse and alien to our clemency be removed; any and everyone who bears a desire to observe the religion of the Christians may now finally and plainly do just that without annoyance or molestation. We thought it best to signify these matters fully to your Solicitude, so that you may know that we have given free and absolute toleration to these Christians in attending to their religion. . . .

7. Moreover, we have resolved to proceed in the following manner as regards the (legal) character of the Christians: those places at which they were formerly accustomed to assemble—concerning which definite orders have already been given by means of a letter sent to your office—if any appear to have bought them, whether from our fisc or from any other source whatsoever, let them restore the same to the Christians without charge and with no price on demand, setting aside all deception and doubtfulness. If any shall have received such as a gift, let them return the same to the Christians in like manner and as quickly as possible. But whether they purchased them or received them as a gift, if they would petition anything of our Benevolence let them state their claims to the Vicarius, by whom measures are taken in their behalf also through our clemency. All these things should be handed

over immediately to the corporation of the Christians by your intercession and without delay. And since the said Christians are known to have possessed not only those places in which they were accustomed to meet but others as well, which belong to their corporation, that is, to their churches rather than to individuals, we have included them under the above law, so that you will order them with no doubt or controversy at all to return the same to the Christians, that is to their corporations and conventicles, providing, of course, as was stated above, that those who restore their property without price, as we said, may expect restitution of damages from our benevolence. In all these matters stated above you must show the corporation of the Christians your most effective intercession so that our command may be carried out as soon as possible, by which also in this matter measures may be taken for the public tranquility. . . ."

13. Having set forth these letters, he [Licinius] exhorted (us) with words that the conventicles should be restored to their former state. Thus from the destruction of the churches until their restoration was ten years and about four months.

A Greek translation of the same ordinance is given by Eusebius in *H.E.* 10.5.2–14. For comparative purposes we give here the relevant sections in *H.E.* 10.5.9–11 (= *De mort.* 48.7–10) [ed. Schwartz, GCS], ca. 317.[42]

5. 9. καὶ τοῦτο δὲ πρὸς τοῖς λοιποῖς εἰς τὸ πρόσωπον τῶν Χριστιανῶν δογματίζομεν, ἵνα τοὺς τόπους αὐτῶν, εἰς οὓς τὸ πρότερον συνέρχεσθαι ἔθος ἦν αὐτοῖς, περὶ ὧν καὶ τοῖς πρότερον δοθεῖσεν πρὸς τὴν σὴν καθοσίωσιν γράμμασιν τύπος ἕτερος ἦν ὡρισμένος τῷ προτέρῳ χρόνῳ [ἵν'] εἴ τινες ἢ παρὰ τοῦ ταμείου τοῦ ἡμετέρον ἢ παρά τινος ἑτέρου φαίνοιντο ἠγορακότες, τούτους τοῖς αὐτοῖς Χριστιανοῖς ἄνευ ἀργυρίου καὶ ἄνευ τινὸς ἀπαιτήσεως τῆς τιμῆς, ὑπερτεθείσης [δίχα] πάσης ἀμελείας καὶ

42. A follow-up letter calling for speedy implementation of the above edict is found in Eusebius *H.E.* 10.5.15–17 (Constantine to Anulinus, proconsul of Africa Proconsularis [313]). See No. 35 below. The provisions for restoration of church properties in both the Latin and Greek make it clear that a universal "destruction of the churches" was not the order of the day, but rather the rhetorical symbol among the Christians. It appears instead that search and seizure of the properties was more common; so see below Nos. 34–35 and esp. No. 46.

ἀμφιβολίας, ἀποκαταστήσωσι, καὶ εἴ τινες κατὰ δῶρον τυγχάνουσιν εἰληφότες, τοὺς αὐτοὺς τόπους ὅπως ἢ τοῖς αὐτοῖς Χριστιανοῖς τὴν ταχίστην ἀποκαταστήσωσιν· 10. οὕτως ὡς ἢ οἱ ἠγορακότες τοὺς αὐτοὺς τόπους ἢ οἱ κατὰ δωρεὰν εἰληφότες. αἰτῶσι τι παρὰ τῆς ἡμετέρας καλοκἀγαθίας προσέλθωσι τῷ ἐπὶ τόπων ἐπάρχῳ δικάζοντι, ὅπως καὶ αὐτῶν διὰ τῆς ἡμετέρας χρηστότητος πρόνοια γένηται. ἅτινα πάντα τῷ σώματι τῷ τῶν Χριστιανῶν παρ᾽ αὐτὰ διὰ τῆς σῆς σπουδῆς ἄνευ τινὸς παρολκῆς παραδίδοσθαι δεήσει· 11. καὶ ἐπειδὴ οἱ αὐτοὶ Χριστιανοὶ οὐ μόνον ἐκείνους εἰς οὓς συνέρχεσθαι ἔθος εἶχον, ἀλλὰ καὶ ἑτέρους τόπους ἐσχηκέναι γινώσκονται διαφέροντας οὐ πρὸς ἕκαστου αὐτῶν, ἀλλὰ πρὸς τὸ δίκαιον τοῦ αὐτῶν σώματος, τοῦτ᾽ ἔστιν τῶν Χριστιανῶν, ταῦτα πάντα ἐπὶ τῷ νόμῳ ὅν προειρήκαμεν, δίχα παντελῶς τινος ἀμφισβητήσεως τοῖς αὐτοῖς Χριστιανοῖς, τοῦτ᾽ ἔστιν τῷ σώματι [αὐτῶν] καὶ τῇ συνόδῳ ἑκάστῳ αὐτῶν ἀποκαταστῆναι κελεύσεις, τοῦ προειρημένου λογισμοῦ δηλαδὴ φυλαχθέντος, ὅπως αὐτοὶ οἵτινες τοὺς αὐτοὺς ἄνευ τιμῆς, καθὼς προειρήκαμεν, ἀποκαθιστῶσι, τὸ ἀζήμιον τὸ ἑαυτῶν παρὰ τῆς ἡμετέρας καλοκἀγαθίας ἐλπίζοιεν.

No. 34: Maximinus (Emperor 305–313)
Rescript concerning the Christians (313)
(apud Eusebius, *H.E.* 9.9a.11, 9.10.10–11 [ca. 317])
[ed. Schwartz, GCS 9 (1903)]

[With reference to Maximinus's first gesture toward the Christians, a letter drafted just after the "Edict of Milan" (cf. *H.E.* 9.9.12f), Eusebius comments on the negligible effects of the gesture.]

9a.11. οὔκουν ἐτόλμα τις τῶν ἡμετέρων σύνοδον συγκροτεῖν οὐδ᾽ ἑαυτὸν ἐν φανερῷ καταστήσασθαι, ὅτι μηδὲ τοῦτ᾽ ἤθελεν αὐτῷ τὸ γράμμα αὐτὸ μόνον τὸ ἀνεπηρέαστον ἡμῖν ἐπιτρέπον φυλάττεσθαι, οὐ μὴν συνόδους ἐπικελεῦον ποιεῖσθαι οὐδ᾽ οἴκους ἐκκλησιῶν οἰκοδομεῖν οὐδ᾽ ἄλλο τι τῶν ἡμῖν συνήθων διαπράττεσθαι.

Translation. . . . Therefore, none of our people dared to put together an assembly or to make himself conspicuous, since the letter did not even permit him this. It gave us only this, namely, assurance of protection against harsh treatment; it did not give orders on holding assemblies, constructing church buildings, or engaging in our customary activities. . . .

[Then after political and military setbacks, Eusebius reports, Maximinus was forced to concede to the Christians and issue an edict of full toleration and restitution.]

10.10. ἵνα τοίνυν εἰς τὸ ἑξῆς πᾶσα ὑποψία ἢ ἀμφιβολία τοῦ φόβου περιαιρεθῇ, τοῦτο τὸ διάταγμα προτεθῆναι ἐνομοθετήσαμεν, ἵνα πᾶσιν δῆλον γένηται ἐξεῖναι τούτοις οἵτινες ταύτην τὴν αἵρεσιν καὶ τὴν θρῃσκείαν μετιέναι βούλονται, ἐκ ταύτης τῆς δωρεᾶς τῆς ἡμετέρας, καθὼς ἕκαστος βούλεται ἢ ἡδέα αὐτῷ ἐστιν, οὕτως προσιέναι τῇ θρῃσκείᾳ ταύτῃ ἣν ἐξ ἔθους θρῃσκεύειν εἵλετο. καὶ τὰ κυριακὰ δὲ τὰ οἰκεῖα ὅπως κατασκευάζοιεν, συγκεχώρηται. 11. ἵνα μέντοι καὶ μείζων γένηται ἡ ἡμετέρα δωρεά, καὶ τοῦτο νομοθετῆσαι κατηξιώσαμεν ἵνα εἴ τινες οἰκίαι καὶ χωρία ‹ἃ› τοῦ δικαίου τοῦ τῶν Χριστιανῶν πρὸ τούτου ἐτύγχανον ὄντα, ἐκ τῆς κελεύσεως τῶν γονέων τῶν ἡμετέρων εἰς τὸ δίκαιον μετέπεσεν τοῦ φίσκου ἢ ὑπὸ τινος κατελήφθη πόλεως, εἴτε διάπρασις τούτων γεγένηται εἴτε εἰς χάρισμα δέδοταί τινι, ταῦτα πάντα εἰς τὸ ἀρχαῖον δίκαιον τῶν Χριστιανῶν ἀνακληθῆναι ἐκελεύσαμεν, ἵνα καὶ ἐν τούτῳ τῆς ἡμετέρας εὐσεβείας καὶ τῆς προνοίας αἴσθησιν πάντες λάβωσιν.

Translation. Therefore, so that for the future all fear or doubt of fear may be removed, we have decreed that this ordinance be set forth so that it may be clear to all that those who wish to follow this sect and religious observance are permitted by this our gift, as each one wishes or it pleases him, thus to join this religious rite which he observes out of custom. And they are given concessions so that they might construct their dominical houses [private *kyriaka* = church buildings]. Moreover, that our gift might be even greater we have determined to decree this as well: that if any houses or lands which formerly belonged legally to the Christians have passed into the fisc, or have been seized by any city, or have been given to someone as a gift as a result of the edicts of our parents, we have ordered that all these things be restored to the original right of the Christians, so that in this matter also all may perceive our piety and forethought.

[Eusebius concludes the section by stating that after this edict, "by the grace of the all-ruling God the renovation of the churches from the foundations was begun" (τὰ μὲν τῆς τῶν ἐκκλησιῶν ἀνανεώσεως ἐκ θεμελίων . . . ἠγείρετο), cf. *H.E.* 9.11.1 and 10.4.1.]

No. 35: Constantine (Emperor 306–337)

Letter to Anulinus, proconsul of Africa (ca. 313/14)
(apud Eusebius, *H.E.* 10.5.15–17 [ca. 324])
[ed. Schwartz, GCS 9 (1903)]

15. . . . Χαῖρε Ἀνυλῖνε, τιμιώτατε ἡμῖν. ἔστιν ὁ τρόπος οὗτος τῆς φιλαγαθίας τῆς ἡμετέρας, ὥστε ἐκεῖνα ἅπερ δικαίῳ ἀλλοτρίῳ προσήκει, μὴ μόνον μὴ ἐνοχλεῖσθαι, ἀλλὰ καὶ ἀποκαθιστᾶν βούλεσθαι ἡμᾶς, Ἀνυλῖνε τιμιώτατε. 16. ὅθεν βουλόμεθα ἵν', ὁπόταν ταῦτα τὰ γράμματα κομίσῃ, εἴ τινα ἐκ τούτων τῶν τῇ ἐκκλησίᾳ τῇ καθολικῇ τῶν Χριστιανῶν ἐν ἑκάσταις πόλεσιν ἢ καὶ ἄλλοις τόποις διέφερον [καὶ] κατέχοιντο νῦν ἢ ὑπὸ πολιτῶν ἢ ὑπό τινων ἄλλων, ταῦτα ἀποκατασταθῆναι παραχρῆμα ταῖς αὐταῖς ἐκκλησίαις ποιήσῃς, ἐπειδήπερ προῃρήμεθα ταῦτα ἅπερ αἱ αὐταὶ ἐκκλησίαι πρότερον ἐσχήκεσαν, τῷ δικαίῳ αὐτῶν ἀποκατασταθῆναι. 17. ὁποτε τοίνυν συνορᾷ ἡ καθοσίωσις ἡ σὴ ταύτης ἡμῶν τῆς κελεύσεως σαφέστατον εἶναι τὸ πρόσταγμα, σπούδασον, εἴτε κῆποι εἴτε οἰκίαι εἴθ' ὁτιουνδήποτε τῷ δικαίῳ τῶν αὐτῶν ἐκκλησιῶν διέφερον, σύμπαντα αὐταῖς ἀποκατασταθῆναι ὡς τάχιστα, ὅπως τούτῳ ἡμῶν τῷ προστάγματι ἐπιμελεστάτην σε πειθάρχησιν παρεσχηκέναι καταμάθοιμεν. ἔρρωσο, Ἀνυλῖνε, τιμιώτατε καὶ ποθεινότατε ἡμῖν.

Translation. Greetings, Anulinus, our most honored Sir.[43] It is the custom of our benevolence that whatever belongs rightly to another we wish not only to go unharmed but also to be restored, most honored Anulinus. Wherefore, we will that when you receive this letter, if any of those things that belong to the Catholic Church of the Christians in each of the cities or even in other places is now in the possession either of citizens or others, you should cause them to be restored immediately to these very churches, since

43. On Anulinus's role in the persecutions, see the *Acta Saturnini et socii*, No. 21 above.

we have determined that whatever these same churches formerly possessed by right ought to be restored to them. Since, therefore, your Devotedness perceives that the order of this our command is most explicit, whether gardens or houses or whatever rightly belonged to these same churches, see that they are restored to them with all dispatch, so that we may learn that you have obeyed our order most carefully. Fare well, Anulinus, our most honored and esteemed Sir.

Section II

Archaeological and Documentary Evidence: Christian

▲ ▲ ▲

Two types of data will be found in this collection. The first is archaeological data, that is, archaeological sites in which pre-basilical Christian meeting places can be observed. The archaeological sources have been sifted and rewritten for each site in the form of architectural histories in order to provide the greatest light on the physical process of architectural adaptation. All relevant illustrations are assembled within each entry. A schematic summary of this material may also be found in table 1, (p. 27 above) in the introduction. An additional discussion of other archaeological sites from which the evidence is dubious or as yet untested is contained in Appendix A. The second type of data contained herein comes from documentary texts, that is, inscriptions and papyri. All items in this collection are listed according to geographical categories in order to provide the closest contextual links with the comparative material collected in Section III, the Jewish and Mithraic evidence. A complete listing of these items according to type (i.e., archaeological, papyrological, and epigraphic) may be found in Appendix B, table 3. The geographical framework of the Roman provincial administration is schematized in Appendix B, table 5. A map and site location gazette may be found in table 4.

Catalogue

PROVINCE: Syria (Parapotamia)
LOCATION: Dura-Europos (Es-Salihiyeh)

No. 36: The Christian *Domus Ecclesiae* (ca. 241–256)
(Figures 1-3)

First discovered in 1931, the building was excavated from 1932 to 1933. The location is on the west wall of the city (Block M8, fig. 1) immediately east of Gate 17 and just south of the main gate. Excavations revealed a private house that had been renovated once for use as a Christian *domus ecclesiae*. While it has been conjectured that the unrenovated house might have been used by the Christians as a house church (i.e., prior to the identifiable Christian adaptations), no evidence exists to support or deny this possibility. It is best to remain cautious. The house was built in 232/3 CE, was renovated as a Christian *domus ecclesiae* in 241, and remained in use up to the final destruction of the city in 256 CE.

Literature: C. H. Kraeling, *The Christian Building* (Excavations at Dura-Europos, Final Report VIII.2; New Haven: Dura-Europos Publications, 1967). M. Rostovtzeff, *DEP* 5: Fifth Season, 1931–1932 (New Haven: Yale University Press, 1934) 238–88. P. V. C. Baur, "The Christian Chapel at Dura-Europos," *AJA* 37 (1933) 377–80. J. P. Kirsch, "La *Domus Ecclesiae* cristiana del III. secolo a Dura-Europos en Mesopotamia," in *Studi dedicati alla memoria di Paolo Ubaldi* (Milan, 1937) 73–82. W. Seston, "L'Eglise et le baptistere de Doura-Europos," *Annales de l'école des hautes-études de Gand* (Gand, 1937) 161–77. J. Lassus, *Sanctuaires chrétiens de Syrie* (Paris: P. Geuthner, 1947). A. von Gerkan, "Zur Hauskirche von Dura-Europos," in *Mullus*: *Festschrift Theodor Klauser*, *RAC,* Ergänzungsband I (Münster-Westfalen: Aschendorff, 1964) 143–49.

On the general history of the city and the site, see also M. Rostovtzeff, *Dura-Europos and Its Art* (Oxford: Clarendon, 1943); and A. Perkins, *The Art of Dura-Europos* (Oxford: Clarendon, 1973).

For the art of the Christian baptistry, see the works cited above plus the following special studies: J. Quasten, "Das Bild des Guten Hirten in den altchristlichen Baptisterien und in den Taufliturgien des Ostens und Westens," *Pisciculi* (Münster, 1939) 220–44. E. Dinkler, "Dura-Europos III, Bedeutung für die christliche Kunst," RGG^3 2:290–92.

[The following is based primarily on the preliminary and final Excavation Reports and on the author's own work in the Yale collections.]

The Dura Christian building is a true *domus ecclesiae*, insofar as it was a converted private house, which after remodeling ceased to be used for domestic functions. It was renovated from a private house whose plan and outward appearance were very common at Dura; it had several rooms grouped around a central court with an unobtrusive entrance to the street (fig. 2a). An inscription in Room 4B,[1] etched in an undercoat of wet plaster and subsequently covered over, gives the date 232/233 CE.

This date probably represents the construction of the private house. Kraeling drew this conclusion based on the evidence of use of the land prior to the construction of the present building.[2] The trapezoidal plot of land occupied by the house was larger than usual for Durene domestic architecture.[3] It measured 17.35–17.45 m on its east–west axis and 18.58–20.18 m on its north–south axis. Stratigraphic survey of the plot indicates that until the mid-first century CE it was vacant; in fact, Wall Street had not been extended into this area south of the main gate. During the first century, an earlier building (perhaps also a private dwelling) was erected, but by the beginning of the second century it had been destroyed. The lot must have lain fallow for a number of years, as a deposit of earth and sand 1.30 m deep was found mixed with debris of ashes and brittleware. The nature of the debris suggests a date for the construction of the next private house in this block at some time well after the Roman takeover, that is, after 165 CE. The house was bordered by other structures only on its east side; the area to the south (Lots J and K) remained vacant to the end. For this reason a date for subsequent constructions falling after the military buildup of the third century (ca. 209–211) is preferred. The present structure shows no signs of extensive, long-term use; therefore, the date of the graffito (232/233) may be taken to reflect the construction of the private house. In keeping with this dating, the renovation for Christian use would have occurred probably in ca. 240/241.

The structural alterations undertaken by the Christian owners of the building seem to have been done all in one campaign. The most important

1. C. H. Kraeling, *Christian Building,* 92 (= No. 10). See n. 6 below for text.
2. Ibid., 34–39.
3. Ibid., 34.

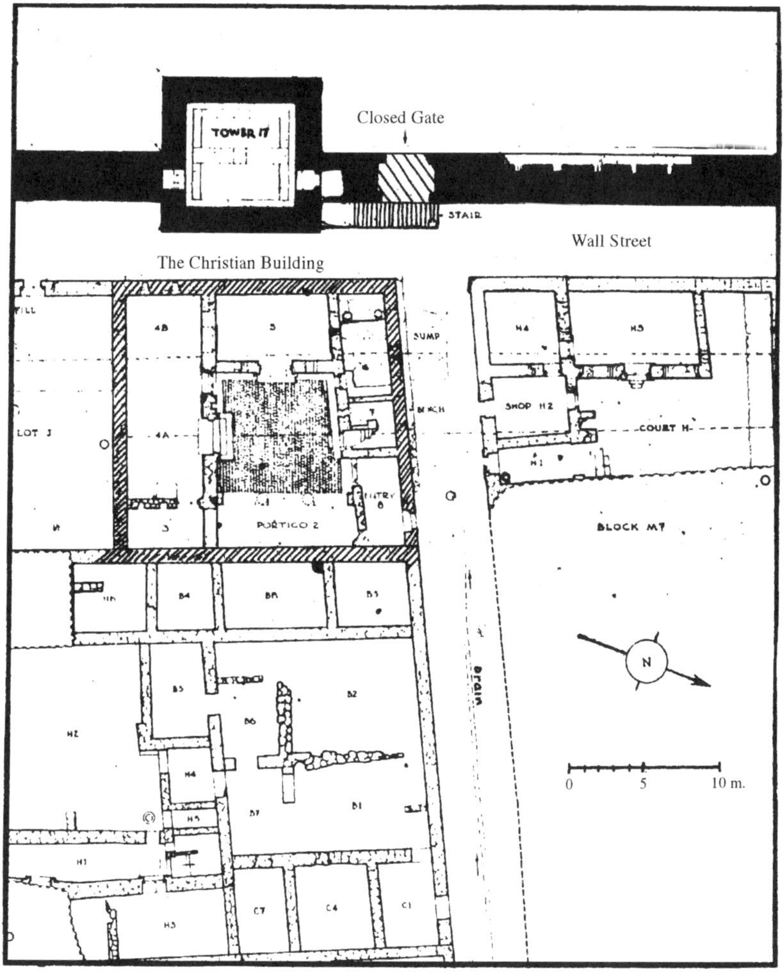

Fig. 1
Syria, Dura-Europos. Block M8 and the Christian building.
Field plan (after H. Pearson)

features of the remodeling took place in the south suite of rooms (Rooms 4A and B) and in the west suite (especially Room 6). Then the courtyard and vestibule were embellished as the common entrance to these two suites. From the street the vestibule, Room 8 (L.5.68; W.ca.2.50 m), led to an

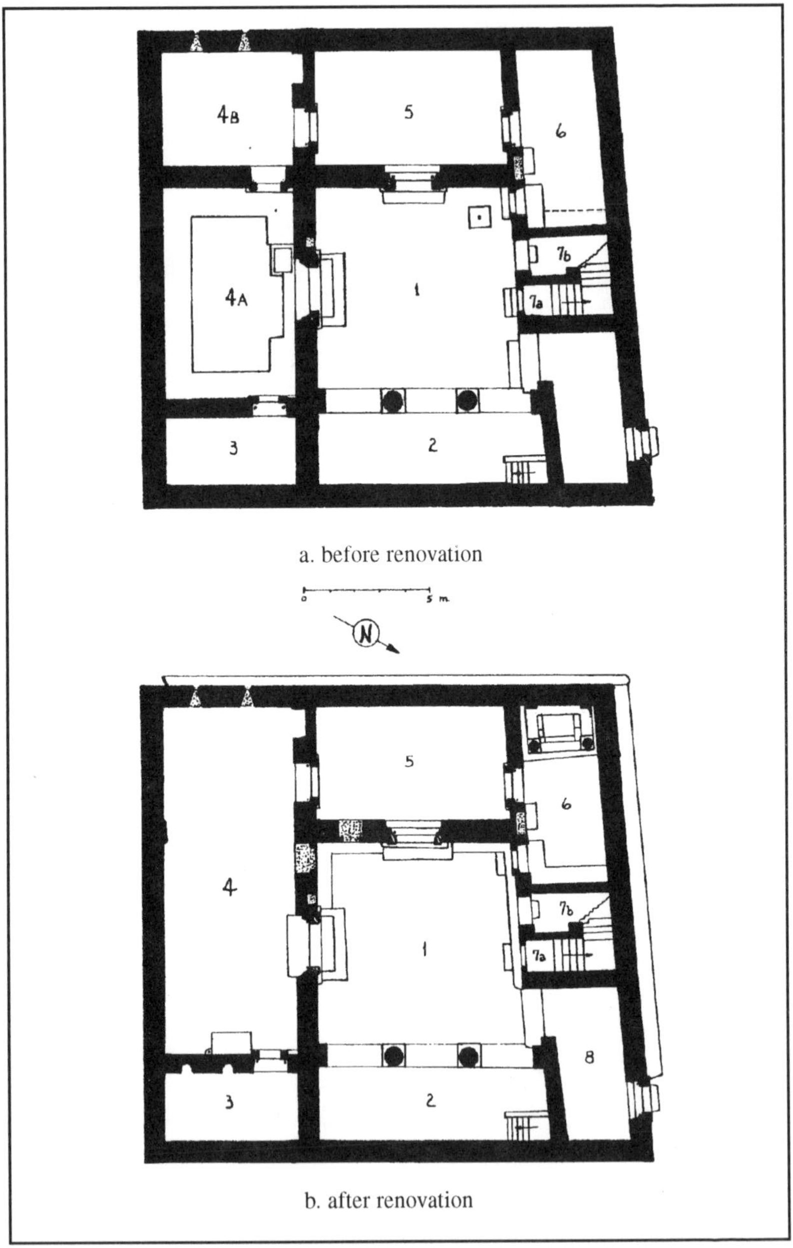

Fig. 2

Syria, Dura-Europos. Christian building, 231–256 CE. Plan reconstruction before and after renovation as *domus ecclesiae*

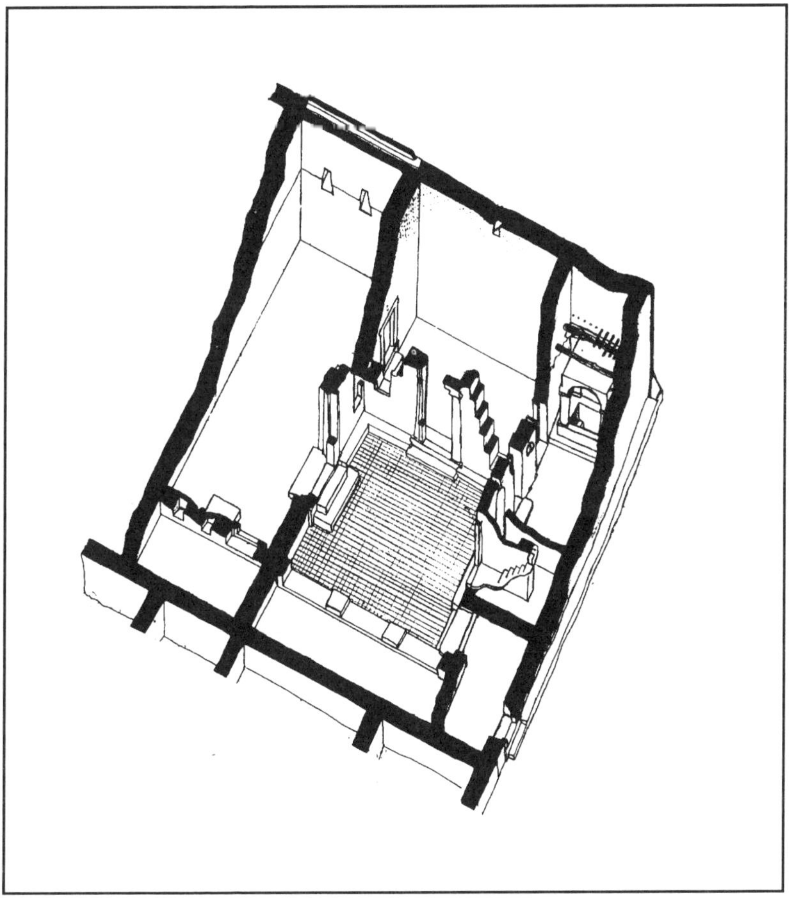

Fig. 3
Syria, Dura-Europos. Christian building, ca. 256 CE.
Isometric reconstruction (based on Pearson)

arched entrance (W.1.75 m), down two low steps to the courtyard (L.7.70; W.7.70-8.55 m). Below the vestibule was a cellar reached by steps from Room 2. When the courtyard was renovated, the packed-earth floor was raised 0.08 m and covered with cinders, plaster, and tiles (0.195 m square). The fill in the floor sealed up the cesspool in the northwest corner. It also covered the lower steps of the vestibule, at the entrance to Room 6, and at the stairs (Room 7A). Around the walls two L-shaped sections of rubble and plaster benches (H.ca.0.50; Br.0.42 m) were installed in the northwest and southwest corners. New steps were constructed in front of the bench at the entrance of Room 6 and the stairs (7A).

To the east off the courtyard lay Room 2, a portico (L.8.90-9.15; W.2.65-2.68 m). A rubble stylobate of the same thickness (0.90 m) as the west wall of the courtyard supported two evenly spaced columns (Diam.0.75 m). Common proportions for such architectural features at Dura would make the height of the ceiling ca. 4.00 m in Rooms 2 and 3, and perhaps a little lower in the vestibule (Room 8).

From the courtyard a formal doorway (W.1.60 m at base) led to the row of chambers on the south side. Originally there were three rooms (3, 4A, and 4B). Of these three, Room 4A was the largest (L.8.00; W.5.15; H.ca.5.07 m); it was the *diwan* or dining room (*triclinium*) of the house. The floor level was 0.46 m higher than that of the court; the doorway was surmounted by two steps on the exterior (both H.0.375; Br.0.50 m) and a low step on the inside. Around the walls were benches made of rubble and plaster (H.0.17; Br.l.00-1.10 m) and there was a brazier box (L.0.90; Br.0.70) set on the west side of the door against the step. On the north wall a portion of a band of Bacchic frieze was found in situ to the west of the door at a height of 2.06 m above the floor. Room 3 (L.2.55; W.5.15 m) had no other access except through Room 4A and probably served as a storage area for the dining room. Room 4B (L.4.25; W.5.15 m) was probably used for some storage as a row of peg-holes and a recessed niche (W.1.45; D.0.45; H.1.75 m) in the northwest corner would indicate. At the same time Room 4B also provided access to and from the west suite, through Room 5.

When the structure was remodeled (see fig. 2b) the partition between Rooms 4A and 4B was removed down to foundation level (although remnants of the wall were found on the south and north walls). Then the floor was filled in to the height of the benches and covered with plaster. (The floor level in 4B was originally 0.15 m lower than that of 4A.) When finished, the new floor of the combined Room 4 sloped slightly, rising 0.07 m higher at the west end. On the east end of the room beside the door to Room 3 stood a small rubble dais or platform (W.1.47; Br.ca.0.97; H.0.20 m). To the south of the dais a plaster socket (W.ca.0.20; H.0.09 m) with an aperture 0.12 m in diameter was set in the floor. This installation suggests a platform for a reader (or, less likely, a cathedra), and the floor socket suggests a holder for a torch or lampstand. On the north wall beside the door to the courtyard, a low, shuttered window (W.ca.0.90-1.00; H.1.75 m) was cut through at 0.55 m above the level of the new floor. The walls were treated with a thin overcoat of new plaster, but no decorations were undertaken. The room thus created comprised the large (L.12.90; W.5.15 m) assembly hall of the Christian community. Room 3 probably continued to serve as storage for equipment and utensils. Vertical depressions in the west wall of Room 3 might have supported a wooden chest of some type.

On the west side of the courtyard another formal doorway (W.1.50 m at base) led to Room 5 (L.ca.7.35-7.60; W.4.22 m). Because of its size, its access, and its formal entrance, Room 5 must have comprised with Room 6 the private quarters, perhaps one serving as the *gynaikeion,* or women's quarters, of the house. The renovation involved several steps. First, a low, shuttered window (W.ca.0.80; H.1.15 m) was set in the southeast corner of the room facing onto the courtyard at a height of 1.53 m above the floor (or ca. 0.40 m above the comparable window in Room 4). Second, the doorway to Room 6 (W.1.35 at base; H.2.00 m) was embellished with an elaborate trim quite unusual for such interior, connecting doors. The elaboration of the doorway gave a more formal character to the entrance to Room 6 from Room 5.

Room 6 was originally only an ancillary chamber to Room 5, as indicated by its lower floor level (H.0.085 m above the courtyard) and its irregular shape. (The angle of the northwest corner was 94°31'; the dimensions were 6.80 m along the north wall, 6.87 on the south, 3.16 on the east, and 3.132 on the west.) The room could be entered through two doors (from the courtyard and Room 5). When renovated by the Christians, Room 6 received a more thorough transformation than any other in the house. The ceiling of the room was originally of the same height as Rooms 4 and 5 (ca.5.22 m). The first step in the remodeling of the room was to divide the space vertically into an upper and a lower chamber by setting beams in the walls at a height of 3.45 m from the floor (see fig. 3). Next, the west end of the room was excavated down to bedrock to receive the font construction.

The font basin and canopy comprised a single masonry construction. The basin (W.2.57; Br.1.583 on north and 1.830 m on south), constructed of brick and mortar, had walls 0.34 m thick front and back and 0.47 m on the sides. The interior dimensions were L. 1.63 m and Depth 0.955 m (of which 0.508

m was above the floor level). Once in place, the floor around the font was raised to a height 0.04 m above the original level. On the outer edge of the basin was set a low step (Br.0.29; H.0.165 m), and the area between the sides of the basin and the walls was filled in to the same height. The canopy of the font was constructed of bricks and plaster carried by two rubble pilasters against the wall (H.1.075 m) and two rubble and plaster columns (Diam.0.45; H.1.44 on south, 1.47 on north). The superstructure was a barrel vault along its east–west axis with arched openings sprung from the pilasters and columns on the sides. The frontal arch of the vault had a span of 1.74 m and reached its crown 0.253 m below the new ceiling (H.3.20 m from the floor). The walls were replastered, and a low bench/step (H.0.22; Br.0.51 m) was constructed at the east end of the room. The bench connected with the lower step of the entrance from the courtyard. Finally, a rectangular niche in the south wall between the two doors was arcuated. Apparently there was also some sort of low table extending from the wall below this niche beside the door from Room 5.

After the structural modifications in Room 6 were completed and the ceiling finished, the entire room was decorated with frescoes. On the font the decorations consisted of geometric designs and foliate motifs. The columns were painted to look like marble. In the lunette of the vault on the west wall a single composition was painted. The other three walls of the room were divided into horizontal zones and painted with narrative scenes. The ceiling of the room and that of the canopy vault were treated with white stylized stars on a blue field. The decoration of the ceiling is very similar to that found in the final stage of the Dura mithraeum (see below No. 58). In addition, the decoration of the canopy of the font bears similarities to the decoration of the Torah Shrine of the later synagogue. These tendencies suggest that the decorative work might have been done by local workshops or artisans on contract.

Although it is not possible here to go into a detailed analysis of the artistic program of the baptistry room, at least some observation may be made regarding its apparent programmatic quality.[4] It appears that all the scenes of the east and north walls of the baptistry portray the characters (or narrative

4. For a complete discussion of the design, see Kraeling, *Christian Building*, 45–88 and plates XVII–XLVI. For Kraeling's suggestions regarding the narrative compositional design, see *Christian Building*, 158, 163–68.

flow) in postures of motion from right to left, that is, moving toward the font end of the room. The observation applies to both the upper and lower registers of the north wall, and thus to the scenes of Jesus' miracles. Yet it is especially noticeable in the movement of the female figures in the lower register of the east wall and continuing around the north wall as the women approach the tomb. The scene of the south wall immediately beside the font (depicting the "Woman at the Well") continues this movement, as it were, through the font and out the other side toward the doors on the south wall. This pattern of narrative flow is consistent with Kraeling's observation of the basic axial orientation of the room toward the font; however, it suggests that there may have been a conscious design of the artistic program of the room to conform to some liturgical pattern of usage in conjunction with baptismal ritual. It appears that the processional movement in the room would have been in a counterclockwise direction commencing at or near the door from the courtyard and culminating after the baptism proper before the arcuated niche between the doors, and thus before the "David and Goliath" scene with its commemorative graffiti. (On the graffiti, see No. 37 a and b below.)

The final alterations made in the Christian renovation of the building appeared on the exterior. On the west wall facing Wall Street a flange was constructed of rubble 0.50 m wide at the base and tapering to a point on the west wall 1.40 m above the base. Apparently it buttressed the wall and protected it from the rising level of the street. On the north wall of the building and integral in construction with the flange was a bench (Br.ca.0.50; H.0.50 m), that faced onto the side street and ran from Wall Street to the doorway at the east end of the wall.

PROVINCE: Syria
LOCATION: Dura-Europos

No. 37a-c: Commemorative Graffiti (ca. 241–256)

a. Proclus, a patron (?)

Graffito found in Room 6 (the baptistry) of the Christian *domus ecclesiae* (No. 36) on the south wall (now in Yale University Art Gallery) in the decorative framing band at the top of the David and Goliath panel, which is situated between the two doors and just below the arcuated niche. Letters are coarsely scratched in the plaster coating, which has suffered some damage, although almost all letters were visible at the time of discovery. Letters, H.0.04-0.05 m.

Literature: First published *DEP* 5. 241–42, no. 596; see pp. 283ff. The text below follows that edited by C. Bradford Welles in C. H. Kraeling, *The Christian Building* (Final Report VIII.2; New Haven: Dura-Europos Publications, 1967) 96, no. 18.

τὸν Χ(ριστὸ)ν Ἰ(ησοῦ)ν ὑμεῖν. Μṿ[ή]σκεσθẹ. [. . . Πρ]όκλου.

Translation: Jesus Christ (be) with you.[5] Remember[6] Proclus.[7]

---

5. Welles understands the first phrase as distinct from the second, a Christian version of a common religious formula: τὸν θεόν σοι (*Christian Building*, 96 and n. 7).

6. ΜΝ̣[Η]CΚΕCΘΕ̣. The verb was virtually complete when first seen by Clark Hopkins in 1931. The present state of the plaster is as represented in the trace of Welles (*Christian Building*, 96, fig. i, and pl. XLI: ΜΝ̣[Η]C̣ΚΕCΘ̣[Ε]. Variations of the μνηθῇ/μνήσκεσθε formula are quite common at Dura and are used in a number of contexts (see *DEP* 9. 3:33–4 and *Yale Classical Studies* 14 [1955] 143–48). It is not restricted to funerary usage, though it may indicate a posthumous dedication on behalf of the departed. In this regard, consider the Greek building inscription from the Dura synagogue, No. 61b below.

The use of the formula in another graffito from the Christian building is quite different. It seems to use the same language as part of the construction work, that is, giving the name of the artisan/worker and the date of the work. This is the case for the important inscription dated to 232/233 from the west wall of Room 4 found on an earlier layer of plaster (see No. 36 above and n. 1). It reads: Ἔτους δμφ' (544 =232/233 CE). Μν(ησθῇ) Δωρόθεος. Dorotheos is probably the artisan who performed the work of plastering the walls of the earlier house at the time of its original construction. In this light we may also compare the use of the formula in a sixth-century mosaic inscription from the Beth Alpha synagogue (*CIJ* 2. 1166) which commemorates the work of the mosaicists. In other cases the commemoration seems to take the place of the normal pagan dedication formulae, for example, in the Aramaic inscriptions from the Beth Gubrin and Na'aran synagogues (see E. Sukenik, *Ancient Synagogues in Palestine and Greece* [London: Oxford University Press, 1934] 72–76). The three more clearly Christian graffiti from the Dura Christian building that use the μνησθῇ formula (see No. 37b-c below) have usually been considered funerary in nature. But the range of possibilities for the use of the term at Dura alone make such a reading less likely. See nn. 9 and 11 below.

7. The name Proclus is well attested at Dura, especially among the Roman military records.

b. Siseon, an artisan (?)

Graffito found in Room 6 (the baptistry of the Christian *domus ecclesiae*) on the south wall (now in Yale University Art Gallery) centered in the dado panel to the left of the arcuated niche between the two doors. The graffito in three lines occupies a space (L.0.29; H.0.08 m) of unpainted plaster, which is badly defaced. The letters are deep and coarse (perhaps executed while the plaster was still wet?), H.0.09-0.02 m.

Literature: First published *DEP* 5. 240, no. 594. The text below follows C. Bradford Welles, in C. H. Kraeling, *The Christian Building* (Final Report VIII.2; New Haven: Dura-Europos Publications, 1967) 95–96, no. 17.

τὸν Χρισ(τὸν). Μνήσκεστε
2 Σισε͂ον τὸν ταπ(ε)ι-
νόν.

Translation: Christ (be with you).[8] Remember[9] Siseon (or Sisaeus) the Lowly.[10]

---

8. TON XPIC (mur.). On the basis of the fuller formula in No. 37a, Welles would supply for sense ὑμῖν.

9. MNHCKECTE (mur.). The verb was originally read by C. Hopkins as MNHCKETE, but it should be read with No. 37a as T for θ, that is, as a substitution for μνήσκεσθε.

10. CICEON TON TAΠI/NON (mur.). Welles (in Kraeling, *Christian Building*, 96) comments on the grammatical problem caused by the use of the accusative instead of the genitive with the verb. He thinks the unusual name derives from a Semitic, perhaps even Jewish, root and cites only one other occurrence, also at Dura (*P.Dura* 47.3). On the other hand Comte R. du Mesnil du Buisson in a late article ("L'inscription de la Niche Centrale de la Synagogue de Doura-Europos," *Syria* 40 [1963] 303–14) restores the Aramaic name סיסא (Sisa') for the name of the artisan who constructed the Torah niche in the later synagogue (see below No. 61g; Sec. III, n. 31). He goes on to suggest that Σισε͂ον is the appropriate transliteration of the name and that the same person might have done both jobs (see pp. 312–13). The epithet he takes to be an instance of the common practice among later Christians of calling themselves "the humble." If, however, these two graffiti from the Baptistry (with No. 37a above) are meant to commemorate the actions of these individuals in the renovation or decoration of the Christian edifice, then the epithet may also be taken more literally. The true significance cannot be certain, but the other appearance of the formula in a fragmentary graffito from Room 4 (No. 37c) points in the direction of the latter.

c. Paulos, a bishop (?)

Graffito in two lines (apparently) from north wall of Room 4, just beside the west jamb of the door leading to the courtyard. The letters are incised into the final layer of plaster, which is broken away on the left side, at a height ca. 1.00 m above the floor. Overall (as preserved): L. ca. 0.80; H. 0.17 m; Letter Height: 0.05 m.

Literature: First reported in *DEP* 4. 177 (no. 367); the text below follows that of Welles in C. H. Kraeling, *The Christian Building* (Final Report VIII.2; New Haven: Dura-Europos Publications, 1967) 92, no. 9 and fig. 3), based on his own transcription, but the reading is that of the author.

[ΜΝΗΣ]Θ̣Η ΠΑΥΛΟΣ Κ̣[ΑΙ . . .] Π̣ΑΥΛΟΥ
[ΤΟΝ ΕΠΙ]Σ̣ΚΟΠΟΝ ΚΑ̣[Ι . .]Λ̣ΑΙΝ̣

Translation: (Christ be with you.)[11] Remem]ber Paul and [. . .], son of Paul . . . .
. . . . the bishop[12] and (people ?). . . .

---

11. I have supplied the formula based on the two texts from the baptistry (Nos. 37a and b above). If this parallelism is correct, then it suggests something of the original length of the first line of the graffito, which would be missing between eleven and sixteen letters.

12. Welles (in Kraeling, *Christian Building*, 92) argued that the apparent use of ἐπί]σκοπον is not likely to be read as a reference to the Christian bishop because of the early date. Why this title would not have been in use in the middle of the third century among Christians of provincial Syria is not apparent to me, especially given the roughly contemporaneous material preserved in Eusebius, *H.E.* 7.30.18 (cf. No. 20b above). Welles tried to interpret the term instead as an epithet for the Christian God ("the one who attends or watches over"). I would prefer to restore the second line as follows: ΕΠΙ]Σ̣ΚΟΠΟΝ ΚΑ[Ι Λ]Α̣ΩΝ, and hence as some sort of reference to the Christian community and its leadership. This reading would cohere not only with the spatial proportions of the inscription but also with the sense of dedicatory formulae by members of the community on behalf of the work. Read in this way, the fragmentary inscription from Room 4 and those from the baptistry (Nos. 37a and b) would seem to come from patrons and/or artisans who participated in the renovation and decoration of the building for Christian usage. Unfortunately, the precise context is entirely lost.

PROVINCE: Syria (Coelesyria, Cynegia Chora)
LOCATION: Qirqbize

No. 38: Villa and Church Complex (late third to sixth centuries)
(Figures 4–5)

The deserted village of Qirqbīze sits atop a ridge of the *Gebel il A'la* overlooking the *Plaine de Self* to the east (see Tchalenko, *Villages,* vol. 2, plates XC, C, CI) in an area of arable land terraced for growing grain and olives. The architecture was first surveyed by the Princeton expedition under H. C. Butler in 1899–1900. The village proper seems to have been founded only in the later third century. The oldest monument on the site is the large villa (A) at the north edge of the village datable to the end of the third century. Most likely the villa denotes the founding of a plantation estate for growing olives. During the fourth to sixth centuries the village grew out (primarily to the south) from the first villa. The village reached its full extent before the seventh century and was abandoned by the Middle Ages. To the west of the first villa and as a dependency of it, a modest church was constructed in the early part of the fourth century. Tchalenko suggests that this may be one of the earliest known monuments from northern Syria specifically constructed as a church building. It went through four subsequent stages of renovation and/or embellishment carrying through the mid-sixth century.

Literature: AAES (1899) I:10-14, 87, 118; II:114f, 269. G. Tchalenko, *Villages antiques de la Syrie du Nord* (3 vols.; Bibliothèque archéologique et historique de l'institut français d'archéologique de Beyrouth 50; Paris: J. Gabalda, 1953–1958) I:319–42; II: plates X, XIII, XC, C–CVII, CCXI. Cf. J. Lassus and G. Tchalenko, "Ambons Syriens," *Cah. Arch.* 5 (1951) 75–122.

[The following summary is based primarily on the analysis of Tchalenko, *Villages*. For the purposes of the present study, the first stage is by far the most significant, but the later stages are summarized.]

a. Stage 1: Establishment of the Villa and Church (late third to early fourth century)

The villa A (see fig. 5) comprised a walled rectangular court with the large house of the owner to the north. This house opened through the court from a columned portico with gallery above. On the south side of the court another building provided apartments probably for two families who shared in the operation of the plantation. Gates opened from either end of the south building, and a cistern stood outside the south wall.

H. C. Butler had originally identified the edifice (B) immediately to the west of this earliest villa as another villa of very similar plan and construction.[13] The edifice is constituted as a walled court facing a colonnaded portico before a rectangular building; another large room with its own court lay to the west. The room and the court to the west Tchalenko dates to a later addition, and he calls the court and hall of B a very modest church building. He dates its construction probably to the first third of the fourth century. The hall proper (L.14.75; W.6.40; H.ca.6.55 m) was an aisleless nave. The single indication of interior orientation and division of the earliest structure was the slightly elevated platform (Br.3.15 m) across the east end. There was a low bench or step on this platform against the east wall (see fig. 4a). Two doors opened from the long south wall down one step onto the portico of six columns with either end (east/west) closed by the walls of the courtyard. The raised floor of the portico was surmounted by two steps: one set before the platform and the second set in the intercolumniations. In the court immediately before the third column from the east stood a large cistern (Diam.ca.4-5 m), covered with five flagstones in the center of which was a square opening.[14]

According to Tchalenko, the plan and construction of the west edifice (B) and even the layout of the main hall would have been very difficult to identify as a Christian church building were it not for the more formal liturgical embellishments added in later stages. The main door to the church complex was in the east wall of the court at the southeast corner, that is, facing the west wall of the villa complex. The entrance was a very large doorway with stone jambs and an ornamental cornice. The door matches those of the villa, but the cornice is unique to the church. The two buildings were separated by a narrow alleyway which later carried a roof at the church entrance. The church is considered by Tchalenko to belong to the very earliest development of the village after the foundation of Villa A. For this reason he argues that the church was built as a dependency by the owner(s) of the villa for

13. See AAES 2. 117f.

14. See Tchalenko, *Villages*, 1. 46.

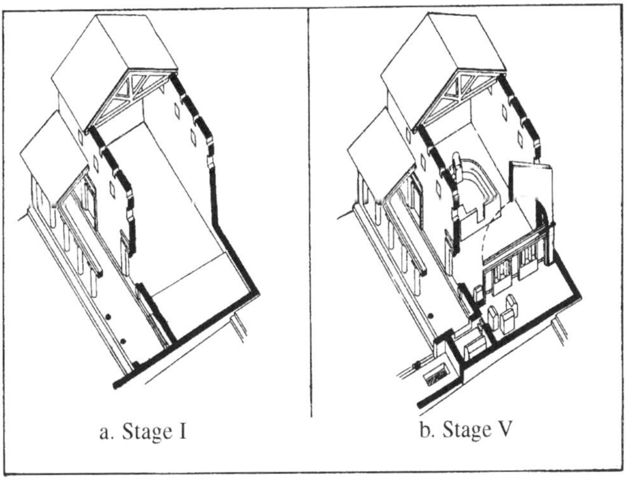

Fig. 4
Syria, Qirqbize. Christian church, fourth–sixth centuries.
Isometric reconstruction in stages (after Tchalenko)

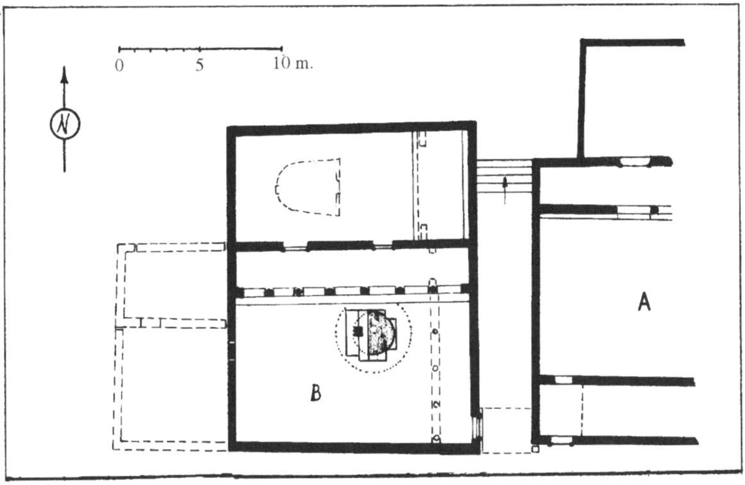

Fig. 5
Syria, Qirqbize. Christian church, fourth–sixth centuries.
Plan reconstruction, composite (based on Tchalenko)

their use (and that of any other indigenous Christian population). He considers the construction of even the modest first church building to be one generation later than the foundation of the villa, hence his date in the first third of the fourth century.[15]

b. Stage 2: Creation of the Sanctuary (later fourth century)

The second stage of renovation in the church occurred in the second half of the fourth century with the introduction of a "triumphal arch" on the raised platform at the east end of the hall as the primary internal feature (see fig. 4b). Tchalenko attributes this embellishment to the influence of the first basilical planning (with apse) in Syrian church construction in the mid-fourth century.[16] The Qirqbize church was fitted with a sanctuary by supporting the stonework arch on two piers set against the wall near the west edge of the platform. [The piers are not bonded to the walls.] The decorative motifs of these piers (acanthus leaves carved on the capitals and the molding of the bases) support a later-fourth-century dating in that they resemble features in basilicas at Batuta and Burǧ Heidar which belong to the same period.[17]

c. Stages 3 and 4: Remodeling of the Sanctuary and Introduction of the Bema (fifth century)

In the next stages the entire platform of the sanctuary was raised to the height of the low step/bench against the east wall (the same height as the bases of the pillars for the arch). The platform came to an end at the front edge of the pillar bases, creating a two-step ascent to the sanctuary. The sanctuary was formally closed off from the nave by fitting the arch with a screen. The crossbar of the screen was carried by two colonettes supported on a low chancel with a central opening. At about the same time the monumental ambo (L.3.77; W.3.04-3.77 m) was introduced in the center of the nave (lying on the east–west axis 4.80 m from the sanctuary and 3.10 m from the west wall). The bema (fig. 4b) probably replaced some earlier

15. Ibid., 1. 332.

16. Compare the churches in the villages of Behyo and Bankusa; see Tchalenko, *Villages*, 1. 333, and vol. 2: plate X.

17. Ibid., 1. 329 and n. 2.

wooden structure now lost. The stonework ambo was curved on the west side and opened on the east; a bench row was placed on the side walls and around the curved back wall where a central cathedra was elevated. The date of these additions is placed at the beginning of the fifth century.[18]

Stage 4 brought further embellishment of the sanctuary screen. A triportal was created in the screen by opening it on either end of the chancel. At the same time the screen was transformed into a partition by placing two colonnettes on either side of the central doorway to carry the partition cross-structure. The south door of the triportal opened to a "martyrial chapel" in the south portion of the sanctuary. The "chapel" consisted of three reliquaries arranged so that they open toward the nave (see fig. 4b). This arrangement Tchalenko dates to the mid-fifth century, since it appears elsewhere in northern Syrian around 430.[19]

d. Stage 5: Constructions in the Portico and Courtyard (sixth century)

The final form of the church (as in fig. 4b) was achieved in the sixth century. The elements of renovation included rebuilding the fourth-century entrance to the courtyard after earthquakes in 526 and 528. To the same period may be attributed piercing the south wall of the sanctuary with a doorway and the installation of a martyrion on the east end of the portico (see fig. 4b).[20] The martyrion was constructed by closing the space between the last portico column on the east and the pilaster of the east wall. Then an arch was constructed carried on two pillars set against the same last column and against the south wall of the sanctuary (beside the new doorway). A sarcophagus was placed in this martyrion. Another martyrial structure was added in the sixth century with the construction of an entry portico along the east wall of the courtyard. The platform of the portico was surmounted by two steps, and on its north end it contained a sunken tomb. Presumably about the same time, the complex was expanded to the west by the addition of a room off the portico with a separate court to the south. The new room could be entered either from the west end of the portico or from the court. The construction of this annex probably meant that the west wall of the church's courtyard was

18. Ibid., 1. 327–28, 334 n. 1; see also Lassus and Tchalenko, "Ambons Syriens," 96–97.

19. Tchalenko, *Villages*, 1. 334–35 and n. 2.

20. Ibid., 1. 335.

torn down and replaced with a colonnade, but later the intercolumniations were closed and a single door installed near the north end. Finally, two more reliquaries were set on the step of the sanctuary against the arch pillars. Tchalenko dates these reliquaries to the end of the sixth century.[21]

PROVINCE: Syria (Phoenice, Libanensis)
LOCATION: Lebaba (Deir-Ali)

No. 39: Building Inscription of a "Marcionite Synagogue" (318/319)

From the village of Lebaba found reused in the construction of a modern house in the present village of Deir-Ali, ca. three miles south of Damascus, an inscribed lintel in very good condition (measurements and material unknown). The inscription is in five lines (letter height unknown).

Literature: P. Le Bas and H. J. Waddington, *Inscriptions Grecques et - Latines de Syrie* (Paris, 1898) III.2558. A. Harnack, *Marcion*: *Das Evangelium vom fremden Gott* (2nd ed.; TU 45; Leipzig: Hinrichs, 1924; repr. Darmstadt, 1960) 263*–266*.

[The text reproduced here is after the transcription of Waddington, cited above.]

Συναγωγὴ Μαρκιωνιστῶν κώμ(ης)
Λεβάβων τοῦ κ(υρίο)υ κ[α]ὶ
σ(ωτῆ)ρ(ος) Ἰη(σοῦ) Χρηστοῦ
προνοίᾳ Παύλου Πρεσβ(υτέρου)
τοῦ λχ΄ ἔτους.

Translation: (This is) the synagogue, in the village of Lebaba, of the Marcionists (*sic*) of the lord and savior Jesus Christ (built) under the direction[22] of the presbyter Paul in the year 630 (=318/19 CE).[23]

---

21. Ibid., 1. 336.

22. ΠΡΟΝΟΙΑ. For the term used in the sense of "management" or "plan" of a building project, compare the building inscriptions in PAES III.A.5, nos. 732–33 and no. 734. PAES III.A.5, no. 734 makes it clear that in this context πρόνοια is taken as synonymous with ἐπιμέλεια and σπουδῆ.

23. The date of the inscription (λχ΄) is rendered by Waddington according to

PROVINCE: Syria (Hauran)/later Arabia
LOCATION: Thantia (?) (Umm-el-Jimal)

No. 40: "Julianos' Church" (fourth to fifth century)
(Figures 6–7)

The ancient city, known probably as Thantia, was observed on numerous occasions in the nineteenth century.[24] The city in general (and the basilical "Julianos' Church" in particular) were first surveyed by the Princeton expedition of 1904–1905 led by H. C. Butler. The church is located in an insula of six houses in the northwestern portion of the city (see fig. 6). These first discoveries were subsequently checked, corrected, and supplemented by a survey expedition in 1956 led by Spencer Corbet. The "Julianos' Church" was so identified and dated by Butler on the basis of an inscription (see No. 41 below), of 344 CE, found near the main (south) portal of the basilica.[25] This inscription has since been shown to be a funerary monument used as spoil in the final stage of the church's construction. The inscription does provide a *terminus a quo* for this final stage. Indeed, secondary cruciform decoration of some of the doors of the house complex would substantiate a late-fourth- or early-fifth-century date. But the construction of the church and the insula complex point to prior stages of use that may date from an earlier Christian presence in the city.[26] A flourishing Roman presence is attested by architectural (the "Commodus" gate, ca. 176-180; the barracks and Praetorium, ca. fourth to fifth century) and documentary (the inscription of Flavius Lucianus, ca. 349–361) evidence. Because the complex has only been cleared and surveyed to the floor of the basilica, it is not possible to give a detailed architectural history for the site. The data presented here, therefore, will represent the final phases of construction but with special attention to evidence for earlier stages of development.

Literature: H. C. Butler, PAES II.A.3, "Archeology of Umm-idj-djimal," 173–80; PAES III.A.3, *Greek and Latin Inscriptions*, 515–16. G. U. S.

Seleucid dating, that is, 318/19. The same year according to provincial dating would yield a much later date, 735 CE. There is no mention of the indiction in this case as in PAES III.A.5, no. 677. The earlier dating is preferable.

24. Butler, PAES II.A:151–52; III.A.2(Appendix) xiv.

25. PAES II.A:173.

26. Corbet, "Investigations at 'Julianos' Church' at Umm-el-Jemal," 63–65.

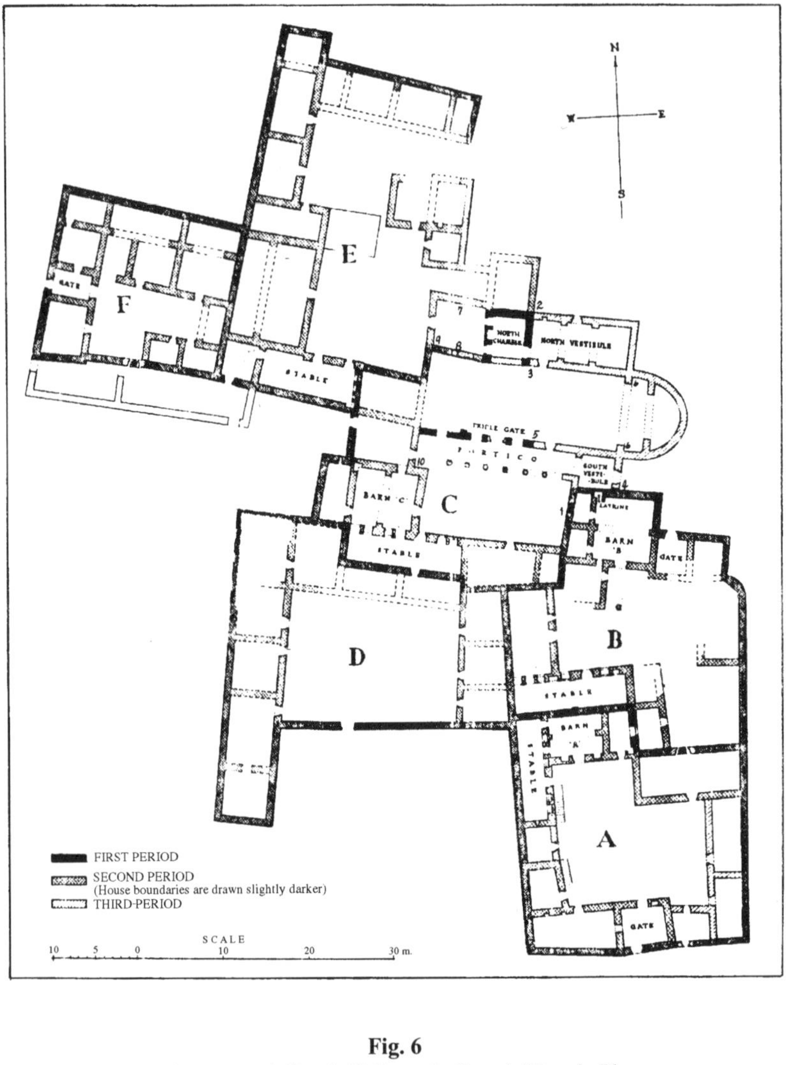

Fig. 6

Syria, Umm el-Jimal, "Julianos's Church." Insula Plan.
(after G. U. S. Corbett, PBSR, XXV, fig. 3)

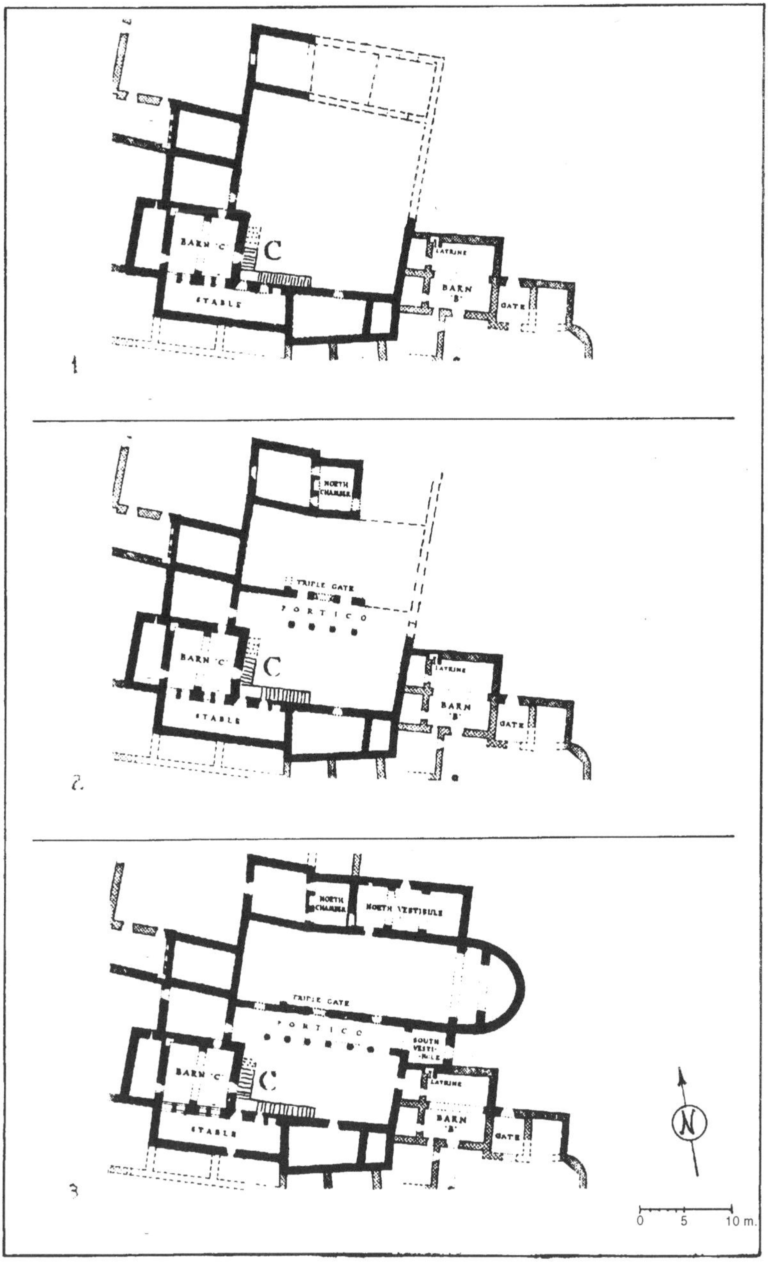

Fig. 7

Syria, Umm el-Jimal, "Julianos's Church," third–fifth centuries.
Plan restoration in stages (conjectural)

Corbet, "Investigations at 'Julianos' Church' at Umm-el-Jemal," *PBSR* 25 (1957) 39–65. Additional note for dating by J. M. Reynolds, "Note on the Inscription of Flavius Lucianus," *PBSR* 25 (1957) 65–67. B. De Vries, "Research at Umm el-Jimal, Jordan, 1972–1977," *BA* 42 (1979) 49–55.

a. The Insula Complex

The six distinct houses of the northwest insula (A-F, fig. 6) conform to the common style of domestic architecture for the city. A typical house consisted of a courtyard reached by a double gateway with a vestibule. Around the courtyard are clustered the stone buildings of the house including mangers, stables, barns with high arched ceilings, and storage rooms. Domestic quarters were usually in a second or third story above these ground-level rooms. A latrine can often be found as a small closet-like room in the corner of the larger barn or stable (see fig. 6 in Barn B). The inclusion of quarters for livestock in domestic structures is most indicative of the generally rural life-style and agrarian economy of the city even during Roman military occupation.

There is evidence of some remodeling in the plans of the houses in the insula. For example, in House A the three small rooms in the southeast corner were probably later additions in what was originally part of the courtyard.[27] This fact is indicated by the narrow interior wall construction contrasting with that of the exterior walls. In addition, the doorways of these three rooms were decorated with crosses carved on the lintels. Also added at a later time were doorways cut through the party walls to interconnect the various houses of the complex (see, for example, the inserted doorway from the small room of the barn of House B to the courtyard of C—the church, fig. 6, locus 1).[28]

b. House C and the Basilica

The construction of the church as an extension of House C left untouched the barn, the stable, and part of the courtyard of the house. Remnants of a stairway suggest that domestic quarters above the barn also remained intact.

27. Ibid., 46.
28. Ibid., 46–47.

Moreover, the west end and the northwest corner of the nave were formed by an interior wall and part of an exterior party-wall of the original house, as suggested by the irregularity with which windows appear in the west wall of the nave and by the bonded northwest corner.[29] The east end of the nave, the north vestibule, and the south vestibule entrance, however, were constructed later as part of the fourth-century basilical plan. The north wall of the north vestibule (fig. 6, locus 2), the north wall of the nave (locus 3), the east wall of the main entrance (locus 4), and the south wall of the nave (at the east portal, locus 5) are not bonded to the earlier house wall. Similarly, the apse is not bonded to the great crossing arch at the east end of the nave (locus 6).

The basilica was constituted as an aisleless nave divided laterally into three sections by chancel screens at both the east and the west ends. In Butler's plan of the church (PAES II.A:174 and PAES III:147) he restored the nave with an arched ceiling in ten bays (W.ca.2.00 m), each "of over seven meters span" sprung from piers (W.0.70 m) extending 0.75 m from the walls. According to Corbet's survey, a flat wooden beam roof with no piers is more likely.[30] The apse, on the other hand, is constructed of two stone arches, which Corbet takes to indicate a lack of expertise on the part of the builders. Corbet concludes, therefore, that apse construction was still a relatively new, unrefined technique for this region as late as 344 CE.[31]

The use of decorative crosses on the lintel stones of several doors (e.g., above the cupboard in the north vestibule, at the north door from the nave) helps support a late-fourth-century date. Similar evidence is provided by a stone reused in the apse wall construction, which bears an inscription, datable to about the same period as the stone bearing the Flavius Lucianus inscription reused in the construction of the apse *synthronon*.[32] It may be, however, that the finishing of the *synthronon* or even its construction belongs to a secondary period of renovation within the basilica. This conclusion is given added weight by the fittings of the east chancel screen and by the fact

29. Ibid., 53.

30. Ibid., 55.

31. Ibid., 64–65; for this date as a *terminus a quo* based on the Julianos inscription, see No. 41 below.

32. Corbet, "Investigations," 64. The inscription is PAES III.A, no. 236. Further dating evidence is provided by the analysis of J. M. Reynolds ("Note on the Inscription of Flavius Lucianus," 65–67).

that the nave floor was originally a polychrome mosaic later covered over with white (or painted red) plaster.[33]

c. Evidence of Earlier Renovation in House C and the Sequence of Construction

These facts deal basically with the construction of the basilica (from the mid-fourth to the early fifth century). The construction on the west and south sides of the nave, however, gives evidence of earlier phases in this building history. The most suggestive feature is the construction of the triportal (what Corbet calls the "Triple Gate"), which formed the main (south) entrance to the nave. Both architectural and masonry analysis shows that the Triple Gate structure is not bonded to the east end of the nave's south wall (fig. 6, locus 5), and, therefore, was not integral with the construction of the basilica.

The Triple Gate was part of an earlier construction within the courtyard of House C. The Triple Gate was faced on the south by a colonnaded portico opening onto the courtyard. In the final form of the basilica, this portico consisted of six columns (Butler's plan called for seven). In an earlier period, however, there were only four columns and their intercolumniation was wider. This alteration in the colonnade probably corresponds to the construction of the basilica, at which time the Triple Gate was also altered. The three south entrances of the basilica were widely spaced—one to the west of the west chancel and one to the west of the south vestibule. The latter was cut into the newly constructed portion of the basilica's west wall. Found blocked up in the older portion of the south wall were two other, more narrowly spaced flanking portals whose dimensions correspond to the four-column layout of the portico.[34] The orientation of the Triple Gate and its portico (an unusually Roman element in the domestic architecture of the city) corresponds to that of the so-called North Chamber. According to Corbet, they may date from the same period and the same monumental construction. The west wall of the North Chamber contains a niche flanked by two doors; the east wall contains a single door. This south door is considerably lower than the floor level of the north vestibule and lower than the sill of the north door

33. Corbet, "Investigations," 59.
34. Ibid., 52, and figs. 9a-b.

from the nave. These proportions suggest something of the original floor level before construction of the basilica.

Corbet concludes that the Triple Gate and the North Chamber represent the remnants of a monumental structure, perhaps a "Nabataean temple," which was the earliest structure in this area and which was then taken over or reused in the construction of House C. He cites as architectural support a supposed Nabataean temple excavated by the Princeton expedition (PAES II.A:155 and map 2). Following the Princeton expedition's restoration, this so-called Nabataean temple also had a triportal entrance and was later incorporated into a domestic structure. The date accorded to this renovation by Butler was later in the Christian period. In contrast to Corbet's reconstruction of the "Julianos" Triple Gate, the Nabataean temple has a prostyle with only two columns on the north side. It should be noted, however, that the new excavations at the site have seriously questioned the identification, form, and date of Butler's "Nabataean temple" (reported in conversation with B. De Vries).

The primary reason, according to Corbet, for assuming that the Triple-Gate building antedates the domestic insula is that "no such monument could ever have been constructed inside the courtyard of a small private house."[35] Corbet does suggest, however, that the entire Triple-Gate building may have stood intact within House C.[36] There it may have served as an earlier meeting place for the Christian community, which no doubt existed before 344 CE (based on the reference to the cemetery in inscription No. 41). Thus, he suggests that the basilica grew out of a reconstruction of the Triple-Gate precinct within House C. Corbet's chronology for the building history is as follows:

(1) A (Nabataean) temple within the Triple Gate existed on the site, which
(2) was later incorporated more or less intact in the construction of House C; subsequently it may have been used as a Christian meeting place.
(3) At some point in the late fourth to early fifth century the north portion c House C (including the Triple-Gate building) was taken over in the c struction of a basilica, which
(4) was later remodeled, perhaps at the same time that the other hou the insula were interconnected (Corbet does not specify the dat

35. Ibid., 62.
36. Ibid., 65.

this renovation, nor does he detail the sequence of building for the other houses of the insulae relative to that of House C).

Corbet's careful survey of the site makes a number of detailed observations regarding the so-called Julianos's church possible, but, in contrast, we may not conclude so quickly that a "monumental" structure could not have been built within the courtyard of a house. After all, extensive construction and renovation in house courtyards for cultic sanctuaries may be seen in the Priene synagogue (No. 69) and the San Clemente mithraeum (No. 87). Moreover, Corbet never gives attention to the orientation and placement of the Triple Gate within the courtyard of House C. Except for House F, the courtyard of House C (as bounded on the north by the Triple Gate) is the smallest courtyard in the entire insula. This fact is somewhat surprising, given Corbet's chronology. If the Triple-Gate building were a preexisting structure, House C would have been among the first domestic edifices constructed in the insula, with Houses B, D, and E growing up around it. The diminutive courtyard is, therefore, incongruous, unless one suggests that the Triple-Gate building was consciously incorporated into the house (perhaps by Christians) as a *domus sanctus*.

Corbet's qualms notwithstanding, a different sequence of construction is plausible. Of course, any evidence for the original form of House C and the Triple-Gate building is buried under the unexcavated floor of the church nave. Nonetheless, the following points emerge. The general size and orientation of House C within the insula remain a puzzle, especially since the plan of the insula as a whole is quite irregular: for example, the north wall of Barn B and the north wall of Barn C form not a straight line but an obtuse angle against the line of the Triple-Gate colonnade. The walls (fig. 6, loci 7-8) of the small room to the west of the North Chamber demonstrate the same irregularity. The two walls (oriented east–west) are parallel to each other but are askew of the line of the Triple Gate, the axis of the basilica, and the north wall of the North Chamber. Yet these walls (7, 8) are well in line with other construction in the insula, especially in House E. The southernmost of these walls (8) was, according to Corbet, the exterior party-wall of House C (with House E), and its earlier date is attested by the bonded masonry angle at its northwest corner.[37] Since there were no subfloor soundings in this area, there is no evidence that these walls (7, 8) were continued to the east. But the

37. So also Corbet, "Investigations," 53.

termination of wall 7 at the North Chamber is abrupt, and the axis of the later nave north wall provides an equally abrupt termination for wall 8. The line of wall 8, if extended to the east meets a line extended north from the exterior wall of Barn B. The area bounded by the extension of these wall lines (see fig. 7a) is quite comparable to the courtyards of Houses A, B, D, and E. Moreover, if wall 7 is extended, the plan begins to look very much like the exterior walls with a row of small chambers, as on the west side of House A or D. The fact that the west wall of the chamber is bonded to wall 7 but not to wall 8 presents no real problem to this conjecture, since other segments of the house were not constructed with bonded walls (e.g., the west wall of the courtyard at the north wall of Barn C, fig. 6, locus 10). A comparison of the floor level (according to Corbet's cross-section, pl. XXIX) on the North Chamber, the courtyard, and the stable and barn of House C might also suggest that the area to the north of the nave had been originally part of the house construction phase.

With these facts in mind an alternative sequence of construction might be suggested, as further excavation is pending (see fig. 7).

Phase I. The first phase of construction (fig. 7a) would have included the construction of the domestic complex, especially Houses B and C and perhaps A, D, and F. The entrance to House C was probably on the east or north side of the courtyard in the area covered by the nave. No firm date can be assigned to this construction, but the general oriental character and relation to the church would suggest some time in the second to third centuries CE.[38]

Phase II. After House C was constructed (Perhaps the third or early fourth century) the "Triple-Gate" building was installed within the courtyard (fig. 7b). The form of this structure and its relation to the North Chamber are not clear.[39] There may have been more than one stage of renovation in the formal edifice constructed in the courtyard. Perhaps the North Chamber was earlier than the Triple Gate, given the higher level of the column bases. Moreover, it would seem that before the construction of the basilica, the structure ençompassed the entire west portion of the courtyard bounded on the south by the extension of the Triple-Gate wall and on the north by wall 8. Paving stones under the nave floor in the west chancel would suggest this expansion. The function of the Triple-Gate building remains equally mysterious, awaiting

38. See Butler, PAES II.A:152–53.

39. See Corbet's proposed reconstruction of the original form of the Triple Gate in "Investigations," 52.

further excavation. Corbet's suggestion that in the third to early fourth centuries it was the meeting place for the Christian community is most intriguing and might help to explain this seemingly unlikely site for the construction of a basilica. But other cultic functions are also possible, not the least of which could be a synagogue. The fact that no evidence of a synagogue was found in the town is intriguing, and Christian basilicas built over synagogues are known elsewhere (e.g., at Stobi, No. 72). While there is no epigraphic evidence for a Jewish community at Thantia, the triportal entrance would not have been uncommon in synagogue architecture in northern Palestine (in the Galilee and the Golan) of the fourth century and later.

Phase III. Beginning in the late fourth or early fifth century (Corbet suggests ca. 400), the Triple-Gate building was incorporated into the construction of the basilica (fig. 7c). The construction included the nave, apse, north vestibule and south vestibule; embellishments included expanding the colonnade and altering the doors of the Triple Gate, mosaic paving for the nave floor, paving the courtyard, and other interior touches, for example, plastering the walls.

Phase IV. Later (in the fifth century?) the basilica was refurbished, but in some ways it was made more austere. The mosaics of the nave floor were removed and plastered over. The two chancels were probably added in the later period, as was the *synthronon* of the apse. In the other houses of the insula a number of interconnecting doors were cut creating one large complex; many of the doors were decorated with crosses. These facts suggest that the insula complex might have been taken over for ecclesiastical functions. The austere decor of this later phase might suggest appropriation and renovation for use by a monastic community. If this were the case, the unusual west chancel might be explained as the area for novices rather than for catechumens, as previously proposed.[40] That the building and insula, perhaps the earliest of the Christian edifices at Thantia, could have been given over entirely to a monastic community (and removed from public Christian use) may be explained in the light of a great proliferation of church buildings in the town in the fifth-sixth centuries (see Butler's plan of the city, PAES II.A, map 2, which identifies eleven basilical "churches").

These suggestions must be considered highly conjectural pending further

40. Ibid., 62.

work on the site. A new series of excavations under the direction of B. De Vries were begun in 1972. New surveys of the site have been produced, and the new evidence is being prepared for publication. It is hoped that soundings in the "Julianos's Church" area, along the lines proposed above, can be included in future seasons. Such examination below the present floor levels will help to clear up a number of matters regarding the building history and dating of the church.

PROVINCE: Syria (Hauran)/later Arabia
LOCATION: Thantia (?) (Umm-el-Jimal)

No. 41: The "Julianos" Memorial (344)

Inscription on a lintel stone discovered on the ground in the church that was erroneously named for it (see No. 40 above). It could not have been (as Butler argued)[41] the lintel of the main door, since that was later found to be in place. The inscription is probably to be understood as a funerary monument, and its presence in the church explained as a spoil. The stone was broken into two pieces (L.overall. 1.58 m; frag.A: H.0.345; L.top.0.905; bottom.0.955 m; frag.B: H.0.345; L.top.0.675; bottom.0.625 m). Letters: H.0.03-0.04 m.

Literature: H. C. Butler et al., PAES II.A.3: *Architecture of S. Syria*, 173-80; III.A.3: *Greek and Latin Inscriptions*, 151–52. G. U. S. Corbet, "Investigations at 'Julianos' Church' at Umm-el-Jemal," *PBSR* 25 (1957) 39–65. Cf. J. M. Reynolds, "Note on the Inscription of Flavius Lucianus," *PBSR* 25 (1957) 65–67. J. Lassus, *Sanctuaires chrétiens de Syrie* (Paris: P. Geuthner, 1947) 26–27, 191.

Ἰουλιανοῦ τόδε μνῆμα, μακρῷ βεβαρημένῳ ὕπνου,
ᾧ Ἄγαθος δείματο πατὴρ κατὰ δάκρυ[ον] εἴ[βω]ν,
κοιμητηρίου παρὰ τέρμα κοινοῦ λαοῦ χρειστοῦ,
ὄφρ᾽ αὐτὸν ἀείδοιεν ἀμείνων εἰς ἀεὶ λαὸς
ἀμφά‹ι›δια, Ἀγάθῳ πάροιθεν πρεσβυτέρῳ
πιστὸν ἐόντ᾽ ἀγαπητόν, ἐτέων ιβ´ ὄντα.
Ἔτο(υς) σλθ´.

41. Butler, PAES II.A.3:174–75.

Translation: This (is) the memorial[42] of Julianos, which Agathus (his) father, streaming with tears,[43] built for him, weighed down with long slumber,[44] at the summit[45] of the common (public?) cemetery of the congregation of Christ, to the end that the better people[46] might ever publicly sing his praise that he was formerly to Agathus, the presbyter, a trusty and beloved (son), being twelve years old. In the year 239 (344 CE).[47]

PROVINCE: Syria (Palestine)
LOCATION: Capernaum (Capharnahum)

No. 42: "The House of St. Peter": Sanctuary and Octagonal Church (fourth–mid-fifth century)
(Figure 8)

The reexcavation in 1968 of the octagonal Byzantine church was directed by Father Virgilio Corbo of the Studium Biblicum Franciscanum. The church

42. MNHMA. Butler (PAES II.A:174) took the term to refer to the church itself, but this is very doubtful. Corbet ("Investigations," 62), therefore, proposed to read the term in its more common, funerary sense.

43. The phrase κατὰ δάκρυ[ον] εἴ[βω]ν is only one indication of the affected Homeric style of these epitaphs (see PAES III.A, no. 160). The phrase is restored by Littmann et al. (PAES III) on the basis of its numerous occurrences in Homer, at the end of a hexameter. See especially *Od.* w. 280, where the phrase occurs as here.

44. The endings of μακρῷ βεβαρυμένῳ and ὕπνου apparently have been transposed, a stone-cutter's error (see PAES III.A:152).

45. τέρμα. Littmann et al. read the word as "boundary," owing to Butler's conviction that the memorial was the church itself standing close to a now-lost cemetery. On the basis of Corbet's arguments ("Investigations," 64) we may read the term in more literal terms of a cemetery layout (see n. 46 below), though the "boundary" is not ruled out.

46. ἀμείνων λαὸς may be a reference to Christians as opposed to non-Christians. However, it may also be read more literally as socioeconomic distinction, taken with παρὰ τέρμα (line 3) and πρεσβυτέρω (line 5) as an indication of the family's standing in civic and Christian circles.

47. ET/OCΛΘ (lapis), inscribed vertically at either edge of the stone. Of the two possibilities for the date, ΛΘ = 39 (144 CE) and CΛΘ = 239 (344 CE), the former seems unlikely since a "public Christian cemetery" (see PAES III.A.3:152) would be doubtful at that early date. On the other hand, if we read for λαοῦ χρειστοῦ "congregation of Christ," the later dating is not absolute. For λαός used in this way among both Jews and Christians, see A. T. Kraabel, "Judaism in Western Asia Minor under the Roman Empire, with a Preliminary Study of Jewish Community at Sardis, Lydia," (Th.D. Thesis, Harvard University, 1968) 214–15.

complex lies only a short distance to the south of the more famous synagogue of Capernaum (which dates from the fourth century); in antiquity the two were separated only by a few blocks of what were originally residential buildings. Corbo's analysis of the evidence has indicated at least three phases of architectural development—two main strata of construction in the area beneath the level of the octagon. The octagonal church (Phase 3) is dated to the mid-fifth century; the earliest strata of buildings (Phase 1), which are domestic in nature, belong to the first century. The middle strata (Phase 2), dated by Corbo to the early fourth century, comprise a quadrilateral complex in and on which the later octagon was centered. Corbo identifies this fourth-century structure as the transformation into a formal sanctuary or cultic center from an earlier Jewish-Christian "house church" located in the actual house of St. Peter at Capernaum. While the later stages of usage as a holy site devoted to the tradition of Peter in the Gospels is apparent from the subsequent constructions, the claims of usage prior to the early fourth century, and specifically of an early "house church," are not demonstrable on the basis of any current evidence.

Literature: G. Orfali, *Capharnaum et ses ruines* (Paris: Boccard, 1922). B. Bagatti, "Oggetti inediti di Cafarnao," *Liber Annuus de Studium Biblicum Franciscanum* 14 (1964) 261–72. V. Corbo, *The House of St. Peter at Capharnaum, a preliminary report of the first two campaigns of Excavations* (trans. S. Saller; Publications of the Studium Biblicum Franciscanum, Collectio Minor 5; Jerusalem: Studium Biblicum Franciscanum, 1969). Emmanuele Testa, *I graffiti della casa di S. Pietro* (Studium Biblicum Franciscanum 18; Jerusalem: Studium Biblicum Franciscanum, 1972). V. Corbo, *Cafarnao I: Gli edifici della citta* (Studium Biblicum Franciscanum 19; Jerusalem: Studium Biblicum Franciscanum, 1975). S. Loffreda, *Recovering Capharnaum* (Studium Biblicum Franciscanum Guides 1; Jerusalem, 1985). On the Capernaum excavations in general, see the review article by James F. Strange, "The Capernaum and Herodion Publications," *BASOR* 226 (1977) 65–74. E. M. Meyers and J. F. Strange, *Archaeology, the Rabbis, and Early Christianity* (Nashville: Abingdon, 1981) 128–30. G. F. Snyder, *Ante Pacem* (Macon, GA: Mercer University Press, 1985) 71–72.

[The only published reports on the site are of a preliminary nature and are lacking in quite a number of important details that would provide more substantiation for interpretations and conclusions. In this particular case, one of the most notable deficiencies is the lack of a thorough stratigraphic analysis as evidence of the layers of architectural history. As a result, no detailed summary of the construction or architectural history can be presented here. Instead, we must be content with Corbo's own summary of the major discoveries with some attempt to evaluate specific claims regarding the so-called Jewish-Christian house church.]

a. Literary Evidence

The identification of the Capernaum church with the "house of St. Peter" is based largely on two sources: (1) a literary tradition derived from fourth- and fifth-century texts connected with the beginnings of Christian pilgrimage traffic to the holy land,[48] and (2) circumstantial material evidence in the excavated site (to be discussed later). The latest of these literary texts is the report of an anonymous pilgrim from Placentia (Piacenza) in northern Italy (dated ca. 570) who reports seeing a church "in Capernaum in the house of the blessed Peter, which is in the form of a basilica" [*Item venimus in Capharnaum in domo beati Petri, quae est modo basilica*].[49] A late anonymous report (of approximately the sixth century) preserved in the *Liber de Locorum Sanctorum* of Peter the Deacon (twelfth century) thought by some[50] to be based on the diary of Egeria (late fourth century), mentions "a church that had been built from the house of the Prince of the Apostles" [*ex domo apostolorum principis ecclesia facta est*].[51] Nonetheless, these texts are not uniform in their location of sites associated with stories in the Gospels.[52] The earliest but least clear reference comes from Epiphanius's

48. The basic collection used by Corbo is that of D. Baldi, *Enchiridion Locorum Sanctorum* (Jerusalem: Studium Biblicum Franciscanum, 1935) s.v. Capharnaum.

49. Baldi, *Enchiridion Locorum Sanctorum*, no. 436 [=Antoninus Placentinus 7, in *Itinera Hierosolymitana* Saec. III-VIII, ed. P. Geyer, CSEL 39. 163].

50. So Baldi, *Enchiridion*, 354 n. 2.

51. Ibid., no. 412 [= Petrus Diaconus, in *Itinera Hierosolymitana*, ed. Geyer, CSEL 39. 112)].

52. Baldi's entry for the text in n. 51 above, however, does not include that portion of the text (CSEL 39. 113) in which the anonymous excerpt refers to the house of Peter as the place where the paralytic was healed (*Ibi paraliticum Dominus curavit*), a reference to Mark 2:1 (cf. Matt 9:1). In other words, a key aspect of the holy site in the text preserved by Peter the Deacon (but not considered by Baldi and Corbo) was

Panarion 1.30.110.[53] It mentions Capernaum among cities in Galilee where Constantine had granted permission to build churches (οἰκοδομῆσαι ἐκκλησίας) for a certain convert, Joseph of Tiberias. Yet a specific connection of a church on the house of Peter is not given.

b. The Proposed Architectural History and the so-called "House Church"

On the basis of this literary tradition[54] Corbo draws a conjectural scenario regarding the architectural history of the site. He says the following in support of fact that "the Christian church at Capharnaum, [was] constructed over the house of St. Peter.

> (1) A complex of habitations of the first century of our era has been found in the entire area of the excavation.
>
> (2) In the complex of very poor habitations one hall was venerated in a special way from the first century onwards by the local community of Jewish Christians, who transformed this area into a place of cult, whilst they continued to live in the other rooms next to this one.
>
> (3) From the late Roman period (about the fourth century) onwards the community of Jewish Christians of Capharnaum enlarged the primitive house church by adding to the venerated hall an atrium on the east and dependencies on the north end by enclosing the entire small "insula" of the house of Peter within a sacred precinct.
>
> (4) The belief of the community of Jewish Christians of Capharnaum and of pilgrims in the sanctity of the place, indicated as the house of St. Peter by tradition, finds expression in incisions of symbols and graffiti on the walls of the venerated hall.
>
> (5) A church with a central plan (two concentric octagons with a portico on 5 sides and sacristies and subordinate loci on 3 other sides) was constructed at Capharnaum towards the middle of the fifth century over the venerated house of St. Peter."[55]

---

that it had been the location of a particular miracle of Jesus and could be correlated directly with the story of the Gospels. Other earlier literary sources, however, place this same event in a different location (see Baldi, *Enchiridion*, no. 439) thus indicating later conflation of divergent traditions.

53. Baldi, *Enchiridion*, no. 433 [= *PG* 41. 425]. Despite a number of elaborate details of Joseph's foundations in *Pan*. 1.30.112, no other mention is made of a church at Capernaum.

54. For Corbo's discussion of these texts, see *House of St. Peter*, 17, 53 n. 16.

55. Ibid., 71.

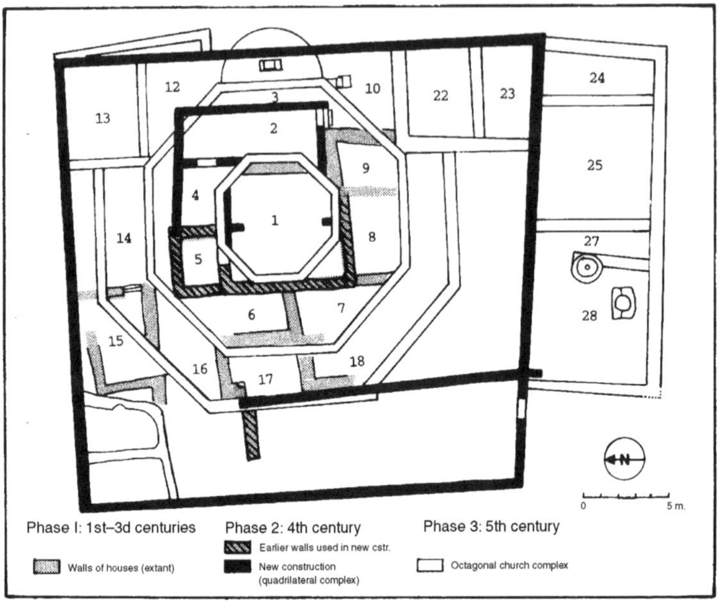

Fig. 8
Palestina, Capernaum. "House of St. Peter," fourth–fifth centuries.
Plan restoration, composite (based on V. Corbo).

The main archaeological point for Corbo lies in the successive layers of construction centered on the spot he calls the "venerated hall" (Room 1; see fig. 8). He discusses in some detail the construction in this area of the complex with special attention to the layers of pavement. In his final analysis it is the position of the central octagon of the Byzantine church (Phase 3) over this room in its fourth-century state (Phase 2) that allows him to make claims regarding the earlier Christian use of the site going back to the first century. But beyond this apparent relationship between the fourth- and fifth-century buildings (and the support of the literary traditions), there is no clear evidence of Christian presence on the site prior to Phase 2 of construction. Despite the lack of evidence for earlier usage, the later buildings seem clearly to be in Christian use, if Corbo's evidence is accurate in all points. Among the evidence in this regard are a number of small artifacts and fragmentary graffiti from the wall plaster of the Phase 2 hall which support Christian identification and usage from the fourth century, by which it would seem that the site was by then thought to be connected with the tradition of Peter.[56] It is to the form of the Phase 2 building that we now turn our attention. For Corbo says, "With the transformation of the house of Peter into a sanctuary . . . we have at Capharnaum one of the most ancient house churches (perhaps the most ancient) which is known."[57]

c. Phase 2: The Quadrilateral Complex (fourth century)

The complex of buildings from Phase 2 constituted an outer enclosure of quadrilateral plan (ca. 27 x 27-30 m; see fig. 8), with a small grouping of rooms in the center. The complex was entered from the south near the southwest corner. There seems to have been a partition beside the door creating a corridor (or portico?) along the west side of the enclosure (L.ca.16; W.5.40-5.80 m). The outer walls of the enclosure were 0.80 m thick at the foundation and 0.60 m higher up. Corbo calls this the "sacred precinct," as he thinks it only an enclosure for the buildings in the center of the complex. The central area consisted of several rooms (1, 2, 4, 5) that owe their location and form, in part at least, to the plan of the buildings below. The largest of these chambers, Room 1 (the "venerated hall"), measured 7.00 m (east to west) by 6.50 m (north to south). In Phase 2 it received a new pavement in lime (5.80 x 6.45 m, D.7-8 cm) at a level several centimeters [exact measurements not given] above that of the first-century buildings. The original walls seem to have been used at least to a certain height, and they were reinforced with piers against the north and south walls to carry a higher, arched ceiling. The walls of the room were finished in white plaster with painted polychrome decoration.

Around Room 1 other chambers were similarly developed. It is not clear from the stratigraphy to what extent the earlier habitations (Rooms 6-9, 14-

56. Ibid., 68–69 and figs. 21–22. A fuller discussion of the graffiti is found in Testa, *I graffiti della casa di S. Pietro,* passim, esp. 138–41. All the graffiti analyzed by Testa point to a fourth-century date—thus after the construction of the Phase 2 enclosure and sanctuary (to be discussed below). None can be associated with use of the earlier "house" at any date prior to this, though Testa and others are optimistic that such evidence will eventually be found.

57. Corbo, *House of St. Peter,* 53.

18) might have been preserved in this period. Corbo thinks that only Rooms 2, 4, and 5 were used; the rest were leveled to become an open courtyard. The area covered by Rooms 2 and 4 in Phase 2 had originally been an open courtyard in the Phase 1 habitations. In the Phase 2 construction Room 2 was transformed into an atrium (L.9.73; W.2.50 m). A door with steps in the southeast corner provided the main entrance from Room 2 to the central complex. The atrium was paved in lime (7.00 x 2.50 m) as was Room 1. From Room 2 a door led to Room 4 (ca.4.20 x 2.50 m), also paved in lime, which probably opened directly onto Room 1 via a door in their common (north/south) wall. The form of Room 5 was preserved from earlier periods.

d. Phase 3: The Octagonal Church Complex (fifth century)

When the later octagonal plan was superimposed on the site several features of the Phase 2 structure were incorporated. The octagon was founded on a fill of red earth or *humrah* (D.ca.0.87 m in loci 10 and 12). The east wall of the quadrilateral enclosure was preserved intact (height uncertain) as were portions of the north and south walls (on the east). The walls of the Phase 2 complex circumscribed the sacristies (Rooms 10 and 12) and the interior dependencies of the octagon (Rooms 13, 22, and 23). Other dependencies (Rooms 24-28) were established on the east exterior. The central rooms (especially Room 1) provided the foundation for the central octagon; a portion of the west corridor partition served as foundation for the octagonal portico on that side.

e. Analysis

As one would expect, it is the layering of these architectural stages that is most important to the excavators, especially since it permits the claim of continuous Christian usage associated with the name of St. Peter. Despite these claims, the first clear evidence of Christian usage occurs in the fourth century quadrilateral structure (Phase 2). From the architectural and material evidence, it appears that in this period the site was thought to have been the house of the apostle and was thus venerated. Nonetheless, there are two problematic areas in the proposals made regarding earlier identification and usage. First, there is no evidence of any sort that the buildings of Phase 1 were actually used by Christians prior to the beginning of the fourth century, either as a holy site (associated with Peter) or as a place of Christian assembly. The construction of the Phase 2 complex would appear to come from the period of Constantine's patronage in developing sacred sites in the holy land. As a result, it also makes Corbo's conjectures about the site as the locus of an early "Jewish-Christian" congregation highly questionable. Second, it is quite inappropriate to use the term "house church" of this site in any of its phases, since there is no evidence that the domestic edifices of Phase 1 were ever used as a place of Christian meeting. Nor is it appropriate to call the Phase 2 Quadrilateral Complex a *domus ecclesiae*, since nothing in its architectural form suggests renovation from or for an assembly space. It appears to be a *de novo* Christian construction for explicitly religious functions from the post-Constantinian period. In the final analysis, it would be better to describe this Phase 2 complex as a sanctuary, *memoria*, or holy place associated with the tradition of St. Peter and the Gospels. That tradition of usage was then preserved and further elaborated architecturally in the construction of the Phase 3 Octagonal church. Even if one maintains a cautious skepticism toward the claims of pre-Constantinian use and development, it must be noted that this site and its relationship to the synagogue[58] in the fourth to seventh centuries is nonetheless significant for understanding later developments in Judaism and Christianity (and their interaction) in the Homeland.

58. There are similar problems with the dating claims made for the Capernaum synagogue edifice also. The present synagogue edifice cannot be dated ealier than the fourth century (though some might say late third). For the current state of the discussion on this site (with corrections of the earlier dating claims), see Gideon Foerster, "Notes on Recent Excavations at Capernaum," *IEJ* 21 (1971) 207–11; and S. Loffreda, "The Late Chronology of the Synagogue at Capernaum," *IEJ* 23 (1973) 37–42. Pursuant to these criticisms, the Franciscan excavators at Capernaum claim to have found evidence of an earlier foundation course below the present synagogue building, which they would date to the first or second century. However, thus far no technical archaeological reports have been produced nor have more substantial excavations below the present edifice been detailed, so that these claims can be evaluated. The excavators' claims for seeing archaeological evidence of a continuous interaction between proximate Jewish (rabbinic) and Jewish-Christian congregations, while intriguing, remain entirely conjectural in the light of the available evidence.

PROVINCE: Egypt (Thebais)
LOCATION: Panopolis

No. 43: Papyrus List of Buildings (ca. 298–341)
P.Gen.Inv. 108 [=SB VIII (1967), 9902], Col. D, Lines 8–17

Extensive fragments preserve some twenty columns of a comprehensive list of buildings (perhaps for tax purposes) in the city of Panopolis, in the Thebaid. The list is important as a witness to the topography of the Greco-Roman town site; for the survey was recorded by streets (see col. D, line 8), corners (see C.11; D.3, 12; E^2.3), and other common physical landmarks. Among the buildings noted are shops (λινουφίον, γναφεῖον), a mill (μυλών), a refuse dump (κοπριώδους), and even vacant lots (ψιλός). But by far the most common references are to houses (usually οἰκία) listed by the name of an owner or inhabitant. In some cases the houses may also contain shops, for example, the house of the mat-weaver (σχοινοπλόκου, B^3.8). Occasionally buildings are noted as houses that are used for other purposes, such as a storehouse (col. F.9).

In this connection we may consider a portion of column D (lines 8–17) in which a church (ἐκκλησία) is apparently mentioned (line 11). The text was originally published by V. Martin, who dated it on paleographical grounds to the mid-third century. For this reason he rejected the idea that ἐκκλησία could mean "church building."[59] Such an assumption may not be appropriate, given other papyri that point to property acquisitions by churches by the mid- to later-third century (see No. 44 below). Moreover, further paleographic study of the text has suggested a dating between 298 and 341, at which time a house that is known to belong to the church is certainly demonstrable from comparable papyrological sources (see Nos. 45 and 46 below).

The key feature of this text, in addition to the clear acknowledgment of church property by public officials, is the fact that the reference is clearly to a domestic quarter of the city, since all of the other edifices mentioned in this region are houses. The church property is apparently in the middle of a block that had four houses facing onto the street, at least as the recorder listed the properties. Still, it is difficult to know the precise configuration, since these domestic insulae often had entrance ways from a street into the inner areas of the complex. The property of the church is either in the private house identified, or this house is somehow a dependency of the church building

59. V. Martin, in *Recherches de Papyrologie* 2 (1962) 66.

proper. If the latter is the correct reading, it is possible that the house was not contiguous to the church building, since it is not mentioned in the census. Still, it would mean that, at this time in Panopolis, there was public knowledge of both a church building and property owned by the Christian community. Unfortunately, the right edge of the column, which would have given the exact relationship of the οἰκία to the ἐκκλησία, is lost.

Literature: V. Martin, *Recherches de Papyrologie* 2 (1962) 37–73. SB= *Sammelbuch griechischer Urkunden aus Ägypten* (Wiesbaden: Harrassowitz, 1967) 8 (1967) 9902. J. D. Thomas, "Chronological Notes on Documentary Papyri," *ZPE* 6 (1970) 177–80. H. C. Youtie, "P. Gen. Inv. 108," *ZPE* 7 (1971) 170–72. Reedited by Z. Borkowski, *Une description topographique des immeubles à Panopolis* (Warsaw, 1975). E. A. Judge and S. R. Pickering, "Papyrus Documentation of Church and Community in Egypt to the Mid-Fourth Century," *JAC* 20 (1977) 61 and n. 21.

ἀπέβημεν εἰς ῥύμην π[. . . ,
οἰκία μητρὸς Ὑιοθεοῦ[. . .
υἱῶν
ἄλ(λη) οἰκία Σερηνοῦ Πασινο̣[. . .
οἰκία ἤτοι ἐκκλησίας σ̣[. . .
ἄλ(λη) ἐπιγώνιος θεοδώρον [. . .
μυλὼν Κύρου Ἄραβος [. . .
οἰκία Ἥρωνος κεραμ[εως . . .
καὶ κοι(νωνῶν)
ἄλ(λη) Σενπνούθου
ἄλ(λη) Κλαυδίου βαλανέω[ς . . .

Translation: As we turn onto ____ street, the house of the mother of Huiotheos . . . , next the house of the sons of Serenus Pasino[. . .] . . . , (next) the house which is also[60] the ____ of the church;[61] another (house), on

60. οἰκία ἤτοι. Following Martin's reading, the other use of this formula from the same papyrus, while still fragmentary, suggests that it was used by the recorder(s) to designate a domestic edifice known to have been used for some other purpose as designated, for example, in col. F.9, a storehouse: οἰκ(ία) ἀποθ[ήκη . . .]. In other papyri, however, a similar formula seems to indicate a "house which also includes" other appurtenances or features, such as cisterns or wells. See *P.Oxy.* I.43 verso, line 13 (= No. 45 below).

61. ἐκκλησίας σ[. . . (Pap). The letter just before the page breaks off is not defi-

the corner, that of Theodorus . . . ; the mill of Cyrus the Arab; the house of Heron the potter and his partners (or associates); another (house), that of Senpnouthos; another, that of Claudius the Bath-man. . . .

PROVINCE: Aegyptus (Arcadia)
LOCATION: Oxyrhynchus

No. 44: Private Letter (late third century)
***P.Oxy.* XII (1916), 1492**
(ed. Grenfell and Hunt) 22.6 x 10.3 cm

Since its discovery, this private letter has been considered one of the earliest Christian documents from Egypt and certainly contains some interesting features. One of these, the introductory formula (lines 4–6) is unique among the known early Christian letters. The letter is addressed to a certain Demetrianus, who is called a "holy son" by the writer Sotas (see line 1 and the address on the verso). The tone of the letter, however, lacks the intimacy that one would expect between a natural father and son, even in the case of a business letter. It is possible, therefore, that the designation "holy son" is based on a special relationship between the two as Christians, and the fatherly tone of Sotas may be due to his ecclesiastical rank. Two other papyri from Oxyrhynchus [*PSI* 3 (1914), 208, and *PSI* 9 (1929), 1041] bear the name of the bishop Sotas as the writer. The present letter is dated on paleographic grounds and on the basis of its content to the end of the third century or the very beginning of the fourth. It is compared by the editors to *P.Grenf.* II.73, which clearly dates to the Diocletianic period (see A. Deissman, *Light*

---

nitely to be read as Σ according to Martin. If it were not, then the Σ attached to ἐκκλησία might be the first letter of the next word and not the genitive ending. This variable provides us with two basic ways of understanding the relationship between the church and the house. (a) Reading ἐκκλησία σ[. . .], it should probably be taken as "the house which is the church (of?) *such-and-such* (or *so-and-so*) . . ." or "the house which is the *such-and-such* church." This latter reading is much like the references to the north and south churches in *P.Oxy.* I.43 verso (No. 45 below). (b) Reading the text printed above, it is probably to be taken as "the house which is the *such-and-such* of the church." For supplying the latter lacuna, four unprovable but intriguing candidates suggest themselves. The reading σ [. . .] may be supplied as: (1) συναγωγή, (2) σύνοδος, (3) σχολή, or (4) συγκύροντος (= a dependency or adjacent structure; see *CIJ* 2. 1442, 1443).

from the Ancient East [London: Hodder & Stoughton, 1928] 213ff.). The most interesting feature of the letter is the subject of the discussion—Sotas's instructions on what appears to be a donation of land to the church, designated as ὁ τόπος (line 11). The designation of the recipient of the donation and the specification of provisions for future disposition deserve further consideration. If ὁ τόπος is to be understood as "the church," as seems likely, then it is a case of transferring the identity of the Christianity community to the place of assembly, and then back again, as a corporate entity capable of (quasi-) legal property ownership. But note that the provision for subsequent disposition of the property (which might have involved either continued farming or sale) with the proceeds to go to the church, reflects the actions of community members or decisions of community as a whole.

Literature: For other publications of the text and additional discussion, see G. Bovini, *La proprietà ecclesiastica e la condizione giuridica della chiesa in età preconstantiniana* (Milan: Università di Roma, 1948) 148–50. H. Leclercq in *DACL* 8.2:2784–85; 13.1:1423.

Χα[ῖ]ρε, ἱερ[ὲ υἱὲ
Δημητρι[ανέ. Σώτας
σε πρ[οσαγορεύω.
τὸ κοινὸν . . [. . . . . .
ε̣ὔδηλον καὶ τὸ κο̣ι̣[νὸν
σωτήριον ἡμῶν [. . . ,
ταῦτα γάρ ἐστιν τὰ̣ ἐ[ν τῇ
θείᾳ προνοίᾳ. εἰ οὖν ἔ-
κρεινας κατὰ τὸ π̣α̣λ̣[αιὸν
ἔθος δοῦναι τὴν ἄ̣ρ[ο]υ̣-
ραν τῷ τόπῳ, ποίησον
αὐτὴν ἀφωρισθῆναι
ἵνα χρήσωνται, κ[α]ὶ ὡς
ἐὰν κρείνῃς περὶ τοῦ ἔ̣[ρ]γ̣[ου
θάρρει. πάντας τ[ο]ὺ̣[ς
ἐν τῷ οἴκῳ σου ἅπα̣ν̣τ̣[ας
προσαγόρευε. ἐρρῶ-
σθαι ὑμᾶς εὔχομαι

τῷ θεῷ διὰ παντὸς
καὶ ἐν παντί.

On the verso

τῷ ἱερῷ υ[ἱ]ῷ μ[ο]υ Δημητριανῷ π(αρὰ) Σώτου.

Translation: Greetings, (my) holy son Demetrianus, Sotas addresses you. Our common . . . is plain and our common salvation is . . . (sure, secure?),[62] for these are the objects of divine providence. If, therefore, you have decided according to the ancient custom[63] to give the *arura* of land to the place, see that its boundaries are marked off so that they may make appropriate use of it. Whatever you decide concerning the work be confident (or of good cheer). Greet all those in your house, every one. I pray God on your behalf for every good in all things.

(Address, on the reverse:) To my holy son Demetrianus from Sotas.

PROVINCE: Aegyptus (Arcadia)
LOCATION: Oxyrhynchus

No. 45: Churches and Streets (ca. 295)
***P. Oxy.* I (1898), No. 43 verso**
(ed. Grenfell and Hunt) [selections] 25 x 90 cm

The recto of this document is a military record of supplies provided to various troops and accompanied by copies of receipts from the persons concerned. The date of the papyrus is determined from the end of this account. The verso is undated but probably belongs to a date not long after the recto, that is, not long after 295. The verso contains a list of the guards or street-watchmen distributed throughout the major portions and buildings of the

62 The editors of *P.Oxy.* XII suggest as a possibility for filling the lacuna at the end of line 6 something like ἀσφαλέν ("sure, secure") to balance the adjective ending of the parallel phrase in line 5. Similarly, we should expect the missing noun in the first clause to be something like πιστόν (with the sense of "faith") to match the usage of σωτήριον in the second.

63. κατὰ τὸ παλ[αιὸν] ἔθος. Since the phrase clearly refers to the decision to donate property, it probably alludes to the idealized picture of Acts 4:34–37. Compare the use of the phrase [κ]ατὰ τὸ ἔθος in connection with the exercise of hospitality in *PSI* 3 (1914) 208.

city. The record is made up of five columns of which columns III and V are unfinished.

The document is of interest for the topographical terms used and because of the ways in which the street wardens were named. Some streets were named according to the residents, for example, Shepherd's Street or Libyan Street. Some streets bear the names of specific individuals, for example, Street of Apollonius, presumably the most illustrious property owner in the neighborhood. But the most common forms of street names derive from some prominent building or house which they contain or adjoin. The record generally gives the name of the street, the name of the watchman, and where he is stationed or is housed. Of particular interest are the references to two streets known by buildings called ἐκκλησία; one is in the northern portion of the town, and the other is in the south. These two references are given in the following selections from the papyrus (col. I.7–16; col. III.17–21).

Column I

. . . .

ρ̣(ύμη) τῇ οἰκίᾳ κνα[φέω]ς κ[. .]   . . [
Ὧρος [. . .]ι[. . . .]ν[. .]υ. [. .]ς, [κατα-
μένων ἐ[ν] τ(ῷ) αὐτῷ τόπῳ.
ρ̣(ύμη) τῇ βοριν[ῇ] ἐκκλασίᾳ,
Ἀπφοῦς θέωνος.
οἰκων ἐν τῷ στάβλῳ τῆς Αἰωνίας.
καὶ ρ̣(ύμη)[64] τῇ οἰκίᾳ Χορταικοῦ ἤτοι
καμαρῶν καὶ μικροῦ φρέστος,
Ἑρμείας Ἡρᾶτος,
καταμένων ἐγγύς.

. . . .

Column III

. . . .

καὶ ρ̣(ύμη) τῇ νοτινῇ πύλῃ,
Παῦλος Ὀννώφριος

64. ρ̣(ύμη). The square bracket in I.13, thus ρ̣[ύμη], in the 1898 edition is doubtless a printer's error and should be read as a parenthesis, as printed here.

καὶ ῥ(ύμη) τῇ νοτινῇ ἐκκλησίᾳ,
Ἀμόις Παράμμωνος, καταμένων
ἀντικρὺς οἰκίας Ἐπιμάχου κηρωματικ(οῦ).
. . . .

Translation: Column I: . . . [The watchman for] the street of the fuller's house . . . , Horos . . . , who is stationed in his own place. For North-Church street,[65] Apphous Theonos, who lives in the stable of Aeonia. And for the street of the house of Chortaikos including the vaulted (channels?) and the small cistern, Hermias Heratos, who is stationed nearby . . .

Column III: . . . And for South-Gate Street, Paulos Onnophrios. And for South-Church Street,[66] Amois Parammonos, who is stationed directly opposite the house of Epimachos the wax-salve dealer . . .

PROVINCE: Aegyptus (Arcadia)
LOCATION: Chysis (in Oxyrhynchite nome)

No. 46: Declaration of Church Property (5 February 304)
***P.Oxy.* XXXIII (1968), 2673 (ed. Rea) 12 x 26 cm**

The document is an official record consisting of three copies (designated A, B, C) bound together. It illustrates the forms of compliance in Egypt to Dio-

65. According to E. A. Judge, Von Wilamowitz (GGA=*Göttingische gelehrte Anzeigen* 160 [1898] 676) took ἐκκλησία (I.10 and III.19) simply as places of public assembly. But since the streets regularly take their names from buildings or houses, this seems less likely. Moreover, *P.Oxy.* XI (1915), no. 1315 (ed. Grenfell and Hunt) (sixth century) makes reference to a "southern" church. Judge argues, therefore, following Grenfell and Hunt's original reading, that the terms should be read as meaning church buildings that are well established and recognized to the extent that they dominate the identity of the streets on which they stand. The fact that two such structures (and perhaps more) could have existed in the city before the end of the third century is most intriguing. See E. A. Judge and S. R. Pickering, "Papyrus Documentation of Church and Community in Egypt to the Mid-Fourth Century," *JAC* 20 (1977) 60–61. The property declaration of a church building from the nearby village of Chysis, barely nine years later, gives further evidence that such buildings were already known publicly. See No. 46, following.

66. The proximity of the references to South-Gate Street and South-Church Street probably reflect a specific indication of the location of the church building near the southern city gate; however, there is nothing more definite to bear this out.

cletian's edicts concerning the Christians. The report was attested by a lector or reader (ἀναγνωστής) of the church at Chysis; it provides a declaration of the church's property. Apparently, the church building (ἐκκλησία, line 15) had already been confiscated earlier (see ποτε, lines 9, 15), and this document is intended to record the official registration during the search of the property. The declaration claims no possessions save a bronze item (line 22), which had been sent by local officials to Alexandria after confiscation. The search and seizure may suggest a correlation with the first edict of Diocletian (February 303) as reported by Eusebius, *H.E.* 8.2. The fact that no other property was declared need not be taken as a sign of the church's poverty; however, that this was in all likelihood a Coptic-speaking Christian community is perhaps indicated by the fact that the lector is said to be illiterate in Greek (line 34), despite his Greek name. Finally, it should be noted that there is no reference to the edifice being destroyed.

Literature: For further discussion, see E. A. Judge and S. R. Pickering, "Papyrus Documentation of Church and Community in Egypt to the Mid-Fourth Century," *JAC* 20 (1977) 59 and n. 17. [Note that the date given on p. 59 (3 February) is incorrect, while the date is listed correctly on p. 49.] J. R. Rea, "P. Oxy. XXXIII.2673.22: ΠΥΛΗΝ to 'ΥΛΗΝ!" *ZPE* 35 (1979) 128.

[The text provided below is that of copy A of the document (after the edition of *P.Oxy.* XXXIII) with corrections and emendations supplied from copies B and C where necessary.]

ἐπὶ ὑπάτων τῶν κυρίων ἡμ̣[ῶν αὐτοκρατόρων
Διοκλητιανοῦ τὸ ἔνατον καὶ Μαξ[ιμιανοῦ
τὸ η´ Σεβαστῶν
Αὐρηλίοις Νείλῳ τῷ καὶ Ἀμμωνίῳ γυμ[( ) βουλ(ευτῇ)
ἐνάρχῳ πρυτάνει καὶ Σαρμάτῃ καὶ Ματρίνῳ ἀμφ[οτέροις
γυμ( ) βουλ(ευταῖς) συνδίκοις τοῖς πᾶσι τῆς λαμ(πρᾶς)
καὶ λαμ(προτάτης)
Ὀξυρυγχιτῶν πόλεως (vac.)
Αὐρήλιος Ἀμμώνιος Κοπρέως ἀναγνωσ-
τὴς τῆς ποτε ἐκ‹κ›λησίας κώμης Χύσεως
ἐπ̣ιθεμένων ὑμῶν ἐμοί ἀκολούθως
τοῖς γραφ‹ε›ῖσι ὑπὸ Αὐρηλίου Ἀθανασίου ἐπιτρό-

που πριουάτης ὡς ἐκ κελεύσεως τοῦ δια-
σημ(οτάτου) μαγίστρου τῆς πριουάτης Νερατίου
Ἀπολλωνί‹δ›ου περὶ τοῦ παραστῆσαι ἅπαντα
τὰ ‹ε›ἴδη τὰ [ἐ]ν τῇ αὐτῇ ποτε ἐκ‹κ›λησίᾳ κα̣ὶ ἐ̣μοῦ
προενεγ᾽καμένου μὴ ἔχειν τὴν ‹αὐτὴν› ἐκ‹κ›λη-
σ{ε}ίαν μήτε χρυσὸν μήτε ἄσημον
μήτε ἀργύριον μήτε ἐσθῆτα μήτε τετρά-
ποδα μήτε ἀνδράποδα μήτε οἰκόπαιδα
μ̣ήτε ὑπάρχοντα μήτε ἀπὸ χαρισμάτων
μηδ᾽ α̣ὖ ἀπὸ διαθηκῶν εἰ μὴ μ̣όνην
τὴ̣ν ε̣ὑ̣[ρε]τ̣ῖσαν χαλκῆ̣[ν] ὕλην καὶ παραδο-
τ̣ῖ̣σαν τῷ λογιστῇ πρὸς τὸ κατενεγ᾽χθῆναι
ἐπὶ τὴν λαμ(προτάτην) Ἀλεξάνδριαν ἀκολούθως τοῖς γρα-
φ‹ε›ῖσι ὑπὸ τοῦ διασημ(οτάτου) ἡμῶν ἡγεμόνος Κλωδίου
Κο‹υ›λκιανοῦ καὶ ὀμνύω τὴν τῶν κυρίων ἡμῶν
αὐτοκρατόρων Διοκλητιανοῦ καὶ Μαξιμιανοῦ Σεβασ̣(τῶν)
καὶ Κωνσταντίου καὶ Μαξιμιανοῦ τῶν ἐπιφανεστάτων
καισάρων τύχην ταῦθ᾽ οὕτως ἔχειν καὶ μηδὲν διε-
ψεῦσθαι ἢ ἔνοχος εἴην τῷ θείῳ ὅρκῳ
(ἔτους) κ´ καὶ ιβ´ τῶν κυρίων ἡμῶν Διοκλητιανοῦ καὶ
Μαξιμιανοῦ
Σεβαστῶν καὶ Κωνσταντίου καὶ Μαξιμιανοῦ τῶν ἐπιφανεστάτων
καισάρων Μεχεὶρ [ι´·

(second hand)

Αὐρήλιος Ἀμμώνιος ὤμοσα τὸν ὅρκον
ὡς (πρόκειται)· Αὐρ(ήλιος) Σερῆνος ἔγρα(ψα) ὑ(πὲρ) αὐτοῦ
μὴ εἰ̣(δότος) γρά(μματα)

Translation: In the consulship of our lords the emperors, Diocletian—for the ninth time— and Maximian—for the eighth time—the Augusti.

To Aurelius Neilus, also known as Ammonius, gymnasiarch, city councillor, prytane in office, and to (Aurelius) Sarmates and (Aurelius) Matrinus, both (ex?)gymnasiarchs, city councillors, and syndics, all of whom are of the glorious and (most) glorious city of the Oxyrhynchites, Aurelius Ammonius, son of Copreus, reader of the former church of the village of Chysis swears:

Whereas, you gave me orders in accordance with the published decree of

Aurelius Athanasius the *procurator rei privatae*, by virtue of a command of the most illustrious *magister rei privatae*, Neratius Apollonides, concerning the surrender of all the goods that were in the said former church, I reported that the said church had neither gold nor silver nor money nor clothes nor beasts nor slaves nor lands nor property either from grants or bequests, excepting only the bronze vessel[67] that was found and delivered to the *logistes* to be carried down to most glorious Alexandria in accordance with the edict of our most illustrious praefect, Clodius Culcianus.

I also swear by the fortune of our lords the emperors Diocletian and Maximian, the Augusti, and Constantius and Maximian (Galerius), the most noble Caesars, that these things are so and that I have falsified nothing, or may I be liable to the divine oath.[68]

67. ὕλην (line 22). In the published *editio princeps* Rea had read the word πύλην in copy A, even though ὕλην was clearly discernible in copies B and C. Rea translated the text as a reference to dismantling the building. In his 1979 note in *ZPE*, Rea retracted this reading in favor of ὕλην, as printed above. In the light of this change, he went on to suggest that the nature of the declaration attests to a more private "house-chapel" for the form of the confiscated building (*ZPE* 35 [1979] 128). He suggested that the term ὕλην be read as "bronze vessels" used in the church and confiscated by the authorities as valuable items. Compare the record of search and seizure at Cirta, Numidia (19 May 303), Section I (No. 31) above, in which the presence of a number of implements is detailed.

68 The apparent willingness of the lector of the church to swear an oath by the genius (here literally the fortune) of the emperors might give some indication of the procedures during the persecution that would give rise to charges of lapsing, as in the Donatist controversy in North Africa. Still, it is interesting that no other church officials were named or required to participate. All this assumes, of course, that Aurelius Ammonius, son of Copreus (whose name suggests native Coptic origins; cf. P.Mich. XIV.676.21, dated 272 CE from Oxyrhynchus), is correctly understood as "reader" of the church (and thus himself a Christian leader). In any case, the closing statement that the "reader" is illiterate is perplexing, unless Chysis is understood as a predominantly Coptic-speaking village. On this phrase compare the identical wording in two other papyri from Oxyrhynchus, P.Mich. XIV 675.24 (dated 241 CE) and P.Mich. XIV.676.27 (dated 272 CE), and see H. C. Youtie, "*Hypographeus:* The Social Impact of Illiteracy in Graeco-Roman Egypt," *ZPE* 17 (1975) 201–21; "'Because they do not know letters,'" *ZPE* 19 (1975) 101–8. The name Copres, denoting a local Christian from Oxyrhynchus, also appears in a letter of 303 (P.Oxy XXXI [1966] 2601), in which he reports having to sacrifice by imperial decree as part of a legal proceeding. It is not clear whether this could be the named father of Aurelius Ammonius, but the circumstances are proximate. For the names Aurelius Athanasius and Neratius

In the 20th and 12th years of our lords the emperors Diocletian and Maximian, the Augusti, and Constantius and Maximian (Galerius) the most noble Caesars. Mecheir, the 10th.

(2nd hand) I, Aurelius Ammonius (of Chysis), swore the oath as said above. I, Aurelius Serenus, wrote on his behalf because he does not know letters.

[trans. after Rea, *P.Oxy.* XXXIII, p. 107, adapted]

PROVINCE: Aegyptus (Arcadia)
LOCATION: Oxyrhynchus

No. 47: A Christian Building as Social Center (early fourth century, before 337) *P.Oxy.* VI (1908), 903 recto, lines 15–21 (ed. Grenfell and Hunt) 27.2 x 21.6 cm

The recto of this document contains an elaborate account in thirty-seven lines of the marital dispute of an unnamed couple. It was submitted by the wife (a Christian), apparently as an affidavit for her indictment of the husband and as a petition to the courts for redress. The selection given below (lines 15–21) contains references to involvement by church leaders (ἐπισκόπων, line 15) and to the role of the church building itself (κυριακόν, line 19) as a social as well as religious center. The wife had apparently gone to the church building as a place of refuge and for other assistance from church officials, who were functioning in a public capacity (lines 19–21).

καὶ ὤμοσεν ἐπὶ παρουσίᾳ τῶν ἐπισκόπων καὶ τῶν ἀδελφῶν αὐτοῦ
ὅτι ἀπεντεῦθεν οὐ μὴ κρύψω αὐτὴ‹ν› πάσας μοῦ τὰς κλεῖς καὶ
τοῖς δούλοις καὶ ἐπέχω,
αὐτοῦ ἐπίστευσεν κἀμοὶ οὐκ ἐπίστευσεν[69]
οὔτε ὑβρίζω αὐτὴν ἀπεντεῦθεν. Καὶ γαμικὸν γέγονεν, καὶ μετὰ
τὰς συνθῆκας ταύτας καὶ τοὺς ὅρκους ἔκρυψεν πάλιν ἐμὲ τὰς κλεῖς

Apollonides in other property confiscations of the time at Oxyrhynchus, see P.Oxy. XXXIII (1968) 2665: the confiscation of property belonging to a certain Paul. Despite the similarities, it is not possible to say definitively that Paul was a Christian (so Judge in *JAC* 20:60, following J. E. Rea).

69/69a. The insertion above (line 17) is apparently a parenthetical explanation of the phrase οὐ μὴ κρύψω . . . κλεῖς καὶ τοῖς δούλοις καὶ ἐπέχω in line 16.

εἰς ἐμέ. Καὶ ἀπελθούσας [εἰ]ς τὸ κυριακὸν ἐν Σαμβαθῷ, καὶ ἐποίησεν τὰς ἔξω θυράς αὐτοῦ ἐνκλισθῆναι ἐπάνω μου λέγων ὅτι διά τι ἀπῆλθας εἰς τὸ κυριακόν; . . .

Translation: . . . He swore in the presence of the bishops and his own brothers, "Henceforward I will not hide all my keys from her and give (them) to the slaves"—he trusted his (slaves), but he would not trust me—[69a] "nor will I insult her anymore." Whereupon a marriage contract was made. Yet after this agreement and these oaths, he again hid the keys from me. And when I had gone to the church building on the Sabbath day[70] he had the outside doors locked against me saying, "Why did you go to the church building?". . .

PROVINCE: Asia (Phrygia/Pisidia)
LOCATION: Laodicea Combusta (*Laodikeia Katakekaumene* [Ladik])

No. 48: The Epitaph of M. Julius Eugenius (ca. 307–340)
***MAMA* 1. 170**

Inscription in a framed, recessed tabula (H.0.57; W.0.92) on the side of a blue limestone sarcophagus (H.1.32; W.2.63) found half buried in a field so that the letters of the upper portion show considerable weather damage. The panel was broken into two parts vertically through the inscription after the eighth or ninth letters of each line. The greatest damage occurs in the three lines at the bottom. The nineteen lines of Greek would seem to be from an artisan's workshop. The fact that a number of the lines overlap the borders of the framing elements (lines 4–14, 16) indicates that the sarcophagus was not made with the inscription in mind. Letters: Lines 1–16, H.0.035-0.02; lines 17-19, H.0.015-0.025 m.

This text is particularly important for the information it provides regarding the social location of Christians in central Asia Minor just before and

70. ΕΝΣΑΜΒΑΘΩ (Pap., line 19). The phrase was originally read by the editors of *P.Oxy.* VI as a place name, ἐν Σαμβάθῳ ("to the church at Sambatho"). The corrected reading of ἐν Σαμβαθῷ was suggested first by W. Schubart in his *Einführung in die Papyruskunde* (Berlin, 1918) 371. See also the discussion in *CPJ* 3, no. 457d. For a general discussion of the term, see the article entitled "The Sambathions," in *CPJ* 3. 43–56; see *CPJ* 3, nos. 457a–c.

after the Great Persecution. First, it shows a Christian aristocrat who had been serving in the military *officium* of the provincial governor, and was thus moving through the *cursus honorum* for provincial aristocracy. Laodicea Combusta (also called Laodikea Katakekaumene) was one of the Roman colonies of provincial Phrygia/Pisidia. This social status is also indicated by the fact that Eugenius (and/or his father) served on the Laodicean city council, a sign of decurional rank, and by the fact that he married the daughter of another local aristocrat, a man of senatorial rank (perhaps from Antioch-toward-Pisidia).[71] Second, this aristocratic Christian, having earned honors as a "martyr" (confessor) during the persecutions, was then made bishop and turned his familial status and wealth to the rebuilding of the church edifice. This inscription thereby represents one of the key documentary data for observing the process of renovation both in architectural terms and in terms of the social location of the leadership behind it at a date before the Constantinian building programs. Third, recent discussions (based on other related epigraphic materials) have suggested that Eugenius (together with his predecessor as bishop and the Christians of Laodicea Combusta) might have been of a Montanist (or Novatianist-Montanist) sectarian bent.[72]

71. On the colonial organization of the region and the *cursus honorum,* see Barbara Levick, *Roman Colonies in Southern Asia Minor* (Oxford: Clarendon, 1967) 18, 52, 108–20. In fact, by returning to Laodicea Combusta to serve as a local decurion, Eugenius did not entirely abandon the *cursus*, even though his retirement from the military must have negated (or presumably would have in pre-Constantinian times) the higher reaches of consular service and senatorial rank. Also on the individuals mentioned in the text: Cyrillus Celer (PLRE 1. 238); G. Julius Nestorianus (PLRE 1. 625); Flavia Julia Flaviana (PLRE 1. 343). See also nn. 72 and 75 below.

72. So William Tabbernee, *Montanist Inscriptions and Testimonia: Epigraphical Sources Illustrating the History of Montanism* (Macon: Mercer University Press, 1996) no. 65; also discussed in his unpublished paper "The Social Identity of the Montanists: The Epigraphic Data," 6. In the latter, Tabbernee notes that the family of Eugenius is of unusually high social standing relative to most of the epigraphic and literary data for Montantist membership. For the Montanist identification, Tabbernee classes Eugenius as "likely" (but not definite), still leaving open the matter of the particular strain of Montanism that might be represented.

This identification was first suggested by W. M. Calder ("The Epigraphy of the Anatolian Heresies," *Anatolian Studies* (Manchester: Manchester University Press, 1923) 67–74). Nothing in the Eugenius inscription itself even remotely hints at a Montanist connection. Calder's hypothesis was based on the discovery in 1911 of another inscription from the environs of Laodicea; see Calder, "Studies in Early

Literature: W. M. Calder, "A Fourth Century Lycaonian Bishop," *The Expositor* (1908) 385–93. W. M. Ramsay, "A Laodicean Bishop," *The*

Christian Epigraphy," *JRS* 10 (1920) 42–59. This second inscription (*MAMA* 1. 171 = Tabbernee, *Montanist Inscriptions and Testimonia*, no. 66) is in ten lines on a large marble plaque and dates from the end of the fourth century. It commemorates the illustrious careers of two bishops, Severus and his successor Eugenius. The text reads as follows:

Τόν Χ(ριστο)ῦ σοφίης ὑποφήτορα, τὸν σοφὸν ἄνδρα,
Οὐρανίου γενέτου κύδιμον ἀθλοφόρον,
Σ]εβῆρον πόλεων πανεπίσκοπον ἡγητῆρα
Λ]αοῦ σακκοφόρου μνῆμα κέκευθε τόδε·
Λεί]ψανον Εὐγενίου τε θ(εο)υδέος ὃν κατέλιψεν
Ποιμ]νῆς πνευματικῆς ἄξιον ἡνίοχον.
Ἁγνὸν] καὶ ζώντες ἑαῖς π[ληγαῖς ὄνομ᾽ ἔσχον
Νῦν τ᾽ εὐ]άσκητον μνῆ[μ᾽ ἔχει ἀμφοτέρους.
[Two lines lost.]

Calder ("Studies in Early Christian Epigraphy," 47–50; "The Epigraphy of the Anatolian Heresies," 70–72) concluded (1) that the Eugenius mentioned in *MAMA* 1. 171 is the same as M. Julius Eugenius of *MAMA* 1. 170; (2) that the plaque represents the transfer of the relics of Severus to some sort of shrine or chapel associated with Eugenius's rebuilt church at Laodicea; and (3) that the Severus inscription clearly uses Montanist terminology. In support of the last point, Calder noted two main features of the Severus inscription: his designation as a regional bishop (line 3: πόλεων πανεπίσκοπον ἡγητῆρα) and the use of the term λ]αός σακκοφόρος (line 4). (See Tabbernee, "Montanist Regional Bishops," 254–55.) Calder argues that the latter term, here taken to mean "sackcloth-wearing people," was a peculiarly Montanist self-designation. Further evidence for Montanist congregations in the vicinity of Laodicea Combusta is found in three other inscriptions, all epitaphs dating to the latter part of the fourth century (ca. 375 or later). Calder classifies them as clearly Novatianist. These are discussed by Calder, "The Epigraphy of the Anatolian Heresies," 75–81, and on that basis he further posits sectarian leanings (i.e., either Montanist or Novatianist, or some mixed form) for up to six other epitaphs (ibid., 81–91). On the other hand, it must be noted that all these texts are later and much of the technical vocabulary employed by Calder comes from fifth- and even sixth-century inscriptions. Of all the Christian inscriptions from the vicinity of Laodicea Combusta, the earliest date assigned on the basis of epigraphic analysis is that of M. Julius Eugenius.

A Montanist identification for the Severus inscription (*MAMA* 1. 170 = Tabbernee, *Montanist Inscriptions and Testimonia*, no. 66) appears quite likely; however, the case of M. Julius Eugenius is less clear. Tabbernee ("Social Identity of the Montanists," 6) thinks it unlikely (albeit not impossible) that M. Julius Eugenius's parents

Expositor (1908) 409–13, 546–51. Idem, *Luke the Physician* (London: Hodder & Stoughton, 1908) 339–46. W. M. Calder, in *The Expositor* (1909) 307–12. A. Harnack, in *TLZ* (1909) 165. F. di Cavalieri, "Note agiografiche," *Studi e Testi* 22 (1909) 59–62. W. M. Ramsay, in *The Expositor* (1910) 51–53. W. M. Calder, in *Klio* 10 (1910) 233–34 [including facsimile and trace]. A. Wilhelm, *Klio* 11 (1911) 388–89. W. M. Calder, "Studies in Early Christian Epigraphy," *Journal of Roman Studies* 10 (1920) 42–59. W. M. Calder, "The Epigraphy of the Anatolian Heresies," in *Anatolian Studies Presented to Sir W. M. Ramsay* (Manchester: University Press of Manchester, 1923) 59–91 (esp. 67–74). *PLRE* 1. 293. W. Tabbernee, "Montanist Regional Bishops: New Evidence from Ancient Inscriptions," *JECS* 1 (1993) 249–80. Idem, *Montanist Inscriptions and Testimonia: Epigraphical Sources Illustrating the History of Montanism* (Macon, GA: Mercer University Press of Manchester, 1996) nos. 65–66.

[The following text is after *MAMA* 1. 170, checked against the new reading by W. Tabbernee. The latter's book, *Montanist Inscriptions and Testimo-*

---

and in-laws were Montanists. It must be noted that the core of the argument is based on reading the Eugenius who succeeded Severus as identical with M. Julius Eugenius. While this is indeed a plausible reading of the evidence, it is not the only reconstruction. The following considerations must be kept in mind. First, there is no clear dating or succession in the Severus inscription, and it remains something of a puzzle to me that, given the honors later accorded to Severus as martyr and bishop, his successor (if we were to take M. Julius Eugenius in this way) should not have mentioned such a famous predecessor in commissioning his own funerary monument. Second, this is not the only Eugenius known from inscriptions in the immediate vicinity. Calder himself published an epitaph from the region of nearby Sarayönü to a presbyter Eugenius, whom he considers Montanist (or Novatianist), who was a wealthy and prominent overseer in the church and who died young (see "Epigraphy of the Anatolian Heresies," 76–78; however, this text is not mentioned by Tabbernee in his collection). While this last Eugenius does not accord precisely with the one mentioned in the Severus inscription, it ought to cause us to be cautious. Third, there is the matter of the early dating (not to mention the career and family) of the M. Julius Eugenius inscription. It seems to me entirely possible that the Severus inscription, which clearly comes from a period later than that of the M. Julius Eugenius inscription, might have been intended to co-opt the latter figure for a claim of Montanist succession and that this represents a later turn toward Montanism (or Novatianist-Montanism) on the part of churches in this region. Or it is possible that the Eugenius mentioned in the Severus inscription is a different individual from a later period.

nia, was not yet published at the time of this revision, but I wish to thank Dr. Tabbernee for making some of the materials available to me.]

Μ(ᾶρκος) Ἰού(λιος) Εὐ[γε]νιος Κυρίλου Κέλερος Κουησσέως
βουλ(ευτοῦ/-τῆς?)[73]
στρατευσ[ά]μενος ἐν τῇ̣ κατὰ Πισιδίαν ἡγεμονικῇ τάξι
καὶ γήμα[ς] θυγατέρα Γαίου Νεστοριανοῦ συνκλητικοῦ
Φλ(αουίαν) Ἰ[ο]υλ(ίαν) Φ[λ]αουιανὴν καὶ μετ᾽ ἐπιτει[μ]ίας
στρατευσάμενον
ἐν δὲ τῷ μ̣εταξὺ χρόνῳ κελεύσεως [φ]οιτησάσης ἐπὶ Μαξιμίνου
τοὺς Χρ[ε]ιστιανοὺς θύειν καὶ μὴ ἀπα[λ]λάττεσθαι τῆς
στρατεί[α]ς πλείστας δὲ ὅσας βασάνου̣[ς] ὑπομείνας
ἐπὶ Διογέ̣νους ἡγεμόνος σπουδάσας [τ]ε ἀπαλλαγῆναι
τῆς στρατείας τὴν τῶν Χρειστιανῶν πίστιν φυλάσσων
χρόνον τ[ε] βραχὺν διατρείψας ἐν τῇ Λαοδικέων πύλι
καὶ βουλή̣σει τοῦ παντοκράτορος θεοῦ ἐπίσκοπος
κατασταθ[εί]ς καὶ εἴκοσι πέντε ὅλοις ἔτεσιν τὴν ἐπισκοπὴν
μετὰ πολ[λ]ῆς ἐπιτειμίας διοι[κ]ήσας καὶ πᾶσαν τὴν ἐ‹κ›κλησίαν
ἀνοικοδο[μ]ήσας ἀπὸ θεμελίων καὶ σύνπαντα τὸν περὶ αὐτὴν
κόσμον τ̣ο̣ῦτ᾽ ἔστιν στοῶν τε καὶ τ[ετ]ραστόων καὶ
ζωγραφιῶ[ν] καὶ κεντήσεων κὲ ὑδρείου καὶ προπύλου
καὶ πᾶσι τοῖς
λιθοξοϊκοῖς ἔργοις καὶ πᾶ̣[σι ἁπ]αξαπλῶ(ς) κατασκευά[σας
λειψόμε]νός τε τὸν τῶν ἀνθρώπων
βίον ἐποίησα ἐμαυτῷ πέ[λτα τ]ε̣ καὶ σορὸν ἐν ῇ τὰ
προ[γεγραμμένα] ταῦτα ἐποίησα ἐπιγρ(α)φῖνε
[εἰς κόσ]μον τῆς τε ἐ‹κ›κλ[ησίας κ]ὲ τοῦ γένους μου.

73. Calder's text (as printed above and followed by Tabbernee) takes the abbreviated term βουλ(ευτοῦ) [= "city councillor"] to refer to Eugenius's father (as indicated by the genitive ending). It should be noted that this syntactic ending was Calder's resolution of the abbreviation; however, both on form and on epigraphic convention, the abbreviation might as easily be resolved in the nominative βουλ(ευτής), thus as the office of Eugenius himself. This, his last public office, would open his *cursus honorum* and parallel στρατευσ[ά]μενος in the following line. It is also possible that the title stands in an intentionally ambiguous position, reflecting the common practice of passing down admission to the local decurionate from father to son among the local aristocracy.

Translation: Marcus Julius Eugenius, son of Cyrillus Celer of Kouessos, a member of the (Laodicean) council, having been stationed (as a military officer)[74] in the *officium* of the governor of Pisidia and having married Flavia Julia Flaviana, daughter of Gaius (Julius) Nestorianus, a man of (Roman) senatorial rank; and having served with distinction; and when command had meanwhile been issued by Maximinus that Christians (in the military) offer sacrifice and not be released from the service,[75] having endured many tortures under Diogenes, the governor (of Pisidia), and having contrived to quit the service in order to maintain the faith of the Christians; and having spent a short time in the city of the Laodiceans[76] and having been made bishop by

---

74. ΣΤΡΑΤΕΥΣΑΜΕΝΟΝ (line 4, lapis). Apparently an engraver's error for -ΝΟΣ (so Calder, "Studies in Early Christian Epigraphy," 45).

75. This document (lines 5–9) provides the only evidence for an edict of Maximinus requiring soldiers to sacrifice. The reference to the governor (Valerius) Diogenes makes it possible to date these events before 311. Ramsay suggested (*Luke the Physician*, 344f) that the edict was a supplementary one issued between 303 and the edict of Galerius in 311, but most probably between 307 and 310. This conclusion allows us to deduce the chronology of the rest of Eugenius's career. The style and construction of the sarcophagus and the inscription indicate a *terminus ante quem* of ca. 335–340. Eugenius's accession to the episcopate must have been about 310–315, with the rebuilding of the church very shortly thereafter.

76. Eugenius does not indicate the reason for his stay in Laodicea Combusta. His career in the service of the governor would probably have meant a residence in Antioch-toward-Pisidia. The same location is probable for a man of Roman senatorial rank such as his father-in-law, Julius Nestorianus. Quite a number of provincial aristocrats from the colony of Antioch were adlected to the senate, beginning in the early second century (see Levick, *Roman Colonies in Southern Asia Minor*, 102–10). It is likely, therefore, that Laodicea Combusta, his hometown, became the chosen place of Eugenius's retirement during the persecution and after his decommissioning from the military. The "short" stay refers to the time prior to his election as bishop. The fact that he passed through or over other ecclesiastical offices is attributable to his status as a martyr/confessor, but may also be due to his social position. That Laodicea had at some point become his family's home is indicated by the reference to them (line 19) and to his (and/or his father's) membership in the Laodicean council (line 1). At what point the family moved to Laodicea from their native Kouessos (line 1) is not known. There is no indication, however, that his episcopal office in any way conflicted with his membership on the council. In this way, by the early part of the fourth century we begin to see Christian bishops, many of whom already possess higher social status, serving in the standard capacities of local patrons and decurions. Here compare the case of Phileas of Thmuis (No. 22 above).

the will of Almighty God, and having administered the episcopate for 25 full years with great distinction; and having rebuilt the entire church from its foundations and all embellishments around it,[77] which contain stoai and tetrastoa, paintings, mosaics,[78] a fountain, and an outer gateway, and having furnished it with all the masonry construction and, in a word, with everything; and being about to leave the life of humankind, I had made for myself a tomb enclosure (or platform)[79] and a sarcophagus, on which I had the above inscribed for the adornment of the church and of my family.

---

77. Ramsay made much out of the references to the rebuilding and decoration of the church (see his "A Laodicean Bishop," *The Expositor* [1908] 409–11, 586–89; and *Luke the Physician*, 339–41). He argues on the basis of Eusebius's description of the church at Tyre (*H.E.* 10.4) that Eugenius's construction was an elaborate basilica built over the ruins of the church destroyed in the Great Persecution. It must be noted, however, that the inscription, in sharp contrast to the rhetoric found in Eusebius, does not mention a destruction or even a confiscation of the previous church building. The phrase "rebuilt from the foundations" (ἀνοικοδο[μ]ήσας ἀπὸ θεμελίων, line 14) is regularly found in reference to renovation projects. Nor is there any indication in this document of a move toward formal basilical architecture. It may represent the enlargement of the edifice along the lines of an *aula ecclesiae*, a suggestion I have made also for Eusebius's description of the rebuilt church of Paulinus at Tyre. Perhaps the closest parallels in date and form are S. Chrisogono at Rome (No. 55 below) and the Church of Bishop Theodore at Aquileia (Appendix A, No. 8a below).

78. κεντήσεων (line 16). Calder and Ramsay originally read the word as meaning a carved wooden screen or lattice-work (see *The Expositor* [1908] 413). Calder corrected the reading on the basis of a discussion with M. Gregoire as noted in "Studies in Early Christian Epigraphy," 45.

79. πέλτα (line 18). The term was not readily identified by Calder in 1908, but the meaning "base for a sarcophagus" was provided by an inscription from Iconium (see "Studies in Early Christian Epigraphy," 46). According to the supplement to LSJ (117b) two other inscriptions from Lycaonia (SEG VI.307 and 431) give the meaning "tomb," "tomb platform," or "tomb enclosure." The question that arises from this reading is whether the "tomb" should be considered a shrine in or somehow connected with the church. This is the way it was taken by Calder based on the discovery of the epitaph for the two bishops Severus and Eugenius (*MAMA* 1. 171; see n. 71 above; see Calder, "Studies in Early Christian Epigrpahy," 47–49; idem, "The Epigraphy of the Anatolian Heresies," 67–72). Even though the Severus inscription was a later addition, it is possible to read the Eugenius epitaph as the patron setting up some sort of sepulchral monument to himself near his rebuilt church. Thus, I have taken the phrase εἰς κόσ]μον τῆς τε ἐ‹κ›κλ[ησίας (line 19) in the more common sense as "adornment" or "embellishment," a parallel to its use in line 15 above. Compare also the use in synagogue inscriptions from Sardis (No. 67a) and Akmonia (No. 65).

PROVINCE: Greece (Macedonia)
LOCATION: Philippi

No. 49: Hall Church and Octagon (fourth–sixth centuries)
The "Basilica" of Paul
(Figures 9–10)

New excavations at Philippi were undertaken in 1958 under the direction of Stylianos Pelekanidis of the University of Thessaloniki and sponsored by the Greek Archaeological Society, Athens. The new work focused on the area immediately adjacent to (on the southeast) the Forum of the imperial period and bounded (on the north) by the so-called Via Egnatia. In this area they discovered early imperial buildings around some Hellenistic remains (including a tomb) and a Byzantine Octagonal church complex (fifth–seventh centuries). Upon further investigation the latter was found to have been built over the earliest (early fourth century) Christian edifice known to date from Philippi. During the same period, the Forum itself, usually dated to Antonine period rebuilt over an earlier Hellenistic agora, has been undergoing new excavations under the direction of Michel Sève of the École Français, Athens.[80] After the death of Pelekanidis in 1980, work on the area of the Octagonal church complex was continued by a five-person team of longtime participants in excavations at Philippi from the Ephoreia of Byzantine Antiquities for Eastern Macedonia and Thrace (at Kavala) under the direction of the current Ephoros, Charalambos Bakirtzis. The aim of the team is to finish the work and publish the complex.

Literature: For yearly excavation reports, see "*Anaskaphe Oktagonou Philippon*," in *Praktika Archaiologikes Etaireias* (*ΠΑΕ*) 1958–1979 (by S. Pelekanidis), esp. 1978:69–73 (for building history and plans for the Hall, Octagon A and Octagon B), and 1981–83 (by G. Gounaris, A. Mentzos, and Ch. Bakirtzis). S. Pelekanidis, "Excavations in Philippi," *Balkan Studies* 8 (1967) 123–26. Idem, "Kultprobleme in Apostel Paulus-Oktagon von Philippi im Zusammenhang mit einem ältern Heroenkult," *Atti IX CIAC* (Rome, 1978) II:393–99. Idem, "*Palaiochristianikos taphos en Philippois*," in

80. For annuals on the excavations in the Forum, see Sève's *rapports* in "Chronique des Fouilles," in *BCH*, beginning in 1979. Note especially *BCH* 104 (1980) 699–716; 105 (1981) 918–23; and 106 (1982) 651–53. See also M. Sève and P. Weber, "Le Côte Nord du forum de Philippes," *BCH* 110 (1986) 531–81.

Meletes palaiochristianikes kai Byzantines archaiologias (Thessaloniki, 1977). Idem, *Hoi Philippoi kai ta christianika mnemeia tous, Aphieroma Tessarokontaeteridias Etaireias Makedonikon Spoudon* (Thessaloniki: Society for Macedonian Studies, 1980). G. Gounaris, *To Balneio kai ta Boreia prosktismata tou Oktagonou ton Philippon* (Thessalonika: Society for Macedonian Studies, 1987). Ch. Bakirtzis, "*To Episkopeion ton Philippon,*" in *Proceedings of the Second Symposium on Kavala and its Environs (1986)* (Kavala: Center for Historical Studies, 1987) 149–57. V. Abrahamsen, "Bishop Porphyrios and the City of Philippi in the Early Fourth Century," *VC* 43 (1989) 80–85. D. Feissel, *Recueil des inscriptions chrétiennes de Macédoine du IIIè au VIè siècle* (BCH Supplements 8; Paris: Boccard, 1983).

[This description is based on the author's observation on site and the published excavation reports. I wish to express my thanks for the hospitality and assistance of Charalambos Bakirtzis, the Ephor of Byzantine Antiquities for Eastern Macedonia and Thrace, and his staff.]

a. Earlier Structures to the Southeast of the Forum

Work in the area to the southeast of the Antonine Forum revealed (Fig. 9) the course of another major roadway (called the South Decumanus), which ran between the Forum and the later Basilica B (to the south). This wide, paved roadway ran parallel to the so-called Via Egnatia (now better called the North Decumanus), which ran through the Hellenistic agora and formed the northern boundary of the Antonine Forum. In the newly excavated area to the east was found a complex of buildings dating from as early as the Roman period (second century CE) and continuing in use until the seventh-century decline of the city. The westernmost of these structures lay contiguous to the eastern perimeter of the Forum. The original character of the region was of three consecutive U-shaped insulae facing along the North Decumanus. Thus, the development of this area arose with the Roman orientation of the urban street plan around the area of the Forum. The middle insula (fig. 9, locus D) was dominated by a Roman-period thermal establishment. The remaining areas of the insulae were comprised of private quarters and shops. In the earlier Roman period, the easternmost portion on the south side of this area seems to have been largely unoccupied. In this area the Octagon would later be built.

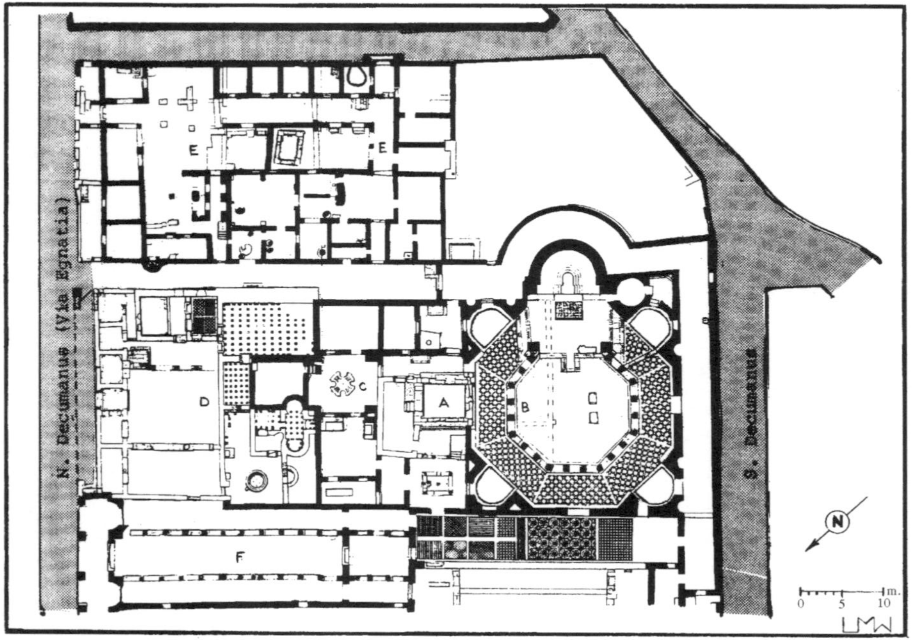

Fig. 9
Greece, Philippi. Octagonal Church complex and Episkopeion.
Plan restoration of last phase (based on field plan of S. Pelekanidis)

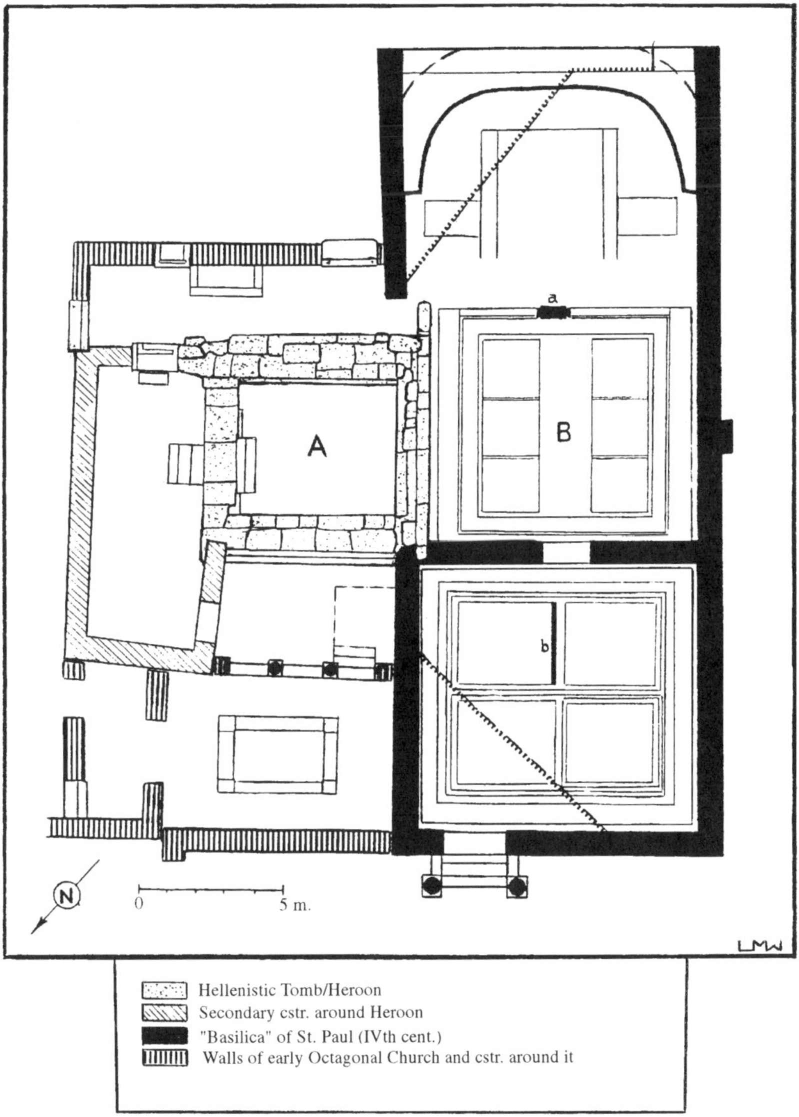

Fig. 10

Greece, Philippi. Fourth-century Hall Church and Heroon, beneath the Octagonal Church complex. Plan restoration (based on plan of S. Pelekanidis.)

The Roman-period edifices of the middle insula were built over or around some earlier Hellenistic remains, of which only a little is known. The earliest structure in this area (locus A in figs. 9 and 10) was a chamber-tomb of the Hellenistic period. Originally, the terrain in this area had sloped off sharply toward the South Decumanus, so that the tomb entrance would have been exposed on this southern slope. Above the tomb proper was constructed a *naos,* which was reached by stairs through an antechamber to the north. This room was on a level higher than the entrance of the tomb (see fig. 10, locus A). Based on an inscription, it has been hypothesized that the burial was associated with a child-priest (*mystes*) of the Temple of the Cabieri (or Samothrakeion) at Samothrace. The tomb became a *Heroon*, the center of a hero cult, attached to the name of the child, Εὐέφηνες Ἐξεκέστου.[81]

b. The Later Christian Buildings:
The Octagonal Complex and Episkopeion

Contiguous to the Heroon (on its southwest face) was found an extensive ecclesiastical complex dominated by an elaborate Byzantine Octagonal church (fig. 9), dating from the fifth-sixth century and extending to the boundary of the South Decumanus. The floor of the Octagonal church stood some 2.5 m above the roadway, and the perimeter wall served as a terrace or retaining wall, running along the South Decumanus, for the fill used to level the earlier slope. Of particular interest from the first discovery was the proximity of the church to the Heroon. The latter was incorporated into the ecclesiastical complex. The baptistry of church, in fact, was built off of the Heroon (to the north) and made use of the warm water of the Roman bath (see fig. 9, locus C). On the west side of the Heroon a small atrium and portico were installed. The presence of steps off this later atrium and other construction around the Heroon related to the building of the Octagon indicate that the platform on top of the tomb itself (originally a small shrine) continued to be used in the physical plan of the church. These rooms adjacent to the Heroon interconnect the entry area (or narthex) from the west with the area of the baptistry, and from there into the area behind the apse of the

81. See S. Pelekanidis, "Kultprobleme in Apostel Paulus-Oktagon von Philippi im Zusammenhang mit einem älteren Heroenkult," *Atti IX CIAC* (Rome, 1978) 2. 393–99.

Octagon. The main entrance to the Octagonal church complex, at least in its final form, was from the North Decumanus down a long colonnaded portico (fig. 9, F) to a narthex paved in *opus sectile*. This broad colonnade was a later remodeling of this area, which had originally been a narrow street between the first and middle insulae. The later narthex stood at the same height as the floor of the Octagon and ca. 1.00 m above the earlier street at the entrance to the narthex from F. To the west of the narthex, the area of houses adjacent to the southeast corner of the Forum was converted into a courtyard. Among the scattered finds in this area were a number of marble architectural slabs, clearly from earlier pagan contexts, which had been reused in the Christian edifice (as indicated by the presence of Christian inscriptions cut on the backs).

The easternmost insula facing onto the North Decumanus was converted into the Episkopeion (or bishop's residence and audience chambers) associated with the Octagon. It too had a narrow street that gave access from the North Decumanus to the Episkopeion and to the areas behind the apse of the church. It now appears that the Octagonal church complex served as the cathedral of the Bishop of Philippi at least from the fifth to the seventh centuries, and probably from the fourth as well. During this period the ecclesiastical complex of the Octagon came to dominate physically the region to the east of the Forum.[82] Both the Octagonal church and the Episkopeion continued in use until damaged in a severe earthquake, probably sometime in the eighth century.

c. The Earlier Hall Church: The "Basilica" of Paul

In the excavations it was discovered that the present Octagon (now called Octagon B) represented a subsequent rebuilding of an earlier, simpler Octagonal church underneath (Octagon A, dating to the fifth century) of the same basic plan. These renovations involved enclosing the earlier Octagon with a quadrilateral exterior wall. From the interior, four apsidal exedrae were set into the corners of this quadrilateral. Octagon B was then given a new chancel and synthronon and a new floor in *opus sectile*. Octagon A had had a

82. See Ch. Bakirtzis, "*To Episkopeion ton Philippon*," in *Proceedings of the Second Symposium on Kavala and its Environs (1986)* (Kavala: Center for Historical Studies, 1987) 149–57.

simpler paved floor, but the octagonal stylobate of the colonnade was set on the same plan as the later.

Beneath the left (N) aisle of the earlier Octagon A was found the paved mosaic floor of a simple hall church (L.29; W.10.25 m). The plan of this earlier edifice was a rectangle divided into roughly three equal bays. The two bays on the east comprised a large hall with no other internal divisions. The third bay was partitioned by an intervening wall as a sort of entry chamber. The entrance was from the west, off the narrow street between the first and middle insulae. Because of the slope of the street down toward the South Decumanus, a stair was installed up to the level of the floor of the hall. From the door one entered into the first room, and from there into the hall proper. The floor of the hall was paved in a very fine mosaic with bird and floral patterns in distinct registers. (The basic geometric design is indicated in the plan of fig. 9.) The design of the mosaic pavement in the hall itself shows a kind of central aisle leading toward the front (east end) of the room and reflecting the longitudinal axis. The mosaic design in the entry chamber is more of a quadrifoil, with its central border oriented on the doorway to the main hall.

At the east end of the hall the pavement shows a squarish apsidal design, perhaps demarking a synthronon; however, it appears that the external walls of the edifice were quadrilateral. Unfortunately, the later construction and renovations of the Octagonal buildings destroyed the eastern termination of the hall. On the north long side of the hall, the Heroon was used for part of the construction by splicing the newly constructed walls of the hall onto it. Thus, it appears that the Heroon edifice was integrated into the physical plan of the church from the first stage, but there is no evidence for how it might have been used in this stage.

The hall church structure is datable to before ca. 343/344 by an inscription in the mosaic floor (see section e. below for texts). Since the text commemorates the paving of the floor by the bishop, it is likely that the hall itself was built somewhat earlier, but by exactly how much is difficult to guess on the basis of available evidence. A date in the early fourth century is a safe estimate.

Thus, it has been concluded by Pelekanidis, Bakirtzis, and the others that the hall church, called the "basilica of St. Paul" (where basilica has no technical architectural significance) was the first church built in this region of the city and became the episcopal see. The fact that it clearly incorporated the existing Heroon suggests that by the fourth century the cult of a Christian "martyr" (perhaps something to do with Paul himself) in local Christian lore had become associated with the site of the tomb.[83] The form of the hall is also significant, since it marks probably the earliest extant remains of a Christian edifice in this region of Greece. It suggests further that true basilical architecture (in the technical architectural sense) was a later arrival in northern Greek regions of Christianity, since the remaining four basilicas in the city are from the fifth and sixth centuries or later.

d. The Inscriptions from the Hall Church

Two inscriptions were found in the mosaic pavement of the hall church. The first identifies Bishop Porphyrios (a signator of the Council of Serdica in 343/344), who dedicated the mosaic paving of the hall. It provides a *terminus ante quem* for the construction of the hall church. Whether the same Bishop Porphyrios was also responsible for the building of the hall church itself cannot be determined on the basis of the present data. The inscription is found in mosaic, in a *tabula ansata* (H.0.33; L.1.195 m overall; L.0.875 m without the ansae), in the border pattern of the pavement between the first and second bays of the hall (fig. 10, locus a). In addition, the dedicatory formula identifies the edifice as a "basilica" devoted to St. Paul. The term "basilica" here cannot have a technical architectural significance; it merely refers to the "hall" of the church. The text reads as follows:

Inscription 1

ΠΑΕ 1975:101 (= *BCH* 100 [1976] 685 and fig. 236; Feissel, *Recueil*, no. 226). Letters: H.0.09 m.

[The letters were done in blue tessarae, except the words underlined, which were done in gold-leaf tessarae.)

ΠΟΡ[ΦΥ]ΡΙΟC ΕΠΙCΚΟ-
2 ΠΟC ΤΗ[Ν Κ]ΕΝΤΗCΙΝ ΤΗC ΒΑCΙΛΙΚΗ-
C ΠΑΥΛΟ[Υ ΕΠ]ΟΙΗCΕΝ ΕΝ Χ(ΡΙCΤ)Ω

83. See Pelekanidis, "Kultprobleme," 398.

Translation: Porphyrios, the bishop, made the mosaic of the basilica of Paul, in Christ.

The second inscription was found in the outer or entry room of the hall, also prominently displayed in a border of the mosaic (fig. 10, locus b). It identifies a certain Priscus (Priskos), probably a wealthy donor who paid for the paving work of this room. Since the program of the mosaic seems to be of single design between the two areas, it suggests that Bishop Porphyrios and this prominent figure Priscus oversaw the project together. The text reads as follows:

Inscription 2
ΠΑΕ 1976:128 (= *BCH* 101 (1977) 617 and fig. 242; SEG 26:732; Feissel, *Recueil*, no. 227). Letters: H.0.10 m.

[Χ]ΡΙϹΤΕ ΒΩΗΘΙ ΤΟΥ ΔΟΥΛΟΥ ϹΟΥ
ΠΡΙϹΚΟΥ [Ϲ]ΥΝ ΠΑΝΤΙ ΤΟΥ ΟΙΚΟΥ ΑΥΤΟΥ

Translation: Christ, help your servant Priskos together with all his household.

PROVINCE: Venetia (Istria-Venetia)
LOCATION: Parentium (Parenzo or Poreč)

No. 50: Hall Church (fourth century) and Basilica (fifth century)
(Basilica Eufrasiana, sixth century)
(Figures 11–12)

The present church called the Eufrasiana at Poreč, Croatia (known in Italian as Parenzo), is a sixth-century complex named after its founding bishop, Eufrasius (ca. 550–559 CE). This Justinianic complex has largely survived intact.[84] Examinations of the site at the end of the nineteenth century

84. A mosaic donor portrait with inscription from the apse of the present basilica (dating from the sixth-century Eufrasian complex) credits the bishop Eufrasius with the foundation. The name of the bishop of Parentium is also mentioned in a letter of Pope Pelagius I dating to 559. On the mosaics see A. Šonje, "I mosaici parietali del complesso architettonico della basilica Eufrasiana a Parenzo," *Atti del centro di ricerche storiche di Rovigno* 12 (1982–83) 65–138. On the dating based in part on

revealed that this monumental complex stands over a fifth-century complex of nearly the same dimensions (cf. fig. 12). Further excavation indicated that this somewhat unusual fifth-century complex (especially in the area now designated the North Site, see fig. 11b) stood over another earlier Christian structure. The earlier complex included two parallel, rectilinear halls and what may have been a baptistry. This early "hall church" is dated to the fourth century, and it was found to incorporate elements of earlier Roman buildings dating from the third century.

Literature: O. Marucchi, "Le recente scoperte del Duomo de Parenzo," *NBAC* 2 (1896) 9–10. W. Gerber, *Altchristlichen Kultbauten Istriens und Dalmatiens* (Dresden, 1912) 37–41. D. Frey, "Neue Untersuchungen und Grabungen in Parenzo," *Mitteilungen der K. K. Zentralkommision für Denkmalpflege* 5–6 (1914) 118, 179. A. Gnirs, "Zur Frage der christliche Kultanlagen aus der ersten Halfte des IV Jahrhundert," *Jahrsheft des Österreich. archäologische Institut in Wien 19–20* (1919) [Beiblatt] 165–81. B. Tamaro, "Parenzo-Mosaica presso la basilica eufrasiana," *Notizie degli Scavi di antichità* 4 (1928) 411–12. F. Forlati, "Gli ultimi restauri nella Basilica Eufrasiana de Parenzo," *Atti e memorie della Società istr. di archeologia e storia patr.* 42 (1930) 43–44. M. Mirabella Roberti, "Notizie di Parenzo," *Atti e memorie* 51–52 (1942) 289–90. B. Molajoli, *La Basilica Eufrasiana di Parenzo* (2d ed.; Padua, 1943). Ante Šonje, "Arheoloska istrazivanja na prodrucju Eufrazijeve bazilike u Poreču," *Jadranski Zbornik* 7 (1969) 249–51. Idem, "Il complesso della prima basilica nella zona della basilica Eufrasiana a Parenzo," *Atti VI CIAC* (1962) 799–806. Idem, "Contributo alla soluzione della problematica del complesso della basilica Eufrasiana de Parenzo," *Felix Ravenna* 97 (1968) 27–65 [includes a history of the excavations and substantial bibliography]. Idem, "Mosaici parietali della basilica Eufrasiana a Parenzo," *Atti del centro di ricerche storiche di Rovigno* 12 (1982–83) 65–138. Ann Terry, "The Architecture and Architectural Sculpture of the Sixth-Century Eufrasius Cathedral Complex at Poreč." (Unpublished Ph.D. Thesis; Champaign-Urbana: University of Illinois, 1984). Idem, "The *Opus Sectile* in the Eufrasius Cathedral at Poreč," *DOP* 40 (1986) 147–64. Idem,

artistic comparisons with other Justinianic buildings, see A. Terry, "The *Opus Sectile* in the Eufrasius Cathedral at Poreč," *DOP* 40 (1986) 147, 159–64. For the text of his inscription, see below n. 111.

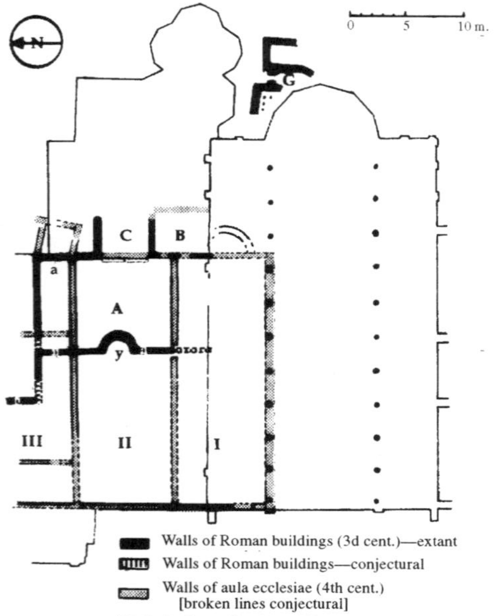

a. Earlier building in the area of the North Site, restored plan

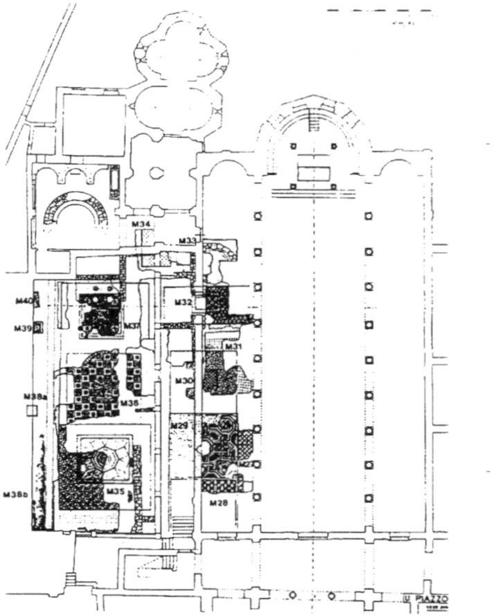

b. Arrangement of mosaic pavements beneath the basilica floor showing the North Site. After the plan of Piazzo, 1939 (from A. Terry, 1995)

Fig. 11

Istria, Parentium. Roman buildings and *aula ecclesiae* beneath the Basilica Eufrasiana.
Plan restoration, composite and siting plan of mosaics (based on Gilmore Eaves and Piazzo)

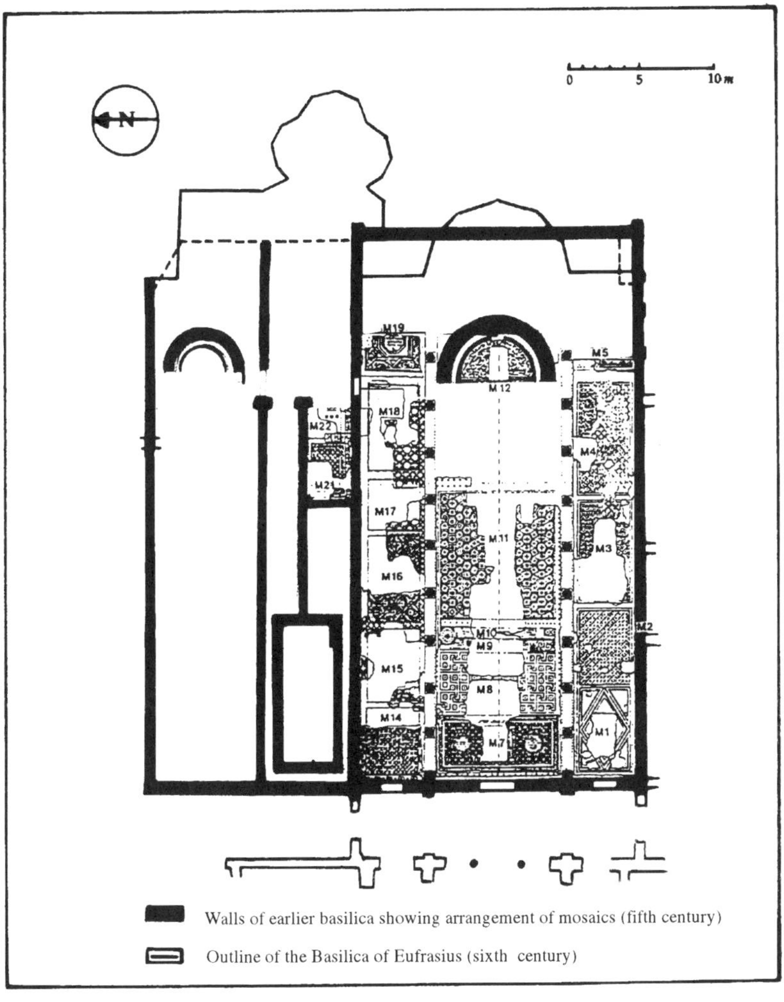

Fig. 12

Istria, Parentium. Fifth-century basilica beneath the Eufrasiana.
Plan restoration showing mosaics (based on Šonje and Piazzo, adapted)

"The Sculpture at the Cathedral of Eufrasius in Poreč," *DOP* 42 (1988) 13–64. Idem, "The Conservation History of the Mosaic Pavements at the Cathedral Site of Poreč," *Hortus Artium Medievalium* 1 (1995) 176–86. Ffiona Gilmore Eaves, "Annulling a Myth: A Reassessment of the Earlier Phases of the Eufrasian Basilica at Poreč, and the Evidence for *Domus Ecclesiae*" (Unpublished Ph.D. Thesis, Nottingham, University of Nottingham, 1993).

[While a long tradition holds that there was a *domus ecclesiae* here from the late third century, the archaeological record does not substantiate this claim. The following summary is based on the reports of work by Ante Šonje, listed above, who made numerous suggestions for the existence of a third-century *domus ecclesiae* on the site. I am very grateful to Dr. Ann Terry and Dr. Ffiona Gilmore Eaves, who have worked extensively in recent years on the Eufrasian complex, its decoration, and the complicated architectural history of the site and its archaeological recovery. Their forthcoming study of the site will unveil these complexities. Because detailed archaeological reports of the Roman complex remain incomplete or in preparation, the present historical reconstruction will only attempt to demonstrate the basic chronology of the earliest Christian strata of use in the "hall church" or *aula ecclesiae.*]

a. Construction History: The Roman Buildings and the Aula Ecclesiae

The earliest archaeological strata in the area occupied by the Eufrasian complex seems to be from the second to early third centuries. The dating, suggested by artifacts (especially ceramic ware) found at the first of three levels of Roman construction, would coincide with the earlier stages of Roman occupation in the Istrian peninsula.[85] The form of the first Roman structure on the site is uncertain due to the fragmentary and irregular nature of the remains, and little more can be said of the second stratum.[86]

The third stratum of Roman occupation on the site contains remains of

85. See Šonje, "Contributo alla soluzione della problematica del complesso della basilica Eufrasiana di Parenzo," *Felix Ravenna* 97 (1968) 29 (and n. 10), 36.

86. No attempt has been made to show these earlier Roman remains on the accompanying figures. The figures presented here take into account Šonje's reconstructions from the articles "Contributo alla soluzione," Tav. I and "Il complesso della prima basilica nella zona della basilica Eufrasiana a Parenzao," *Atti VI CIAC* (1962) 801–2 and Tav. II as checked against other plans and photographs currently under study by Drs. A. Terry and F. Gilmore Eaves.

what appears to be a third-century Roman edifice located adjacent to the north wall of the city (areas A–C in fig. 11a). Possibly associated with this stratum is a hypocaust establishment (area G) located just to the east and running under the apse of the sixth-century basilica. The precise nature and and extent of the building (or buildings) cannot be determined. It is not clear whether the hypocaust (G) was integral with the edifice in A–C. There is some evidence of a natural spring in the area to the northeast of area A. Šonje argued that all these remnants were part of one large complex, a Roman villa that was later converted into a *domus ecclesiae* by the late third or early fourth century.[87] Šonje's reconstruction of the domestic structure and its Christian renovation is not demonstrable on archaeological grounds in the view of the current research.[88] As a result, earlier Christian usage of the edifice, while not impossible, must be considered speculative.

87. See Šonje, "Il complesso della prima basilica," 800; "Contributo alla soluzione," 32–36. Šonje identified the "villa" as a large hall-like room (A), oriented on the north–south axis; he thought it was probably the *triclinium* of the house. Area A measures approximately 20 m (north–south) by 8.45 m (east–west). Šonje also posited other domestic quarters located to the east in area C and another smaller "hall" in B (see fig. 11a). The apsidal structure in A (at locus y) was thought to be an atrium with pool or fountain (a nymphaeum?), with a vestibule (*prothyrum*) to the west and other rooms to the north of it. In his later work Šonje had pushed the date of the Christian renovation of this "villa" back earlier into the third century. See Ffiona Gilmore Eaves, "Annulling a Myth: A Reassessment of the Earlier Phases of the Eufrasian Basilica at Poreč, and of the Evidence for Domus Ecclesiae," (Ph.D. Thesis, Nottingham, University of Nottingham, 1993) 93–95. While the basic wall structures identified by Šonje have been confirmed in more recent archaeological work (as reflected in fig. 11a), the domestic form and the Christian usage of the site before the fourth century have been called into question.

88. The study that has most critically revised the traditional claim is the dissertation of Gilmore Eaves, noted above. A significant piece of evidence for Šonje's argument was the mosaic pavement in areas M37 and M34 (see fig. 11b), which were thought to belong to areas A and B, and thus pointing to the domestic character of the edifice. He also thought it pointed to a Christian adaptation of the villa, since M37 contained fish symbols, and thus was the prime evidence for identification of the site as a *domus ecclesiae.* These mosaics were actually found *in situ* in the paving of the fourth-century stratum, that is from the floor of the Christian *aula ecclesiae* that was built over the earlier Roman edifice. Following the older tradition of O. Marrucchi (over against Tamaro, Molajoli, and later excavators), Šonje proposed that these mosaics had been preserved from the earlier domestic structure. So B. Tamaro, in an article in *Notizie degli Scavi di antichità* 4 (1928) 11, had already suggested that the mosaic sections M35–37 were a unitary installation. B. Molajoli noted that M37 con-

The first demonstrable evidence of Christian usage of the site occurs in the building program of the fourth century. A few elements of the earlier Roman edifice were used as footings or architecturally incorporated in this construction. The new edifice was an *aula ecclesiae,* which Šonje called "il complesso della basilica primitiva."[89] While a mosaic inscription from this stratum (section M35 in fig. 11b, to be discussed below) does use the term *basilica* in reference to the church building, it does not carry a technical archtectural sense of later basilical planning.[90]

The architectural form of the building can be determined archaeologically from limited wall remains and the layout of the mosaic pavements (see fig. 11b).[91] It was configured as two contiguous rectilinear halls (I and II in fig. 11a), oriented on an east–west, longitudinal axis. The halls are slightly irregular: Hall I measures ca. 8.5 x 23–24 m; Hall II ca. 8–9 x ca. 23 m. The three

---

tained older elements stylistically in the composition of the mosaic, but he did not think it could be separated from M35–36, which clearly came from the later hall sturcture. Thus the evidence for earlier walls was treated separately. See Molajoli, *La Basilica Eufrasiana di Parenzo* (2d ed.; Padua, 1943) 12–13, and the discussion of the archaeological interpretations by Gilmore Eaves, "Annulling a Myth," 92–96. The fish symbols taken together with the wording of the funerary inscription of Bishop Maurus (to be discussed below) were central to Šonje's argument that the villa had already been converted into a *domus ecclesiae.* See "Contributo alla soluzione," 43. In the earlier tradition the area of M37 was associated with a chapel dedicated to St. Maurus and had been equated with the reference to an "oratory" in his own house, drawn from the inscription. See Gilmore Eaves, "Annulling a Myth," 92. Šonje also argued that locus a was already in Christian usage as a baptistry by the beginning of the fourth century, since a basin was found preserved under the font of the later fourth-century building.

89. Šonje, "Contributo alla soluzione," 36. In other cases it is just referred to as "prima basilica." The notion of an "original" or "primitive" (*primitiva*) basilica may come from Šonje's reconstruction of three parallel halls, resembling, in his view, a central nave and two side aisles. On the incorporation of earlier wall elements see Gilmore Eaves, "Annulling a Myth," 108–12.

90. Compare the use of the term *basilica* in a mosaic floor inscription from the early fourth-century *aula ecclesiae* at Philippi (No. 49 c–d, above) and in a memorial inscription from Altava, Mauretania (No. 56, below).

91. On the significance and complexity of these mosaic pavements in the archaeology of the site, see the article by Ann Terry, "The Conservation History of the Mosaic Pavements at the Cathedral Site of Poreč: 1862–1990," *Hortus Artium Medievalium* 1 (1995) 76–86 and the discussion of Gilmore Eaves, "Annulling a Myth," 92–93. A new study of the evidence for these phases is in preparation jointly by Terry and Gilmore Eaves.

main east–west carrying walls seem to be new construction for this project, but at a number of points they were founded on older wall segments from the Roman edifice. Both halls were paved with mosaics: Hall I in four sections or bays (M28, 29, 30, 31/32) and Hall II in three sections (M35, 36, 37). Section M37 contained fish symbols, while sections M35, 36, 28, and 32 contain donor inscriptions for the paving project.[92] At this point Hall II appears to be the main hall of the church, and the orientation of the symbols and inscriptions in all three bays indicates axial orientation toward the east. It is assumed, therefore, that the main entrance was on the west end of Hall II; however, there is some indication of another entrance into Hall I from the south (in section M28). There is evidence of additional rooms to the east (as marked by the paving in areas M33 and M34 in fig. 11b) and what may be an external apsidal wall (Th. ca. 66 cm) on the central axis of Hall I (see figs. 11a and 11b).10 The function of this apsidal structure or its relation to the halls cannot be determined.

Area III was first assumed by Šonje to be a third, narrower hall, which he labeled the *catachumeneum* and baptistry of the church.[94] A supposed baptismal font (a) was found in a small partitioned room with mosaic floor (sections M39–40) on the east end of area III. The northern terminating walls of

92. The nature of these inscriptions suggest donations by leading families or individuals. Unfortunately nothing more is known about the people named. See the text and discussion of the inscriptions below in No. 50b.

93. On the south doorway see Inscription 4 below. The remnants of this apsidal structure are visible in the older site plans (just to the east of M32 in fig. 11b) but have generally been dismissed in most of the discussions to date. Its existence and the measurements have been confirmed in conversations with Dr. Ann Terry. While it appears that the apsidal structure may belong to the fourth-century stratum, it is possible that it came from the earlier Roman edifice. The fact that the mosaic in M33 (clearly from the fourth-century edifice) does not conform to the apsidal structure is suggestive of an earlier date for the apsidal edifice. If so, it would be similar in size and form with the apsidal structure at locus y. Given the current reservations regarding the domestic character of the third-century structure, we may take note of possible similarities to nymphaea and/or bath buildings, and thus potentially connected to the hypocaust edifice at G. See Gilmore Eaves, "Annulling a Myth," 78–80.

94. Šonje, "Contributo alla soluzione," 39–42 and Tav. LV. Šonje assumed a narrower, parallel hall running the full length of halls I and II but subdivided horizontally into three rooms. The three rooms seem to be based on the three different types of paving found in the excavated areas immediately to the north of Hall II. See n. 95 following.

this area were not discovered, and the precise extent and architectural form of these areas remain uncertain.[95]

Šonje dated the construction of the hall complex (or "prima basilica") to the early part of the fourth century based on his assumption of a direct continuity with the third-century *domus ecclesiae* as correlated with the Maurus inscription. The inscription (see below) refers to the repair or renovation of "his first church building" (*primitiva ecclesiae*).[96] Since the bishop Maurus was thought to be a martyr (confessor) of the pre-Constantinian period, Šonje thus dated the initial construction of the hall complex to the early Constantinian period with completion and installation of a martyrium (identified with Hall I) by ca. 386.[97] It is now thought by current researchers that the entire hall complex was a single project completed some time in the later fourth century, but the evidence of the Maurus inscription still suggests that it was closely associated with his name. Coins found beneath the paving in halls I and II dating from the time of Valens (364–78) and Gratian (375–383) provide a *terminus a quo* for this construction, or at least the installation of the mosaic pavements.[98]

---

95. Only the small "baptistry" room is identifiable. The area at M38a was paved in plain black and white tesserae, while the section in M38b was left paved in large brick slabs. These brick paving slabs appear to be more typical of an exterior covered protico or some less formal area, although it is possible that this was intended as a temporary measure. Terminating walls and evidence of functions in these areas are lacking. See Gilmore Eaves, "Annulling a Myth," 184–215, esp. 191–210. There is now little evidence to suggest direct continuity to fonts in area a of the earlier edifice; see ibid., 97–112.

96. Šonje, "Contributo alla soluzione," 43–44. The tradition of St. Maurus as bishop and confessor was preserved in the apse mosaic of the later Eufrasian basilica (sixth century). In the earlier excavations of the nineteenth century, the fish mosaic in M37 was thought to be the original pavement from the room that had served as the chapel or martyrium of Maurus. A shrine or memorial to Maurus is now thought to be possible, but not confirmed, in the fifth- and sixth-century strata but located in a different area. It appears that the same traditions underlie the notion that the mosaic pavement in M37 had come from the house of Maurus which had been renovated for a church.

97. Ibid., 38. Šonje and others had first dated Maurus to the Diocletianic persecution, but gradually the date was pushed back to the time of Decius or Valerian. It must be noted, however, that Maurus is only called a "confessor." Without any other evidence the assumption of a Diocletianic date is possible but by no means certain, since it ignores other circumstances throughout the fourth century. On the date see the discussion below in 50c and n. 112.

98. Also reported by Šonje in ibid., 43.

In the first half of the fifth century the so-called "primitive basilica" or *aula ecclesiae* complex was replaced by the construction of a monumental, three-aisle basilica (see fig. 12). It may be, however, that a number of features of this structure preserve earlier planning. The left colonnade of the nave was founded on the southern terminating wall of Hall I. The large rectangular nave has only an internal apse structure.[99] The dependencies of this fifth-century basilica are located in two parallel halls to the north which are superimposed over the earlier buildings on the North Site. In the sixth-century renovation this earlier North Site complex was further modified when the monumental complex of bishop Euphrasius was constructed.

b. Inscriptions from the Aula Ecclesiae *(fourth century)*

Five main inscriptions were preserved *in situ* in the sections of mosaic pavement associated with the fourth-century stratum, three from Hall II (sections M35, 36) and two from Hall I (sections M28, 32). Each refers to donations made by individuals or familial groups for the mosaic work. They are here identified by the sections in which they were located (according to fig. 11b). [I am grateful to Ann Terry for making available to me the portions of her study (in preparation) on the Eufrasian complex that deal with the mosaics and inscriptions.]

Inscription 1: From Hall II, section M36, in an inset rectangle in the center of the panel. The text is on one line at the top and two lines at the bottom with a crater (or *cantharus*) and vines in the center. Read facing east.[100]

> [Lu]picinus et Pascasia p(edes) CCCC f(ecit)
> Clamosus, mag(ister) puer(orum),[101] et Successa p(edes) C
> Felicissimus cum suis p(edes) C

99. This feature is not uncommon among churches of this period in Venetia and Istria; see the study of G. C. Menis, *La Basilica nelle diocesi settentrionali della metropoli d'Aquileia* (Studi di Antichita cristiana XXIV; Rome: Pontificio instituto di archeologia cristiana, 1958).

100. The text is from A. Degrassi, *Inscriptiones Italiae* X.2 (Rome, 1934) no. 58 (Tab. III, II). A photograph of the inscription is also shown in F. van der Meer and C. Mohrmann, eds., *Atlas of the Early Christian World* (London: Nelson, 1966) 65 (plate 141).

101. Note that the same name and title appear in a donor inscription from the

Translation: Lupicinus et Pascasia made 400 feet (of mosaic); Clamosus, master of the children, and Successa, 100 feet; Felicissimus, together with his household, 100 feet.

Inscription 2: From Hall II, section 35, five lines in a central clippeus set in an octagonal medallion. Read facing east.[102]

> Infaṇ[tius]
> et Innoc̣[entia][103]
> ex suo p[avimentum][104]
> basị[licae]
> tes(sellaverunt) p(edes) [. . .]

Translation: Infantius and Innocentia tessellated the pavement of the basilica[105] from his (their?) own funds, ______ feet.

Inscription 3: From Hall II, in a section of mosaic found between M36 and M37. Read facing east.[106]

> Memorius et Valeria p(edes) L.

Translation: Memorius and Valeria (gave) 50 feet.

---

mosaic pavement of the fifth-century basilica (section M10, fig. 12b), but the wife's name in the latter text is Victorina. See also n. 103 below.

102. Text from Degrassi, *Inscriptiones Italiae,* no. 57 (Tab. II, I).

103. As noted by Degrassi, the endings of the names are conjectural because of the missing portions of the text. The names were possibly abbreviated owing to the space. They might have also been intended as Infan[tia] and Innoc[ens] or Innoc[entius]; however, given the parallel constructions in M36, 32, and 28 (and used regularly in the later fifth-century inscriptions), the combination of a masculine followed by a feminine name, suggesting a husband and wife, is reasonable. Nonetheless, it may be noted that the name Innocentius, a deacon, also appears in an inscription from the mosaic floor of the fifth-century basilica (in section M7, text at n. 135 below). See also n. 101 above.

104. So Degrassi; however, due to the available space the word *pavimentum* might have been abbreviated, thus: p[avim(entum)].

105. As noted above (n. 90), the term "basilica" here means hall or church building with no technical architectural signification.

106. Text from Degrassi, *Inscriptiones Italiae,* no. 59.

Inscription 4: From Hall I, in section M28. Read facing north.[107]

Castus et Ursa pedis centum fecerunt.

Translation: Castus and Ursa had 100 feet made.

Inscription 5: From Hall I, in section M32. Read facing east.[108]

. . .]s et Spectata famuli f(ecerunt) C.

Translation: [NN (masc.)] and Spectata, slaves, had 100 feet made.

c. The Maurus Inscription

An inscription from what is thought to be a sarcophagus was found reused in the fifth-century basilica beneath the Eufrasian church complex. The inscription names the martyr/confessor and bishop Maurus, whose body had been translated from a previous burial site to a special room set aside, presumably in the context of the church building. Since the inscribed stone was reused as a spoil in the paving of the medieval floor of Eufrasian cathedra, it appears to come from the fifth-century basilica. It has traditionally been suggested that it came originally from the earlier hall church, where a *martyrium* was installed at some point in the remodeling.[109] The designation of Maurus as a confessor is generally assumed to point to a date in the Great Persecution (ca. 303–313), but this is by no means certain.[110] The inscription itself is undatable on any archaeological grounds. It also identifies the edifice as "his first church" (*primitiva ecclesiae*). The remaining fragment of the marble panel (broken off to the right, left, and bottom) measures 0.93 x 1.18 m and is 0.11 m thick. [Letter quality and measurements are not available.]

107. Text from Degrassi, *Inscriptionses Italiae,* no. 60 (Tab. II, IV). On the basis of the orientation of this text it has been conjectured that there was a doorway into Hall I from the south in the westernmost bay. See above at n. 93.

108. Text from Degrassi, *Inscriptiones Italiae,* no. 63 (Tab. III, VII).

109. The sarcophagus was considered by Šonje to be the reliquary of the fourth-century *martyrium* (which he thought was located in Hall I) of the "Hall Church" (cf. No. 50a, above and fig. 11).

110. Šonje had gradually pushed the date back to the time of Decius or Valerian. It seems to me that a date up to the middle of the fourth century is equally possible. There were sporadic outbreaks of persecution under Licinius in the east until 324 and again under Julian in 360–361 that might as easily account for the status of Maurus

Literature: A. Šonje, "Il complesso della prima basilica nella zona della basilica Eufrasiana a Parenzo," *Atti VI CIAC* 799–806 (the text is on 804, n. 10). Idem, "Contributo alla soluzione della problematica del complesso della basilica Eufrasiana di Parenzo," *Felix Ravenna* 47 (1968) 33–44. Idem, "Sarcofagi paleocristiani dell'Istria," *Atti VIII CIAC* (1969) 490–93. G. Cuscito, "*Hoc cubile sanctum:* contributo per un studio sulle origini cristiane in Istria," *Atti e memorie della Società istr. di archeologia e storia patr.* ns. 19 (1971) 77–99. Idem, *Cristianesimo antico ad Aquileia e in Istria.* Fonti e studi per la storia della Venezia giulia. Serie secondo, III. Trieste, 1977. Idem, "I santi Mauro e Eleuterio di Parenzo l'identità, il culto, le reliquie," *Atti di centro di ricerche storiche Rovigno* 16 (1985–86) 31–46. Idem, "Vescovo e cattedrali nella documentazione epigrafica in occidente," *Acta XI CIAC (1988),* in *Studi di Antichità cristiana* 41 (1989) 741–49.

[Text after *Atti VI CIAC,* 804 n. 10.]

Hoc cubile santum confessoris Maur[i] nibeum contenet corpus[111]
[H]aec primitiva eius oratibus reparata est ecclesia
[H]ic condigne translatus est
ubi episcopus et confessor est factus
ideo in honore duplicatus est locus [. . .]m
s(ub)actus [. . .]s.

Translation: This chamber contains the holy, shrouded body of the confessor Maurus. This, his first church was restored[112] for prayers (as an ora-

as confessor. It is also possible that his status as confessor arose out of heresy accusations and reprisals associated with the period between 325 and 381. See n. 96 above.

111. The wording and grammar of the inscription seem to be awkward due to the employment of an affected poetic style or meter. For some similarities of wording compare the later altar inscription of bishop Eufrasius from the sixth-century basilica, discussed in the appendix by F. R. Trombley in the article by A. Terry, "The Sculpture at the Cathedral of Eufrasius in Poreč," *DOP* 42 (1988) 59–60. The text is from Degrassi, *Inscriptiones Italiae,* no. 92 (= Diehl, *ILCV* 1854) and reads:

+Famul(us) D(e)i Eufrasius antis(tes) temporib(us)
suis ag(ens) an(num) XI a fondamen(tis) D(e)o io-
bant(e) s(an)c(t)e aec<c>l(esie) catholec(e) hunc loc(um)
cond(idit).

112. There are two ways of taking the chronological implications of this phrase in conjunction with the construction terminology in line 5. Šonje's view was that the sarcophagus itself (thus identical to *hoc cubile*) was installed in a *martyrium* located

tory?), and his body was worthily translated from where the bishop and confessor had been taken. For this purpose, the locus was enlarged in his honor . . . (and) prepared. . . .

PROVINCE: Istria (Venetia-Istria)
LOCATION: Aquileia
No. 51: The Hall Church of Bishop Theodore (ca. 317–319).
(Figure 13)

In 1893 during construction on the campanile of the eleventh-century cathedral of Aquileia several portions of ancient mosaic were brought to light. Following the discovery concentrated excavations resulted in the restoration of the well-known double-church of bishop Theodore, which dates to the

---

in Hall I of the fourth-century church and reused in the fifth-century edifice; therefore, he argued that the "restored" and "enlarged" locus referred to the fourth-century hall church, and that "his first church" referred to Maurus' own house, the third-century *domus ecclesiae.* On the contrary, if the "restored" and "enlarged" locus referred to another edifice (so also *hoc cubile*) from the fifth century or to the basilica itself, then "his first church" would refer to the fourth-century *aula ecclesiae.* This suggests that the sarcophagus was from the actual burial of Maurus; it was relocated to the church and inscribed at the time of the construction of the fifth-century basilica. Since the inscription is undatable on its own terms, we must be cautious of the dating implications relative to the construction history of the site. On the basis of the evidence presently available, the second chronological reconstruction is preferrable. It suggests that we should date the *aula ecclesiae* to the middle or later fourth century, at which time it could properly be called the church of bishop Maurus. The fifth-century basilica would have carried the same identity in his memory, as reflected in the wording of the text above. Given the names that appear in some of the mosaic inscriptions from the floors (see nn. 101 and 103 above), it is possible that the interval between the paving of the fourth-century *aula ecclesiae* and the construction of the fifth-century basilica was less than one full generation. Then in the sixth century the entire complex was rebuilt "from the foundations" by bishop Eufrasius, whose name came to be attached to the cathedral. But it is noteworthy that the legacy and identity of bishop Maurus, together with another bishop Eleutherius, with hagiographical exaggeration of the episcopal succession, were preserved in the decoration of the apse of the Eufrasian basilica. In general on the chronological implications of the inscription for Istrian Christianity, see the work of G. Cuscito cited above. Also, on the lateness of the development of episcopal sees in this region, see the comment of Adolf Harnack, *The Mission and Expansion of Christianity in the First Three Centuries* (2d. ed; London: Williams & Norgate, 1908) 2. 258–60, citing passages from Ambrose, *Ep.* 1.63 and *The Life of Ambrose* by Paulinus of Milan (*Vita Ambrosii* 14).

early fourth century. In addition, it has been claimed that this pre-basilical church might have stood on an even earlier *domus ecclesiae.* While the latter claim is not supported by the archaeological evidence, the hall constructed by bishop Theodore in ca. 314–319 does represent an early stage of church building in the form of a large rectilinear hall or *aula ecclesiae,* in the period following the Diocletianic persecutions.

Literature: C. Cecchelli, "Gli edifici e i mosaici paleocristiani nella zona della Basilica," in *La Basilica di Aquileia* (Bologna, 1933) 109–245. G. Brusin, Gli scavi di Aquileia (Udine, 1934). M. Mirabella Roberti, "Considerazioni sulle aule teodoriane di Aquileia," in *Studi aquileiesi offerti Giovanni Brusin* (Aquileia, 1953) 209–43. J. Fink, *Der Ursprung der ältesten Kirchen am Domplatz von Aquileia* (Münster, 1954). G. Brusin and P. L. Zovatto, *Monumenti paleocristiani di Aquileia e di Grado* (Udine, 1957). G. U. S. Corbett, "A note on the arrangement of the Early Christian Buildings at Aquileia," *Riv.AC* 32 (1956) 99–106. H. Kähler, *Die spätantiken Bauten unter dem Dom von Aquileia und ihre Stellung innerhalb der Geschichte des frühchristlichen Kirchenbaues* (Saarbrücken, 1957). G. Brusin, "La piu antica 'domus ecclesiae' di Aquileia e i suoi annessi," *Memorie storiche Forogiuliesi* 43 (1958/59) 33–60. H. Kähler, *Die Stiftmosaiken in der konstantinischen Südkirche von Aquileia* (Cologne, 1962). B. Forlati Tamaro, "Ricerche sull'aula Teodoriana nord e sui battisteri di Aquileia," *Aquileia Nostra* 34 (1963) 86–98. K. Gamber, *Domus Ecclesiae: Die ältes Kirchenbauten Aquilejas sowie im alpen- und Donaugegiet bis zum Beginn des 5. Jahrhunderts liturgiegeschichtliche untersucht* (Regensburg, 1968). [A brief discussion of the various hypotheses may be found in C. H. Kraeling, *The Christian Building* (New Haven, 1967) 134–36.] G. Bovini, *Le Antichità cristiane di Aquileia* (Bologna, 1972). Sergio Tavano, *Aquileia christana* (Udine, 1972). G. Snyder, *Ante Pacem* (Macon, 1985) 73–75. L. Bertacchi, "Architettura e mosaico," in *Da Aquileia a Venezio,* ed. B. Forlati Tamaro (2d ed.; Milan, 1986) 95–332. V. Fiocchi Nicolai "Notizario delle scoperte avvenute in Italia nel campo dell'archeologia cristiana degli anni 1981–1986," *Studi di Antichità cristiana* 61.3 (1989) 2221–44. C. Jäggi, "Aspekte der städtebaulichen Entwicklung Aquileias in frühchristlicher Zeit," *JAC* 33 (1990) 158–96. Ffiona Gilmore Eaves, "Annulling a Myth: A Reassessment of the Earlier Phases of the Eufrasian Basilica at Poreč, and of the Evidence for *Domus Ecclesiae,*" (Unpublished Ph.D. Thesis, Nottingham, University of Nottingham, 1993).

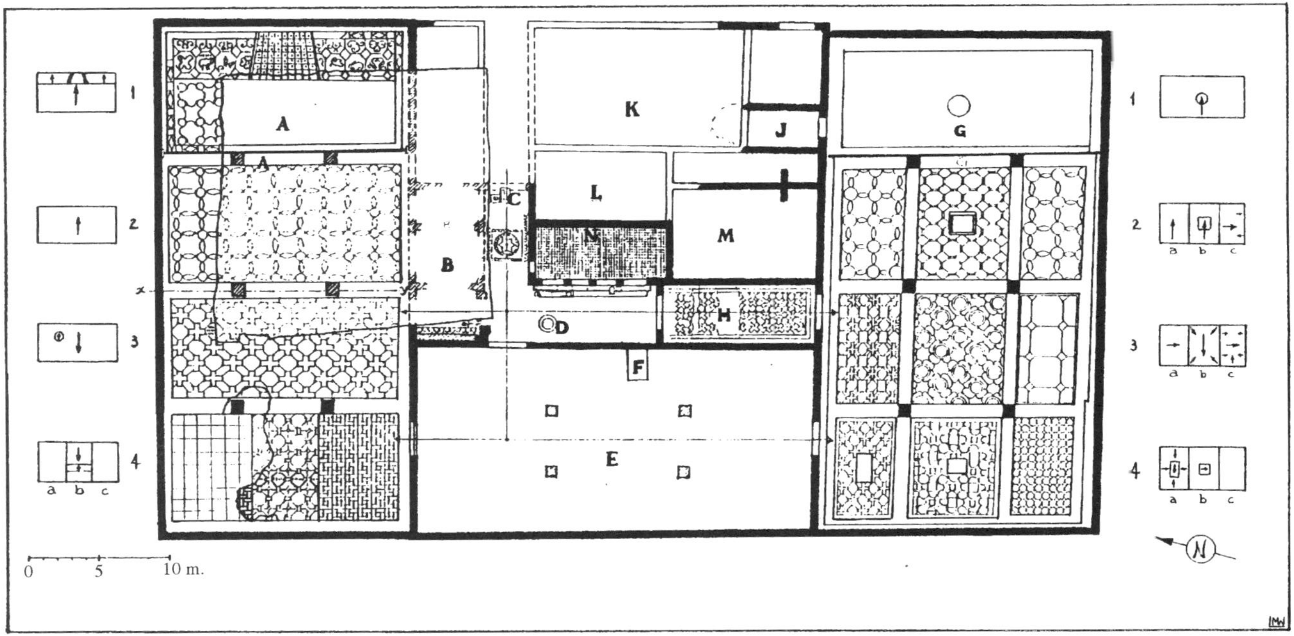

Fig. 13
Istria, Aquileia. Church of Bishop Theodore (early fourth century).
Plan with schematic representation of mosaic orientation

[I am grateful to Dr. Ffiona Gilmore Eaves for her suggestions and additional materials regarding recent archaeological discoveries at Aquileia.]

a. The Church of Bishop Theodore (ca. 314–319)

This moderately scaled complex consists of two parallel halls of rectangular plan oriented on an east–west axis (cf. fig. 13). The north hall (A) measured 37.40 x 17.14–17.25 m; the south hall (G), 37.10–37.37 x 20.10–20.10–20.40 m. Between the two halls other rooms of the complex were arranged around a long, hall-like atrium (D) which provided access to both halls through an entry-chamber on either end (B and H). To the west of the atrium/hallway (D) lay another transverse hall (E), which communicated with both of the main halls (A and G). To the east of D a number of other rooms (J–M) opened off of a peristyle (N) and were accessible from Bay 1 of the south hall G through Room J. It is in no way clear what purpose these rooms served as they are rather poorly preserved; however, a likely solution would seem to be in considering them part of the episcopal residence. The main entrance to the entire complex seems to have been from the east at area C. The dating of this early ecclesiastical complex is difficult and subject to a wide range of interpretations. The identification of the complex is based on an inscription in a roundel of the mosaic in Bay 1 of the south hall (G), to be discussed below, which mentions Theodore.

The name of the bishop Theodore is known among the signatories of the council of Arles (314), and his episcopate is generally dated between 308 and 319/320. These dates are the ones usually assigned to the building of the double-church complex. On the other hand, completion of the complex may have taken longer than the period assigned to bishop Theodore, since a reference from Athanasius of Alexandria mentions an eyewitness report of the church at Aquileia "under construction" during a visit between 336 and 345.[113] As a result of this and other evidence Heinz Kähler suggested a date closer to 325 for the complex; however, an early date of ca. 314–319 is favored by Krautheimer.[114] It is quite possible that one of the halls (probably

113. Athanasius, *Apologia ad Constantium imperatorem* 15 (*PG* 25. 616), written in 357. The reference has been taken in different ways to suggest that the older building was then being rebuilt or was still under construction. On the basis of the evidence discussed below, I will suggest that it refers to the completion of the North Hall (A) or other renovations and decorations within the complex.

114. See H. Kähler, *Die spätantiken Bauten unter dem Dom von Aquileia und ihre*

the south hall, usually thought to be closely associated with the baptismal activities located at J and later F) was built first, and the other (the north hall) added later.[115] Moreover, the mosaics seem to be secondary to the completion of both halls (thus a second or third phase of construction activity that could easily carry down to the time of Athanasius). In either case the Aquileia double-church is often cited as a transitional stage between the renovated *domus ecclesiae* and the monumental Christian basilica, since the halls are not true basilicas in architectural form. They are instead plain halls or *aula ecclesiae.*[116]

Sometime in the later fourth century (up to ca. 400) the north hall was rebuilt. The hall was nearly doubled in length and more than tripled in square-footage by extending it to the east to a length of 73 m and to the south to a width of 31 m. It covered the north hall and a significant portion of the intervening rooms between the two halls, including the original entrance at C and part of the so-called episcopal residence (Rooms H–N). This "post-Theodoran hall," still lacking an apse, would serve as the base plan for the later medieval cathedral complex.[117] A new entrance with quadrangular court was then added to the west end of the hall covering over earlier adjacent houses to the west. A new episcopal residence was also constructed on the annexed property to the north.[118] In the light of the series of later church

---

Stellung innerhalb der Geschichte des frühchristlichen Kirchenbaues (Saarbrücken: Universität des Saarlandes, 1957) 34–40. Kähler, like most others, thought that the North Hall was the earlier. He based his dating in part on the mosaic inscriptions to be discussed below (No. 51c). Krautheimer, *Early Christian and Byzantine Architecture,* 43.

115. G. U. S. Corbett ("A Note on the Arrangement of the Early Christian Buildings at Aquileia," *RivAC* 32 [1956] 99–106) has offered the most persuasive argument, based on the arrangement of the mosaics in the two halls, that the South Hall (G) was the focal point of worship and religious activity in the earlier stages of the Theodoran complex.

116. Compare now the buildings at Qirqbize (No. 38), Philippi (No. 49), Parentium (No. 50). See also Krautheimer, *Early Christian and Byzantine Architecture,* 44.

117. The date of this construction is debated. Krautheimer prefers the end of the fourth century ("Early Christian and Byzantine Architecture," 43–44, 189–90 (which follows Brusin). The extent of the enlarged hall is shown in the plans of Krautheimer (ibid., 44, fig. 9) and Snyder, *Ante Pacem,* 74, fig. 12. On the dating question see especially now L. Bertacchi, "Architettura e mosaico," in *Da Aquileia a Venezio,* ed. B. Forlati Tamaro (2d ed.; Milan: Garzanti, 1986) 218–20.

118. See Bertacchi, "Architettura e mosaico," 349; cf. Sergio Tavano, *Aquileia*

edifices on the site, there have been several proposals regarding the nature of buildings located beneath the early fourth-century complex and their usage.

b. The Earlier Buildings Beneath the Fourth-century Aula Ecclesiae

Two basic pieces of evidence have traditionally been taken to indicate the form and Christian use of the Roman structures beneath the complex; however, little archaeological evidence has been found to corroborate the interpretations of this evidence. The first bit of evidence, as noticed early on by C. Cecchelli, lay in the peculiar orientation of the mosaics of the two main halls and especially those of Hall A (cf. fig. 13 for schematic representation of this orientation).[119] In the north hall (A) it was noted that the mosaics of Bays 1 and 2 were composed so as to be viewed facing east, that is, toward the exedra on the east end. In Bays 3 and 4, however, the mosaics were meant to be viewed facing west, except for the inscription in Bay 4b (discussed below).

The second piece of evidence regarding the earliest stages of the building comes from the succession of fonts (located at F in fig. 13) used in the late fourth-century basilica. Upon examination it was found that this font was built over a basin from the level beneath the transverse hall (E) of the Theodoran complex. It was assumed, therefore, that the basin had been part of a domestic bath establishment associated with the "villa" of which other evidence was discovered in the area between the Halls A, E, and N. The house seems to date from the later first century, but has been variously dated up to the third century.[120]

Several hypotheses have been advanced to explain this evidence in terms of an earlier Christian edifice on the site. First, J. Fink suggested that the halls were originally part of an imperial palace later taken over by the Christians, but the thesis has not been generally accepted.[121] Second, G. Brusin, on the basis of Cecchelli's observations regarding the orientation of the mosaics, proposed what has been the most popular theory regarding the site.

---

cristiana (Udine: Friulane, 1972) 70. Also discussed by Gilmore Eaves, "Annulling a Myth," 299–304.

119. C. Ceccelli, "Gli edifici e i mosaici paleocristiani nella zona della Basilica," in *La Basilica di Aquileia* (Bologna, 1933) 119–20.

120. Bertacchi, "Architettura e mosaico," 182; cf. Gilmore Eaves, "Annulling a Myth," 269.

121. J. Fink, *Der Ursprung der ältesten Kirchen am Domplatz von Aquileia* (Münster, 1954) 57–58, 71–73.

He suggested that Bays 1 and 2 of Hall A (the north hall) were originally part of a single room in a Roman house (measuring ca. 19 x 17 m) and that this room served as the *oratorio* of the earliest Christian edifice, that is, a *domus ecclesiae.* In support of this hypothesis Brusin had conjectured the existence of a west terminating wall for the Roman house on the line xy between Bays 2 and 3 of Hall A.[122]

Mario Mirabella Roberti questioned Brusin's thesis on archaeological grounds: if such a west terminating wall had existed, settling of the mosaics would have made the division apparent. But no such settling or signs of underlying partitions were found. Consequently, the notion of an earlier oratory beneath the eastern part of the north hall was thought unlikely. Thus, Mirabella Roberti put forth a new hypothesis based on the assumption that Hall A was constructed as a unit. He proposed instead that the north hall was constructed over a large urban *domus* with central peristyle and a *tablinum* on the west side, and that this edifice was used as a "community hall" (meaning a *domus ecclesiae*) upon which the Theodoran hall complex was founded.[123] In support of this argument, Mirabella Roberti cited the evidence of continuity betweed the font (F) of the transverse hall, thought to be the main baptistry of the Theodoran complex, and the basin beneath it, thought to be from the house.[124]

More recently, B. Forlati Tamaro undertook analysis of the footing of the north exterior wall of Hall A. She found on the interior face of the wall a foundation wall which, in fact, showed the north hall (A) to be a single construction. In her examination she also discovered that the interior wall footing was constructed as would be normal for the exterior of a wall, that is, with projecting piers or pilasters at regular intervals, and that it belongs to an even longer wall structure that must have stood in the area to the north of Hall A. As a result of these findings, Forlati Tamaro suggested that the

122. Brusin's hypothesis was promulgated in a number of publications. See especially G. Brusin and P. L. Zovatto, *Monumenti paleocristiani di Aquileia e di Grado* (Udine, 1957) 16–19 and plates II and III. The "myth of the Aquileian oratories" is discussed critically by Gilmore Eaves, "Annulling a Myth," 198–226 et passim.

123. M. Mirabella Roberti, "Considerazioni sulle aule teodoriane di Aquileia," in *Studi aquileiesi offerti Giovanni Brusin* (Aquileia, 1953) 218 and fig. 4. Thus, it should be noted from the previous note and other entries in the literature that Brusin continued to espouse his theory of the *domus ecclesiae* even after Mirabella Roberti's objections.

124. Ibid., 220–22.

double-church was actually built using elements of two houses (below the northern aisle of Hall G, areas E–N, and the southern aisle of Hall A) and bridging an intervening street (under what is now the northern two-thirds of Hall A, equivalent to sections a and b of Bay 4, cf. fig. 13).[125]

This important discovery means that Hall A was built in part over a street and could not have been integrally connected to usage of the earlier structures that formed the domestic complex. While this evidence seemed to support Mirabella Roberti's hypothesis regarding the form and domestic character of the earlier structures in the areas to the south of Hall A, more recent discoveries have called this notion into question as well. Subsequent archaeological research has determined that the domestic edifice(s) that lay under areas E–G comes from the later first century. In addition it now has been determined that this domestic stratum was superimposed by an intervening phase of commercial activity prior to the construction of the Theodoran hall complex. The commercial property included a row of shops that ran along the west end of hall E, and included the basin located at F. Consequently, the argument for continuity of usage in the baptistry at F must also be dismissed.[126]

As a result of these archaeological findings it is not possible to make any claims for a direct continuity of usage from the domestic edifice prior to the construction of the Theodoran complex. From an archaeological perspective what now emerges as a key, but as yet unsettled, question regards the circumstances that led to the acquisition of the commercial property, either before or during the episcopate of Theodore. No evidence has been found to indicate Christian usage of any part of the commercial property prior to the construction of the Theodoran complex, even though such a possibility exists in other localities.[127] It is not impossible that some portion of the property was owned by a Christian, even Theodore's family; however, direct evi-

125. B. Forlati Tamaro, "Ricerche sull'aula Teodoriana nord e sui battisteri de Aquileia," *Aquileia Nostra* 34 (1963) 86–98.

126. See Bertacchi, "Architettura e mosaico," 183–84. It has also been determined that the octagonal font at F was not from the Theodoran phase, but from post-Theodoran complex of the later fourth century. The baptistry of the Theodoran complex was found to be situated at the north end of J, but (in contrast to some earlier suggestions) it was found to have no connection to the earlier strata of domestic or commercial use. See Bertacchi, 194–95 and Gilmore Eaves, "Annulling a Myth," 270.

127. Notably San Giovanni e Paolo (No. 52, below) and San Clemente (No. 53) in Rome.

dence is lacking. The area acquired for the construction of the double hall complex was quite extensive and encroached on more than one insula of existing edifices. Immediately to the east of the two halls a commercial granary continued in operation, apparently up until the construction of the post-Theodoran hall, at which time the property was further expanded to the east, north, and west.[128] Thus, the site and planning of the Theodoran *aula ecclesiae* complex suggest a notable step in the fortunes and public presence of the Christian group within the local culture of Aquileia. Their position prior to that time can only be guessed.

c. *Inscriptions from the Church of Bishop Theodore*

Inscription 1: An inscription was found in a roundel in the center of the eastern or first bay of the south hall (G) of the double hall church at Aquileia. It is surrounded by the elaborate Jonah mosaic composition. The text reads:[129]

XP[130]
Theodore Feli[x][131]

---

128. On the site and the areas surrounding the double hall complex, see especially the discussion of Gilmore Eaves, "Annulling a Myth," 299–307.

129. The text is after G. Brusin and P. L. Zovatto, *Monumenti paleocristiani di Aquileia* (Udine, 1957) 111; cf. Kähler, *Die spätantike Bauten,* 35. A photograph of the inscription and the larger mosaic floor is available in both of the above works and in van der Meer and Mohrmann, *Atlas of the Early Christian World,* pls. 139–40, 143.

130. The form of the Chi-Rho monogram here is that of the *labarum* but without an encircling wreath. It may suggest an early Constantinian date (up to 324–325), but the evidence is inconclusive. On the date see the following note.

131. Another inscription from the north hall (A) located in the fourth bay, panel b (see fig. 13) uses the same form. It was read facing east, while the rest of this panel (and all of bay 4) was oriented to be viewed facing west. The text reads:

[Theod]ọre
Felix
hic crevisti
hic felix [. . .]

("Theodore, Happy One, here you have brought forth, here [. . .] happy"). The text is found in Brusin and Zovatto, *Monumenti paleocristiana di Aquileia,* 60; Kähler, *Die spätantiken Bauten,* 34 (and pl. 25).

Kähler argued that the use of the term *felix* in these two texts points to a date after the death of bishop Theodore; cf. *Die spätantiken Bauten,* 34–35. Thus, he places the construction project between 319 and 325. It may well be that he is correct regarding

[a]diuvante Deo
omnipotente et
poemnio caelitus tibi
[tra]ditum[132] omnia
[b]aeate fecisti et
gloriose dedicas-
ti.

Translation: Theodore, Happy One, with the help of the almighty God and of the flock bequeathed to you from heaven, you have made everything happily and dedicated it gloriously.

Inscription 2: An inscription found in the north hall (A) in the third bay under the northwest corner of the later Campanile, and thus partially destroyed (see fig. 13). Read facing east, while the rest of the mosaic was read facing west.[133]

Ianuariụ[s . . ca. 5 . .][134]
de Dei dono[135] ṿ[oto fecit][136]

---

felix as a funerary formula; however, this may only point to the date at which the floor mosaics were commissioned or dedicated, while the rest of the inscription seems clearly to say that the construction project, at least in the south hall, was undertaken during Theodore's life. The parallel inscription in the north hall may be taken to suggest that the mosaics were completed at nearly the same time in the two halls, and that the phrase *hic crevisti* likewise refers back to Theodore's inauguration of the building programs.

132. Brusin (*Monumenta paleocristiana di Aquileia,* 111–12) supplied the lacuna as printed; Kähler (*Die spätantiken Bauten,* 35) also gives this reading. Van der Meer and Mohrmann (*Atlas of the Early Christian World,* 65) offer the alternative reading *[cre]ditum* ("entrusted"]. In either case the meaning is virtually the same.

133. The text is from Mirabella Roberti, "Considerazione sulle aule teodoriane," 231–32; cf. Kähler, *Die spätantiken Bauten,* 32 (and pls. 16, 21).6

134. There is enough space for an abbreviated title, such as *diac(onos).*

135. This phrase clearly means his own personal funds and is commonly used by Christians and Jews. So compare two inscriptions from the mosaic floor (section M7) of the fifth-century basilica at Parentium (Poreč, No. 50 and fig. 12b above). The first reads: *De dunis D(e)i/ s(an)c(t)e e<c>clisie/ Innocentius diaconus/ pro voto suo f(e)c(it)/ p(e)d(es) XC* (Degrassi, *Inscriptiones Italiae,* no. 71). The second reads: *De donis D(e)i et s(an)c(t)e e<c>clesie/ Bassinus diaconus pro votu suo f(e)c(it) p(e)d(es) XC* (Degrassi, *Inscriptiones Italiae,* no. 69). For a similar formula in Greek-speaking Jewish usage from roughly the same period compare the synagogue inscriptions from Sardis (No. 69a) and Stobi (No. 75) below.

136. The reading *v[ovit . . . . . .]* was proposed by Mirabella Roberti, "Conside-

p(edes) DCCCLXXX̣[. . . . .][137]

Translation: Januarius [. . . . .] from the gift of God vowed (or had made according to a vow) 880 feet.

PROVINCE: Italy (Latium)
LOCATION: Rome (Reg. II)

No. 52: *Titulus Byzantis* (third–fourth century) (Church of SS. Giovanni e Paolo)
(Figures 14–15)

The basilica of SS. Giovanni e Paolo is located on the Caelian Hill. Its major axis runs east–west with the apse on the west end facing down the slope of the hill and toward the Palatine. The south wall of the church faces the Clivus Scauri (whose width in ancient times measured ca. 7.00 m); it parallels the church's east–west axis and proceeds down the hill toward the ancient Via Ostiensis (presently the Via di S. Gregorio Magno). The southern façade is a veritable patchwork of masonry, which provided the first glimpses into the building's rich history. The first notice that the basilica actually rested on and incorporated earlier Roman structures came in the late nineteenth century in the work of Father Germano and others.[138] Thereafter more detailed examinations beneath the basilica produced hypotheses regarding pre-Constantinian use of the site by Christians.

The church is associated with the names of two fourth-century martyrs, John and Paul. The hagiography depends on the sixth-century *Passio Johannes et Pauli;* it claims that they were Christian court officials who were martyred under the emperor Julian (ca. 362) and buried "in their palace" on the Caelian. On the other hand, an inscription from the time of Leo I (ca. 440–461) refers to the bishop Pammachius (d. 410) as the founder of the church of SS. John and Paul. The *titulus Pammachi* is mentioned further in

razione sulle aule teodoriane," 231–32. The lacuna might also be restored as *v[oto fecit]* or *v[oluit]*. My own preference is *v[oto fecit];* so compare the inscriptions from Parentium in the previous note.

137. Mirabella Roberti ("Considerazione sulle aule teodoriane," 231–32), following an earlier emendation, read 890 feet and attempted calculations of precisely how much of the actual mosaic floor was meant.

138. A full bibliography indicating the early work on the site may be found in Richard Krautheimer, *CBCR* 1. 267–77.

the signatories of a synod of 499, but its clergy is closely associated with signators from the *titulus Byzantis*. In turn the *titulus Byzantis* is known from an inscription datable to the pontificate of Innocent I (ca. 401–417): TEMPORIBUS SANCTI/ INNOCENTI EPISCOPI/ PROCLINUS ET URSUS PRAESBB/ TITULI BYZANTI/ SANCTO MARTYRI/ SEBASTIANO EX VOTO FECERUNT.[139] As a result of these varied associations, the founding of the church remains confused and clouded. Yet the incorporation of a Roman insula complex into a basilical structure holds interesting possibilities regarding the early Christian use of the site. R. Krautheimer, following the work of A. M. Colini, E. Junyent, A. Prandi, and others, has brought forth the thesis that the insula had become the site of a Christian *titulus* perhaps as early as the last half of the third century and certainly by the beginning of the fourth century. During this period a large hall was created on the second floor of the insula, and it is considered the assembly room, or "hall of the church." For this type of renovation, we may use the term *aula ecclesiae*, since it evolves from the same type of adaptation that produced the *domus ecclesiae*, but it had not yet developed into formal basilical architecture. This *aula ecclesiae* complex was more fully transformed for Christian use during the fourth century; however, it retained its basic form until it was finally superimposed by the present basilical plan around the beginning of the fifth century (ca. 400–410).

Literature: Germano di S. Stanislao, "The House of the Martyrs John and Paul," *AJA* 6 (1890) 201–5; 7 (1891) 25–32. Idem, *La Casa Celimontana dei SS. Giovanni e Paolo* (Rome, 1894). O. Marucchi, "Scoperta (indagini) nella basilica dei SS. Giovanni e Paolo," *NBAC* 7 (1901) 175–76, 226; 15 (1909) 144–49; 21 (1915) 62–63. Germano di S. Stanislao, *La Memoria dei SS. Giovanni e Paolo* (Rome, 1907). F. Grossi-Gondi, "Scoperta della tomba primitive dei SS. Giovanni e Paolo," *Civ. Cat.* 65 (1914) 3. 579–82. J. Wilpert, *Die römischen Mosaiken und Malereien der kirchlichen Bauten vom IV. bis XIII. Jahrhundert* (2d ed.; Freiberg i.B., 1916) 4. 631–36. J. P. Kirsch, *Die römischen Titelkirchen im Altertum* (Paderborn: Schöningh, 1918) 26–32. E. Junyent, *Il titolo di S. Clemente in Roma* (Studi di antichita cristiana VI; Rome, 1932) 107–10. E. Gasdia, *La casa pagano-cristiana del*

139. The text is from Krautheimer, *CBCR* 1. 301 n. 7). For the above references as well as others relating to the later history of the church, see the "Digest" in ibid., 1. 270–71.

Celio (Rome, 1937). R. Krautheimer, "The Beginnings of Early Christian Architecture," *Review of Religion* 3 (1939) 144–51. A. M. Colini, "Storia e topographia del Celio," *Atti Pont. Acad. Rom. di arch.*, ser. III, 7 (1944) 164–70, 182–85. A. Prandi, "Scoperte e restauri nella basilica celimontana dei SS. Giovanni e Paolo," *Atti I CIAC (1950)* (Rome: Pontificio Instituto di archeologia cristiana, 1952) 233–36. Idem, *Il complesso monumentale della basilica celimontana dei SS. Giovanni e Paolo* (Vatican City: Pontificio Instituto di archeologia cristiana, 1953). R. Krautheimer, *CBCR* 1.4: 267–303. G. Snyder, *Ante Pacem* (Macon, GA: Mercer University Press, 1985) 77–80.

[Because of the complicated maze of Roman buildings beneath the fifth-century basilica of SS. Giovanni e Paolo, it would be neither practical nor productive simply to reproduce Krautheimer's lengthy technical analysis of the remains. The following summary is rather an architectural history in stages based on the author's work on site and following Krautheimer's analysis and conclusions. Also consulted for the discussion were the studies of Junyent and Prandi (cited above).]

a. The Oldest Construction (second to mid-third centuries)

The oldest construction in the area is datable to the early second century. There appear to be at least four separate houses constructed in *opus reticulatum* (see fig. 14). These houses likely replaced whatever first-century construction existed in the area.[140] Two of the houses located under the north aisle and under the central portion of the nave were wholly subsumed in third-century construction. The other two (Houses A and B, fig. 14) may have continued in independent use until the construction of the basilica. House A contained at least three stories and continued toward the west along the axis of the Clivus Scauri. There is evidence of renovation in this house in the third and fourth centuries.[141] The pattern of construction in these and later buildings indicates that there was a lane or open court running from the west at an acute angle to the Clivus Scauri.

140. Fig. 14 shows only two of the four: one (A) under the apse and one (B) under the east portion of the nave; for the others see Krautheimer, *CBCR* 1, plate XXVI; cf. 1. 278.

141. See E. Junyent, *Il titolo de S. Clemente*, 106 and fig. 30; Krautheimer, *CBCR* 1. 278.

Another, rather unusual structure (C) was located to the north of this lane. The brickwork construction dates it to the mid-second century. It seems to have contained on its lower levels a thermal establishment, a *balineum* with a private *domus* or apartments in its upper stories.[142] Sometime shortly after the mid-second century this building was expanded to the east (C_2) and west (C_3) along the axis of the lane/court. On the east the addition (C_2) abutted the older *reticulatum* house (B), and there were laid out a trapezoidal court (30) and a small room (29), which were later remodeled. On the west the addition (C_3) created a new façade for House/Bath C facing an open triangular courtyard that was closed off at the west end of the lane. Later still, the northern portion of this courtyard was incorporated into C_3 and a nymphaeum with mosaics and frescoes was installed (last quarter of the second century).

Sometime after the construction and first renovation of House/Bath C (mid to late second century) but before the installation of the nymphaeum in C_3 (end of the second century), a much larger complex (D) was erected between C and House A.[143] The brickwork structure D was most likely an insula with ground-floor shops and at least three (and perhaps as many as five) upper stories. The front of the structure faced the Clivus Scauri at a distance of ca. 6.00 m from the street (area F, later incorporated into D). Along this street-front court were four or five shops (see figs. 14, 15b). Each of the first three units from the west had a back room connected by a doorway. By a small back door (W.1.20 m) the rear apartment of unit 3 opened onto the court between C and D. The ground-floor rooms originally had barrel vaults (H.ca.6.00 m). There was probably a mezzanine floor at H.2.40 m above the floor (at least in unit 1); it was reached by stairs in the northwest corner of the front shop of unit 1. The original plan of the east portions of Insula D are unclear as it was subsequently remodeled. For example, it is not absolutely clear that the original building extended to its present termination point against the west wall of House B. Only a single wall fragment or pier remains in the middle of this area (at the end of wall 23), and there is no indication of the back wall.[144]

---

142. Krautheimer, *CBCR* 1. 279; cf. plate XXVII.

143. Ibid., 1. 280.

144. Krautheimer nowhere discusses the full implications for the upper stories of knocking down ground-floor support walls. Similarly, there is no mention of the fact that the rebuilt rear (north) wall of units 4 and 5 does not continue on the line of the rear wall of units 1-3. Consequently, while some structure on the east end of D is called for, nothing assures us that its plan was like that of the rebuilt units 4 and 5. Is

Early in the third century the east portion of Insula D was rebuilt in a brickwork similar to the original. The changes undertaken in this area (later units 4 and 5) included the following: reconstruction of the partition wall (21) between units 3 and 4, construction of partition walls in the front shop of unit 3 and between units 4 and 5, and reconstruction of the rear wall of units 4 and 5. The reconstruction of this rear (north) wall is most significant because it provided for a vaulted cover spanning the lane and connecting buildings C and D. The height of the vault was at the second-floor level in Insula D. Krautheimer assumes, therefore, that a terrace was extended between the two houses.[145] At the same time the court (30) in the addition (C_2) was vaulted, and a hypocaust room was added over it at the mezzanine level of Insula D. The new complex (consisting of a house, *balineum*, an insula, and shops) was of considerable size. Krautheimer concludes that the owners of C purchased Insula D and introduced the renovations to connect the two.[146]

b. Emergence of the Christian Titulus (mid-third to early fourth century)

Later in the third century more radical renovation of the complex occurred. About the middle of the third century the erection of a brickwork façade along the east portion of the Clivus Scauri marked the construction of a commercial building (E). The front portion of the building contained three barrel-vaulted chambers with a mezzanine level and three more upper levels.[147] The house behind this commercial building remains largely unknown. Room 25 seems to have been a storage cellar behind and below the first chamber. Building E may have incorporated (portions of) the earlier House B; however, there is no indication whether or not the new structure was a dependency of House C (and thus of the entire complex C-D). It is possible that Building E remained an independent unit until the construction of the basilica.

Far more telling for the future of the site was the construction of a façade (area F) along the street front of the insula complex (D). It may be dated

---

it possible that these renovations made possible for the first time the development of upper-level apartments over units 4 and 5 to match the earlier levels above units 1-3?

145. Krautheimer, *CBCR* 1. 281.

146. Ibid., 1. 293.

147. Ibid., 1. 281–82.

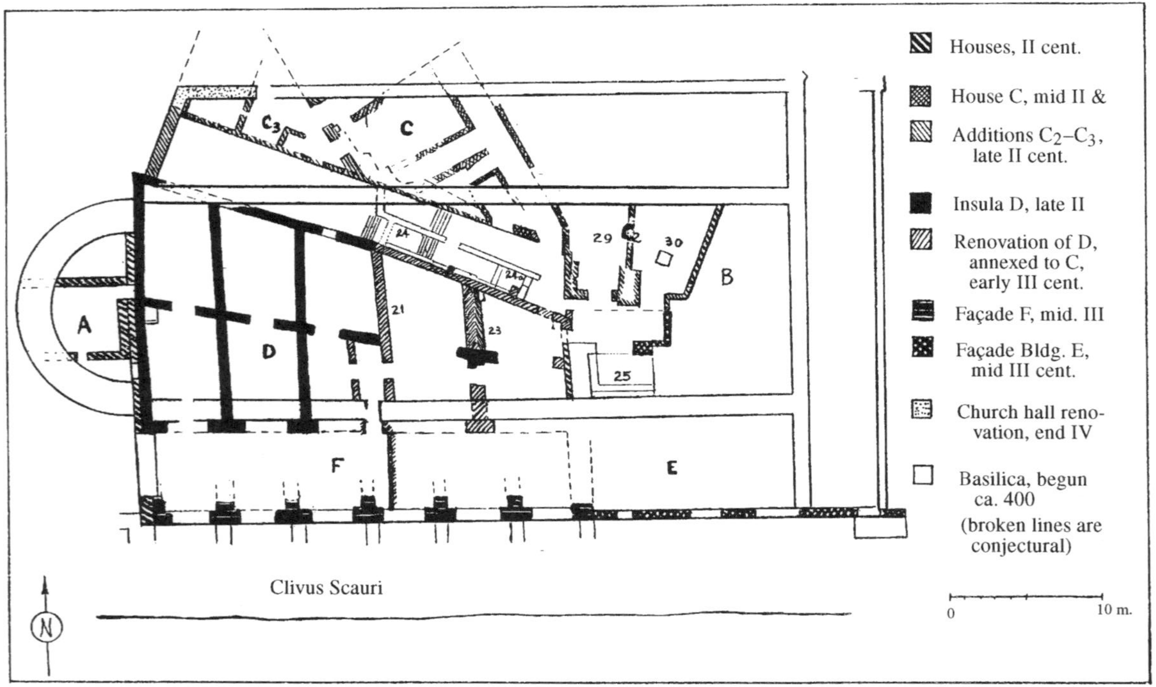

Fig. 14

Italia, Rome. SS. Giovanni e Paolo, third–fifth centuries. Plan restoration, composite in stages of construction (based on Krautheimer, *CBCR* 3)

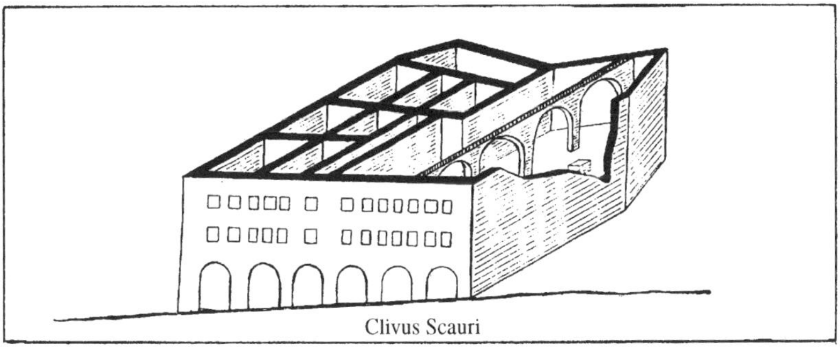

Fig. 15a
Rome. *Titulus Byzantis,* third–fourth centuries.
Isometric reconstruction (after Krautheimer, *CBCR* 3, fig. 158).

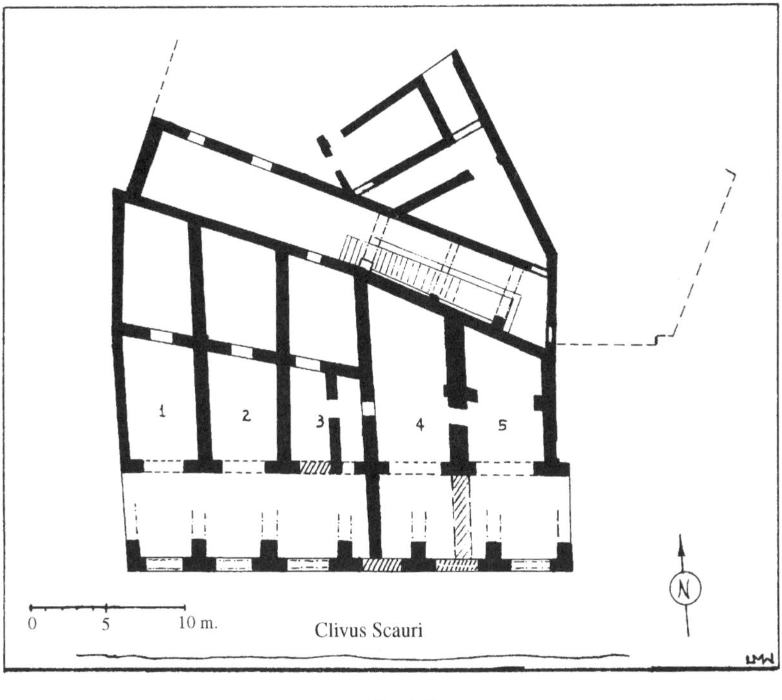

Fig. 15b
Rome. *Titulus Byzantis,* third–fourth centuries.
Plan restoration of renovated insula.

shortly after the middle of the third century and not long after the construction of the façade of Building E. From the ground floor along the south side, the façade (F) opened in six arches onto a portico in front of the shops of D. Above these arches the façade rose in upper elevations matching the upper stories of the insula. This new construction provided more rooms on the street side of D, especially on the west end above units 1-3 (see fig. 15a). Other changes in Insula D occurred in two projects following the incorporation of the façade structure (F). The first was the erection of a number of partition walls in the east portions of the ground floor. One of these partitions (perhaps of a slightly later date) was a massive carrying wall (23) between units 4 and 5 of the insula. The second operation included extending the partition (21) between units 3 and 4 across the portico to the façade. Since this wall interrupts the opening of the fourth arch, it is likely that the arch was sealed. Something similar may have occurred with an extension of wall 23 to the façade (see fig. 14). This means also that communication between the east and west portions of the ground floor was restricted. Also, the front portion of unit 3 was subdivided by the intrusion of wall sections.[148]

In relation to this construction, Krautheimer points to the fenestration of the second- and third-floor levels (as preserved in the church's south façade).[149] He suggests that the arrangement of these windows indicates the interior plan of these upper floors and points to an unusual feature. The five windows on the west side correspond (divided 2 and 3) to units 1 and 2 of the ground floor respectively (see fig. 15a). In the middle of the row of windows, a single opening corresponds to the west subdivision of unit 3 and sets it apart in the second- and third-floor levels. On the east side, however, the fenestration (seven windows of equal size evenly spaced; see fig. 15a) points to a single large hall.[150] He suggests, further, that the later construction of the massive wall 23 was intended to carry a row of pillars or supports in the hall above, probably for a very high ceiling rising through the third-floor level. Krautheimer argues, therefore, that this hall was intended to accommodate a Christian assembly in the later third century.[151]

Christian adaptation of the building is clearly indicated by the early fourth

148. Ibid., 1. 283.

149. Ibid., vol. 1, plate XXVIII.

150. Ibid., 1. 293–94.

151. Ibid., 1. 295.

century, although these measures postdate the construction of the hall facility. The first obviously Christian elements are the frescoes that decorate the back room of unit 3 on the ground floor. Certainly these areas were no longer used as shops. The partitioning of the east portions of the ground floor (see fig. 15b) suggests that the main entrance was from the easternmost arch of the façade through units 5 and 4 to the hallway created in the front room of unit 3. Another adaptation of the structure occurred in the mid-fourth century with the construction of the monumental staircase (24) and the *confessio* (24a). In its final form the staircase leads from the enlarged door at the rear of the painted (Christian) room in unit 3. Enlargement of the door was simultaneous with the construction of the monumental stair, since it caused damage to the frescoes. The stairway was constructed in the southern half of the vaulted cryptoporticus between House C and Insula D. The stairs ascend to a landing at the mezzanine level; from there they turn left and continue above the north half of the cryptoporticus to the second-floor level, that is, to the large hall. At the mezzanine level the landing provided the venue for the *confessio*. The *confessio* was constructed as a deep square shaft rising from the floor of the cryptoporticus up to the second floor, where a mensa likely protruded through the floor to mark the spot. A room below the stairway permitted viewing of the *confessio* from the ground floor.[152] Krautheimer thinks, however, that the landing and the *confessio* (perhaps as the *martyrium* or shrine of SS. John and Paul) were a secondary alteration after the staircase had already been installed.[153] Traces of steps continuing up on the same line as the first flight suggest a monumental ascent directly to the second-floor level. The installation of the *confessio*, then, forced the change in the plan. Originally the staircase would have put the entrance to the hall near the middle of the long east side of the room (see fig. 15b). This may suggest something of the arrangements of the Christian assembly, that is, oriented toward the west as was the later apse. The construction of the staircase belongs to the mid-fourth century, at which time a clearly Christian use of the hall seems likely. The installation of the *confessio* belongs to the later fourth century, quite in keeping with the traditional dates assigned to the martyrdom of SS. John and Paul.

152. Ibid., 1. 285–86.
153. Ibid., 1. 284–85.

c. Construction of the Basilica (ca. 400–410)

At the beginning of the fifth century the entire complex was transformed into a Christian basilica. Yet this transformation occurred in two chronologically proximate stages. The first project, begun probably just at the end of the fourth century, was intended basically to expand the second-floor meeting hall over the same area now covered by the nave and the side aisles. In other words, the initial plan was for an enlargement of the *aula ecclesiae* form through subsequent renovation. This project did not, however, include the foundation walls that now mark the side aisles. Thus, what was envisioned would not appear to be a formal basilica plan. In this first stage the two façades along the Clivus Scauri (areas F and E) were leveled in height and the apertures walled shut with *opus mixtum*. Internally, House E was annexed to the rest of the complex in order to extend the hall to the east. In order to extend the hall to the west the upper floors of House C and the apartments above units 1 and 2 of Insula D were sacrificed. The construction of the new second-floor hall was begun at the northwest corner (at the exterior wall of what is now the north aisle; see fig. 14), but it was soon halted.[154]

Apparently what halted this renovation was a substantial change of plans. What, if any, other factors (such as a collapse or fire) might have prompted the change are unknown. The next project began not long thereafter with the construction of massive brickwork walls cut through the entire length of the complex as foundations for the side aisles. As a result, the ground-floor rooms of the original structures were made inaccessible. An apse was then added on the west end over House A, which till then had remained untouched by the previous constructions. On the east end there was a narthex and probably an atrium. Krautheimer dates the basilica, in keeping with the Pammachius reference, to ca. 400–410. The construction was completed by the mid-fifth century. He further conjectures that the references to two separate *tituli* of Byzans and Pammachius may derive from joining the independent structure E to the Christian complex C–D. The original Christian *titulus* (in C–D) he calls the *titulus Byzantis*. The establishment of the basilica became the *titulus Pammachii*. While the basilica incorporated the *titulus Byzantis*, the latter, because of its traditional association, retained some nominal identity in an attached clergy.[155]

154. Ibid., 1. 297.
155. Ibid., 1. 301.

PROVINCE: Italy (Latium)
LOCATION: Rome (Reg. III)

No. 53: *Titulus Clementis* (third–fourth century) (Basilica S. Clemente)
(Figures i, 16–17)

The present Church of S. Clemente on the Esquiline is a twelfth-century basilica (consecrated in 1128 under Pope Paschal II), which has since been remodeled and redecorated on several occasions. The medieval structure is notable for its unusual orientation, with its apse on the west end and its façade and an atrium on the east. Traditionally the church has been associated with the figure of Saint Clement of Rome, in Christian tradition identified with a certain Flavius Clemens, who was martyred under the emperor Domitian (see Dio Cassius, *Hist.* 67.14; Eusebius, *H.E.* 3.18.4). These traditions were imbued with new interest in 1852, when F. G. Mullooly discovered a second basilica beneath the level of the twelfth-century church. Subsequent excavations determined that this earlier basilica dates to the end of the fourth century. During these excavations yet another level of construction was found (in 1857) to consist of two buildings dating from as early as the first and second centuries, and upon which the fourth-century basilica was based. Finally, in 1867 a mithraeum was discovered in the westernmost of the two buildings, in the area below the apse of the fourth-century basilica (see No. 87 below). The earlier of these two buildings, probably a warehouse, had been thought the property (even a house) of Saint Clement, assuming that Christians might have met there from the first century. This notion remains undemonstrable on the basis of any historical or archaeological data. Careful analysis of the excavations up to the middle of the twentieth century was carried out by Krautheimer. Subsequent excavation work began in 1979 and continues up to the present time, under the direction of the Dominican Fathers of S. Clemente. In addition to providing further clarification regarding the earliest layers beneath the present church, these new excavations are expected to yield fresh finds in the areas around the Roman and early Christian levels. The reconstruction of the building history up to the time that the first basilica was erected is based on fragmentary structural data, since much of it was covered over or subsumed in later layers of construction. But there are indications that the Roman buildings under the earlier basilica were renovated during the third century to serve as a large hall

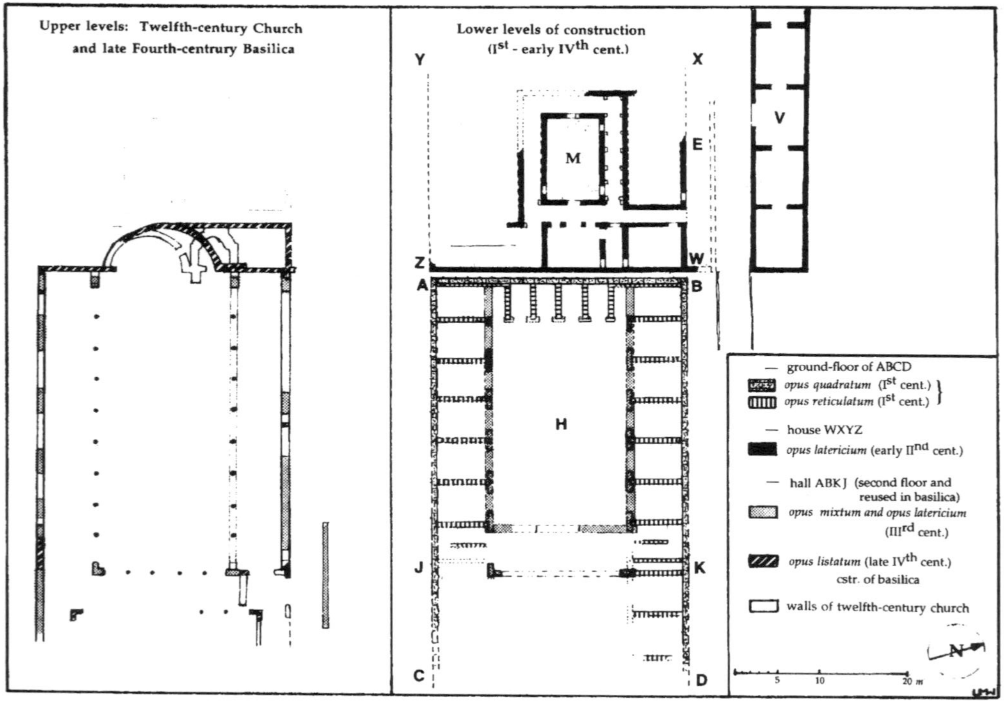

Fig. 16

Italia, Rome. S. Clemente and *titulus Clementis,* second–fourth centuries. Plan restoration, composite with stages of construction (after Guidobaldi, adapted).

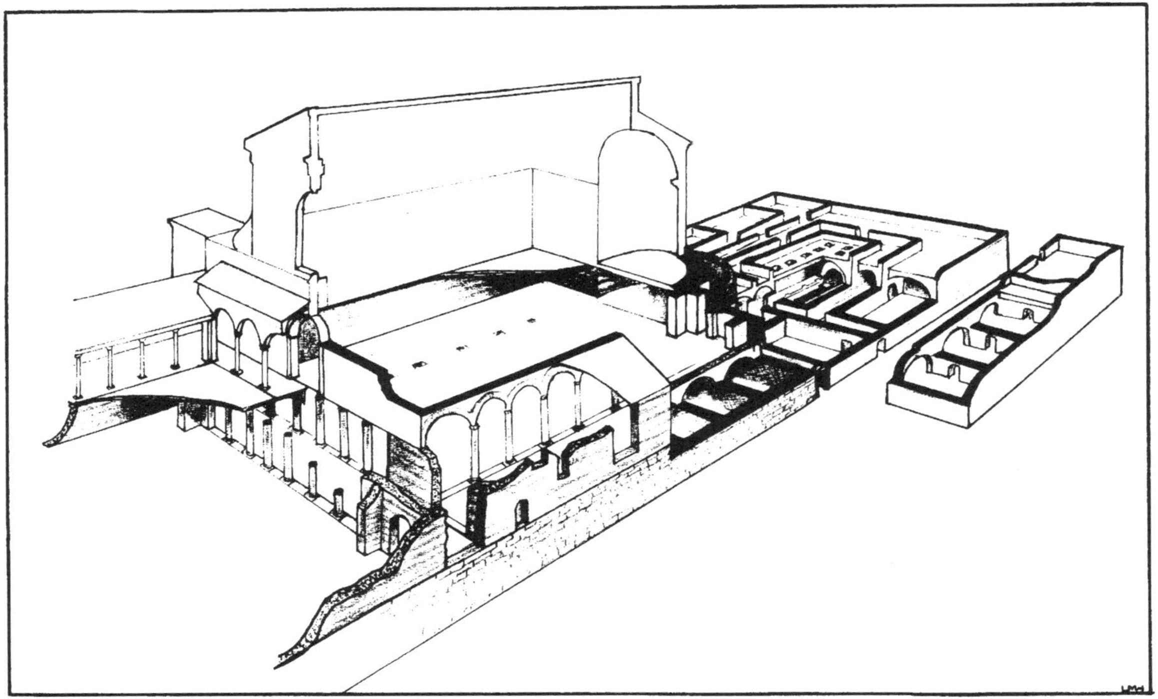

Fig. 17
Italia, Rome. S. Clemente. Isometric reconstruction
(after drawings of F. Corni and V. Consentino, adapted)

and, thus, might well have housed a pre-Constantinian Christian community, at least in the stage just prior to the construction of the first basilica.

Literature: G. de Rossi, "Prime origini della basilica di S. Clemente," *BAC* 1 (1863) 9–13, 25–31 (+ "Appendice" 39, 89–90). Idem, "La pitture scoperte in S. Clemente," *BAC* 2 (1864) 1–7. Idem, "I monumenti scoperti sotto la basilica di S. Clemente studiati nella loro sucessione stratigrafica e cronologica," *BAC* Ser. 2, 1 (1870) 129–53; cf. 125–27 and 153–68. (Also see *BAC* in the years 1874, 1875, 1884–85, 1888–89 for continuing reports.) F. G. Mullooly, *The Church of S. Clemente* (Rome, 1869). Idem, *St. Clement and his basilica in Rome* (2nd ed.; Rome, 1873). J. P. Kirsch, *Die römischen Titelkirchen im Altertum* (Paderborn: Schöningh, 1918) 36–40. L. Nolan, *St. Clement's Tunnel* (Boston, 1914). Idem, *The Basilica of St. Clement* (3rd ed.; Rome, 1925). E. Junyent, "La primitiva basilica di S. Clemente e le costruzioni antiche circostanti," *RivAC* 5 (1928) 231–78. Idem, *Il titolo di S. Clemente in Roma* (Studi di archeologia cristiana VI; Rome: Pontificio Instituto di archeologia cristiana, 1932). Idem, "Nuove indagini sotto la basilica primitiva di S. Clemente," *RivAC* 15 (1938) 147–52 F. Deichmann, "Zur Datierung der Unterkirche von S. Clemente in Rom," *Mitteilungen des deutschen archäologischen Institut,* Römischen Abteilung 58 (1943) 153–56. R. Krautheimer, *CBCR* 1:117–45. G. Snyder, *Ante Pacem* (Macon, GA: Mercer University Press, 1985) 76–77. Leonard Boyle, *St. Clement's, Rome* (1962; repr. Rome: Collegio San Clemente, 1989). Federico Guidobaldi, with appendices by Irene Bragantini and Paul Lawlor, *San Clemente: Gli Edifici Romani, La Basilica Paleocristiana, e le Fasi Altomedievali* (San Clemente Miscellany IV.1; Rome: Collegio San Clemente, 1992). [The last work provides a history of the excavations up to 1990 and a comprehensive bibliography.]

[The reconstruction that follows is based primarily on the work of Krautheimer, *CBCR* 1 (which was based on the previous excavation work up through the time of Junyent's, *Il titolo di S. Clemente*) but has been updated. The present author has examined the site on two occasions, the most recent thanks to the hospitality of the Dominican priory at S. Clemente and the current director of the excavations, Fr. Paul Lawlor, O.P., so that new discoveries have been incorporated, as reflected in the compilation of Guidobaldi, cited above.]

In excavating at the level of the earlier basilica, it was discovered that the south wall and left aisle of the medieval church corresponded exactly to that of the lower basilica. But on the north side the earlier basilica was much wider; the north exterior wall of the medieval structure was on the line of the colonnade of the earlier north aisle, which had been reinforced with brickwork in the intercolumniations (see fig. 16). The arched spanners in the intercolumniations of the right (north) aisle are visible just above the floor level of the upper church, as they were incorporated into the lower course of the right (north) side wall. The span of the arc marking the line of the apse in the earlier building was also much wider. Finally, it was found that the wider north aisle of the earlier basilica (W.6.27 m) was in closer proportion to the south aisle (W.5.82 m) than the north aisle of the later building (W.3.57 m). Thus, the initial investigations of the earlier basilica revealed a wider and more symmetrical edifice. Further investigation revealed that its plan was based on the lines of the earlier building beneath it.

a. The Earlier Buildings (first–third centuries)

The level of construction beneath the earlier basilica was found to consist originally of two separate buildings, both dating from the imperial period (see fig. 1, in the introduction above). The ground floors of these two buildings were used to form the foundation level below the early basilica, while the first floor of each building was incorporated into the construction of the basilica proper. The easternmost of these two buildings, now called the *horreum* (labeled ABCD; see our fig. 16), corresponds to the side walls of the lower basilica. The building to the west (labeled WXYZ), also known as the "house of the mithraeum," formed the west end-wall of the nave, and the apse was erected in what had been the area of several rooms on its first floor.

Edifice ABCD was originally a rectangular structure constructed in heavy walls of tufa block and Travertine (Th.ca.1.05 m). The width on the west end was 29.60 m (or 100 Roman ft.). The overall length cannot be determined since the eastern extremities have been lost to subsequent construction, but it certainly extended well beyond the nave of the earlier basilica. It probably extended to the east end of the current atrium/cloister, or approximately 60-64 m (i.e., ca. 200-210 Roman ft.).[156] This building may be dated by its con-

156. Junyent had proposed a length of 59.20 m (200 Roman ft.); see Krautheimer, *CBCR* 1. 122 and n. 2. Mullooly had originally traced part of the tufa construction to

struction to the late first century, probably in the Neronian rebuilding after the fire of 64 CE. Its character and use, however, remain unclear. The only interior plans that can be determined consist of a row of narrow chambers (L.ca.4.30 m) around the exterior, with a wide, open aisle down the middle. These chambers were separated by partition walls (Th.0.45 m) in *opus reticulatum* interspersed with layers of brick, typical of the later first century. The floor in these chambers was paved with brickwork (*opus spicatum,* or herringbone pattern) typical of lower-grade public or commercial use. These internal arrangements suggest that the building was perhaps a *podium* for some sort of public building or, more likely, a *horreum* or warehouse.[157] Based on references in Roman literature to a mint (*moneta*) in this area of the city, some had thought that this warehouse-type structure might be it; however, this conjecture does not seem likely.[158] Remains of the upper floors of this building are scant, but they indicate brickwork construction dating to the late first or early second century. The internal plan of the upper floors is indeterminate. There is no indication that any part of the ground floor was used for domestic activity, and it is unlikely that the upper floors formed a domestic insula (or apartment building). Consequently, the suggestions that this property was owned by Clement of Rome and was used by Christians for a "house church" near the beginning of the second century are not supported by the archaeological record.

Building WXYZ was separated from ABCD by a narrow passageway (labled tu on fig. 16), sometimes called "Clement's alley" (W.0.80 m). Building WXYZ, which sits ca. 0.50 m above the level of ABCD, was a large private *domus* (with upper stories) constructed in very fine brickwork (*opus latericium*) of the second century.[159] Because of the slope of the hill, the east

the east for several hundred (English) feet, and a length of up to 500 Roman feet (or 148 m) was at one time proposed. The current proposal uses R. Lanciani's plan for a crossing street just to the east of the present church atrium; see F. Guidobaldi, *San Clemente: Gli Edifici Romani, La Basilica Paleocristiana, e le Fasi Altomedievali* (San Clemente Miscellany IV.1; Rome: Collegio San Clemente, 1992) 48–49.

157. On the brickwork, see E. Junyent, "Nuovo indagini sotto la basilica primitiva di S. Clemente," *RivAC* 15 (1938) 147–48. For the podium, see Junyent, *Il titolo di S. Clemente in Roma* (Rome: Pontificio instituto di archeologia cristiana, 1932) 42; for the *horreum,* see Krautheimer, *CBCR* 1. 122 and n. 5. The current excavators have generally verified the latter view; see Guidobaldi, *San Clemente*, 58–64.

158. See Guidobaldi, *San Clemente*, 62, for references and discussion.

159. Krautheimer, *CBCR* 1. 123 and n. 3, contra Junyent, *Il titolo*, 56–57. See also Guidobaldi, *San Clemente*, 73–94.

portions of the ground floor may have been below ground level. A stairway descended to this level from the street that ran along the south side of the two buildings. The floor of the first level above was 0.60 m higher than the ceiling vaults in the later chambers in ABCD. The passageway (tu) was covered with a vault that may have served as a pavement for an entry to the first-floor level of house WXYZ (see fig. 16). The house was organized around a central cortile (M) with a vaulted portico on all sides. During the early to mid-third century this cortile (M) was converted into a mithraeum (see No. 87 below). The full extent of this house remains unknown, especially in its western portions. On the north side, it appears that there was a row of vaulted chambers (labeled E1-8), which may go back to an earlier construction (of Claudian or Neronian date) and were incorporated into the second-century house. Contrary to earlier reconstructions, it now appears that there was a narrow street separating these chambers from another row of chambers to the north (labeled V1-5). This street or passageway seems to have continued to the east along the north side of tufa-block building ABCD and was later incorporated into the construction of the earlier basilica.[160]

b. The "Hall" Building (mid-third century)

At some point after the construction of house WXYZ, the upper stories of tufa building ABCD were replaced by a brick structure datable to ca. 250–275 CE.[161] The type of brickwork in the lower courses and the fact that the new walls were set back from the north wall by ca. 0.50 m suggest that the tufa walls were covered over as a subfoundation below ground level. To support the upper building the entrances to the vaulted chambers in ABCD were sealed with reinforcing brickwork (*opus mixtum*). The brick structure above became the ground floor of a new building, probably constructed as a hall on the lowest level, perhaps with an insula above.

160. See now Guidobaldi, *San Clemente*, 42, 76–77 (and Tav. II, III) contra the plans of Junyent, as used by Krautheimer, which portrayed all these rooms as part of a single edifice.

161. So Krautheimer, *CBCR* 1. 125, based largely on the brickwork. Guidobaldi has now confirmed this basic view with the discovery of a stamped amphora fragment (from Severan period) that was deposited in this construction (*San Clemente*, 115–16). He assigns a *terminus post quem* of 230–240 for the availability of the spoil and, hence, a date in the middle of the third century for the construction of the hall edifice.

The floor level of the new edifice was ca. 0.50 m below the level of the first upper floor of house WXYZ. The north and south side walls of this new building were incorporated into the construction of the earlier basilica. The plan of the hall might have had shops on the street side,[162] while the interior hall on the ground floor may have served related functions, for example, a factory hall.[163] The interior arrangement of this building cannot be determined, but there seem to have been two load-bearing walls and/or rows of piers (or columns) along the east–west axis. This formed a U-shaped area in the middle of the large hall. This type of arrangement would have been typical of guild or commercial halls, where small shops or trading could be conducted in the outer ambulatory area, while the central hall space could be used for larger gatherings. Wall JK (the entrance to the earlier basilica) may contain remnants of a north–south transverse partition, but this is the only such transverse wall discernible. Krautheimer suggests that the transverse wall JK was the entrance to the building,[164] but recent work has confirmed that the building continued to the east, probably to the extent of the earlier levels below. However, the form and use of these eastern portions of the building are not known. The conclusion, therefore, is that the first floor of ABCD was at this time constituted as a large hall (ABJK) with pillars running along the east–west axis (roughly on the lines of the colonnades of the earlier basilica). Above the hall, presumably, would have been other levels containing domestic quarters of the common tenement sort. It is in this hall area that Krautheimer thinks a Christian group might have begun meeting, sometime in the later third century. The strongest evidence in support of this view is the fact that Christians were clearly in possession of the building prior to the construction of the first basilica at the end of the fourth century.

---

162. Junyent had proposed that in the south wall AB were several large arched doors that had been walled up in the fourth-century construction (*Il titolo*, 45–46; see Krautheimer, *CBCR* 1. 124). He proposed further that they opened onto other rooms at street level rather than onto the street itself. The row of vaulted rooms along the north side of WXYZ was considered a proximate analogy. However, Guidobaldi has expressed reservations about the existence of any arched openings in the south wall, though there do appear to be three doorways or openings in this wall (*San Clemente*, 98; cf.Tav. IV).

163. See R. Krautheimer, *Early Christian and Byzantine Architecture* (3d ed.; New York: Penguin, 1979) 30.

164. Krautheimer, *CBCR* 1. 124.

There is evidence of intermediate renovation prior to the construction of the basilica proper that further substantiates this view.[165]

c. The Basilica (ca. 400)

The basilica was erected near the end of the fourth century, probably between 392 and 417.[166] It incorporated the basic scheme and dimensions of this third-century ground-floor hall and its foundation elements. Thus, the line of pillars, reinforced in the subfloor with a rubble wall, became the aisle colonnades. On the east end a narthex (L.4.15; W.28.05 m) and atrium were constructed. On the west end, wall AB was knocked down at the first floor level; the east wall WZ of the "house of the mithraeum" became the west wall of the nave. In order to construct the apse, this wall was pierced and the semicircular foundation was extended out over the ground-floor apartments E and F (which had been access areas associated with the mithraeum) of house WXYZ.

d. Chronology

This reconstruction of the archaeological evidence leads to the following chronological scheme:

1. Construction of tufa building ABCD (late first century)
2. Construction of house WXYZ (end of the first century or early second century)
3. Renovation of cortile (M) of WXYZ for use as a mithraeum (late second or early third century)
4. Rebuilding of ABCD as hall (ABJK) (mid-third century, ca. 250–275)
5. Renovation of ground floor of hall ABJK (with "court" JKCD) and part of house WXYZ to create the Christian basilica (late fourth century, ca. 392–417)

Since the documentary and literary evidence[167] seems to confirm the traditional existence of a Christian community (known as the *titulus Clementis*)

165. Guidobaldi, *San Clemente*, 119–22.

166. Krautheimer (*CBCR* 1. 133–34) first proposed the late-fourth-century date; contrast Junyent's proposed sixth-century date (*Il titolo*, 142). Guidobaldi cites additional evidence for narrowing the range of dates to 392–417 (*San Clemente*, 155–56).

167. These are collected in Krautheimer, *CBCR* 1. 118.

prior to the construction of the basilica, Krautheimer concluded that the ground-floor hall of ABJK was already in use as a Christian assembly hall well before the basilica was constructed.[168] Yet Krautheimer was more cautious that Junyent, who had assumed that the third-century hall was designed from the outset for Christian usage. Krautheimer suggested that the upper floors of the insula (rather than the ground-floor hall) contained the original meeting place. In this case the hall would have been taken over only later and gradually, probably in the late third century. This hall structure would have been minimally adapted for Christian use at first, we might guess, and would thus have formed an *aula ecclesiae*. It continued to function in this form throughout the fourth century, well after the beginnings of basilical construction elsewhere in Rome. In this regard, its chronology is comparable to that of the *titulus Byzantis* (SS. Giovanni e Paolo; see No. 52 above), which was not converted to formal basilical plan until ca. 400–410. In the case of the *titulus Clementis* it is important to notice how the form of the basilica was determined (at a relatively late date) by the constraints of an existing structure already in Christian use. The focal point of the nave in the basilical plan seems to be the area of the earlier third-century "hall." The apse was created by extending out over the "house of the mithraeum," which would seem to have been incorporated structurally only at the time of the construction of the basilica. Unfortunately, there is no direct evidence for who owned the property or how it came into Christian hands.

PROVINCE: Italy (Latium)
LOCATION: Rome (Reg. III)

No. 54: *Titulus Aequitii* (or *Sylvestri*) (early fourth century) (Church of S. Martino ai Monti)

(Figure 18)

The Romanesque church of S. Martino ai Monti lies near the crest of the Oppian Hill with its apse facing northwest down the slope of the hill. The apse itself is some 2 m above the present ground level. To the west (and slightly askew) of the ninth-century basilica lies a complex of rooms (A-L; see fig. 18) that have long been noted for their antiquity. The floor level of this complex is 10 m below the floor of the church; the vaulted ceiling of the

168. Ibid., 1. 134–36.

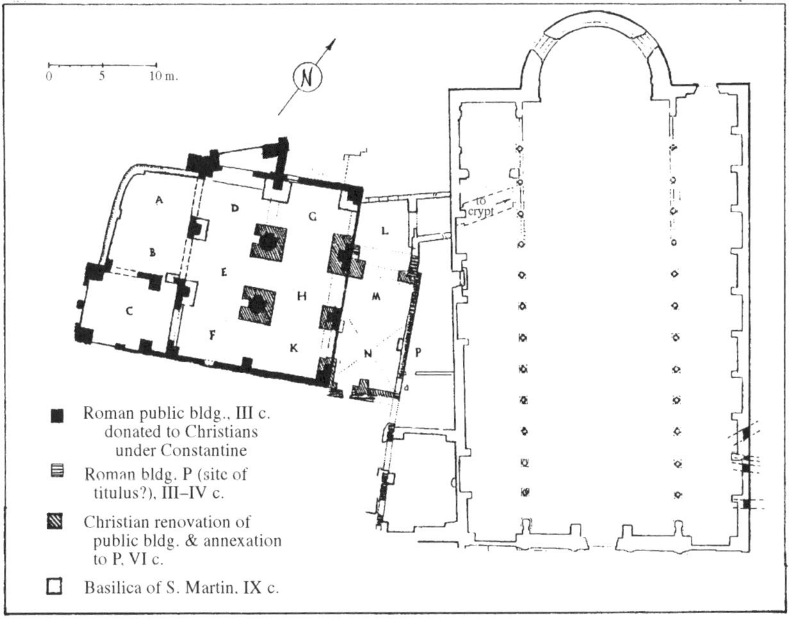

Fig. 18

Italia, Rome. S. Martino ai Monti and the *titulus Equitii,* third–ninth centuries. Plan restoration, composite with stages of construction (based on field plan of Corbett in *CBCR* 3).

complex lies 3 m below the church. In the medieval period a mezzanine and two stories were constructed over the ancient rooms in connection with the monastery that lies to the west of the church. The oldest level of rooms, dating from the second to fourth centuries, was brought to light in 1642–55 during restoration work on the church. At the same time, during work on the crypt, an ancient *confessio* was discovered beneath the old high altar, and it was found to be connected directly to the Roman complex. Traditional identification preserved in the *Liber Pontificalis* made it possible to relate the Church of S. Martin to the Church of S. Sylvester and ultimately to the name of Equitius.[169] According to the tradition, Pope Sylvester (314–334) founded a church near the baths of Domitian on the property of the presbyter Equi-

169. For the texts, see Krautheimer, *CBCR* 3. 89–90; cf. the discussion in R. Vielliard, *Les origenes du titre de Saint Martin-aux-Monts à Rome* (Rome: Pontificio instituto di archeologia cristiana, 1931) 12–14.

tius, and the church was called the *titulus Equitii*; thus the passage from the *Liber Pontificalis* I (ed. Duchesne, p. 170): *Hic fecit in urbe Roma ecclesiam in praedium cuiusdam presbiteri sui, qui cognominabatus Equitius, quem titulum romanum construxit, iuxta termas Domitianus, qui usque in hodiernum diem appellatur titulus Equitii*. . . . In another passage (*Lib. Pont.* I, p. 187) apparently the same dedication of Pope Sylvester is also called the *titulus Silvestri*.[170] On the basis of these texts and the archaeological analysis of the Roman building, René Vielliard reconstructed his picture of the *titulus Aequitii* as a third-century house church in the central rooms of the older Roman complex. Further analysis by Krautheimer and others has challenged this; these rooms do not seem to have served as a Christian meeting place as such, prior to the construction of the basilica. Nonetheless, Krautheimer argues that, as part of a semipublic building (shops or an insula), they may have served as the entry chambers for an early Christian meeting place located in the area beneath the present basilica. Unfortunately, no archaeological work has been done in the area beneath the basilica to explore these suggestions further.

Literature: R. Muñoz, "Chiesa di S. Martino ai Monti," *NBAC* 17 (1911) 109. S. Silvagni, "La basilica di S. Martino: l'oratorio di S. Silvestri e il titolo constantino," *Arch. Soc. Rom. Stor. Patr.* (1913) 329–32. Idem, "Il titolo constantiniano di Equizio," *NBAC* 19 (1913) 167–70. J. P. Kirsch, *Die römischen Titelkirchen im Altertum* (Paderborn: Schöningh, 1918) 41–48. René Vielliard, *Les origines du titre de Saint Martin-aux-Monts à Rome* (Studi di antichita cristiana IV; Rome: Pontificio Instituto di archeologia cristiana, 1931). R. Krautheimer, *CBCR* 3.87–124. C. Davis-Weyer and J. Emerick, "The Early Sixth-Century Frescoes at S. Martino ai Monte in Rome," *Römisches Jahrbuch für Kunstgeschichte* 21 (1984) 1–60.

[It will not be necessary to reproduce the lengthy archaeological analysis of Vielliard and Krautheimer, since it generally points to construction of the fifth century and afterward, all associated with the basilica. We shall rather summarize Krautheimer's reconstruction of the architectural history and use in the third to fourth centuries.]

170. On the vexed question of dating and authenticity in the composition of the *Liber Pontificalis,* see the discussion in Vielliard, *Les origines*, 15 and n. 4, but compare Krautheimer, *CBCR* 3. 121–23.

In its original state the Roman building consisted of a central hall (L.17.20; W.14.20 m) that was divided by piers into six cross-vaulted bays (D, E, F, G, H, K; see fig. 18). The entrance to the building was by a vestibule and a large arched doorway in the north wall of D. The areas to the south and east (Rooms L, M, and N) were originally open yards, and there were windows in the south and east walls of H and K. The west boundary of D and E was similarly a wall facing onto an open court (A-B). Bay F was faced on the west by an antechamber (C).

In contrast to Vielliard, Krautheimer sees no direct evidence of Christian adaptation in this building for a place of assembly. The first indications of Christian renovations in the hall for ecclesiastical purposes do not occur until the beginning of the sixth century.[171] On the basis of the original layers of masonry, Krautheimer dates the first building to the early third century, as does Vielliard.[172] The public nature of the building's plan suggests for Krautheimer something like a market hall or other commercial building.[173]

At a distance of 6.20 m to the east of the exterior wall of H and K was located the west wall line of a separate building (P) datable to the late third century. This west wall of P runs parallel to the east wall of the hall complex, which suggests that the later building was sighted on the same axis as the earlier one. (The axis of the basilica is roughly 12° west of the common axis of the hall complex and P.) Only a portion of the west wall of P is now extant, as most of the building is lost under the Romanesque nave. The north extremity of building P seems to have been ca. 10.50 m south of the north wall line of the hall complex. Between the hall and P was an open court area, and P opened by a door (a) onto the southeast corner of this court. Further data regarding the structure of P are completely lacking except for a few remnants of third-century wall construction in the substructure of the east wall of the Romanesque basilica.[174] These remnants suggest the presence in the later third century of other buildings oriented on roughly the same east–west axis as the Roman hall and P. Other third-century masonry found at the level of the basilica floor indicates further that P contained levels above the ground floor of the hall. Sometime after the initial construction of

171. See Krautheimer, *CBCR* 3. 115.

172. Ibid., 97–98; see Vielliard, *Les origines*, 28.

173. See J. B. Ward-Perkins, "Constantine and the Origins of the Christian Basilica," *PBSR* 22 (1954) 69–72.

174. See our fig. 18, which is based on Krautheimer, *CBCR* 3, plate III.

P, the court area (N) between it and the hall (Room K) was roofed over with a square cross-vault. The north portion of the court (M) was covered with an open-ended barrel-vault; on the north the new Room M opened (presumably by a gate) onto the street. This covered court now formed an elaborate vestibule for the enlarged entrance (a) to P. The east wall of the hall complex was directly affected in this construction, especially as the east fenestration of H and K was closed. Beyond this structural connection, however, there is no evidence in the earliest stages that the two buildings were physically interdependent.[175]

In a second stage of renovation the two buildings were interconnected by piercing the east wall of H and K with arched doorways. This modification of the structural design of the hall necessitated buttressing the vault arches of H and K. Krautheimer sees in this renovation the establishment of an entry complex leading to what must have been the Christian assembly hall in P. Access was provided from the north entrance in D leading through the vaulted rooms (D, E, F, H, K) of the hall complex to the inner vestibule (M, N). The hall was further elaborated to enhance its function as an antechamber to the assembly hall in P, probably to serve as a martyrium. Krautheimer dates this ultimate transformation of the Roman building to ca. 500 under Pope Symmachus.[176] Features of this renovation included installation of cross arches (at G/L, L/M, and K/N), wall and ceiling decoration (e.g., a gemmed cross in the vault of E), and mosaics (e.g., that of S. Sylvester in F). The Christian "hall" P (its character uncertain) was finally overlaid by the ninth-century basilica of Sergius II. But in the interim further renovation and modification of P are likely.

Krautheimer concludes, then, that the *titulus* associated with the property of Equitius must have been located in building P just before and/or during the Constantinian donations, beginning in 314. It is not unlikely that this property would have been adapted for Christian use, probably as some sort of hall, under the auspices of Pope Sylvester during the early to mid-fourth century. The site known in the sixth-century documents (as reflected in the *Liber Pontificalis*) may be equated with the incorporation under Symmachus of the Roman hall (now to be called the *titulus Sylvestri*, because of the mosaics) into the church complex beginning to be known under the name of

175. Krautheimer, *CBCR* 3. 116.
176. Ibid., 3. 122–24.

S. Martin.[177] This reconstruction of the data provides a useful view of the consolidation of ecclesiastical property after Constantine; however, the form and character of an original Christian meeting place (the *titulus Aequitii*) remain inferential. No evidence exists prior to the Constaninian period, and any direct evidence of Christian adaptation of an earlier meeting place, if it exists at all, is most likely buried under layers of subsequent construction beneath the basilica.

PROVINCE: Italy (Latium)
LOCATION: Rome (Reg. XIV)
No. 55: *Titulus Chrysogoni* (ca. 310)
(Basilica S. Crisogono)
(Figures 19–20)

The present Church of S. Crisogono is a twelfth-century basilica situated on one of the main streets of the Trastevere (the ancient Via Aurelia). To the south of the basilica proper lies a monastery that was partially removed in 1878–80 when the first hints were found that an ancient basilica might lie beneath it. Systematic excavations were begun in 1906–8 after O. Marucchi had made a significant discovery of ancient wall structures. The excavations were resumed (after a nine-year hiatus) in 1923 under G. Mancini. During this phase of research, the lines of the earlier basilica were discovered. Like the medieval structure, the earlier basilica had a western apse, but the entire lower structure was parallel but further to the south along this east–west axis (see fig. 20a). Thus, the south aisle columns of the medieval basilica were supported in part by the north exterior wall of the earlier structure. The plan of the earlier basilica (dated to the late fourth or early fifth century) shows a number of irregular or, one might say, "primitive" features. Not the least of these features is the presence of an aisleless nave. In reconstructing the history of this structure, R. Krautheimer has proposed that the basilica was constructed by incorporating a large rectangular hall of an earlier date. He dates this hall to the beginning of the fourth century, and he considers it to be a pre-Constantinian hall structure used as a "church building." By the mid-fifth century it had come to be associated with a certain Chrysogonus, a martyr from Aquileia.

177. Ibid., 3. 123.

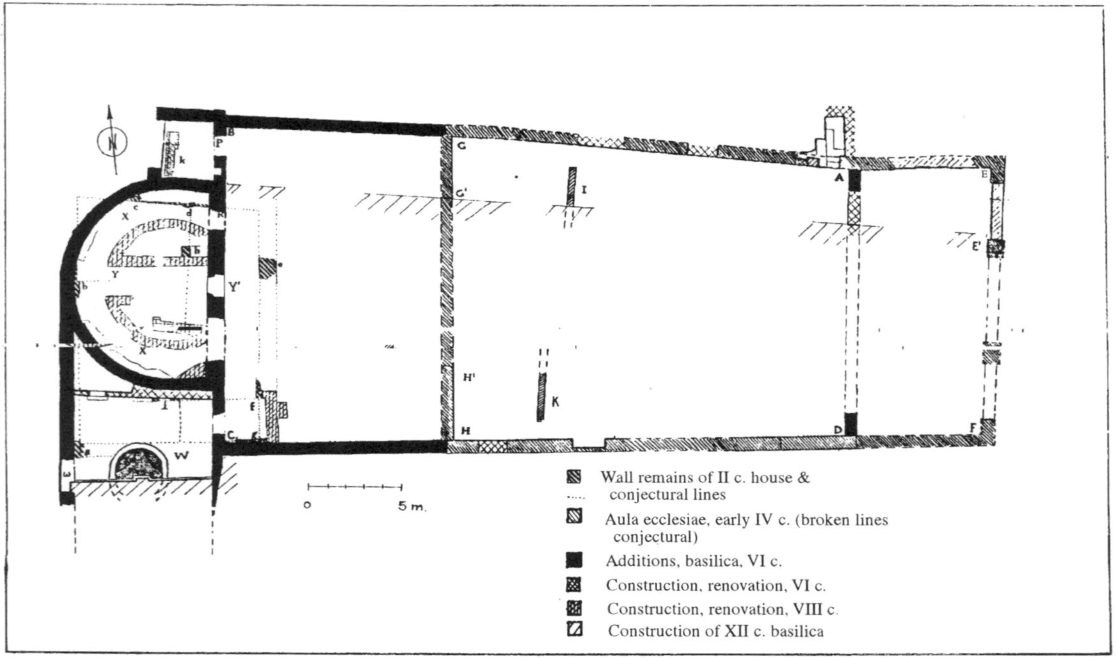

Fig. 19

Italia, Rome. S. Crisogono and *aula ecclesiae,* fourth–sixth centuries.
Plan restoration, composite with stages of construction
(based on field plan of W. Frankl in *CBCR* 1).

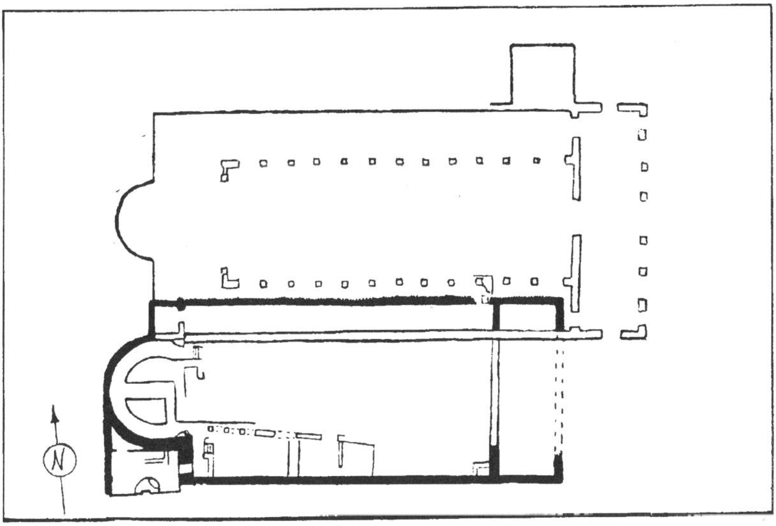

Fig. 20a
Italia, Rome. S. Crisogono. Siting plan of fourth–sixth century church beneath medieval basilica.

Fig. 20b
Italia, Rome. S. Crisogono. Isometric reconstruction of first church building (*aula ecclesiae*), ca. 310 (after Krautheimer, *Rev. of Rel.*, 3)

New excavations have only recently (1993–94) been undertaken on the earlier buildings beneath S. Crisogono, focusing initially on further investigation of Krautheimer's proposals. No notices of the work have yet been published, but according to reports from knowledgeable sources in Rome some interesting discoveries have been made that will tend to verify Krautheimer's basic views. Yet indications are that some modifications will be proposed regarding the plan of the early-fourth-century Christian hall.

Literature: O. Marucchi, "Scoperta dell'antica basilica di S. Crisogono," *NBAC* 14 (1908) 149–50, 259–62. Idem, "La recente scoperte . . . di S. Crisogono," *British and American Archaeological Society* 4 (1908–9) 280–84. Idem, "L'antica basilica di S. Crisogono," *NBAC* 17 (1911) 5–9. J. P. Kirsch, *Die römischen Titelkirchen im Altertum* (Paderborn: Schöningh, 1918) 108–11. G. Mancini, "Gli scavi sotto la basilica di S. Crisogono," *Atti della pont. Acad. rom. di Arch.* 2 (1923–24) 137–41. M. Mesnard, *La basilique de Saint Chrysogone à Rome* (Studi di antichita cristiana IX; Rome: Pontificio instituto di archeologia cristiana, 1935). R. Krautheimer, "The Beginnings of Early Christian Architecture," *Review of Religion* 3 (1939) 144–59. Idem, *CBCR* 1. 144–64. Idem, *Early Christian and Byzantine Architecture* (3d ed.; New York: Penguin, 1979) 37–38. B. M. Apollonj-Ghetti, *S. Crisogono* (Chiesa illustrate XCII; Rome, 1966).

[The reconstruction of the pre-Constantinian building derives wholly from the archaeological analysis of the fourth-to-fifth-century basilica. The following analysis is based on the works of Mesnard (*La Basilique*) and Krautheimer (*CBCR* 1). Based on reports of the yet unpublished recent work, some further indications will be incorporated here. But these must for now be considered tentative and preliminary.]

The early basilica (fig. 19, bldg. ABCD) was constituted as an aisleless rectangular nave of irregular proportions (L.35.35; W. at AD 17.25; at BC 19.25 m). On the east end there was a portico (ADEF) (L.7.25; W.17.25 m); on the west a horseshoe apse (L.8.25; W.max.10.75 m) with an annular crypt. The apse was flanked by a small room to the north and a larger one (W) to the south. Room W (L.ca.7.69 m) was cut by the medieval foundation walls, but if the door (w) was in the center of the room (as the position of the font would suggest), then W may have been as wide as 10.65 m. In the center of the room stood the circular font (Diam.2.50 m), likewise bisected by the medieval wall. Composition of the basilica as discovered clearly included elements from as early as the fourth-fifth centuries and as late as the seventh and eighth centuries. It was apparent, therefore, that the earlier basilica had undergone periodic renovation and remodeling.

Several peculiar architectural features were discovered in the composition of this basilica:

First, in excavating below floor level, several wall sections (H.ca.0.51 m) were found at points H and G and some slightly higher ones at points K and I. The walls of Room W were found to be of similar construction to the south nave wall adjacent to it (HC). In the apse and Room W a number of wall fragments (founded at 5.61 m below the medieval building) of brickwork construction (loci a-i, fig. 18) indicate the existence of an earlier structure datable to the second century (perhaps a house).

Second, in examining the composition of the nave walls it was discovered that the north wall was not a homogeneous construction. The west end (from G to B and including the apse and the north side chamber) was of *opus mixtum* datable to the late fourth or early fifth century. It was founded at a level 4.55 m below the datum line of the upper church. The east portion of the north nave wall (from G to E), however, was a single brickwork construction (L.29.50 m). It was founded at the 5.06 m level below the datum line of the upper church (or ca. 0.5 m below that of the apse area). Its brickwork dated from the early fourth century. At G and E corners were found to indicate that this north wall construction was originally integral with the wall segments found under the nave floor (GG'). The composition of the south nave walls on the east (at H and D) and the subfloor wall HH' were of the same brickwork composition as the north nave wall (GE). It was noted further that the two subfloor sections (GG' and HH') were cut down to precisely the level (4.55 m from the datum line of the upper church) at which wall BG was founded. Finally, it was noted that the east wall of the nave (AD) was raised on two pillars (at A and D) of the same *opus mixtum* construction as the walls in the west portion of the nave. The rest of the extant portions of wall AD are of still later construction in *opus mixtum* (perhaps from the seventh century with other subsequent reinforcement work).

On the basis of these findings Krautheimer (following Mesnard) identified six different levels of construction in the early basilica. They range from the early fourth century to the eleventh century; however, only the first three of these levels are of primary concern here. The first level (Krautheimer's level α)[178] is undoubtedly the most significant, for it represents the construction of a simple rectangular building (EGDH) (L.29.50; W.17.25 m) with brickwork walls (Th.0.725 m). Of the side walls, EG on the north seems to have been completely closed; the south wall (FH) had two doorways. The main entrance was from the east end.

Based on limited evidence of an arch in the eastern wall (at EE') Krautheimer suggested a triple-arch (or triportal) façade.[179] Although yet unconfirmed, the recent archaeological work on corner E has verified the basic lines of this eastern termination; however, it does not appear that there were three openings in the eastern façade. On the basis of the masonry, Krautheimer dates this first building to the beginning of the fourth century, possibly ca. 310.[180] There is no evidence of interior partitioning, as there are uninterrupted wall paintings extant from this first period. The existence of wall supports suggests a beamed roof construction over the entire hall.

The central portion of the west wall (HG) is not extant. While there was almost certainly no formal apse, a small niche or exedra (though unlikely) is not entirely ruled out.[181] It is also possible that an exedra could have been added in a second phase of this building. Such remodeling is indicated in the west portions of the hall, where two thin (Th.0.35 m) partitions were constructed on a slightly raised floor (I, K). This is Krautheimer's level α', and it may represent a raised bema on the west end of the hall. While the two sections (I, K) do not form a continuous lateral line (K is 0.75 m west of I), Krautheimer thinks they represent the division of the hall by a choir screen, with entrance provided at either end and perhaps in the center. At the same time, three openings were made in the north wall conceivably onto some kind of portico or court. Any such structure, if it ever existed, was lost in the medieval construction. Krautheimer surmises in any case that at least by the time of the first renovation, but more probably from its construction, the hall was used for Christian assembly.[182] He thinks, therefore, that the lateral divi-

178. *CBCR* vol. 1, plate XXI.1.

179. Ibid., 1. 153; cf. our fig. 20b. This reconstructed drawing will now need to be modified on the basis of the current archaeological work.

180. Ibid., 1. 157; see Mesnard, *La Basilique*, 29.

181. *CBCR* 1. 153; see Mesnard, *La Basilique*, 32.

182. *CBCR* 1. 155, 166–68.

sion of the nave and the creation of side doors were for segregation of the clergy. To Krautheimer's reconstruction of this phase one further qualification may be added. If the west wall (HG) had not originally contained an apse, as seems likely, then the apparently liturgy-oriented renovations of the second phase (sometime in the mid to late fourth century) might well be expected to include the installation of an apse or niche fixture on the raised platform of the west end. Any such fixture is, however, purely conjectural.

The radical transformation of the building occurred in the third stage (Krautheimer's level β). At this time the entire west wall (HG) was knocked down to 0.51 m, and the hall was extended 12.22 m by the construction of the *opus mixtum* wall extensions GB and HG. The west end of the new building was completed with the construction of the apse and its two side chambers. It is not clear whether the second-century structure under the apse (loci a-i) had already been destroyed or was intentionally dismantled to make room for the apse. The latter appears more likely, given the preservation of some of the features of this earlier structure; however, evidence of a direct connection (or relationship) of this earlier house (?) to the first rectangular hall is lacking. The floor of the new apse was raised 0.46 m above that of the nave using the support wall RS. In front of the apse was a *confessio* at Y'.

As noted above, the apse itself was built over and partially incorporated remnants of the second-century house (Krautheimer's level ζ), most significantly at locus e in the construction of the *confessio*. It would appear that by this time, the nearby house had come to be associated with the name of the martyr Chrysogonus, but whether there was an earlier connection one cannot determine. At this stage the large chamber W was entered only from door w; the font belongs to this stage as well. On the east end of the building (at a distance of 7.25 m from wall FE) partition AD was constructed, perhaps with intermediate columns. It serves to divide the nave from a narthex, which had not previously existed in this building. The construction may be dated no later than the middle of the fifth century on the basis of the masonry.[183] At this point, it appears that there were conscious attempts to make the older, more "primitive" hall edifice conform to formal features of basilical planning.

In later stages in the sixth-eighth centuries the basilica was remodeled further with the addition of the annular crypt in the apse and the reconstruction

183. *CBCR* 1. 159; see Mesnard, *La Basilique,* 61.

of the choir with a bema above the *confessio*. Full treatment of these later developments may be found in Krautheimer and Mesnard.

PROVINCE: Mauretania Caesariensis
LOCATION: Altaua (Altava)

No. 56: Memoria and "Basilica" (309-334) From a Sepulchral Inscription

Discovered at Altava some 300 m northeast of the city in what appears to be the cemetery, now in the Musée d'Oran, a limestone *mensa* (H.1.68; W.1.05; Th.0.50 m) broken at the top right and badly defaced along the top and in the lower corners. The text mentions not only the martyr Januarius, in whose memory the *mensa* was dedicated, but also a *confessio*, a *memoria*, and a "basilica" built by the bishop L. Tannonius Rogatus to commemorate honored individuals from the congregation. The inscription is given in three portions: (A) two lines at the top on the surface of the stone; (B) four lines centered in a large recessed panel in the center of the stone (H.0.88; W.0.72 m); (C) five lines in a recessed panel along the bottom (H.0.26; W.0.88 m). Letters: (A) H.0.045; (B) H.0.10; (C) H.ca.0.05.

Literature: J. Marcillet-Jaubert, *Les Inscriptions d'Altava* (Aix-en-Provence: Éditions Ophrys, 1968) 32–35 (= no. 19), and plates 7–9.

[The following reading is after Marcillet-Jaubert with corrections and alternative reconstructions according to published photographic plates.]

A [———] DOM [$^{2-3}$———][184]
[———]
B Mẹ(n)sa Iaṇ-
uarị Maṛ-
ṭỵris. P[i]-
ẹ Zeseṣ.[185]

---

184. DOM (lapis, line 1). The text of A is beyond recognition except for the three letters. They suggest that some sort of address to Christ as Lord (*Dominus*) may have provided the heading, which was along the top edge of the *mensa*.

185. P[i]E ƷESEṢ (lapis, lines 5–6): Marcillet-Jaubert's suggestion to take this as a latinized reading of the Greek πιὲ ζήσῃς is warranted and in keeping with the clear

C [Confe]ssione sancti et basilica dominica
[et] memoria b(eatorum) v(irorum), Honorati
Ẹp(iscopi), Ta[n-
n]oni Victori Z(aconi), et Tannoni R[ufini]-
ani Ẹp(iscopi), fecit L. Tannonius Rog[atus]
[Epi]s(copus) IIII ab Honorato, a(nno) p(rovinciae) CCLXX[.....]

Translation: [———the Lord (?)———]. (This is) the mensa of the martyr Januarius. Drink and you shall live. The *confessio*[186] of the saint, the dominical basilica, and the *memoria* of the(se) blessed men[187]—Honoratus the bishop,[188] Tannonius Victor the deacon, and Tannonius Rufinianus the

---

use of the Greek ζ (in a script form ʒ, in line 6) and in the latinized *z(akonus)* (line 9; see n. 188 below). Marcillet-Jaubert also cites the discussion of F. J. Dölger, in *ΙΧΘΥΣ* 5 (1943) 74, 83 for support in reading this as a standard formula in Christian funerary reference. Given the reference to the martyr Januarius (about whom nothing is known), we may also consider the phrase an allusion to "drinking the cup of martyrdom," which produces "life."

186. In lines 7–8, for *confessione, basilica,* and *memoria* Marcillet-Jaubert would read the accusative, the *m* having been omitted.

187. BB VV (lapis, line 8). The doubling of the letters ensures the plural reading, *beatorum virorum*, but the number is unspecified.

188. Line 8: ẸP (lapis). Marcillet-Jaubert had originally read in this line LP, which he was then forced to leave as an unintelligible abbreviation. Close examination of the photographs provided by Marcillet-Jaubert makes it possible that the first letter is actually an "E" with only a hint of the upper and middle strokes remaining (see esp. pl. 8). If this reading is accurate, it allows a more consistent reading of the rest of the text. In line 10 we have probably an elided version of the same abbreviation (Ᵽ) also in very poor condition. Taken together with the general use of ecclesiastical terminology it is easy to understand these as abbreviations for *episcopus*, a latinized form of the Greek. This is also in keeping with the Greek in the abbreviation for deacon in line 9. There the stone gives Σ (a Greek sigma with a bar) which is taken as a technical abbreviation for *zaconus=diaconus.* [Note also the use of the Greek in lines 5–6; cf. n. 185 above.] Finally, in line 11 the lacuna at the beginning is, in this light, understandable as another abbreviation for *episcopus*, the stone having originally read EPIS or ⱣIS. Marcillet-Jaubert mentions the possibility of reading "P" or "LP" before the S, but he demurs to make any reconstruction. I think the meaning is clear.

This means, further, that the designation of Tannonius Rogatus as the fourth bishop since Honoratus places him in a clear succession of local bishops going back into the third century. Further, if one looks carefully at the other names in this list of "blessed men," all of whom hold ecclesiastical office, it appears that there is a likely

bishop — L. Tannonius Rogatus, the fourth bishop from Honoratus, made in the year of the province 270 (?).[189]

---

familial relationship, perhaps a father and son(s). Given the likely date of the inscription (see n. 189), this pushes the line of succession at least to the Diocletianic period (as would seem likely in the case of the martyr Januarius) and probably well before into the third century. For other cases where familial succession in church offices may be observed in the Diocletianic period see No. 21 (n. 30) and No. 47 (n. 68) above.

189. CCLXX[. . . . .] (lapis, line11). The date accepted by Marcillet-Jaubert is that of the stone without emendation, 270. The most natural reading of the text would be to mark the date of the dedication of the *mensa* by L. Tannonius Rogatus. It would mean, therefore, that the other building projects mentioned (the *confessio* and the *memoria*, both of which were presumably close to the "basilica" or church edifice) would have been either previously completed or part of the same project commemorated in the *mensa* itself. That it was part of a single project is suggested by taking the *confessio sancti* as a dedication to the same martyr, as indicated by the syntax. Thus, we may have here a partial record of a larger building project undertaken by the bishop sometime near the end of the Diocletianic persecution. Still, some further considerations must be addressed.

The provincial date 270 would be equivalent to 309 CE. If correct, this early date would be of great significance. It should be noted, however, that the last X and the rest of the line are damaged. While it is not necessary for the date to occupy all the remaining space, there is enough room for the reading CCLXXXX (et) V. This would give us a maximal provincial date of 295 (=334 CE). Of course, there are other combinations of numbers that would fit the remaining space and would fall between 309 and 334. A date sometime after 313 (when Constantine's edicts for return of Christian property were issued in letters to the proconsul of Africa, No. 35 above) is quite feasible).

The use of the term "basilica," if taken in its technical architectural sense, would be impossible for the earlier date, and even at the later would be one of the earliest known uses of the term in North Africa. Therefore it is best taken without technical architectural signification. It most likely refers to an early church building of some simpler form, such as a large plain hall now being adorned with *confessio* and *memoria*. If the martyrdom of Januarius is placed in the persecution of Diocletian, the date 309 could possibly be taken as the time of his death; however, this does not seem the most natural reading of the text. This means that the fourth bishop, L. Tannonius Rogatus, represents a familial succession going back into the third century. While this is somewhat surprising for such a locality, it is not impossible. It may help to explain why a single, very prominent and wealthy family should have been so central to the leadership of the local Christian community over a long period of time. Nonetheless, given these factors it is prudent to give the dates 309–334 as the clear limits within which the inscription may be dated.

PROVINCE: Britannia
LOCATION: Lullingstone (Eynsford, Kent)
No. 57: Roman Villa and Christian *Domus Ecclesiae* (ca. 280–390)
(Figures 21-23)

The site of the Roman Villa, known from its discovery at the north edge of Lullingstone Park near Eynsford in Kent, was in antiquity one of a number of Roman settlements along the fertile Darent Valley. Other such settlements have been found every few miles along the river, such as at Stone-by-Faversham. The presence of Roman ruins and artifacts near the river at Lullingstone Park had been noted since the eighteenth century and again in 1823 and 1939. Systematic excavations in the area were conducted from 1949 to 1961 under the direction of Col. G. W. Meates, with the support of the Kent Archaeological Society. The excavations yielded elaborate evidence of a Roman estate, founded near the end of the first century CE. The villa went through three stages of occupation, construction, and elaboration before a Christian "chapel" was installed in one room on the north end of the house. At this time, the rest of the house continued in domestic use. The initial construction of the chapel is dated to the mid-fourth century. Later, toward the end of the fourth century, it is possible that the house and chapel were given over to the Christian community, since domestic use seems to have diminished. Thus, despite its relatively late date, this site provides one of the few cases where incremental stages of adaptation in a domestic edifice can be observed archaeologically (i.e., where only part of the edifice was renovated for specifically religious function). The entire estate was destroyed by fire in the early fifth century and abandoned.

Literature: Yearly excavation reports published by G. W. Meates et al. in *Archaeologia Cantiana* 63 (1950) lff.; 64 (1951) 160; 65 (1952) xlvii, 26ff.; 66 (1953) xlii, 15ff.; 68 (1954) xliv, 206ff.; 69 (1955) xlv, 201ff.; 70 (1956) 249; 71 (1957) xlv; 72 (1958) xlviii; 73 (1959) xlviii; 76 (1961) l[L]. The entire find up to 1954 was published in a lengthy reconstruction and summary by G. W. Meates, *The Lullingstone Roman Villa* (London: William Heinemann, 1955). Idem, "Lullingstone Roman Villa," in *Recent Archaeological Excavations in Britain*, ed. R. L. S. Bruce-Mitford (London: Routledge & Kegan Paul, 1956) 87–110. An updated summary report was issued following the completion of the excavations: Meates, *Lullingstone Roman*

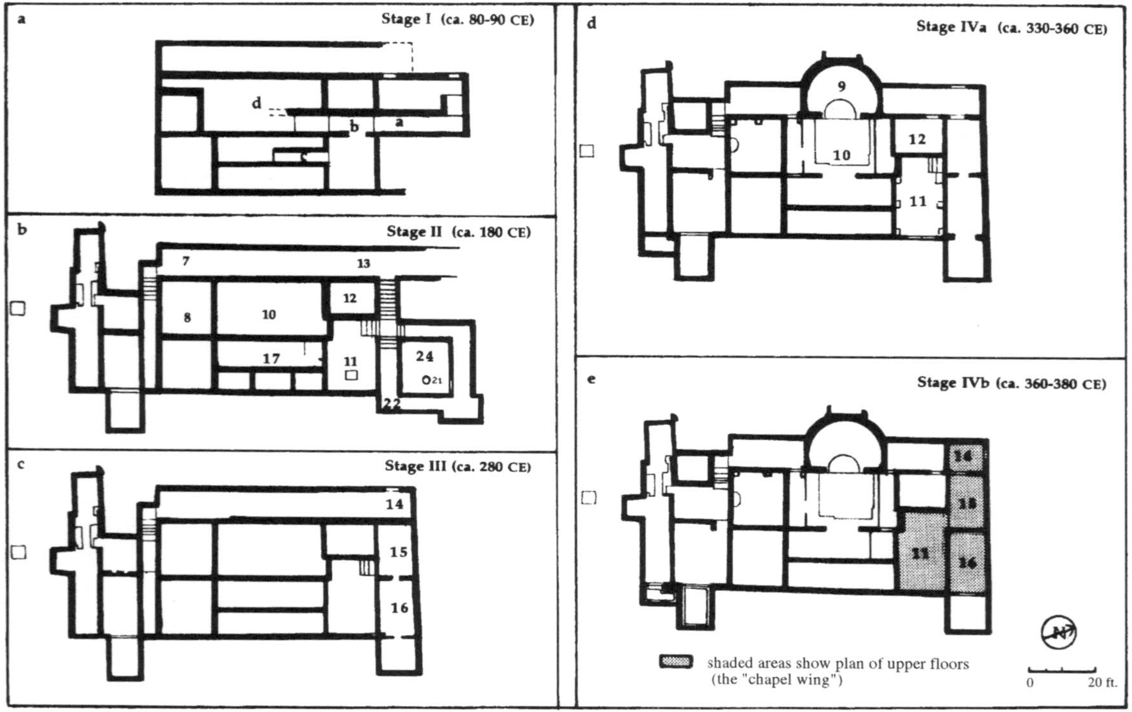

Fig. 21

Britannia, Lullingstone. Roman villa and Christian chapel, first to fourth centuries.
Plan restoration in stages of construction (after Meates).

Villa (Dept. of the Environment Guide; London: HMSO, 1963). The final reports of the site were prepared after further study by G. W. Meates et al., *The Roman Villa at Lullingstone* (2 vols.; Chichester: Phillimore, 1979, 1987). [The second volume was completed after the death of Col. Meates.] J. Liversidge and M. Weatherhead, "The Christian Paintings," in Meates, *The Roman Villa,* 2. 11–40. R. Reece, "The Roman Coins," in Meates, *The Roman Villa,* 2. 48–51. R. Morris, *Churches in Landscape* (London: Dent, 1989). D. Watts, *Christians and Pagans in Roman Britain* (London: Routledge, 1991). F. Gilmore Eaves, "Annulling a Myth: A Reasessment of the Earlier Phases of the Eufrasian Basilica at Poreč, and the Evidence for *Domus Eccclesiae*" (Ph.D. Thesis, Nottingham: University of Nottingham, 1992) 276–89.

[The following reconstruction is based primarily on the longer treatments of Meates, *The Lullingstone Roman Villa* (1956), the Department of the Environment Guide (1963), and the final reports (1979, 1987). The yearly excavation reports, especially after 1954, have been included for more detailed information wherever necessary. All measurements are given in feet and inches after the manner of the original excavation reports. Where it has been possible for the present author to check measurements based on work at the site, these are reported in metric notations. The illustrations used here, again based on the earlier reports (as these are still used in later publications), have been updated according to later findings wherever possible, and especially the plan in fig. 22. It has not been possible, however, to make the isometric reconstruction drawing (fig. 23) conform to the latest details of the plan.]

a. Stage I: The Early House (ca. 90–ca.175) [Figure 21a]

There is evidence of farming activity on the site from before the Roman occupation, in 43 CE. Later in the first century there was an expansion of Roman rule under Domitian. In Britannia, under the Roman governor Agricola, there seems to have been a conscious process of romanization for native Britons who could be absorbed into the provincial mentality. Meates suggests, therefore, a date near the last decade of the first century for the construction of the first building at Lullingstone as part of this program of expansion. The house was a rectangular plan (fig. 21a) made of flint (locally available) and mortar. It originally stood on or very near the bank of the river (to the east) and was set against and into the side of a low hill (to the west). The main entrance was from the area to the north of the so-called Deep Room, which faced onto the river. An entry ramp (a) descended from the hill to the north down to the platform area (b) behind and ca. 2 ft. above the Deep Room. From there wooden steps ascended to the level of the main quarters (d). The floor of the Deep Room lay some 8 ft. below the main levels of the house and only 1 ft. above the level of the river bank. The floor was finished with a layer of natural flint gravel. Meates first suggested that the so-called Deep Room was used originally as a water dock and entrance to the house.[190] A wooden construction (c) of a platform set on beams opening onto the Deep Room at a height 4 ft. above the floor could then be explained as a loading platform or pier, or some sort of stair up to the main house from the landing. It appears, however, that the area of the Deep Room was originally some sort of storage room, perhaps for grain, with access by ramp and stairs up to the main house. (It should be noted that another granary was built later in third century [Stage III], as discussed below.) The internal features of the house at this period are little known, but they were probably none too lavish. The remains suggest more of an agricultural estate than a country villa, and a romanized Briton rather than a Mediterranean owner.

The pottery record from the site indicates clearly that the first stage lasted well into the Trajanic or Hadrianic period, probably up to ca. 120.[191] There is, however, a gap in such material objects for the middle portions of the second century. Evidence for continued Stage I activity beyond 120 is found in the construction of a small circular temple on the terrace above and behind the house. It dates to the second half of the second century. It was constructed with a flint-and-mortar outer wall (Th.0.51 m), and the interior measured some 15 ft. (actual Diam.5.02 m). The entrance was from the east by a wooden stair, and the interior floor was tesselated (in red and yellow). A small slab on the floor opposite the entrance served as the base for some sort of cult image, and there is evidence of ritual fires just inside the entrance. These features point to use as a Celtic-type temple, but no specific cult images have been found to confirm the precise nature of the activity. This Circular Temple remained in use until Stage IV, when it was apparently dismantled in favor of the so-called Temple Mausoleum (see below).

---

190. Meates, *Lullingstone Roman Villa,* 63–64.

191. Ibid., 90.

b. Stage II: The Roman House and Cultic Annex (ca. 180–200) [Figure 21b]

The nature and appearance of the buildings were to be altered dramatically in Stage II. In the last quarter of the second century (ca. 180) it is apparent that a new owner took over the property. At this time the earlier structure was remodeled and enlarged (see fig. 21b). The central domestic quarters (Rooms 7, 8, 10, 12, 13) retained their basic rectangular plan and continued to form the core of the house. Completed excavation of the site showed that the second-stage house was expanded to the west [not fully excavated] so that the kitchen area (Room 7/13) comprised a room (or rooms) of ca. 30 x 20 ft.[192] The entire house was refurbished on the interior. On the south end of the domestic complex was added a hypocaust bath wing with furnaces for heating two of the rooms and water provided from a nearby well.

On the north end of the complex more changes were made. The Deep Room (fig. 21b, Room 11) was filled and the floor paved. Its southern access to Room 10 was through a new partition wall. At first it was thought that the Deep Room was constituted as a new garden entrance to the house (in keeping with the earlier assumptions that it had been an open "dock" area). Only later was it discovered that the south wall opened onto Room 17 by a ramp. In Stage II this entrance was closed and a niche was installed in the new wall segment. The richly decorated room served as a nymphaeum and so attests to the romanization of the estate. A fresco in the niche showed three water nymphs, presumably associated at least in part with the nearby river.[193] In addition, two Roman-style portrait busts were found associated with this period of construction. These busts were executed in an eastern Mediterranean style in Pentelic marble (one Hadrianic in date and the other Antonine) and further attest to the "Roman" tastes of the new owner, both in artistic style and in preservation of the Roman cult of the ancestors (*manes*).[194]

192. See Meates et al., in *Archaeologia Cantiana* [hereafter *Arch. Cant.*] 73 (1959) xlix.

193. Meates, *Lullingstone Roman Villa*, 91, corrected following subsequent excavations, as reported in *Arch. Cant.* 71 (1957) xlvi; 72 (1958) xlviii; cf. G. W. Meates, *Lullingstone Roman Villa* (Department of the Environment Guidebook; London: HMSO, 1963) 11–15 [hereafter cited as *Lullingstone Guidebook*]; idem, *The Roman Villa at Lullingstone* (2 vols.; Chichester: Phillimore, 1979, 86) 1. 33–35 [hereafter cited as *Roman Villa*]. On other *nymphaea* in Roman sites of Britain, see Martin Henig, *Religion in Roman Britain* (London: Batsford, 1984) 47–49, 173.

194. Meates, *Roman Villa*, 1. 21–30, 36.

The installation of the nymphaeum in the Deep Room coincides with the addition of a quadrangular annex on the northeast end of the complex, adjacent to the nymphaeum room. The access to this area was from the rear areas of the house through Room 13 and down a flight of tiled steps to a landing. From this landing, another set of steps led down at a right angle (to the south) into the nymphaeum (Deep Room, 11). From the landing another set of tiled stairs replaced the entry ramp leading out through the north passageway and there connected to a new passageway on the north exterior of the house. The third set of stairs ascended a short distance to the east to another passageway that continued at a right angle to the north. This newly added wing in the northeast corner of the complex formed a set of rooms (21–24). The plan of this area was a squarish central chamber (24), with a pit (21) in the center, and with an ambulatory (22) around it. This layout is fairly typical of what is now called a "Romano-British" or "Romano-Celtic Temple" type, and it suggests that this area was configured for cultic purposes as well.[195] (Whether the ambulatory was open to the outside [as is often the case in other temples of this type] on either of the two exterior walls [on the north and east] cannot be determined, since the upper levels were later destroyed in the subsequent renovations. Yet it should be remembered that the main entrance to the house had earlier been located at the ramp and landing taken over in Stage II as part of the Cultic Annex, from which access was gained by stairs to Room 13 and the rest of the house.)

Artifacts from this period bear witness to a great deal of domestic activity, but almost no farming. The quantity of dishes indicate elaborate dining. Meates suggests, therefore, that in Stage II the house became the country estate of a wealthy Roman of Mediterranean descent, living in the province and probably based in Londinium. The two marble busts were found (in the

195. The so-called Temple Mausoleum constructed on the terrace behind the house in Stage IV is of basically the same plan. (See below.) Regarding the identification of this temple type, see Henig, *Religion in Roman Britain*, 36–48; see W. Rodwell, ed. *Temples, Churches, and Religion* (British Archaeological Reports 77; London: Oxford University Press, 1980). Good examples are found at Springhead (Kent), Uley, and Lydney Park. The blending of Roman and native Celtic deities is seen frequently in this period, with perhaps the best known case being the spa and cult center at Bath dedicated to Sulis-Minerva. See Henig, *Religion in Roman Britain*, 43–45. More generally on the development of "Roman" villas in Britain, see A. L. F. Rivet, ed., *The Roman Villa in Britain* (London: Routledge, 1969), and M. Todd, ed., *Studies in the Romano-British Villa* (Leicester: Leicester University Press, 1978) s.v. "Lullingstone."

Deep Room) disused in a later period, which Meates (following J. M. C. Toynbee) attributes to the second-stage house and its lavish decoration. This affluence was, however, apparently short-lived as the house was abandoned and partially destroyed by ca. 200.

b. Stage III: The Farming Estate (ca. 280–330) [Figure 21c]

The villa seems to have been untouched for much of the early to mid-third century; it was rebuilt and reoccupied late in the century probably by a wealthy romanized Briton who used it as a country villa and agricultural estate. The rebuilt plan was of a slightly smaller scale as a result of truncating the north wing and the abandonment of the Cultic Annex. The entire north end of Stage II (the Cultic Annex of the northeast wing) was razed, and a new exterior wall was constructed as the north boundary of Rooms 14, 15, and 16 (see fig. 21c). At the same time the north entrance stair to the Deep Room was blocked by construction of a partition wall. The floor of the Deep Room was covered with a layer of clay, and the two busts from Stage II were deposited on the steps. Rooms 14, 15, and 16 were thereby created as the north wing of the house and were arranged with a hypocaust installation, although it is not clear that it was ever extensively used. The earlier steps and landing (now located in Room 15) were covered with fill; Room 16 was designed as the furnace. Whatever the purpose of this north hypocaust, the bath wing on the south was not neglected but was remodeled.[196]

The main new feature of this period of construction (Stage III) was the erection of a large rectangular barn (L.80'; W.33') situated just east of the north end of the house and lying perpendicular to its north–south axis. The size and unique plan of the barn point to the period of growth in provincial agriculture at the end of the third century. It is likely, therefore, that the new furnace room (hypocaust) on the north end of the house was intended to function in some capacity related to the farming.

d. Stage IVa: The Temple Mausoleum and the Later Roman Villa (ca. 300–360) [Figure 21d]

Sometime near the beginning of the fourth century, the older Circular Temple on the terrace to the north and west of the house was dismantled. The

196. There are signs of a small fire in the south bath wing near the beginning of the fourth century. This event might have been the cause for some of the renovations. See Meates, *Lullingstone Roman Villa*, 108–10.

terrace was further leveled, and a new cultic edifice (called by the excavators the "Temple Mausoleum") was constructed. The mausoleum was designed over the burial place of a young man and woman, which were set several feet down in a rock lined tomb beneath the crest of the terrace. The two bodies were covered in gypsum and deposited in decorated lead coffins with some grave goods. While the manner of burial has affinities with some Christian practice in Britain, the grave goods and orientation indicate that this was still a pagan burial.[197] The coffins were then enclosed in a wooden sarcophagus (2.45 x 2.20 m), which was anchored to the cutaway hillside and then enclosed in the chamber. The chamber was sealed with twelve layers of alternating chalk and gravel deposit, nearly 2 m deep. On top of this fill was constructed the new edifice, a square plan very much like the "Romano-Celtic Temple" type. It was built in large chalk-block masonry. On the exterior was a half-open ambulatory (W.1.8 m) with an low outer wall of stonework supporting its roof. In the center was the square cella (5.55 m on a side) with a domed ceiling. The plan of this upper building was of the "Romano-Celtic Temple" type and seems to have perpetuated some aspect of the young couple's memory as part of its cultic activity. However, since no other burials took place here, it is not likely to have been simply a cemetery. This "Temple Mausoleum" continued in use to the latter part of the fourth century before it was despoiled and abandoned.

The estate continued in this form for some time. Then, about 330 the domestic quarters of the house were once again altered radically (Stage IVa; see fig. 21d). Apparently, the destruction of the north entrance during Stage III had already necessitated moving the main entrance to the long east face of the house. Although no remnants were actually found, Meates postulates a grand wooden stair to ascend from the garden facing the river up to the main level of the house. Later, then, the central portions of the house were reoriented on this new axis and made more formal areas of reception and dining. Meates thinks this remodeling coincides with the era of prosperity and imperial favor beginning under Constantine.[198]

The remodeling included (fig. 21d) the construction of an apsed dining room (9) on the west side and the creation of a partitioned entry chamber

---

197. Meates, *Roman Villa*, 1. 122–32; cf. C. J. S. Green, "The Significance of Plaster Burials for the Recognition of Christian Cemeteries," in *Burial in the Roman World*, ed. by R. Reece (CBA Research Report 22; London, 1977) 46–57.

198. Meates, *Lullingstone Roman Villa*, 116–17.

(10) down one step before it.[199] Both Rooms 9 and 10 were decorated with mosaic floors. Room 10 contained a square pavement depicting Bellerophon slaying the chimera (center) flanked by personifications of the four seasons (corners). Room 9 was paved with plain brick around the outer apsidal concourse (W.3.12 m), while the central lunette (W.6.03 m) opening onto Room 10 was a mosaic scene of Europa and the Bull. The brick border was probably the seating/reclining area for the dining room. The mosaic scene was designed to be viewed from the west, that is, from the position of those reclining in the dining hall. An inscribed Latin verse completed an allusion to the Aeneid: *Invida si* [*Tauri*] *vidisset Ivno natatus / iustius Aeolias isset ad vsqve domos* ("Had Juno in her jealousy seen the bull swimming thus, might she more justly have flown even to the halls of Aeolus").[200]

Food for the dining room was provided from two kitchen areas, one in the northwest corner of the house (Room 14) and the other in the courtyard (8). The kitchen in Room 14 seems to be the earlier of the two having been put out of use by ca. 350, when the rooms to the north were converted to use as a Christian chapel (Stage IVb, below). Room 12 served as a bedroom; however, the space for private quarters and sleeping is very limited in the house. Meates postulated, therefore, that the owner actually slept in the dining area.[201]

---

199. Other rooms were later found to extend to the west behind the apse, but the full extent of these rooms was never found. See fig. 21 and *Arch. Cant.* 69 (1955) 201–2.

200. See Meates, *Lullingstone Roman Villa*, 36; *Lullingstone Guidebook*, 26. As a small qualification to Meates, who presupposes an exclusively pagan setting for these scenes, it should be noted that the house (perhaps also a *domus ecclesiae*?) at Hinton St. Mary's near Dorsett, England, shows the same Bellerophon scene in a mosaic floor which contains what is generally considered to be a representation of Christ. This site also dates from the mid- to later-fourth century. See Appendix A, no. 12, below, for discussion and bibliography. It suggests, therefore, that while the scenes might have originated from a pagan dining context, they could be carried over without much hesitation into a Christian context through allegorical or symbolic reinterpretation. On the possible relevance of these particular pagan scenes in a Christian context, see also J. Huskinson, "Some Pagan Mythological Figures and their Significance in Early Christian Art," *PBSR* 42 (1974) 68–97 (esp. 73) and R. T. Eriksen, "Syncretistic Symbolism and the Christian Roman Mosaic at Hinton St. Mary: A Closer Reading," *Proceedings of the Dorset Natural History and Archaeology Society* 102 (1980) 43–48.

201. Meates, *Lullingstone Roman Villa*, 119.

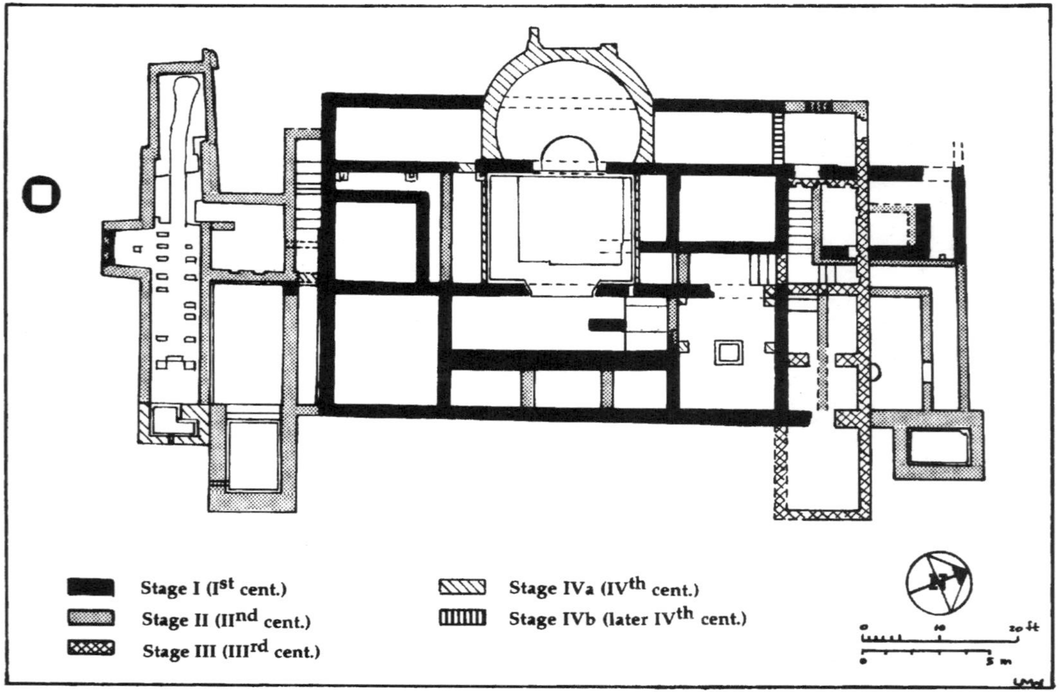

Fig. 22
Britannia, Lullingstone. Roman villa and Christian chapel, fourth century.
Plan restoration in stages (after Meates).

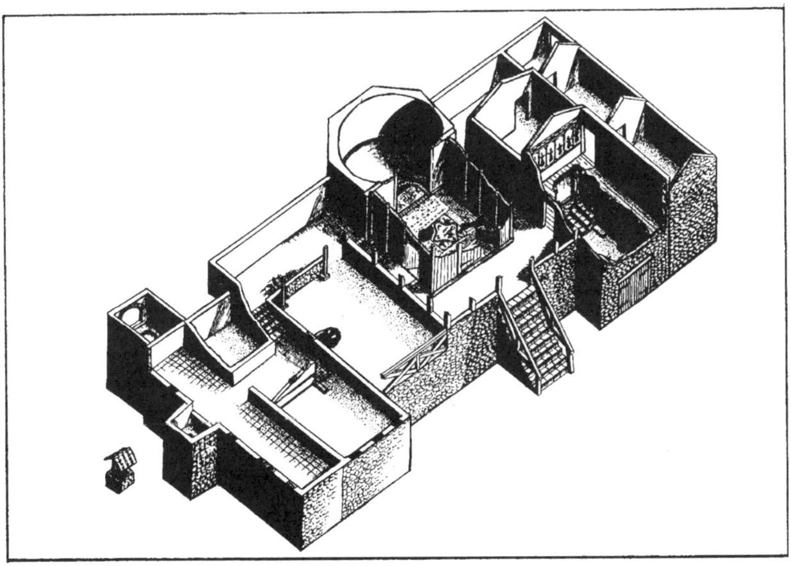

Fig. 23
Britannia, Lullingstone. Roman villa and Christian chapel, ca. 390.
Isometric reconstruction (after Meates, *Lullingstone Roman Villa,* fig. 4a).

At about this time (ca. 330) the north hypocaust (Rooms 15-16) was turned to a new purpose. There is little evidence of extensive heat or burning in Room 15, but there is a layer of ashy residue (D.ca. 2'). To explain this residue Meates looked to the position of a number of postholes found in the floor. He took their arrangement to indicate some sort of portable frame, which he interpreted as a rack for drying cloth over a low flame, that is, as some sort of dyeing establishment.[202] There is some evidence of decline through neglect for all areas of the villa during the rest of the fourth century. The lack of upkeep may point to dwindling resources or an absentee owner in the later stages.

202. Ibid., 114–16.

e. Stage IVb: The Christian Chapel and Domus Eccesiae *(ca. 360–390) [Figure 21e]*

About the middle of the fourth century the final adaptation (Stage IVb) of the house was made in the north wing. It involved the construction of a Christian "chapel" or assembly hall in the area above the Deep Room (11) and Rooms 15 and 16. The dating of the renovation and continued usage is based almost exclusively on numismatic evidence. In the carbonized fill of Room 15 were found twenty-one coins from the period of Constantine (i.e., up to 337), six coins from just after 337, and two more from the period 350-354 (Constantius Gallus and Magnentius). These finds suggest the period from at least 337 to the early 350s for the use of Room 15 as a dyeing establishment. The installation of the chapel entailed constructing wooden floors (at about the level of Room 10) in Rooms 11, 15, and 16. In Room 15 this wooden floor lay just over the layer of fill, and the floor construction included a trench dug into this fill for placement of supports. In this trench was found a coin of Constantius II (ca. 345-361). The construction of the wooden floor for the Christian hall, therefore, was dated by Meates to ca. 360.[203] When Christians actually began using this part of the house (whether before or simultaneous with these renovations) cannot be determined more precisely. The renovation of the chapel room is the only clear indication of Christian presence. Yet, insofar as the proclivities of the owner and his/her family were likely part of the change, it may suggest an earlier Christian presence. On the other hand, it is clear that the nymphaeum and pagan shrine in the Deep Room (below the Christian chapel) continued in use throughout much of the fourth century, even after the Christian chapel was installed above.[204]

The Christian rooms were initially only a part of the house (figs. 21e, 23) but encompassed the entire north wing of the villa, including Rooms 14, 15*, 16*, and 11* (over the Deep Room). (The asterisk denotes upper floor in the plan of fig. 21e.) Most of the construction has been determined in

203. Ibid., 144, 146. Cf. Meates, *Roman Villa,* 1. 53, 38. Redating of some of the coins may suggest a later date. Nine coins from Room 14 are dated to the "house of Theodosius" (379–395; so Meates, *Roman Villa,* 1. 57). But R. Reece ("The Roman Coins," in Meates, *Roman Villa,* 2. 49) suggests that these indicate that the earth floor in it was still in use up until ca. 390. Thus, the date range for the construction and use of the wooden floor is ca. 360/361–390.

204. Meates, *Roman Villa*, 1. 39. For further discussion see now Gilmore Eaves, "Annulling a Myth," 279–80.

detail. The form of the "chapel" room (11*) was determined by that of the Deep Room beneath it. Its width on the interior was just over 12 ft. along the west end (because of the offset position of the earlier partition wall from Stage II) and nearly 14 ft. at the east end (actual measurment 4.308 m). Its interior length was just over 22 ft. (7.04 m). The north and east walls (Th.0.69 m) were constructed of flint and mortar up to the roof. The west and south walls were light partitions consisting of a wooden frame (like that in Room 10) covered with baked clay and chalk. All the interior walls of Room 11* were finished in white plaster and then decorated with mosaics (see below). The main entrance to the hall was by a door in the northwest corner of 11* leading from Room 15*.[205] Room 15* (L.ca.16'; W.ca.10'), then, served as an antechamber for the main hall and also afforded access to Room 16* (L.ca.14'; W.ca.10' [actual 3.04 m]). The function of Room 16* in this period is completely unknown though Christian usage is almost certain.

Room 15* adjoined Room 14 (the earlier kitchen) to the north, and the latter provided access to the chapel wing. At the time of the chapel construction the floor of Room 14 was filled with a layer of packed earth and gravel completely covering the kitchen and pit. The original outside door in the west wall of Room 14 was sealed, and a new door opened to the outside on the north. At the same time a partition was erected in the corridor (13) closing off Room 14 from the rest of the house. Room 14 (L.ca.l0'; W.ca.7½') became a vestibule providing outside access to the chapel wing. This fact suggests that more than just household members used the chapel. Indeed, later excavations on the hill above the house to the west brought forth the remains of a small Romano-British community of houses and numerous other buildings including as many as four pagan temples.[206] Thus, the chapel wing should more properly be seen as a partial *domus ecclesiae* serving not only the extended household of the estate itself but also other members from the surrounding community.[207]

A number of interior appointments for the assembly hall were found in the

205. Meates at one point hypothesized a second door to 11* leading from the entry corridor before Room 10, but there is no direct evidence of such a door mentioned in any of the later reports (see *Lullingstone Roman Villa*, 52 and fig. 4a). Once the full scale of the wall decorations in 11* was discovered, it made such a door very doubtful. But the possibility has now reemerged in recent discussions.

206. These are discussed in *Arch. Cant.* 69 (1955) 201–2; 76 (1961) l[L].

207. This suggestion was first made by Meates but has been questioned recently by Gilmore Eaves, "Annulling a Myth," 284.

debris that had collapsed into the Deep Room when the house burned. Among the charred remains were numerous fragments of painted wall plaster. The evidence suggests an elaborate decorative program in fresco for the chapel/hall proper. The main features of this decorative program that have been reconstructed are from the west and south walls of the chapel. On the west (or back) wall was a row of six orans figures standing between pillars of a portico. These include a man, a woman, a younger man, and a child with two other badly damaged (and therefore less identifiable) figures. The style of the portraiture is considered to reflect influences of early Byzantine notions of frontality and portraiture. The dress depicted of these figures is of a expensive quality and may also reflect late Roman style. While the posture of one of the six was thought perhaps to represent a martyr, it appears rather that the whole group comes from a single family. Given the quality of the dress and the depiction of the individuals, it is likely that they represent the owner of the house (and the patron of the church) together with his family.

On the south side wall of the "chapel" room facing the doorway from 15* and at the corner adjacent to the Orans figures (at the west end) was a large Chi-Rho monogram encircled by a wreath (Diam.ca.3'). A similar monogram was painted on the south wall of Room 15* adjacent to the entrance to the chapel, and a third one was found in the fill on the east end of the room, now thought to come from the east wall.[208] The remainder of the south wall of the chapel seems to have contained a landscape with clear (though fragmentary) elements suggesting a house by a river, probably the villa itself. The east wall of the chapel was apparently decorated with a geometric (fleur-de-lis) pattern arranged around two (?) splayed windows.[209] The decoration of the north wall is completely unknown.

Other accouterments of the chapel included a heavy slab of pink concrete (or *opus signinum*)(L.ca.2½' [0.75 m]; W.ca.1.5' [0.53 m]; Th.ca.6" [0.10 m]) placed somewhere along the south wall near the east end [a bema or dais?]. A large water jar (H.ca.12") was found in the northwest corner, and a small beaker (H.5") at the southeast end. The most intriguing interior element found (in the northeast corner) was a group of chalk blocks carefully tooled and mortared to form an arch (interior Diam.ca.2-3'). Meates has suggested

208. *Arch. Cant.* 72 (1958) xlviii. See now J. Liversidge and M. Weatherhead, "The Christian Paintings," in Meates, *Roman Villa,* 2. 12–13, 16–18.

209. Only one window was actually found, and it was quite large and deep; see *Arch. Cant.* 70 (1956) 249–50.

an arched doorway from Room 16* or, placed horizontally, a piscina or font.[210] It is possible, however, that the arch served as a niche construction below or between the windows of the east wall. If this is the case, then it is quite possible that the third Chi-Rho fresco stood in this niche. The other possibility that has been suggested is that the arch framed another doorway into the "chapel" room from the vestibule of the house (Room 10a). This possibility suggests that the other areas of the house, including the dining room, were used in conjunction with the "chapel" room.[211]

The Christian chapel [*domus ecclesiae*], as attested by numismatic finds (coins of Theodosius, 379-395) in the floor fill of Room 14, remained in use until about the beginning of the fifth century. But the rest of the villa and the barn suffered neglect and ruin. The bath wing of the house continued to be used up to ca. 380, at which time it was filled in. About the same time the barn seems to have been abandoned except for minor use. This date corresponds closely to the evidence for cessation of cooking in the kitchen of Room 8. Meates thinks that this evidence points to a complete stop in domestic activities at a time when the owners no longer actively inhabited the villa. It was in all likelihood given over completely to the Christian community, which used only the chapel wing and (to a limited extent) the central quarters (Rooms 9, 10, 12, 13). There is evidence that someone continued to sleep in the bedroom (12), and this suggests the presence of a Christian caretaker or a resident ecclesiastic in the later stages of occupation. The villa was finally destroyed by fire in the early fifth century. Meates had at one point posited destruction during the period of barbarian invasions, but the causes of the fire are indeterminate. After the destruction the villa seems to have been completely abandoned, although life in the neighboring village(s) might have continued.[212]

---

210. Meates, *Lullingstone Roman Villa*, 150–51; cf. *Roman Villa*, 1. 42–43.

211. See the discussion of Gilmore Eaves, "Annulling a Myth," 285–87, who thinks that the "chapel" resembles a funerary or martyrial chapel (rather than a *domus ecclesiae* proper) and that the dining room/living room areas continued to be the main areas of assembly for a family's activities. While use of the living quarters for Christian activities seems likely, the argument that the "chapel" room does not constitute a *domus ecclesiae* on the grounds of size (or because it was familial) is not convincing.

212. For this phenomenon in the period of change from Roman to non-Roman rule in Britain, with special attention to the persistence of Christianity and of "romanization," see Charles Taylor, *Christianity in Roman Britain to A.D. 500* (London: Batsford, 1981).

SECTION III

Comparative Archaeological and Documentary Evidence: Mithraism and Diaspora Judaism

▲ ▲ ▲

Following the same geographical order as was employed in Section II (cf. Appendix B, Table 4), this chapter will provide a selection of comparable sources for Mithraism and Diaspora Judaism. Because the range of materials is so much more extensive in these areas than in the early Christian sources, only a representative sample can be included here, though it will be noted the Jewish evidence is much more complete than the Mithraic. An effort has been made to include evidence proximate both in date and in location to the Christian evidence. In a manner similar to the procedure in Section II, all archaeological reports have been rewritten as architectural histories, and relevant illustrations are assembled. Also included are the texts and the author's translations of representative inscriptions. A classified listing of all items is provided in Appendix B, Table 3.

Catalogue

PROVINCE: Syria (Parapotamia)
LOCATION: Dura-Europos (Es-Salihiyeh)

No. 58: The Mithraeum (ca. 168–256)
(Figures 24–27)

Discovered in 1934 by the joint expedition of Yale University and the French Academy of Inscriptions and Letters, the mithraeum was located on the west wall of the city between Gates 23 and 24 (Block J5). The excavations revealed four stages of construction on the site, three of which were for use as a Mithraic sanctuary (to be designated as early, middle, and late). Originally thc edifice was a private house, in which one room was later renovated for use as the sanctuary. In subsequent stages the house was extensively remodeled and expanded so that the mithraeum occupied the entire edifice. The site was in use up to the destruction of the city in 256 CE.

Literature: M. Rostovtzeff, "Das Mithraeum von Dura," *Mitteilungen des deutschen archäologischen Instituts*, Römische Abteilung 49 (1934) 180–207. F. Cumont, "The Dura Mithraeum," ed. and trans. E. D. Francis, in *Mithraic Studies* (2 vols.; Manchester: Manchester University Press, 1975) 1. 151–214. M. Rostovtzeff, F. Brown, and C. B. Welles, et al., *The Excavations at Dura-Europos: Preliminary Report of the Seventh and Eighth Seasons* (New Haven: Yale University Press, 1939) 62–134 [hereafter *DEP* 7–8]. E. D. Francis, "Mithraic Graffiti from Dura-Europos," in *Mithraic Studies* (Manchester: Manchester University Press, 1975) 2. 424–45. Vermasaren, *CIMRM* 1, nos. 34–70. For a general history of the site and the city, see also M. Rostovtzeff, *Dura-Europos and Its Art* (Oxford: Clarendon, 1943), and A. Perkins, *The Art of Dura-Europos* (Oxford: Clarendon, 1973).

a. The House and Early Mithraeum (ca. 168–71)

The mithraeum was originally erected in one room of an older private house (in Block J5, fig. 24) whose foundations date from the later stages of the Parthian period of the city's history (ca. 113 B.BCE to 165 CE). This area of the city was adjacent to the northern end of the main (or west) city wall near

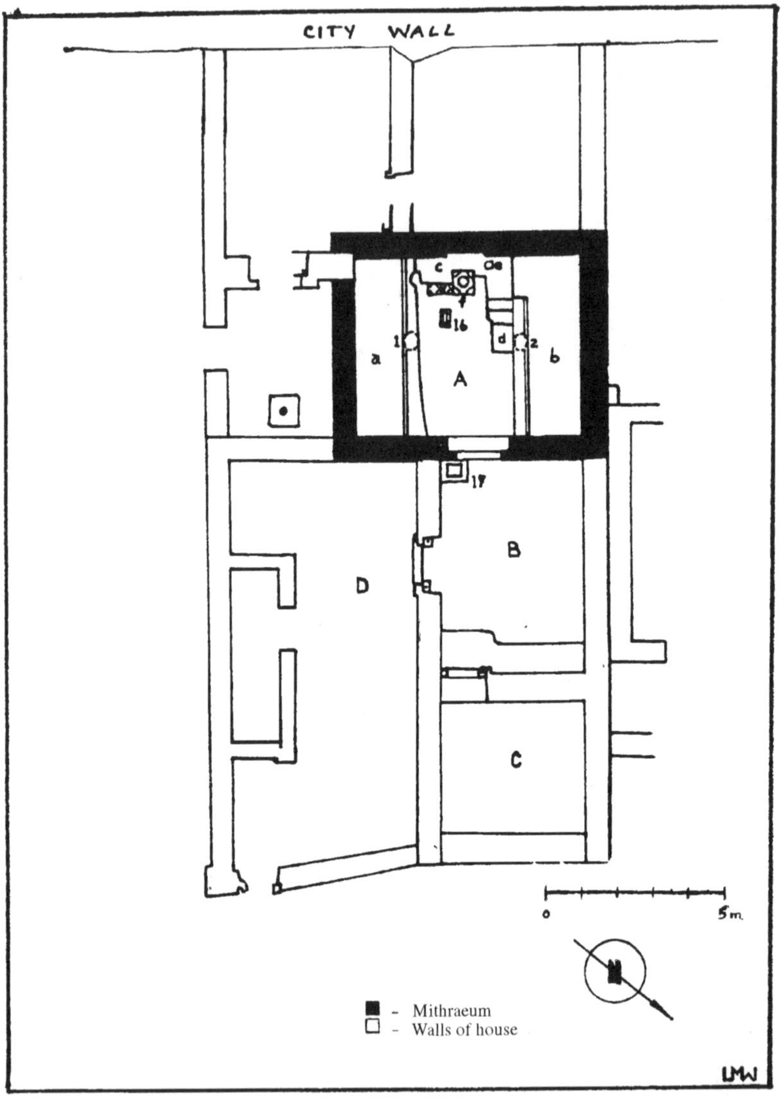

Fig. 24
Syria, Dura-Europos.
Early mithraeum and Parthian-period house, ca. 168–171 CE
Plan restoration (based on Pearson)

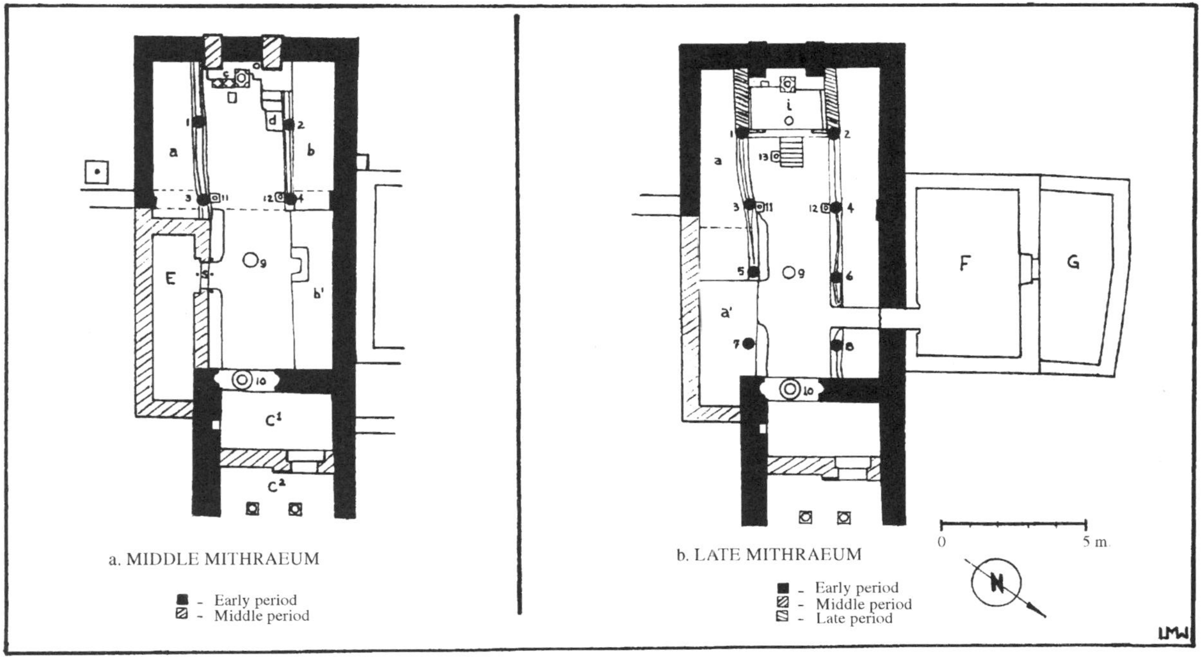

Fig. 25
Syria, Dura-Europos. Mithraeum, ca. 209–256 CE.
Plan restoration or middle and late stages of renovation

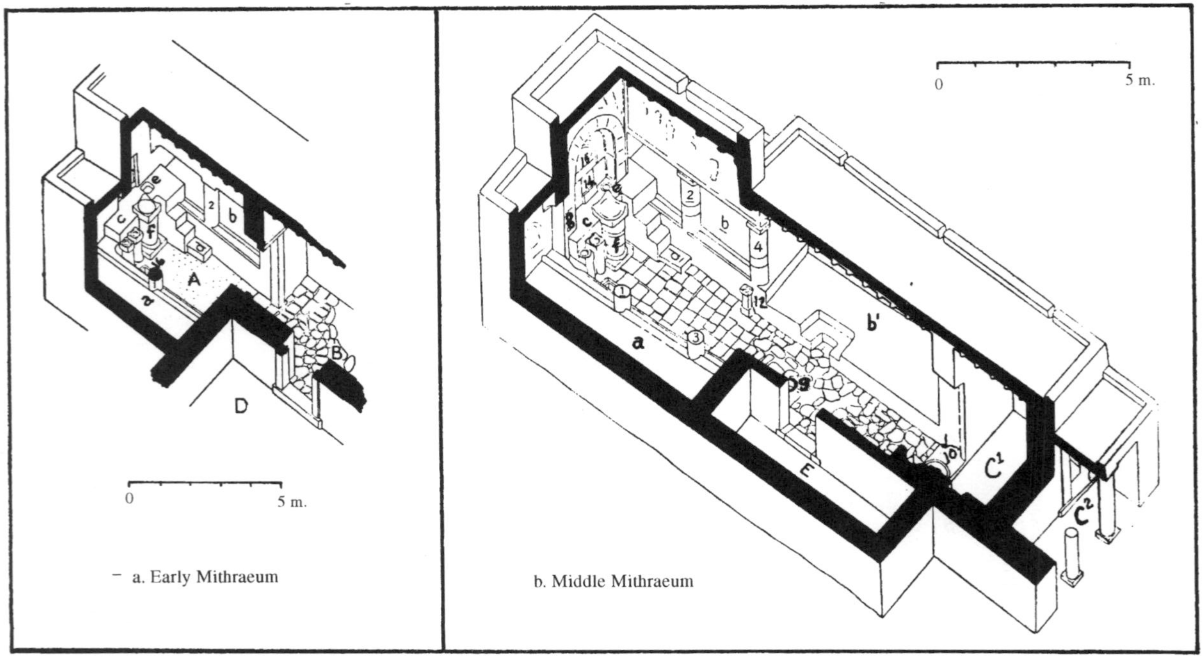

Fig. 26

Syria, Dura-Europos. Early and middle mithraeum, ca. 167–209 CE.
Isometric reconstruction (after H. Pearson)

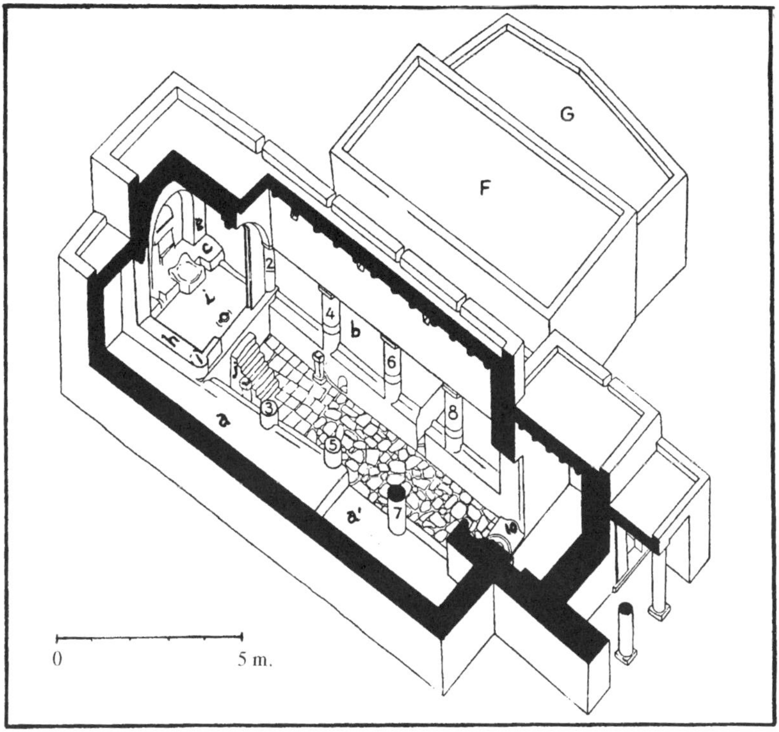

Fig. 27
Syria, Dura-Europos. Late mithraeum, ca. 256 CE.
Isometric reconstruction (after H. Pearson)

the precinct of the Temple of Bel (or the Palmyrene gods). Inscribed stones found reused as building materials in the later mithraic construction indicate that other houses and small sanctuaries occupied this general area during the later Parthian period, and specifically during the period of Roman control under Trajan (116–118 CE).[1] The house continued in use after the initial

1. Two texts (*DEP* 7–8, nos. 868–69) were found in the area, and record the dedications of construction of a small sanctuary to an unnamed god by a father and son, who successively held the office of herald of the city. The second of these was reused in the construction of the altar table in the middle mithraeum (ca. 209–211; see below). Since no formal temple complex was found in this area of the city, it is likely

construction of the Mithraic sanctuary but was eventually taken over entirely in later renovation and expansion of the sanctuary.

Inscriptions on the two central *tauroctone* reliefs (preserved in the later stages of the mithraeum) indicate that this initial construction took place not long after the city came under Roman control in the campaign of Lucius Verus, ca. 168–171 CE.[2] The house (figs. 24, 26a) was entered from the street through court D which, opened onto the central chamber B (L.5.75; W.3.50 m), probably the *diwan* or living/dining room of the house. From B the two anterooms A (L.4.64; W.5.80 m) and C (L.3.50; W.3.50 m) were accessible. In order to create the Mithraic sanctuary, room A was divided into three parts along its long axis, with two podia (a and b) (H.0.72; Br.ca.1.70 m) on either side of a central aisle. The ceiling was probably not modified at this stage. So there were no columns in the room, and any upper floors that might have existed in the house likely continued in domestic use.[3]

On the west wall of room A a central altar table was erected. It consisted

(and in keeping with the wording of the inscriptions) that the "sanctuary" was of a more private sort, perhaps installed in a house. It cannot be determined whether the house referred to in these earlier texts is the same used for the building of the early mithraeum, but it remains an intriguing possibility. See the discussion in *DEP* 7–8. 168 and in my *Building God's House in the Roman World* (Baltimore: Johns Hopkins University Press, 1990) 40–44 (esp. 44 and nn. 66–67).

2. The reliefs were located in the arched niche at the front end of the hall (loci 14 and 15 in figs. 26b, 27) in the middle and late mithraea. It is most likely that they occupied the same position in the early mithraeum, since the altar and niche constructions in the later stages preserved the location of the *naos* or cult center from this first sanctuary. For the texts and photographs, see *CIMRM* 1, nos. 39 and 41, and see further below.

3. In the reconstruction of H. Pearson (*DEP* 7–8. 63–65) it was suggested that columns 1 and 2 were installed at this time to support a slightly elevated ceiling over the central aisle (ca. 1.60 m higher than over the sides). His unpublished excavation notes claim more emphatically a clerestory construction. This is the plan of the upper elevation of the room reflected in fig. 26a, based on the drawing by Pearson. On the other hand, Rostovtzeff strongly opposed this reconstruction (*DEP* 7–8. 80), and Cumont agreed that it was unlikely that there was anything more than the original flat-roof construction without columns. See F. Cumont, "The Dura Mithraeum," in *Mithraic Studies*, ed. J. Hinnels (2 vols.; Manchester: Manchester University Press, 1975) 1. 163 and n. 61; cf. E. D. Francis, "Mithraic Graffiti from Dura-Europos," in ibid., 2. 427 and n. 14. A graffito on column 1 (*CIMRM* 1, no. 54) datable to the reign of Caracalla would seem to support Rostovtzeff's view.

of a narrow platform (c) (H.0.88; Br.0.58 m) reached by four steps (d). A well (e) (Diam.0.32 m) was molded in the plaster of the top. In front stood the main altar and, perhaps, two side altars to the south. Two pits (16 and 17) were found dug to the original floor level; one and perhaps both of them were used as receptacles for the bones of birds and small animals. Above c in a square recessed niche cut in the west wall were set the two rectangular reliefs (loci 14 and 15, fig. 26b) depicting Mithras slaying the bull. Traces of paint (e.g., on the columnar base of the altar, which was painted to resemble marble) would indicate the presence of decoration on the front and side walls, but no other clues exist as to what the program might have been, since much of the building was destroyed in later renovations.

The inscriptions on the two *tauroctone* reliefs indicate that the first sanctuary was built by elements of a Palmyrene military detachment (a *numerus* of archers) that had been part of the II Ulpian Cohort in Lucius Verus's campaign. Apparently these Palmyrene archers were then stationed in the garrison at Dura. The donors of the two reliefs, Ethpeni and Zenobios, were officers (*stratēgoi*) of this detachment. The dedication of Ethpeni (*CIMRM* 1, no. 39, dated 168) is in Palmyrene with a semitized Greek heading line. This was a smaller rectangular plaque and, given the date, probably represents the establishment of the cult. The dedication of Zenobios (*CIMRM* 1, no. 41, dated 171) comes from the upper relief. It is a larger lunette relief with iconographic similarities to some western *tauroctones*; the inscription is entirely in Greek. It is clear that the plaque of Zenobios was meant to supersede that of Ethpeni. Given these texts, it is likely that the first Mithraic conventicle was made up predominantly of members of this same military detachment, that is, eastern personnel of upper and middle rank.[4] Since the rest of the house remained in domestic use, it is also likely that its owner had connections with the cult group. Thus, it is quite possible that the house was acquired either by Ethpeni or Zenobios, but probably the latter.[5]

4. See *DEP* 7–8. 80–136. For a full discussion of the prosopography, see Francis, "Mithraic Graffiti," 424–45 (esp. 429–30).

5. I base this suggestion on the following observations: (1) It is assumed in all the reports that these two reliefs were in the same position in the early mithraeum (and preserved out of reverence in the later stages); therefore, their positioning in the wall had to have come at the time of the later of the two, the dedication of Zenobios. (2) The installation of the reliefs was coincidental with the renovation of the room as a sanctuary. (3) Even though the Mithraic conventicle might have been meeting for

This building was largely destroyed especially along the south side before it was renovated in the middle period. The exact circumstances of the destruction are not clear. It is possible that the strong military presence during the campaign of Lucius Verus (ca. 165–68 CE) was later diminished, or the detachment of Ethpeni and Zenobios transferred, leaving the mithraeum to fall into disuse. Or it may be that the dismantling of significant portions was a conscious architectural decision in preparation for remodeling. In any case, much of the northwest portion of the city was also razed and rebuilt in ca. 209–11, when an enlarged military garrison was to be constructed.

b. The Middle Mithraeum (ca. 209–11)

Along with the general renewal of the north quadrant of the city the mithraeum was rebuilt in ca. 209–11 CE. The renovation corresponds to a massive reinforcement of the garrison at Dura in preparation for Caracalla's Persian campaign. In the sanctuary room the walls were knocked down to bench level along the sidewalls. On the back (west) wall of the room, the wall was preserved up to the height of the naos platform, presumably including the implacement of the *tauroctone* reliefs. Thus, the basic plan and some of the physical elements were consciously preserved in the construction. In the rest of the house, especially on the south side, the walls were razed to sill level. New walls were then extended to the east to create the elongated hall.

An inscription (No. 59 below) indicates that the rebuilding was inaugurated by Antonius Valentinus, the *centurio princeps* of the newly arrived *vexillationes* from the IV Scythica and XVI Flavia Firma legions. The size of the mithraeum proper was more than doubled by taking in what had been

---

several years after these Palmyrene soldiers were stationed in Dura (i.e., beginning with the dedication of Ethpeni), the construction of the first (albeit modest) mithraeum in House J7 might have come three years later. Where they would have been meeting previously is impossible to know. The same house is possible. (4) The name Zenobios appears in two other graffiti (= IM Dur. 121) from House D in Block C3 (near the Roman Baths), and these suggest further acquisition of domestic properties. Whether it is the same Zenobios cannot be ascertained definitely. See also Francis's comments ("Mithraic Graffiti," 436) regarding the fact that the Greek name Zenobios is probably the hellenized form of the Palmyrene *Zebida* or *Zabbai*. Since the Ethpeni dedication names his father as Zabde'a, it is very possible that Zenobios is the hellenized form. But then is the Zenobios of the second relief the father (or perhaps another relative) of Ethpeni?

most of the earlier house (see fig. 25a). The physical size of the new sanctuary and the numerous graffiti indicate that the Mithraic community had grown significantly, probably as a result of the military reinforcements and the general growth of the city. Rostovtzeff thought this reflected a radical shift to a more Roman membership in the cult; however, it is still probably a mixed group with the inclusion of some nonmilitary residents.[6]

The alterations consisted of annexing room B by knocking out the partition wall. Since the partition was a carrying wall, columns 3 and 4 were installed on its foundations to support the ceiling. It was apparently at this time that the abbreviated clerestory was constructed over the central aisle, extending from the naos to columns 3 and 4 (see fig. 26b). Columns 1 and 2 were also added at this time.[7] The north podium b was extended (b') through the length of room B but at a slightly lower level (H.0.40 m). On the south side the exterior wall of room A was extended by a new construction to the middle of room C. The small room E (L.5.60; W.1.65 m) was created by rebuilding the earlier north wall of D in a thinner construction and intersecting it with a new partition on the west end. Finally, room C was converted into a vestibule or *pronaos* (C^1) and an entry portico (C^2) with two columns. The door from C^1 was widened and set with a recessed trim, and a basin (10) was set in the step. Another basin (9) (Diam.0.32 m) was situated in the central aisle as a receptacle for animal bones. It stood opposite a rectangular, recessed step in the newly constructed north podium.

The *naos* was also elaborated at this time. First, when the west wall of the *naos* was rebuilt, it included as an integral part of its brickwork construction an arched arcosoleum rising up into the clerestory. On the interior the arch was faced with plaster to frame cult reliefs 14 and 15. At the same time the level of the plaster altar table was raised 0.08 m and a jar was set in the platform over the well (e). Extensive plaster work in the niche was used as preparation for a complete reworking of the interior decoration. Among other things, the upper portion of the topmost relief (15—a rectangle carrying statue heads of Sol and Luna on the top edge and [in the corners] personifications of winter [left] and summer [right]) was covered over with plaster to form a lunette corresponding to the shape of the arch (compare fig. 26a–c). Two more altars (11 and 12) were installed at the bases of columns 3

6. See *DEP* 7–8. 88, and Francis, "Mithraic Graffiti," 428, 434–37.

7. See n. 3 above.

and 4. Finally, the walls and perhaps the ceiling were painted with a symbolic, decorative program. On the side walls were figures in processional posture. In the reveal of the arch were painted white stars on a blue field. The ceiling may have been decorated to complete the desired effect of creating a *spelaeum* iconography.

c. The Late Mithraeum (ca. 240–56)

The final stage of reconstruction in the mithraeum began in ca. 240 CE, only some sixteen years before the destruction of the entire city. The most striking feature of this renovation was the construction of a vaulted canopy in the clerestory over arch g (see figs. 25b, 27). Its side walls extended out to and incorporated columns 1 and 2. The narrow platform c was enlarged in a corresponding way by constructing a platform (i) at a height 0.08 m lower than c. The platform engulfed the main altar, and the earlier well e was covered over and replaced by a jar set in i between the altar and the steps. The new *naos* was reached by a central stair of seven narrow steps (Br.0.15 m). Another small altar (13) was placed beside the stair. The construction of the vault would have probably entailed removing the ceiling, and at this time the clerestory was extended the full length of the sanctuary.

On the south wall, podium a was extended by knocking down the walls of room E to 0.40 m and filling them with rubble and plaster. Two more columns (5 and 7) were installed on the south bench to carry the extended clerestory. The new podium a' was the same height as the earlier section (a) as far as column 5, but from that point it was slightly lower. On the north side the podium extension b' was raised to the same height (0.72 m), and two more columns (6 and 8) were added for the extended clerestory. A passageway was cut through the north podium between columns 6 and 8. This passageway led to a door newly cut through the north wall to provide access to two chambers (F [L.3.25; W.6.00 m] and G [L.ca.2.50; W.6.00 m]). The prior history of these rooms is uncertain, and no previous connection to the mithraeum can be demonstrated. Their foundations are quite old, certainly antedating the construction of the first mithraeum and perhaps going back to the original construction of the block.

Some new decorations were added in this period, but the program of redecoration was largely confined to the area of the new *naos* in keeping with the structural modifications. The name of one of the artists, Mareos, is given in graffito accompanying the central arch scene of Mithras slaying the bull (*CIMRM*, 1, no. 42).[8] The walls of the altar canopy were likewise painted with hunting scenes, and the ceiling was treated with white stylized stars on a field of blue to create a "canopy of the heavens" motif in the vaulted *spelaeum*.

PROVINCE: Syria
LOCATION: Dura-Europos

No. 59: Building Inscription (209–11) (The Middle Mithraeum)

Inscription in a *tabula ansata* of white marble (H.0.33; W.0.63–0.65 m) set in the west wall of the *pronaos* (room C^1) of the middle mithraeum (cf. No. 58b above), now in the Yale University Art Gallery, broken in five pieces, of which one (from the center bottom) is missing. The letters carefully incised and painted (probably red) are widely spaced in lines 1–2 but compressed in lines 3–4 and especially in line 5. Letters: H.0.042 m.

Literature: *DEP* 7–8. 85 (no. 847); cf. pl. XLIX,l. *CIMRM* 1. 53. E. D. Francis, "Mithraic Graffiti from Dura-Europos," in *Mithraic Studies* (Manchester: Manchester University Press, 1975) 2. 428.

[The following transcription is after *DEP* 7–8. 85 as checked against the photograph in pl. XLIX,l and the plaque itself in the Yale Art Gallery. It may, therefore, be considered an accurate correction of *CIMRM* 53.]

Pro sal(ute) et incol(umitate) d(ominorum)
n(ostrorum) imp(eratorum) (duorum/ [[trium]])
L. Sep(timi) Severi pii
Pert(inacis) et M. Aurel(i) Antonini [[L. Sept(imi)
Geta[e]]] Aug(ustorum) (duorum/ [[trium]]) templum dei Solis invicti Mithrae sub Minic(io)
Martiali proc(uratore) Aug(usti)
rest(itutum) ab Ant(onio) Valentino (cent.)
princ(ipe) pr(aeposito) ve[x(illationum)

8. For a description of the painted scenes from the zodiac and the myth of Mithras around the arch and in the reveal, see *CIMRM* 1, nos. 42–47. All these items are in the Yale University Art Gallery, where I was able to study them extensively.

leg(ionum) III]I Scyt(hicae) et XVI Fl(aviae)
F(irmae) p(iae) f(idelis).

Translation: For the safety and well-being of our Lords,[9] the two/[[three]] Emperors, L. Septimius Severus Pius Pertinax and Marcus Aurelius Antoninus [[and L. Septimius Geta]], the two/[[three]] Augusti, the temple of Sol Invictus Mithras was restored under Minicius Martialis, the imperial procurator, by Antonius Valentinus *centurio princeps*,[10] commander of the vexillations of the most loyal legions, the IVth Scythian and the XVIth Flavia Firma.

PROVINCE: Syria
LOCATION: Dura-Europos

No. 60: The Synagogue (late second century, 256)
(Figures 28–30)

The synagogue was discovered in 1921 and excavated from 1922 to 1933 by the joint expedition of Yale University and the French Academy of Inscrip-

9. DD⟦D⟧/NN⟦N⟧ IMPP⟦P⟧ (lines 1–2, lapis). The abbreviations are still to be resolved in general terms as d(ominorum) n(ostrorum) imp(eratorum), but the multiplication of the ending letters was originally intended to denote the number of honorees in the salutary formula. The erasures are to be explained with the *damnatio memoriae* of Geta as in line 3. Note also the erasure in line 3, AVGG ⟦G⟧.

The inclusion of Geta and the subsequent erasure give a clear indication of the date. The inscription was originally produced between 209 and 211, during which time the three would have been named together as "emperors" (*Imperatores*, line 2). Inscriptions using the same opening formula (*Pro salute* ...) from before 209 designated Geta as "Caesar"; cf. *CIL* 6^1. 3768, dated 207/8 (text given in n. 162 below). The erasure of the name of Geta and the correction of the imperial titles (lines 1–3), all still legible, are undoubtedly a later, but none too thorough, alteration owing to the *damnatio memoriae* of Geta after 212/13.

10. The name Antonius Valentinus appears elsewhere at Dura. The *centurio princeps* at this period held the same rank in the city as the later tribunes of the *Cohors XX Palmyrenorum*. It is not the case, however, as reported by M. J. Vermaseren, that this same person dedicated the Dolicheneum; rather it was his freedman, a certain Agathocles (see *DEP* 9, inscription no. 970). See also Francis, "Mithraic Graffiti," 428). Other inscriptions preserve the names of a mithraist named Antoninus (*DEP* 7–8, no. 855 and 858=*CIMRM* 1. 57, 60). For a mithraic inscription in the Dolicheneum by a soldier of the XVI Flavia Firma see *DEP* 9, no. 974 (=*CIMRM* 1.70).

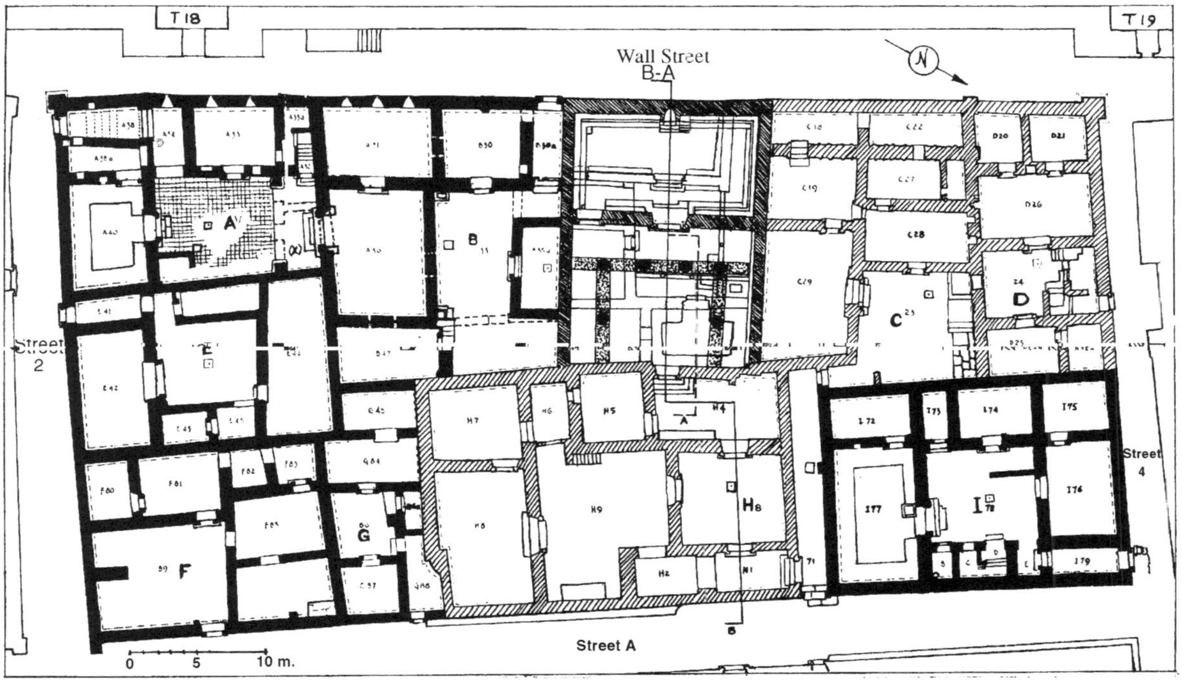

Fig. 28
Syria, Dura-Europos. Block L7 and the synagogue, ca. 160–256 CE.
Plan restoration in stages of construction (based on field plan of Andrews)

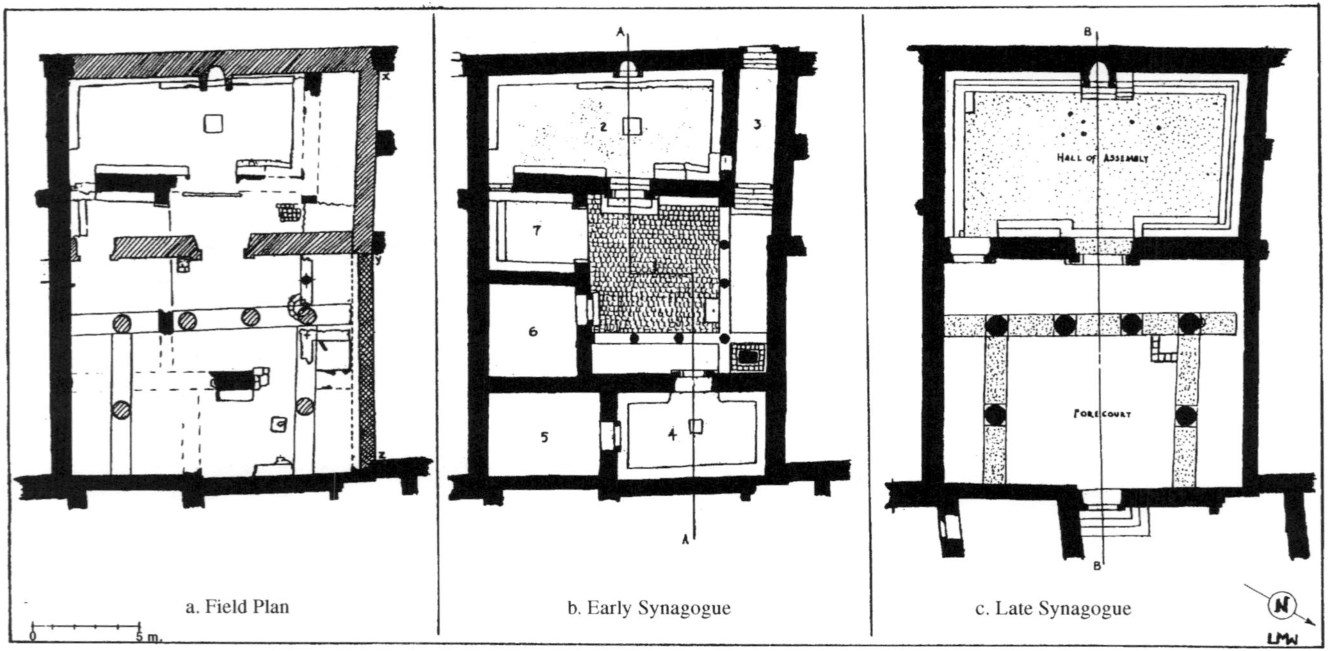

Fig. 29
Syria, Dura-Europos. Synagogue. Field plan (a) and plan restoration in stages (based on excavation field plan of Pearson)

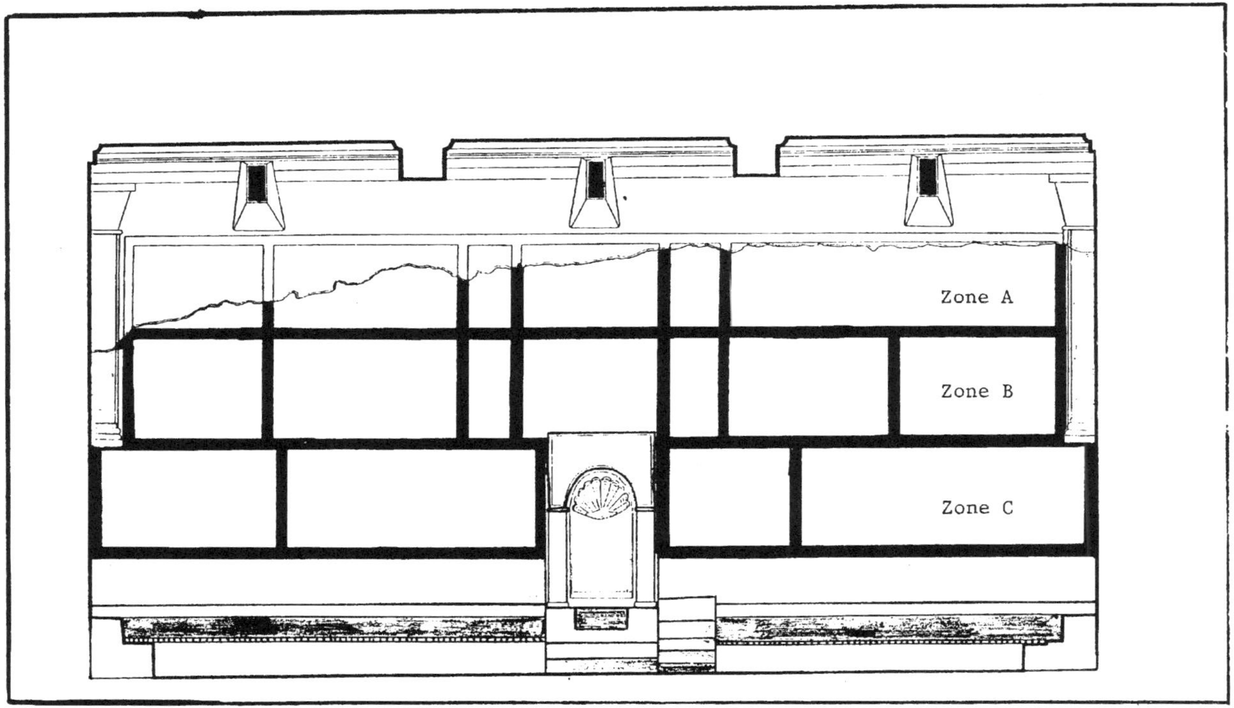

Fig. 30
Syria, Dura-Europos. Late synagogue, ca. 256 CE.
Diagram of west wall of Hall of Assembly (based on Kraeling)

tions and Letters. The structure was located in a block [designated L7; see fig. 28) of private dwellings on the west wall of the city between gates 19 and 20. The excavations revealed three stages of construction in the site. In the latter two stages the building was reconstructed as a synagogue (designated early and late). The site was in use up to the destruction of the city in 256 CE.

Literature: C. B. Welles et al., *DEP* 6 (1933). C. Hopkins and Comte du Mesnil du Buisson, "La Synagogue de Doura-Europos," *CRAI* (1933) 243–54. M. Rostovtzeff, "Die Synagoge von Dura," *RQ* 62 (1934) 203–18. C. H. Kraeling, *The Synagogue. The Excavations at Dura-Europos* (Final Report VIII.l; New Haven: Yale University Press, 1956). E. R. Goodenough, *Jewish Symbols in the Graeco-Roman Period,* vols. 9–11 (New York: Pantheon, 1961–65). A. T. Kraabel, "The Diaspora Synagogue: Archaeological and Epigraphic Evidence since Sukenik," *ANRW* 2.19.1 (1979) 477–510.

For the paintings of the synagogue, see above plus the following special studies: Du Mesnil du Buisson, *Les peintures de la synagogue de Doura-Europos, 244–256 après J.-C.* (Paris: Collège de France, 1939). A. Grabar, "La Theme religieux des fresques de la Synagogue de Doura (245–256 après J.-C.)," *RHR* 123 (1941) 143–92; 124 (1941) 5–35. E. G. Kraeling, "The Meaning of the Ezekiel Panel in the Synagogue at Dura," *BASOR* 78 (1940) 12–18. R. Wischnitzer-Bernstein, "The Conception of Resurrection in the Ezekiel Panel ot the Dura Synagogue," *JBL* 60 (1941) 43–55. Eadem, "The Samuel Cycle in the Wall Decorations of the Synagogue at Dura-Europos," *Proceedings of the American Academy for Jewish Research* 11 (1941) 85–103. R. Wischnitzer, *The Messianic Themes in the Paintings of the Dura Synagogue* (Chicago: University of Chicago Press, 1948). J. Gutmann, ed., *The Dura-Europos Synagogue: A Reappraisal (1932–1972)* (Missoula, MT: Scholars Press, 1973).

[The following reconstruction is based primarily on the preliminary excavation report (*DEP* 6) of the sixth season at Dura (1933), on the final report of Kraeling (*The Synagogue)*, and on the three volumes (9–11) devoted to Dura in Goodenough's *Symbols*. Some additional observations are gleaned from the study of A. Seager, "The Architecture of the Dura and Sardis Synagogues," in *The Dura-Europos Synagogue: A Reappraisal (1932–1972)*, 79–

116. The author has also worked in the archives at Yale and in the collections of the Yale Art Gallery, which include *in situ* copies of the paintings.]

a. Phase I: The House and Early Synagogue (ca. 165–200)

The first synagogue (figs. 28, 29b) was constructed by renovating one of the private houses in the middle of block L7 of the city, on the Wall Street side (west) of the block. The size of the plot was 21.50 X 15.50 m. The house was originally constructed at the same time as Houses A and B (see fig. 28) in the earliest period of development for this area of the city, that is, sometime during the later Parthian occupation (between 50 and 150 CE). The synagogue house was of integral construction with House B to the south and probably had a very similar plan. The renovation of the house for use as a synagogue occurred in the city's early Roman period, that is, ca. 165–200 CE. This dating is indicated in part by the fact that the entrance passageway (room 3) was raised (by 1.75 m) to the height of the fill in Wall Street when the building was remodeled. It was raised by setting poles in the side walls across its width and by covering them with planks, earth, and plaster. (A similar method was used to raise the level of the passageway to House B at this same time.) Access to the central court (room 1) was gained from Wall Street by descending a short step to the level of the new passageway 3 (L.5.50; W.1.75 m) which opened onto the court with another stair. The passageway platform construction created an open storage area underneath, which was reached by a small opening in the north wall of room 2 (fig. 28b).

The central court, room 1 (L.6.55; W.6.05 m) was originally an open area around which the other rooms of the house were clustered. This plan is typical in Durene domestic architecture. In the renovation it was paved with small square tiles (ca.0.22–0.26 m on a side) laid over a bed of ashes. On the west side this paving came to an end against a plaster bench (W.0.40 m) that ran along the exterior of room 2. On the north and east sides of the court a portico was created by mounting five columns (Diam. ca.0.42 m) on two perpendicular stylobates (W.0.525; H.0.265 m). The stylobates intersected in the northeast corner of the peristyle to frame a square basin (D.0.08 m). The basin was drained through the stylobate by a channel leading to the cesspool of the earlier house (fig. 28a, locus 36).

From the court, access was gained to the other rooms of the house, again in keeping with the common type of house plan found at Dura. While the walls of the rooms in the east portion of the house were largely destroyed in the later reconstruction, their positions can be generally determined by a few remnants and projections along the party wall with House H (see fig. 28a, loci 42–44, 48, 49). In all likelihood, then, there were two rooms (4 and 5) on the east side of the house. Room 4 (L.6,85; W.4.15 m) took the common form of a *diwan* or dining room with plaster benches (H.0.22; W.ca.0.49 m) around the walls (fig. 26a, locus 44–44). In the center of the room a plaster block (L.0.67; W.0.62; H.0.27 m) served probably as the brazier stand.[11] Less is known about room 5 (L.5.15; W.4.15 m), but it was probably an anteroom or a pantry for the *diwan*, since such are commonly found in Durene houses. Similarly, the original form of room 6 is uncertain. From the remains (fig. 28a, loci 33, 41), it would appear to be an irregular room (L.ca.4.25–4.30; W.ca.3.87–4.10 m) opening directly onto the courtyard. These houses were typically two stories, at least in certain areas. (Notice the stairway in House A: room A32.) However, any indication of such features in the house of the synagogue was destroyed in the later remodeling.

The more significant renovations for adapting the house to the needs of synagogue community occurred in rooms 2 and 7, since these became the areas for assembly and formal activity. In the original house plan, room 2 may have been composed of two rooms (compare fig. 27, House B: rooms 31 and 30 or House I: rooms 75 and 76). Whether there was originally such a partition, in the early synagogue room 2 was a large irregular quadrilateral (L.10.65–10.85; W.4.60–5.30 m). The main entrance to the room was a door (W.1.50 m at base) from the courtyard. The interior of room 2 had a raised floor of packed earth (H.0.46–0.48 m above the court yard). Around the walls there were plastered mud-brick benches (W.0.39–0.45 m) ranging in height from 0.22 m (fig. 28a, locus 7) to 0.34 m (fig. 27a, loci 12, 16) to 0.45 m (fig. 28a, loci 17, 18) where a footrest (H.0.14; Br.0.30 m) was added. The floor was finished in plaster mixed with pebbles over a layer of red earth (D.0.03–0.05 m). In the middle of the floor a patch of unmixed plaster (0.82 x 0.86 m) was used to fill a hole in the floor. The patch probably represents the removal later (but still in the early period) of some kind of contrivance that had been installed when the room was first renovated.

On the west wall of room 2 (north of center but directly in line with the door and the patched floor) the remains of the earlier benches showed a

11. See Kraeling, *The Synagogue*, 28, but contrast Goodenough, *Symbols*, 9. 27.

number of peculiar features when examined by the excavators: (a) the footrest here showed an inordinate amount of wear (fig. 28a, loci 4–4); (b) the bench at this point was constructed of stone rather than mud-brick; (c) there were slight projections from the bench and traces of paint; (d) finally, two small gypsum colonnettes (H.ca.0.48; Diam.0.12–0.15 m), with an abacus and echinus for each one, were found in the debris in this area. These facts suggest that there was an *aedicula* constructed on the bench of the west wall at this point (locus 3). Given the position, it is almost certainly to be understood as a Torah Shrine of some sort. Even so, its precise pattern of use remains unclear, since it is too small to have accommodated the entire scriptures, and even the entire Torah might have been too large.[12] It cannot be determined whether there was also a niche cut into the wall (as in the late synagogue and in the usual reconstructions of the early one; see fig. 28b). A graffito in a portion of the plaster from the earlier building, found preserved in the construction fill in the later synagogue, might be the design for this first *aedicula*.[13]

---

12. See the suggestions of E. M. Meyers, "The Niche in the Synagogue at Dura-Europos," *BA* 47 (1984) 174, and his reference to usage in the slightly later synagogues of the Galilee in E. M. Meyers, A. T. Kraabel, and J. F. Strange, *Ancient Synagogue Excavations at Khirbet Shemaᶜ, Israel (1970–72)* (Durham, NC: Duke University Press, 1976) 53. Meyers thinks that the Dura Torah Shrine, even in the later period, was used not as a permanent repository for the scrolls but rather as a display only during the service. Here he is following Goodenough's interpretation of room 7 (in the earlier phase), on which see n. 18 below. Meyers is at least partially correct. It must be remembered, however, that any Torah Shrine posited for the first synagogue at Dura would make it the earliest known from archaeological evidence, whether in the Homeland (even earlier than En Nabratein) or from the Diaspora. I suspect that the actual usage of the Dura Torah niche was more determined by local traditions than by rabbinic norms from the Homeland that appear only later.

There are indications from the later period at Dura that the scrolls were kept in a portable wooden chest that could have been carried into the assembly and set in the Torah niche, ready for use in the service. This wooden chest would have been considered the "holy ark" (Heb. *ʾārôn haqqodeš*), not the niche itself. The niche, at least by the time of the construction of the later synagogue, was actually called the "house of the ark" (*bît ʾārônâ*). For a graffito from the later Torah Shrine found on the niche itself that gives this terminology, see No. 61g below. Further exploration of this pattern of usage may illumine the liturgical and processional activities that were conducted in the synagogue building, which of course must also be correlated with the paintings in the synagogue.

13. Kraeling, *Synagogue*, 320 (inscr. no. 71–72, from the south bench in room 2 of

At the south end of room 2 a small door (W.ca.1.00 m) led to room 7. Only the west wall (the partition from room 2) of this room is actually discernible, but the line of the north wall can be determined as it must have abutted the cinder fill of the courtyard (fig. 25a, locus 34). The room was thus approximately 3.85–3.97 m long and 3.75 m wide. Elements of an arch having a span of ca. 2.70 m were discovered; it must have served as an expanded doorway of room 7 from the courtyard. This room, too, had low benches around the walls (west wall, H.0.25; W.0.40 m; south wall, H.0.26; W.0.40 m) and on the south wall a low footrest (H.0.06; W.0.36 m). The plaster step between these benches at the S, door to room 2 showed signs of heavy usage.

Both room 2 and room 7 show signs of decoration indicating their formal character. The walls of room 2 were divided into three horizontal zones. The lowest zone (H.0.87 m) was painted in imitation of a marble plinth. The highest zone seems to have been mostly blank (as far as can be determined) and was finished in white plaster. The middle zone (H.1.38 m), a portion of which was found *in situ* behind the later bench of the south wall, consisted of a band of dado.[14] On the west wall the middle zone probably would have framed the *aedicula*. The plaster ceiling (H.ca.4.90 m) was painted in imitation of a tiled or coffered ceiling.[15] The decorations of room 7 are not well attested, but they were probably of a more modest sort. The scant evidence suggests two horizontal zones divided by a red band at a height of 1.05 m from the floor. The upper zone was decorated with a continuous floral motif, while the lower register was left white. The ceiling was painted in a tile pattern with floral designs.[16] The formal character of room 7 seems clear, but its exact function remains uncertain. At first it was assumed that the room was set aside for women, but such segregation is not found in other synagogues

the early synagogue). Kraeling suggested that this *aedicula* from the first synagogue might have been a secondary addition and that its construction might have been the occasion for removing whatever was in the center of the floor (see *DEP* 6. 334). It is quite plausible and is still in keeping with other considerations in the patterns of movement between rooms 2 and 7, as suggested in nn. 12 and 18.

14. See Kraeling, *Synagogue*, plate XLIX.

15. Ibid., plate L. It should be noted that the late synagogue had an actual coffered ceiling. This fact may suggest some local aesthetic or stylistic tendencies that provided continuities between the first and second stages.

16. Ibid., plate L.

of this early period.[17] Goodenough argued instead that it served as a sort of "sacristy" (probably for the storage of the biblical scrolls) used in conjunction with worship in the assembly hall (room 2).[18] Goodenough's argument is the more plausible.

b. Phase II: The Late Synagogue (ca. 244/5–56)

Circumstances in the early third century, both in the general growth of the city and in the specific fortunes of the Jewish community, made possible an extensive rebuilding project in the synagogue edifice. Inscriptions both in Aramaic and in Greek (No. 61 below) place this event in the year 244/5. The building program comprised three major phases or projects, which were completed in successive stages: (1) reconstruction and enlargement of the earlier edifice, (2) annexation of House H, and (3) appointment and decoration of the hall of assembly (in two stages).

1. The Reconstruction of the Earlier Edifice

The most extensive structural modifications took place in the area occupied by the earlier synagogue house. These modifications consisted primarily in transforming the whole interior space of the house plan into an enlarged hall of assembly and a monumental court. (The physical relation-

---

17. As reflected in Kraeling, *Synagogue*, 31–32. On the absence of such segregation in both Homeland and Diaspora synagogues of this period, see Bernadette Brooten, *Women Leaders in the Ancient Synagogue* (Brown Judaic Studies 36; Chico, CA: Scholars Press, 1982) 103–38.

18. Goodenough, *Jewish Symbols*, 9. 32–34. It is worth noting here (as even Kraeling was aware) that several Aramaic graffiti were found in the area of room 7 from the layer of plaster dating to the early synagogue. These are published in Kraeling, *Synagogue*, inscr. nos. 20–22; two of the three use some formula of remembrance for the person named, a pattern typical at Dura for contributors or those who regularly make use of something. All the names in these graffiti are of men. I suspect that the scrolls (and any other liturgical equipment) were kept in room 7 and were carried in procession to the assembly hall for worship. One problem is that no such clearly articulated area is apparent in the late synagogue, but one suspects that a room in House H (the synagogue annex) might well have served a similar function as the sacred storage area, and that the procession of the scrolls (if such occurred) would have come through the forecourt. See my comments in n. 12 above.

ship of the plan of the early building to that of the later one can be seen in figs. 28 and 29a, b.)

In order to accomplish this renovation, it was necessary to destroy virtually all of the earlier edifice and to erect new walls from the foundations. The interior walls of the early synagogue were entirely destroyed down to floor level (except for a few remnants as shown in fig. 29a). Likewise, the entire west wall of the building (facing onto Wall Street) was knocked down. The benches along the wall were left in place, but the wall line itself was dug down to foundation level (below street level). The north wall (the party-wall with House C) was similarly destroyed from x to y (i.e., in rooms C18 and C19). The south wall (the party-wall with House B) was knocked down to a height of ca. 1.75 m above floor level (i.e., to the height of the raised level of the passageways in House B and the early synagogue). [The north wall from y to z, if it was knocked down at this same time, was probably handled in the same way as the south wall. It is clear, however, the the wall segment y–z was removed at some time; see below.] From these foundation courses new, monumental exterior walls were erected to a height of ca. 7.00 m for the enlarged hall of assembly. To carry the structure, the west wall was increased to a thickness of 1.04 m; the north (segment x–y) and south walls remained 0.92 m in thickness. [The north wall segment y–z was thinner and was probably reconstructed at a still later time; see below.]

The shell thus created was cut into two parts by the construction of a heavy crossing wall (Th.1.04 m, the same as the new west wall) intersecting the north wall at y. The thickness of these two was meant to carry the high, coffered ceiling over the entire expanse. The large rectangular chamber (L.13.65; W.7.68 m) in the western half of the edifice became the hall of assembly. Two doors were opened in its east wall. The main entrance (W.ca.2.02 m at base, ca.1.70 m at top, H.ca.4.35 m) was mounted with two massive wooden doors opening toward the interior of the room. The smaller south door (W.ca.1.35; H.ca.2.75 m) employed a similar double-door arrangement. [The ceiling, floors, and benches of the room will be discussed along with the appointment and decoration of the hall of assembly.]

The east compartment created by erecting the partition wall at y became the monumental forecourt of the hall of assembly. The area was an unroofed courtyard (L.[north–south axis] 13.30, W.[east–west axis] 10.25– 10.40 m), walled in on all four sides. The court was embellished with colonnaded porticoes on three of its sides (west, north, south). This *tristoon* was arranged with six large columns set on a heavy rubble and stone stylobate (W.ca.1.00 m) laid in three sections. The west stylobate was laid across the entire width of the forecourt (ending some 0.17 m from the thinner north wall section; see fig. 29a, locus 37).[19] The north and south stylobates were set perpendicular to the west stylobate. The six rubble columns (Diam. ca.0.96 m at base) with gypsum bases and capitals were placed on the three stylobate sections: one each at the midpoint of the north and south sections, one at each of the intersections on the west stylobate, and two central columns on the west stylobate. The last-named, central columns framed the main door of the assembly hall, but the door itself is slightly north of center (0.51 m) on the east wall (on the axis of the west wall *aedicula*). The columns (according to their diameter) must have been ca. 5.50–6.00 m in height to support a flat roof reaching just above thc main door of the hall of assembly. The floor of the court had been filled with earth and covered with a layer of ash to make a bed (D.ca.0.60 m) for tiles (ca. 0.22–0.26 m square). A drain through the west stylobate leading to the original cesspool suggests the existence of a basin in the northwest corner of the open court. Another small half-basin of plaster was attached to the north side of the northwest column.

2. Annexation of House H

In order to enlarge the hall of assembly, the entryway of the earlier structure (fig. 29b, room 3) had been incorporated in expanding the room to the north party-wall with House C. Since the planned expansion necessitated the elimination of what had been the only entrance to the synagogue proper, integral with this expansion was a provision for a new entrance leading through the forecourt to the main door of the assembly hall. In its final stage the new entrance to the peristyle court was cut through the party-wall from

19. In addition to the gap at the north end of the west stylobate, it should be noticed that the edge of the stylobate and those of the earlier water basin and stylobate are aligned (see fig. 29a, loci 37–39). This point suggests that at the time of the construction of the peristyle for the later synagogue forecourt the original north wall (at least at the base) was still in place in the segment y-z. Wall y-z, therefore, must have been demolished and replaced by the thinner construction at a later time. See n. 20 below.

House H, room 4. House H was thus remodeled and annexed to the synagogue. It is not clear whether this remodeling occurred simultaneously with the completion of the forecourt or slightly later.[20]

The plan of House H is unique among private dwellings at Dura, and this fact may be attributed to its annexation for use by the synagogue. The plot of H was quite large and irregularly shaped (L.25.70–27.00; W.17.75–18.50 m). When adapted for use as an entrance to the synagogue forecourt, House H was comprised of two interconnected suites of rooms. From the entrance off Street A through the common alley (fig. 28, room 71) the entryway of H was divided into two chambers (rooms Hl and H2) leading to two open courts (H3 and H9). The two courts were also connected by a door, and rooms H4 and H5 were similarly related. In their final arrangement and use, however, Hl, H3, and H4 constituted a suite of entry rooms leading to the synagogue forecourt. The other rooms of the house (H2, H9, H5–8) were more private, domestic quarters, with H8 being the *diwan*. In room H4 (L.9.15; W.4.60 m) a flight of steps led to a doorway cut through the east wall of the forecourt at a height 0.60 m above the floor level of House H. A plaster bench stood along the east wall of H4, and a pier or pedestal projected into the room 0.33 m from its west wall.

20. It is usually assumed (for want of any other evidence) that the entrance from House H was the planned route from the time that the renovations for the later synagogue began. But the later wall restoration in the forecourt (section y-z on the north wall) remains a puzzle. One possible (but highly conjectural) explanation might be that the new entrance to the forecourt at the time of the renovation came not from House H but from the party-wall with House C in room 29. The reasons for the conjecture are as follows: (a) House C is generally thought to have been owned by a member of the Jewish community, since the construction so radically affected party-walls [it belonged perhaps to the presbyter Samuel, named in the inscriptions, Nos. 61a and 61d below]. (b) At some point House C was interconnected with House D by cutting a doorway between rooms C23 and D24, thus providing a direct line of access to room C29 (either from Street 4 or Street A through room C23). (c) Finally, the party-wall with House H was never demolished or altered except for the installation of the door when it was annexed. It seems reasonable to conjecture, therefore, that the first entrance to the new forecourt was by a door (or doors?) cut through wall y-z from room C29 at a time when House H had not yet been readied as the annex/entryway (or had not yet come into possession of the synagogue or one of its members). Then, when House H was acquired and made the new avenue of entry into the forecourt, the wall section y-z was demolished and replaced with the ill-fitting thinner partition.

3. Appointment and Decoration of the Hall of Assembly

In the structural adaptation of the synagogue, provisions were made for formal adornments, especially in the hall of assembly. On the west wall of the assembly hall the height of the foundation courses was ca. 3.00 m above the floor level, owing chiefly to the rising level of Wall Street. As a part of this rubble-work foundation there was inset a block of rubble-work masonry (H.2.80; W.1.56 m). Its center was 0.10 m north of the east–west axis of the hall, and it projected 0.41 m into the room. In the block a recess was pre-cut to form a niche (H.1.51; W.0.83; Br.0.91 m). A central step (Br.0.33 m) flanked by pedestals (H.0.30; W.0.40; Br.0.31 m) extended from the block 0.43 m below the floor of the niche (and 0.71 m above the floor of the room). Two steps (H.0.26; Br.0.26, H.0.20; Br.0.33 m) were set against the base step. On this core was constructed the *aedicula* for the Torah Shrine by applying an ornamental facade. Two rubble-work columns (Diam.0.26; H.1.13 m), plastered and painted to resemble marble, were set on the flanking pedestals of the top step. These columns carried a heavy rubble-work arch (H.1.06; W.1.47;Th.0.26 tapering to 0.05 m at the top) extended 0.40 m above the rubble-masonry core of the *aedicula*. At the head of the niche, the decorative fluting of a conch was executed in plaster and the entire niche-interior was painted. On the back of the façade was found a graffito (No. 61g below) that alludes to its construction.

Flanking the *aedicula* and extending around the room (interrupted only by the two doors on the east), benches were constructed. These benches were made of rubble and coated with plaster to form two steps (lower: H.0.29–0.47 m; upper: H.0.29–0.38 m). Along the west and north walls and the east wall (north of the main door) these benches were provided with a footrest (H.0.06; Br.0.23 m) set along the rear of the lower bench. The width of benches without footrests was ca.0.40 m; those with footrests were 0.51–0.57 m wide.

At some time after the initial construction of these benches the area immediately to the north of the *aedicula* was overlaid with a rubble and plaster construction of five steps (W.0.76 m) rising 0.28 m above the top bench, that is, 0.97 m above the floor. (The steps from bottom to top measure: H.0.12; Br.0.16, H.0.18; Br.0.20, H.0.18; Br.0.23, H.0.23; Br.0.30, H.0.36; Br. 0.43 m).

As in the bench construction, two stages are in evidence in the floor. When the monumental hall was first constructed, the floor was filled in at a height of 0.24–0.30 m above the earlier floor level (covering over the benches of room 2). This floor was finished in plaster mixed with pebbles. Then at a later time another, more carefully prepared mixture of pebbles and plaster (D.0.10 m) was laid over a bed of sand. The wear patterns of this last floor level would indicate that there was a traffic zone (W.ca.1.40 m) just inside the line of the benches. In contrast, the central floor area shows little sign of wear. Along the east, north, and south walls were grouped holes of various sizes, molded when the floor was laid, for numerous appurtenances, for example, lampstands and, perhaps, a bema (set 1.60 m from the west bench just south of the Torah Shrine).

The ceiling of the hall of assembly was fitted with rows of baked clay tiles (ca. 0.41 m square; Th.0.045 m) laid upon joists. The vast majority of these tiles (numbering about 450 in total) bore artistic designs (e.g., persons, animals, astral symbols, flowers, or fruit) and were apparently produced in local workshops. Six other tiles bear inscriptions (three in Aramaic and three in Greek) detailing the dedication and history of the building (Nos. 61–62).

The final element of the interior furnishings of the hall of assembly consists of the magnificent frescoes that decorated the four walls. These paintings, likewise, constitute two phases of decoration. In the first phase (following upon the structural renovation) the Torah Shrine was painted both on the interior of the niche and on the facade. Apparently the wall area directly above the Torah Shrine (known in the later decorative program as the "reredos") was one of the first painted (and repainted on several occasions). Around the walls a two-zone design (at heights above the benches of 1.15 and 0.60 m respectively) must have been intended to reproduce something on the order of the decorative elements of the first synagogue (i.e., a marble plinth with dado above). Kraeling also suggests that in the last stage the painted pilasters at the four corners of the room and the architrave pictorially supported above them were elements held over from this first decorative stage.

The interior decorations of the assembly hall were next redone beginning about 251, and the work must have continued almost to the final destruction of the building in 256. The walls were divided vertically into five zones of unequal height (see fig. 30). The highest zone was a painted architrave of about 0.70–1.00 m. The lowest zone was the elaborate dado rising 0.70 m above the upper benches. The three intermediate zones (from top to bottom, A-B-C respectively) were treated with the elaborate narrative scenes. Of these, register B was the broadest (ca.1.50 m), A the narrowest (ca.l.l0 m), and C intermediate (ca.1.30 m). The reredos above the Torah Shrine were repainted in a two-zone arrangement corresponding to registers A and B. Flanking the reredos were four "wing-panels" (numbered I–IV) in registers A and B depicting male figures in monumental scale.[21]

PROVINCE: Syria
LOCATION: Dura-Europos

No. 61: Synagogue Inscriptions (244/45) (The Later Synagogue)

The date of the renovation of the later synagogue (No. 60b, above) is fixed by inscriptions found on six ceiling tiles from the hall of assembly. Three of the tiles (No. 61a–c) bear Aramaic texts; the other three (No. 61d–f) are inscribed in Greek. All of the tiles preserve essentially the same legend, a commemoration of the construction of the later synagogue. The Aramaic tiles preserve the full version of this dedication in two parts (Tiles A and B). Aramaic Tile C carries an abbreviated form of the first lines of Tile A in two separate inscriptions. The three Greek tiles reproduce in abbreviated form the content of the Aramaic commemorative, that is, with the names and offices of the leading synagogue officials from Tile A. The final text included here is a graffito from the Torah Shrine that refers to its construction. Pertinent data regarding each text will be given below.

Literature: C. Hopkins and Comte du Mesnil du Buisson, "La Synagogue de Doura-Europos," *CRAI* (1933) 202–3, 243–54. Du Mesnil du Buisson, "La nouvelle decouvertes de la synagogue de Doura-Europos," *RB* 43 (1943) 546–63. *DEP* 6 (1932–33) 384–95. C. C. Torrey, "The Beginning of the Dura-Europos Synagogue Inscription," *JQR* n.s. 28 (1938) 295–99. Du Mesnil du Buisson, *Les Peintures de la Synagogue de Doura-Europos, 244–256 apres J.-C.* (Paris: Collège de France, 1939) 158. J. Obermann, "Inscribed Tiles from the Dura-Europos Synagogue," *Berytus* 7 (1942) 89–138.

21. For the arrangement of the final phase of decorations, see fig. 30; for descriptions, plates, and discussions of the contents of the frescoes, see especially Kraeling, *Synagogue,* pp. 70–239 and plates, and Goodenough, *Jewish Symbols*, vols. 10–11, passim and plates.

C. H. Kraeling, *The Synagogue*. (Final Report VIII.1; New Haven: Yale University Press, 1956): Aramaic inscriptions by C. C. Torrey [pp. 261–76]; Greek inscriptions by C. Bradford Welles [pp. 277–82]. B. Lifshitz, *Donateurs et Fondateurs dans les Synagogues juives* (Cahiers de la RB 7; Paris: Gabalda, 1967), nos. 58–60.

[The following reconstructions are based primarily on the discussions of Torrey and Welles in Kraeling, *The Synagogue* (Final Report VIII.l) and of Obermann in *Berytus* 7. All reference numbers are given according to the edited texts in Kraeling, *The Synagogue*.]

61a–c: The Aramaic Commemorative

a. Aramaic Tile A: Kraeling, *Synagogue*, 263–65 (inscr. no.la) (Compare *CIJ* 2. 828b, and Obermann, *Berytus* 7:97)

The tile (ca.0.42 x 0.42 m) is broken off in the lower left corner and cracked from the center top down to the breakline. The text of fifteen lines is a dipinto in black. Letters, H.0.016–0.028 m.

ה
1 הדין בית אתבני
2 בשנה חמש מאה חמשין
3 ושית דאִינין שנת תרתן לפלפוס
4 [[יוליס]] קסר בקשישותה דשמואל
5 כהנה בר ידעי ארכון. ודקמו
6 על עיבידה הִדין אברם גיזב-
7 רה ושמואל [בר] סִפִרה ו . . . .
8 גיורה. ברוח [מיתרעיה שוין למיבני]
9 בשנת שית וחמשין אִיִלין ושדרו ל..
10 . .ר . . . . ורהטו . . . .
11 . . . . .ב . . . . תה ועמלו ב . . .
12 . . . . ברכתה מן שביה
13 וכל בני . . . . עמלו ולאיִן . . .
14 שלמה [להון ולנ]שִיהון ובניהון כלהון.
15 וכשים

b. Aramaic Tile B: Kraeling, *Synagogue*, 265–66 (inscr. no. la) (Compare Obermann, *Berytus* 7:113; not included in *CIJ*)

The tile (ca.0.42 x 0.42 m) is unbroken but badly defaced. The text of nine lines is a dipinto in black. Letters, H.ca.0.020 m.

1 וב
2 וכשים כלהון דעמלו [כך אחיהין] . . .
3 כלהון דבכספה . . . .
4 ובחמידת נפ[שהון]
5 אגרהון כלמה . . . . עלמה [ההבא]
6 דאתי ה . . . .
7 קימה להון . . . . שמ . . . .
8 בכל שבת . . . . פרסין [ידיהון]
9 בה׳

Translation: (Tile A) This house was built in the year 556, this corresponding to the second year of Philip Julius Caesar; in the eldership of the priest Samuel son of Yedaʿya, the Archon.[22] Now those who stood in charge of this work were: ʾAbram[23] the Treasurer, and Samuel son of Sapharah, and ..... the proselyte. With a willing spirit they [began to build] in this fifty-sixth year; and they sent .... and they made haste ....[24] and they

22. ארכון (line5). A simple transliteration of the Greek *archon,* but the title does not appear in the Greek inscriptions (cf. Greek Tile 1 = No. 61d below).

23. The fact that the name of the father of "Abram the treasurer" is not given has led Torrey to ask whether the genitive ʼΑρσάχου in Greek Tile 3 (= No. 61f below) might be his father, the καὶ being an error (cf. Kraeling, *Synagogue*, 265). On the other hand, Obermann (*Berytus* 7. 107) had read the name Tedros, son of Arsach (וטדרוס/בר ארסח) in lines 9–10. Torrey thinks this unlikely and postulates for lines 9–10 an allusion to the Targum on Exodus 35:21, a reference to the "spirit" in which the Tabernacle was built (cf. *Synagogue*, 265).

24. For lines 10–12, (where Torrey reads ורהטו . . . / . . . תה ועמלוב . . / . . .. Obermann had reconstructed this portion of the text as follows:

ועמ]לו רהיטי / [לבי]תה במזטבתה ועמלו בבו״׳ / וכ[רטי]סא . . .

and he translates, "And they provided for columns for the house on its porch and they provided for murals and the scroll." Obermann admits that the reading is highly conjectural (*Berytus* 7. 97, 108, 111). Despite the intriguing possibilities, the reference to

labored in .... a blessing from the elders and from all the children of .... they labored and toiled .... Peace to them, and to their wives and children all. (Tile B) And (in the second part) like all those who labored[25] [were their brethren ....], all of them, who with their money .... and in the eager desire of their souls .... Their reward, all whatever .... that the world which is to come .... assured to them .... on every sabbath .... spreading out [their hands (in prayer)] in it.

[Text and translation after C. C. Torrey, in Kraeling, *Synagogue*, 263–64.]

c. Aramaic Tile C: Kraeling, *Synagogue*, 267–68 (inscr. no.lb,c). (For no. lb, compare *CIJ* 828a; for both, see Obermann, *Berytus,* 7. 93–95)

The tile (ca. 0.42 x 0.42 m) is chipped on the lower right corner and broken (but with little damage) on the upper right corner. On close examination the tile was found to contain two inscriptions, both in Aramaic: in the upper quadrant of the tile a graffito of six lines (Letters, H.0.008–0.010 m; across the center of the tile a dipinto in black of five lines, Letters, H.0.0l0 m). It was found that both texts reproduce, with very few changes, the first portion of the text in Tile A given above. Inscr. no. lb contains lines 1–5; inscr. no.lc contains lines 1–7. The more complete readings given for these lines provided for the more certain reconstruction of the first lines of Tile A. For this reason the texts of inscrs. lb and lc will not be given here.

"murals" would be difficult to correlate with the conclusion of the excavators that the paintings were executed later than the rebuilding (see No. 60b above).

25. וב / וכשים (lines 1–2, lapis). Obermann (*Berytus,* 7. 113) had read תקנים for the beginning of the text of Tile B. He interpreted the entire inscription, independent of Tile A, as a liturgical text—a prayer for the dead (see *Berytus,* 7. 116). Torrey's reconstruction makes Tile B the continuation of Tile A, as it is rendered above. In addition to the general content of the text (surmised from the few remnants still readable), Torrey cites as support for his reconstruction the beginning words of Tile B. The first line he thinks consisted only of the two letters וב, which he takes to mean "and the second (part)" as an indicator that the text is a continuation. Then he argues that וכשים כלהון intentionally picks up the last words of the text in Tile A.

61d–f: The Greek Dipinti

d. Greek Tile 1: Kraeling, *The Synagogue*, 277 (inscr. no. 23) (cf. *CIJ* 829)

The tile (ca. 0.42 x 0.42 m) contains a painted wreath encircling a dipinto of five lines in black. The upper left corner is chipped, but the text is completely legible. Letters, H.ca.0.028 m.

Σαμουὴλ
Εἰδδέου
πρεσβύτερος
τῶν Ἰουδέ-
ων ἔκτισεν.

Translation: Samuel, son of Idaeus, presbyter of the Jews, built (the synagogue).

e. Greek Tile 2: Kraeling, *Synagogue*, 277 (inscr. no. 24) (cf. *CIJ* 2. 831)

The tile (ca. 0.42 x 0.42 m) contains a painted wreath encircling a dipinto of five lines in black. The tile is broken (five pieces), causing some damage to line 4. Letters, H.0.028 m.

Σαμουὴλ
Βαρσαφάρα
μνησθῇ ἔκ-
[τ]ισεν ταῦ-
τα οὕτως.

Translation: Samuel, son of Sapharas, may he be remembered, built[26] this (building) thus (as you see).[27]

---

26. ἔκ/[τ]ισεν (line 3). The same term is used for the work of this second Samuel as for the first in Greek Tile 1. In Aramaic Tile A (No. 61a), however, Samuel son of Sapharah is placed among the overseers of the project along with the persons mentioned in Greek Tile 3. The distinctions may refer instead to the rebuilding project itself, as opposed to the decoration and painting of the hall of assembly. See also the following note.

27. The text of Aramaic Tile A will not admit the interpretation once advanced that Samuel son of Idaeus built the earlier synagogue and Samuel son of Sapharah the

f. Greek Tile 3: Kraeling, *Synagogue*, 278 (inscr. no. 25)
(cf. *CIJ* 830)

The tile (ca. 0.42 x 0.42 m) contains a painted wreath encircling a dipinto of five lines in black. The tile is cracked down the middle, but the text is completely legible. Letters, H.0.028 m.

῎Αβραμ
καὶ ᾽Αρσά-
χου καί Σιλᾶς
κὲ Σαλμάνης
ἐβοήθησαν

Translation: Abram and (the son of?)[28] Arsaches and Silas[29] and Salmanes assisted.[30]

g. An Aramaic Graffito: Kraeling, *Synagogue,* 269 (inscr. no. 2)
(Cf. Comte du Mesnil du Buisson, “L’inscription de la niche centrale de la synagogue de Doura-Europos,” *Syria* 40 [1963] 310–16)

A graffito in two lines on the facade of the *aedicula*, just below the base of the menorah. Letters, H.ca.0.01 m. The text records the names of special

later. The date 244/5 CE given in Aramaic A must refer to the later synagogue. The difference suggested vaguely in the final phrase (ταῦτα οὕτως) may refer to the embellishment or finishing of the hall of assembly, as opposed to the renovation of the entire complex attributed to Samuel son of Idaeus. It has also been suggested that House C of Block L7 belonged to this Samuel son of Idaeus because of its integral relationship to the synagogue structure and because it was so directly affected in the remodeling of the later synagogue (see No. 60b above and fig. 28).

28. On the genitive ending of the name Arsaches and its relation to Aramaic A, see No. 61a, n. 23, above.

29. Obermann (*Berytus* 7. 106) suggested that the missing name of the proselyte in Aramaic Tile A (line 7) should be filled in with either Silas or Salmanes (he favored the former).

30. That all of the names mentioned in these dedications refer to those who participated in the major parts of the renovation project (either the building or the decoration) may be inferred from another Aramaic graffito found on the face of the Torah Shrine, which clearly indicates who assisted in its construction. This text is given as No. 61g below.

contributors or, perhaps more likely, the artisans who worked on the *aedicula*. The two lines are in the same hand.

The following is Torrey's reading of the text, based on Kraeling's trace.

..... אנא עזי עבדת בית ארונה

מ
יוסף ברה דאבא עבר ב... ה

Translation: I, ʿUzzi, made the repository of the Torah Shrine. Joseph son of ʾAbba made the.... (Torrey's translation).

Comte du Mesnil du Buisson, one of the original excavators for the French Academy, in a later and little known article ("L'inscription de la niche centrale dc la synagogue de Doura-Europos," *Syria* 40 [1963] 310–16) provided a substantially complete reading of the last half of the graffito, reconstructing the names not as ʿUzzi and Joseph but as Martin and Sisaʾ. His version of the remainder of the first line agrees for the most part with that of Torrey. His reading is as follows:

מרתין דע[בד] עבדת בית ארונה
[ו]סיסא ברה̣ דארום הקדש.

Translation: Martîn made the paintings of the "house of the ark"; Sisaʾ made the holy ark. (My translation, with some alteration, from Du Mesnil du Buisson.)[31]

31. Du Mesnil du Buisson offered the following translation: "Martin qui a fait l'ouvrage (les peintures) à la niche de l'Armoire (beit ʾarôn), [et] Sisaʾ (qui a fait) la façon (ou la sculpture) de l'Armoire sainte (ʾaron haqqôdesh)." He then goes on to suggest that the person named Sisaʾ was likely a (Jewish?) artisan of the city. He also suggests that this might be the same individual identified by the Greek name Sisaeon. He thinks, therefore, that this might be the same Sisaeon who is memorialized as a Christian and who executed some of the work in the baptistry of the *domus ecclesiae* (see No. 37b above). So Du Mesnil du Buisson, "L'inscription de la niche," 313–14.

PROVINCE: Judea (Palestina [prima])
LOCATION: Jerusalem

No. 62: Ophel Synagogue Inscription (first century [?])
(*CIJ* 1404; *SEG* 8. 170)

Inscribed on a rectangular limestone tile, the text contains ten lines set in a recessed plaque with frame. It was discovered during the excavations in the City of David in 1913–14 under the direction of Raimond Weill. The discovery was reported in the area of what were then identified as baths dating to the pre-70 period. This particular stone was found deposited in the cisterns; consequently, it must be considered without identifiable context.[32] The stone is badly weathered with a sizable lacuna in the center of the text plaque. Two lines of erosion or wear run vertically through the text at the right center and along the left edge (after the first letter of each line). The upper right corner is badly defaced, but some letters are discernible.

Literature: R. Weill, "La cité de David, Campagne de 1913–1914," *REJ* 69 (1919) 186–90, and *Annexe*, plate XXVa; cf. *REJ* 71 (1920) 30–34; 71 (1920) 186–90. T. Reinach, "L'inscription de Theodotos," *REJ* 71 (1920) 46–56. H. Lietzmann, "Notizen: Ein Synagogen-Inschrift aus Jerusalem," *ZNW* 20 (1921) 171–73. A. Deissmann, *Licht vom Osten* (4th ed.; Tübingen: J. C. B. Mohr [Paul Siebeck], 1923) 378–80 [= *Light from the Ancient East* (1978 ed.) 439–41]. H. Leclercq, *DACL* 7. 240–47. E. L. Sukenik, *Ancient Synagogues in Palestine and Greece* (London: Oxford University Press, 1934) 69–72. *SEG* 8. 170. *CIJ* 2. 1404. B. Lifshitz, *Donateurs et Fondateurs*

32. The date of the inscription is usually given as first century CE (before the destruction of Jerusalem in 70) owing to the assumed proscription of Jewish worship in the city after 70. So the discussion in Deissmann, *Light from the Ancient East*, 439 n. 2, 441 (citing E. Schürer, *A History of the Jewish People in the Age of Jesus Christ [175 B.C.–A.D. 135]* [rev. ed.; Edinburgh: T & T Clark, 1973] regarding the prohibitions after 70). Because of the lack of an identfiable context, however, this date is far less certain than is often assumed. A date up to the time of the second revolt (132–35 CE) is also possible, as would be a date in the late fourth–fifth centuries. I suspect that the provisions within the text for pilgrimage to Jerusalem have too easily been ascribed to a pre-70 date without adequate critical evaluation of later possibilities.

dans les Synagogues juives (Cahiers de la RB 7; Paris: Gabalda, 1967) no. 79.

Θ[ε]όδοτος Οὐεττήνου, ἱερεὺς καὶ
ἀ[ρ]χισυνάγωγος, υἱὸς ἀρχισυν[αγώ]-
γ[ο]υ, υἱωνὸς ἀρχισυν[α]γώγου, ᾠκο-
δόμησε τὴν συναγωγὴν εἰς ἀν[άγν]ω-
σ[ιν] νόμου καὶ εἰς [δ]ιδαχ[ὴ]ν ἐντολῶν, καὶ
τ[ὸ]ν ξενῶνα, κα[ὶ τὰ] δώματα καὶ τὰ χρη-
σ[τ]ήρια τῶν ὑδάτων εἰς κατάλυμα τοῖ-
ς [χ]ρήζουσιν ἀπὸ τῆς ξέ[ν]ης, ἣν ἐθεμε-
λ[ίω]σαν οἱ πατέρες [α]ὐτοῦ καὶ οἱ πρε-
σ[β]ύτεροι καὶ Σιμων[ί]δης.

Translation: Theodotos, son of Vettenos,[33] priest and archisynagogos, son of an archisynagogos, grandson of an archisynagogos, built the synagogue for the reading of the Law and for instruction in the commandments. (He built) also the guest house, the rooms, and the water facility as a lodging for travelers in need.[34] Of this synagogue his fathers, the elders, and Simonides laid the foundations.

33. It is clear from the wording (see n. 34 below) that this synagogue was intended to serve pilgrims and, therefore, was built by and for Diaspora Jews, who would have come to Jerusalem out of piety (whether before or after the destruction of the Temple). Deissmann (*Light*, 440 n. 1), following H. Lietzmann (in *ZNW* 20 [1921] 172), proposed that Vettenos had received Roman citizenship from a member of the *gens Vettena*, over against those who read it as the name of a freedman of the same *gens*. The latter reading had been taken to suggest that this was somehow associated with a synagogue of imperial freedmen from Rome and was thus taken to be identical with the "Synagogue of the Libertines (Freedmen)" mentioned in Acts 6:9. Deissmann concluded that such an identification was possible but not likely; however, this assertion is still made without critical comment.

34. For this phrase (line 6) compare the Galilean dedication of the third–fourth centuries in Aramaic (*CIJ* 2. 979): בית דה דאורחותה דמיך קדם "(the) house (or hostelry) which is beside the door [of the synagogue]"); see S. Klein, "Das Fremdenhaus der Synagoge," *Monatschrift für Geschichte und Wissenschaft der Judentums* 79 (1932–33) 545–57, 603–4. Deissmann proposed reading "rooms, chambers" for δώματα. Compare the usage in the Ostia synagogue inscription below, No. 84.

PROVINCE: Egypt (Cyrenaica)
LOCATION: Berenike (Benghazi)

No. 63: Jewish Building Inscriptions (first century BCE/CE)

No. 63a: Honors for Decimus Valerius Dionysius for renovation work (ca. 8–6 BCE) (I.Berenike 18)

A marble stele (H.0.77; W.0.37–.39; Th.0.11 m) tapering slightly toward the top, with a gabled molding and akroteria. The text is in twenty-six lines. The face of the inscription is badly worn. Letters: H. 0.012–17 m.

Literature: J. and G. Roux, in *REG* 62 (1949) 281–96 and plate III. J. A. Lloyd, R. Reece, J. M. Reynolds, et al., *Excavations at Sidi Khrebish, Benghazi (Berenice)* (2 vols.; Supplements to Libya Antiqua 5; Tripoli: Libya Antiqua, 1977, 1979) 1. 243–54 (inscr. no. 18, ed. J. M. Reynolds). G. Lüderitz, *Corpus jüdischer Zeugnisse aus der Cyrenaika* (Wiesbaden: Reichert, 1983) 148–51 (no. 70). S. Applebaum, *Jews and Greeks in Ancient Cyrene* (Leiden: Brill, 1979) 160–67. R. Tracey, "Jewish renovation of an amphitheatre," *NDIEC* 4 (1987) 202–9 (no. 111).

(ἔτους) [ ]γ´. Φ[αμ]ένωθ ε´ ἐπὶ ἀρχόντων Ἀ̣ρ̣ίμμα τοῦ
[*7 letters*]ος Δωρίωνος τοῦ Πτολεμίου
Ζ̣ε̣λ̣α̣ι̣ου τοῦ [Γ]ναίου Ἀρίστωνος τοῦ Ἀραξα-
[. .]ν̣τ̣ο̣ς Σ̣αρα[πί]ω̣νος τοῦ Ἀνδρομάχου Νικία
τ[οῦ *9–10 letters*]Α̣[.]Σ̣Α̣[. . . .] τ̣ο̣ῦ̣ Σίμωνος. ν. ἐπεὶ
[Δέκ]μος Ο[ὐαλέριος Γ]αίο[υ Διον]ύσιος Π̣Ρ̣ΗΠ̣ΟΤΗΣ
[±*9*] Ω̣Γ̣Η̣Σ̣ ἀνὴρ καλὸς καὶ ἀγαθὸς ὢν δια-
τελε[ῖ ?λόγῳ καὶ ἔργῳ καὶ αἱρ]έσε̣ι̣ καὶ ποιῶν ἀγαθὸν
[ὅτι] ἂ̣[ν] δ[ύνηται καὶ κοι]ν̣ᾶι καὶ ἰδίαι ἑκάστωι τῶν
π̣[ο]λ̣ί̣τ̣[ων] καὶ δ[ὴ καὶ] ἐκονίασεν τοῦ ἀνφιθεάτρου
τ[ὸ ἔδ]α̣φος καὶ το̣ὺ̣[ς] τ̣οίχους ἐζωγράφησεν
ἔ[δοξε τοῖς ἄ]ρχουσι καὶ τῶι πολιτεύματι
τ̣[ῶν] ἐ̣ν̣ Β̣ε̣ρ̣ν̣ι̣κ̣ί̣δ̣ι̣ Ἰ̣ο̣υ̣δαίων καταγράψαι αὐτὸν εἰς
τὸ τ̣ῶ̣ν̣ τ[±*6*]ΕΥΕΙ̣Σ̣Υ̣Δ̣Ι̣Ο̣Υ̣ κ̣α̣ὶ̣ εἶεν ἀλειτούρ-
γητο[ν πά]σης [λε]ιτουρ[γί]ας [ὁ]μοίως δὲ καὶ στε-
φα[νοῦν α]ὐτὸν καθ᾽ ἑκάστην σύνοδον καὶ νουμ̣η̣-
νία̣ν̣ σ̣τ̣ε̣[φ]άνωι [ἐλ]αίνωι καὶ λημνίσκωι ὀνομαστί

τὸ [δ]ὲ ψήφισμα τόδε ἀναγράψαντες οἱ ἄρχον[τες]
[εἰ]ς στήλην λίθου Παρίου θέτωσαν εἰς τὸν ἐ[πι-]
[σημ]ότατον [τόπ]ον τοῦ ἀμφιθεάτρου.
λευκαὶ πᾶσαι
vac.
Δέκμος Οὐαλέριος Γαΐου Διονύσιος
τὸ ἔ̣[δ]α̣[φ]ος ἐκονίασεν καὶ τὸ ἀμφι-
θέατρον καὶ ἐζωγράφησεν τοῖς
ἰδίοις δαπανήμασιν ἐπίδομα
τῶι πολιτεύματι.

Translation: In the year [.]3, on the 5th of Phamenoth, in the archonship of Arimmas son of […], Dorion son of Ptolemaios, Zelaios son of Gnaios, Ariston son of Araxa[…], Sarapion son of Andromachos, Nikias son of [… , (and) …] son of Simon. Whereas Dec(i)mus Valerius Dionysius son of Gaius … (of the synagogue?)[35] remains an honorable and good man in word, in deed, and in purpose, and doing whatever good he is able, whether in public or private matters (dealing rightly) with each of the citizens, and in particular, (whereas) he has plastered the floor of the amphitheater[36] and painted

35. No attempt has been made to resolve the lacuna in lines 6–7 in most studies. However, it appears to me that the line should read τῆς [· · · συναγ]ωγῆς. Thus, the sense seems to be a title of Dionysius in connection with the synagogue. For the badly damaged term in line 5: ΠΡ̣Η̣ΠΟ, I would suggest reading πρηπό(σιτος), a transliteration from the Latin *praepositus,* a standard term for a prefect. If this conjecture is accurate, it suggests that Dionysius holds an honorific place or *proedrion* in the congregation; see lines 13–15 below and n. 38.

36. The editors, J. and G. Roux (*REG* 62. 292–93) and others have concluded that the term "amphitheater" must refer to the place where the Jews themselves met, that is, their synodal hall or synagogue. The term is thus taken to connote an architectural shape rather than a specific type of public building. (Cf. J. and L. Robert, in *Bull.epigr*. [1951] 246; Applebaum, *Jews and Greeks in Ancient Cyrene*, 264–66.) J. Reynolds, however, maintained that it still refers to a public building, in which the Jewish *politeuma* must have been allowed to meet; see *Excavations at Sidi Khrebish, Benghazi (Berenice)*, 1. 247. In either case, some measure of autonomy in the use of the building must have fallen to the Jewish *politeuma*, since the renovation and decoration funded by Valerius Dionysios were clearly directed at them and they were able to grant (or secure) exemption from liturgies. It is not impossible, given this obviously public role of the Jewish *politeuma* in local civic life, that at this early stage there was no separate "synagogue" per se as a place of exclusively Jewish worship

the walls,[37] it is hereby resolved by the archons of the *politeuma* of the Jews in Berenike to inscribe (or enroll, register) him in the [...] of the [...][38] and (it resolved) that he be exempted from all liturgies whatsoever, and moreover to crown him with an olive crown and a wooden nameplate at each synod and new moon. Wherefore, the archons, having inscribed this resolution on a stele of Parian marble, are to set it up in a very visible place in the amphitheater. (The vote:) All whites (i.e., unanimous).

(vac.)

Dec(i)mus Valerius Dionysius, son of Gaius, plastered the floor and (*sic of*) the amphitheater and painted (it) at his own expense as a gift to the *politeuma* (of the Jews).[39]

No. 63b: Honor Roll of Contributors to Synagogue Renovation (ca. 56 CE) (REG 72 [1959] 514)

An inscribed stele of Parian marble.

Literature: G. Caputo, *Parola des Passato* (1957) 132–34. J. and L.

---

and assembly. A generation or two later, however, we hear of the renovation of such a synagogue for the Jewish community; see No. 63b below. On the role of the *politeuma* and its relations with local civic leaders, see also n. 39 below. On the basis of the available evidence, it is not possible to say conclusively whether the "amphitheater" is the same as the synagogue edifice or not; however, a place of regular Jewish meetings (at least for public functions) is clearly indicated.

37. The term for "painting" refers to decoration with paintings, i.e., painted scenes. See the discussion in *NDIEC* 4. 204–7.

38. The missing phrase suggests either a list of honorees and benefactors in the Jewish *politeuma* or appointment to some public office, which would then carry exemption from other public liturgies. Decimus Valerius Dionysius would seem to be Jewish and a Roman citizen. The corrupted portion of line 14 is probably to be restored with some form of the word ('Io)υδ(α)ίου.

39. Another inscription from the year 24/5 (*I. Berenike* 17 = *REG* 62 [1949] 283–89) was also set up in the amphitheater. It records the honors paid by the Jewish *politeuma* to a Roman official named Marcus Tittius, who had acted favorably toward the Jews in granting special public concessions. This text suggests that the use of the amphitheater as a place of meeting by the Jews continued for several decades and that they had certain rights of decoration and display in it. This inscription uses the term ἐφάνη as a formula for decrees as is found also in the later text of the Berenike synagogue (No. 63b), line 3.

Robert, in *Bull. epigr.* (1959) 514. B. Lifshitz, *Donateurs et Fondateurs dans les Synagogues juives* (Cahiers de la RB 7; Paris: Gabalda, 1967) no. 100.

[Text after Lifshitz.]

(Ἔτει) Β´ Νέρωνος Κλαυδίου Καίσαρος Δρούσου
Γερμανικοῦ Αὐτοκράτορος χοϊάχ ις´
ἐφάνη τῇ συναγωγῇ τῶν ἐν Βερνεικίδι
Ἰουδαίων τοὺς ἐπιδιδόντες εἰς ἐπισκευ-
ὴν τῆς συναγωγῆς ἀναγράψαι αὐτοὺς εἰστή-

λην λίθου Παρίου	Ἀλέξανδρος
Ζηνίων Ζωίλου ι´	Εὐφράνορος ε´
Εἰσίδωρος Δωσειθέου ἄρχων ι´	
Δωσείθεος Ἀμμωνίου ἄρχων ι´	Εισιδώρα
Πρᾶτις Ἰωναθᾶ ἄρχων ι´	Σεράπωνος ε´
Καρνήδας Κορνηλίου ἄρχων ι´	Ζωσίμη Τερ-
Ἡρακλείδης Ἡρακλίδου ἄρχων ι´	πολίω ε´
Θαλίαρχος Δωσιθέου ἄρχων ι´	Πόλων
Σωσίβιος Ἰάσονος ἄρχων ι´	Δωσιθέου ε´
Πρατομήδης Σωκράτου ἄρχων ι´	
Ἀντίγον(ο)ς Στράτωνος ἄρχων ι´	
Καρτισθένης Ἀρχία ἱερεὺς ι´	
Λυσανίας Λυσανία κε´	
Ζηνόδωρος Θευφίλου κη´	
Μ̣α̣ρ̣ι̣[ων......]ος κε´.	

Translation: In the second year of the emperor Nero Claudius Caesar Drusus Germanicus, on the 16th of Chorach. It pleased the congregation of the Jews in Berenice that (the names of) those who contributed to the renovation of the synagogue be inscribed on a stele of Parian marble.

(First Column) Zenion, son of Zoilos, 10 (drachmae); Isidoros, son of Dositheos, archon, 10 (drachmae); Dositheos, son of Ammonios, archon, 10 (drachmae); Pratis, son of Jonathan, archon, 10 (drachmae); Carnedas, son of Cornelius, archon, 10 (drachmae); Heracleides, son of Heracleides, archon, 10 (drachmae); Thaliarchos, son of Dositheos, archon, 10 (drachmae); Sosibios (son of) Jason, archon, 10 (drachmae); Pratomedes, son of

Socrates, archon, 10 (drachmae); Antigonos (son of) Straton, archon, 10 (drachmae); Cartisthenes, son of Archias, priest, 10 (drachmae); Lysanias (son of) Lysanias, 25 (drachmae); Zenodoros, son of Theophilos, 28 (drachmae); Mari[on, son of ...]os, 25 (drachmae).

(Second column) Alexander, (son of?) Euphranoros, 5 (drachmae); Eisodora, (daughter of) Serapeon, 5 (drachmae); Zosime, daughter of Terpolios, 5 (drachmae); Polon, son of Dositheos, 5 (drachmae).[40]

PROVINCE: Asia Minor (Caria)
LOCATION: Aphrodisias

No. 64: Honorific for Contributors by a Jewish *Dekany* (third century) (Aphrodisias Inventory No. 76.1)

A slightly tapered marble block (H:2.80; W:0.43–45; D:0.425–46 m) was found loose and hence despoiled of its original context. There is damage to the stone top and bottom, which eradicated part of the text at the top of face b. The stone is smoothed on three faces (a, b, c), but rough dressed on side d, which is on the left as one looks at face a. The stone is inscribed on faces a and b (each in a different hand) with three columns totaling eighty-eight lines. The conclusion that the text is Jewish is predicated on the high proportions of Semitic names and references to offices or status of individuals, for example, "proselytes" (col.i,17, 22), "Benjamin the psalmologue" (col.i,15), and "Samuel the Elder" (col.i,margin). Most notable is the use of the term "God-fearer" (col.i,19, 20; col.iii,34). The presence of a Jewish community at Aphrodisias is confirmed by a number of other inscriptions.

Literature: *Editio princeps*: Joyce M. Reynolds and Robert F. Tannenbaum, *Jews and Godfearers at Aphrodisias: Greek Inscriptions with Commentary* (Cambridge Philological Society, Supplements 12; Cambridge: Cambridge Philological Society, 1987). Also published in *SEG* 36 (1986)

---

40. The sum of the individual contributions listed is 208 drachmae. The family of Dositheos (lines 6, 9, 13), if one may assume that these are a father and sons, seems to be heavily represented in the list, and most hold offices in the synagogue. The total of their donations is 35 drachmae. Three more contributions (lines 18–20) totaled 78 drachmae. These two groups made up more than half of the total.

no. 970. The inscription has also been discussed prior to official publication in the following: A. T. Kraabel, "The Disappearance of the 'Godfearers,'" *Numen* 28 (1981) 113–26. Robert F. Tannenbaum, "Jews and God-Fearers in the Holy City of Aphrodite," *BAR* 12 (1986) 54–57; Louis H. Feldman, "The Omnipresence of Godfearers," *BAR* 12 (1986) 58–63, 64–69; Robert S. MacKinnon and A. T. Kraabel, "The God-Fearers — A Literary and Theological Invention," *BAR* 12 (1986) 46–53, 64. Since publication: M. H. Williams, "The Jews and Godfearers Inscription from Aphrodisias — A Case of Patriarchal Interference in Early 3rd Century Caria?" *Historia* 41 (1992) 297–310.

Face a
Col. i

Θεὸς Βοηθός, πατέλλα̣? δο̣[.1 or 2.]
Οἱ ὑποτεταγμέ-
νοι τῆς δεκαν(ίας)
τῶν φιλομαθῶ̣[ν]
τῶν κὲ παντευλογ(--ων)
εἰς ἀπενθησίαν
τῷ̣ πλήθι ἔκτισα[ν]
ἐξ ἰδίων μνῆμα
Σα — Ἰαηλ προστάτης.
μου — *v.* σὺν υἱῷ̣ Ἰωσούα̣ ἄρχ(οντι?)
ἠλ — Θεόδοτος Παλατῖν(ος?) σὺν
πρεσ — *v.* υἱῷ̣ Ἱλαριανῷ̣ *vac.*
βευ — Σαμουὴλ ἀρχιδ(έκανος?) προσήλ(υτος)
τὴς — Ἰωσῆς Ἰεσσέου *vacat*
Περ- — Βενιαμὶν ψαλμο(λόγος?)
γε- — Ἰούδας εὔκολος *vacat*
ούς — Ἰωσῆς προσήλυ(τος)
Σαββάτιος Ἀμαχίου
Ἐμμόνιος θεοσεβ(ής) *v.v.*
Ἀντωνῖνος θεοσεβ(ής)
Σαμουὴλ Πολιτιανοῦ
Εἰωσηφ Εὐσεβίου προσή(λυτος)
κα[ὶ] Εἰούδας Θεοδώρ(ου)
καὶ Ἀντιπέος Ἑρμή(ου?)

καὶ Σαβάθιος νεκτάρις
⟦[?κα]ὶ Σαμο[υ]ηλ πρεσ-
βευτὴς ἱερεύς⟧

Face b (at a slight angle to col. i and in a different hand)

Ṇ Ṃ Δ̣

Col. ii

[? *one line completely lost*]
[. . *c*. 8 . . Σ]εραπίωνος *v.* [*v.*]
⟦*one line completely erased*⟧
[Ἰωση]φ Ζήνωνος *vacat*
[Ζή]νων Ἰακωβ *stop* Μανασῆς Ἰωφ *sic*
Ἰ̣ούδας Εὐσεβίου *vacat*
Ἑορτάσιος Καλλικάρπου *vacat*
βιωτικὸς *stop* Ἰούδας Ἀμφιανοῦ
Εὐγένιος χρυσοχόος *vacat*
Πραοίλιος *stop* Ἰούδας Πραοιλίου *v.*
Ῥοῦφος *stop* Ὀξυχόλιος γέρων
Ἀμάντιος Χαρίνου *stop* Μύρτιλος
Ἰακω προβατον(όμος?) *stop* Σεβῆρος *vacat*
Εὔοδος *stop* Ἰάσων Εὐόδου *vacat*
Εὐσαββάθιος λαχα(νοπώλης?) *stop* Ἀνύσιος
Εὐσαββάθιος ξένος *stop* Μίλων
Ὀξυχόλιος νεώτερος *vacat*
Διογένης *stop* Εὐσαββάθιος Διογέν(ους)
[Ἰού]δας Παύλου *stop* Θεόφιλος *vac.*
[Ἰ]α̣[κ]ωβ ὁ κὲ Ἀπελλί(ων?) *stop* Ζαχαρίας μονο(πώλης?)
[Λε]ό̣ντιος Λεοντίου *stop* Γέμελλος
[Ἰο]ύ̣δας Ἀχολίου *stop* Δαμόνικος *vacat*
Εὐτάρκιος Ἰούδα *stop* Ἰωσηφ Φιληρ(?)
Εὐσαββάθιος Εὐγενίου *vacat*
Κύρυλλος *stop* Εὐτύχιος χαλκο(τύπος?)
Ἰωσηφ παστι(λλάριος?) *stop* Ῥουβην παστ(ιλλάριος?)
Ἰούδας Ὁρτασί(ου) *stop* Εὐτύχιος ὀρν(ιθοπώλης?)
Ἰούδας ὁ κὲ Ζωσι(?) *stop* Ζήνων γρυτ(οπώλης?)
Ἀμμιανὸς χιλᾶς *stop* Αἰλιανὸς Αἰλια(νοῦ)

Αἰλιανὸς ὁ καὶ Σαμουὴλ Φίλανθος
Γοργόνιος Ὀξυ(χολίου) *stop* Ἑορτάσιος Ἀχιλλέ(ως)
Εὐσαββάθιος Ὀξυχ(ολίου) *stop* Παρηγόριος
Ἑορτάσιος Ζωτικοῦ Συμεών Ζην(?)
vacat

Face b
Col. iii *vacat*
Καὶ ὅσοι θεοσεβῖς *stop* Ζήνων βουλ(ευτής)
Τέρτυλλος βουλ(ευτής) *stop* Διογένης βουλ(ευτής)
Ὀνήσιμος βουλ(ευτής) *stop* Ζήνων Λονγι(ανοῦ?) βου(λευτής)
Ἀντιπέος βουλ(ευτής) *stop* Ἀντίοχος βουλ(ευτής)
Ῥωμανὸς βουλ(ευτής) *stop* Ἀπονήριος βουλ(ευτής)
Εὐπίθιος πορφυρ(ᾶς) *stop* Στρατήγιος
Ξάνθος *vacat* Ξάνθυς Ξάνθου *v.*
Ἀπονήριος Ἀπον(ηρίου) *stop* Ὑψικλῆς Μελ(?) *stop*
Πολυχρόνιος Ξάν(θου) *stop* Ἀθηνίων Αἰ(λιανοῦ?)
Καλλίμορφος Καλ(λιμόρφου?) ΙΟΥΝΒΑΛΟΣ
Τυχικὸς Τυχι(κοῦ) *stop* Γληγόριος Τυχι(κοῦ) *v.*
Πολυχρόνιος Βελ(?) *stop* Χρύσιππος
Γοργόνιος χαλ(κοτύπος?) *stop* Τατιανὸς Ὀξυ(χολίου?)
Ἀπελλᾶς Ἡγε(μονέως?) *stop* Βαλεριανὸς πενα(κᾶς?)
Εὐσαββάθιος Ἡδ(υχρόος?) ?Μανικιος Ἀττά(λου?) *vac.*
Ὀρτάσιος λατύ(πος?) *stop* Βραβεὺς *vacat*
Κλαυδιανὸς Καλ(λιμόρφου?) *stop* Ἀλέξανδρος πυ(?)
Ἀππιανὸς λευ(?) *stop* Ἀδόλιος ἰσικιάριος
Ζωτικὸς ψελ(λός?) *stop* Ζωτικὸς γρύλλος
Εὐπίθιος Εὐπι(θίου) *stop* Πατρίκιος χαλκο(τύπος)
Ἐλπιδιανὸς ἀθλη(τής?) *stop* Ἡδυχροῦς *vacat*
Εὐτρόπιος Ἡδυχ(ρόος) *stop* Καλλίνικος *vac.*
Βαλεριανὸς ἀρκά(ριος?) *stop* Εὔρετος Ἀθηναγ(όρου)
Παράμονος ἰκονο(γράφος?) *stop* *vacat*
Εὐτυχιανὸς γναφ(εύς) *stop* Προκόπιος τρα(πεζίτης?)
Προυνίκιο γναφ(εύς) *stop* Στρατόνικος γναφ(εύς)
Ἀθηναγόρας τέκτω(ν) *vacat*
Μελίτων Ἀμαζονίου *vacat*
vacat *vacat*

Translation:(Face a, col. i) God, helper. The donors of the *patella* (?).[41] Listed below are the (members of the) *dekany* of "Lovers-of-Learning," also called the "All-Blessing,"[42] who, for the relief of suffering (or grief) in the community, built (this building) from their own resources, as a memorial.

41. For possible reconstructions of lines 1–3, see Reynolds and Tannenbaum, *Jews and Godfearers at Aphrodisias: Greek Inscriptions with Commentary*, 41. It must be pointed out that the commentary on the Jewish elements in the text, authored by Tannenbaum, read much of the language in terms of later rabbinic norms and mishnaic or talmudic terminology. The expressed assumption is that this reflects direct influence from the patriarchate in the Homeland, but this view faces a number of difficulties. It is better to read the text in the light of local traditions and conventions. See also the criticism of M. H. Williams, "The Jews and Godfearers Inscription from Aphrodisias — A Case of Patriarchal Interference in Early 3rd Century Caria?" *Historia* 41 (1992) 297–310. I had earlier expressed some of the same reservations in an unpublished paper, and this view is reflected in my discussion in *Building God's House in the Roman World*, 89–90.

On the term πατέλλα (or perhaps πατελλαδο[. .]) the key issue is whether it should be understood as some sort of charitable "soup kitchen." The term πατέλλα (used in Greek and Latin) meant a small, flat dish or pan often used in conjunction with incense offerings and especially associated (though by no means exclusively) with Bacchic rites. While it is still possible to read the phrase as "donors to the soup kitchen," especially given the reference to seemingly charitable activities in lines 6–7, one must not assume that this is an official synagogal institution, as suggested by Tannenbaum. At the very least it would appear to be a mixed Jewish and non-Jewish social group or perhaps a *collegium*, even if charitable functions were also at work. Williams ("The Jews and Godfearers Inscription," 307) suggests a funerary association and reads the term πατελλαδο[. .] as a reference to their banquets. (Williams translates line 1 as "God our Helper. Put [food] on the plate" [p. 309].) This is more plausible than the formal institution proposed by Tannenbaum, but one final alternative reading suggests itself thus: "God our Helper. Giver (or accepter) of Offerings." In any case, the text is a decree of honors enacted by the members of the *dekany* for those who contributed to the construction either of the memorial itself or (more likely) the collegial hall in front of which it stood.

42. I see no reference to study of Torah (as suggested by Tannenbaum, *Jews and Godfearers*, 41). Both names should be taken as formal self-designations or epithets of the collegium that is being represented by its chosen council, here designated by the common term *dekany*. For δεκανία as a collegial association, see Reynolds and Tannenbaum, *Jews and Godfearers*, 28–30; cf. Williams, "The Jews and Godfearers Inscription," 305. In my view these epithets reflect the common practice of adopting lofty titles of self-designation through word-coinage by collegial and cultic groups in the Greek cities. In this way the terms might well be taken by Jews in the light of allusions to "law" or "scripture," but on the surface they are intentionally neutral and for public consumption by the broader population of the city. On the same ground,

Jael, the President.[43] (from margin) Samuel, the Elder, Pergaios (or a Pergean), with (his) son Joshua, Archon; Theodotos, Palatinos (or Officer of the Court), with his son Hilarian; Samuel, *archidekanon*, a proselyte; Joses, son of Jesse; Benjamin the Psalmologue; Judas Eukolos ("good tempered"); Joses, a proselyte; Sabbatios, son of Amachios; Emmonios, a God-fearer; Antoninos, a God-fearer;[44] Samuel, son of Politianos; (second

apparently, Williams reads the second title in terms of funerary eulogies, in support of her suggestion that this is really a burial association (p. 307). Other types of collegial associations might also be considered, however. So, compare the pagan (!) cult of angel worshipers from Yayla Baba Köy in Galatia, which calls itself "The Association of Friends/Lovers of the Angels" (Φιλαγγέλων συμβίοσις); see A. R. R. Sheppard, "Pagan Cults of Angels in Roman Asia Minor," *Talanta* 12–13 (1980–81) 88.

43. There is an incised horizontal line above the left third of line 9. I take it together with the text in the margin and read it as the end of the honorific preamble and the beginning of the list of honorees. The first name, that of Jael, the President of the *dekany*, however, remains in a category distinct from all the rest in the lists, deserving of special honor. The marginal insertion is in a second hand and may be a correction for the erasure in lines 26–27. I have read the name of the son in line 9 with the marginal insertion, rather than with the name Jael. In addition, it must be noted that the name Jael in biblical tradition is feminine, even though it would be the only name of a woman in this entire list. Bernadette Brooten argues that it is feminine here ("Ἰαηλ Προστάτης in the Jewish Donative Inscription from Aphrodisias," in *The Future of Early Christianity: Essays in Honor of Helmut Koester,* ed. B. Pearson (Minneapolis: Fortress, 1991) 149–62). A female patron and president of an otherwise all-male *collegium* is perhaps rare but not impossible. Nonetheless, nothing within the Aphrodisias inscription itself makes a clear determination possible regarding Jael.

44. The term "God-fearer" θεοσεβής (which occurs twice in the preamble and again later in the heading to col. iii) as it appears in this text has received considerable attention and speculation since it was first reported. The traditional understanding of the term as a designation for semi-proselytes in the synagogue has been argued by some and denied by others. Since the body of this inscription does not refer to a synagogue congregation per se (as was supposed also in the reading of Tannenbaum), I do not think that the appearance of the term here can be taken in support of the traditional reading. Instead, I would read it as an intentionally neutral term of piety that Jewish members of the *collegium* could use conscientiously of their non-Jewish fellow members. The designation of piety would also be appropriate, given the number of decurions (city councillors) and prominent merchants that appear in the list of col. iii. It may or may not, therefore, have anything to do with whether these individuals participated in the Jewish worship. The fact that two individuals from this group were on the board of the *dekany* simply means that there was a concerted effort for representation across the membership, even if the bulk of the group or its base of operations was Jewish.

hand)[45] Joseph, son of Eusebius, a proselyte; and Judas, son of Theodoros, and Antipios, son of Hermeos, and Sabathios Nektaris ("sweet"), ⟦and Samuel, the Elder, priest.⟧

vacat

(Face b, col. ii) . . . . . (S)erapion; . . . .(Jose)ph Zenon, son of Zenon; Jacob; Manases Joph (*sic*); Judas son of Eusebius; Heortasios, son of Kallikarp; Biotikos; Judas, son of Amphianos, Eugenios, goldsmith; Praoilios; Judas, son of Praoilios; Rouphos; Oxycholios, the aged; Amantios, son of Charinos; Myrtilos; Jaco(b), shepherd; Severos; Euodos; Jason, son of Euodos; Eusabbathios, greengrocer; Anysios; Eusabbathios, the foreigner; Milon; Oxycholios the younger; Diogenes; Eusabbathios, son of Diogenes; Judas, son of Paul; Theophilos; Jacob, also called Appellion; Zacharias, merchant; Leontios, son of Leontios; Gemellos; Judas, son of Acholios; Damonikos; Eutarkios Judas; Joesph Philar(?); Eusabbathios, son of Eugenios; Cyryllos; Eutychios, bronzesmith; Joseph, confectioner (?); Judas, son of Hortasios; Eutychios, poulterer; Judas, also called Zosi; Zenon, rag-dealer; Ammianos, mat-maker (?); Ailianos, son of Ailianos; Ailianos, also called Samuel, Philanthos; Gorgonios, son of Oxycholios; Paregorios, Heortasios, son of Zotikos; Symeon, son of Zenon (?).

vacat

(Face b, col.iii) And as many (of the rest) as are God-fearers: Zenon, councillor; Tertullos, councillor; Diogenes, councillor; Onesimos, councillor; Zenon, son of Longinos, councillor; Antipeos, councillor; Antiochos, councillor; Romanos, councillor; Aponerios, councillor; Eupithios, purple-seller; Strategios; Zanthos; Zanthos, son of Zanthos; Aponerios, son of Aponerios; Hypsikles (son of?) Mel(ito?); Polychronios, son of Zanthos, Athenion, son of Ai(lianos ?); Kallimorph, son of Killimorph; Iounbalos (?); Tychikos, son of Tychikos; Glegorios, son of Tychikos; Polychronios, (son of) Bel (?); Chrysippos; Gorgonios, bronzesmith; Tatianos, son of Oxycholios; Apellas, son of Hegemon; Valerianos, tablet maker; Eusabbathios, (son of?) Hedychroos (?); Manicios, son of Attalos; Hortasios, stone cutter;

45. A second hand begins at line 22, but may also include line 21. All of face b is in a different hand. Lines 26–27 have been erased. It is likely that they were carved incorrectly and were corrected in the marginal insertion (n. 43 above), also in a second hand.

Brabeus; Klaudianos, son of Kallimorph; Alexander, (doorkeeper?); Appian, marble worker (?); Adoloios, minced-meat maker; Zotikos, armlet maker (?); Zotikos, swineherd (or pork dealer);[46] Eupithios, son of Eupithios; Patricios, bronzesmith; Elpidianos, athlete; Hedychrous; Eutropios, son of Hedychrous; Kallinikos; Valerianos, treasurer; Heuretos, son of Athenagoros; Paramonos, sculptor; Eutychianos, fuller; Procopios, moneychanger; Prunicios, fuller; Stratonikos, fuller; Athenagoros, carpenter; Melito, son of Amazonios.

vacat

PROVINCE: Asia Minor (Phrygia)
LOCATION: Akmoneia (Ercis)

No. 65: Honors for Julia Severa: Donation and Renovation of a Synagogue Building (late first century) (*MAMA* 6. 264, *CIJ* 2. 766)

The honorific is inscribed on a rectangular slab of white marble (H.0.49; W.0.58; Th.0.15 m). The letters are somewhat coarsely rendered and carelessly placed. The original transcription of the text was by W. M. Ramsay in 1888 when he found it used as the support for a porch column of a modern house. The surface of the stone has suffered greatly from the misuse, but the text remains largely intact. Letters: H.0.0175–0.0225 m.

Literature: W. M. Ramsay, *Cities and Bishoprics of Phrygia* (2 vols.; Oxford: B. Blackwell, 1895, 1897) 1. 2, no. 559. Idem, "Deux jours in Phrygie," *Revue des Études anciennes* 3 (1901) 272. Idem, "Nouvelles remarques sur les textes d'Acmonie," *Revue des Études anciennes* 4 (1902) 270. *IGRR* 4. 655 (Cagnat-Lafaye). E. Schürer, *Geschichte* (4th ed.; Paris: Hinrichs, 1909) 3. 20–21. *MAMA* 6. 264 (Buckler-Calder). *CIJ* 2. 766. L. Robert, "Inscriptions grecques de Side," *Rev. Phil.* 32 (1958) 41 and n. 1. B. Lifshitz, *Donateurs et Fondateurs dans les Synagogues juives* (Cahiers de la RB 7; Paris: Gabalda, 1967) no. 33. A. T. Kraabel, "Judaism in Western Asia Minor

46. Line 52: *Gryllos* (Γρύλλος) is either a nickname ("Porky") or, more likely, an occupational designation (as occurs frequently in the list) and is meant to distinguish the two men of the same name mentioned in this line. In either case, it must be thought unusual in any "typical" sense of Jewish sympathizers.

under Roman Rule, with a Preliminary Study of the Jewish Community at Sardis, Lydia" (Th.D. Thesis, Harvard University, 1968) 71–80. B. Brooten, *Women Leaders in the Ancient Synagogue* (Chico, CA: Scholars Press, 1982) 144, 158.

Τὸν κατασκευασθέντα οἶκον ὑπὸ
Ἰουλίας Σεουήρας Π. Τυρρώνιος Κλά-
δος, ὁ διὰ βίου ἀρχισυνάγωγος καὶ
Λούκιος Λουκίου ἀρχισυνάγωγος
καὶ Ποπίλιος Ζωτικὸς ἄρχων ἐπεσκεύασαν ἔκ τε τῶν ἰδίων καὶ τῶν συν-
καταθεμένων καὶ ἔγραψαν τοὺς τοί-
χους καὶ τὴν ὀροφὴν καὶ ἐποίησαν
τὴν τῶν θυρίδων ἀσφάλειαν καὶ τὸν
λυπὸν πάντα κόσμον, οὕστινας κα[ὶ]
ἡ συναγωγὴ ἐτείμησεν ὅπλῳ ἐπιχρύ-
σῳ διά τε τὴν ἐνάρετον αὐτῶν δ[ι]άθ[ε]-
σιν καὶ τὴν πρὸς τὴν συναγωγὴν εὔνοιάν
τε καὶ σπουδήν.

Translation: The edifice,[47] which was constructed by Julia Severa,[48] Pub-

47. The term οἶκος is now understood rightly to mean "edifice" and could refer to buidings of various architectural types. Going back to H. Kohl and C. Watzinger (*Antike Synagogen in Galiläa* [Leipzig: Hinrichs, 1916]), it was a presupposition in dealing with this inscription and the comparable one from Phocaea (No. 68 below) that οἶκος meant "hall of assembly"; see L. Robert, "Inscriptions grecques de Side," *Rev. Phil.* 32 (1958) 41 (n. 1) and 47 (n. 1). Robert had criticized Frey's rendering of the text because he had not consulted the edition in *MAMA* 6. He also called J.-B. Frey's translation, "L'edifice" for οἶκος (*CIJ* 2. 766) imprecise and "vague." Lifshitz, on the other hand, reads with Frey, but he understands the more general terminology to be a reference to "l'edifice de la synagogue tout entier" (see *Donateurs*, 35). In the final analysis, Frey's "imprecision" was justifiably cautious. The arguments of Kohl and Watzinger, L. Robert, and Lifshitz were predicated on the erroneous assumption that οἶκος meaning "hall of assembly" or "synagogue" in a formal architectural sense could be demonstrated archeologically by the Polycharmos inscription from the basilica at Stobi (see Nos. 72–73 below). At the time the basilica, later found to be Christian, was thought to be the synagogue edifice described in the inscription. The inscription turned out to be a reused spoil from an earlier building on the site, and the term "house" turned out to be literal.

48. Julia Severa is known from several other inscriptions in the provenance of

lius Tyrronios Clados, archisynagogos for life, Lucius son of Lucius,

---

Akmoneia as a very prominent pagan woman. She was not, as once assumed, Jewish, nor was she even a Jewish "sympathizer." She was of Galatian royal ancestry and a cousin of senator Aulos Julius Quadratus from Ephesus. She was the wife of Italian equestrian Lucius Servenius Capito, and their son L. Servenius Cornuts was adlected to the senate under Nero. She was also a municipal archontess and priestess in the local imperial cult. (Cf. PIR[1] S, 104; B. Levick, *Roman Colonies in Southern Asia Minor* [Oxford: Clarendon, 1967] 106–7.) Coins bearing their legend and references to their joint archonship under Nero and Agrippina make possible a dating between 60 and 80 CE (cf. the lengthy discussion of the evidence in Ramsay, *Cities and Bishoprics*, 1.2. 649f. and no. 550). Ramsay assigned the present inscription to the same period, i.e., the end of the first century.

E. Schürer (*Geschichte* [4th ed.] 3. 21) argued that a distinction should be made between the original construction of the edifice (using the Greek term κατασκευασθέντα) by Julia Severa and its renovation (ἐπεσκεύασαν) under the three named Jewish leaders that follow (lines 2–5). Following P. Groag (in the article "Julia Severa," PW 10.l. 946–48) Schürer argued (against Ramsay) that Julia Severa was not likely Jewish or even a "sympathizer." The latter view has prevailed. In consequence of this observation, also, Schürer placed the renovation of the synagogue at a later time. See also the discussion in Kraabel, "Judaism in Western Asia Minor," 72–75. However, given the fact that Julia Severa is still being honored in the inscription, probably for having donated the building to the Jewish leaders who then renovated it, the date of the inscription should not be placed too much later, probably not later than the early second century, when her kin were still known to be prominent figures in Akmoneia.

Given the distinction in terminology noted by Schürer, the edifice erected by Julia Severa does not mean the construction of a synagogue proper. Instead it refers to the construction of some other private building, potentially even a house. See n. 47 above. There is nothing in the text to indicate that Julia Severa was a patroness of the synagogue itself, only that she owned the building which was later renovated as a synagogue. What one misses from the text (especially when compared to the honorific from Phocaea, No. 68 below) is an explicit statement as to how the property came into the hands of the Jews. It may be assumed that the building was not a synagogue when originally constructed and that the rather meager mention of Julia Severa refers only to her largess (or that of her heirs) in donating their private property at a later time (though the circumstances are not given). The bulk of the honors in the inscription are directed at the three named Jewish leaders who oversaw and paid for the renovation of the edifice for use as a synagogue. The present commemoration, then, is properly construed as a slightly later event wherein the building was being converted from its original form into a synagogue of a more formal type.

A final question regarding Julia Severa's patronage of the Jewish community should address her relationship to the three named Jewish leaders. The names Lucius (Julia's husband Lucius Servenius Capito) and Tyrronios (Tyrronios Rapo, *IGRR,* 4.

archisynagogos, and Popilios Zoticos, archon, have renovated from their own funds and from the community treasury. They have decorated the walls and the ceiling, and they made the security of the gates and all the rest of the decoration. The congregation (of the Jews) honors these individuals with a gold shield on account of their excellent leadership and their kindly feelings and zeal toward the congregation.

PROVINCE: Asia Minor (Lydia)
LOCATION: Sardis (Sart)
No. 66: The Synagogue (third to sixth centuries)
(Figures 31–33)

The Sardis synagogue was discovered in 1962 by the Harvard-Cornell expedition; it was excavated and restored through 1972. The structure was prominently located in a large hall on the south side of the monumental Roman bath-gymnasium complex (fig. 31) in the northwest portion of the city. The hall was bounded on the north by the *palaestra* of the gymnasium and on the south by a row of shops facing onto the city's main street. The original foundations of the bath-gymnasium complex date to ca. 17 CE, but the complex was not completed in its present form until the end of the second century. Apparently, further expansion of the south hall was planned but unfulfilled. There were four stages of construction in the hall; in Stages III and IV (dating from the third to the sixth centuries) it was definitely used as a synagogue. The principal form of the edifice as a synagogue is that of Stage IV and dates to the fourth century. This edifice seems to have been modified slightly thereafter and was used continuously by the Jewish community up to the destruction of the city by the Persians in 616 CE.

655) are attested in connection with Julia Severa's family and archonship at Akmoneia (cf. Groag, *PW* 10.1. 947; Kraabel, "Judaism in Western Asia Minor," 76–77; Ramsay, *Cities and Bishoprics*, 1.2. 648–49). One wonders, despite the lack of any direct evidence, whether Tyrronios and Lucius were Jewish freedmen, or descendants of freedmen, in her service. Such a relationship would certainly help to explain why such a prominent pagan, a municipal archontess and a priestess in the Akmoneian imperial cult, would make such an arrangement with the local Jewish community. The benefaction may be construed then as an act of patronage to her own familial clients. The renovations undertaken by the three Jewish leaders, in turn, constituted their act of patronage toward the Jewish community. Thus, one sees a tiered set of relationships.

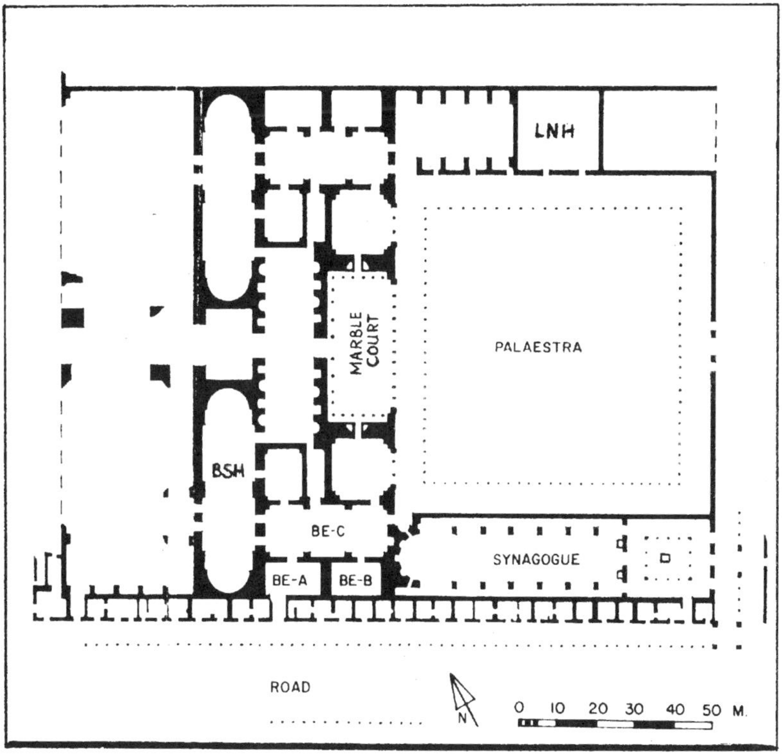

Fig. 31
Lydia, Sardis. Municipal complex and synagogue, ca. fourth century.
Plan restoration (Seager, 1972)

Literature: Yearly excavation reports by G. M. A. Hanfmann, A. Ramage, J. C. Waldmann, D. G. Mitten, et al. in *BASOR* 170 (1963) 38ff.; 174 (1964) 30ff.; 177 (1965) 17ff.; 182 (1966) 34ff.; 187 (1967) 9ff., 60ff.; 191 (1968) 26ff.; 199 (1970) 45ff.; 206 (1972) 20ff., 33ff. Cf. G. M. A. Hanfmann, *Letters from Sardis* (Cambridge: Harvard University Press, 1972). D. G. Mitten, *The Ancient Synagogue of Sardis* (Archaeological Explorations of Sardis; New York, 1965). Idem, "A New Look at Ancient Sardis," *BA* 29 (1966) 61–68. G. M. A. Hanfmann, "The Ancient Synagogue of Sardis," *IVth World Congress of Jewish Studies* (1967) 1. 37–42. E. R. Goodenough, *Jewish Symbols in the Graeco-Roman Period* (New York: Pantheon, 1965)

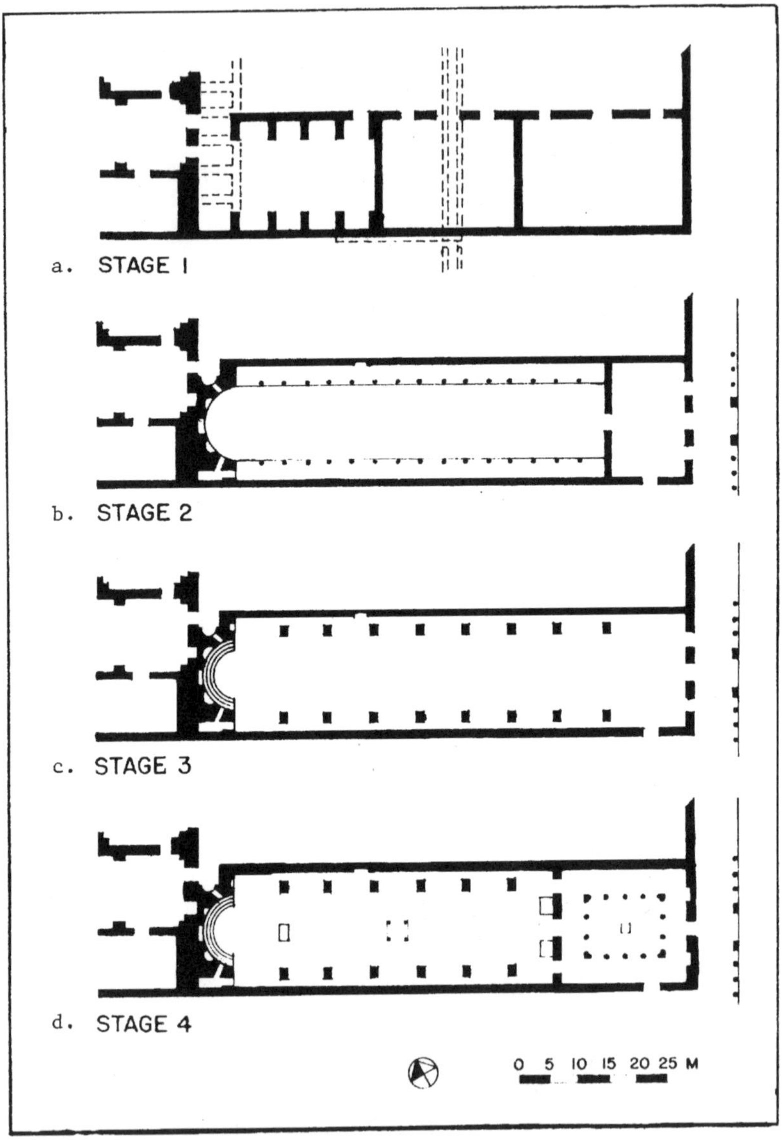

Fig. 32
Lydia, Sardis. Synagogue. Plan restoration in stages
(Seager, 1972)

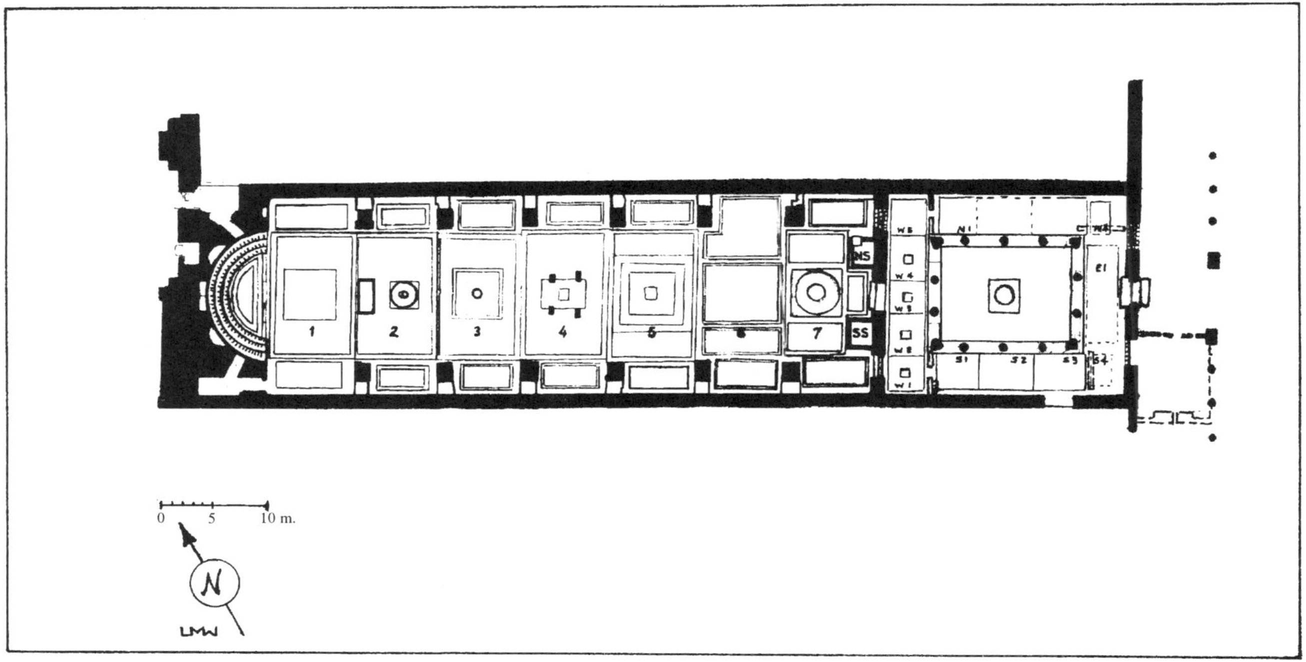

Fig. 33
Lydia, Sardis. Synagogue stage IV. Plan restoration showing arrangement of floor mosaics.

12. 191ff. Y. Shiloh, "Torah Scrolls and the Menorah Plaque from Sardis," *IEJ* 18 (1968) 54–60. A. T. Kraabel, "Judaism in Western Asia Minor under Roman Rule, with a Preliminary Study of the Jewish Community at Sardis, Lydia," (Th.D. Thesis, Harvard University, 1968). Idem, "*Hypsistos* and the Synagogue at Sardis," *GRBS* 10 (1969) 81–93. Idem, "Melito the Bishop and the Synagogue at Sardis: Text and Context," in *Studies Presented to G. M. A. Hanfmann*, ed. D. G. Mitten et al. (Fogg Art Museum Monographs in Art and Archeology 2; Cambridge, MA: Harvard University Press, 1971) 77–85. A. R. Seager, "The Building History of the Sardis Synagogue," *AJA* 76 (1972) 425ff. Idem, "The Architecture of the Dura and Sardis Synagogues," in *The Dura-Europos Synagogue: A Reevaluation (1932–1972)*, ed. J. Gutmann (Missoula, MT: Scholars Press, 1973) 79–116; reprinted in *The Synagogue: Studies in Origins, Archeology, and Architecture*, ed. J. Gutmann (New York: KTAV, 1975) 149–93. A. T. Kraabel, "The Diaspora Synagogue: Archaeological and Epigraphic Evidence since Sukenik," *ANRW* 2.19.1 (1979) 477–510. A. R. Seager and A. T. Kraabel, "The Synagogue and the Jewish Community," in *Sardis: From Prehistoric to Roman Times*, ed. G. M. A. Hanfmann (Cambridge, MA: Harvard University Press, 1983). H. Botermann, "Die Synagoge von Sardes: Eine Synagoge aus dem 4. Jahrhundert?" *ZNW* 81 (1990) 103–21. M. P. Bonz, "The Jewish Community of Ancient Sardis: A Reassessment of Its Rise to Prominence," *Harvard Studies in Classical Philology* 93 (1990) 343–59. Eadem, "Differing Approaches to Religious Benefaction: The Late Third Century Acquisition of the Sardis Synagogue," *HTR* 86 (1993) 139–54. A. R. Seager, A. T. Kraabel, and J. H. Kroll, *The Synagogue at Sardis* (Archaeological Explorations of Sardis 5; Cambridge, MA: Harvard University Press, forthcoming).

a. Stage I: Prehistory of Synagogue Hall (first–third centuries CE*)*

The bath-gymnasium complex was built on an artificial earthen terrace at a level several meters above the Hellenistic constructions of this area of the city. The terracing and layout of the foundations occurred in the first century CE after an earthquake in 17 CE had leveled much of the city. When the actual construction of the bath-gymnasium complex began is unknown, but apparently it was under construction for a long period. Based on a dedicatory inscription to Lucius Verus, the western portions of the complex were completed after ca. 166.[49] The eastern portions of the complex, including the Marble Court and the *palaestra,* were not completed until the early third century, dated by an inscription to ca. 211/212. The south wing (LSH) of the *palaestra* (later to become the hall and synagogue) was completed by about the beginning of the third century.

According to the original plan this south wing comprised three rooms which opened onto the baths to the west and the *palaestra* to the north, perhaps as dressing rooms or *apodyteria* (see fig. 32a). In form, then, the south suite of rooms (LSH or "Long South Hall") was paired symmetrically with the wing on the north of the *palaestra* (designated LNH or "Long North Hall").

b. Stage II: Conversion to an Apsidal Hall (early third century)

At some point the LSH wing was transformed architecturally into a formal hall (L.82.50; W.18.00 m) with a colonnaded nave, an (apsed) exedra on the west, and an entry chamber on the east. Based on the epigraphic evidence, the completion of this hall may be dated to ca. 225 (or not long thereafter). This construction involved extensive foundation work, which included digging down more than 4.00 m into the terrace fill for the rubble foundation of the exedra. An "inner" foundation was constructed running along the east–west axis from the exedra foundation to that of wall 16 (fig. 32b). These foundation walls carried the ceiling supports of the nave. The extent of the foundation work indicates changes in the plan (i.e., for carrying a much heavier elevation plan) and the move toward the construction of a monumental hall.

There is some evidence to suggest that the transformation to the plan of Stage II occurred before the construction of Stage I had been completed, perhaps before the end of the second century.[50] It would seem that the building

49. According to D. G. Mitten ("A New Look at Ancient Sardis," *BA* 29 [1966] 61–62; cf. Hanfmann in *BASOR* 154 [1959] 14; and 158 [1960] 7–9), room BSH (in the southwest portion of the complex [fig. 31]) was the first completed, in ca. mid-second century but before 166. Now, however, the date assigned to this portion is after 166, based on the Lucius Verus inscription.

50. A. R. Seager, "The Building History of the Sardis Synagogue," *AJA* 76 (1972) 432; cf. Seager and Kraabel, "The Synagogue and the Jewish Community," in *Sardis: From Prehistoric to Roman Times*, ed. G. M. A. Hanfmann, 173.

(originally intended as part of the *palaestra* complex) was not to be transformed into a civil (court) basilica; however, the exact function of this first hall remains uncertain. It had not been taken over by the Jewish community at this stage (as was conjectured early on). Marianne Bonz has conjectured that this apsidal hall was intended to serve as the meeting place of the civic *gerousia*.[51] When the hall was laid out, there were niches and passageways leading from the exedra to other rooms (BE–B, BE–C) in the complex. Thus, the hall remained integrally related to the functions of the municipal bath-gymnasium complex. The hall seems to have functioned in this capacity to ca. 270.

c. Stage III: The First Synagogue (late third century)

The precise circumstances of the acquisition of this hall by the Jewish community remain unclear. Bonz proposed that it resulted from a monetary crisis

51. For the original speculations on the nature of the new plan, see R. Detweiler in *BASOR* 187 (1967) 23. For the discussion of the relationship to the *gerousia,* see M. P. Bonz, "Differing Approaches to Religious Benefaction," *HTR* 86 (1993) 142–44. The proposal is based on the wording of an inscription found in the earlier excavations of Sardis (from the 1930s); in a list of municipal water supplies, it mentions a building called γυμνάσιον γερουσιάκον. While there were other gymnasia in Sardis, if this were the one designated by that name, she conjectures, then this apsidal hall would be the only suitable place of assembly for such a group. She would date the change of plan to the late Antonine period (consistent with the rise of such institutions in other Greek cities of the region), and the completion of the apsidal hall ("The Gerousia") to ca. 225.

This hypothesis is somewhat different from the proposals of both Seager and Kraabel. Seager had proposed that the enormously expensive building project for the baths proper at some point met with a lack of civic funds to complete it; therefore, there may have been some negotiation for subsidy or purchase of the space even before the first stage was completed (see Seager, "Building History," 432 and n. 25). Kraabel had taken a Hebrew inscription found elsewhere in the city (IN 62.79) to commemorate the acquisition of the hall by the Jewish community at the time of the visit of Lucius Verus in 166 ("Judaism in Western Asia Minor," 213–14; cf. Kraabel, "Impact of the Discovery of the Sardis Synagogue," in *Sardis: From Prehistoric to Roman Times*, ed. Hanfmann, 179 and n. 9). This dating for the Jewish acquisition seems most unlikely. In general on the dating problem, see M. P. Bonz, "The Jewish Community of Ancient Sardis: A Reassessment of Its Rise to Prominence," *Harvard Studies in Classical Philology* 93 (1990) 343–59.

in the city in the 260s and that the building was given or sold to the Jewish community as a measure of financial relief after the function and significance of the civic *gerousia* had declined.[52]

After acquiring the portion of muncipal property, the Jewish community used the space as it was, that is, in its Stage II basilical form, but some renovations were begun. The full extent of these renovations is not clear, but they probably include the following measures (see fig. 32c):

(1) In Stage II the apse-exedra (W.12.00; D.5.50 m) had a central rectangular niche and two flanking hemispherical ones (W.2.25; Br.1.25 m). The apse was fitted with a large ashlar podium (H.1.30–1.40 m constructed of limestone and marble blocks). The niches were later blocked up, as were the two narrow passages (L.2.70; W.1.10 m) leading to rooms BE–B and BE–C in the bath complex. The sealing of these passages may correspond to the construction of three tiers of benches (H.0.48–0.52; Br.0.75 m average) in the apse. The benches were constructed of brick and rubble, and among the rubble were scattered numerous column fragments.[53] These benches were found to rest on fragments of an earlier mosaic floor that has been dated to the end of the third century. The walls of the apse were revetted.

(2) It is possible that the column fragments found in the bench composition were from the basilical ceiling supports from Stage II of the hall. If so, this fact would mean that the pier construction of the nave belongs to this third stage (and may suggest further monumentalization of the structure). The position of the first bay of nave mosaics (see below) indicates that the piers were in place and the architectural scheme of the west end of the nave was set before the mosaics were executed. The nave pillars measure 1.50–1.75 m on the east–west face and 1.25 m on the north–south face; they stand 1.20 m from the side walls to which they were tied at the base by a low

52. Bonz, "Differing Approaches to Benefaction," 145–48. In effect, Bonz has taken a conjecture of Seager (discussed in the previous note) for an economic motivation for the change of plan at the end of the second century (between Stages I and II; so his "Building History of the Sardis Synagogue," 432), but has applied it to the change between Stages II and III. She connects this to the economic crisis of the third century. It must be pointed out, however, that there is considerable debate now among historians whether there really was such a crisis, or at least whether it affected the cities of Asia as severely as was once thought. Thus, any suggestion must be based on the archaeological evidence for a "crisis" in the environs of Sardis proper. G. M. A. Hanfmann and C. Foss do not think Sardis felt the crisis so sharply.

53. Seager, "Building History of the Sardis Synagogue," 430.

platform. The pillars stood 6.25 m apart (with six on each side) and may have been as much as 8.00 m in height.

(3) The mosaic "carpet" of the third bay (see fig. 33) at the west end of the hall was executed in the late third (or early fourth?) century; some portions of bays 1 and 2 may have been placed at this time and repaired in Stage IV.[54] Similarly, parts of the walls were embellished with *opus sectile* and may be reflected in the epigraphic evidence (see No. 67a below). Reconstruction of the dedications from the wall revetments of the apse and the west end of the nave further support a third-century dating for this renovation and decoration.[55]

(4) At the east end of the hall the walls show signs of an earlier marble revetment which indicate that the partition wall (wall 16, fig. 32b) of the Stage II entry chamber was removed.[56] Other evidence for the appearance of the east end in Stage III was destroyed by the constructions in this area in Stage IV. On the east street front, however, the building was faced by a colonnaded portico (W.ca.7.50 m), which must have extended the length of the *palaestra.* The construction of this portico may date to Stage II of the construction. Two large central columns framed the main door of the synagogue.

d. Stage IV: The Later Synagogue (fourth–fifth centuries)

The synagogue edifice thus created by the limited renovations of Stage III was in use for fifty years or more before any substantial changes were made. Apparently this new work constituted one major building project concentrated largely in the east end of the building with further decorations and embellishments throughout. The project may be commemorated by an inscription from the forecourt balustrade (IN 62.111) which mentions the

54. Ibid., 433; cf. D. Majewski in *BASOR* 187 (1967) 32.

55. The revetment inscription (IN 62.37, 46, 47 = No. 67a below) was at one time dated by the excavators before 212 CE, based on the lack of Aurelian names. These inscriptions are now assigned to the late third century and later. See J. H. Kroll, "The Greek Inscriptions," no. 29. [I wish to thank Dr. Kroll for allowing me to consult his draft of the epigraphic catalogue.] Cf. Bonz, "Differing Approaches to Religious Benefaction," 144 and n. 17. (For illustrations of these decorations and other discussion, see G. M. A. Hanfmann, *Letters from Sardis,* 195–96 and figs. 144, 84, 182, 200, 216, and 217.)

56. Seager, "Building History," 432.

"renovation" (ἀνανέωσις) of a certain Hippasios. The major structural change made at this time was the construction of a colonnaded atrium-forecourt (L.21.60; W.18.00 m) at the east end (see fig. 32d, 33). The forecourt was partitioned off from the nave (producing a length of 59.65 m) by the construction of what is usually referred to as the "shrine cross-wall." The foundation for the wall was constructed by excavating the floor (thus damaging the mosaic in bay 7) and inserting a course of stonework spoils into the subflooring. The cross-wall itself was constructed of large marble and limestone blocks (W.ca.1.25 m) with a triportal opening. The central door was a massive formal entranceway whose threshold measured 2.90 m. The north portal (W.1.97 m) was later walled shut, as were both of the arched side-portals (N: W.2.50; S: W.2.37 m) of the street entrance. The atrium (L.12.00; W.9.00 m) was constructed as a rectangular peristyle with larger heart-shaped columns at the corners (measuring 1.00 m on a side at the base). The sides of the peristyle (east–west) were set with three columns each while the ends (north– south) had two. The stylobate for these interior columns was 0.60 m wide. In the center of the atrium was a large fountain constructed of a crater (Diam.0.80 m) set in a shallow trough. The fountain was fed by water-pipes from the city's water supply.[57]

Upon completion, the forecourt walls were finished in stucco and the floor of the peristyle in mosaic.[58] The mosaics were arranged (like those of the nave) in sections that were dedicated by individual donors (see fig. 33). In addition a balustrade was constructed to close the intercolumniations of the atrium sides. The balustrade, too, carried dedications (IN 62.111). A small ablution basin (H.0.73; L.0.60; W.0.36; D.0.16 m) was set in the south peristyle. At a later time the walls of the forecourt were embellished with a marble revetment.[59]

In the nave, after the shrine cross-wall was constructed and the mosaic of bay 7 repaired, two *aediculae* or Torah Shrines (designated NS and SS) were installed on the west side of the cross-wall flanking the main entrance. The

57. For a discussion of the water system, the water-flow capacity, and the implications, see Kraabel, "Judaism in Western Asia Minor," 238 and n. 1. At a later time the water channels were replaced by a parallel system fed from a roof cistern, but mosaics damaged by this plumbing work were not repaired (see *BASOR* 191 [1968] 29–31).

58. See *BASOR* 187 (1967) 27–32.

59. Seager, "Building History," 434.

aediculae (SS, H.3.36 m) were constituted as square platforms (H.0.55; W.3.00; Br.2.31 m) made of marble and limestone blocks. Two recessed steps (upper, H.0.30; lower, H.0.25; Br.0.32 m) surmounted the platform. On a smaller platform (H.0.30; W.ca.2.31; Br.ca.2.00 m) columns were set. The columns of SS were Doric and carried a Doric entablature and pediment (perhaps spoils). The embellishments of NS were in Corinthian style.[60]

Other additions in the main hall of this period included the construction of a bema in bay 4. The bema was set on four marble slabs inserted into the mosaic of the floor. In bay 1 a great marble table (H.1.225 m) with carved eagles on its supports (the "Eagle Table") stood before the apse benches. The top was a marble slab (W.2.43; Br.1.225; Th.0.33 m) dating from the Augustan period.[61] Two stone lions found in the excavations probably flanked the table. Both the table and the lions were spoils of Hellenistic period temples. The lions, according to an inscription (IN 63.126, 127) were donated by a member of the φυλὴ λεοντίον ("Leontion/Lionine tribe"). Another Hellenistic monument, a circular base with Corinthian columns and architrave (H.1.30 m), was set near the north pier of bay l perhaps as a base for a lamp or menorah. Another smaller table stood 0.80 m before the south shrine (SS). It too was set on marble blocks anchored (1.07 m apart) in the mosaic floor; the top was a marble slab (W.1.14; Br.0.99; Th.0.23 m).

Very few structural modifications were made at the west end of the main hall, but a number of decorative elements were added throughout. Several portions of the mosaic (especially in bays 5–7) date from this period, as does the second layer of marble revetment in the eastern portions of the north and south walls. Numerous dedications are apparent in these areas. A number of the dedicants in both Stages III and IV seem to have been prominent civic and government officials at Sardis (see No. 67b).[62] Further, the floor of the apse was raised and paved with a mosaic (W.7.50; Br.2.25 m) dedicated by two brothers who took the Flavian family name of the Emperor Constantine (IN 63.122).

A few repairs and modifications continued from time to time up until the destruction of the city in 616 CE. These incidental features included the sec-

60. For illustrations of the restored *aediculae,* see Hanfmann, *Letters from Sardis*, figs. 167, 182.

61. See *BASOR* 174 (1964) 34f.; Kraabel, "Judaism in Western Asia Minor," 227.

62. Kraabel, "Judaism in Western Asia Minor," 9–10, 244–45; Seager, "Architecture of Dura and Sardis Synagogues," 84–85; *BASOR* 187 (1967) 32.

ond revetment of the forecourt and the new water system for the atrium fountain. Some thin partition walls were built within the forecourt and portico. A small room was blocked out in this manner on the south end of the portico, perhaps as a treasury room.[63] Finally, a rise of some 1.20 m in the street level over the years of use necessitated the installation of a marble pavement and a flight of steps at the east entrance from the street. The steps were inserted between the central columns of the porch.

PROVINCE: Asia Minor
LOCATION: Sardis

No. 67: Synagogue Inscriptions (third–fourth centuries)

The following entries represent just two of the numerous inscriptions from the Sardis synagogue. These two may bc considered representative since they, like most of the others, detail gifts of decoration for the hall of assembly and atrium/forecourt.

No. 67a: Donation of Wall Revetment (late third century)
(Sardis IN 62. 37, 46, 47)

Inscription from the south side wall of the Synagogue (now restored in place) on a plaque originally in four sections of marble (overall L.2.10; H.0.405; Th.0.014–0.020 m) now broken into numerous fragments, some of which have not been recovered. The inscription is in three lines (as far as preserved) of very regular letters, H.0.06 m. [See photograph in L. Robert, *Nouvelles Inscriptions de Sardes* (Paris: Librairie d'Amérique et d'Orient, 1964) pl. VI.]

Literature: *BASOR* 187 (1967) 27 = J. H. Kroll, "The Synagogue Inscriptions, a Preliminary Catalogue" (Expedition typescript, unpublished), no. 14. L. Robert, *Nouvelles Inscriptions de Sardes* (Paris: Librairie d'Amérique et d'Orient, 1964) no. 7, pp. 48ff. B. Lifshitz, *Donateurs et Fondateurs dans les Synagogues juives* (Cahiers de la RB 7; Paris: Gabalda, 1967) no. 20. Cf. G. M. A. Hanfmann, *Letters from Sardis* (Cambridge, MA: Harvard University Press, 1972) fig. 24. J. H. Kroll, "The Greek Inscriptions," in *The Synagogue at Sardis* (Cambridge: Harvard University Press, forthcoming), no. 3.

63. Seager, "Building History," 435.

[. . . . . . .]ς μετὰ τῆς συμβίου μου Ῥηγείνης καὶ τῶν
τέκνων μ[ου ca. 7?]
2 [. . . . . . . ἔδ]ωκα ἐκ τῶν δωρεῶν τοῦ παντοκράτορος θ(εο)ῦ
τὴν σκούτλωσιν πᾶσαν (*vacat*)
[τοῦ οἴκο]υ καὶ τὴν ζωγραφίαν.

Translation: I . . . [64] with my wife Regina and my children . . . gave from the gifts of the almighty God[65] the entire marble revetment [vac.] (of the hall?)[66] and the painting (of the walls).

No. 67b: Donation of Floor Mosaic (third–fourth centuries)
(Sardis IN 66. 19)

Inscription in mosaic read facing east from a square frame (H: 0.09; W: 0.69 m) in the center of bay 3 of the synagogue nave, partially lost due to damage of the pavement. Letters in dark tesserae, H.0.055–0.075 m.

Literature: *BASOR* 187 (1967) 29 [revised according to the photograph in *BASOR* 187 (1967) 21 fig. 46]. J. H. Kroll, "The Greek Inscriptions," no. 3.

Αὐρ(έλιος) Ἀλε-
ξ[άν]δρος ὁ

64. Because of the absence of an Aurelian name, common among the synagogue inscriptions, Robert (*Nouvelles Inscriptions*, 52) calls this the earliest datable inscription from the synagogue and places it in ca. 211, that is, before the *Constitutio Antoniana* under Caracalla (see No. 67b). In all probability, then, the donation belongs to the decoration of the hall of assembly in Stage III (see No. 66c above), but Kroll would now assign it to the late third century.

65. As seen in the Polycharmos inscription from Stobi (No. 73 below), this phrase refers to the donors' own funds, rather than the communal treasury.

66. Robert restored this phrase on the basis of two other inscriptions (IN 62.82 [=*Nouvelles Inscriptions*. no. 8b] and *BASOR* 187 [1967] 27 [= *BASOR* 199 [1970] 50]) which refer to the gifts "for the decoration of the edifice" (εἰς τὸν κόσμον τοῦ οἴκου). Cf. Robert, *Nouvelles Inscriptions*, 51. On the other hand, the reference to revetment and wall paintings suggest that the lacuna might be supplied with (τοῦ) τοίχου ("the" or "this wall"). Compare the Jewish inscription from Berenike, Cyrenaica (No. 63a above), which uses the same combination of terms. J. Kroll has now restored it with [τοῦ διαχώρο]υ ("the bay"); cf. "The Greek Inscriptions," no. 29.

κα[ὶ ᾿Ανα]τόλι-
ο[ς Σα]ρ̣δ(ιάνος) Βου-
λ(εύτης) τ[ὸ τρί]τον
διαχώρημα ἐ-
κέντησεν.

Translation: Aurelius Alexandros,[67] also called Anatolios, a citizen of Sardis and city councillor,[68] paved the third bay with mosaic.

---

67. The date of this inscription is suggested by two facts. First, the mosaic is among the oldest of the synagogue hall, as indicated not only by its condition but also by the fact that it is to be read facing east (see *BASOR* 187 [1967] 36ff.). Many of the floor mosaics from the later period were arranged to be read facing west, that is, toward the apse (see fig. 30). According to this arrangement the mosaic of bay 3 should probably be placed in the decoration of Stage III, although it may be a secondary feature in this stage. Second, the name Aurelius, common among the synagogue inscriptions and often associated with members of the Sardis council, indicates that the individual or someone in the family before had become a Roman citizen as a result of Caracalla's grant of 212 CE, the *Constitutio Antoniana*. On the basis of this fact the inscription can be dated no earlier than the middle portion of the third century. See Robert, *Nouvelles Inscriptions*, nos. 4–6, and Kraabel, "Judaism in Western Asia Minor," 218–19. It should be noted that the current thinking is to place these inscriptions in the later range of dates rather than the earlier, as was previously suggested by the excavators. Kroll dates it to the latter third of the century, and this date is confirmed by numismatic evidence. A coin of Claudius Gothicus (ca. 270) was found beneath the mosaic.

68. It is significant that the donor of this mosaic is both a citizen of Sardis and a city councillor (βουλεύτης). A survey of the synagogue inscriptions produces the following list of notables from the city who made donations to the synagogue: a number were citizens of Sardis, and at least four used the term *Sardianos* (see *BASOR* 187 [1967] 27, 29; *Nouvelles Inscriptions*, nos. 14, 17); nine inscriptions identify the donors as city councillors (*Nouvelles Inscriptions*, nos. 13–16); two are identified as clerical workers in the Roman provincial administration (βοηθοὶ ταβουλαρίου; see *BASOR* 187 [1967] 27–32); one was a former procurator (ἀπὸ ἐπιτροπόν; see *BASOR* 187 [1967] 32); one was a count (κόμης; see *BASOR* 206 [1972] 20); and two brothers had taken the Flavian family name of the emperor Constantine (IN 63.122, the apse mosaic = *BASOR* 187 [1967] 32). For discussion of the prosopography and its implications, see *BASOR* 187 (1967) 27–32 [based on two unpublished reports by J. H. Kroll and L. Robert from the 1966 season], and Kraabel, "Judaism in Western Asia Minor," 218–20. A full discussion of the prosopography is expected with the final publication of the inscriptions by J. Kroll, "The Greek Inscriptions" (to appear in the final report of Seager, Kraabel, and Kroll, *The Synagogue at Sardis*, forthcoming).

PROVINCE: Asia Minor (Lydia/Asia)
LOCATION: Phocaea

No. 68: Honors for Tation, Donor of the Synagogue Building (third century) (*CIJ* 1. 738; *IGRR* 4. 1327)

Inscription first published by S. Reinach after an earlier discovery which left no indication of original provenance except the modern city of Phocaea, though the ancient site of Phocaea near Cymae is preferred by Reinach. [No indication of condition or measurements given.]

Literature: S. Reinach, "Synagogue juive à Phocée," *BCH* 10 (1886) 327–35. Idem, "Un nouvelle synagogue à Phocée," *REJ* 12 (1886) 236–43. E. Schürer, *Geschichte* (4th ed.; Paris: Hinrichs, 1909) 14. *IGRR* 4. 1327. H. Leclercq, *Manuel d'archéologie chrétienne* (Paris, 1907) 1. 347. *DACL* 8. 250–51. S. Krauss, *Synagogale Altertumer* (Berlin: Akademie-Verlag, 1922) 231. H. Kohl and C. Watzinger, *Antike Synagogen in Galiläa* (Leipzig: Hinrichs, 1916) 144. L. Robert, "Inscriptions grecques de Sidé," *Rev. Phil.* 32 (1958) 46–47 n. 1. *CIJ* 1. 738. B. Lifshitz, *Donateurs et Fondateurs dans les Synagogues juives* (Cahiers de la RB 7; Paris: Gabalda, 1967) no. 13. B. Brooten, *Women Leaders in the Ancient Synagogue* (Chico, CA: Scholars Press, 1982) 144, 157.

[Text after *IGRR* 4. 1327 checked against Reinach.]

Τάτιον Στράτωνος τοῦ Ἐν-
πέδωνος τὸν οἶκον καὶ τὸν
περίβολον τοῦ ὑπαίθρου κατασκευ-
άσασα ἐκ τῶ[ν ἰδ]ίων
ἐχαρίσατο τ[οῖς Ἰο]υδαίοις.
Ἡ συναγωγὴ ἐ[τείμη]σεν τῶν Ἰουδαίων Τάτιον Σ[τράτ]ωνος τοῦ Ἐνπέ-
δωνος χρυσῷ στεφάνῳ
καὶ προεδρίᾳ.

Translation: Tation, wife of Straton the son of Empedon, made a gift to the Jews of the house and the walls of the (peristyle) court which she had built from her own resources. The congregation of the Jews has honored Tation, wife of Straton the son of Empedon, with a gold crown and a seat of honor.[69]

PROVINCE: Asia (Caria/Asia)
LOCATION: Priene
No. 69: House and Synagogue (ca. third–fourth centuries)
(Figures 34–35)

The city of Priene was excavated by the German expedition of T. Wiegand and H. Schrader from 1895 to 1898. Among the discoveries was a converted private house (designated by the excavators House XXIV, see fig. 34) on the main east–west thoroughfare, the so-called *Westthorstrasse*. Originally the excavators identified the structure as a Christian *Hauskirche*, claiming it to be of a fourth- or fifth-century type.[70] The basis of this identification was the discovery of a menorah relief found in the building, which was similar to

69. It is not clear whether Tation is herself Jewish or just a "sympathizer" who acted as patroness to the Jewish community. From the wording, it would appear that her husband either was deceased or had nothing to do with her actions toward the Jewish community. Thus, it is very unlikely that he was Jewish (or a sympathizer) in any case. Tation's "gift to the Jews" was her own act of patronage.

The honors accorded to Tation are typical of those given to wealthy patrons, both male and female, of clubs and collegia. The establishment of a place of honor (the προεδρία or "front seat" of line 9) for such patrons would have been customary for other cults and associations even though it had not usually thought possible in traditional Jewish practice, either for a pagan or for a woman. Clearly such constraints did not apply in this Diaspora congregation.

The nature of the edifice is not indicated by the wording in the inscription (despite attempts in the earlier literature to read it as a normative synagogue architecture). It might well be a house, and it need not have been built exclusively as a synagogue. One simply does not know. It is not inconsistent with the data provided by the present inscription to construe it as the commemoration of the gift of the property and structure from which the synagogue proper was renovated (cf. the Akmoneia inscription, No. 65 above). Or this text may commemorate the renovation project for the synagogue community. If such were the case the inscription itself and the "seat of honor" (line 9) probably should be understood as coming from the synagogue after renovation.

70. T. Wiegand and H. Schrader, *Priene: Ergebnisse der Ausgrabungen,* 480.

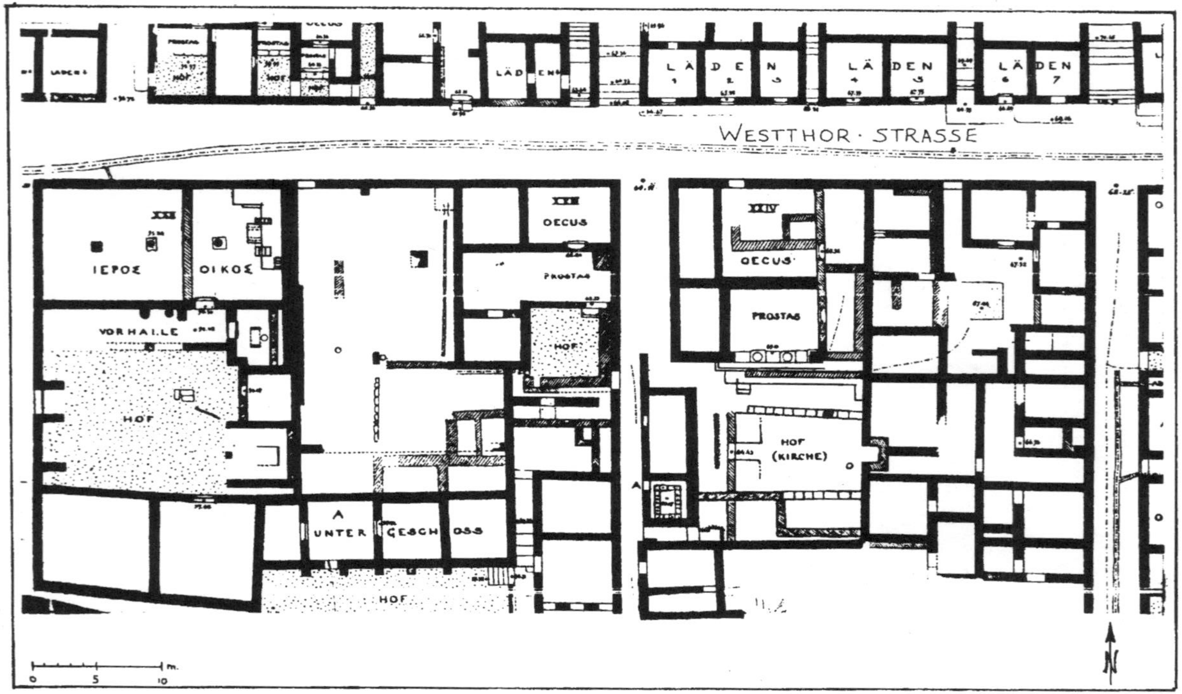

Fig. 34
Asia/Caria, Priene. Insulae XXII–XXIV, containing the *hieros oikos* and synagogue.
Excavation plan (after Wiegand and Schrader, Abschn. XXI, adapted)

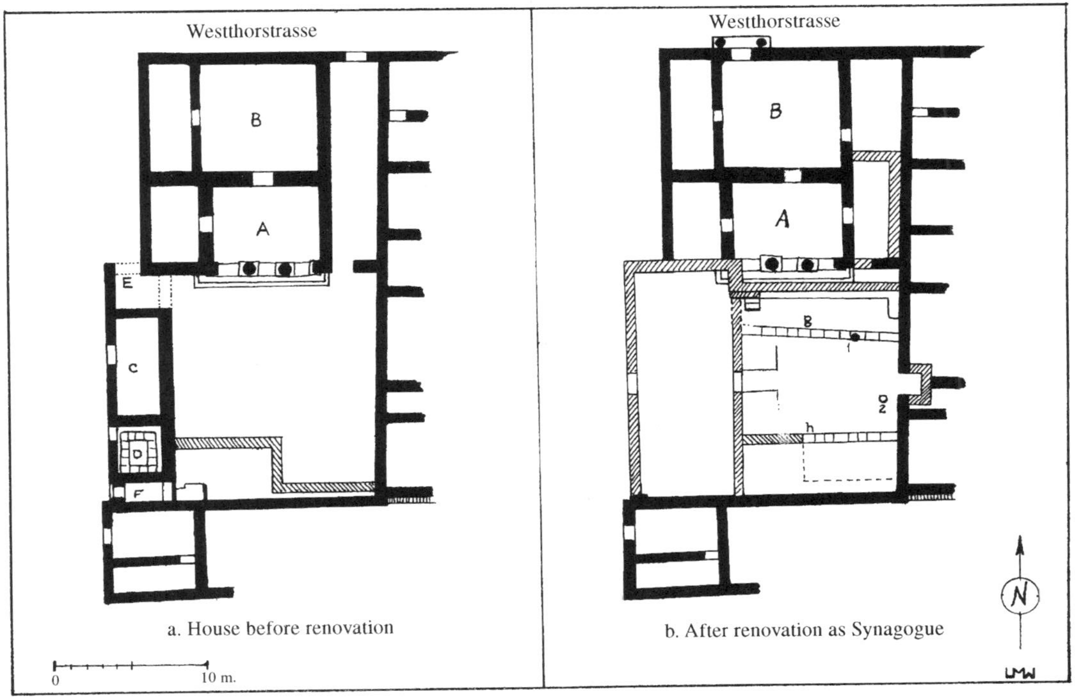

Fig. 35
Asia/Caria, Priene. Synagogue.
Plan restoration in stages

another relief found in the Byzantine *Grossenkirche* next to the theater.[71] Since the latter monument was considered (wrongly) to be of Christian origin owing to its location, the former was taken as an indication of Christian usage of House XXIV. The relief in the *Grossenkirche* may now be confidently identified as a spoil from a Jewish site.[72] Similarly, the so-called house church is more properly to be recognized as a synagogue constructed in one stage through renovation of the courtyard of an existing private house. The original house had been built in the late Hellenistic period; the renovations for the use as a synagogue date to the second or third century CE.

Literature: T. Wiegand and H. Schrader, *Priene*: *Ergebnisse der Ausgrabungen und Untersuchungen in den Jahren 1895–1898* (Berlin: Akademie-Verlag, 1904) 287, 320, 480f.; Abb. 301, 585, 586; Abschn. XXI. E. L. Sukenik, *Ancient Synagogues in Palestine and Greece* (London: Oxford University Press, 1934) 42–43. E. R. Goodenough, *Jewish Symbols in the Graeco-Roman Period* (New York: Pantheon, 1952–65) 2. 77; 2. 878, 882. A. T. Kraabel, "Judaism in Western Asia Minor under Roman Rule, with a Preliminary Study of the Jewish Community at Sardis, Lydia" (Th.D. Thesis, Harvard University 1968) 20–25. Idem, "The Diaspora Synagogue: Archaeological and Epigraphic Evidence since Sukenik," *ANRW* 2.19.1 (1979) 477–510.

[The following is based on the excavation reports of Wiegand and Schrader, with corrections offered by on-site observations of Kraabel and the author's own work at Priene.]

The Hellenistic House XXIV lay on the west side of an insula block that originally comprised at least three such domestic quarters (see fig. 34; the south portion of the block was not fully excavated). A rather large structure

71. The two reliefs are presented in Wiegand and Schrader, *Priene*, 481 [Abb. 586] and 475 [Abb. 582], respectively. The measurements of the two (taken on the site) are respectively: W.0.53; H.0.53 m (extant); and W.0.52; H.0.60; Th.0.105 m. The former appears to be on a jamb or wall slab but in the depiction is roughly the same size as the latter. The carving of the latter is of higher quality and the slab was dadoed along the bottom edge, probably for setting into a channel or slot for a stand.

72. See Kraabel, "Judaism in Western Asia Minor," 22; and his "The Diaspora Synagogue: Archaeological and Epigraphic Evidence since Sukenik," *ANRW* 2.19.1 (1979) 489–90.

(overall L.ca.30.50; W.15.40–17.25 m), House XXIV represented for the excavators a typical upper-class οἶκος for the city.[73] The Hellenistic house plan consisted of a large open court (L.ca.14.80; W.ca.13.00 m) which was entered from the north by a narrow passageway leading from the street (the *Westthorstrasse;* see fig. 35a). The domestic areas of the house lay to the north of the court; they consisted of a stepped, colonnaded *prostas* or vestibule (room A, L.ca.5.30; W.ca.6.70 m) opening onto the *oecus* or main living room (room B, L.ca.7.95; W.7.90 m). Both room A and room B had small antechambers on the west side. A narrow street ran along the west side of the house, sloping sharply as one moves farther to the south. On the west side of the court lay a row of three chambers (fig. 35a, rooms C, D, and F) that were accessible only from the side street. Of these rooms, D has been identified as a latrine and F as a water chamber. Room C was perhaps a shop.[74] The street must have originally been on a lower level to make these shops accessible. It is worth noting also that the floor level at the south end of House XXIII (across the street from C and D) was approx. 4–5 m below that of House XXIV. At the earliest period the court was apparently accessible by an entrance from the side street (at locus E). Given the lower level of the street and of the floor in C, D, and F, it might be conjectured that the entrance at E contained stairs (in an L-shape) to ascend from the street up to the level of the court. It is not altogether clear how the house was used in the early Roman period, but there seem to have been some renovations intro-

73. Wiegand and Schrader, *Priene*, 287: compare Houses XXXIII and XXXIV, Abb. 302, 299, and Abschn. XXII. These other houses also show signs of subsequent remodeling (ibid., 297–300) (most notably in House XXXIII, which had been substantially enlarged in Roman times by incorporating and renovating an adjacent alleyway on one side and another smaller house on the other). Based on the excavators' work, House XXXIII has become the paradigm for discussions of private house construction (or *oecus-prostas* type) at Priene. For further discussions both of the plans and of issues of renovation, see also M. Schede, *Die Ruinen von Priene* (2d ed.; Berlin: de Gruyter, 1964) 96–107 (esp. 105); J. Raeder, *Priene: Funde aus einer griechischen Stadt im berliner Antikemuseum* (Berlin: Gebr. Mann Verlag, 1984) 13–19. Not discussed in these works but well worth noting is House XXII, located just to the west of the synagogue house (XXIV) (see fig. 34). While its plan is somewhat less typical, it is significant that in the *oecus* of this house at some point in time a shrine to the deified Alexander the Great was installed while the adjacent room (labeled *hieros* in fig. 34) was also modifed for cultic use.

74. Wiegand and Schrader, *Priene*, 480.

duced both in the court area and in the house proper. The original south wall of the court appears to have been the irregular wall (abutting to room D) upon which the south stylobate was later set. At some point, either with the construction of the synagogue or before, another wall was built to the south and was then used in the construction of the synagogue.

At some time later, probably in the second–third centuries CE, the house was again renovated.[75] The plot was divided into two sections (north and south) by the construction of a wall between the vestibule colonnade and the court. The entrance from the *Westthorstrasse* was closed off, and the domestic quarters were expanded by converting the passageway into two east antechambers off rooms A and B. A new entrance (steps to a shallow porch with two columns flanking the doorway) was created from the *Westthorstrasse* into room B (see fig. 35b). Room A was converted into a paved court. These renovations suggest that the north quarters lost most, if not all, of their domestic function.

The south portion of the plot (the courtyard) was converted into the synagogue proper (fig. 35b). The renovation consisted of three main steps.

(1) The walls of the street-side chambers (C, D, F) were knocked down to the level of the court, and the lower rooms were covered over or filled in. The opening at locus E was blocked off (if not already done previously). Walls were constructed in this area to create a forecourt (L.ca.6.00; W.14.80 m) facing onto the west street front. It appears that the street level had risen by this time (or was raised further), well above the level of the older shops. The main entrance was made in the west wall of the forecourt from the side street. Although most of the accouterments of the forecourt are now lost, a small rectangular basin can be seen in the northeast corner.

(2) The hall of assembly was constituted as a slightly irregular room (L.[east–west]ca.10.20; W.[north–south]12.59–13.70 m). The floor level in this area was raised by ca. 0.50 m from that of the previous courtyard. Two rows of stone slabs (g, h) were laid along the east–west axis of the floor, probably to serve as a stylobate (the north one being slightly askew of this axis). The slabs in the southern stylobate (h) measure ca. L:0.89–0.965; W:0.61–0.625; Th:0.14–0.15 m. A single column fragment (fig. 35b, locus 1) was found in the area, though not exactly in place.[76]

75. Kraabel, "Judaism in Western Asia Minor," 21.

76. Ibid., 24 (contra Sukenik, *Ancient Synagogues in Palestine and Greece,* 42).

One feature of the layout remains to be considered: from the level of the Hellenistic house (fig. 33) the remnants of an east–west wall are visible on the same line as the south stylobate (h) but continuing in an L-shaped construction. The later west wall of the hall of assembly cuts through the line of this wall and the south stylobate seems to incorporate it as a bedding course or stereobate (at locus h) cut down to the level of the stone slabs. These facts suggest that the east–west wall dates from an earlier period (perhaps the boundary of the court of House XXIV from one of its stages of development; see fig. 34). The wall, then, would have been destroyed at the same time as rooms C, D, and F in the construction of the synagogue. At the same time, the wall remnant was employed in the placement of the "stylobates," and the floor level was filled in. The interior of the new assembly hall (L:10.20; 0:12.50 m) was embellished by the installation of benches, steps, and a seat on the north wall (and perhaps on the south) and (perhaps) two low platforms on either side of the central door.

(3) The third step in the renovation of the house for use as a synagogue was the construction of a square niche or exedra (interior W.1.35; Dp.1.37 m) in the east wall of the assembly hall. Lying just north of center on the east wall, the niche stands in a direct line with the door to the hall of assembly and the entrance from the street. The niche was constructed by knocking out a portion of the party-wall with the adjacent building. Then, the three partition walls were erected to form a chamber that projected into the adjacent structure. This niche is most probably to be recognized as some sort of Torah Shrine. The excavators had originally identified it as the "apse" of the church (assuming a basilical architecture) with "enough space for only one priest."[77] The fact that the niche itself was built outside the original bounds of the house gives even greater weight to the idea that the Jewish community had come into possession of all or most of the houses and buildings in the block.[78]

The domestic quarters of the house (rooms A and B and the four ante-

The assumption that they were stylobates for columns influenced the excavators in their identification of the structure as a basilica (see Wiegand and Schrader, *Priene*, 480). Kraabel at one point suggested that these stone courses were added at a later time after the synagogue had already been constructed ("Judaism in Western Asia Minor," 24), but this now seems doubtful.

77. Wiegand and Schrader, *Priene*, 480.

78. See Kraabel, "Judaism in Western Asia Minor," 25.

chambers) probably served community functions for the synagogue, for example, caretaker's quarters, guest rooms, or a school. The hall of assembly would have been the primary place of communal gathering and worship. Before the niche were found a menorah relief plaque (W:0.52; H.060; Th:0.105 m)[79] and a large rectangular pillar (H:2.20 m) with a roughly incised menorah graffito (ca. 53 cm square). To the right and in front of the niche was placed a marble basin (fig. 34b, locus 2; Diam.0.95 m). It is not clear for how long the synagogue was in use or what brought about its end. The rough graffito of the pillar, seemingly unfinished, may provide one clue to further embellishments that were planned but never realized.[80]

(A number of important features of the construction and renovation are quite unclear owing to the nature of the original excavation reports. An architectural history of the synagogue house has not been written and is needed. Some additional data and observations toward this end have been offered on the basis of the author's fieldwork on the site.)

PROVINCE; Asia/Greece (Insulae Aegeae)
LOCATION: Delos

No. 70: The Synagogue (second century BCE – first century CE)
(Figures 36–37)

The building (designated GD 80 in the *Guide de Délos*) was excavated in 1912–13 by the École Française d'Archéologie under the direction of André Plassart, who was the first to identify it as a Jewish synagogue. The building is situated on the east shore of the island, not far from the alternate harbor at Ghournia (see fig. 36). It is near the gymnasion (GD 76) and stadion (GD 77/78) and shows contact with an adjacent residential quarter (GD 79). The synagogue building was originally a private edifice of some sort, probably a house, which was renovated in two (or more) subsequent stages. The house dates originally from the second century BCE and was probably turned to synagogue use sometime near the beginning of the first century BCE. It was subsequently renovated and embellished once again in the period after the first Mithridatic war (88 BCE). It continued in use until sometime in the late

79. See Wiegand and Schrader, *Priene*, 481 [Abb. 586]; Goodenough, *Jewish Symbols*, 3. 882.

80. See Kraabel, "Judaism in Western Asia Minor," 23.

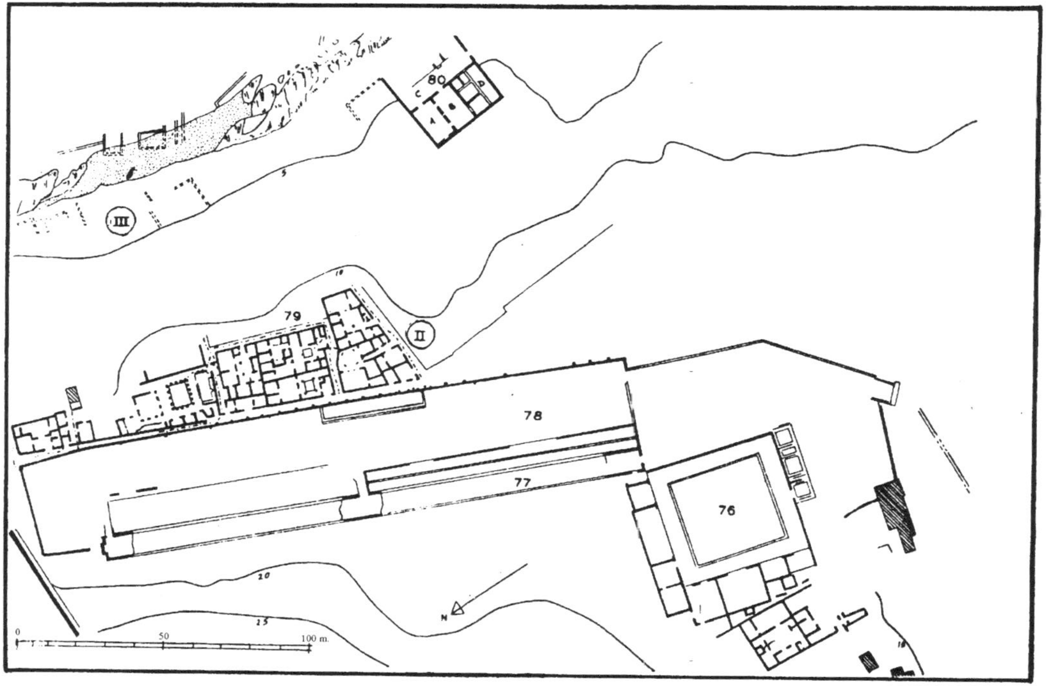

Fig. 36
Insulae Aegeae, Delos. Plan of Stadion Quarter and synagogue
(after Bruneau and Ducat, *Guide de Délos,* pl. III)

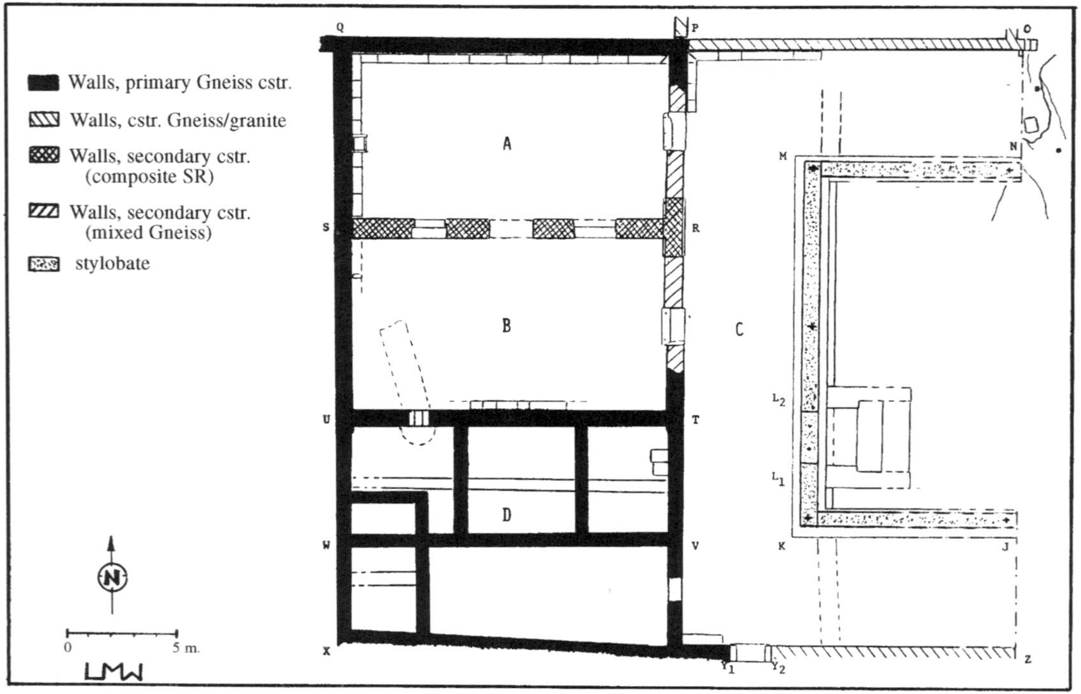

Fig. 37
Insulae Aegeae, Delos. Synagogue. Plan restoration, showing reconstruction (L. M. White)

first or second century CE. Consequently, it is the oldest synagogue building known from substantial archaeological remains, either in the Diaspora or in the Homeland. Still, its identification as a Jewish house of worship has been the subject of some debate over the years. Recent discovery of more inscriptions very near this site (see No. 71 below) has given further weight to its identification as a synagogue, albeit of a very early type.[81]

Literature: André Plassart, "La Synagogue juive de Delos," in *Mélanges Holleaux, recueil de memoirs concernant l'antiquité grecque* (Paris, 1913) 201–15; reprinted in *RB* 11 (1914) 523–34. E. L. Sukenik, *Ancient Synagogues in Palestine and Greece* (London: Oxford University Press, 1934) 37–39; B. D. Mazur, *Studies on Jewry in Greece* (Athens: Hestia Printing Office, 1935) 15–24. G. Kittel, "Der kleinasiatische Judentum in der hellenistisch-römische Zeit," *TLZ* 69 (1944) 16. E. L. Sukenik, "The Present State of Ancient Synagogue Studies," *Bulletin of the Louis M. Rabinowitz Fund* 1 (1949) 1–23. E. R. Goodenough, *Jewish Symbols in the Graeco-Roman Period* (New York: Pantheon, 1952–65) 2. 71–74. Philippe Bruneau,

81. For a survey of the shifting opinions and the relevance of the recent discoveries, see my article "The Delos Syngogue Revisited: Recent Fieldwork in the Graeco-Roman Diaspora," *HTR* 80 (1987) 136–40. A. Plassart's identification of the building as Jewish was originally followed in the influential work of E. L. Sukenik, *Ancient Synagogues in Palestine and Greece,* 38. But after the study of Belle Mazur (1935), Sukenik reversed his position (in an article "The Present State of Synagogue Studies," *Bulletin of the Louis M. Rabbinowitz Fund* 1 [1949] 21–23). The basis for this skepticism, most recently followed by H. Shanks (*Judaism in Stone* [New York: Harper & Row, 1979) 43–44), lay in the fact that the building was a house with peristyle, that the inscribed bases might have held statues, and that the inscriptions (including the epithet *Theos Hypsistos*) might be pagan rather than Jewish. So Mazur had read the phrase ἐπὶ προσευχῇ (in inscr. no. 5 [ID 2329 = *CIJ* 1. 726], below) as a votive formula only, since the building (a house) does not correspond to later notions of synagogue architecture as a place of prayer. By contrast the Jewish identification of the building has been followed by Goodenough (*Jewish Symbols*, 2. 74), Kraabel ("Diaspora Synagogue," 491–94), and most convincingly by Philippe Bruneau (*Recherches sur les cultes de Délos* [Paris: École Française, 1970] 486, 491). At first Bruneau was convinced by the convergence of the epigraphic evidence with the other indications of Jewish presence on Delos. More recently the discovery of clearly Samaritan inscriptions in close proximity to GD 80, which refer to the existence of another building, have given further support to the basic Jewish identification. So Bruneau, "'Les Israelites de Délos' et la Juiverie délienne," *BCH* 106 (1982) 465–504. See No. 71 below, for the Samaritan texts.

"La synagogue juive de Délos," *BCH* 87 (1963) 873–75. Idem, *Recherches sur les cultes de Délos à l'époque hellénistique et à l'époque imperiale* (Paris: École Française, 1970) 480–93. H. Shanks, *Judaism in Stone* (New York: Harper & Row, 1979) 43–44. A. T. Kraabel, "The Diaspora Synagogue: Archaeological and Epigraphic Evidence since Sukenik," *ANRW* 2.19.1 (1979) 477–510. Idem, "The Social Systems of Six Diaspora Synagogues," in *The Ancient Synagogue: The State of Research*, ed. J. Gutmann (Chico, CA: Scholars Press, 1981) 79–90. P. Bruneau, "'Les Israelites de Délos' et la Juiverie délienne," *BCH* 106 (1982) 465–504. L. M. White, "The Delos Synagogue Revisted: Recent Fieldwork in the Graeco-Roman Diaspora," *HTR* 80 (1987) 133–60.

[The following discussion is based on the recent work of Bruneau, which also served as the basis for the author's own fieldwork on Delos as published in a separate article, listed above.]

a. The Original Building (second century BCE*)*

The building (GD 80) is only partially preserved on its east side, as the rising sea level has resulted in damage. In addition, there is evidence from contiguous and bonded walls that the building was part of a larger complex or quarter that extended to the north and west but has never been excavated (see fig. 36 and fig. 37 at loci O, P, and Q). The building seems to have been of private domestic sort in original form, with a court (C) facing the water and several rooms (A/B and D) on the west. The shell of the house (PQXY) was an integral construction in homogeneous masonry of mixed local gneiss.[82] Room D (L.ca.9.50–10:20; W:15.055 m) was subdivided internally into several smaller chambers, one of which was an access to the cistern in the northwest corner of D and running under the floor of room B. As the walls of the shell narrow from 69–71 cm in PQU to only 60 cm in UXY, area D was probably used for storage and shows signs of later partition wall construction on the interior. In the original form of the building the area A/B comprised one large room (L:16.90; W:15.04 m), with three doors from portico C. The central door was 2.20 m wide, while the flanking doors were ca. 1.80 m.

---

82. White, "Delos Synagogue," 147.

At some point the large room A/B was bisected by the construction of a partition wall (SR), made of mixed gneiss and granite with some marble and spoils. Wall SR was thicker (85–87 cm) and was not bonded to the shell at S. At R the partition wall terminated in an integral T-shaped construction which blocked the central doorway from C. The wall section PT, although bonded at the corners, shows signs of having been rebuilt in its middle portions at some later time, probably after ST had been built, using a number of inscribed marble spoils which provide valuable dating information. The spoils, which bear dated inscriptions from ca. 140–110 BCE, clearly come from the gymnasion (GD 76) and were likely acquired for the renovation of GD 80 only after the Mithridatic raid on Delos in 88 BCE resulted in destruction of the gymnasion.[83]

b. Dating and Renovation as Synagogue

These features suggest that the house was originally built in the later second century BCE and went through two subsequent stages of renovation by which it was transformed for synagogue use. The first stage (probably around the end of the second or beginning of the first century BCE) included the renovation of Hall A (and the introduction of wall SR), while the second (sometime after 88 BCE) involved the rebuilding of the front wall PT and perhaps an embellishment of portico C. The first of these is consistent with a reference to a Jewish group on the island in 1 Macc. 15:16–23. The second is consistent with the period of edicts under Julius Caesar preserved in Josephus, *Ant.* 14.214.

In the renovation of area A/B, room A (L:17.85; W:14.40 m) became the main hall of assembly. Room B (L:8.22; W:14.40 m) served as an entry area with a triportal to A. Marble slab benches (W ca. 50 cm), found very commonly in Delos, lined the north and west walls of A, and others stood on the west and south walls of B and at the north corner of C. Set in the middle of west wall of A was a carved marble *thronos*, also similar to others found at Delos.[84] The floor in rooms A and B was paved with *opus incertum*. Apart from the *thronos*, often erroneously referred to as a "Moses Seat," there is little extant articulation or decoration to identify the building as a place of Jewish worship.

83. See Bruneau, "Les Israelites de Délos," 492, with a schematic of placement and discussion of the inscribed spoils.

84. See Bruneau, *Les cultes de Délos*, 491–93.

The main entrance to the synagogue edifice, at least so far as has been excavated, came from the seaside approach through portico C (L:28.01; W:ca.5.00 m), which originally carried a tiled roof. It was at one time postulated that the court area C was a peristyle (typical of Delian domestic architecture), of which the east side had been lost (along the shore).[85] Bruneau's work has confirmed portico C facing on the hall but has questioned whether there was a full peristyle around the court.[86] Recent analysis of the stylobate KM shows it to be a simple doric *krepidoma* construction, common to Delos. A single marble slab (L:2.41; W:0.725; H:0.244 m) from top step (i.e., the stylobate proper, on which stood the columns) is preserved *in situ* at a distance of 3.60 m from the south end of KM. The perpendicular sections MN and KJ (which Bruneau thought were later additions) seem to be integral with the lower courses of the *krepidoma*, and thus form the arms of a tristoa court (as restored in the plan, fig. 37). The hitherto unidentified remains at L appear to be a stair structure as the grand entrance to the building.[87]

c. Inscriptions and Identification

Because of the lack of overtly Jewish symbols or arrangements for worship, the identification of the building as a synagogue has been questioned. The absence of a Torah Shrine is especially noticeable; however, the early date of the site accounts for these features. At this stage a fully developed synagogue service or plan had not yet evolved, even in the Homeland, nor would it for several centuries after the destruction of the Temple. Apart from the form of room A as a hall of assembly, the primary basis for the identification (since Plassart) has been the congruence of several pieces of evidence: (1) the evidence for the presence of Jewish groups in 1 Maccabees and Josephus; (2) two funerary inscriptions that preserve Jewish names and incorporate Septuagint language, including the epithet θεὸς Ὕψιστος (ID 2532 = *CIJ* 1. 725); and (3) several inscribed bases (i–iv) found in GD 80 which carry *ex voto* dedications to θεὸς ὕψιστος. A fifth inscribed base (v), found in a nearby house in the insula at GD 79 (see fig. 36, locus II), repeats

85. Plassart, "Synagogue juive," *RB* 11 (1914) 524; Mazur, *Studies on Jewry in Greece*, 17; cf. Goodenough, *Jewish Symbols*, 2. 72.

86. Bruneau, *Les cultes de Délos*, 483.

87. See White, "Delos Synagogue," 150–51 and figs. for discussion of the evidence and conjectural restoration.

the name Lysimachus found in GD 80 (i) with a dedication "to the house of prayer" (ἐπὶ προσευχῇ). The texts are as follows:

i. ID 2328 (*CIJ* 1. 729)
Λυσίμαχος
ὑπερ ἑαυτου
θεῷ Ὑψίστω
χαριστήριον

ii. ID 2330 (*CIJ* 1. 728)
Λαωδίκη θεῶι
Ὑψιστωι σωθεῖ-
σα̣ ταῖς ὑφ' αὐτο-
υ θαραπήαις
εὐχήν

iii. ID 2331 (*CIJ* 1. 727)
Ζωσᾶς
Παρίος
θεῷ
Ὑψίστω
εὐχήν

iv. ID 2332 (*CIJ* 1. 730)
Ὑψίσ-
τω εὐ-
χὴν Μ-
αρκία

v. ID 2329 (*CIJ* 1. 726)
Ἀγαθοκλῆς
καὶ Λυσίμα-
χος ἐπι
προσευχῆι

i. (*CIJ* 1. 729) Lysimachus (made this) thank-offering to God Most High on behalf of himself.

ii. (*CIJ* 1. 728) Laodice (gave this in fulfillment of) a vow, to God Most High, for having delivered her from her infirmities.

iii. (*CIJ* 1. 727) Zosas, the Parian, to God Most High, (gave this in fulfillment of) a vow.

iv. (*CIJ* 1. 730) To God Most High, Marcia (gave this in fulfillment of) a vow.

v. (*CIJ* 1. 726) Agathocles and Lysimachus (gave this) to the house of prayer.

In consequence, it would appear that after renovation the house took the form of a rather simple collegial hall, similar to others on Delos. It served as a community center for the local Jewish enclave as well as a place for preserving their ancestral worship. Compare the House of the Poseidoniasts, the collegial hall of an association of Syrian shippers from Berytus (GD 57), and the epigraphic evidence for the hall of a Samaritan group on the island.[88]

88. No. 71 below; cf. White, "Delos Synagogue," 141–47, 153–55 (with bibliography for both).

PROVINCE; Asia/Greece (Insulae Aegeae)
LOCATION: Delos

No. 71: Samaritan Honorifics (second–first centuries BCE)

In 1979–80 two inscribed stelai of white marble were found by a team from the École Français; they were first published (with a discussion of their implications) by Philippe Bruneau in 1982. They were found in an otherwise unexcavated stretch along the east shore of the island parallel to the stadion (GD 78) and insula complex (GD 79) and approximately 90 meters north of the synagogue (GD 80). (See fig. 36, locus III.) Both stelai are decorated with a wreath design above the text of the inscription. The formula of the text and the design are typical of honorifics to benefactors. One of the honorees (Sarapion of Knossos) is clearly from Crete, and the other (Menippos of Herakleion) may well be. The honors are being offered by a group that calls itself "The Israelites (in Delos) who make offerings to hallowed *Argarizein*." Since *Argarizein* is an attested Greek rendering for the sanctuary of Mt. Gerizim, the identity of the group as an enclave of Samaritans is certain. The honorifics celebrate the benefactions of two pagans who provided for the construction and upkeep of the assembly hall or προσευχή of the Samaritan enclave. The two texts are roughly dated on paleographic grounds by Bruneau. He places No. 71a between 250–175 BCE and No. 71b between 150–50 BCE. Analysis of the texts confirms this basic periodization. As discussed below, based on the appearance of the formula "in Delos" only in No. 71b, I would place 71a before 166 BCE (the Athenian takeover) and 71b after, but perhaps only twenty-five to fifty years apart.

Literature: Philippe Bruneau, "'Les Israelites de Délos' et la juiverie délienne," *BCH* 106 (1982) 465–504; A. T. Kraabel, "New Evidence of the Samaritan Diaspora has been found on Delos," *BAR* 10 (1984) 44–46; L. M. White, "The Delos Synagogue Revisited: Recent Fieldwork in the Graeco-Roman Diaspora," *HTR* 80 (1987) 133–60 (esp. 141–47).

No. 71a The Menippos Honorific (before 166 BCE)

Bruneau, Inscription no. 2 (*BCH* 106. 471/474). White marble stele (H: 0.70; W[base]:0.56; W[top]:0. 53; Th: 0.06–0.095; letter height ca. 0.12 m).

[Οἱ ἐν Δήλῳ][89]
Ἰσραηλῖται οἱ ἀπαρχόμενοι εἰς ἱερὸν ἅγιον Ἀρ-
γαριζεὶν ἐτίμησαν *vac.* Μένιππον Ἀρτεμιδώρου Ἡρά-
κλειον αὐτὸν καὶ τοὺς ἐγγόνους αὐτοῦ κατασκευ-
άσαντα καὶ ἀναθέντα ἐκ τῶν ἰδίων ἐπὶ προσευχῇ τοῦ
θε[οῦ] ΤΟΝ [- - - - - - - - - - - - - - - - - - - -]
ΟΛΟΝΚΑΙΤΟ [- - - - - καὶ ἐστεφάνωσαν] χρυσῷ στε[φά-
νῳ καὶ [- -]
ΚΑ - -
Τ - -

Translation: The Israelites who make offerings to hallowed, consecrated *Argarizein*,[90] honor Menippos, son of Artemidoros, of Herakleion, both himself and his descendants, for constructing and dedicating to the *proseuche* of God,[91] out of his own funds, the ... [building?] and the walls[92] and the ..., and crown him with a gold crown and ....

No. 71b: The Sarapion Honorific (after 166 BCE)

Bruneau, Inscription no. 1 (*BCH* 106. 469). White marble stele, with the top broken off across the upper part of the wreath design (H[preserved]:0.48;

89. The phrase ἐν Δήλῳ does not appear on the stone. Bruneau thought to supply it, but I disagree. See White, "Delos Syngogue," 145–46 and n. 93 below.

90. Ἀργαρίζειν. The orthography is unusual but finds an exact parallel in the textual tradition of the Samaritan historian Pseudo-Eupolemus, frg. 1. 4–6. See the discussion in White, "Delos Synagogue," 145.

91. ἐπὶ προσευχῇ τοῦ θε[οῦ] (lines 4–5). Bruneau had originally read this as a votive formula, but I am taking it as a dedication "to the prayerhall of God," that is, to the Samaritans' "synagogue" building, which is the subject of the construction and dedication language in lines 4–6. This reading of the formula is parallel to one of the inscriptions from the synagogue building (GD 80) (White, "Delos Synagogue," 142); cf. 70e (v) above.

92. OLONKAITO (line 6, lapis). The ends of both lines 5 and 6 are damaged beyond reconstruction. Bruneau (*BCH* 106. 474) had originally read ὁλὸν καὶ τὸ ("the whole ___ and the ___"); however, on the basis of similarities to the Phocaea synagogue inscription (No. 68) I suggest the following reconstruction of lines 5–6 with τὸν [-----περίβ]/ολον καὶ τὸ, that is, a reference to the construction of the building and its walls. Thus, while we do not know what the Samaritan edifice was like architecturally, we might well guess that it would have been on the same order of the synagogue building at GD 80, that is a renovated house used as a collegial hall. See White, "Delos Synagogue," 143–44.

W[base]: 0.456; W[top]: 0.33; Th: 0.075–0.11; letter height: ca. 0.10–0.15 m).

Οἱ ἐν Δήλῳ Ἰσραελεῖται οἱ ἀ-
παρχόμενοι εἰς ἱερὸν Ἀργα-
ριζεὶν στεφανοῦσιν χρυσῷ
4 στεφάνῳ Σαραπίωνα Ἰασο-
νος Κνώσιον εὐεργεσίας
ἕνεκεν τῆς εἰς ἑαυτούς.

Translation: The Israelites in Delos[93] who make offerings to hallowed *Argarizein* crown with a gold crown Sarapion, son of Jason of Knossos,[94] for his benefactions toward them.

---

93. The use of the term "in Delos" has a technical significance that was not recognized by Bruneau. Since citizenship in the Delian *demos* was restricted to native-born landholders (after the model of a Hellenistic *polis*), this term was used to confer a status of enfranchisement as "foreigners with special rights" along the lines granted to select foreign individuals and groups in the period of Athenian and then Roman domination. See Marie-François Baslez, "Déliens et étrangers domiciliés à Délos (166–155)," *REG* 89 (1976) 343–60. As Baslez demonstrates, this epithet was coined for such groups only after 166 BCE, and it granted a special status not open to all foreigners. At least some of the broader "Jewish" groups on the island (notably the Samaritan enclave) held "in Delos" status. This kind of special residency status is likely the point of a reference to multiple Jewish groups on Delos in an edict under Julius Caesar (preserved in Josephus, *Ant.* 14.213): οἱ Ἰουδαῖοι ἐν Δήλῳ καί τινες παροίκον Ἰουδαίων ("The Jews 'in Delos' and certain other Jews who are 'dwellers' [resident aliens] there"). This text suggests that not all the Jewish groups on the island had this status. In other words, there was differing social or legal status for the several "Jewish" groups on the island reflected in the edict of Julius Caesar. Included among them might well be the Samaritan enclave and their benefactors (so White, "Delos Synagogue," 146, 152–55).

94. On the basis of the father's name, Bruneau had suggested that Sarapion himself was Samaritan ("Les Israelites des Délos," 481) and that it points to a larger Jewish "ghetto" (his term, *Juiverie*) on the island (ibid., 486–89). Given the proximity of the Samaritan evidence to the synagogue at GD 80 (see No. 70 above), where connections to neighboring domestic insulae are known as well, the notion of multiple enclaves residing in a particular region is possible; however, I doubt that we should take the notion of a "ghetto" too literally. On the other hand, there is no compelling evidence to conclude that the benefactors were themselves Samaritans or members of the Samaritan group. It should be noticed that neither has any reference to an office

PROVINCE: Macedonia/Paeonia
LOCATION: Stobi (near Gradsko)

No. 72: House, Synagogue, and Basilica Complex (second–sixth century)
(Figure 38)

Lying at the juncture of the Crna and Vardar rivers, the ancient town of Stobi (near modern Gradsko, Makedonia, formerly part of Yugoslavia) has been known since the mid-nineteenth century from the existence of ancient ruins. Systematic excavations under the direction of J. Petrovic of the Serbian National Academy were conducted from 1924 to 1934, continuing on a smaller scale to 1939. The most extensive building remains were found in the central portions of the town. Among these was a series of five parallel structures, oriented northwest to southeast, situated side by side on what would appear to be a major street through the town. A column (discovered in 1931) from the peristyle court (fig. 38, locus 1) of the central building in this series, a three-aisle basilica, bore an inscription that detailed the gift of a certain Claudios Tiberios Polycharmos for a synagogue building (see No. 73). As a result of this inscription, the basilica was then designated as the "Polycharmos Synagogue." The terminology used in the inscription and the form of the structure in which it was found gave rise to a number of theories regarding norms for synagogue architecture in the Diaspora which have persisted until recent times.[95]

---

or title within the group, as one would expect of such a benefactor who was also a member. Thus, such benefactions by nonmembers may well point to the social contacts and social location of the Samaritan group. It appears that they represent trading networks from Crete, where there is other evidence of both Jewish and Samaritan groups. These trade contacts and the benefaction by Cretan notables might also lie behind the favorable residence status granted to the Samaritan group (see n. 93 above). In general on the distribution of Samaritan enclaves, see the two articles by P. W. van der Horst: "The Samaritan Diaspora in Antiquity," and "The Jews of Ancient Crete," in *Essays on the Jewish World of Early Christianity* (Göttingen: Vandenhoeck & Ruprecht, 1990) 136–47 and 148–65 (respectively). (The Delos inscriptions are mentioned on pp. 143–44 and 149–50.)

95. This older consensus, following the work of Krauss and others, prior to new discoveries is perhaps best summarized by the report on the Stobi synagogue in R. Wischnitzer, *The Architecture of the European Synagogue* (Philadelphia: Jewish Publication Society, 1964) 6–9.

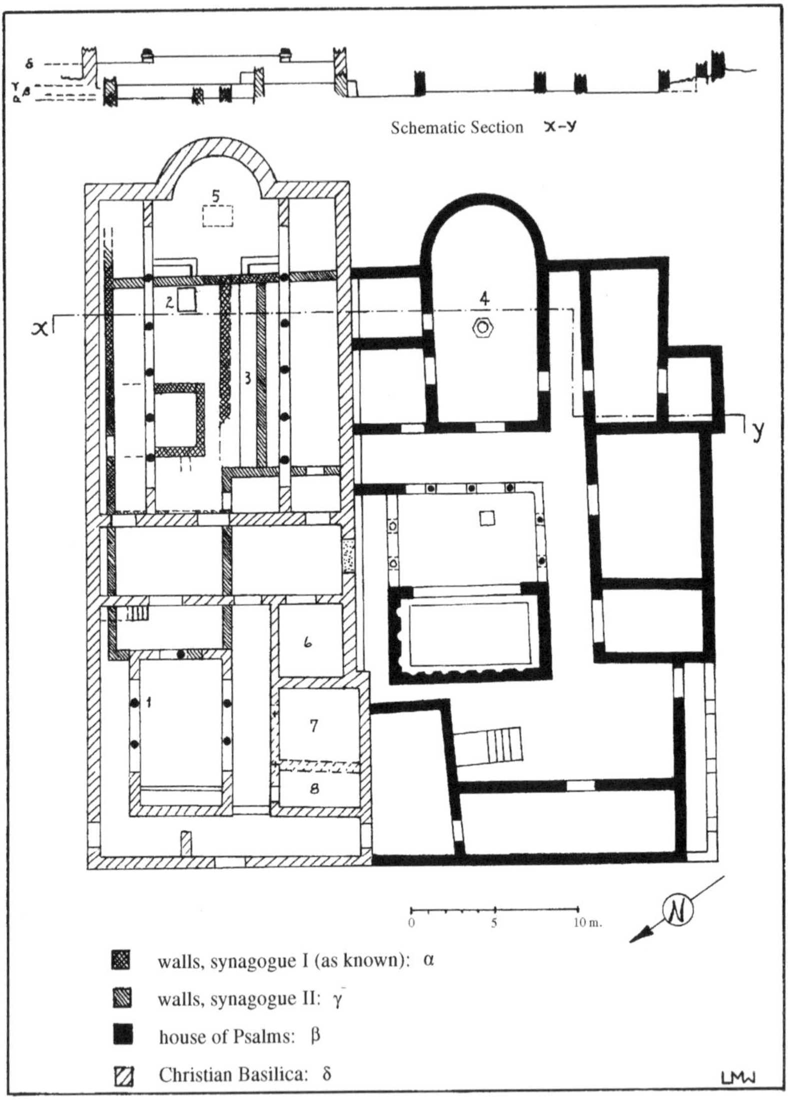

Fig. 38
Macedonia, Stobi. Synagogue complex.
Plan restoration, composition in stages of construction.
(L. M. White, based on Wiseman)

One of the first to question the dating and identification of the basilica as a synagogue was Ernst Kitzinger.[96] Kitzinger's cautions proved accurate when, during restoration work (1965–69), Z. Vincic of the Conservation Institute of Macedonia found direct evidence that the basilica was Christian and that there was an earlier structure below the basilica that communicated with the neighboring building, originally called the "Summer Palace" (now designated the "House of Psalms"). In digging beneath the floor of the basilica Vincic found remains of a rectangular hall with mosaic pavement. As a result of these discoveries, a new series of excavations was begun under the joint Yugoslav-American direction of J. Wiseman and Djordje Mano-Zissi. Continuing excavations on the site have unveiled two architectural strata (designated Synagogues I and II) below the level of the Christian basilica (now designated the Central Basilica). Discovery of painted decoration and dipinti in the floor of Synagogue I (see No. 73) made it possible to place the Polycharmos donation in renovation of Synagogue I. In turn, this earlier synagogue and the adjacent House of Psalms were found to be part of a large private villa complex belonging to Polycharmos. The synagogue proper was constructed by renovating sections of this villa for use as a place of assembly. Later, further renovation and enlargement created the second synagogue, and it was finally superimposed by the construction of a Christian basilica.

Literature: A survey of the early excavation reports and scholarly discussions prior to 1946 may be found in E. Kitzinger, "A Survey of the Early Christian Town of Stobi," *DOP* 3 (1946) 121–30 [includes plans and careful evaluation of the data then available]. M. Hengel, "Die Synagogeninschrift von Stobi," *ZNW* 57 (1966) 145–83; reprinted in *The Synagogue: Studies in Origins, Archaeology, and Architecture*, ed. J. Gutmann (New York: KTAV, 1975) 110–48. B. Lifshitz, *Donateurs et Fondateurs dans les Synagogues juives* (Cahiers de la RB 7; Paris: Gabalda, 1967) no. 10. J. Wiseman and Dj. Mano-Zissi, "Excavations at Stobi, 1970," *AJA* 75 (1971) 395ff. Idem, "Excavations at Stobi, 1971," *AJA* 76 (1972) 407ff. Idem, "Excavations at Stobi, 1972," *AJA* 77 (1973) 391ff. Dj. Mano-Zissi, "Stratigraphic Problems

96. In his review article "A Survey of the Early Christian Town of Stobi," *DOP* 3 (1946) 129–36. This more conservative assessment was also followed by Martin Hengel in his treatment of the inscription (see No. 73).

and the Urban Development of Stobi," in *Studies in the Antiquities of Stobi, 1*, ed. J. Wiseman (Belgrade, 1973) 185–224. J. Wiseman and Dj. Mano-Zissi, "Excavations at Stobi, 1973–1974," *JFA* 1 (1974) 117–48. J. Wiseman, *Guide to the Excavations at Stobi* (Boston, 1975). J. Wiseman and Dj. Mano-Zissi, "Stobi: A City of Ancient Macedonia," *JFA* 3 (1976) 269–302. Dean L. Moe, "The Cross and the Menorah," *Archaeology* 30 (1977) 148–57. J. Wiseman, "Stobi in Yugoslavian Macedonia: Excavations and Research, 1977–1978," *JFA* 5 (1978) 391–95. A. T. Kraabel, "The Diaspora Synagogue," *ANRW* 2.19.1 (1979) 488–509. Dean L. Moe, "The Stobi Synagogue," (paper presented at SBL Annual Meeting, New York, 1979).

[The following reconstruction attempts only to synthesize the findings of the recent excavations in order to sketch, as far as is possible, the architectural history of the complex. No final report on the synagogue/basilica complex has yet been published.]

a. Stages 1–2: The Earlier Houses and Synagogue I (second–third centuries)

Because of the complicated stratification of the site and the exacting nature of the excavations, very little has been determined to date regarding the earliest buildings on and from which the later synagogues and Christian basilica were erected. The pre-Roman history of the site includes what was probably a Hellenistic house and shop complex, as evidenced from ceramic artifacts and a massive coin hoard from the second and first centuries BCE.[97] The first Roman building (designated here as Stage 1) remains obscure except for the discovery of a flagstone pavement (on layers of earth and gravel) at the 136.701 m level.[98] The Hellenistic remnants lay below this structure at the 134.362 level.[99] The first synagogue (which we will provisionally label Stage 2b), according to the inscription (No. 73), was renovated from the house(s) of Polycharmos (here designated Stage 2a). Unfortunately the level of the Polycharmos structure (which for the purposes of the present study is

97. See J. Wiseman and Dj. Mano-Zissi, "Excavations at Stobi, 1971," *AJA* 76 (1972) 411.

98. Following the convention of the official excavation reports for Stobi, all stratigraphic readings are given as altimetric readings in meters above sea level, the city's datum line.

99. Wiseman and Mano-Zissi, "Excavations at Stobi, 1970," *AJA* 75 (1971) 408.

the most important) has been reached by the excavators at only a few points, while the analysis of upper levels continues.

Discoveries to date indicate that the house (Stage 2a) was built as part of or, at least, directly over the first Roman building (Stage l). Set into the flagstone paving (down to ca. 136.200) was a main east–west wall (Th.0.60 m) of the Polycharmos structure (see fig. 38; located directly beneath the center of the later basilica). What seems to be the main floor of the first synagogue (designated here Stage 2b) lies at the 137.200 level above the earlier pavement of the Stage l house. The identification of the synagogue level is made certain by a painted floor which contains dipinti honoring the name of Polycharmos.[100] This discovery also means that the inscribed column reused later in the atrium of the basilica (fig. 38, locus 1) belongs to Stage 2b, the renovation of Polycharmos's house(s) for use as Synagogue I.

Other discoveries include walls of what is probably a small room under the nave area and portions of two parallel walls. It appears now also that the established north wall and a portion of the west wall of Synagogue II (Stage 3) had been part of the earlier Roman house and Synagogue I edifice (Stage 2a–b).[101] Other wall fragments from the same level below the area of the east narthex were perhaps part of a basement of one of the earlier buildings (either the Hellenistic shop or the Roman "house" of Stage l).[102] The floor level in the west portions of Synagogue I (Stage 2b) lay above these walls at the 137.500 level. Little else is known as yet about the form of Synagogue I, except that it was connected to the adjacent southern portions of the house (see fig. 38, to be discussed later as the House of Psalms). Given the provisions of Polycharmos's bequest as specified in the inscription, it is assumed that this was the area of his house that was not immediately renovated for synagogue use and was retained as private domestic quarters for his family.

Other artifacts found at this same level indicate that Polycharmos was not the only benefactor of the renovation project. A copper plaque (W.0.079; H.0.047 m) records the votive offering of a pious woman named Posidonia: Πο[σ]ιδ/ονία Θε(ῷ)/῾Αγίω(ι) / εὐχήν (Stobi Inv. no. 1-70-61).[103]

100. For the text of the dipinti, see n. 123 below.

101. J. Wiseman, "Stobi in Yugoslavian Macedonia: Excavations and Research, 1977–1978," *JFA* 5 (1978) 393.

102. Wiseman and Mano-Zissi, "Excavations at Stobi, 1971," *AJA* 76 (1972) 409.

103. Wiseman and Mano-Zissi, "Excavations at Stobi, 1970," *AJA* 75 (1971) 409.

The date of the first synagogue is most likely the late second or early third century, as indicated by artifacts (especially ceramic and numismatic) found at the level of the fresco floor. This date generally agrees with the paleographic dating of the Polycharmos inscription.[104] The first synagogue may have been destroyed (partially?) by fire, as suggested by a layer of burned debris resting on the level of the fresco floor but beneath the mosaic pavement of Synagogue II.

b. Stage 3: Synagogue II and the House of Psalms (late third–fourth century)

The second synagogue seems to have arisen as a massive building project that included the construction (or perhaps restoration) of the contiguous house (first called the "Summer Palace" now designated the "House of Psalms"). The reason for the building project would seem to lie in the evidence for a fire in the destruction of Synagogue I. Otherwise, the construction project would run counter to the legal provision set forth in the donation of Polycharmos. The construction of Synagogue II involved setting new exterior walls at least on the north and east sides of the synagogue building. These walls were founded at the 136.190 level (i.e., at roughly the same level as the wall footing of Synagogue I).

These new walls were bonded at the northeast corner but were spliced onto the older section of the east wall (from Synagogue I) at the juncture of the main east–west wall (fig. 38).[105] In Stage 3 the east wall continued to the south (as it had probably done in Stage 2b), where it connected with the party-wall between Synagogue II and the House of Psalms (later the east aisle wall of the basilica).[106]

The newly constructed sections of the north wall of Synagogue II extended to the east to an unknown termination point; its west extension has

104. The various proposals for dating the inscription on internal grounds are discussed in n. 122 below. However, Wiseman has proposed that a late-second-century date is also possible for the construction of Stage 2b; see "Stobi: Excavations 1977–78," *JFA* 5 (1978) 393.

105. Wiseman and Mano-Zissi, "Excavations at Stobi, 1970," *AJA* 75 (1971) 408. It also reused sections of the north wall of Synagogue I, as mentioned above (see Wiseman, "Stobi: Excavations 1977–78," *JFA* 5 [1978] 393).

106. In the reports to date, the southeast corner of Synagogue II has not been examined to determine exactly the chronology of construction between the two buildings.

been found to provide the plan of a long, (approximately) rectangular structure (L.overall ca.21 m).[107] The main hall of the synagogue was larger at the east end (W.7.85 m) as a result of an offset east–west partition that formed the south wall of the main hall. Against the entire length of this partition was a low bench (fig. 37, locus 3, Br.1.25 m) set on flat paving stones.[108] Also, the entire floor of the hall was paved with mosaic and *opus sectile* (at the 137.735 level), and the walls were decorated with frescoes.[109] The narrower west end of the main hall may have been partitioned off (at ca. 13.30 m from the east wall) by a wall on the line of the later nave/narthex wall.[110] The main door to the hall would appear to be that found in the west wall (beneath the north atrium wall of the later basilica). Another door was centered on the north wall, while a third door opened onto a room (usually designated the "Southwest Room") which adjoined the House of Psalms and provided access to it by a door in the east party wall. The floor level in the Southwest Room lies at the 137.770–137.820 level. Another small chamber lay to the east of the Southwest Room between the main hall and the House of Psalms. It was entered by a door from the Southwest Room. Discovery of a fragmentary menorah graffito etched in the plaster beside this doorway confirms that the Stage 2 building was designed and constructed as a synagogue.[111] The single piece of evidence as to the orientation of the main hall of Synagogue II is the stepped bema (fig. 38, locus 2) constructed against the east wall roughly on the east–west axis of the room at its widest. The date for the construction of the second synagogue is in the early fourth century.[112]

Synagogue II communicated directly with the House of Psalms (hereafter abbreviated H.Ps.); however, the floor of Synagogue II was slightly higher

107. Wiseman and Mano-Zissi, "Stobi: A City of Ancient Macedonia," *JFA* 3 (1976) 294.

108. Wiseman and Mano-Zissi, "Excavations at Stobi, 1970," *AJA* 75 (1971) 410.

109. Wiseman and Mano-Zissi, "Excavations at Stobi, 1973–1974," *JFA* 1 (1974) 148.

110. The existence of such a partition was originally suggested by Wiseman and Mano-Zissi ("Excavations at Stobi, 1970," *AJA* 75 [1971] 410). It has not yet been confirmed; however, its placement is suggested in the plan of Synagogue II by F. P. Hermans in Dean Moe, "The Cross and the Menorah," *Archeology* 30 (1977) 154–55.

111. See Wiseman and Mano-Zissi, "Stobi," *JFA* 3 (1976) 292–94; Moe, "Cross and Menorah," 154.

112. So Moe, "Cross and Menorah," 153; cf. Wiseman and Mano-Zissi, "Excavations at Stobi, 1971," *AJA* 76 (1972) 409.

than that of H.Ps. (see the schematic section in fig. 38). It is probable, therefore, that H.Ps. was already in existence when the Polycharmos synagogue was destroyed by fire.[113] From the door in the south party-wall of Synagogue II access was provided to most areas of H.Ps. from a corridor surrounding a *tristoon* court opening onto a central chamber with benches on all four walls and multiple niches on the north and west walls. The main living area of the house was organized around a rectangular *triclinium* with east apse (fig. 38, locus 4). The dining hall floor had a fountain in its center and was paved with mosaic throughout. The central mosaic panel was meant to be viewed from the east by those seated in the apse area.[114] The main scene of the mosaic included possibly biblical symbolism; hence the designation "House of Psalms." The main entrance to H.Ps. was from a portico at the southwest corner. Stairs in the entry area indicate the presence of upper floor(s) at least on the west end. The structure suggests an extensive and opulent complex not unlike the one implied by the Polycharmos inscription. If indeed H.Ps. dates to the period of Synagogue I, it is most likely that it represents (at least in part) the house of Polycharmos mentioned in the bequest to the synagogue.

c. Stage 4: The Christian Basilica (late fourth to fifth century)

Sometime near the end of the fourth century, Synagogue II was "deliberately supplanted" by the construction of the basilica.[115] The synagogue was apparently still in very good condition, having been maintained through regular repair. In fact, the basilica was built while the synagogue hall was still standing.[116]

113. See Wiseman and Mano-Zissi, "Excavations at Stobi, 1970," *AJA* 75 (1971) 411, but such cannot be confirmed at the present time. On this point see also the brilliant assessment of the earlier evidence by Kitzinger, "The Early Christian Town of Stobi," 139; on the recent work, see Mano-Zissi, "Stratigraphic Problems and the Urban Development of Stobi," in *Studies in the Antiquities of Stobi, 1*, ed. J. Wiseman (Belgrade, 1973) 208–9.

114. See the photograph in Wiseman and Mano-Zissi, "Excavations at Stobi, 1973–1974," *JFA* 1 (1974) 146 and fig. 32.

115. Moe, "Cross and Menorah," 153.

116. Ibid., 153. The suggestion that the synagogue was still standing is based on cases of inverted stratigraphy between elements of the synagogue and elements of the basilical construction. The fact that the synagogue remained in good repair was reported by Moe in an unpublished paper, "The Stobi Synagogue" (1979).

The construction process for the basilica as suggested by Moe is as follows: (1) removal of the synagogue roof, (2) laying wall foundations for the basilica in trenches cut through existing walls down to bedrock, (3) beginning to lay courses of basilica walls, (4) destruction of synagogue walls, (5) filling synagogue floor with rubble, debris, and packed earth. Because of the unusual relationship between the synagogue and the basilica and as a result of the long-standing assumptions about the basilica prior to recent excavations, it was not possible to demonstrate conclusively that the basilica was really a Christian building (though it had been strongly suspected since Kitzinger). Proof of this fact came only in 1975 with the discovery of a clearly Christian reliquary crypt set in the floor of the basilica beneath the chancel area, just below the spot where the altar would have been. It was dug into the level of Synagogue II. (See fig. 38, locus 5).[117]

The basilica (L.overall 44.00; W.15.60–16.55 m) lies for most of its length contiguous to H.Ps. The basilica proper (interior L.18.31; W.14.10 m) constituted a nave (W.7.40 m) with east apse (W.5.30; Br.2.65 m) and two side aisles (W.2.55 m) separated from the nave by stylobates (W.0.80 m) carrying five columns (interaxial L.2.70 m). The original floor of the nave was at the 138.959 level, but in a second phase of construction (probably still in the fifth century) the floor level was raised with slate paving stones to 139.308.[118] The basilica was entered from a narthex (L.3.85; W.14.10 m) through a triportal entrance. From the narthex the basilica continued to communicate with H.Ps. by a door in the south wall and down a large step (ca. 2.00 m) to the level of the house. To the west of the narthex was an irregular complex of rooms dominated by an asymmetrically placed atrium (L.8.40; W.5.10 m) with colonnade on three sides and surrounded by a corridor. On the south side of the atrium were three rooms: 6 (L.4.30; W.3.30 m) entered from the narthex; 7 (L.4.05; W.4.00 m) and 8 (L.3.40; W.4.00 m) entered from the south corridor of the atrium.[119] There seems to have been an upper story above the atrium, as indicated by the presence of stairs in the northeast corner of the east atrium corridor.

---

117. Wiseman and Mano-Zissi, "Stobi," *JFA* 3 (1976) 219–21.

118. Wiseman and Mano-Zissi, "Excavations at Stobi, 1970," *AJA* 75 (1971) 411.

119. The plan of the basilica (by F. P. Hermans in Moe, "Cross and Menorah," 152, which is the basis for this area in our fig. 38) indicates that rooms 7 and 8 were at some point a single chamber entered from the atrium corridor through a colonnade of two (or perhaps three) columns.

Precisely under what circumstances the synagogue edifice came into Christian hands is not known. One obvious possibility would be that the acquisition of the property and the construction of the basilica were examples of Christian "triumphalism" and, perhaps, even anti-Semitism (coming especially after the Theodosian edicts of 388 CE). Yet, direct evidence of a hostile takeover has not been found.[120]

PROVINCE: Macedonia/Paeonia
LOCATION: Stobi

No. 73: The Polycharmos Inscription (late second–early third century) (*CIJ* 1. 694)

(Figure 38)

An inscription of thirty-three lines was found on a column *in situ* in the northeast corner of the peristyle atrium in the basilica (see fig. 38, locus 1).

120. A hostile takeover is assumed by Moe ("Cross and Menorah," 156–57) and Kraabel ("Diaspora Synagogue," 496–97). One cannot help being impressed by the effort and expense of the transformation from Synagogue II to the Christian basilica. At the same time, certain questions remain unanswered regarding both the form of the earlier buildings and architectural stages. The fact that the Stage 3 building has been definitely identified as a synagogue (II) at the time of its initial construction is significant, but this fact must be reevaluated in the light of future excavations on two points. First, the exact relationship between H.Ps. and the buildings to the north (Stages 2b–3) must be determined in order fully to understand the social circumstances of the Jewish community at Stobi. Second, while Synagogue II was clearly designed as a place of Jewish assembly and worship (in conjunction with the House of Psalms), to date no evidence has been advanced to indicate precisely when these structures came into Christian hands. The operating assumption has been that the construction of the basilica represents the Christian takeover. On the other hand, one way of explaining the care with which Synagogue II was dismantled in the process of building the basilica (as noted by Moe, "Cross and Menorah," 153) would be to suggest that (roughly by the mid-fourth century) the synagogue building was already being used as a Christian place of assembly, but without substantial renovation. Such a scenario might yield a different view of the history of Jewish–Christian relations in this locality. The construction of the basilica would then constitute a secondary Christian renovation. Unfortunately, there is no clear archaeological evidence on these matters to date. Still, it may be significant that the column bearing the Polycharmos inscription (from Stage 26—Synagogue I) must have been preserved and reused in Stage 3—Synagogue II, before being taken over and reused again in the construction of the atrium of the basilica (Stage 4).

The column of white marble (H.2.48; Diam.0.98 m) was at some time cut off at the top, as the first line of the inscription is all but obliterated and remains illegible. When it was first discovered in 1931–32, the assumption was that the dedicatory inscription referred to the building in which it was then housed. New excavations of the site begun in 1970 have proven that the column (with its inscription intact) was a spoil reused in the construction of the basilica and that it originally came from the first of the two synagogue structures beneath the church.[121]

Literature: First published by J. Petrovic in *Starinar* (1932) 82. N. Vulic in *Spomenik* of the Royal Serbian Academy 80 [=2d ser., 55] (1931) 238. Idem, "Inscription grecque de Stobi," *BCH* 56 (1932) 291–98. H. Lietzmann, "Note," *ZNW* 32 (1933) 93–94. S. Klein, "Neues zum Fremdhaus der Synagoge," *Monatsschrift für Geschichte und Wissenschaft des Judentums* 77 (1933) 81–84. C. M. Danov, "Notizen zur grossen Synagogeninschrift aus Stobi," *Bulletin de l'Institut archéologique Bulgare* 8 (1934) 101–5. E. L. Sukenik, *Ancient Synagogues in Palestine and Greece* (London: Oxford University Press, 1934) 79–80. Frey, *CIJ* 1. 694. A. Marmorstein, "The Synagogue of Claudius Tiberius Polycharmus in Stobi," *JQR* n.s. 27 (1937) 373–84. E. Kitzinger, "A Survey of the Early Christian Town of Stobi," *DOP* 3 (1946) 129–61. F. M. Heichelheim, "Mind and Spade," in *The Jewish Standard* [Toronto] May 15, 1953. M. Hengel, "Die Synagogeninschrift von Stobi," *ZNW* 57 (1966) 145–83; reprinted in *The Synagogue: Studies in Origins, Archaeology, and Architecture*, ed. J. Gutmann (New York: KTAV, 1975) 110–48. B. Lifshitz, *Donateurs et Fondateurs dans les Synagogues juives* (Cahiers de la RB 7; Paris: Gabalda, 1967) no. 10. J. and L. Robert, *Bull. epigr.* (1968) 478–79. B. Lifshitz, "Prolegomenon," in *CIJ* 1. 2d ed. (New York, 1975) 76–77.

. . . .
[Κλ.] Τιβέριος Πολύ-
χαρμος ὁ καὶ Ἀχύρι-
ος ὁ πατὴρ τῆς ἐν
Στόβοις συναγωγῆς
ὅς πολειτευσάμε-
νος πᾶσαν πολειτεί-

121. See No. 72 and nn. 100 and 120 above.

αν κατὰ τὸν Ἰουδαϊ-
σμὸν εὐχῆς ἕνεκεν
τοὺς μὲν οἴκους τῷ
ἁγίῳ τόπῳ καὶ τὸ
τρίκλεινον σὺν τῷ
τετραστόῳ ἐκ τῶν
οἰκείων χρημάτων
μηδὲν ὅλως παραψά-
μενος τῶν ἁγίων, τὴν
δὲ ἐξουσίαν τῶν ὑπε-
ρώων πάντων πᾶσαν
καὶ τὴν δεσποτείαν
ἔχειν ἐμὲ τὸν Κλ. Τιβέρι-
ον Πολύχαρμον καὶ τοὺς
«καὶ τοὺς» κληρονόμου
τοὺς ἐμοὺς διὰ παντὸς
βίου, ὃς ἂν δὲ βουληθῇ
τι καινοτομῆσαι παρὰ τὰ ὑπ᾽
ἐμοῦ δοχθέντα, δώσει τῷ
πατριαρχῇ δηναρίων μυριά-
δας εἴκοσι πέντε· οὕτω γάρ
μοι συνέδοξεν, τὴν δὲ ἐπι-
σκευὴν τῆς κεράμου τῶν
ὑπερώων ποιεῖσθαι ἐμὲ
καὶ κληρονόμους
ἐμούς.

Translation: [....][122] I Claudius Tiberius Polycharmus, also called

122. When the column was cut off (probably for use in the basilical construction), the letters of the first line were obliterated at the top rendering them indecipherable. Vulic ("Inscription grecque de Stobi," *BCH* 56 [1932] 282, 292) attempted to reconstruct the lost letters according to the plausible conjecture that the shorter first line contained a reference to the date. He proposed, therefore, to read ΕΤΟΥC ΤΙΑ or ΡΙΑ. According to this rendering, the dates would be, as interpreted by Marmorstein ("The Synagogue of Claudius Tiberius Polycharmos," *JQR* ns. 27 [1937] 381–82), as follows: according to Macedonian calculations: ΤΙΑ (311)= 163 CE; according to Roman calculations: ΡΙΑ (111)=79 CE, ΤΙΑ (311)= 279 CE. Unfortunately, working

Achyrios, father of the synagogue[123] at Stobi, having lived my whole life according to Judaism,[124] in accordance with a vow (gave) the (my) houses to the holy place[125] along with the *triclinium* and its *tetrastoa* out of my household accounts without touching the sacred (treasury). However, (I retain) the ownership and disposition of all the upper chambers for myself, Claudius Tiberius Polycharmus, and for my heirs for life. If anyone seeks to make

---

with these possible dates and with the mistaken presupposition that the basilica was the synagogue of Polycharmus has led a number of scholars into hasty and unfounded conclusions. Apart from these conjectures as to the restoration of the first line, the dating of the inscription ranges from the first or second century CE (so Vulic, Frey, Marmorstein), to late second-early third century (so Lietzmann, Danov), and, finally, to the mid- or later third century CE (so Heichelheim, Hengel, Lifshitz). The later third-century date seems most probable on the basis of three other considerations from within the text. First, Heichelheim made the point that the practice of writing the *gentilicium* Claudius before the name Tiberius is a late imperial practice. He suggested, then, that Polycharmus had received his citizenship under Claudius II Gothicus (268–70). Second, the point has been made that the office of patriarch suggests a later date (see M. Hengel, "Die Synagogeninschrift von Stobi," *ZNW* 57 [1966] 152–54). Third, the inflated scale of the penalty provision is thought by Heichelheim, Hengel, and Lifshitz to come from the third century. However, see Wiseman, "Stobi: Excavations 1977–78," *JFA* 5 (1978) 393–95 for recent archaeological support of a second-century date for Synagogue I. On this basis, it would probably be best to assign a general date in the late second to early third centuries.

123. The association of the benefaction of Polycharmos with the renovation of the house for use as Synagogue I (i.e., Stage 2a–b of the building history of the site as discussed in No. 72a above) has been confirmed by the discovery of a fresco floor in the first level of ruins. Discovered in 1970, the fresco floor was found to contain four or five dipinti in *tabulae ansatae*, in regular patterns around the room. All the inscriptions found repeat the same basic legend (Letters, H.0.004–0.02): [ΠΟΛ]ΥΧΑΡΜΟΣ/ [Ο] ΠΑΤΗΡ/ [Ε]ΥΧΗΝ ("Polycharmos, the Father, in accordance with a vow"). For the texts, see Wiseman and Mano-Zissi, "Excavations at Stobi, 1970," *AJA* 75 (1971) 408 (also pl. 90 and fig. 21). The title "father of the synagogue" is now recognized to denote a wealthy benefactor who is also a leading member of the congregation.

124. For parallels and discussion, see Vulic (*BCH* 56 [1932] 82), Lietzmann (*ZNW* 32 [1933] 93f.), and Hengel ("Die Synagogeninschrift von Stobi," *ZNW* 57 [1966] 178–80).

125. For this phrase as a designation for the synagogue structure, compare *CIJ* 2. 867 (Gerasa, fifth century CE); *CIJ* 2. 1437 (Egypt, date uncertain, probably late Hellenistic); cf. *CIJ* 1. 781 (Side, fourth century CE); and Lifshitz, *Donateurs*, no. 73a (Gaza, sixth century CE).

changes[126] beyond what has been set down by me, he shall give the patriarch two hundred fifty thousand[127] denarii; for this have I agreed. As for the upkeep of the rooftiles of the upper chambers, it will be done[128] by me and my heirs.

PROVINCE: Greece/Achaia (Insulae)
LOCATION: Aegina

No. 74: Synagogue Building Inscriptions (fourth century)

An elaborate floor mosaic preserves the only remains of a synagogue from the island of Aegina. The mosaic was discovered in construction beneath areas of the present town. It was removed and installed for display outdoors at the local museum, located next to the temple of Apollo. The size and basic outline of the floor indicate a moderately sized hall, perhaps with apse on one end, but no interior colonnade. The date is fourth century or later. In the mosaic were set two inscriptions, one immediately above the other, which commemorate the donations of a father and son for the building. The donation of the father (Theodorus the elder) was probably for the construction of the synagogue building. That of the son (Theodorus the younger) was for the mosaic itself, in which both acts were memorialized.

No. 74a: Building Inscription of Theodorus the Elder
(CIJ 1. 722; *CIG 9894b; IG* 4. 190*)*

Inscription in mosaic set in *tabula ansata* frame in the floor near the entrance to the hall of the assembly of the synagogue.[129]

Literature: S. Krauss, *Synagogale Altertumer* (Berlin: Akademie-Verlag,

126. Vulic was the first to argue that the reference here is not to changes in the building (as it was taken by Frey, *CIJ* 1) but to changes in the legal provisions of the benefaction. This view has been supported by Heichelheim, and by L. Robert and Lifshitz (Prolegomenon to *CIJ* 1². 77).

127. ΝΥΡΙΑ (line 27, lapis).

128. ΠΟΙΕΙCΘΑΙ (line 31, lapis), literally, "made."

129. Cf. Sukenik, *Ancient Synagogues*, plate XI; R. Wischnitzer, *Architecture of European Synagogues* (Philadelphia: Jewish Publication Society, 1974) 4–5 and fig. 1–2. H. Shanks, *Judaism in Stone* (New York: Harper & Row, 1979), fig. 42.

1922) 243. A. Kermopoullos, in *Ephemeris Archaiologika* (1932) Chron. 5–6. *CIJ* 1. 722. E. L. Sukenik, *Ancient Synagogues in Palestine and Greece* (London: Oxford University Press, 1934) 44. L. Robert, "Inscriptions grecques de Side," *Rev. Phil.* 32 (1958) 39 and n. 4. Idem, *Nouvelles Inscriptions de Sardes* (Paris: Librairie d'Amérique et d'Orient, 1964) 49, no. 3. Goodenough, *Jewish Symbols in the Graeco-Roman Period* (New York: Pantheon, 1952–65) 2. 75–77; 3. 881. B. Lifshitz, *Donateurs et Fondateurs dans les Synagogues juives* (Cahiers de la RB 7; Paris: Gabalda, 1967) no. 1. J. and L. Robert, *Bull. Epigr.* (1969) 53.

[For a general discussion of the synagogue and the inscriptions, see Sukenik and Goodenough (cited above), and B. D. Mazur, *Studies in Jewry in Ancient Greece* (Athens: Hestia Printing Office, 1935), 25–33.]

θεόδωρος ἀρχ[ισυνάγωγ(ος) φ]ροντίασας ἔτη τέσσερα
ἐχ θεμελίων τὴν σ[υναγωγ(ὴν)] οἰκοδόμησα· προσοδεύθ(ησαν)
χρύσινοι πε´ καὶ ἐκ τῶν τοῦ θ(εοῦ) δωρεῶν χρύσινοι ρε´.

Translation: I, Theodoros, archisynagogos, having served as steward[130] for four years, (re)built the synagogue[131] from the foundations. The funds

130. φ]ροντίσας (line 1). Frey (*CIJ* 1. 722) translated this word "y ayant mis mes soins," but L. Robert ("Inscriptions grecques de Side," *Rev. Phil.* 32 [1958] 39 and n. 4) suggests that the word ought to be taken in connection with the substantive φροντιστής ("curator") as found in the synagogue dedication at Side. In this same vein we may note the derived meaning of the verb form as "to be steward or balif (of property)" in a second-century papyrus (*BGU* 300. 4; cf. L-S-J, 1957). Taken together with the word προσοδεύθησαν (line 2) we may also understand the sense to be as "overseer" of the building project or with the word προσοδάρχον as "treasurer" (of a religious association).

131. I have printed above the most common reconstruction of the lacuna in line 2, as in *CIJ* 1. 722. But Krauss (*Synagogale Altertumer,* 243, following the reading in *IG* 4. 190), based on the letters then visible, resolved the lacuna as τὴν σ[υναγ(ωγὴν) ἀν]οικοδόμησα. The compound ἀνοικοδομεῖν ("to rebuild") is quite common with the phrase ἐκ τῶν θεμελιῶν ("from the foundations") and regularly denotes a renovation project. Compare No. 48 above. This reading may be given further weight by the fact that there was supposedly another floor (apparently unpaved) below the level of the present one and on the same plan. This was the interpretation of Sukenik (*Ancient Synagogues*, 44), but it is apparently based on the supposition that the mosaic was completed at the time of Theodorus the elder. If I am correct in suggest-

collected (from contributions), 85 pieces of gold, and that (given by me) "from the gifts of God,"[132] 105 pieces of gold.

No. 74b: Donation of the Mosaic
(CIJ 1. 723; CIG 9894a; IG 4. 190)

A second inscription in the mosaic floor was set immediately above (or behind as one would have entered the hall) that in No. 74a. It is also framed in a *tabula ansata*. The inscription was badly damaged, and the reconstruction depends heavily on an early partial reading pieced together with later scattered finds.

Literature: See the works cited in No. 74a above. Also L. Robert, in *Hellenica* 10–12 (1960) 394. Lifshitz, *Donateurs*, no. 2.

---

ing that Theodorus the younger is the one who commissioned the mosaic floor, then it would have naturally been laid over whatever floor would have been installed when the synagogue was built by his father. Hence, I see no way to choose between the two readings of line 2 ("built" or "rebuilt the synagogue") on the basis of the available evidence.

132. Frey (*CIJ* 1. 722) understood the first sum mentioned to refer to the synagogue treasury, while he rendered the second as "*dons faits à Dieu (= Les collectes)*," that is, a special collection for the building project. Here he was following the translation of Sukenik: "offerings unto God" (see *Ancient Synagogues*, 44). But L. Robert (*Nouvelles Inscriptions de Sardes*, p. 49 n. 2) has noted that the similar phrase at the Sardis synagogue and among Christian inscriptions, is a formula referring to one's own possessions. (Compare No. 67a above.) Lifshitz (*Donateurs*, 14) nonetheless expressed some reservation regarding Robert's reading, since the formula usually contains an active personal construction. It would seem that this problem is mitigated in the present case by the fact that personal agency is already indicated by the verb of the first clause (ἀν)οικοδόμησα. Such a reading is even clearer if (as suggested above) the term φροντίσας is understood as meaning the "steward of the building project." In each part of the second phrase, therefore, one may supply an understood statement of agency (e.g., ὑπ' ἐμου, or the like) regarding the funds amassed for the building. In this way, the first clause refers to funds collected from others in the congregation, while the second refers to what Theodorus had contributed of his own funds. Theodorus himself was the major donor to the building project, having given over half (55.3 percent) of the total cost of the construction.

θεοδώρου νεω(τέ)ρ(ου) φροντίζοντ(ος) [ἐκ τῆς πρ]ο[σ]όδου τῆς συναγ(ωγῆς) ἐμουσώθη. Εὐλογία πᾶσιν ṭο[ῖς εἰσ]ε[ρ]χ[ο]μένοις.

Translation: Under the stewardship of Theodoros the younger this (mosaic)[133] was elegantly accomplished from the funds of the synagogue. Blessings be upon all who enter.[134]

PROVINCE: Greece/Achaia
LOCATION: Mantineia
No. 75: Building Inscription: Pronaos of the Synagogue (fourth century)
(*CIJ* 1. 720; *IG* 5^2. 295)

Inscribed on a round marble *cippus* (H.0.81; Diam.0.28 m) found near the Byzantine chapiteaux at the Museum at Tegrae. [No letter height given.]

Literature: G. Fougeres, "Inscriptions de Mantinée," *BCH* 20 (1896) 159–61. I. Levi in *REJ* 34 (1897) 148. S. Krauss, *Synagogale Altertumer* (Belin: Akademie-Verlag, 1922) 243. *CIJ* 1. 720, with an addendum on this text in the prolegomenon by B. Lifshitz in *CIJ* 1^2. 86. E. R. Goodenough, *Jewish Symbols in the Graeco-Roman Period* (New York: Pantheon,

133. There are basically two ways of understanding the implied subject of the sentence: either (a) as the floor mosaic itself, a later addition; or (b) as the completion of the renovation project itself, having begun under the older Theodorus and finished with the mosaic, that is, the subject being supplied from τὴν συναγωγήν in the first inscription (line 2). The latter reading does not seem to me to fit well with the verb, which has the sense of embellishment, elegance, or adornment, as in poetry or flowery prose. It is a fitting description of the mosaic decoration. Hence, I have followed the reading of Frey, and I take No. 74b as a reference exclusively to the occasion of paving the floor with mosaic, which was accomplished out of the congregational treasury now under the leadership of the younger Theodorus, and with appropriate commemoration of the earlier building project under Theodorus the elder.

134. The restoration of the lacuna at the end of the second line is that of Frey (*CIJ* 1. 723) following Krauss (*Synagogale Altertumer*, 243). Sukenik (*Ancient Synagogues*, 44) had restored it with παρ]ε[σ]χ[η]μένοις, which he translated, "Blessing be upon all the donors." Lifshitz favors Frey's reading (see *Donateurs*, 14), and I concur, especially given the placement at the entrance of the hall.

1952–65) 2. 76–77. L. Robert, in *Hellenica* 10–12 (1960) 295. B. Lifshitz, *Donateurs et Fondateurs dans les Synagogues juives* (Cahiers de la RB 7; Paris: Gabalda, 1967) no. 9. J. and L. Robert, *Bull. epigr.* (1969) 53.

[Text after *CIJ* and *IG*.]

Αὐρ(ήλιος) Ἐλπίδυς
πατὴρ λαοῦ
διὰ βίου δῶρον
το(ῦ) προνάου
τῇ συναγωγῇ.

Translation: Aurelios Elpidus,[135] father of the community for life, made a gift of the pronaos[136] (vestibule) for the synagogue.

Province: Pannonia (Pannonia Superior)
Location: Siscia (Sisak)

No. 76: Dedication for Construction of a Mithraeum (third century?)
(*CIMRM* 2. 1478; *CIL* 3. 3960)

Inscription on a plaque found in the area of the castle at modern Sisak, at the Sava River southeast of Zagreb in Croatia (formerly Yugoslavia). [No other information given.]

Literature: *CIMRM* 2. 1478. *TMMM* 2. 2.352.

D(eo) I(nvicto) M(ithrae) s(acrum)
Iucundus Aug(usti) n(ostri),
disp(ensator) p(rovinciae) P(annoniae) s(uperioris)
porticus et ap[p]aratorium ex voto fec(it).

---

135. Frey (*CIJ* 1. 720) emended the name to Ἐλπίδ(η)ς, but the change is unnecessary; so Robert, *Bull. Epigr.* (1969) 53 and Lifshitz, “Prolegomenon,” in *CIJ* 1^2. 86.

136. ΤΟ ΠΡΟΝΑΟΥ (lapis). Krauss (*Synagogale Altertumer*, 243) corrected to read τὸ προνάο(ν). Lifshitz (*Donateurs*, 17) followed Frey in reading το(ῦ) προνάου, as printed above. J. and L. Robert (*Bull. Epigr.* [1969] 53) favor the accusative; however, the sense remains the same in either case.

Translation: To the god Invictus Mithras. Jucundus, the treasurer of our (lord) the Augustus[137] for the province of Pannonia Superior, made a sacred gift of the portico and the *apparatorium* (lobby)[138] from a vow.

PROVINCE: Noricum (Noricum Mediterraneum)
LOCATION: Virunum

Nos. 77–78: Dedications of Construction by Mithraists

Several inscriptions discovered in the environs of Virunum in the Zollfeld (near Klagenfurt in the Carinthia of Southern Austria) seem to represent successive stages of renovation of a single mithraeum in the Roman city. The building has not yet been discovered, but continuing archaeological work is finding new evidence.

No. 77: Dedication of Hilarus and Epictetus (239)
(CIMRM 2. 1438; CIL 3. 4800)

Inscription on an altar found at Toltschach am Zollfelde. The stone is broken off across the lower right corner damaging the end of lines 6–9. [No measurements given.]

137. *Augusti nostri*. The date of the inscription is uncertain, but this form of reference to the emperor may suggest a date in the late second or third century, based on usage in the later Antonine and Severan periods. So compare the datable example in No. 59 above (*CIMRM* 1. 53) and especially that in No. 77 below (*CIMRM* 2. 1438 = *CIL* 3. 4800), which uses the precise terms (line 7) in a reference to Gordian. Another inscription from Siscia, assuming it is from the same mithraeum, gives a date under either Marcus Aurelius or, more likely, Caracalla. So see *CIMRM* 1. 1476 (=*CIL* 3. 3958).

138. *porticus et apparatorium* (line 4). This is one of the few clear references to a room constructed and designated as an *apparatorium* (literally a "preparation room"). That its construction is linked with that of a porticus suggests that it was situated near the entrance of the mithraeum, that is, as a "waiting room" (or what we might typically call a "lobby") before moving into the sanctuary proper. Compare the position of the room designated as an *apparatorium* in the so-called Mitreo del Palazzo dei Musei at Rome; see *CIMRM* 1. 434 and fig. 120 (room E). But one should also take note of the usage in another inscription *CIMRM* 1. 747 (=*CIL* 5. 810): ... *speleum cum omni apparatu fecit*. The text is important since it reflects formal dedication of a partial renovation or addition to the building.

Literature: *CIMRM* 2. 1438. *TMMM* 2. 2.405.

[The text given below is that from *CIL* 3. 4800 and should be taken as a correction to the text in *CIMRM*.]

Pro salute Aug(usti)
in honorem d(omus) d(ivinae) Soli
Invicto Mythr(ae) Hilaru[s]
Aug(usti) lib(ertus) tab(ularius) p(atrimonii?)
r(egni) N(orici) et Epictetus
ark(arius) Aug(usti) n(ostri) tem(plum)
vestustate conl[ap]s(um)
sumpto suo cum pictura refe[c(erunt)]
imp(eratore) d(omino) n(ostro) Gordiano Aug(usto)
et Aviola c[o(n)s(ulibus)]
sacerdot(e) Licin(io) Marcello pat[re sac(rorum)?]
Dedicatum VIII kalendas Iulias Q. Viv. . . .

Translation: For the well-being of the Emperor, in honor of the divine house, to Sol Invictus Mithras. Hilarus,[139] a freedman of the Emperor, notary of the regnal patrimony of Noricum, and Epictetus, treasurer of our (lord) the Emperor, at their own expense renovated, along with the painting, the temple, which had collapsed with age, in the reign of our lord the emperor Gordianus Augustus and Aviola the consuls,[140] when the priest Licinius Marcellus was father of the rites. Dedicated on the 8th day of July (?) . . . .

No. 78: Dedication of Aurelius Hermodorus (311)
(CIMRM 2. 1431; CIL 3. 4796)

Inscribed on a white marble slab, probably a dedication plaque, which would have been mounted on the wall of the sanctuary or the pronaos (H.0.60; W.1.00; Th.0.15 m). Letters: H.0.04 m.

---

139. A close variant (Hilarinus) of the same name (perhaps suggesting a son) is found on a Mithraic dedication from nearby Waggendorf; *CIMRM* 2. 1444.

140. A discrete date is rendered by the consular dating under the emperor Gordian (line7): *Gordiano Aug(usto) et Aviola c[o(n)s(ulibus)*, in the year 239 CE.

Literature: *CIMRM* 2. 1431. *TMMM* 2. 2.401.

D(eo) I(nvicto) M(ithrae) templum vetusta(te)
conlabsum quot fuit
per annos amplius
L desertum Aur(elius)
Hermodorus v(ir) p(erfectissimus) pr(aeses)
pr(ovinciae) N(orici)
m(edi)t(erranei) a novo restitui fecit
quot edificatum est divo
Maximiano VIII et Maximino it[e]r(um)
Augustis con(sulibus) Quar(tinio) Ursiniano
cur(ante).

Translation: To the god Invictus Mithras. Aurelius Hermodorus, a man most excellent, governor of the province of Noricum Mediterraneum, rebuilt anew the temple, having collapsed with age, which had been deserted for more than 50 years.[141] It was constructed in the reign of the Augusti, the

---

141. *templum vetustate conlabsum quot fuit per annos amplius L desertum*. Whether or not this mithraeum is to be identified with that restored earlier at Virunum by Hilarus and Epictetus (No. 77 above) is uncertain since no edifice has so far been found. Yet there are certain features of these dedications which suggest that they may belong to the same site.

Of the nine inscriptions from the Virunum area given by Vermaseren and Cumont (*CIMRM* 2. 1431–40 = *TMMM* 2. 2.401–9), five of the dedications (*CIMRM* 2. 1431, 1432, 1434, 1438, 1439) are clearly by members of the provincial administration. In two of the dedications not from provincial officials, the emperor designated *pro salute* would seem to be Caracalla (*CIMRM* 2. 1433 and 1440). Given shifts in the provincial administration, it seems entirely possible for there to have been a mithraeum at Virunum from as early as 212/213 (when Caracalla became sole emperor) which could have suffered neglect under less favorable bureaucrats and was restored on two different occasions. New support for this reconstruction of the vicissitudes of the local Mithras cult has been found in a recently discovered inscription from Virunum. It gives evidence of a fire that destroyed the mithraeum and necessitated rebuilding and is datable to the later second century. See Gernot Piccottini, *Mithrastempel von Virunum* (Klagenfurt: Geschichtsvereins für Kärnten, 1994). The text of the new inscription was not yet available to me at the time of this publication. I am grateful for the reference to Dr. Susanne Zabehlicky-Scheffenegger of the Austrian Archeological Institute, Vienna, who has participated in the recent work at Virunum. See also my discussion in *Building God's House,* 56–57.

divine Maximianus, consul for the eighth time,[142] and Maximinus, for the second, under the direction of Quartinius Ursinianus.

PROVINCE: Italia (Latium)
LOCATION: Ostia (Reg.I,Is.III.3)

No. 79: Mithraeum of Callinicus (late second century) (*Mitreo della Casa di Diana*)

(Figures 39–40)

The site was excavated in 1914–15 and was first reported by G. Calza. The insula known as the *Casa* (or *Caseggiato*) *di Diana* dates from the early Antonine period (probably under Antoninus Pius, 138–60 CE). It is located in the heart of the city on a prominent street (now called the *Via di Diana;* see fig. 39), just east of the Capitolium. The insula is typical of the multi-storied apartment buildings with ground-floor shops that served the urban population of Rome and Ostia.[143] The Mithraic sanctuary was a secondary construction at a later time. It was set in two windowless, vaulted rooms on the ground floor in the northeast corner of the insula. The mithraeum seems to have been in use at least into the early third century.

Literature: G. Calza, "Un nuova santuario mitriaco nella casa detta di Diana," *Notizie degli Scavi di Antichità*, S.5, 12 (1915) 324–30. G. Becatti,

---

The time interval indicated in the latest of these inscriptions (No. 78) in no way conflicts with the dating of earlier ones if this reconstruction of the sequence is followed; see the note below. Nonetheless, a more complete chronology must await further evidence and analysis.

142. *divo Maximiniano VIII.* The inscription may be dated in the year 311 CE sometime shortly after the death of Maximinianus in May. The period of dilapidation and desertion may be dated then to the late 250s, or not long after it was previously restored by Hilarus and Epictetus (No. 77 above). Given the preservation of the inscriptions, one may guess that the 50-year interval cited in the last inscription was calculated from the imperial names given in No. 77.

143. In general on the urban and suburban insulae of Ostia and Rome, see A. G. McKay, *Houses, Villas, and Palaces in the Roman World* (London: Thames & Hudson, 1975) 80–99. On their place in social life, see J. Packer, "Housing and Population in Imperial Ostia and Rome," *JRS* 57 (1967) 80–95. Both works use the Casa (or Caseggiato) di Diana for examples.

Scavi di Ostia, vol. 2: *I Mitrei* (Rome, 1954) 9–28 [hereafter cited as *Mitrei Ostia*]. *CIMRM* 1. 216–19.

The large suburban insula known as the *Casa di Diana* (fig. 39) was located in a block (Reg.I.Is.III) of buildings made up mostly of other large apartments, warehouses, and shops. The street front to the south (on the *Via di Diana*) and that to the west (on the *Via dei Balconi*) of the house were faced by rows of shops (no. 4). The main entrance to the gound floor of the insula, then, was by a passage from the south side between shops. The rooms (including the streetside shops) on the ground floor were clustered around a central cortile (3), which extended through the upper stories. The building (no. 5) to the north of the *Casa di Diana* was also an insula with shops on the west street front. In this building (known as the *Caseggiato del mitreo di Lucrezio Menandro;* see *CIMRM* 1. 224–25) another mithraeum (dedicated by a certain Lucretius Menander) was located in the southeast portion of the building separated only by a small room from the rear (north) wall of the mithraeum in the *Casa di Diana*. To the east of the *Casa di Diana*, separated by a narrow alleyway (no. 2), was another building (no. 1) made up mostly of shops and apartments that faced onto the prominent *Via dei Molini*, just across from the Grand Horreum. The number of shops, tavernae, and warehouses in this area indicate its central place in the commercial life of the city.[144]

The original use of the vaulted rooms (A and B) in the northeast corner of the insula is uncertain; however, they were paved with mosaic (remnants of which are visible under what would have been the benches in room A; see fig. 39). The two rooms were of roughly the same size: room A (L.3.74; W.6.10 m), room B (L.3.96; W.5.95 m). Room A was entered from the outer portions of the house by a south door (W.1.05 m); it once communicated with another larger room to the west by a second door (W.1.14 m), which was later sealed. Room A was divided from room B by a partition wall, which originally had a door (W.1.10 m) on its east end (at 0.75 m from the east wall). In the middle of this partition wall there was apparently a high window.

In order to produce a mithraeum some modest structural changes were made. First, the central window in the partition wall was made into a door

144. For its place within the city of Ostia, see R. Meiggs, *Roman Ostia* (1963; 2d ed.; Oxford: Clarendon Press, 1972) 270–78, 235–62.

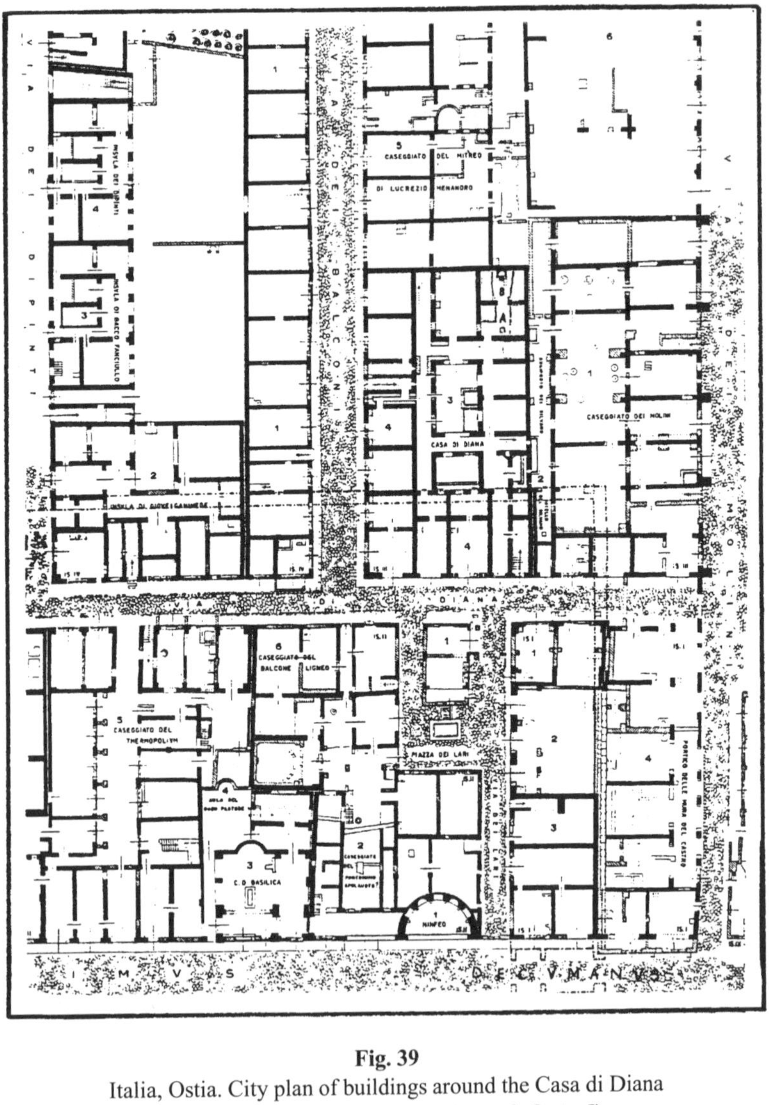

Fig. 39

Italia, Ostia. City plan of buildings around the Casa di Diana (Reg. I, Is. I–IV) (after Calza, *Scavi di Ostia,* I)

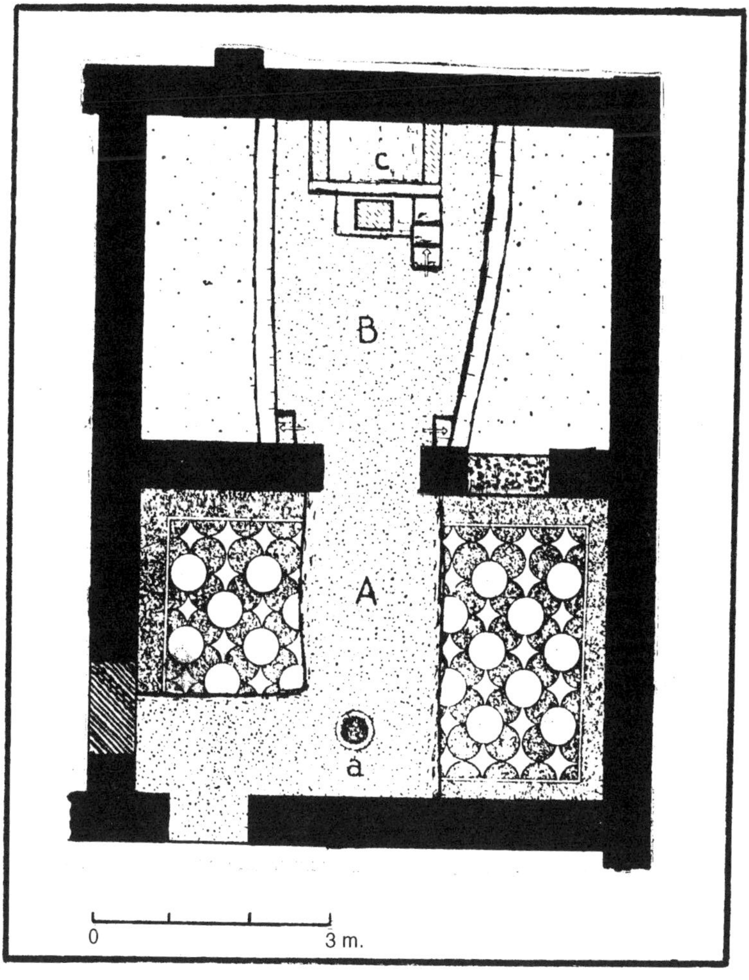

Fig. 40
Italia, Ostia. Mithraeum of Callinicus (*Mitreo della Casa di Diana*). Plan restoration (after Becatti, *Mitrei Ostia*)

(W.1.16 m). Second, benches (H.0.50–0.54 in B, Br.2.30 m in A narrowing to 1.60 m at the north end of B) were installed in both rooms. On the east wall the bench was continuous except for the intervening wall, but the former door at the east end became a passage between the two bench sections. On the west side of room B a narrow bench (H.0.50; Br.1.66–1.74 m) was set off completely from the bench in A. In room A a wider, abbreviated section of bench (L.2.45; Br.1.90 m) made allowance for a narrow passage from the door to the central aisle. The benches were constructed (at least as far as can be determined from room A) of brick and sand with some rubble; they sloped slightly toward the walls. In each room the benches were ascended by a small step (W.ca.0.40 m) on each side at the end of the bench. From the entrance in room A, the aisle (W.1.60 m) turned down the center of the room where a small round basin (Diam.0.33; D.0.15 m) was set in the aisle (a). In room B the aisle widened immediately beyond the door to 2.35 m and gradually enlarged to 2.55 m at the north end.

Against the north wall of B a platform-base (c) (H.1.45; W.1.68; Br.0.88 m), finished in white stucco, was ascended by a stair of three steps (H.0.80; W.0.33 m). The base supported an arched niche (H.1.75 m) in white plaster rising in total 3.20 m into the vault of the room. The fronts of the niche sidewalls were bracketed for the placement of small decorative columns. The ceiling of the arch was treated with pumice and painted blue to complete the *spelaeum*/canopy effect. The niche probably housed a cult relief, though none was found in the excavations. Before the niche base and beside the stair stood a marble altar (H.0.78; W.0.35; Br.0.44 m) atop a low base (H.0.40; W.0.45 m). The altar bears the inscription of the *pater* of the sanctuary, a certain M. Lollianus Callinicus (*CIMRM* 1. 219–20).

Lollianus Callinicus was probably the person who built and outfitted the mithraeum. The same individual, along with a certain M. Caerellius Hieronimus (*CIMRM* 1. 223), who are called *sacerdotes*, constructed a *thronum* which probably belonged to the same sanctuary. M. Caerellius Hieronimus provides a date for the dedication around the year 198 CE as he is known from another inscription (*CIL* 14. 4569) to have belonged to the construction guild (*collegium fabrarum tignuariorum*) located just across the Decumanus Maximus (Reg.I,Is.XII,l). Because of the limited number of inscriptions, the small size of the sanctuary, and the fact that some of the same individuals show up later in connection with other mithraea in Ostia, it is possible that the mithraeum in the *Casa di Diana* went out of use at some point in the third century.[145]

PROVINCE: Italia (Latium)
LOCATION: Ostia (Reg. II,Is.I.2)
No. 80: Dedication of Mithraeum (late second century)
(*CIMRM* 1. 233; *CIL* 14. 4314)

Inscribed on a marble plaque (H.0.59; W.1.64 m) attached to the front of the platform base (H.0.68; W.2.12 m) which sits against the back wall of the so-called Aldobrandini mithraeum (*CIMRM* 1. 232). G. Becatti calls the construction the altar, but it may have served as the base for the cult relief. Thus, it served as the niche platform, as the two projections resembling low *anta* might suggest. The inscription plaque covered the entire front of the platform. Letters: H.0.07 m (line 1); 0.06 (line 6); 0.035–0.05 (lines 2,3,4, 5,7,8).

Literature: *CIMRM* 1. 232–33. G. Becatti, *Mitrei Ostia*, 40. [The reading of *CIMRM* has been corrected below.]

Deum vetusta(te) religione
in velo formatum et umore obnubi-
latum marmoreum cum
throno omnibusq(ue) ornamentis
a solo omni impendio suo fecit
Sex(tus) Pompeius Maximus Pater
q(ui) s(upra) s(criptus) est
et praesepia marmoravit p(edes) LXVIII
idem s(ua) p(ecunia).

145. This same M. Caerellius Hieronimus (designated *patri et sacerdoti suo eosoue antistes*) also made a dedication (*CIMRM* 1. 282) to the *Mitreo degli Animali* (Reg.IV,Is.II.ll) which is still farther to the south within the city (see *CIMRM* 1. 278). For the implications of movement from one mithraeum to another, see also No. 81 (n. 151) and No. 82a (n. 152) below.

Translation: The god, having been represented on a hanging in a most ancient act of veneration and having been defaced with moisture, Sextus Pompeius Maximus, the Father,[146] executed in marble together with the throne and all the decorations at great expense to himself alone; he, who has been inscribed above,[147] also paved the hall[148] with marble for 68 feet at his own expense.

PROVINCE: Italia (Latium)
LOCATION: Ostia (Reg.III,Is.I.6)

No. 81: The Mithraeum of Caelius Ermeros (late second century) (*Mitreo delle pareti dipinte*)

(Figures 41–42)

The mithraeum building was discovered during excavations in the campaigns of 1938–42; it was thoroughly studied by Becatti beginning in 1945.

146. Line 6: *Pater*. With regard to the donor's name and office we may note also the later inscription from the same mithraeum, *CIMRM* 1. 235 (=*CIL* 14. 403): *Sex(to) Pompeio Sex(ti) fil(io)/ Maximo/ sacerdoti Solis in/victi Mit(hrae)/ patri patrum/ q(uin)q(uennali) corp(oris) treiec(tus) toga/tensium sacerdo/tes Solis invicti Mit(hrae)/ ob amorem et meri/ta eius. Semper habet.* This text, along with many others, shows that the leading members, almost always the patrons and donors, of the Mithraic group often held several of the chief offices and/or grades. In this case the donor is being honored for his benefactions, of the type described in his own dedication plaque.

147. The abbreviation in line 7: Q . S . S. EST (lapis) may be read in two ways. Becatti (*Mitrei Ostia*, 42) proposed the reading printed above: *q(ui) s(upra) s(criptus) est*, while Calza had earlier proposed *q(ui) s(acerdos) s(olis) est*. Following Becatti's restoration, the reference is probably to another inscription that would have been placed above the tauroctone relief and altar. On it presumably would have been (in prominent letters) the name of the patron. This kind of arrangement can be seen at Ostia in the case of the *Mitreo delle sette sfere* (Reg.II,Is.VIII.6; *CIMRM* 1. 239) the inscriptions from which (*CIMRM* 1. 245–47) are given at No. 86 below.

148. *praesepia* (from *praesaepe, -es,* literally, "manger, stalls"). Becatti (*Mitrei Ostia*, 42) discusses the relative merits of taking the term either as the Mithraic hall itself or as the benches. Becatti favored the benches, since the excavations showed them to have been revetted with marble. On the other hand, at the front end of the aisle was a T-shaped area between the benches and the altar area. This area was also paved with marble with a square section of *opus sectile* design in the center at the head of the aisle. I wonder if the term refers more particularly to the aisle (though it might mean both the aisle and benches). See *CIMRM* 1. 232 for description and plan.

The sanctuary was located in the rear portions of a private house (fig. 40, bldg. 6) just west off the *Via della Foce* (Reg. III,Is.I). The house was a long rectangular structure lying between a large market (bldg. 7) to the north and a portion of a Flavian bath (bldg. 3) to the south. Later, a Christian basilica (or baptistry) was erected over the earlier structures to the west (bldgs. 4–5), which had originally been part of the Flavian bath complex. The house of the mithraeum was originally built in the later Republican period (perhaps as early as end of the second century BCE), but was extensively remodeled in the Augustan period and again in the second century CE. The mithraeum was installed in a room and part of the peristyle court in the northwest corner of the house in the late second century CE. It may have been enlarged at a later time.

Literature: Becatti, *Mitrei Ostia,* 59–68. *CIMRM* 1. 264–70.

[The description and analysis below are based on Becatti and the author's own work on the site.]

The Augustan period house (fig. 42) was entered from the street by a narrow passageway that led past several rooms (probably shops) at the front of the lot. Portions of the front of the house show some rebuilding but retain their basic Republican form. The core of the Augustan house was constructed in *opus reticulatum*, seen mainly in the rear (or western half) of the lot around the court and *tablinum*. This Augustan renovation probably occurred in conjunction with the construction of the market building to the north (bldg. 7). Further modifications likely continued as a result of the construction of the Flavian bath complex (bldgs. 3–4).[149] This can be seen in the angled rear wall of the house, since it served as a party-wall with the bath

149. The dating of these buildings is somewhat difficult. The Republican structure that became house 6 may be the earliest edifice in this area. The market (bldg. 7) dates to the Augustan period, and its construction probably occasioned the renovation of the house. The shops to the north of the market (bldg. 8), however, date to the middle Hadrianic period. The baths (bldgs. 3–5) date to the Flavian period. On this chronology of Ostian building programs, see Meiggs, *Roman Ostia*, Appendix IX (n. 144 above). The dating of brickwork is based on the two studies of M. E. Blake, *Roman Construction in Italy from Tiberius through the Flavians* (Washington: CASVA, 1959) and *Roman Construction in Italy from Nerva to the Antonines* (Philadelphia: CASVA, 1973).

Fig. 41
Italia, Ostia. City plan of Reg. III, Is. I around *Mitreo della pareti dipinte* (after Calza, *Scavi di Ostia,*I)

edifice and has a bonded corner with the north party-wall between the bath and the market. The precise relationship of the front areas of bldg. 6 to the private quarters in the rear is unclear.

The private quarters were entered through a peristyle court paved in *opus spicatum*. The roof of the peristyle was carried by brickwork columns (at the corners, and with two each on interior of the east and west sides but only one each on the north and south sides). To the west of the court was the *tablinum* (or main living room, E) flanked by two rooms (A, F) whose original use is

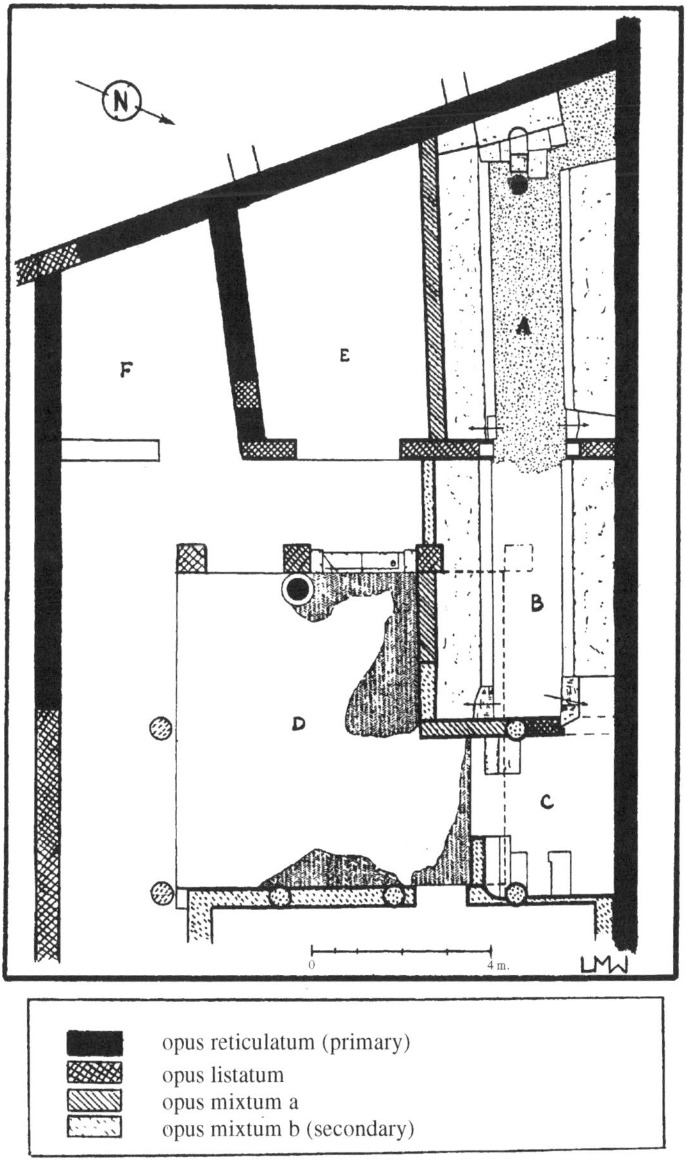

Fig. 42
Italia, Ostia. Mithraeum of the Painted Walls (*Mitreo della pareti dipinte*).
Plan restoration, composition (adapted from Becatti, *Mitrei Ostia*)

uncertain. The *tablinum* had originally been one large room in the areas of rooms A and E. The front wall of the *tablinum* was constructed in a different masonry (*opus latericium*, Th.0.61 m), and a smaller side aperture (W.0.63, at a distance of 0.45 m from the floor) between rooms E and F was filled using the same masonry. These features indicate that at some point the walls of the *tablinum* and the west side of the peristyle were remodeled. It may have been at this time, or perhaps a little later, that the *tablinum* was divided into the two rooms (A and E) by constructing a partition wall in *opus mixtum* (Th.0.47 m). In the renovation, the two interior columns of the west peristyle were replaced with square *opus latericium* pillars (0.59 x 0.59 m) to frame the entrance of the *tablinum*. A threshold was set between these central pillars, and a basin (Diam.0.685 m) stands before the southernmost. The outer columns of the west side of peristyle were replaced with slightly smaller (ca. 0.40 x 0.40 m) pillars. These features suggest that the portico on the west side of the peristyle was given a more elaborate roofing treatment of some sort than that on the other three sides. Thus, the west corridor of the peristyle seems to have been more clearly defined as a vestibule in relation to the *tablinum* entrance.

Later in the second century the peristyle was again remodeled to accommodate the construction of the mithraeum. The inner sanctuary was installed in the large irregular room (A) to the north of the *tablinum*. The pillar of the peristyle in the northwest corner stood immediately before the entrance of the mithraeum. As a result it was removed and an L-shaped partition was constructed (incorporating one of the central, entry pillars of the west peristyle and the center column of the north peristyle) to replace it. This created the outer room (B) of the mithraeum. This wall was constructed in several independent sections of different thickness, suggesting that there was originally a door on the south wall directly from the court into room B. The construction would have also required a new roofing treatment, at least on the north side of the peristyle.

The mithraeum was laid out according to usual lines but adapted to the surroundings. The inner sanctuary (A) (L.6.08–8.00; W.4.00 m) had two benches (H.ca.0.85; Br.ca.l.l0 m) sloping toward the walls with small ledges (Br.0.23 m) along the front. At the rear of each podium was a step. In the side of each podium at floor level was a square niche (H.0.35; W.0.20; Br.0.30 m), and another pair of niches was cut into the door facings of the partition wall with room B (H.0.35; W.0.30; Br.0.30 m). On the back wall of this inner hall was erected a platform and a *thronum* connected with the south podium. The platform (H.1.15; W.1.80; Br.0.60 m) had a niche (H.0.25; W.0.30; Br.0.16 m) in its center. This platform was placed against the west wall of the room, standing at the same oblique angle to the axis of the sanctuary. In front of this dais, however, the *thronum,* altar, and steps were constructed so as to square the face of the niche edifice on the axis of the hall. The *thronum* (H.0.90; W.0.45 m) stood immediately before the niche and took the form of a recessed *incassatura* (W.0.35; Br.0.30; D.0.30 m). Two inscription plaques were set into this construction: one (*CIMRM* 1. 265) refers to the donation of the cult niche by an imperial freedman; the other (*CIMRM* 1. 266) refers to the donation of the *thronum* by L. Sempronius. Before the *thronum* stood the marble altar (H.0.60; W.0.45; Br.0.35 m) on a base (H.0.85 m), and steps stood beside the altar. Behind the platform the wall must have been painted with a large scene of Mithras (a tauroctone, perhaps), and the side walls were completely decorated in zones of painted scenes.[150]

The outer room (B) of the mithraeum (L.5.50; W.4.00 m) was likely part of the original installation of the mithraeum; however, its arrangement might have resulted from a secondary conversion at a later time, that is, from an entry hall to the aisle-podium plan. The sequence cannot be demonstrated conclusively. It is clear, however, that the podia of the inner room (A) were lengthened at some point, and it seems safe to suggest that such an expansion would coincide with the addition of new benches as in B. The construction of the benches in B is slightly different from that in A; in B they do not slope toward the wall. In addition, the door between rooms A and B was widened at some point; logically, the measure would seem to be an accommodation for visibility from the benches in B. The benches in B, although of similar masonry do not correspond exactly to those in A: the left bench is narrower, the right bench is wider, and the mensa of both is wider than the corresponding elements in A. At this time a new entry to the sanctuary was provided on the east side of B through a small vestibule (C) (L.3.50; W.3.50 m) created by closing off the northeast corner of the peristyle and installing small benches. At the same time, apparently, the east colonnade of the peristyle was walled in using *opus mixtum* to complete the transformation of the peristyle into a cortile (or *cortiletto;* so Becatti). In conjunction with the renovation of the court, two doors were opened: one in the east wall from the

150. *CIMRM* 1. 268.

mithraeum vestibule opening onto the newly constructed chamber (C) to the east, and the other at the southeast corner opening onto the long corridor leading to the street. These provisions led Becatti to raise questions regarding the continued relations of the east portions of the house and the cortile-mithraeum area. One would guess that most domestic activity had ceased in the rear portions of the house.

These facts suggest that the mithraeum was originally installed in one room of the house, with an aisle of the peristyle made to serve as a pronaos (B). Later, the sanctuary was enlarged by transforming this pronaos and integrating it physically into the hall proper. New benches were installed, and a new entry was created from the court at the back of room B, through the new vestibule (C). The execution of the paintings would seem to coincide with this enlargement of the mithraeum, since they run along the walls in both rooms A and B. The dating of this enlargement may be from the end of the second century, as suggested by Becatti's dating of the paintings. The date of the installation of the altar and the first renovation of room A is ca. 162, as provided by the name of C. Caelius Ermeros in an inscription (see No. 82a below). Further insights to the building history of this mithraeum and its eventual disposition are also provided by donations of Caelius Ermeros. It appears that this mithraeum went out of use by the mid-third century, at which time the membership seems to have moved to a newly built mithraeum (the so-called *Mitreo dei Palazzo Imperiale*) located in the Maritime Baths (Reg.III,Is.XVIII).[151]

PROVINCE: Italia (Latium)
LOCATION: Ostia (Reg.III)

No. 82: Mithraic Dedications of Caelius Ermeros and Fl. Hermadion (ca. 160–212)

The following inscriptions show the role of patrons in the construction and decoration of two mithraea in the same area of Ostia. They are proximate in date, and both mithraea were renovated in existing private houses. In each case, donations by the same individual show up in other Mithraic sanctuaries

151. For discussion of the prosopography and the relationship with another mithraeum at Ostia, see n. 152 below.

or locations. Given the patterns of renovation and use of these mithraea at Ostia (see Nos. 79 and 81 above), such movement is noteworthy.

No. 82a: C. Caelius Ermeros, for Construction of the Mithraeum of the Painted Walls (ca. 162) (CIMRM 1. 269)

Inscription on a marble cippus from room A of the *Mitreo della pareti dipinte* (Reg.III,Is.I.6; see No. 81 above). The tapered cippus measures H.0.305; W.0.12–0.65 m. Letters: H.0.013–0.021 m.

Literature: Becatti, *Mitrei Ostia,* 67 and pl. XIII,1. *CIMRM* 1. 269.

C. Caelius E[r]-
meros
Antis-
tes h[ui]-
us loc[i]
fecit
s(ua) p(ecunia).

Translation: C(aius) Caelius Ermeros,[152] Antistes of this place, made it out of his own funds.

---

152. The date (162 CE) is provided by a consular notation in another inscription by the same individual from the *Mitreo della Palazzo Imperiale* located in the Maritime Thermes (Reg. III,Is.XVIII); see *CIMRM* 1. 250. There he donated two statues of Cautes and Cautopates. From the base of the statues comes the following (*CIMRM* 1. 255 = *CIL* 14. 58–59): [on the front] *C. Caelius / Ermeros / ant/istes huius lo/ci fecit sua / pec (unia).* [on the left side] *Positi xv k(alends)/ febrarias / Q. Iunio Rus/tico / L. Plaut[io] / Aquilin[o] / co[(n)s](ulibus).* [*Translation*: C(aius) Caelius Ermeros, Antistes of this place, made this (statue) from his own funds. Deposited on the 15th day of February, in the consulship of Q. Iunius Rusticus and L. Plautius Aquilinus.] For the consul Q. Iunius Rusticus, who as urban praefect heard the case of Justin Martyr, see also No. 7b above.

Still another inscription from the *Mitreo della Palazzo Imperiale* identifies Caelius (H)ermeros as the donor of a small altar that stood before a tauroctone statue. These items were built into the platform of the cult niche. The text (*CIMRM* 1. 259 = *CIL* 14. 57) reads similarly: *C. Caelius Hermaeros / Antistes huius loci / fecit / sua pec(unia).*

No. 82b: Dedication for the Plantapedis Mithraeum by Florius Hermadion (160–68/207–12 CE*)*
(CIMRM 1. 273)

Inscribed on a marble slab (H.0.37; W.0.75 m) in the middle step of revetting on the rear wall of the cult niche of the *Mitreo della plantapedis* (Reg. III,Is.XVII.2). Letters: H.0.03 m in lines 1 and 4, 0.05 m in lines 2 and 3.

Literature: Becatti, *Mitrei Ostia*, 77–78. *CIMRM* 1. 272–76.

That the same individual could have held the identical office in two different mithraea simultaneously seems odd. Moreover, the mithraeum in which these other items were found is from a later date. (It cannot have been built earlier than the end of the reign of Septimius Severus, when the Maritime Thermes were constructed. The mithraeum was installed by secondary renovation.) Thus, it is likely that the statues and altar were moved here from another place. Given the identical wording regarding the office of Caelius Ermeros in the inscriptions from the *Mitreo della pareti dipinte*, it is likely that the marble set (a tauroctone, altar, and the torchbearers) was originally commissioned as a cultic installation at the time of the construction of the *pareti dipinte* mithraeum. (Thus, the dissociated cippus of No. 82a was also most likely part of this grouping in its original location.) As the donor of this set, and given his title, Caelius Ermeros was one of the major donors (if not the major donor) of the *Mitreo della pareti dipinte* at the time of its construction. Whether Caelius Ermeros was also the owner of the house cannot be determined, but it is a reasonable guess in the absence of other data. For other fragmentary dedications from the mithraeum, see *CIMRM* 1. 265, 266, 270. Only one of these has a high Mithraic title, a *sacerdos* (no. 265, probably by an imperial freedman), and none bears the title of *pater*. Hence Caelius Ermeros's title of *Antistes* (which means "presiding priest" or just "president") is the most prominent among those preserved from the *Mitreo della pareti dipinte*. On the title *Antistes* as equivalent of the title *pater* and *pater sacrorum,* see below No. 88a,b (and nn. 182, 184).

The reuse of the statue grouping also suggests that at some point in the middle Severan period these items were removed to a new and more oppulent mithraeum, to which Ermeros (or whoever had taken possession of the *Mitreo della pareti dipinte*) had become attached. Some features of the placement of these items in the new sanctuary (the *Palazzo Imperiale* mithraeum) suggest that the cult platform, or *naos,* was consciously designed with them in mind. These facts, particularly the removal of the tauroctone and the formal planning for its reinstallation, may suggest that the remaining membership had also moved to the new sanctuary and that the *Mitreo della pareti dipinte* had for all intents and purposes ceased operation by this time. For a similar suggestion regarding another mithraeum at Ostia, see n. 145 above.

Pr(o) sal(ute) Aug(ustorum duorum)
S(oli) I(nvicti) M(ithrae)
Florius Hermadio(n)
sacerdos s(ua) p(ecunia) f(ecit)

Translation: For the welfare of the two Emperors,[153] to Sol Invictus Mithras, Florius Hermadio(n),[154] the priest, provided it from his own resources.

PROVINCE: Italia (Latium)
Location: Ostia (Reg. IV, *f.l.m.*)
No. 83: The Synagogue (late first–fourth century)
(Figure 43)

The synagogue building was discovered in 1961 and excavated in 1961–62 under the direction of Maria Floriani Squarciapino, then superintendent of the Ostia excavations. The remains were unearthed in a previously unexcavated area in what was thought to be out of the archaeological zone of Ostia during construction on the new expressway from Rome to Fiumicino and Leonardo da Vinci Airport. The building stood very near the ancient shoreline and faced onto the Via Severiana, the Roman road that ran from Portus south toward Laurentium. This area of Ostia stood outside the western or Porta Marina gate in an area of extramural (or, in Italian, *f.l.m.*) suburban sprawl and a few hundred meters south of the Porta Marina baths (Reg. IV,Is.VIII–X). Much of this area developed beginning near the end of the

153. AUGG (line 1, lapis). According to Becatti (*Mitrei Ostia*, 82), the two emperors were likely one of the following pairs: Marcus Aurelius and Lucius Verus, Marcus Aurelius and Commodus, Septimius Severus and Caracalla, or Caracalla and Geta. These pairs yield the possible dates. A date around 192 (plus or minus a few years) is probable for another dedication from the same mithraeum; see *CIMRM* 1. 275.

154. A similar name, L. Fl. Hermadion, appears in the dedication of a statue of Mithras's birth from the rock presumably found at Rome; see *CIMRM* 1. 590–91 (= *CIL* 6. 731). Despite the fact that the abbreviation FL should normally be rendered as *Flavius,* the possibility that it is the same individual should be strongly considered. This statue was found in Rome in 1662 but devoid of any archaeological context. One wonders whether it came from Rome itself or had been removed there from Ostia during the same century.

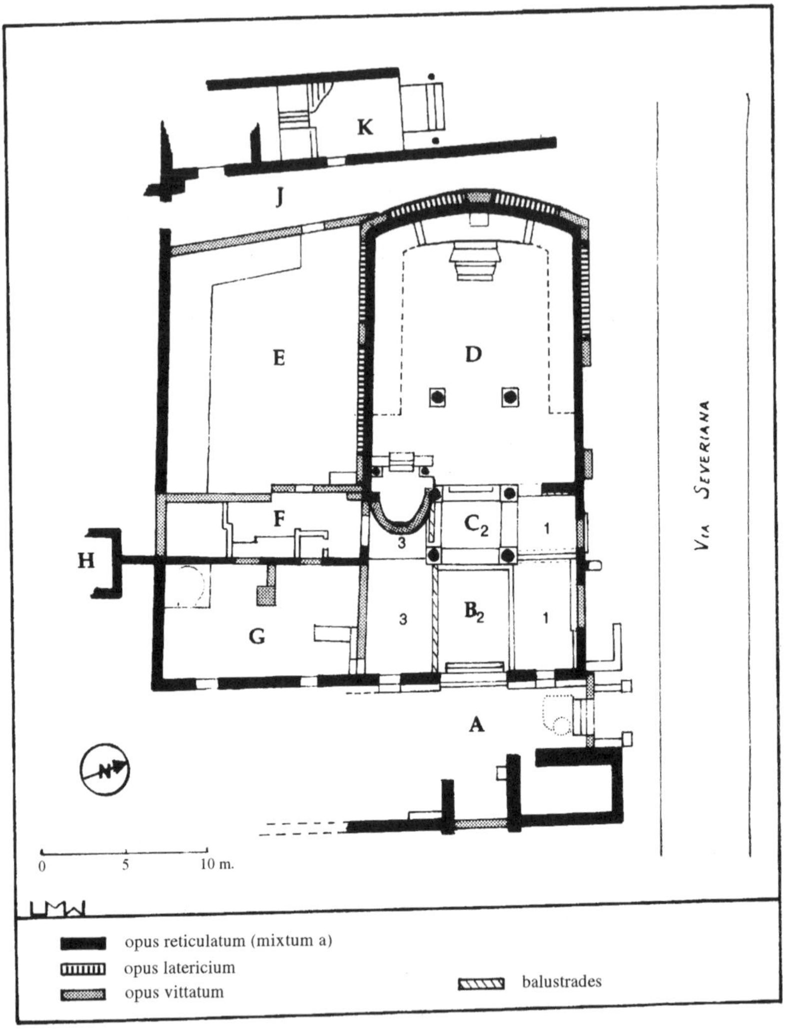

Fig. 43

Italia, Ostia. Synagogue, ca. second–fourth centuries.
Plan restoration, composite showing types of construction.

first century, but was primarily a product of expansion under Trajan and Hadrian in the early second century, and again later in the fourth century. The structure consists of several rooms (measuring in total 36.60 x 23.50 m) in a residential and commercial quarter. Most of the area surrounding the synagogue remains unexcavated, although some recent work has uncovered an adjacent building to the west and a row of commercial buildings across the street stretching northward along the Via Severiana. The masonry work of the synagogue structure points to two distinct types of construction. The original building, constructed in *opus reticulatum*, has generally been dated to the late first century CE. Other masonry indicates renovations of the building in the late third or fourth centuries; mosaic work and the *opus sectile* of the later floor levels likewise point to a fourth-century date for the final stage of the synagogue. The architectural history is probably to be read in four stages. No evidence has yet been presented regarding the fortunes of the site beyond the fourth century, but it seems to have been abandoned by the fifth century, at a time when Ostia itself was in decline. Based on the masonry the original excavators identified the building as a synagogue edifice from its first stage of construction in the first century CE. This conclusion requires further discussion in the light of the architectural history of the site.

Literature: M. Floriani Squarciapino, "La sinagoga di Ostia," *Bolletino d'arte* (1961) 326–37. Idem, "La sinagoga recentemente scoperta ad Ostia," *Rendiconti della Pontificia Academica Romana di Archeologia*, ser. 3, 34 (1961–62). Idem, "Die Synagoge von Ostia antica," *Raggi. Zeitschrift fur Kunstgeschichte und Archäologie* 4 (1962) 1–8. Idem, "La sinagoga di Ostia: Secondo campagna di scavo," in *Atti VI CIAC* (Vatican City: Pontificio Instituto di archeologia cristiana, 1965) 299–315. Idem, "The Synagogue at Ostia," *Archeology* 16 (1963) 194–203. Idem, *La sinagoga di Ostia* (Rome, 1964). H. L. Hempel, "Synagogensfunde in Ostia Antica," *ZAW* 74 (1962) 72–73. F. Zevi, "La sinagoga di Ostia," *Rassegna mensile di Israel* 38 (1972) 131–45. R. Meiggs, *Roman Ostia* (2d ed.; Oxford: Clarendon, 1971) 587–88. R. Wischnitzer, *The Architecture of the European Synagogue* (Philadelphia: Jewish Publication Society, 1974) 5–6 and fig. 3. A. T. Kraabel, "The Diaspora Synagogue: Archaeological and Epigraphic Evidence since Sukenik," *ANRW* 2. 19.1 (1979) 477–510. H. Shanks, *Judaism in Stone* (New York: Harper & Row, 1979) 162–63. Carlo Pavolini, "Ostia (Roma): Saggi lungo la via Severiana," *Notizie degli Scavi di Antichità* (Atti della Accademica Nazionale dei Lincei) ser. 8, 35 (1981) 115–43. L. M. White,

"Synagogue and Society in Imperial Ostia: Archaeological and Epigraphic Evidence," *HTR* 90 (1997, forthcoming).

[No final report of the synagogue excavations has been published to date. This reconstruction of the archaeological data is concerned primarily with the present (final) stage of the remains. But there is evidence of earlier stages, from which the building history may be surmised. The archaeological summary is based on the excavation reports of M. Floriani Squarciapino in *Atti VI CIAC* (1962) and in *Archaeology* 16 (1963), with some discussion based on Kraabel's observations in "The Diaspora Synagogue." The present discussion has also taken into account the recent finds adjacent to the synagogue building (as published by Carlo Pavolini), which were unknown at the time of the original excavation reports, and is based on the author's own work on the site, as reflected in the forthcoming article noted above.]

The architectural remains of the edifice clearly indicate that the building was in Jewish usage in its final stages, as there was a menorah relief inscribed on each of the extended corbels of the architraves of the apsidal niche on the south side of the main hall. Further evidence of Jewish activity at an earlier stage was discovered in an inscription (No. 84 below) found reused in the final floor of the hall. Finally, another inscription (No. 85 below) would seem to reflect the activities of a well-established Jewish community at Ostia, although it cannot be definitively associated with this particular building. Given the nature of the archaeological evidence, one must work backward from the final form of the building, when it was clearly in use as a synagogue. The later stages of renovation are discernible from the type of brickwork used (see fig. 43). The core of the original building was constructed in *opus reticulatum* of a sort common in the late first and early second centuries. Also called *opus mixtum A,* the reticulate facing is reinforced at intervals with a triple course of brick; an interlocking frame of lateral tufa blocks (in a regular three-row offset pattern) is found at all corners and jambs. The masonry of the later stages (seen especially in the brickwork of the apsidal Torah Shrine) is of a "brick-and-block" type known as *opus vittatum B* (with some *opus latericium*), typical of the late third and fourth centuries at Ostia.[155]

---

155. On the brickwork and dating at Ostia, see especially Meiggs, *Roman Ostia*², Appendix IX; M. E. Blake, *Roman Construction in Italy from Tiberius through the*

a. The Later Synagogue (fourth–fifth centuries)

In its final form the synagogue (fig. 43) was entered by a group of rooms forming the vestibule (A) (ca. 23.50 x ca. 3.80 m, as far as it was excavated) down steps from the Via Severiana. At the foot of the steps a cistern had been covered over with a stone slab and a well. While some of these rooms in A come from the earlier period of construction, the layout of the entry chambers was a later renovation, since it employs *opus vittatum* in some walls and in the framing of the steps. These steps also partially blocked the earlier cistern.

From this vestibule a broad central door flanked by two narrower ones opened onto an inner court (B) (W.12.50 m). Room B had a mosaic floor in three aisles, corresponding to the three doors from A (B_1: 5.85 x 3.37; B_2: 5.37 x 4.15; B_3: 7.40 x 3.35 m). Facing B on the west was an inner "gateway" (C) (W.12.50 m), which was also divided into three parts. The middle section (C_2) contained an imposing structure of four columns in grey marble on a raised platform. The columns were arranged in pairs framing the entrance from the vestibule (at B_2); this "gateway" provided the main access (L.4.30; W.3.20 m) into the hall of assembly (D). The columns were ca. 6.00 m tall including the top of the order. The main hall (D) (L.ca.15.00; W.12.50 m) was paved in *opus sectile* culminating on the west end in a slightly curved wall. On the curved west wall of the assembly hall was constructed a tiered bema (W.6.20; Br.1.25; H.0.79 m) faced with a smaller platform and steps. The interior walls of the hall were plastered, but evidence of wall decorations has not been preserved. The external wall in room D shows extensive masonry support. The original wall in *opus reticulatum* was reinforced with an encasing shell along the south, west, and half of the north sides. This

---

Flavians (Washington: CASVA, 1959) 66. One edifice cited by Meiggs as clearly dating from this later period of renovation (and showing similar patterns of masonry and decoration) is the so-called House of Cupid and Psyche (Reg.I,Is.XIV.5), dated in the early fourth century; see Meiggs, *Roman Ostia,* 259–62. Another example of the fourth-century renovation comes from the House of Fortuna Annonaria (Reg.V,Is.II.8). This edifice was originally built under Antoninus Pius (138–60 CE) but was remodeled in the fourth century using *opus vittatum;* see Meiggs, Roman Ostia, 254, 545 and pl. XIVb. The most recent work on the Ostian masonry confirms this process of renovation. See J. Boersma, *Amoenissima Civitas* (Assen: Van Gorcum, 1985), esp. 138–59, 201–20. Boersma uses some different terminology for the masonry than that used here, but the construction patterns are consistent.

encasing wall was constructed in *opus latericium* with piers in *opus vittatum B*. Taken together with the height of the columns, it is evident that in their final form these walls were meant to carry a high ceiling (over 6.00 m) over a wide span over the Hall D. At some point the left aisle of the inner court and gateway (B_3–C_3) was further modified. In its final stage area C_3 of the "gateway" was blocked off by the construction of an apsidal edifice in *opus vittatum*; on the interior the shrine was fitted with a platform faced by a stair of four steps. The north side wall of the apse edifice partially incorporated the southwest column of C_2. Hence, the four columns at the corners of area C_2 were earlier than the apse-edifice. From the top of the apse side-walls, architraves (ending in corbels) extended into the main room. At the front, the architraves were carried by two small colonnettes with composite capitals. Originally these columns stood on the floor before the apse podium, but at some subsequent point the podium seems to have been enlarged, thus incorporating the colonnettes into the podium structure.[156] Thus, there is evidence of ongoing renovations. The architraves likely carried a pediment making the entire structure an *aedicula* with apsed niche.

At the same time as the construction of the *aedicula*, several other partitions were constructed in the colonnade. Prior to the construction of the *aedicula* the room (F) to the south could be reached directly from the inner gateway (C). One partition (or balustrade) blocked off the apse structure from the main entryway (C_2). Another screen closed off C_1 from the main hall, but a door fitted with a metal grate provided access through this aisle. Further, between C_1 and D is the remnant of an earlier wall in *opus reticulatum*. Low balustrades were constructed between aisles B_2 and B_3, as well. In the final form, then, B_3 was completely blocked off from the main entryway through B_2 and C_2 to the main hall, so that the only access to the south chambers (rooms E–G) was through vestibule A by way of the door in B_3. Remnants of similar partitioning were found in the rubble composition of the apse podium and under the balustrade of C_1. It is probable, therefore, that the symmetrical arrangement of the entry areas belongs to a period earlier than

156. For discussions of the apsidal form of the Torah Shrine, the synagogue inscription from Side (*CIJ* 1. 781) is usually cited. It refers to a structure in the Sidé synagogue called the "simma," presumably meaning an edifice in the form of the Greek lunate sigma, that is, "C". See Squarciapino, "The Synagogue at Ostia," *Archaeology* 16 (1963) 198; Kraabel, "Diaspora Synagogue," 498; and L. Robert, "Inscriptions grecques de Sidé," *Rev. Phil.* 32 (1958) 36–47.

the construction of the present *aedicula*, but later than the original building plan (see below).

From the left aisle (B_3), access was gained to the other rooms of the complex. A partition wall of the same *opus vittatum* construction as the apse edifice separated these rooms from the main hall and entryway. Two doors in this partition wall from B_3 opened onto rooms F and G. Room G (6.20 x 10.32–10.50 m) was also accessible by two narrow doors (with steps) from vestibule A. The presence of *opus reticulatum* in rooms G and E indicate that they too were from the earliest stages of construction but that they had been modified. The most prominent features of G were the marble table (near the door) and the oven (located in the southwest corner), which identify it as some sort of kitchen. In its final state the floor of G was covered with a layer of ash, earth, and mixed marble and terra-cotta fragments. Under this floor level, however, was found a mosaic floor arranged in sections much like that of the entryway (B). Room F (2.73–3.23 x 10.50 m) seems to have been little more than a corridor leading from the entry area to the large side room (E). The masonry shows, however, that several small doors from G had been blocked in the later construction and that the partition wall between F and E was a new construction. There were several appurtenances in F including a low bench and what appear to be bins or closets. Room E (L.13.90; W.10.18 m) was a large hall with benches (Br.1.83 m) along its west and south walls. The west wall of this room was a new construction in *opus vittatum,* while the south wall was in *opus reticulatum*. This room, too, was decorated with a mosaic floor. It has generally been considered to be some sort of dining hall or hostelry.

b. Evidence of Earlier Stages

The evidence for the earlier stages of the building is fragmentary but highly suggestive. First, it is possible to distinguish between the *opus vittatum* wall construction of the later period and the *opus reticulatum* core of the earlier building. The *opus vittatum* is to be found primarily in the apse edifice, the south wall of B_3, and the balustrades, and in rooms E and F. The original structure in *opus reticulatum* seems to have comprised only the areas of the main hall (D), the entry court (B/C), the cooking room (G), and portions of areas A and E.

It is also worth noting that since the publication of the original reports the excavation of additional buildings to the west and north (as noted above) provides parallel stages of masonry forms of construction and renovation. The edifice immediately to the west of the synagogue hall (K in fig. 43) was also constructed in *opus reticulatum* and *opus latericium*. It had an entrance recessed from thc street that gave access to stairs and in the rear quarters what appears to be a small oven or baking establishment. The position of the stairs clearly shows that there was a prominent upper-story construction closely associated with the synagogue building. (This point will be important later.) The rear wall of this edifice is integral with the original *opus reticulatum* wall that forms the south wall of room E (the dining room) of the synagogue. Likewise, the buildings along the other side of the Via Severiana show some early, small sections in *opus reticulatum* with more extensive later buildings in *opus vittatum* and *opus latericium*.[157] In other words, the entire stretch along this southern section of the Via Severiana shows signs of having been built originally about the same period (at the end of the first century or early in the second) and having been remodeled and expanded extensively in the fourth century. It appears that insulae of commercial and residential edifices were part of this area.

Second, in area B/C, later divided into sections and paved with mosaic, a lower floor level was found to be of *cocciopesto* (i.e., a packed floor of crushed pottery or earthenware mixed with earth or plaster). This flooring was found to extend over the entire area B/C, apparently without further division, at least at first. Squarciapino reported evidence of a low "bench" (W.1.93 m) found in the southwest corner of B/C, in the area of the later *aedicula*. She conjectured that this might have been an earlier form of the Torah Shrine, and she equated it with the "ark" dedicated by Mindis Faustus, known from the inscription (No. 84).[158] Other remains suggest an intermediate stage of remodeling in area B/C; it included the construction of partitions. There is also a layer of *cocciopesto* flooring beneath the mosaic floor of the cooking room (G). The vestibule (A) in its present form is not from the original building; however, the well is certainly much older than the later building. The well, therefore, was probably an external feature of the earlier building. Thus, the vestibule (A) and the tri-portal entry in B/C were part of the later structure.

Third, the main door (at B_2) of the later synagogue and the two doors to G

157. See Pavolini, "Ostia (Roma)," 120–21, 127. See also White, "Synagogue and Society in Imperial Ostia," fig. 2.

158. Squarciapino, "La sinagoga di Ostia," *Atti VI CIAC,* 314–15.

from the east go back to the earliest period. The two flanking doors from A at B_1 and B_3 were cut through the *opus reticulatum* wall at a later time, as is clearly shown by their buckwork jambs. In contrast, two large doors in the north wall (opening from the street onto C_1 and perhaps B_1 respectively), belong to the original form of the building but were later blocked with *opus vittatum* construction. It would appear, therefore, that the original entrance to the building was directly from the Via Severiana through the entrance in C_1 and that area C served as a lateral corridor that continued directly into room F. This plan is further confirmed by a remnant of a partition wall in *opus reticulatum* between C_1 and room D. Other earlier partition walls in D and E are not known, however. In any case, the original orientation of the building was on a north–south axis through C. In the later structure the axis of the building was reoriented east–west, along the axis of room D through C_2 and B_2 to the vestibule (A). This reorientation corresponds to the partitioning of area B/C and the creation of the tri-portal entry in B, but antedates the construction of the apse-edifice in C_3. Hence, the primary orientation of the new plan would have been toward the bema on the west end of the hall of assembly (D).

In the main hall the four columns of C_2 were found to rest on foundations set into the earliest level of construction. These foundations might have been original, or they could have been dug down to lower levels for support. There is some evidence that they were shifted or rearranged at some point. Fragments of two more columns of the same general proportions were found in the hall, although not precisely aligned with those of the "gateway." Beneath the level of the later *opus sectile* floor in D were found traces of benches along the north, west, and south walls.

Taken together these data suggest that there were at least three phases of use and remodeling in the building.

c. *The Architectural Chronology of the Site*

On the basis of the sketchy evidence then available Squarciapino initially proposed the following chronology for the synagogue structure:[159]

(1) First century: The structure in *opus reticulatum* consisted of three rooms (D, B/C, and G). The curved west wall of D and the presence of side

159. Squarciapino, "The Synagogue at Ostia," *Archaeology* 16 (1963) 197–98.

benches and the bema (which were taken to be original to the construction) confirmed her assumption that it was designed as a synagogue at the time of construction.

(2) Late second to early third centuries: Remodeling of the structure included division of B/C by partition walls and the construction of the torah ark (*keibotos*) of Mindi(u)s Faustus, mentioned in an inscribed plaque found reused in the later floor (see No. 84 below).

(3) Fourth century: Substantial rebuilding produced the present structure with additional rooms (A, E, and F) and more elaborate decoration.

(4) Late fourth century (?): The present *aedicula* was constructed.

In his discussion of the site, A. T. Kraabel questioned Squarciapino's chronology with regard to her third and fourth phases.[160] The presence of some sort of Torah Shrine already in Stage 2 would suggest that an *aedicula* ought to be present in Stage 3 as well. Yet according to the chronology above no such structure was included in the renovation of Stage 3. It might be assumed that an older Torah Shrine continued in use from Stage 2 to Stage 3; however, the elaborate reconstruction that took place in Stage 3 (especially the reorientation of the axis from A) would make this less likely. Kraabel, therefore, would prefer to place the construction of the *aedicula* in Stage 3 and see its siting (in the area of an earlier "bench" construction) as related to the "ark" of Mindi(u)s Faustus. While Kraabel does not take into account the evidence for secondary enlargement of the *aedicula* (as described above), such minor embellishments would not be out of keeping with his proposed Stage 4, predicated on the major renovation occurring in Stage 3.

This basic four-stage building history seems plausible. Still some caution ought to be exercised in the interpretation of the data at several points. There are further indications of renovation that need to be taken into account.

First, it seems hasty to identify the remains of the "bench" structure beneath the later *aedicula* as just an earlier form of the Torah Shrine. Given its location in what would have been the entry corridor of the original building, it could easily have been a stair. This would make it parallel and similar to the corridor and stairway in the adjacent building (K) to the west. Moreover, there is evidence of upper stories in the earlier stages of the synagogue building (to be discussed below), which would necessitate a stairway some-

160. Kraabel, "Diaspora Synagogue," 499–500.

where. It will be suggested below that the later renovation to the present plan caused such a stair to be replaced.

Second, several features of the building plan in its final stage point to a monumentalization of the structure from its earlier form. Most notable in this regard are the six columns of C_2 and D, which must have carried a high ceiling (over 6.00 m) over the "vestibule" and assembly hall. Whereas the four columns of C_2 were thought by the excavators to be original to the building, I have doubts, and the two columns in D are clearly later. However, one of the columns in C_2 appears to be a spoil that was broken and repaired in antiquity before being used in the synagogue edifice. Thus, the monumental elevation of the hall of assembly (D) was (at least in part) a later renovation of the plan. I would suggest that the introduction of the columns was contemporary with the "monumentalization" of the plan in one of the later stages.

In keeping with this, it should be noted that the exterior walls of the original shell (in *opus reticulatum*) on the north, west, and south sides of the main hall (D) were reinforced with *opus vittatum* and *opus latericium*. This remodeling came most likely just before or at the same time as the addition of rooms E and F, at which time also the entry through A was finished and the earlier doors to B_1 and C_1 were sealed. Also, there was additional reinforcement work on the exterior of room D using piers of *opus vittatum* that rose to the roof, a height of six meters or more (see fig. 43).[161] What has not been analyzed thoroughly in previous discussions is the fact that these *opus vittatum* piers blocked several upper windows in the *opus reticulatum* shell. A remaining section of the wall from the northwest corner of D indicates quite clearly that these windows were from a second-floor level, which must have been removed when the columns of D were installed. The masonry of the original shell is quite distinctive on this point, since it shows an integral wall construction in *opus reticulatum* with a triple course of ceramic bricks at a distance of 3.20 m from the present floor. Just above this course, at some interval windows framed in tufa block were set in the upper portion of the *opus reticulatum* wall. This combination of masonry is from the original construction of the building. The presence of an upper story is, in my view, also consistent with the suggestion that the original entrance to the building was from the Via Severiana through the door in C_1 and that there were stairs in C_3 (beneath the *aedicula*).

161. Squarciapino, "La sinagoga di Ostia," 306–7.

Thus, in keeping with the Mindi(u)s Faustus inscription (No. 84 below), the original form of the building seems to have been a two-story edifice (an insula, perhaps) that was subsequently renovated for synagogue use. In recent work at Ostia another building (K) immediately to the west of the synagogue (and facing onto the Via Severiana) has been partially excavated. The two buildings were separated by a narrow alley (J, ca. 2.0–2.6 m wide), which would have provided access to the small rear door of room E. At the juncture of the south wall of room E, it is clear that the two buildings share a common wall, part of the original *opus reticulatum* structure. The neighboring building (K) contains both *opus reticulatum* and *opus latericium* masonry and has an oven (or baking establishment) in the rear (also reached by the alleyway). Most notable is the fact that one enters this building from the Via Severiana and faces a set of stairs to an upper floor, much as suggested above for the original form of the synagogue building. The nature of this building would suggest a private insula complex containing both private quarters and shops. It is not impossible that the two buildings were originally part of some larger complex and that they remained interrelated even after the renovation of the synagogue.

In this light we suggest the following provisional construction history for the synagogue building:

(1) *Phase 1*: Construction of the insula complex as part of the general expansion of the Porta Marina *f.l.m* quarter to the south down the Via Severiana. The original construction dates from the end of the first century or early in the second, probably under Domitian or Trajan. While it is possible that a Jewish group might have used these buildings from early on, there is no direct evidence of this prior to subsequent renovations.

(2) *Phase 2*: First renovations for synagogue use. These were probably internal modifications, as no major structural changes seem to be indicated. They included the basic layout of the assembly hall (D) with the bema on the west end and benches lining the wall. This is probably the project accomplished or continued under the patronage of Mindi(u)s Faustus. The installation of an "ark" as mentioned in the inscription could be a wooden chest set on the bema at the west end of the hall.[162]

162. For depictions of this type of "ark" from a proximate context in Rome, see *CIJ* 1. 315, 327, 337, 343, 401, 460. The decorative glass plates from Rome show a similar depiction (*CIJ* 1. 515–22), as does a fresco from the Jewish arcosoleum of the

No other formal Torah Shrine seems to have been constructed at this time. The date of this renovation is late second or early third century.

(3) *Phase 3a*: The major renovation project of the building to create the "monumental" synagogue hall. It included several distinct projects: (a) construction of new walls to incorporate areas A, F, and E into the building; (b) monumentaliztion of the hall and elevation of the ceiling through the second story, which involved installation of the columns and the external supporting (encasing) walls; (c) partitioning of area B/C, creation of the tri-portal entry from A, and reorientation of the axis to the west. This renovation dates from the end of the third century or early in the fourth (probably the latter). It is possible that the Mindi(u)s Faustus inscription belongs to this phase.

Phase 3b: The installation of the *aedicula* is secondary to this major renovation project. At least initially, it must be assumed, the earlicr "ark" of Mindi(u)s Faustus continued in use on the west-end bema. Then at some later point (which we will provisionally designate Stage 3b) the new Torah Shrine was built in the area C_3, thus necessitating further modifications in the entry court (B/C). It should be noticed that the introduction of the *aedicula* had the effect of reorienting room D from west to east. The date of this renovation is early to mid-fourth century.

(4) *Phase 4*: Further embellishment and decoration, perhaps precipitated or inaugurated by the installation of the new Torah Shrine. It included enlargement of the *aedicula* podium as well as decorative floor treatments and other minor alterations. This process began after the middle of the fourth century and continued to the abandoment of the building.

Via Nomentana catacomb. All of these stylized depictions from Rome are of a rather consistent date (late third and fourth centuries) and form; thus, they may represent a distinctive local development different from that known in Roman Palestine. The depiction seems to represent a two-door wooden chest with arched top. The exterior may be decorated with paint, gilding, inlay, or the like. Inside are several shelves on which scrolls are kept. It is possible that the chest was portable (as a piece of furniture), even if left stationary, rather than a fixed implacement. The introduction of such a chest cannot be documented at Rome prior to the third century. The shift from this type of wooden chest to a fixed architectural edifice (in which a chest might still be used) represents a further significant development in the architectural symbolism of synagogue planning. It would appear that notions of normative orientation of synagogues are also correlated to some extent with the introduction of this latter type of Torah Shrine.

PROVINCE: Italia (Latium)
LOCATION: Ostia

No. 84: Synagogue Inscription of Mindi(u)s Faustus (late second–early third century)

Inscribed plaque found reused as a repair tile in the final stage floor of the synagogue (see No. 83 above). The inscription has not been formally published, but a cursory transcription was given by M. Floriani Squarciapino in her reports on the excavations to 1963. No other data were given.

The plaque is now in the Ostia Museum, and a plaster cast is in the Jewish Museum of Rome. The plaque measures: H.ca.0.299; L.ca.0.545 m. Letters: Line 1: 0.041; Line 2: 0.035; Line 3: 0.034; Lines 4–5: 0.03; Lines 6–7: 0.032. Lines 6–7 show a clear erasure with a correction in a second hand.

Literature: M. Floriana Squarciapino, "La sinagoga di Ostia: Seconda campagna di scavo," in *Atti VI CIAC (1962)* (Vatican City: Instituto di archeologia cristiana, 1965) 314. A. T. Kraabel, "The Diaspora Synagogue," *ANRW* 2. 19.1 (1979) 498. L. M. White, "Synagogue and Society in Imperial Ostia: Archaeological and Epigraphic Evidence," *HTR* 90 (1997, forthcoming).

[The following is transcribed from the plaque in the Ostia Museum. I also wish to thank Mrs. Anna Blie, Director of the Jewish Museum of Rome (*Comunità Ebraica di Roma*) for allowing me to study the cast.]

Pro Salute Aug(usti)[163]

---

163. Line 1 is in Latin, and the rest is in Greek, but the hand is the same for both, down through line 5. Lines 6–7 show an erasure corrected in a second hand. Most notable is the change from a square M in the first five lines to a curved form (ꟽ), especially in the name Mindi(u)s Faustus. The E at the end of line 6 was not corrected.

The formula of line 1 may also give a clue to the dating of the inscription, most likely from the late Antonine or early Severan period. So compare the Mithraic inscriptions from Ostia: *CIMRM* 1. 273 (= No. 82b above, from the Planta pedis mithraeum, Reg. III.xiii.2, in the Porta Marina quarter, probably under Marcus Aurelius) and from Rome: *CIMRM* 1. 510 (= *CIL* 6. 727, under Commodus). Compare No. 59 (*CIMRM* 1. 53), dated ca. 209–211 and No. 77 above (*CIMRM* 2. 1438 = *CIL* 3. 4800), dated to 239. Also for Rome, note the salutary to the emperor Septimius Severus and his sons (datable to 207/8) probably by an imperial client, *CIL* 6. 3768:

Pro Salute et Victoria et Reditu

οἰκοδόμησεν κε αἰπό-[164]
ησεν ἐκ τῶν αὐτοῦ δο-
μάτων καὶ τὴν Κειβώτον
ἀνέθηκεν νόμῳ ἁγίῳ
Μίνδι(ο)ς Φαῦστος ΜΕ-[165]

Impp . Caesar . L . Septimi . Severi . Pii
Pertinacis . et . M . Aureli Antonini Augg
[et P Septimi Getae nobilissimi Caesaris] et Iuliae
Aug m(atris) k(astrorum) totiusq(ue) domus divinae numeroque eorum
L . Accius Iustus ex voto d(onum) d(at) c(um) s(uis).

164. For ΑΙΠΟΗCEN (line 2, lapis) we read ἐποίησεν.

165. All previous publications of the inscription have listed the name of the donor as Mindis Faustos. I have corrected the name to Mindi(u)s Faustus, based on other inscriptions from the immediate environs of Ostia. Mindius must have been a fairly common name. It occurs in a list of the members of the *Corporis Fabrum Navalium*, an association of shipwrights at Ostia (found at Portus, *CIL* 14. 256, line 246). Two texts from Isola Sacra bear special notice in this regard. For the texts see especially Hilding Thylander, *Inscriptions du port d'Ostie* (Skrifter Utgivna av Svenska Institutet i Rom; Lund: C.W.K. Gleerup, 1952). Thylander No. A181 (from tomb N.73) gives the name L. Mindius Diocas (and his wife Julia Zoe) and is datable to the time of Antoninus Pius. Thylander No. A182 (from tomb C = *CIL* 14. 5026) gives the name L. Mindius Dius (and his three "wives" Genucia Tryphaena, Lucceia Januaria, and Annia Laveria) and is datable to the time of Hadrian. The complete text of the latter is as follows:

L. Mindius Dius
fecit sibi et Genuciae
Tryphaenae coniugi
incomparabili cum qua
vixit annis xxiiii mens iii
et Lucceiae Ianuariae ma-
ritae et Anniae Laueriae contuverna-
li suae sanctissimae
et libert(is) libertab(usque) suis pos[ter(is)q(ue)] eor(um).
H(oc) m(onumentum) e(xterum) h(eredem) n(on) [s(equetur)]
In fronte p(edes) xxx, in agro [p(edes) xx]xi.

While both inscriptions are in Latin, the names of the wives show some Greek influences. The mid-second-century dating for both is significant. Moreover, the names Dius and Diocas could even be related cognates to one another. In this light we observe the badly damaged portions of lines 6 and 7 in our Jewish text, which yield portions of two more words Me[. . .] and Dio[. . .]. The similarity to the two names from Isola Sacra is striking. There is, of course, no way of being certain, but it would be typical of the form of such inscriptions if lines 6–7 would have given the name of

[. . . ca. 7–8 . . . .]ΔΙΩ[. 3–4 .]

Translation: For the well-being of the Emperor. Mindius Faustus [. . . . DIO . .] constructed (the synagogue) and made it from his own gifts,[166] and he dedicated (set up) the "ark"[167] for the sacred law.

PROVINCE: Italia (Latium)
LOCATION: Ostia

No. 85: Honorific for C. Julius Justus by the Jewish Gerusia (mid-second century)

(*CIJ* 1. 533)

This Latin inscription is on a marble plaque found originally at Castel Porziano, south of Ostia on the Via Severiana, and first published in 1903.

---

important relatives (or patrons). It is not impossible that our Mindius Faustus was somehow related or attached to the families of Mindius Diocas and/or Mindius Dius. For a discussion of the implications, see White, "Synagogue and Society in Imperial Ostia," n. 47.

166. The term δομάτων (line 3) would usually mean "gifts," but could be read as the derived meaning "funds" (presumably given for the project). Still, the use of this term is unusual, and another option suggests itself. Given the generally poor orthography found in the text, we might well read the omicron for an omega, hence δωμάτων, a variant found in some papyri (see P.Petr. 3. 42, so Moulton-Milligan), and common among Greek epitaphs from Rome. (See P. W. van der Horst, *Ancient Jewish Epitaphs: An Introductory Survey* [Kampen: Kok-Pharos, 1991] 26). This spelling would seem a natural substitution also in a Latin context, given the regular use of the loanword *domus* in Greek as δόμος (for δῶμα). Read in this way, then, the phrase would refer to the house or rooms from which the synagogue was renovated. A similar use of the term δώματα as "rooms" associated with a synagogue building (as hostelry) may be found in the Ophel synagogue inscription (*CIJ* 2. 1404 = No. 62 above). Finally, in either case, it is not possible to read the term ἐποίησεν merely as an auxiliary verb with ἀνέθηκεν (as in the reading of Squarciapino, "The Synagogue at Ostia," *Archaeology* 16 [1963] 203). In general the orthography and usage of this inscription are similar to that typically found in the Jewish epitaphs from Rome. See H. J. Leon, *The Jews of Ancient Rome* (Philadelphia: Jewish Publication Society, 1960) 76–77, 79–89, and van der Horst, *Ancient Jewish Epitaphs*, 25–34. See also L. V. Rutgers, *The Jews in Late Ancient Rome: Evidence of Cultural Interaction from the Diaspora* (Leiden: Brill, 1995) 176–201.

167. For ΚΕΙΒΩΤΟΝ (line 4, lapis), read κιβώτον (so Kraabel, "Diaspora Synagogue," 498, with parallel references on the usage).

Recent work by the British School at Rome has begun to examine other Roman architectural remains from Castel Porziano that suggest at least some elements of an elite life from imperial times. These findings, however, are as yet in a very early stage. This inscription has traditionally been associated directly with Ostia. Unfortunately, the left third of the stone is now completely lost. According to the reconstructed text, it refers directly to a Jewish community "dwelling in the colony of Ostia" (line 2). The names in the text support this identification. Nonetheless, it is not possible to say with any certainty that the Jewish congregation reflected in this text is the same one that met in the known synagogue edifice at Ostia (No. 83 above). The form of the inscription is a typical *titulus* that would have been affixed to the front of a houselike tomb in a necropolis, such as at Isola Sacra. The date is probably mid-second century, Hadrianic to early Antonine periods. The stone is now in the Museo Nazionale della Terme, Rome.

Literature: *CIJ* 1. 533. L. M. White, "Synagogue and Society in Imperial Ostia: Archaeological and Epigraphic Evidence," *HTR* (forthcoming).

[The transcription below is based on the text of Frey, *CIJ,* and on photographs of the stone, with some emendations by the author.]

[Universitas or Collegium?] Iudeorum
[in col. Ost. commor]antium qui compara
[verunt ex conlat]ione locum C. Iulio Iusto
[gerusiarchae ad m]unimentum struendum
[donavit rogantib]us Livio Dionisio patre et
[col(legii) patro]no gerusiarche et Antonio
[..... diab]iu anno ipsorum consent(iento) ge[r]
[us(iae), C. Iulius Iu]stus gerusiarches fecit sibi
[et coniugi] suae lib(ertis) lib(ertabusque) posterisque eorum
[in fro]nte p(edes) XVIII, in agro p(edes) XVII.

Translation: The Community (Collegium or Synagogue?)[168] of the Jews

168. The term *universitas* (line 1) is supplied by Frey. Given the tone of the text, I suspect that either *collegium* or *synagogē* might as easily fit. My own preference (since certainty is out of the question), given the tone of the rest of the text and the kind of honors being bestowed, would lean toward *collegium*, which I have also restored below in line 6.

dwelling in the colony of Ostia, who from the collection[169] acquired a place (or plot) for C(aius) Julius Justus,[170] gerusiarch,[171] so that he might construct

169. *[ex conlat]ione* (line 3) is Frey's restoration. The reading *ex compositione* ("by agreement") would also fit the space and the sense, if the preceding verb were abbreviated *comparaver* (vel sim.). The latter reading provides a slightly different sense and points to the fact that such plaques regularly display the means by which the property was acquired as a kind of legal deed. For the formulas and comparable inscriptions from Isola Sacra see White, "Synagogue and Society in Imperial Ostia," nn. 58, 60, 64–65. Also compare the form in n. 165 above, which confirms the mid-second-century date.

170. Both Julius Justus and Livius Dionysius appear to be Roman citizens. How they came to Ostia or achieved this status is not clear. Their names suggest local origins as suggested by onomastic similarities to local families at Ostia. As John H. D'Arms has noted, as these names passed on through layers of freedmen, they tended "to cluster and repeat themselves, especially within the *collegia*" (*Commerce and Social Standing in Ancient Rome* [Cambridge: Harvard University Press, 1981] 137). Cf. Meiggs, *Roman Ostia*^{2}, 323.

Both C. Julius Justus and Livius Dionysius were possibly the descendants of aspiring Jewish freedmen of Ostia with at least some social prominence. The onomastic C. Julius indicates direct linkage to other prominent Ostian families of imperial freedmen. At Ostia at least four individuals with this onomastic held the office of *Augustalis*, the highest municipal office open to freedmen. See D'Arms, *Commerce and Social Standing*, 127; 137 n.82 and App. 1, nos. 62–65 (cf. *CIL* 14. 369, 461, and 5322). At least two of these (D'Arms, nos. 63 and 65) also married outside of their *gentilicium*, which gives further testimony to their social prestige (see D'Arms, 134 and App. 2). The onomastic Livius similarly evinces linkages through freedmen of another aristocratic Ostian family, the A. Livii. Decurions of this family held magistracies under Trajan and Antoninus Pius. More than forty freedmen with this onomastic (over several generations) are known from Ostia. Meiggs, *Roman Ostia*^{2}, 202; D'Arms, *Commerce and Social Standing*, 138 and App. 1, nos. 68–74. See the discussion in White, "Synagogue and Society in Imperial Ostia," nn. 67–72.

171. For *gerusiarchs* (or *gerousiarchs*) at Rome, see Leon, *Jews of Ancient Rome*, 180–83. I am in complete agreement with Leon (pp. 168–70, following Schürer and Frey) that the *gerusia* did not represent a central council of elders over all the Jewish congregations in a city (except perhaps Alexandria), and especially not in the city of Rome. Instead, it seems that it represents the volition of individual congregations to adopt for themselves a collegial organization (and appropriate titles) in imitation of other collegial groups in their immediate locality. If this inscription comes from the same Jewish community at Ostia as the edifice and Mindius Faustus inscription (Nos. 83–84 above), then it may well suggest that the earliest form of the building was more like other collegial halls in its earliest phases. For comparable honorific Jewish texts see B. Lifshitz, *Donateurs et Fondateurs dans les Synagogues juives* (Cahiers de la RB 7; Paris: Gabalda, 1967) passim. See also for the title *pater/mater* and other

a monument, (hereby) have donated it to him at the request of Livius Dionysius, father (and patron of the collegium?), gerusiarch, and of Antonius (archon?) for life, in the year of their office, by consent of the gerusia. C. Julius Justus, gerusiarch, made (this monument) for himself and his wife, together with their freedmen and freedwomen and their descendants, in width, 18 feet; depth, 17 feet.[172]

PROVINCE: Italia (Latium)
LOCATION: Ostia
No. 86: Mithraic Dedication of Decimius (third century?)
(*CIMRM* 1. 246–47; *CIL* 14. 60–61)

A large figure of Mithras as tauroctone is dedicated with two inscriptions. The monument probably comes from the so-called Mithraeum of Petrini, now known by its floor decoration as the *Mitreo delle sette sfere*, first excavated by R. Lanciani in 1886 (Reg.II,Is.VIII.6; cf. *CIMRM* 1. 239–44). The monument is a large relief in white marble (H.1.09; W.1.17 m) which probably stood in a circular recessed niche on the rear wall of the sanctuary. The two dedications were walled in above and below the niche; they proclaim the renovations not only of the cult relief but of the mithraeum itself by the patron Aulus Decimius Decimianus.

Literature: G. Labus, *Biblioteca Italiana* (Milan, 1816) 3. 49 (no. 2) and plate III. L. Paschetto, *Ostia, Colonia Romana* (Rome, 1912) 387–89. Cumont, *TMMM* II, Mon. 82, fig. 70, inscr. 134. Becatti, *Mitrei Ostia*, 123–24 and plate XXXIV,l. *CIMRM* 1. 245–47. *CIL* 14. 60–61.

---

social implications the discussion by B. Brooten, *Women Leaders in the Ancient Synagogue* (Chico, CA: Scholars Press, 1982) 57–72 (the Castel Porziano inscription is mentioned on p. 70).

172. Julius Justus makes provision for his own freedmen and freedwomen who were his dependents and clients. This fact indicates something of the prominence and status he had achieved, and it probably correlates with his position within the Jewish *gerusia* and as a patron of the congregation. It is a typical provision in funerary *tituli* at Ostia and Rome among the higher classes. For the formulas and the significance of the measurements in both legal and economic terms see White, "Synagogue and Society in Imperial Ostia," nn. 74–76. Compare nn. 5, 169 above.

No. 86a: CIMRM 1. 246 = CIL 14. 60.

Above the relief in a semicircular plaque formed of five pieces of white marble. The plaque forms an arch over the circular niche, and the inscription is in one line. This text served as the main honorific for the benefactor who restored the mithraeum. The text below the tauroctone (No. 86b) provided the precise nature of his act of beneficence. [Letter height not given.]

A. Decimius A(uli) f(ilius) Pal(atina) Decimianus
s(ua) p(ecunia) restituit.

Translation: A(ulus) Decimius Decimianus, son of Aulus Decimius, of the tribe Palatina, restored it from his own funds.

No. 86b. CIMRM 1. 247 = CIL 14. 61.

Below the relief in a rectangular plaque of blue marble (H.0.125; L.0.88 m). An inscription in three lines. [Letter height not given.]

A. Decimius A(uli) f(ilius) Pal(atina) Decimianus aedem
cum suo pronao ipsumque deum solem Mithra
et marmoribus et omni cultu sua p(ecunia) restituit.

Translation: A(ulus) Decimius Decimianus, son of Aulus Decimius, of the tribe Palatina, from his own resources restored the sanctuary with its *pronaos*, and (the figure of) the God himself, Sol Mithras, (he restored) in marble and in all splendor.

PROVINCE: Italia (Latium)
LOCATION: Rome (Reg.III)

No. 87: Mithraeum under S. Clemente (early–mid-third century)
(Figure 44, cf. 1, 16, 17)

In 1867 a mithraeum was discovered during excavations under the basilica of S. Clemente. Beginning in 1852 F. Mullooly had discovered that a late-fourth-century basilica (below the level of the present basilica; see No. 53

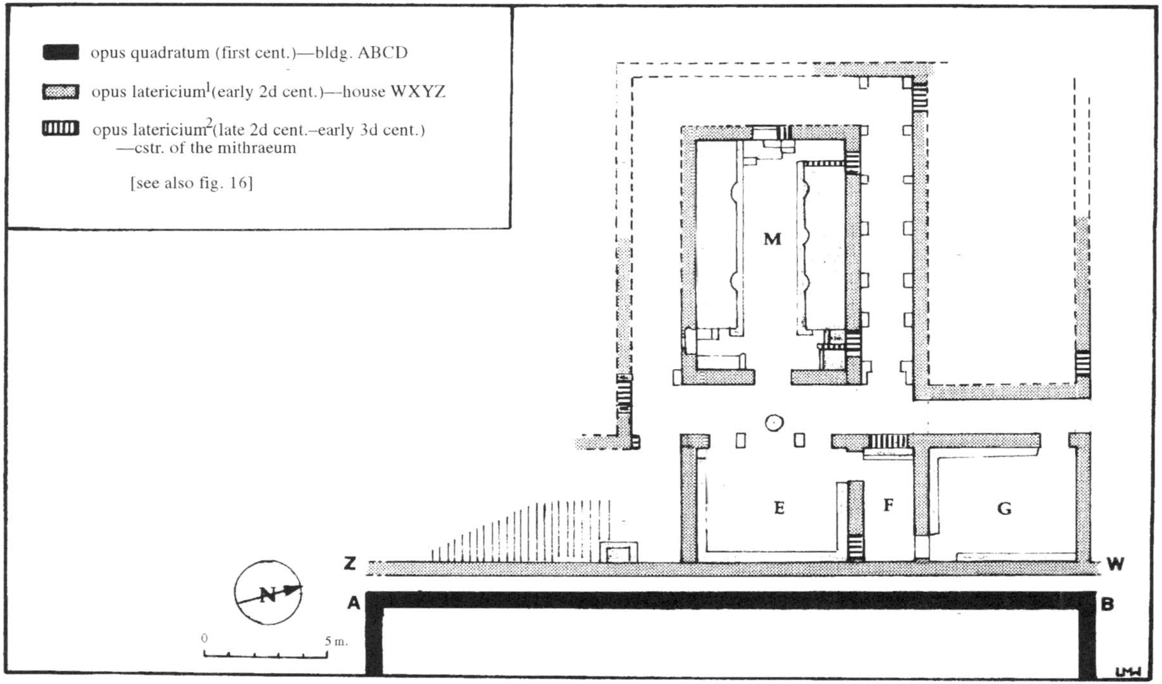

Fig. 44
Italia, Rome. Mithraeum beneath Church of S. Clemente. Plan restoration (after Guidobaldi, adapted). (See figs. 16–17 above.)

above) was actually founded on top of a level of first–third-century Roman buildings (see figs. i and 16). The excavation and reexamination of the lower levels produced the reconstructed history of the pre-Constantinian church, the *titulus Clementis* (No. 53). During the excavations, it was discovered that the fourth-century basilica was actually built over one large building complex, while the apse extended out over what was originally a separate building to the west. It was in this second building, just a few meters below and to the west of the apse that the mithraeum was discovered (see fig. 16). The so-called house of the mithraeum was initially excavated in 1869–70. The mithraeum was constructed in the central cortile of the house. The house itself dates to the beginning of the second century; the mithraeum was installed by the late second or early third century. In addition to the Mithraic hall proper, at least two other rooms from the house were used by the Mithraic group. Most of the northern and western portions of the house were never excavated, but recent work has produced some new information regarding the north side of the building. The mithraeum remained in use up to the late fourth century, when the property was taken over in the construction of the basilica.

Literature: G. de Rossi, "Scoperta di un insigne speleo mitriaco sotto l'antica basilica di S. Clemente," *BAC* 1 (1870) 125–27. Idem, "Dello speleo mitriaco testé scoperto sotto la basilica di S. Clemente," *BAC* 1 (1870) 153–68. F. Gori, "Il santuario del dio persiano Mitra ultimamente scoperto a S. Clemente in Roma," in *Il Buonarrotti* (s.II) 5 (1870) 289–301. T. Roller, *Saint-Clément de Rome: Description de la basilique récemment découverte* (Paris, 1873). F. Gori, "Sorgenti vive nei mitrei e nel mitreo di S. Clemente," *Revue archéologique* 44 (1892) 189–90, 313. Cumont, *TMMM* 2.3. 203–5 (no. 19). L. Nolan, *St. Clement's Tunnel* (Boston, 1914). Idem, *The Basilica of S. Clemente in Rome* (3d ed.; Rome, 1925). J. P. Kirsch, *Die römischen Titelkirchen im Altertum* (Paderborn: Schöningh, 1918), 36–40. F. Cumont, "Découvertes nouvelles au Mithréum de Saint-Clément à Rome," *CRAI* (1915) 203–11. E. Junyent, "La primitiva basilica di S. Clemente e le costruzioni antiche circostanti," *RivAC* 5 (1928) 231–78. Idem, *Il titolo di S. Clemente in Roma* (Studi di antichità cristiana 6; Rome: Pontificio instituto di archeologia cristiana, 1932) 55–81. Idem, "Nuove indagini sotto la basilica primitiva di S. Clemente," *RivAC* 15 (1938) 147–52. F. Deichmann, "Zur Datierung der Ünterkirche von S. Clemente in Rom," *Mitteilungen des* *deutschen archäologischen Institut, Römische Abteilung* 58 (1943) 153–56. R. Krautheimer, *CBCR* 1. 119–27. M. J. Vermaseren, "Het Mithraeum onder de Kirk van S. Clemente," *Mededelingen van het Nederlands Histor. Inst. te Rome* (R.3) 6 (1950) ciii–cxviii. Vermaseren, *CIMRM* 1. 338–48. F. Guidobaldi, "Il complesso archeologico di S. Clemente: Risultati degli scavi più recenti e riesame dei resti architettonici," in *Art and Archaeology*, ed. L. Boyle, E. Kane, and F. Guidobaldi (S. Clemente Miscellany 2; Rome, 1978) 215–309 (= 5–99). Idem, "L'Edificio del Mitreo," in *San Clemente: Gli Edifici Romani, La Basilica Paleocristiana, e Le Fasi Altomedievali* (S. Clemente Miscellany 4; Rome, 1992) 73–94. I. Bragantini, "Le decorazioni parietali dell'Edificio del Mitreo," in ibid., 317–26.

[The reconstruction that follows is based primarily on the following: Junyent, *Il titolo di S. Clemente*; Krautheimer, *CBCR* 1. 123–27; *CIMRM* 1. 338; Guidobaldi, "L'Edificio del Mitreo;" and the author's work at the site.]

The so-called house of the mithraeum (fig. 16, bldg. WXYZ) was a fine brickwork structure in *opus latericium*, datable to about the beginning of the second century CE.[173] The house was situated just to the west of the large building in tufa construction (*opus quadratum*) considered to be a *horreum* or public building of the first century. The two edifices were separated by a narrow (W.0.80 m) alleyway (fig. 16, locus tu) that was bridged by a barrel-vault that was intended to serve as the pavement for a passageway into the upper floor of the house. Shortly after the construction of house WXYZ, another building was constructed above the tufa building (ABCD) to the

173. Cumont ("Découvertes nouvelles au Mithréum de Saint-Clément," 203–11; cf. *TMMM* 2. 3.203–5) had suggested (on the basis of what he assumed was an Augustan *gens* in a dedication; cf. *CIMRM* 1. 340) that the house must date to the Augustan period. Junyent had arrived at a first-century date on archaeological grounds. But based on an observation of C. C. van Essen — that the house rests on a layer some 4 m deep which dates from the fire of Nero — Vermaseren argued for a date in the early second century (see Vermaseren, "Het Mithraeum onder de Kirk van S. Clemente," cv–cix and the note to *CIMRM* 1. 340). Krautheimer (*CBCR* 1. 123) likewise concluded from this fact and the nature of the brickwork an early second-century date. Most recently, F. Guidobaldi (*San Clemente: Gli edifici Romani, la Basilica Paleocristiana, e le Fasi Altomedievali,* 41, 85) has proposed a *terminus post quem* at the end of the reign of Domitian (ca. 90–96), based on the use of Flavian styles. Nonetheless, the house is generally referred to as early second century.

east, and from this edifice the early Christian titular church would emerge (see No. 53 above).

Because of the slope of the hill (from east to west) the east end of house WXYZ was originally below ground level with other floors above. The south side of the ground floor *domus* was largely domestic quarters, while the north side may have housed shops. In the center of the domestic quarters was a walled cortile (M) opening onto a *cryptoporticus* on all sides. Stairs at the southeast corner (Z) of the building provided access from the street level. It was in this central court (M) (L.9.60; W.6.00 m) that the mithraeum was eventually constructed (figs. 16, 44).

The court, originally open, was at some point roofed with a barrel-vault having eleven openings. Of the six original doors into the court, all but one (on the east from D, W.1.50 m) were walled shut. The central door to the west was sealed to only half the wall thickness from the outer side to create a simple niche on the inside of M. Apparently not long after the construction of the house the cortile was transformed into a nymphaeum, with its focus on the west wall of M.[174] The ceiling of the vault was treated with tufa to resemble a grotto, and there is evidence of mosaic work in the openings.

At some point later, probably in the latter half of the second century, the nymphaeum (M) was converted into a mithraeum. In addition, rooms E and G (and probably room F) were altered to serve some function in conjunction with the Mithraic cult. The sanctuary proper (in M) was laid out as a plastered central aisle (W.2.15 m) with two side benches. The benches began at a short distance (1.05 m) from the east wall where two low steps surmounted each bench. The south bench (H.0.82; Br.1.64 m) continued to the west wall where it met the dais for the cult niche at a right angle. The north bench (H.0.84; Br.1.60 m) stopped 1.00 m short of the west wall where a low stucco wall (H.1.60 m) set against the end of the bench partitioned off a narrow space to the north side of the niche. Each bench was faced by a wide rim (W.0.30 m) set slightly lower than the front edge of the bench; from this rim each bench was relieved by several semi-circular recesses (Diam.0.35 m).[175] In the front

174. Guidobaldi, *San Clemente*, 84, citing the appendix by I. Bragantini, "Le decorazione parietali dell'Edificio del Mitreo," 317–26.

175. Junyent, *Il titolo di S. Clemente,* 68 and fig. 18 (see our fig. 43) reports six such recesses, three on each side; however, Vermaseren (*CIMRM* 1. 338) says that there were only two on the left side. The latter position has been confirmed in more recent work. See Guidobaldi, *San Clemente*, Tav. I.

of each bench at ca. 3.00 m from the cult niche and at the floor level rectangular compartments were cut out (W.0.60; H.0.35–0.40; Br.0.27 m).

The base for the cult niche was connected by an L-shaped extension (H.0.82; W.0.75 m) from the south bench. Two low steps set at the corner with the bench made it possible to ascend the platform from the left side. Beside these steps stood a large base (H.1.00; W.1.00; Br.1.00 m), which was hollow and could be covered by a terra-cotta lid. Another stair of three steps (H.1.00; W.0.80; Br.1.00 m) ascended this base/pit from the right (north) side, thus creating a platform (W.2.25 m) across the end of the central aisle. Behind the central base rose the arched niche (H.0.97; W.ca.1.50; Br.0.75 m) created by sealing the west doorway to M from the outside but leaving half of its depth open on the inside.

Before the base stood two smaller bases, one almost square (H.0.52; W.0.40; Br.0.44 m) and the other round (H.0.20; Diam.0.30 m). On the first of these stood a square altar (H.1.12; W/Br.0.63 m) with a tauroctone relief and dedicated by Cn. Arrius Claudianus, the *pater* of the mithraeum.[176] On the other base (or perhaps in the niche) stood a small statue (H.0.63 m) of Mithras born from the rock.[177] At the rear of the sanctuary stood two smaller benches, one on the east wall beside the main entrance and the other in the northeast corner of the room. Above these benches and flanking the door, shallow niches were cut into the wall, probably for statues of the torchbearers.[178]

The small rooms (E, F, and G) opposite the mithraeum to the east have been claimed to be part of the mithraeum.[179] The walls of both were lined with benches, and F was decorated with mosaic floors and a painted stucco ceiling. In G the walls were seven niches of varying sizes containing reliefs, frescoes, or (perhaps later) graffiti. Because of the decoration and layout of

176. *CIMRM* 1. 340: *Cn(aeus) Arrius Claudianus / pater posuit.* The altar itself is *CIMRM* 1. 339. This Arrius Claudianus was probably a descendant of a freedman of the prominent *gens Arrii.* The emperor Antoninus Pius was also a member of this *gens* on his mother's side. This fact may also correlate with a mid- to late-second-century date for the establishment of the mithraeum.

177. *CIMRM* 1. 344.

178. *CIMRM* 1. 341–42.

179. Vermaseren was less than certain on this point; see *CIMRM* 1. 157 (no. 338). Guidobaldi (*San Clemente*, 85) and Bragantini ("Le decorazioni," 323–24) are more confident.

this room it has been labeled the "school" of the mithraeum, on the assumption that some sort of instruction and preparation prior to initiation took place here. Room G communicated through a doorway in its southeast corner to room F, and another doorway led to room E. The exact function of the room, however, cannot be determined. The walls of G were painted in fresco, the style of which bears striking similarities to the frescoes of S. Maria Capua Vetere mithraeum. The date of the decoration of this room seems to be ca. 180–200 CE.[180] Evidence of how other areas of the cryptoporticus and the house might have been used in connection with the mithraeum is lacking.

It is probable that the mithraeum was decommissioned by the time that the first basilica was constructed in the late fourth century.[181] At this time the west wall of the nave was constructed above the east wall (ZW) of the "house of the mithraeum." Hence, the earlier alleyway (tu) and wall AB were incorporated into the foundation. Then the apse was constructed by extension out into the second-floor apartments above rooms E and F of house WXYZ. (See also figs. 16 and 17 and the discussion in No. 53 above.)

PROVINCE: Italia
LOCATION: Rome (Reg. IX)

No. 88: Foundation of a Mithraeum by Aebutius Restitutianus (date?)

Two inscriptions were found in conjunction with the fragmentary remains of a mithraeum under the Basilica San Lorenzo in Damaso, which is now part of the *Palazzo della Cancelleria*. The inscriptions (one from the altar of the sanctuary) record the donations of the presiding priest and patron of the cult for the construction and decoration of the mithraeum.

No. 88a: Dedication of the Altar
(CIMRM 1. 422)

Inscribed in a rectangular plaque on a cylindrical marble altar (H.0.725; Diam.0.41 m) which sits on a square base (W.0.40 m). Letters: H.0.035–0.04 m.

---

180. Ibid., 325.

181. So Krautheimer, *CBCR* 1. 134–35; cf. Junyent, *Il titolo di S. Clemente*, 159–60. See Guidobaldi, who dates the abolition of the cult to 392, at which time the construction of the basilica began (*San Clemente*, 93).

Literature: First published by B. Nogara, *Monumenti romani scoperti negli anni 1938–1939 nell'area del Palazzo della cancelleria* (Quaderni di studi romani 9; Rome, 1941) pl. Ia. *CIMRM* 1. 422.

Aebutius Restituti-
anus qui et Proficen-
tius antistes dei
Solis Invicti Mithrae
aram d(onum) d(edit)

Translation: Aebutius Restitutianus, also called Proficentius, *Antistes*[182] of the god Sol Invictus Mithras, donated the altar.

No. 88b: Construction of the Mithraeum (CIMRM 1. 423)

The dedication of the sanctuary is in the form of a verse in nine lines composed by the same priest who dedicated the altar in No. 88a above. It is inscribed in a rectangular marble slab (H.0.395; W.0.65 m) which seems to have been designed to be fastened to a wall (by a hole in the middle of the stone). The stone itself seems to have been a reused spoil. Letters: H.0.022 m.

Literature: B. Nogara, *Monumenti romani scoperti negli anni 1938–1939 nell'area del Palazzo della cancelleria* (Quaderni di studi romani 9; Rome, 1941) pl. 1. *CIMRM* 1. 423.

Hic locus est felix, sanctus, piusque benignus,
Quem monuit Mithras mentemque dedit
Proficentio patri sacrorum
Utque sibi spelaeum faceret dedicaretque
Et celeri instansque operi reddit munera grata
Quem bono auspicio suscepit anxia mente
Ut possint syndexi hilares celebrare vota per aevom
Hos versiculos generavit Proficentius
Pater dignissimus Mithrae.

182. The title *Antistes* means "presiding priest" or simply "president." Compare No. 82a (and n. 152) above and n. 184 below.

Translation: Happy, sacred, and holy is this auspicious spot which Mithras designated and put into the mind of Proficentius, the father of the rites, that he should build and dedicate a cave to the god. So, acting quickly because of the good omen but with an anxious mind, he presided over the work as a pleasing gift, so that rejoicing *syndexi*[183] might ever be able to celebrate their vows (to the god). Proficentius, the most worthy father[184] of Mithras, composed this little verse.

PROVINCE: Italia (Latium)
LOCATION: Rome (Reg. XIII)

No. 89: The Aventine Mithraeum Beneath Basilica S. Prisca (ca. 195–400)

(Figures 45–46)

The mithraeum was originally discovered during excavations by the Augustinian Fathers beneath the basilica in 1935. It was found to be situated in a group of underground rooms (a cryptoporticus) of a large Roman house. Excavations of the mithraeum proper were conducted from 1952 to 1959. The findings showed that the house itself went through several stages of reconstruction before the mithraeum was introduced ca. 195. The mithraeum was later remodeled and enlarged in ca. 220. It was destroyed in ca. 400 (if not earlier) when Christians, who inhabited another portion of the same house, broke in and ravaged the sanctuary. The rooms were then filled with rubble and debris to form foundations for the basilica, which was then built over the site.

---

183. The term is a transliteration from the Greek (συνδεξίοι) and literally means "those who join right hands." It is clearly an in-group designation for the members of the Mithraic conventicle. So compare the usage in Greek from a graffito in the Dura-Europos mithraeum (*CIMRM* 1. 54).

184. *Proficentio patri sacrorum* (line 3). Taken together with the preceding inscription (No. 88a), this text indicates that Proficentius held the offices and/or titles of *pater sacrorum*, *antistes*, and *Pater (dignissimus)*. These offices seem to have less to do with any assumed "rank" of initiation (as is traditionally supposed in discussions of Mithraism). Instead, it appears that they come from the simple fact that he was the founder, the principle donor of the mithraeum, and its self-appointed poet laureate. One wonders whether this activity in the cult had anything to do with his adopted name.

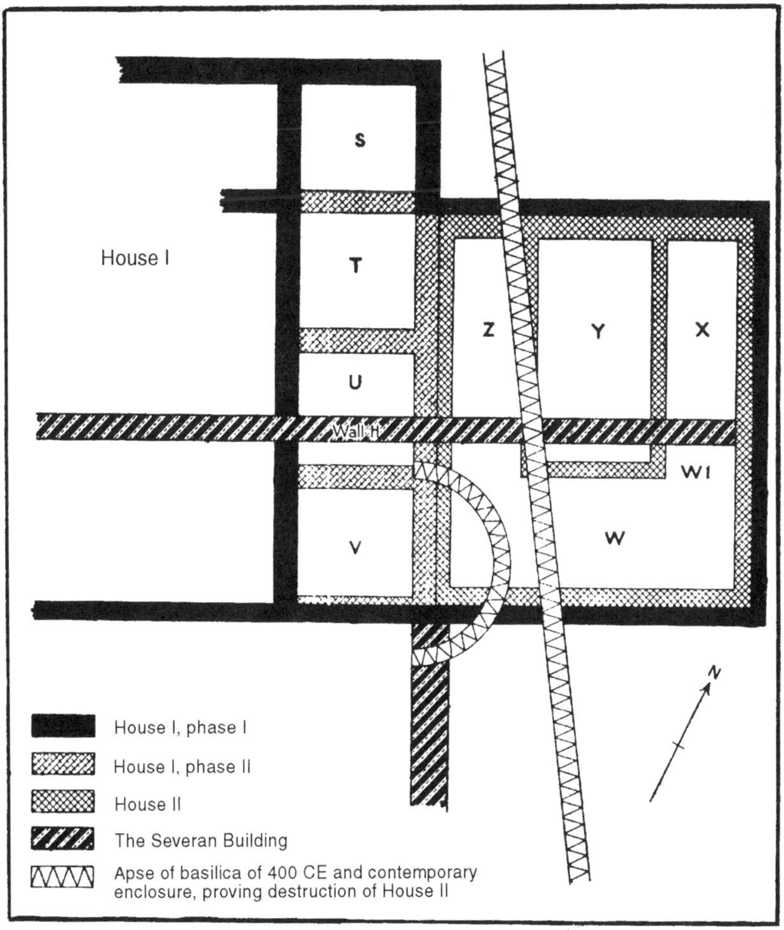

Fig. 45
Italia, Rome. Aventine mithraeum.
Plan restoration, composite in stages of construction of the house
(after Vermaseren and Van Essen)

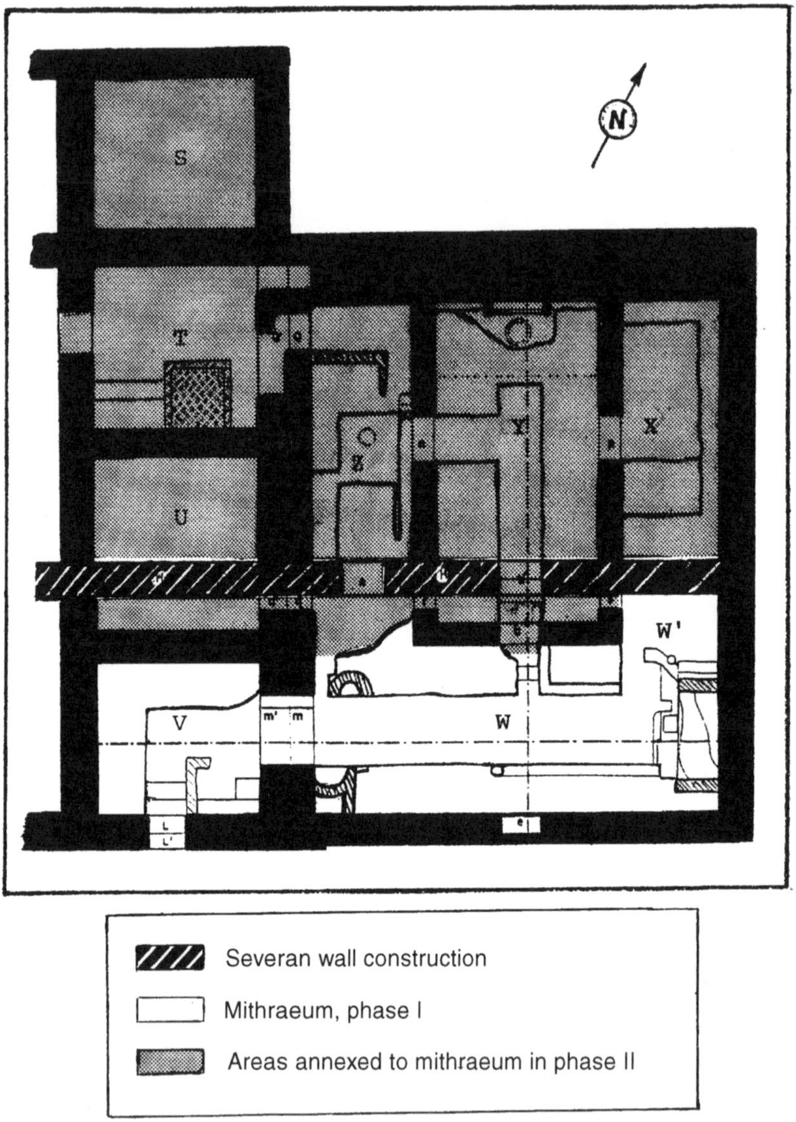

Fig. 46
Italia, Rome. Aventine mithraeum. Plan restoration, composite (after Vermaseren and Van Essen)

Literature: G. Lugli, *I monumenti antichi di Roma Suburbio* (Rome, 1938) Suppl. 3. 56. A. Ferrua, "Mitreo Prisca," *Bulletino della Commissione archeologica del Governatorato di Roma* 68 (1940/41) 59–64. Idem, in *La Civilta Catholica* 17.2 (1940) 298–304. F. Cumont, "Rapport sur une mission à Rome," *CRAI* (1946) 386–90. M. J. Vermaseren, "The Aventine Mithraeum adjoining the Church of St. Prisca," *Antiquity and Survival* 1 (1955) 3–12. *CIMRM* 1. 476–500. M. J. Vermaseren and C. C. Van Essen, *The Excavations in the Mithraeum of the Church of Santa Prisca in Rome* (Leiden: Brill 1965).

[The following reconstruction is based primarily on the final excavation report of Vermaseren and Van Essen and on the author's work at the site.]

a. The Site Before ca. 195

The area around the Church of Sta. Prisca was in the region of the Aventine destroyed in the fire of July, 64 CE under Nero. The site remained vacant for some thirty years until ca. 95, when the oldest portions of the present substructure were built (i.e., House I: phase 1; see fig. 45). It is possible that Trajan was already the owner of the property before he became emperor, since the site was traditionally known as the *privata Traiani*.[185] A few years later, perhaps shortly after Trajan's accession in 98, a terrace was added to the east garden (House I: phase 2). In the west porticus around the garden, four chambers (S, T, U, V) were constructed to serve as a substructure for the terrace overlooking the garden.

Again, a few years later (but still under Trajan), the entire east garden adjacent to S-T-U-V was taken over in the building of House II, as an expansion of the palace. In the new construction the windowless, vaulted rooms W-X-Y-Z formed the basement of House II. Air and light holes in the vault of Y would indicate a central cortile in the domestic quarters above. Apparently rooms V and T (and perhaps U) of the terrace substructure were incorporated into the plan of House II at this time. These modifications rendered the terrace above S-T-U-V useless; therefore, a new terrace was constructed along the south side of House I, where a nymphaeum (in area CC) had already been constructed. The vaulted rooms (AA-FF) formed the substruc-

185. See Vermaseren and Van Essen, *Excavations in the Mithraeum of the Church of Santa Prisca in Rome,* 14–15, 109–10.

ture for this south terrace. It is likely that this construction continued up to the early years of Hadrian's reign (117–38 CE).[186]

The buildings remained basically in this condition until the end of the second century, when the so-called Severan Building was constructed. About 194/5 the complex (consisting of Houses I and II) was radically altered. It is possible that the estate was inherited by the new emperor, Septimius Severus.[187] In this rebuilding, the south portions of both Houses I and II were sacrificed. A trench running from east to west across the plot was cut down to the foundation/basement level. The new north wall (H) of the building (House Ia, fig. 45) was set in this trench; the new south wall was made to rest on the arcaded exterior walls of the south terrace substructure (AA-GG). The exact nature and use of the new building are not clear. The north portion of the older complex (House IIa, fig. 45) probably remained in domestic use. The basement (W-X-Y-Z) was likely unchanged except for the intrusion of the support wall (H), which was built to include doorways with relieving arches for access to all areas of the basement (fig. 45). Sometime after this major renovation, probably shortly, the basement was given over to the Mithraists.[188]

b. Mithraeum I (ca. 195)

At the very beginning the Mithraists seem to have occupied only rooms W-W' of the basement (fig. 46). While all the rooms may have been at their disposal, construction was limited in the first period to this one area. Originally there were several points of access to the basement rooms; doors e and m/m' led directly to room W. Room V (L[north–south]:4.10; W[east–west]:4.60 m) was an anteroom or vestibule for the basement sanctuary with an entrance from the outside through door L/L' into Q and then down five steps. Door m/m' (W.1.00 m) was the main entrance to the sanctuary and was later widened; door e was later sealed. The sanctuary (room W) (L.11.25; W.4.20 m) was constituted as a narrow central aisle (W.1.65 m) flanked by two sloping benches (H.1.00; Br.1.35 m). The right (south) bench was interrupted by door e; the left (north) bench was similarly interrupted by a passage leading

186. Ibid., 112.

187. Ibid., 105–6.

188. And soon afterward (according to Vermaseren) the Christians moved into the west portion of the Severan period House IIa (see Appendix A, No. 10d).

to door b/b' and room Y. On the south bench at the entrance m/m' was a semicircular niche (H.1.75; Diam.0.90 m) that was connected vertically to the south wall by a small partition. A similar niche (H.1.75; Diam.0.66 m) was set at the west end of the north bench but at a distance of 0.40 m from the wall, leaving a narrow access for door a and room Z. Thus, the north niche was erected freestanding above the bench. The first section of the bench on the north originally ended at a distance of 0.42 m from the west jamb of door b/b'; later the bench was extended 1.08 m taking up more than half of the entry area in front of b/b'. The second bench section on the north side ends at the corner of walls K2–K3, or at a distance of 2.70 m from the east wall. The benches on both sides were stuccoed white; the front sides were painted red along with door m/m' and the fronts of the two niches. The inside of the niche on the north bench was painted purple, while that on the south was painted orange; they undoubtedly housed the statues of the torchbearers Cautopates and Cautes respectively.

At the east end of the aisle a large niche (H.2.44; W.2.36; Br.1.22 m) was constructed. The base was a brick wall (H.1.22 m). Before the base and immediately beside the right podium were three steps (Br.0.65 m). The stucco side walls (*antae*) of the niche carried a shallow arch constructed of tiles. The front of the *antae* were painted to look like pilasters (with Corinthian capitals and acanthus tendrils) supporting the *aedicula*. The entire structure was stuccoed and painted. On the back wall tufa or pumice was embedded to give the appearance of a grotto. The ceiling tiles were painted blue with gold/yellow stars. In the niche on the back (east) wall was affixed a relief in stucco of the tauroctone. Another small stucco relief was executed (by the same artist) on the right wall of the niche; it portrays Mithras in the act of catching the bull. On the left wall a raven was represented. The entire podium-floor of the niche was occupied by a large reclining statue of Caelus-Oceanus that contained the conduit for a fountain.[189]

The side walls of the central aisle of room W were painted with three processions of the *mystae* with lines of verse in dipinti at the top.[190] Other deco-

189. For discussions of the statue and its interpretation, see Vermaseren and Van Essen, *Mithraeum of Santa Prisca*, 131–32, 37–38 and Vermaseren, "Aventine Mithraeum," 15–18.

190. See *CIMRM* 1. 484–85. Both the painting and the text represent features of a Mithraic meal and procession. For discussion, see also H. D. Betz, "The Mithraic Inscriptions from Santa Prisca and the New Testament," *NT* 10 (1968) 62–80.

rative scenes and geometric designs adorned the walls of the room. The area W' (L[north–south]:1.55; W[east–west]:2.70 m) to the left of the cult niche contained an irregular block of stone in its northeast corner, and five large amphorae were embedded in the ground along wall H. On the outside of the left *anta* of the niche facing into W' was a graffito,[191] below which were a bench and a ledge or shelf (0.64 m above the latter).

c. Mithraeum II (ca. 220)

About 220 the entire mithraeum was enlarged and refurbished. At this time rooms V, Z, Y, and X (fig. 46) were incorporated architecturally into the cultic activity of the sanctuary. In addition, the interior of room W was embellished and redecorated. First, the anteroom (V) was added to the sanctuary proper making the overall length 17.50 m. An L-shaped section of bench (H.1.00; Br.ca.1.50 m) was constructed in the northwest corner of room V. Door m/m' was widened (later perhaps) by 0.70 m to the north to provide greater visibility for those on the bench in V. In the southeast corner of V, adjacent to the steps from L/L', a small enclosure was created with a narrow entrance (W.0.34 m) and one step down. Inside the enclosure on the east wall stood a base or altar platform (H.1.10; W.0.63; Br.0.63 m). On the south wall was a low ledge above which a large stucco figure (probably a *gigant* with reptilian legs) was fastened to the wall.

In the sanctuary (W), the benches were raised and given a mensa (in those sections closer to the niche). Portions of the bench fronts were revetted with marble slabs. In the left bench (at a point ca. 0.45 m west of the passageway to b/b') a deep, narrow opening was cut out (though it may date from a later stage of the first period). On the south side entrance e was sealed in the outer half of the doorway (thus creating a niche), and the bench was made continuous at this point. On the bench a small brick seat (H.0.60; W.1.50; Br.0.70 m) was constructed in the expanded door frame of e creating a *thronos* that looked directly through door b/b' to the north wall of room Y. A terra-cotta vase (Diam. 0.40 m) was set in a semicircular opening in the bench before the *thronos*. The cult niche was embellished slightly with the addition of a

191. *CIMRM* 1. 498 (Letters: H.0.05–0.06 m): *Natus prima luce / duobus Augg. co(n)s(ulibus) / Severo et Anton[ino] / XII k(alendas) decem[bres] / dies Saturni / luna XVIII.* The date is 20 November 202 CE.

brickwork basin and a low table beside the steps and with the construction of a little wall from the north *anta* closing off the access to W' to a width of 0.45 m. The entire decorative program of the sanctuary was repainted with new processional scenes and dipinti verses.

At this same time the three rooms X, Y, and Z were put to use in the service of the cult. In all three rooms benches were constructed indicating various types of assembly and seating. The layout of room Y (L.6.85; W.4.55 m) was much like that of W, with a central aisle (W.1.23 m) leading from door b/b'. The orientation of this room was such that a person seated on the *thronos* (at the newly constructed niche e) of the south bench in W would have been looking directly down the central aisle of Y toward a cult niche on its north end wall. On either side of the aisle was a low bench (H.0.30; Br.ca.1.65 m); the left (west) bench was interrupted by a passageway leading to door n and room Z. The north wall of Y was fitted with a niche. At a distance of 1.10 m from the wall (A) the low bench (H.0.35 m) extended across the width of the room. The niche itself was placed on another narrow elevation (H.0.55 m from the floor). The niche (H.1.82; W.1.85; Br.0.27 m) was very shallow with two *antae* (W[left]:0.25; W[right]:0.20 m) supporting a rather flat, arched canopy. Before the niche was an irregularly shaped, raised platform (max. H.0.75 m) that was rounded toward the front. In it was set a shallow basin (Diam.0.71 m). In the niche was affixed a stucco relief (badly damaged) apparently depicting the head of Sol surrounded by a circle, probably of the zodiac. The room shows almost no signs of decoration except a white stucco finish for the walls. The fronts of the niche *antae* were painted red; the interior, greenish-blue.

Room Z (L.6.85; W.2.75 m) was entered directly by door n from room Y or by door a from room W. From door a (W.1.19 m) along the wall (I_1) there was a bench (H.0.85; Br.0.78 m) that met at a right angle with another bench (Br.1.42 m). The north section of bench met the east wall (K_1) at door n, where three narrow steps (W.0.32 m) surmounted the podium. Behind the north bench stood a crude stucco wall (constructed later, probably after 306); it rises 1.32 m from the bench and almost entirely closes off door o/o' leading to room T.[192]

---

192. Vermaseren and Van Essen concluded that, since Christian incursions into the mithraeum (beginning after ca. 306) were likely made through room T and door o/o', this wall was built as some sort of screen for privacy and protection (see *Mithraeum of Santa Prisca*, 142).

In the area before the benches in Z a lower platform of packed earth (L.2.10; W.1.59; H.ca.0.35 m) was created. Set in the lower platform was an inscribed *dolium* (H.0.72; W.0.56 m) that contained a terra-cotta vase (H.0.22; W.0.31 m).[193] Along the east edge of this lower podium was a stucco wall (W.0.22 m) extended to a distance 0.67 m from wall H creating a passageway (W.0.45 m) beside door n. This passage from n and the area just inside door a were dug out to the floor level of the Trajan house. Thus, there was created a pit (L.1.70; W.1.39 m) between the platform and door a, which Vermaseren identifies as a symbolic grave for ritual performances.[194] There is little sign of other decoration in the room.

Room X (L.6.80; W.2.70 m), unlike Y and Z, could only be reached by one approach, door p from room Y. The entrance through p was not a passage through the bench in Y but was made over the bench and down into X by a step. Around the other walls were benches that on the north and east slope forward: north bench (H.[front]0.67;[rear]0.82; Br.0.60 m); south bench (H.0.82; Br.1.20 m). Before the south bench and extending out to the south door jamb was a lower podium (H.0.40; Br.1.40 m). The appearance of the room was very plain with little or no decoration and a packed clay floor. The benches and perhaps the walls were finished in white stucco.

The later mithraeum apparently continued in use up into the fourth century, and Vermaseren thinks up until its final destruction in ca. 400. There were probably attacks on the sanctuary by Christians beginning in ca. 306. At the end the Christian community meeting in the northwest portion of the Severan complex broke through room T (and door o/o'). They demolished the sanctuary interior and damaged a number of the statues and paintings. Then they used the existing airholes in the ceiling vaults to fill the basement with rubble and debris. That they could fill so much debris from above probably means that the rooms above the basement had already been destroyed by the Christians in preparation for construction of the basilica. The east end of the basilica was set above room V using wall G as support for the east wall of the nave. The apse was then extended out over what had been the mithraeum (see fig. 45).

---

193. *CIMRM* 1. 495.

194. Vermaseren and Van Essen, *Mithraeum of Santa Prisca*, 142–43.

PROVINCE: Italy (Etruria/Tuscia)
LOCATION: Nersae (Nesce, Aequiculi)

No. 90: Rededication of a Collapsed Mithraeum (ca. 172)

Three inscriptions by the same individual were found below the modern town of Nesce; they reflect the fortunes of a mithraeum from the Roman town of Nersae. A certain Apronianus, a provincial administrator (*arkarius rei publicae*), rebuilt the mithraeum after it had apparently fallen into disrepair and disuse. The two inscriptions given below reflect the rededication of this building after repair. He also provided a new tauroctone relief and other furnishings (*CIMRM* 1. 650–51, not given here).

No. 90a: CIMRM 1. 647 (= CIL 9. 4109, cf. TMMM 2.2.152).

Invicto Mithrae
Apronianus arkar(ius)
rei p(ublicae) d(onum) d(edit).
Dedicatum VII kal(endas) Iul(ias)
Maximo et Orfito co(n)s(ulibus)
per C. Arennium Rea-
tinum patrem.

Translation: To Invincible Mithras. Apronianus, state treasurer (for the province), made this gift. Dedicated on the 7th of July in the consulship of Maximus and Orfitus,[195] through C(aius) Arennius Reatinus, father.[196]

No. 90b: CIMRM 1. 648 (= CIL 9. 4110; cf. TMMM 2.2.153).

[..spelaeu]m Solis invic[ti]
[Mithrae pro salut]e ordinis et pop[uli]

195. The consular notation yields the date 172 CE.

196. It is significant that there is a local official, the *pater* (who would typically be a patron) of the Mithraic group (C. Arennius Reatinus), while no mention is made of Apronianus's own Mithraic "rank." It is possible that Apronianus's benefaction came as a result of his public office rather than his attachment to the cult. So note the references to the civil magistracy in the following inscription. He is known from another inscription as *r(ei) p(ublicae) Aequicul(orum) ser(vus),* who dedicated a sanctuary to Isis and Serapis (*CIL* 9. 4112).

[Apronianus arka]rius rei p(ublicae) vetustate [collap]sum
[perm(issu) ordin(is) de] sua pecunia restit[uit]

Translation: For the well-being of the magistracy and the people, Apronianus, state treasurer (for the province), restored [this] cave of Sol Invictus Mithras, since it had collapsed with age,[197] from his own resources by permission of the (civil) magistracy.

PROVINCE: Italy (Etruria/Valeria)
LOCATION: Aveia Vestina

No. 91: Mithraeum Dedication (213)
(*CIMRM* 1. 652; *CIL* 9. 3608)

Inscription found on an altar discovered at the modern town of Fossa.

Imp(eratore) Severo Antoni-
no Aug(usto) IIII co(n)sule T. Fl. Lucilianus
eq(ues) pub(licus) et T. Avidiaccus Furianus eq(ues) pub(licus) speleum
Soli invicto consumma-
ver(unt) cur(am) ag(ente) P. Peticen(o) Prim(o).

Translation: For the Emperor Severus Antoninus Augustus, consul for the fourth time,[198] Titus Flavius Lucilianus and Titus Avidiaccus Furianus,

197. *vetustate [collap]sum...restit[uit]* (line 5). Compare a third-century inscription from Ostia, *CIMRM* 1. 308 (= *CIL* 14. 4315): *[Na]ma Victori Patri / Aur(elius) Cresce[n]s / Aug(usti) lib(ertus) / fratres ex / speleo dilap/so in melio/ri restaura/vit.* See also Nos. 77–78 above.

198. The emperor referred to is somewhat unclear. According to Vermaseren this inscription is placed with references to Septimius Severus. But the unusual name is more like that of Caracalla (Marcus Aurelius Antoninus; see *CIMRM* 1. 53, 407, 630, 800; 2. 1433, 1440). Likewise, the consular dating is apparently that of Caracalla, that is, 213 CE (see *CIMRM* 2. 1227 = *CIL* 13. 6754; *CIMRM* 2. 1793 = *CIL* 3. 3384). Such a date would also explain the absence of references to Septimius Severus and Geta. On the date, see the brief notation of Cumont, *TMMM* 2. 2. 154, and *CIL* 9. 3608.

magistrates of the equestrian order, completed the *spelaeum* for Sol Invictus (Mithras) under the management[199] of P. Peticenus Primus.

PROVINCE: Italy (Umbria/Umbria)
LOCATION: Sentinum (Sentino)

No. 92: A List of the "Patrons of Mithras" (ca. 260) (*CIMRM* 1. 688; *CIL* 11. 5737)

The inscription gives a list of members of the mithraeum at Sentinum who are designated patrons. It is in the form of a roster of the cult in the form of a *collegium* inscribed on a marble tablet (H.0.46; W.0.57 m), which presumably would have been displayed prominently in the sanctuary or its *pronaos*. The inscription would seem to commemorate some project undertaken by those members listed. Whether this list represents the entire membership of the cult cannot be determined. Beneath the centered first line of the title (with the name of the president of the *collegium* below) are given three columns listing the names of the members. Column I contains fourteen lines; Column II, thirteen lines; and Column III, nine lines with space for some five more between line 7 and line 8. Letters: Line l: H.ca.0.05 m; lines 2–14 H.ca.0.03 m.

[Text according to *CIL* 11. 5737.]

Cultores d(ei) S(olis) I(nvicti) Mithrae
Patroni, prosedente C. Propertio Profuturo

(I)	(II)
Coiedius Proculus	Pompon(ius) Victor
Ligurius Theodotus	Statius Velox
Mussius Vindex	Vassiden(us) Verus
Coiedius Hilarianus	Helvenat(ius) Celer

199. *curam agente* (line 6). For the phrase as used of military leadership, see *CIMRM* 2. 1805 and *CIL* 3. 10429. For *cura* as oversight in matters of the Mithraic cult, see *CIMRM* 1. 564 (= *CIL* 6. 745) and *CIMRM* 1. 722; compare No. 78 above.

Sentin(as) pater leonum Ianuarius
Titius Castor
Pompe(i)us Pompeianus
Gessius Optabilis
Ligurius Clementinus
Plotius Fortunatus
Licinius Faustus
Aetrius Romanus
Asinius Commo[dus]
Visenn(ius) Quinqu[ennalis]

Carfan(ius) Achille(s)
Cassidius Rufin(us)
Antist(ius) Benign(us)
Aetrius Irenaeus
Helven(atius) Gemellin(us)
Sentin(as) Valentin(us)
Iulius Victorin(us)
[Ca]ecil(ius) Sozo[n . . .]
Ve[recundus . . .?]

(III)

Rantif(ius) Verus
Caesoni(us) Dexter
Ianuarius Sent(inatum)
Aelius Ylas
Coied(ius) Pamphilus
Aduren(us) Theseus
Coied(ius) Auxa(n)on
...
...
... (vacat)
...
...
D(edicatur) menesterio
T. Sevio Felice

Translation: The worshipers of the god Sol Invictus Mithras, the patrons, under the presidency of C. Propertius Profuturus.[200]

200. Line 2: *patroni, prosedente C. Propertio Profuturo*. The same office and a similar name are given in another dedication from the Sentinum mithraeum, *prosedente C. Propertio Augurino sacerd(ote)*, which is datable to 210 CE (*CIMRM* 1. 687 = *CIL* 11. 5736; cf. *TMMM* 2. 2.156). The present inscription, however, likely comes from a slightly later period in the life of the Sentinan cult. Thus, the later president may be a relative (a son?) of the earlier one. The dating of this text is based on certain names in the list. According to a decree (*CIL* 11. 5748) three of the names

(Column I) Coiedius Proculus, Ligurius Theodotus, Mussius Vindex, Coiedius Hilarianus, Januarius Sentinanus, father of the lions,[201] Titius Castor, Pompeius Pompeianus, Gessius Optabilis, Ligurius Asinius Commodus, Visennius, the quinquennal magistrate.

(Column II) Pomponius Victor, Statius Velox, Vassidenus Verus, Helvenatius Celer, Carfanius Achilles, Casidius Rufinus, Antistius Benignus, Aetrius Irenaeus, Helvenatius Gemellinus, Valentinus Sentinanus, Julius Victorinus, Caecilius Sozon…, Verecundus.…

(Column III) Rantifius Verus, Caesonius Dexter, Januarius the Sentinate, Aelius Ylas, Coiedius Pamphilius, Adurenus Theseus, Coiedius Auxanon.…

This (plaque) is dedicated by direction of T. Sevius Felix.

---

listed above (Aetrius Romanus, Casidius Rufinus, and Statius Velox) appear in a roster of a *collegium fabrum* datable to the year 260 CE.

Other indications of the history of the membership of the cult at Sentinum may be derived tentatively from the names in the other inscriptions from the site. Two names have already been cited as presiding in the collegium; a third occurs on an altar dedication, *prosedente Sevio Facundo* (*CIMRM* 1. 689 = *CIL* 11. 5735; cf. *TMMM* 2. 2. 158). With this name compare that of the last line. A certain Rufinus is given in this same inscription as one of the donors of the altar (along with Aemilianus). It may be the case that the members of the cult are drawn from a number of prominent members of the city along with their freedmen and other clients. This notion is suggested by the fact that two of the *cultores* are called *Sentinas*; that is, they are either decurions or freedmen of the city. So note Januarius (col. I.5, cf. col. III.3) and Valentinus (col. II.10). It is also conceivable that the cult membership of the later date is drawn from descendants of those persons mentioned in earlier inscriptions, for example, Rufinus (*CIMRM* 1. 689) and Casidius Rufinus (col. II.6).

Cumont (*TMMM* 2.2. 157 n. 3) suggested that the list given in the text is not the full roster of members of the Sentinan cult but only those who had been designated patrons. Presumably what is meant by this designation is that the individuals named made gifts to the collegial treasury, though for what purpose is not clear. One may compare the similar, but fragmentary, list from Portus, which is called an *album sacrato[rum]*, with two columns of names and grades (*CIMRM* 1. 325 = *CIL* 14. 286; *TMMM* 2. 2. 140).

201. *pater leonum* (2. 6). On the stone written in the line but in smaller letters with *pater* above *leonum*.

PROVINCE: Africa/Numidia)
LOCATION: Cirta (Constantine)

No. 93: Dedication of a Mithraeum by P. Ceionius Caecina Albinus, *v.c.* (ca. 364–67) (*CIMRM* 1. 129; *CIL* 8. 6975)

Inscribed on a rectangular slab of limestone (H.0.43; W.0.82 m). The stone is broken off along the right edge. Letters: Lines 1–2: H.0.07 m; line 3: 0.065 m; line 4: 0.06 m.

Speleum cum [sig]-
nis et ornamen[tis]
Publilius Ceion[ius]
Caecina Albinu[s v(ir) c(larissimus)]

Translation: This cave with its figures and decoration Publius Ceionius Caecina Albinus,[202] *vir clarissimus* (dedicated or built).

---

202. Publius Ceionius Caecina Albinus was a member of an old aristocratic family from Rome. He served as *praeses consularis* of Numidia early in his public career under Valentinianus and Valens (364–367), and it was apparently at this time that he dedicated the mithraeum in Cirta. Given the place of Cirta in the Diocletianic persecution of Christians (see No. 31 above) and also during the Donatist controversy, this foundation of a mithraeum at such a late date and under nominally Christian emperors is of some interest. Thus, it is worth noting that the donor was involved in the pagan–Christian rancor at Rome (ca. 380–400) associated with the leadership of Aurelius Symmachus. For his life, see *PLRE* 1. 34 ("Albinus" 8). Jerome's *Ep.* 107 (from ca. 401) makes direct reference to him because of his pagan influence. By 401 Albinus was about to become the maternal grandfather of a baby named Paula; his son-in-law, the baby's father, was the son of Jerome's patroness Paula, both devout Christians. Apparently Albinus's wife and daughter were also Christians. His son, however, remained staunchly pagan and served as urban and praetorian praefect of Rome (as had Albinus's father and brothers). One of his brothers was also intermarried with Christian families and would be the grandfather of the noted ascetic Melania the younger. For the prosopography and relationships, see my article "Finding the Ties that Bind: Issues from Social Description," in *Social Networks in the Early Christian Environment: Issues and Methods for Social History*, ed. L. M. White (*Semeia* 56; Atlanta: Scholars Press, 1992) 3–15. For Jerome's letter and his relations to the Christian members of this family, see J. N. D. Kelly, *Jerome: His Life, Writings, and Controversies* (New York: Harper & Row, 1975) 273–75.

PROVINCE: Germania (Germania prima)
LOCATION: Gimmeldingen

No. 94: Dedication of a Mithraeum (325) (*CIMRM* 2. 1315)

Inscription from a red limestone monument (H.0.37; W.2.35; Th.0.20 m) that stood on a base and supported the central cult relief. The stone is broken in three parts. It comes from the poorly preserved mithraeum at Gimmeldingen. The first part of the inscription (lines 1–5) appears in a *tabula ansata*. Letters: H.0.045.

Literature: F. Sprater, "Mithrasdenkmäler von Gimmeldingen," *Pfälzische Heimatkunde* 16 (1926) 1–5. H. Finke in *Bericht der Römisch-Germanischen Kommission* 17 (1927) 52–53 (no. 62). *CIMRM* 2. 1315.

In h(onorem) d(omus) d(ivinae)
deo inviht[o] Midre
Maternin[i]us Faustinu(s)
carax fan[um] cum solo inviht[o]
in suo fecit c[onsac]ratus XI k(alendis) Feb(ruariis.)
Fanus consacrat(us)
per Potentianum
patrem co(n)s(ulibus)
Paulino et Iuliano
l(ibens) l(aetus) m(erito).

Translation: In honor of the divine house (of the emperor), to the god Invictus Mithras (*sic!*). Materninius Faustinus, corax (*sic!*), set up the sanctuary with the Invictus (*sic!*) alone in his own (place, house?),[203] consecrated

203. *in suo* (line 5). I have supplied *domo* or *loco*, a locative use of *in* to be understood with *fanum*. In this sense it is possible to read *cum solo inviht[o]* not as the agency of the god but as a reference to the cult relief, that is, the *invictus* is the tauroctone (see *CIMRM* 1. 747). Read this way the inscription is a commemoration of the founding of the mithraeum in new quarters or of the installation of a new cult niche within an existing mithraeum, depending on the way one construes the antecedent of *suo* (line 5), that is, the dedicator or the god. Given the use of the term *fanum,* I tend to think it refers to the mithraeum proper.

on the 11th day of February. The sanctuary was consecrated by the father, Potentianus in the consulship of Paulinus and Julianus,[204] rightly willing.

PROVINCE: Britannia (Valentia)
LOCATION: Brocolitia (Carrawburgh)
No. 95: Carrawburgh Mithraeum (third–fourth century)
(Figure 47)

The mithraeum was discovered in 1949 during the excavations at the Roman fort at Carrawburgh on Hadrian's Wall. This was the seventh fort from the east along the wall, and the station was known as Brocolitia (previously called Procolitia). The sanctuary was an independent construction some thirty yards [NB] south of the southwest corner of the fort on the slope of a marshy valley. It was not dug into the hillside but was oriented with the natural slope perpendicular to the main axis (southeast to northwest). The sanctuary went through three major stages of structural renovation and two minor phases of remodeling during its existence from the late second to the early fourth centuries. It was finally destroyed and largely covered over by the marshy surroundings.

Literature: I. A. Richmond and J. P. Gillam, *The Temple of Mithras at Carrawburgh* (Newcastle on Tyne: Newcastle, 1951). I. A. Richmond, "The Carrawburgh Mithraeum," *JRS* 41 (1951) 122–30. *CIMRM* 1. 844–45. I. A. Richmond, "The Cult of Mithras and its Temple at Carrawburgh," in *Recent Archeological Excavations in Britain*, ed. R. L. S. Bruce-Mitford (2d ed.; London: Routledge & Kegan Paul, 1957) 65–69. C. M. Daniels, *Mithras and His Temples on the Wall* (2d ed.; Newcastle on Tyne: Hill, 1967).

The other possibility is to take the entire phrase (*cum … suo*) instrumentally. Given the number of orthographic "barbarisms" in this text, it is possible to read *in suo* for the common patronage language of *de suo* or *(de) sumptu suo*, hence: "with the (aid of the god) Invictus alone, at his own expense." Compare *CIMRM* 2. 1361–62, 1438. This also seems to be the use of *in suo* at Augusta Treverorum (Gallia), precisely where one would normally expect *de suo* (see *CIMRM* 2. 986, 987 [suppl.]).

204. The date was 22 January, and, according to the consular dating, the year was 325.

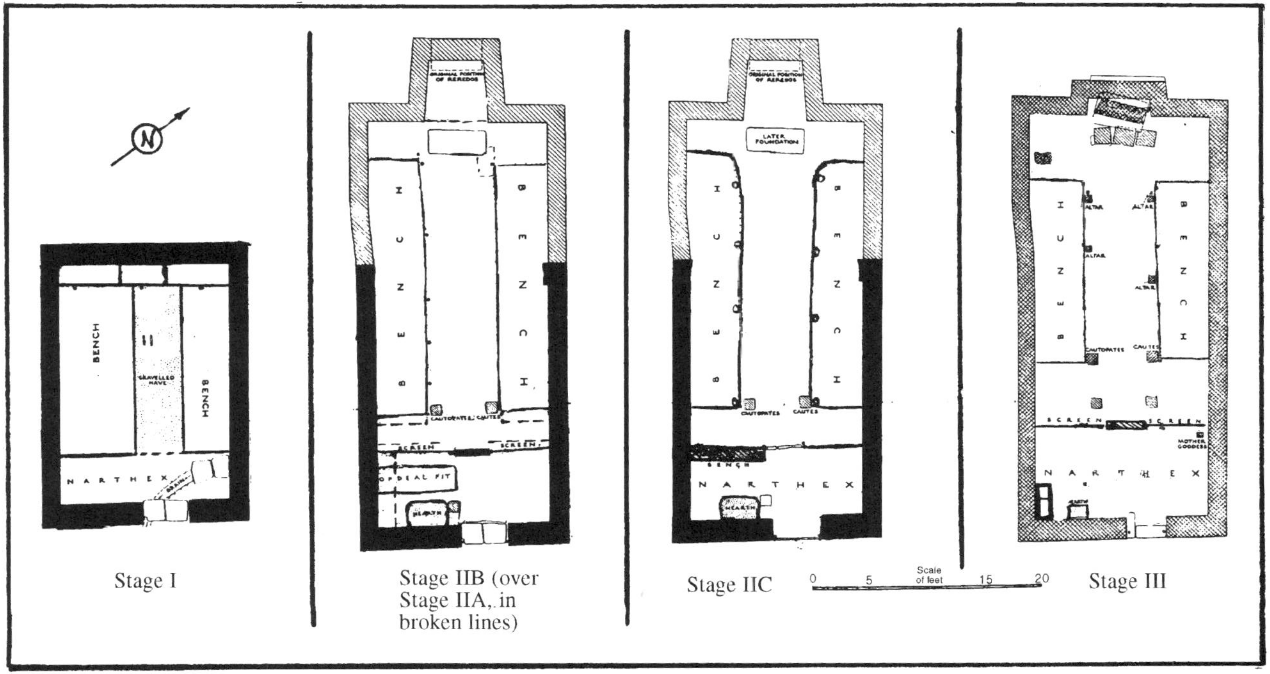

Fig. 47
Britannia, Brocolitia. Carrawburgh mithraeum. Plan restoration in stages of construction and renovation (based on Richmond and Gillam)

[The following reconstruction is based primarily on the official excavation report by Richmond and Gillam (1951).]

[N.B. The measurements given in the original excavation report are all in feet/inches, and this practice will be followed here.]

a. Stage I (ca. 205)

The earliest mithraeum (fig. 47a) was a modest rectangular building (L.ext.26'; W.18'3"); it was substantially constructed of clay-bound rubble walls faced with freestone blocks (Walls Th. north/south 24", east/west 19"). The entrance in the south wall (W.4'2") was offset toward the east by 21 in.; however, it was in line with the central aisle, which had been set 15 in. north of center on the axis of the building. The reason for this asymmetry seems to have been as a provision for a larger open space just to the left inside the entrance.[205] The pronaos (called a "narthex" by Richmond and Gillam) originally had a packed earth floor (L.4'2"; W.15') and was presumably separated from the sanctuary proper by a wooden screen at the back of the benches (of which two posts remain on the east side). There was some flagstone paving in the pronaos, which covered an open drain in the floor.

The main sanctuary chamber (L.17'6"; W.15') had a central aisle (L.ca.14'6"; W.4'2"), paved in gravel, and side benches. The benches were of clay revetted with wattlework, and the one on the west was wider (L.ca.15'; Br.5'3") than the one on the east (L.ca.15'; W.4'2"). At the north end, the benches presumably came to an end against a timber revetment (Br.2') running the width of the chamber. In the middle of this dais, remains suggest the placement of a low stonework platform, probably an altar table or base. The area beside the altar table seems to have been left open and used for storage, perhaps for the pinecones used as fuel.[206]

The excavators estimate that the sanctuary could have scarcely accommodated more than a dozen members. The date of this stage is determined largely from the more certain dates (from coins and inscriptions) of the later

205. The excavators point out that this same provision for a space just inside the entrance can be seen in each stage of renovation. See Richmond and Gillam, *Temple of Mithras at Carrawburgh,* 5.

206. Ibid., 6–7, and Appendix I–II.

stages and from an altar datable to the end of the second or beginning of the third century.[207]

b. Stage II, Phase A (ca. 213–22)

From the modest beginnings in the first stage, the Mithraic community must have grown considerably. For the sanctuary was more than doubled in size by renovations of the second major stage. The first phase of this renovation included most of the structural modifications (fig. 47). In order to enlarge the existing building, the north wall of the sanctuary was knocked down (leaving only a spur at the east corner), and the east/west walls were extended by some 14 ft. 3 in. The new walls were of a slightly cruder form, and it would appear that the addition was constructed in counterclockwise progression beginning at the northeast corner. Thus, after extending the east wall, the north wall was built (L.18'11") with a central, trapezoidal apse (D.5'6"; W.front 5'7", back 4'9"). Finally, the west wall was constructed moving from north to south.

This progression of the construction is suggested by the fact that the northwest corner of the addition is ca. 8 in. to the west, and the wall extension on that side had to be adjusted during the course of construction. The addition created a building with internal measurements L.37'5" and W.15'. In addition, it should be noted that the apse was not set on trench foundations (as in both the older side-walls and the extensions); instead it was carried on a slab foundation made of stones and rounded from the corners of the apse to the corners of the sanctuary. A similar stone pavement was used as a subfloor for the extension of the central aisle. The "nave" or aisle of the new sanctuary was centered on the axis of the building (L.29'; W.6'). At the south end of the building the pronaos (narthex) was likewise expanded to the north (L.7'3"; W.15'). Along its west wall a stone bench (H.18"; Br.21") was erected, and a wooden screen was set at the end of the benches to separate the pronaos from the sanctuary proper. The floor of the pronaos and the central aisle were covered with a thin layer of yellow gravel and with a course of

207. Ibid., 37, 47–48. The altar is the one identified as the west altar in Stage III below (= *CIMRM* 1. 846), which yields a date between 198 and 208 CE. The date 205 has become more accepted in recent discussions; see Daniels, *Mithras and His Temples on the Wall.*

paving stones at the main entrance and at the entrance to the sanctuary. There seems to have been a place for a stone hearth to the west of the main door on the south wall of the pronaos.

In the sanctuary, the podia were surmounted by a step with flagstone foundation just inside the screen on each side. The benches were regularized in form at the same width as the earlier east bench (W.4'2"); they were revetted with timbers and finished in plaster. The benches must have extended to the north wall, or very nearly so. At the south end of each bench (just beyond the steps) a square base (W./Br.12"; H.31") served (probably) as platforms for statues of Cautes and Cautopates. At the north end of the east bench another square base (W./Br.18") held some other appurtenance. Beside the west bench a stone foundation (L.4'; W.3') likely supported a low entry stair to the apse. The apse floor was fitted with a low platform or dais (H. unknown) set on a foundation of stone slabs. In the back of the apse a large rectangular slab (L.3'; W.4'6") was embedded in the north apse wall extending into the apse as a shelf (perhaps for the cult relief). It is possible that, of the three altars found in the mithraeum from Stage III, the middle one was installed in the apse at this time.[208]

c. Stage II, Phase B (ca. 250 [?])

Following upon the major structural changes made in Stage IIA, in the next period the internal layout and appointment were given much attention (see fig. 46c). First, the length of the pronaos was shortened (from 7'3" to 6'6"), and a new screen was constructed. The benches were unchanged, so that there was now more room at the south end of each bench. At the north end the benches were cut back from the walls at a distance of 3'8". Large posts at the south end of each bench and others along the fronts suggest a reinforcement for the sagging gabled roof (of timbers and thatch), which had been extended in Stage IIA. The floor of the vestibule and the central aisle were paved: with flagging up to about 10 ft. north of the screen and with cobbling from that point on. These floors were also covered (though perhaps a little later) with a carpet of heather or leng. Thus, the floor level was increased a good deal (as in Stage IIA), but the bench height was raised only slightly making the steps for the benches unnecessary (see fig. 47b).

208. *CIMRM* 1. 845, dated 212–222 CE.

In the pronaos the paving was 18" above the previous floor level, so that the bench along the west wall was completely covered over. A hearth was still placed against the south wall of the pronaos with a raised stone bollard at its northeast corner used as a barrier from the door. At a distance of 15" north of the hearth a long trough was cut down to the previous floor level (L.7'; W.19"; D.18"). Against the west wall the trough cut through the now covered bench (but at a narrower width, 13"). The excavators identified this trough as a coffin-shaped "ordeal pit" in which the initiate reclined, head to the west, during some ritual.[209]

d. Stage II, Phase C (ca. 275–96/7)

As in the previous period, Stage IIC represents an internal remodeling with little external reconstruction (fig. 47d). Once again the screen of the vestibule was moved, shortening the pronaos from 6'6" to 6'3". The floor level was raised, covering over the "ordeal pit" and rising to the height of the door sill. The new floor was of clay, and a hearth was placed in the same position. Against the west screen section another bench (W.12") was constructed. The area between the screen and the backs of the benches was now 3–4 ft. wide. The benches themselves had been raised considerably (ca. 8") and were revetted with wattle-work. At their north ends the benches had been rounded off on the interior corners. The floor of the sanctuary had been raised only slightly and was finished in clay set with planks (W.3–4") up to 4' in length. The benches were faced now by evenly spaced (interval 2'6" to 3') posts that supported a restructured roof, perhaps even a clerestory construction. The apse area was unchanged except that a few appurtenances, for example, amphorae and a brazier stand, were added to the dais. The building was destroyed in 296/7, perhaps after a period of desertion, when the sanctuary was invaded, pillaged, and parts of it (e.g., the screen) burned.

e. Stage III (early fourth century)

Following the destruction of the mithraeum at the end of the third century, and perhaps after a period of neglect, the sanctuary was entirely recon-

209. Richmond and Gillam, *Temple of Mithras at Carrawburgh*, 19. In their opinion, the bench of stage IIA probably served some comparable purpose, and it may relate to the use of the open space to the west of the door from the very first stage. As for the apse area, no real changes were determined.

structed. The old walls were knocked down to the level of the benches, and the central aisle was filled in to the same height to form the foundation. New walls were then raised on the bedding provided by the old ones, so that the new building followed the same plan as that of Stage IIA–C, except for an abbreviated apse (see figs. 47c,d). Coins found in the levels of construction of this period associate the renovation work with the third period of Hadrian's wall (i.e., 297–367), probably to ca. 308.[210]

In the walls the same irregularity in the west wall extension was preserved, and the walls were generally of poorer quality, using clay masonry and reused blocks. The apse was an opening of the same width (5'6") from the sanctuary, but it was terminated at a depth of only 18". For this reason the appurtenances of the earlier periods were installed in the central aisle just before the "apse" (now more properly a niche). The pronaos (narthex) of this period reached its maximum size (L.8'2"; W.15'). The main door retained its same basic position but was reconstructed as a much wider entrance (W.3'5") with a new threshold of massive blocks (Th.9"). The hearth in the pronaos was narrower than before and stood on a small platform (Br.3') running from the doorway to the west wall. The floor of the pronaos was randomly paved, mostly with building spoils and clay. The pronaos was divided from the sanctuary by a wooden screen which framed the entryway. The screen did not extend to either side wall, but the frame was substantial enough to carry a partition or curtain. In the northeast corner of the pronaos a small pedestal (H.16") was set; it carried a statue of the Mother goddess with child.

In the sanctuary proper the floor level was raised so that it was even with the benches of Stage IIC coming up to the crown of the pedestals for the dadophori. New benches were constructed above the floor level (H.ca.9"; L.16'; Br.4') beginning at a point 6' from the pronaos screen. The benches were revetted with wattle-work and plaster, and they were faced with roof posts set at intervals of 5' (the last pair being the center posts of the pronaos screen). Also on the face of each bench was a pair of altars (H.15–20") which had been plastered into the finish of the benches. The floor of the central aisle was randomly paved with reused stones set in clay. At the north end of the central aisle the niche was fitted with the reused shelf slab from the earlier apse, but because of its size it extended through the wall onto the exterior of the building. Before the niche, the three altars were set on a

210. Ibid., 34.

rubble foundation covering a "ritual deposit" in a deep pit.[211] Flanking the altars at the heads of the benches were two stonework pedestal bases (perhaps as large as L.3'6"; W.1–1'6"). According to Richmond and Gillam these pedestals probably carried statuary, for example, the lions of the Königshoffen mithraeum, but another possibility might be the construction of a *thronum* on each side associated with the bench.[212]

The final stage, begun in the early years of the fourth century, must have been soon abandoned, as suggested by the total absence of Constantinian coinage. The fate of the building must have been sealed by rising water and silt from the marshy surroundings; such seepage finally filled the sanctuary to the tops of the benches. The demise was accelerated by the collapse of the roof and, later, by the disintegration of the claybound walls. Finally, the plot was incorporated in the mid-fourth century into a refuse tip and was later pillaged (either by robbers or Christians).[213]

---

211. For the altars, see *CIMRM* 1. 845–47. For the contents of the "ritual pit," see Richmond and Gillam, *Temple of Mithras at Carrawburgh*, 35–36. The three altars probably belong to three earlier stages in the building's history reused together in the final stage. The last altar, however, may in fact be from the dedication of the final stage (*CIMRM* 1. 847–48); see the discussion by E. Birley in Richmond and Gillam, *Temple of Mithras at Carrawburgh*, 45–51.

212. Ibid., 39.

213. Ibid., 42.

Appendix A

Catalogue of Other Christian Archaeological Sites

▲ ▲ ▲

This catalogue includes two types of material: (a) sites that have been alleged (on the basis either of tradition or earlier archaeological work) to represent an early (especially pre-Constantinian) church building but where further archaeological analysis has disproved the claim, and (b) sites that may hold potential as early or pre-basilical church buildings (or places of assembly) based on limited archaeological evidence to date or where further analysis or discussion is warranted. The catalogue is organized geographically according to the same provincial organization followed in the main collection of materials in Sections II and III above; see also Tables 4 and 5, below.

1. Province: Syria (Hauran/Arabia)
   Location: Umm el-Zētûn

A small rectangular building with domed roof has been erroneously called a Christian oratory from the pre-Constantinian period. The designation and the dating derive from two inscriptions found *in situ* in the building (in Butler, PAES III.A.5, nos. 765^{12} and 765^{13}). The first of these inscriptions indicates that the structure was built in 282 during the reign of the emperor Probus. The second calls the building a "sacred cell" and thus provided for the ostensible Christian attribution. The relevant portion of the second inscription (no. 765[13]) reads: τὸ κοινὸν τῆς κάμης καὶ/τοῦ θεοῦ τὴν ἱερὰν· καλύβην/ἔκτεσαν δια[. ... It appears, however, that the term κοινόν does not refer to the Christian community. The deity in question is probably Kronos according to the editors of PAES III.A.5. See Bovini, *La proprietà ecclesiastica*, 31 (continuation of n. 3, p. 28).

2. Province: Palestina (Judaea)/Palestina prima
   Location: Nicopolis/Emmaus (Amwas)

A basilica (L.46.40; W.24.40 m) with polygonal apse (W.9.67; Br.5.50 m) and a baptistry had been called a pre-Constantinian church by its excavators, H. L. Vincent and F. M. Abel (*Emmaus, sa basilique et son histoire* [Paris: E. Leroux, 1932]), who dated the structure to ca. 220. The dating was erroneously based on the type of brickwork, and the basilica is probably from the later fourth century. It is the case, however, that the basilica stands on the foundations of an earlier Roman villa or palazzo, but no clear indications of Christian use have been advanced. See C. Ceccelli, "Il problema della basilica cristiana preconstantiniana," *Palladio* 7 (1943) 1–5; and J. P. Kirsch's review of Vincent and Abel (noted above) in *RivAC* 10 (1933) 138–43. Cf. G. Bovini, *La proprietà ecclesiastica e la condizione giuridica della chiesa in età preconstantiniana* (Milan: Università di Roma, 1948) 28 n. 3.

3. Province: Egypt (Arcadia)
   Location: Oasis Minor (Bahria Oasis)

Near the modern village of Al-Hayz in the southern portion of Bahria (or Bahriyah) Oasis, remains of a basilical church and a nearby village are preserved. The plan and construction are comparable to other remains datable to the fifth century, but this building may be of a later date.

For the general survey of the area, see A. Fakhry, *The Oases of Egypt*, Vol. 2, *Bahriyah and Farafra Oases* (Cairo: Services des Antiquités de l'Égypte, 1974) 3–124.

At a distance of some 500 m south of the church a number of large houses from perhaps as early as the second century indicate the presence of a Romano-Egyptian village. Among the houses are what has been called a military fortress and a large mansion, also called the "palace." Two other houses suggest the presence of a Christian community in later Roman times. In one of the houses, although there is no direct Christian evidence, a large rectangular hall in the house was fitted with what appears to be an apsed exedra (see A. Fakhry, *Oases* 2. 120 and fig. 55.). In another house a large chamber was embellished with a decorated arch on its eastern wall. In the arch was painted a large cross which Fakhry takes to be a representation of the crucifixion. This Christian use is dated to the fourth or fifth century. Before the arch was a mud-brick altar, and it would appear that an adjacent longitudinal chamber was also available for assembly purposes (see Fakhry, *Oases* 2. 121–24 and figs. 57–58). It has also been suggested that these houses might have been used for monastic communities. For a discussion of the renovated houses in the history of Egyptian monasticism, with mention of this site, see also the study of C. C. Walters, *Monastic Archaeology in Egypt* (Warminster, England: Aris & Phillips, 1974) 29–30.

4. PROVINCE: Greece (Macedonia)
   LOCATION: Philippi

Excavations were begun in the area under the Byzantine Octagonal Church, first discovered in 1958 in the area east of and contiguous to the Antonine Forum. The upper octagonal church dates from the sixth century, but was found to have been built over and from an earlier octagonal church dating from the fifth century. Further excavations in the adjacent areas revealed an extensive complex surrounding the Octagon, which has now been identified as the episcopal complex (or *Episkopeion*) of Philippi. Also, some older buildings just to the north of the Octagon were found to have been incorporated into its construction. Among these were a portion of a bath complex, dating to the late second or third century, and a Heroon (or Hero tomb/shrine), dating to the late Hellenistic period. Beneath the floor level of the earlier Octagonal Church was found yet another mosaic pavement, lying immediately contiguous to and partially integrating the south wall of the Heroon. The plan and decoration of this pavement reveal a rectangular hall, subdivided into two rooms along the longitudinal axis. Inscriptions in the mosaic make it possible to date the paving of the floor to 343/4 CE. The hall itself, while perhaps somewhat earlier, seems to be an early-fourth-century construction, and hence the earliest of the known church buildings in Philippi, and was dedicated to St. Paul.

[For a fuller discussion of the plan see now Section II, no. 49.]

5. PROVINCE: Greece (Achaia)
   LOCATION: Athens

A Roman house dating from the fifth century located on the north slope of the Agora seems to have been renovated for use by Christians in the late fifth or sixth century. The rooms of the house contain rich decoration including mosaic floors, and in one of the rooms an apsed projection contained a basin. Detailed description may be found in the yearly excavation report on "The Athenian Agora," *Hesperia* 40 (1971) 266–70; cf. *The Athenian Agora* XIV (Athens, 1972) 215 n. 23; *Hesperia* 42 (1973) 156–64.

For discussion of recent suggestions that the Metroon on the west side of the Agora may have been converted (at least in two rooms) to the use of a synagogue in the third–fifth centuries, see the addendum in A. T. Kraabel, "The Diaspora Synagogue: Archaeological and Epigraphical Evidence since Sukenik," *ANRW* 2.19.1 (1979) 505–6.

6. PROVINCE: Dalmatia
   LOCATION: Salona

Of the numerous churches in and around the city of Salona at least two have been claimed as pre-Constantinian martyria later converted into cemeterial basilicas. Of these sites one in particular, the Manastirine complex, has also been claimed as a *domus ecclesiae* because of the architectural forms discovered in excavation of the fifth-century basilica from 1917 to 1926. The complex lay outside the ancient city walls on the road leading north from city gate III. In the official excavation report of R. Egger (*Forschungen in Salona*, Vol. 2, *Die altchristliche Friedhof Manastirine* (Vienna: Beck'schen Universitäts-Buchhandlung, 1926), the oldest building level of the complex was identified as a Roman villa dating from the third century. The "villa" had already housed a funerary chamber by the end of the third century, but Egger concluded that it continued to be used for domestic purposes of an influential family (see *Forschungen* 2. 10). The significant point for the early

Christian use of the site lies in the discovery of a sarcophagus bearing the name of Domnio, the first bishop, who died in the Diocletianic persecutions in 304 (see *Forschungen* 2. 75f. and inscription no. 82). The sarcophagus was placed in room 1 of the Manastirine "villa" in what is termed the second stage of its history. In any case this early history of the site is significant, but E. Dyggve, the director of the Salona excavations, later differed with Egger on the interpretation of the earliest buildings. In a paper Dyggve has argued that the so-called villa was not a domestic edifice at all but a family tomb that was adopted for a Christian martyrium ("Salona Cristiana: Aperçu historique du développement de la ville et des constructions sous l'époque paleochrétienne," in *Atti III CIAC*, 245–50; cf. his fuller treatment, *A History of Salonitian Christianity* [Oslo: Van Gorkum, 1951) 30, 71–73 and fig. IV.5). See also E. Ceci, *I monumenti christiani di Salona*, vol. 2 (Milan: Edizioni Pleion di Bietti, 1963), and G. Snyder, *Ante Pacem* (Macon, GA: Mercer University Press, 1985) 89–91.

7. PROVINCE: Istria
   LOCATION: Orsera

A Roman building discovered in 1935 has been claimed as a Christian *domus ecclesiae* dating from the mid-fourth century by M. Mirabella Roberti (*La sede paleocristiana di Orsera* [Trieste, 1944]). The structure has been identified as a peristyle house which overlooked the sea and which was given over to the local clerics as an ecclesiastical residence. [The study of Mirabella Roberti has not been available; therefore, these remarks are based on the brief notice of the site and the bibliographical note found in G. Bovini, *La proprietà ecclesiastica e la condizione guiridica della chiesa in età preconstantiniana* (Milan: Università di Roma, 1948) 55 and n. 1.]

8. PROVINCE: Istria
   LOCATION: Aquileia

In 1893 during construction on the campanile of the eleventh-century cathedral of Aquileia several portions of an ancient mosaic were brought to light. Following the discovery, concentrated excavations resulted in the restoration of the well-known double church of Bishop Theodore, which dates to the early fourth century. In addition, it has been claimed that this pre-basilical church might have stood on an even earlier *domus ecclesiae*. While the latter claim cannot be supported, the hall constructed by Bishop Theodore in ca. 317 does represent an early stage of monumental buildings after the persecutions.

[For complete description of the site and the evidence for the early phases see now No. 51 above.]

9. PROVINCE: Italia (Latium)
 LOCATION: Ostia

a. Excavation of a large house (Reg. III, Is.vii, outside the Porta Marina gate) overlooking the water near the ancient shoreline produced some interesting discoveries. The house was found to date originally from the late first (or early second) century CE but was renovated extensively in the fourth century. In the latter stage, the house retained many of its domestic arrangements, but one room was converted into something of a "collegial hall." The room (L.7.45; W.6.60 m) was fitted with an exedra and a "false aedicula" and was decorated (including a representation of Christ). These adaptations were taken by the excavators to indicate that it served some special Christian function while still in the possession of a wealthy patron. No other evidence was discovered to substantiate such a claim, and so it must be treated with caution. See the excavation report of G. Becatti, *Scavi di Ostia* 6: *Edificio con opus sectile fuori Porta Marina* (Rome: Lib. dello Stato, 1969) 236–50, and the review article by A. Frazer in *AJA* 75 (1971) 319–20.

b. Another Ostian house (in Reg. IV, Is.iii), called the *Domus dei pesci*, has a basin and a mosaic depicting a chalice and a fish. The house was built sometime in the early third century. On this basis some (especially Becatti and Calza) have called it a *domus ecclesiae*; a semicircular basin is further identified as a baptistry. This usage is thought to date from the late third century. However, with no other indications of Christian identity, symbolism, or use, it is difficult to make such a claim. See G. Calza, "Nuovo testimonianze del cristianismo a Ostia," *Rendiconti della pontificia accademia romana di archeologia* 25–26 (1949–50); followed by G. Becatti, *Scavi di Ostia* 4 (Rome, 1962) 181–83. Cf. P.-A. Février, "Ostie et Porto à la fin de l'antiquité," *Mélanges d'archéologie et d'histoire* 70 (1958) 295–330, and G. Snyder, *Ante Pacem* (Macon, GA: Mercer University Press, 1985) 116–17.

10. PROVINCE: Italia (Latium)
LOCATION: Rome

The so-called titular or ("parish") churches of Rome are linked by tradition and legend to the early pre-Constantinian congregations of the city. According to the *Liber Pontificalis,* there were twenty-five of these titular churches by the fifth–sixth centuries. Several of these have been discussed in the main catalogue in Section II above, where the evidence does indeed point to some early Christian presence on the site of the later church buildings. In the case of several more, they were found, upon excavation, to rest upon Roman foundations dating from as early as the second century. But in most cases there is little or no evidence to claim pre-Constantinian use of the site by Christians apart from tradition. Of those that were founded on earlier Roman structures, the following have at least some evidence for a direct Christian use, though not likely before the period of Constantine. In most cases they are later, and no direct evidence of Christian usage can be demonstrated prior to the construction of the church building proper (as noted).

a. Church of S. Pudenziana (*titulus Pudentis*, Reg. VI), a second-century bath complex taken over and renovated as a basilica in the second half of the fourth century. See R. Krautheimer, *CBCR* 3. 277–98 and pl. XIV; and G. Snyder, *Ante Pacem*, 82.

b. Church of S. Anastasia (*titulus Anastasiae*, Reg. X), a third-century insula complex converted in mid to later fourth century to a basilica. See E. Junyent, "La maison romaine du titre de Sainte Anastasie," *RivAC* 7 (1930) 91–106. R. Krautheimer, *CBCR* 1.1. 42–48. G. Snyder, *Ante Pacem*, 80.

c. S. Balbina (*titulus Tigridae*, Reg. XII), a large hall later converted into a basilica, but with no clear indication of Christian use prior to the construction of the basilica. See R. Krautheimer, *CBCR* 1.1. 82–88.

d. S. Prisca (*titulus Priscae*, Reg. XIII), a large urban domus on the Aventine that had been renovated at the beginning of the third century. It is thought perhaps to have been an imperial family residence. In the third century, a mithraeum was installed in the cryptoporticus, which was subsequently renovated and enlarged (see No. 89 above). The excavators also found an adjacent room in the area off the same cryptoporticus which appeared to have housed a Christian conventicle in the late third or fourth century. See R. Krautheimer, *CBCR* 3. 260–68, but see more recently M. J. Vermaseren and C. C. Van Essen, *The Excavations in the Mithraeum of the Church of S. Prisca in Rome* (Leiden: Brill, 1965) esp. 107–16, 242–49.

e. S. Cecilia (*titulus* ?, Reg. XIV). Excavations showed the substructure to follow the line of a Roman house dating from as early as the first century BCE and in use to the fourth century CE. See P. Crostarosa, "Scoperte in S. Cecilia in Trastevere," *NBAC* 6 (1900) 143–46; R. Krautheimer, *CBCR* 1.2. 94–110.

f. S. Sebastiano *f.l.m.*, a fourth-century basilica in the area traditionally called *ad catacumbas* and under which was a necropolis. The site is one attested by tradition (going back to the third century) as the burial place for the bones of both St. Peter and St. Paul. This site is marked by an early *memoria*. Among the structures of the necropolis, and near this *memoria,* was a quadrangular roofed hall, with open side walls, called the *triclia*. Apparently it served for funerary *refrigeria*, and direct Christian usage is demonstrated by a number of graffiti dating from the mid-third century. See A. Prandi, *La memoria apostolorum in catacumbas* (Vatican City, 1936). R. Krautheimer, *CBCR* 4. 114–42; and G. Snyder, *Ante Pacem*, 98–104.

g. S. Sinfrosa *f.l.m.*, basilica converted (in the fifth century) from a tri-apsidal funerary chapel which is claimed to be pre-Constantinian. See R. Stapleford, "The Excavations of the Early Christian Church of S. Sinfrosa in Rome," *AJA* 77 (1973) 228–35.

7. PROVINCE: Africa (Tripolitania)
   LOCATION: Henschir Taglissi (el-Msufiin, in the W. Gebel)

An unusual edifice that is clearly shown to be used for Christian assembly in the mid to late fourth century by an inscription:

[L]audes [D]omino om[nipote]nti Deo et
Christo ei-
[us] cuiu[s] aspiration[e et prae]stantia Ae-
[mil]ian[u]s disposuit
i[nstitui]t et perfecit.

The building seems to have retained a number of peculiar arrangements and is clearly not a basilica in design. J. B. Ward-Perkins cautiously refers to it as a possible *domus ecclesiae*. See J. B. Ward-Perkins and R. G. Goodchild, "The Christian Antiquities of Tripolitania," *Archaeologia* 95 (1953) 1–84, esp. 39–41 and fig. 19; cf. J. B. Ward-Perkins, "Recent Work and Problems in Libya," *Atti VIII CIAC*, 219–36, esp. 232.

12. PROVINCE: Belgica (Prima)
LOCATION: Augusta Treverorum (Trier, Treves)

According to early medieval tradition, the cathedral at Trier was dedicated by Constantine and was built over (or from) a palace of his mother, Helena. Excavations on the site revealed an extensive complex dating to the fourth century, usually called the double church. This edifice was found to have been built over two domestic insulae. One of these insulae may go back to the early Roman occupation (first century CE), while the other probably dates to the early third century. Both buildings suffered extensive damage during the later third century. They were apparently rebuilt in the early fourth century. At this time the eastern insula was extensively renovated, including installation of new floors, wall plaster, and ceilings. Numerous fragments of painted plaster were also found. Although very little evidence exists regarding the initial adaptation for Christian usage, some indications are evident in the south part of the western insula. In one suite there appears to be an apsidal installation that may date from as early as the end of the third century, and later renovations may have developed from this area. Further elaboration began in the first decade of the fourth century, with the construction of a three-aisled building (Building I) in the area of this apsidal edifice. A second building (B.II), also a three-aisled hall, was begun in the second decade (ca. 315) over the area of the eastern insula. These were completed by the 330–40s, and a third building (B.III) was added later. While the construction of the fourth century clearly reflects Constantinian building programs, the suggestion of an earlier space already in Christian use remains an intriguing possibilty. Further work to identify the nature and use of this space more clearly, and particularly with regard to direct evidence of Christian usage, would be welcome.

See Winfried Weber, "Antike Kirche im Bereich von Dom und Liebfrauen," in *Die Römer in Rheinland-Pfalz*, ed. H. Cüppers (Stuttgart: A. Drückenmüller, 1990) 632–35. Idem, "Die Anfänge des Trierer Dom," *Trierer Theologische Zeitschrift* 2 (1989) 147–55. Jochen Zink, "Die Baugeschichte des Trierer Doms von Anfängen im 4. Jahrhundert bis zur letzten Restaurierung," in *Der Trierer Dom*, ed. F. J. Ronig (Neuss: Rheinland. Vereins, 1990) 17–111. I am grateful to Dr. Janice E. James, who has been working on the Trier evidence, for her assistance in securing these reports.

13. Province: Britannia
    Location: Hinton St. Mary [in Dorset]

A fourth-century villa in the Roman settlement was found to have a mosaic floor in two rooms. The plan of the house is largely unintelligible except for what can be discerned from the floor. The mosaic in one room portrays a scene of Europa and the bull (compare the Lullingstone villa in Sec. II, No. 57 above). The connecting mosaic in the other room has a central roundel showing a male bust with an Chi-Rho monogram behind the head. J. M. C. Toynbee and K. S. Painter have both suggested that this was more than just private Christian decoration. The possibility of a "house church" or *domus ecclesiae* still remains but cannot be demonstrated on other archaeological grounds.

See K. S. Painter, "The Roman Site of Hinton St. Mary, Dorset," *British Museum Quarterly* 32 (1968) 15–31. Idem, "Christianity in Roman Britain: Recent Finds, 1962–1969," *Atti VIII CIAC* (Barcelona, 1969) 373–74. Idem, "Villas and Christianity in Roman Britain," *British Museum Quarterly* 35 (1971) 156–75. For discussion of the mosaic with plans, see J. M. C. Toynbee, "The Christian Roman Mosaic, Hinton St. Mary, Dorset," *JRS* 54 (1964) 7–14. Idem, "The Christian Roman Mosaic, Hinton St. Mary, Dorset," *Proceedings of the Dorset Natural History and Archaeology Society* 85 (1964) 116–21. R. T. Eriksen, "Syncretistic Symbolism and the Christian

Roman Mosaic at Hinton St. Mary: A Closer Reading," *Proceedings of the Dorset Natural History and Archaeology Society* 102 (1980) 43–48.

14. PROVINCE: Hispania
    LOCATION: Bruñel, Merida, Torre de Palma

A number of newly excavated or recently discovered Christian sites indicate the transformation of rural villas to a basilical plan. Though the villas generally date from the third and fourth centuries, the construction of the churches dates generally to the fifth century or later. In some cases, however, it has been suggested that these villas were already in use as "house churches," especially at Bruñel and Merida.

See Pedro de Palol, "Les monumentas de Hispania en la arqueologia palcocristiana," *Atti VIII CIAC* (Barcelona, 1969), 167–85; P. de Palol and M. Sotomayor, "Excavations in la villa de Bruñel (Quseda) de la provincia de Jaen," *Atti VIII CIAC* (1969) 375–81; D. Fernando de Almeida and J. L. Martine de Matos, "Notes sur quelques monuments paléochrétiens du Portugal," *Atti VIII CIAC* (1969) 239–46 (cf. esp. Torre de Palma villa); José-Ramón Melida y Alinari, *Catalogo monumental de España, provinces de Badahoz (1907–1910)* (Madrid, 1925) 1. 185–97 (Merida: the so-called "Casabasilicas").

Appendix B

Tables

▲ ▲ ▲

Table 3
Classified List of Archaeological and Documentary Evidence

1. Christian Archaeological Sites (Excavated Buildings)

No.	36	Syria, Dura-Europos: Christian *Domus Ecclesiae*
	38	Syria, Qirqbize: Villa and Church Complex
	40	Syria/Arabia, Umm el-Jimal: "Julianos' Church" Complex
	42	Palestina, Capernaum: "House of St. Peter" Complex
	49	Greece, Philippi: Hall Church and Octagon
	50	Istria, Parentium: Hall Church and Basilica (Eufrasiana Complex)
	51	Istria, Aquileia: Hall Church of Bishop Theodore
	52	Italia, Rome: *Titulus Byzantis* (SS. Giovanni e Paolo)
	53	Italia, Rome: *Titulus Clementis* (S. Clemente)
	54	Italia, Rome: *Titulus Aequitii* (S. Martino ai Monti)
	55	Italia, Rome: *Titulus Chrysogoni* (S. Crisogono)
	57	Britannia, Lullingstone: Roman Villa and *Domus Ecclesiae*

2. Christian Inscriptions and Graffiti

No.	37	Syria, Dura-Europos: Commemorative Graffiti
	39	Syria, Lebaba: Building Inscriptions of a "Marcionite Synagogue"

	41	Syria/Arabia, Umm el-Jimal: "Julianos" Memorial
	48	Lycaonia, Laodicea Combusta: Epitaph of M. Julius Eugenius
	49e	Greece, Philippi: Inscriptions from the Hall Church
	50b–c	Istria, Parentium: Inscriptions from the Maurus Memorial
	50c	Istria, Aquileia: Inscriptions from Church of Bishop Theodore
	56	Mauretania, Altava: Memoria and "Basilica" (From a Sepulchral Inscription)

3. Documentary Papyri

No.	43	Egypt, Panopolis: Papyrus List of Buildings (*P.Gen.Inv.* 108)
	44	Egypt, Oxyrhynchus: Private Letter of Bishop Sotas (*P.Oxy.* XII,1492)
	45	Egypt, Oxyrhynchus: Papyrus Record of Streets and Churches (*P.Oxy.* I.43 verso)
	46	Egypt, Chysis: Papyrus Declaration of Property (*P.Oxy.* XXXIII.2673)
	47	Egypt, Oxyrhynchus: A Church Building as Social Center (*P.Oxy.* VI.903 verso)

4. Mithraic Archaeological Sites (Excavated Buildings)

No.	58	Syria, Dura-Europos: Mithraeum
	79	Italia, Ostia: Mithraeum of Callinicus (*Mitreo della Casa di Diana*, Reg.I,Is.III.4)
	81	Italia, Ostia: Mithraeum of Caelius Ermeros (*Mitreo della pareti dipinte*, Reg.III,Is.I.6)
	87	Italia, Rome: S. Clemente Mithraeum
	89	Italia, Rome: Aventine Mithraeum (Sta. Prisca)
	95	Britannia, Brocolitia: Carrawburgh Mithraeum

5. Mithraic Inscriptions and Graffiti

No.	59	Syria, Dura-Europos: Donation of Building for Mithraeum by Antonius Valentinus
	76	Pannonia, Siscia: Mithraic Donation of Jucundus

6. Jewish Archaeological Sites (Excavated Buildings)

8. Jewish Inscriptions

74	Achaia (Ins.), Aegina: Building Inscriptions (a–b)
75	Achaia, Mantineia: Donation of a Pronaos for Synagogue
84	Italia, Ostia: Synagogue Inscription of Mindi(u)s Faustus
85	Italia, Ostia: The Jewish Gerusia Honors C. Julius Justus

Table 4
Gazette of Site Locations for Archaeological and Documentary Items

This table provides locations synoptically for all entries in sections II, III, and Appendix A, without differentiation by type of item. The listing follows the same order as the geographical format used internally in each section and is keyed to the numbers on map 1 (see pp. 446–47). It is based on the provincial organization of the Roman Empire before and after 284 CE, moving principally from east to west based on the Roman numbering of the Praefectures after 284, as reflected below in Table 5. Priority of listing in latitude is generally gauged by distance away from main centers of activity or travel in Roman times. This synoptic table presents the data collected in the following manner: the locator number on map 1; the Roman Province (and sub-region) before/after 284, the site location (ancient name, modern name where applicable, and country), the map coordinates, sub-regions of a city (where applicable), and the catalogue entry number(s) as used in Sections II and III above. Entries marked A^1 (etc.) refer to the items in Appendix A (additional and questionable sites) by number within that listing. Some coordinates are nearest possible approximations.

Site Locations Key

The map shows sites for all entries in the catalogue in sections II, III, and appendix A. A complete gazette of site information and catalogue items, using this same numerical key, is provided in Table 4. Items in bold print below are labeled by name.

1. Dura Europos
2. Qirqbize
3. Lebaba
4. Umm el Zeitun
5. Thantia/Umm el-Jimal
6. Capernaum
7. Emmaus
8. **Jerusalem**
9. Oxyrhynchus
10. Bahriya Oasis
11. Panopolis
12. Berenike
13. Laodicea Combusta
14. Aphrodisias
15. Akmoneia
16. Sardis
17. Phocaea
18. Priene
19. Delos
20. Stobi
21. Philippi
22. **Athens**
23. Aegina
24. Mantineia
25. Salona
26. Siscia
27. Virunum
28. Parentium
29. Orsero
30. Aquileia
31. **Rome**
32. Ostia
33. Nersae
34. Aveia Vestina
35. Sentinum
36. Cirta
37. Altava
38. Gimmeldingen
39. **Augusta Treverorum**
40. Lullingstone
41. Hinton St. Mary
42. Brocolitia
43. Augusta Emerita

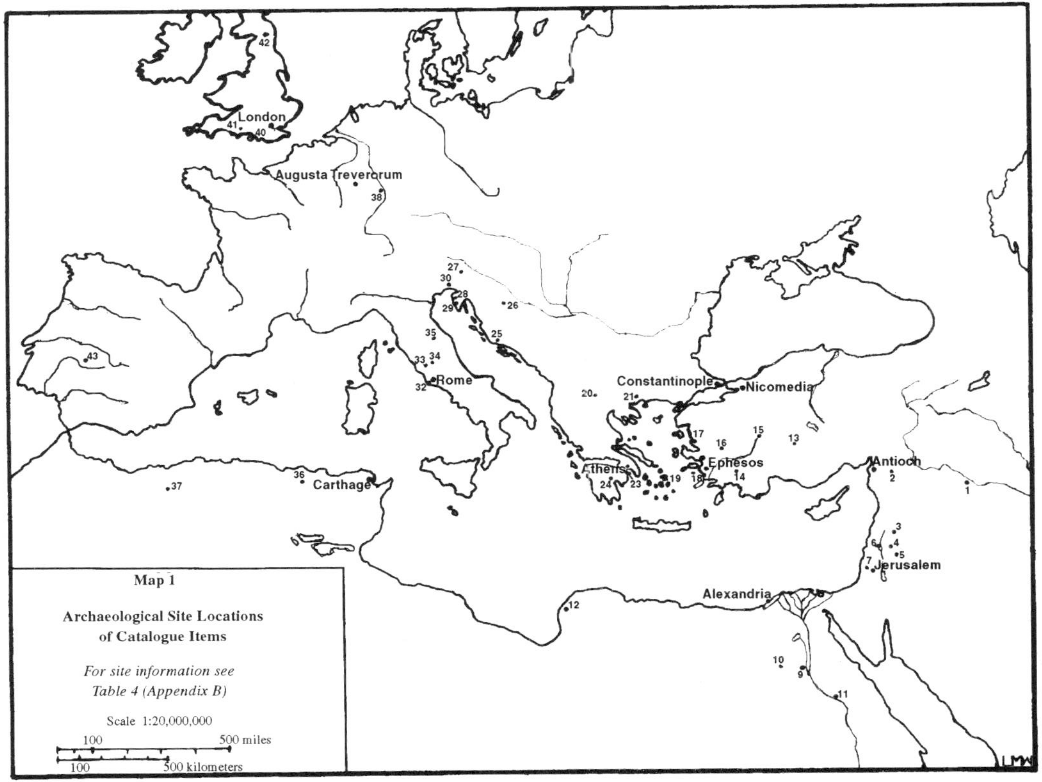

Map 1

Archaeological Site Locations of Catalogue Items

For site information see Table 4 (Appendix B)

Scale 1:20,000,000

100 500 miles

100 500 kilometers

Roman Province	Site Name/Location Ancient (Modern)	Map Coordinates (City Region)	Catalogue No.
1. Syria (Parapotamia)			
	Dura-Europos (Qal‘at Es Salihiyeh, Syria)	34.46N 40.46E	36, 37, 58, 59, 60, 61
2. Syria (Cynegia Chora)			
	Qirqbize (Kirk Biza or Qalb Loze, Syria)	36.12N 36.36E	38
3. Syria /Phoenicia Libanensis			
	Lebaba (Deir ‘Ali, Syria)	33.17N 36.20E	39
4. Syria(Hauran)/Arabia			
	Umm el Zeitun (Zayzun, Syria)	32.43N 35.56E	A[1]
5. Syria (Hauran)/Arabia			
	Thantia?/Umm el-Jimal (Al Jimal, Jordan)	32.20N 36.24E	40,41
6. Palestina (Judaea/Galilaia)/Palestina Secunda			
	Capernaum (Kafrnahum, Israel)	32.53N 35.34E	42

7. Palestina (Judaea)/Palestina Prima			
	Emmaus/Amwas (Imwas, Israel)	31.50N 34.59E	A2
8. Palestina (Judaea)/Palestina Prima			
	Jerusalem/Aelia (Jerusalem, Israel)	31.47N 35.13E	62
9. Aegyptus (Arcadia)			
	Oxyrhynchus (El Banasa, Egypt)	28.33N 30.38E	44,45,46,47
10. Aegyptus (Arcadia)			
	Al-Hayz, Bahriya Oasis (El Heiz, Egypt)	28.03N 28.35E	A3
11. Aegyptus (Thebaid I)			
	Panopolis (Chemmis/ Akhmim, Egypt)	26.35N 31.48E	43
12. Aegyptus (Cyrene)/Libya Cyrenaica			
	Berenike (Benghazi, Libya)	32.07N 20.04E	63
13. Asia (Galatia-Lycaonia)/Pisidia			
	Laodicea Combusta (Yorgan Ladik, Turkey)	38.13N 32.17E	48

Roman Province	Site Name/Location Ancient (Modern)	Map Coordinates	(City Region)	Catalogue No.
14. Asia (Caria)				
	Aphrodisias (Geyre, Turkey)	37.42N 28.41E		64
15. Asia (Phrygia)/Phrygia Pacatiana				
	Akmoneia (Ercis, Turkey)	38.39N 29.50E		65
16. Asia (Lydia)				
	Sardis (Sartmustafa, Turkey)	38.28N 28.02E		66,67
17. Asia (Lydia)				
	Phocaea (Eski Foça, Turkey)	38.40N 26.45E		68
18. Asia (Lydia)				
	Priene (Priene/Güllübahçe, Turkey)	37.38N 27.17E		69
19. Insulae Aegeae				
	Delos (Dhilos, Greece)	37.23N 25.15E		70,71
20. Greece-Illyricum (Macedonia)/Macedonia Salutaris				
	Stobi (Gradsko, Makedonia)	41.33N 21.59E		72,73

21. Greece-Illyricum (Macedonia)/Macedonia Prima			
	Philippi (Philippes/Krinidhes, Greece)	41.01N 24.18E	49
22. Greece (Achaia)/Achaia			
	Athens (Athinai, Greece)	38.00N 23.44E	A5
23. Greece (Achaia, Insulae)/Achaia			
	Aegina (Aiyina, Greece)	37.45N 23.26E	74
24. Greece (Achaia)/Achaia			
	Mantineia (Mantinea, Greece)	37.38N 22.23E	75
25. Dalmatia			
	Salona (Solin, Hercegovina)	43.33N 16.30E	A6
26. Pannonia/Savia			
	Siscia (Sisak, Croatia)	45.30N 16.22E	76
27. Noricum/Noricum Mediterraneum			
	Virunum (Klagenfurt, Austria)	46.38N 14.20E	77,78
28. Venetia/Venetia-Istria			
	Parentium (Parenzo; Poreč, Croatia)	45.14N 13.36E	50

Roman Province	Site Name/Location Ancient (Modern)	Map Coordinates	(City Region)	Catalogue No.
29. Venetia/Venetia-Istria				
	Orsero (Orsera; Rovinj, Croatia)	45.05N 13.40E		A^{7}
30. Venetia/Venetia-Istria				
	Aquileia (Aquileia, Italy)	45.47N 13.22E		51
31. Italia (Latium)				
	Rome (Roma, Italy)	41.53N 12.30E		
			Reg. II	52
			Reg. III	53,87,54
			Reg. VI	A^{10}a
			Reg. IX	88
			Reg. X	A^{10}b
			Reg. XII	A^{10}c
			Reg. XIII	89,A^{10}d
			Reg. XIV	55,A^{10}e
			(*f.l.m.*)	A^{10}f,g
32. Italia (Latium)				
	Ostia (Ostia Antica, Italy)	41.46N 12.18E		
			Reg. I	79
			Reg. II	80

		Reg. III	81,82,
		Reg. III(*flm*)	A^9a
		Reg. IV	86,A^9b
		Reg. IV(*flm*)	83,84
		uncertain	85
33. Italia (Latium)			
Nersae (Nesce/S. Silvestro, Italy)	42.13N 12.29E		90
34. Italia (Valeria)			
Aveia Vestina (Fossa, Italy)	42.24N 12.51E		91
35. Italia (Umbria)			
Sentinum (Sentino, Italy)	43.24N 12.50E		92
36. Africa/Numidia			
Cirta (Constantine, Algeria)	36.22N 6.40E		93
37. Mauretania/Mauretania Caesariensis			
Altava (Altaua; Lamoricière, Algeria)	33.31N 0.20W		56
38. Germania Superior/Germania Prima			
Gimmeldingen (Germany)	49.21N 8.09E		94

Roman Province	Site Name/Location Ancient (Modern)	Map Coordinates (City Region)	Catalogue No.
39. Belgica/Belgica Prima			
	Augusta Treverorum (Treves; Trier, Germany)	49.45N 6.39E	A[12]
40. Britannia/Britannia Secunda			
	Lullingstone (Eynsford, Kent, England)	51.22N 0.13E	57
41. Britannia/Britannia Prima			
	Hinton St. Mary	50.46N 1.43W	A[13]
42. Britannia/Valentia			
	Brocolitia (Carrawburgh, Northumber., Eng.)	55.02N 2.08W	95
43. Hispania/Lusitania			
	Augusta Emerita (Merida, Spain)	38.55N 6.20W	A[14]

Table 5
Geographical Divisions of the Roman Empire

The following lists of the provincial divisions of the empire are keyed to and are followed in the geographical arrangement of items in the catalogues of evidence (archeological and documentary). The dates are based on the following sources: T. Mommsen, *The Provinces of the Roman Empire*, 2 vols., ed. T. R. S. Broughton (Chicago, 1968); A. H. M. Jones, *The Cities of the Eastern Roman Provinces* (2d ed.; Oxford: Clarendon, 1971); F. van der Meer and C. Mohrmann, *Atlas of the Early Christian World* (London, 1966).

Provinces (in regional groupings) before 294	Praefecture organization (diocese and province) after the reform of Diocletian and Constantine
	A. Praefecture of Anatolia
I. Syria-Anatolia	I. The Oriens
1. Mesopotamia/Osrhoene	1. Mesopotamia/Osrhoene
2. Parapotamia	2. Coelesyria
3. Syria (including Decapolis)	3. Phoenice
4. Phoenice	4. Palestina (I, II, III)
5. Judaea (including Galilaia)	5. Arabia (including Decapolis)
6. Arabia	6. Cilicia
	7. Isauria
	8. Cyprus
II. Aegyptus	II. Aegyptus
1. Aegyptus	1. Aegyptus
	2. Arcadia
	3. Thebais
2. Cyrenaica (Cyrene)	4. Libya
	a. Dyrenaica/ Cyrenaica (superior)
	b. Marmorica (inferior)
III. Asia	III. Pontus
1. Armenia	1. Pontus Polemoniacus

	2. Armenia
2. Cappadocia	3. Cappadocia
3. Cilicia (& Isaurai)	
4. Galatia (& Lycaonia)	4. Galatia
5. Bithynia-Pontus	5. Heleno-Pontus
	6. Paphlogonia
	7. Honorias
6. Cyprus	
	IV. Asia
7. Asia (& Lydia, Caria, Pisidia, Phrygia, Mysia Insulae)	1. Lycaonia
	2. Pisidia
	3. Phrygia
	4. Lydia
	5. Caria
	6. Asia
	7. Hellespontus
	8. Insulae
8. Lycia-Pamphylia	9. Lycia
	10. Pamphylia
IV. Illyricum & Greece	V. Thracia
1. Thracia	1. Scythia
2. Moesia (Inf./Sup.)	2. Moesia (Secunda)
3. Dacia	3. Haemimonitus
	4. Rhodope
	5. Europa
	6. Thracia
	B. Praefecture of Illyricum
	VI. Dacia
	1. Dacia
	2. Dardania
	3. Praevalitana
	4. Moesia Prima
	VII. Macedonia
4. Macedonia (& Thessalia)	1. Macedonia (Prima/Salutaris)

5. Achaia	2. Thessalia
	3. Achaia
6. Epirus	4. Epirus
7. Creta	5. Creta
	VIII. Illyricum
8. Dalmatia	1. Dalmatia
	2. Savia (Illyria) Prima
9. Pannonia (Sup./Inf.)	3. Pannonia Prima
10. Noricum	4. Pannonia Secunda
	5. Valeria
	6. Noricum (ripens/mediterraneum)
	C. Praefecture of Italy
V. Italia Settentrional (North of Po River)	IX. Italia Annonaria
1. Raetia	1. Raetia (prima/secunda)
2. Venetia	2. Venetia-Istria
3. Transpadana	3. Liguria-Aemilia
	4. Flaminia-Picenum
	5. Tuscia
	6. Alpes Cottiae
VI. Italia	X. Italia Suburbicaria
1. Liguria	
2. Aemilia	
	1. Umbria
	2. Picenum Suburbicarum
3. Etruria	3. Valeria
4. Latium (Rome & environs)	4. Latium (Rome & environs)
5. Umbria	5. Campania
6. Picenum	6. Samnium
7. Campania	7. Apulia-Calabria
8. Samnium	8. Lucania-Brutium
9. Apulia-Calabria	9. Sicilia
10. Lucania-Bruttium	10. Sardinia
11. Sicilia	11. Corsica

12. Sardinia	
13. Corsica	
VII. Africa	XI. Africa
1. Africa Proconsularis	1. Tripolitania
	2. Byzacena
	3. Africa Proconsularis
2. Numidia	4. Numidia
3. Mauretania	5. Mauretania Sitifensis
	6. Mauretania Caesariensis
	D. Praefecture of Gaul
	XII. Gallia of the Seven Provinces
1. Alpes	1. Alpes Maretimae
a. Maretimae	
b. Cottiae	
c. Graiae	
d. Poeninae	
	2. Viennensis
2. Narbonensis	3. Narbonensis (prima/secunda)
3. Aquitania	4. Aquitania (prima/secunda)
	5. Novem Populana
	XIII. Gallia
4. Lugdunensis	1. Lugdunensis
5. Belgica	2. Belgica (prima/secunda)
6. Germania (Inf./Sup.)	3. Germania (prima/secunda)
	4. Maxima Sequanorum
	5. Alpes Poeninae/Graiae
IX Britannia	XIV. Britannia (prima/secunda)
	1. Valentia
	2. Caesariensis (Flavia-/Maxima-)
	3. Britannia (prima/secunda)

X. Hispania	XV. Hispania
1. Baetica	1. Baetica
2. Lusitania	2. Lusitania
3. Terraconensis	3. Gallaecia
	4. Terraconensis
	5. Carthaginiensis
	6. Mauretania Tingitana
4. Insulae (Libericae)	7. Ins. Baleares

Bibliography

▲ ▲ ▲

Primary Sources

Acta Munati Felicis apud *Gestae apud Zenophilum*. Edited by C. Ziwsa. Corpus Scriptorum Ecclesiasticorum Latinorum 26. Vienna: C. Geroldi filium Bibliopolem, 1893.

Acta Pauli et Theclae. Edited by R. A. Lipsius and M. Bonnet. *Acta Apostolicorum Apocrypha*. 3 vols.Leipzig: Herman Mendelssohn, 1891–1903.

Acta Petri (cum Simoni). Edited by R. A. Lipsius and M. Bonnet. *Acta Apostolicorum Apocrypha*. 3 vols.Leipzig: Herman Mendelssohn, 1891–1903.

Acta Phileae (P. Bodmer XX). Edited by Herbert Musurillo. *The Acts of the Christian Martyrs*. Oxford Early Christian Texts. Oxford: Clarendon, 1972.

Acta Saturnini. Edited by J.-P. Migne. Patrologia Cursus Completus, Series Latina. Paris: Garnier Fratres, 1878ff. Vol. 8, cols. 688ff.

Acta Thomae. Edited by R. A. Lipsius and M. Bonnet. *Acta Apostolicorum Apocrypha*. 3 vols. Leipzig: Herman Mendelssohn, 1891–1903.

Acts of Thomas (Syriac). Edited and translated by W. Wright. *Apocryphal Acts of the Apostles*. 2 vols. London: Williams & Norgate, 1871.

Die apostolischen Väter. Edited by F. X. Funk and Karl Bihlmeyer. Third edition by W. Schneemelcher. Sammlung ausgewählter kirchen- und dogmengeschichtlicher Quellenschriften, second series, I.l. Tübingen: Mohr (Siebeck), 1970.

Arnobius of Sica. *Ad Nationes*. Edited by C. Marchesi. Corpus Scriptorum Ecclesiasticorum Latinorum 4. Vienna: C. Geroldi filium Bibliopolem, 1875.

Augustine of Hippo. *Contra Crescionum*. Edited by J.-P. Migne. Patrologia Cursus Completus, Series Latina. Paris: Garnier Fratres, 1878ff. Vol. 8, cols. 704–68.

Calder, W. M., and W. H. Buckler, eds. *Monumenta Asiae Minoris Antiqua*. 8 vols. Manchester: Manchester University Press, 1928–62.

Clement of Alexandria. *Paedagogus*. Edited by O. Stählin. Die griechischen christlichen Schrifsteller der ersten drei Jahrhunderte. Leipzig: J. C. Hinrichs, 1906.

Clement of Alexandria. *Stromata*. Edited by O. Stählin. Die griechischen christlichen Schriftsteller der ersten drei Jahrhunderte. Leipzig: J. C. Hinrichs, 1906.

Pseudo-Clement (of Rome). *Recognitions*. Edited by B. Rehm. Die griechischen christlichen Schriftsteller der ersten drei Jahrhunderte. Leipzig: J. C. Hinrichs, 1965.

Corpus Inscriptionum Iudaicarum. Edited by J.-B. Frey. Sussidi allo delle antichita cristiani I. 2 vols. Rome: Pontificio Istituto di Archeologia cristiana, 1936–52.

Corpus of Jewish Inscriptions. 2d ed. Volume I with Prolegomenon by Baruch Lifshitz. New York: KTAV, 1975.

Corpus of Jewish Papyri. Edited by V. Tcherikover, A. Fuks, and M. Stern. 3 vols. Cambridge, MA: Harvard University Press, 1957–64.

Cyprian. *De ecclesiae catholicae unitate*. Edited by W. Hartel. Corpus Scriptorum Ecclesiasticorum Latinorum III.l. Vienna: C. Geroldi filium Bibliopolem, 1868.

———. *De ecclesiae catholicae unitate*. Edited by W. Hartel in *Cyprian: On the Lapsed and the Unity of the Catholic Church*. Translated by Maurice Bevenot. Oxford Early Christian Texts. Oxford: Clarendon, 1968.

———. *De lapsis*. Edited by M. Bevenot in *Cyprian: On the Lapsed and the Unity of the Catholic Church*. Oxford Early Christian Texts. Oxford: Clarendon, 1968.

———. *Epistula*. Edited by J.-P. Migne. Patrologia Cursus Completus, Series Latina. Paris: Garnier Fratres, 1878ff. Vol. 4.

———. *Epistula*. Edited by W. Hartel. Corpus Scriptorum Ecclesiasticorum Latinorum 3.2. Vienna: C. Geroldi filium Bibliopolem, 1871.

———. *Epistula*. Edited by W. Hartel in *Saint Cyprien: Correspondance*. Translated by L. Bayard. Sources chrétiennes. 2 vols. Paris: Editions du Cerf, 1974.

Didache. Edited by F. X. Funk and K. Bihlmeyer. *Die apostolischen Väter*.

Sammlung ausgewählter kirchen- und dogmengeschichtlicher Quellenschriften, second series, I.l. Tübingen: Mohr (Siebeck). 1970.

———. Edited and translated by Kirsopp Lake. *The Apostolic Fathers*. Loeb Classical Library. London and Cambridge: Heinemann, 1912–13. 2 vols.

Didascalia Apostolorum. Edited and translated by R. H. Connolly. Oxford: Clarendon, 1929.

———. Edited and translated by Margaret Dunlop Gibson. *The Didascalia Apostolorum in Syriac*. Horae Semiticae I–II. 2 vols. Cambridge: Cambridge University Press, 1903.

Dittenberger, Wilhelm, ed. *Orientis Graeci Inscriptiones Selectae, Supplementum Syllogis Inscriptionum Graecarum*. Leipzig: S. Hirzel, 1905.

——, ed. *Sylloge Inscriptionum Graecarum*. 3d ed. 3 vols. Leipzig: S. Hirzel, 1914–25.

Die edessenischen Chronik. Edited by L. Hallier. Texte und Untersuchungen zur Geschichte der altchristlichen Literatur 9.l. Leipzig: J. C. Hinrichs, 1892.

Epistle to Diognetus. Edited by F. X. Funk and K. Bihlmeyer. *Die apostolischen Väter*. Sammlung ausgewählter kirchen- und dogmengeschichtlicher Quellenschriften, second series, I.1. Tübingen: Mohr (Siebeck), 1970.

———. Edited and translated by Kirsopp Lake. *The Apostolic Fathers*. Loeb Classical Library. 2 vols. London and Cambridge, MA: Heinemann, 1912–13.

Eusebius Pamphilii, bishop of Casarea. *Historia Ecclesiastica*. Edited by E. Schwartz. Die griechischen christlichen Schriftsteller der ersten drei Jahrhunderte. 3 vols. Leipzig: J. C. Hinrichs, 1903–9.

———. *Historia Ecclesiastica*. Edited and translated by K. Lake and J. E. L. Oulton. *Eusebius: The Ecclesiastical History*. Loeb Classical Library. 2 vols. London and Cambridge, MA: Heinemann, 1926–32.

———. *Historia Ecclesiastica*. Translated by H. J. Lawlor and J. E. L. Oulton. *Eusebius, bishop of Caesarea: The Ecclesiastical History and the Martyrs of Palestine*. 2 vols. London: SPCK, 1954.

———. *Vita Constantini. Laus Constantini*. Edited by I. A. Heikel. Die griechischen christlichen Schriftsteller der ersten drei Jahrhunderte. Leipzig: J. C. Hinrichs. 1902.

Grant, Frederick Clifton, ed. *Ancient Roman Religion*. New York: Bobbs Merrill, 1957.

——, ed. *Hellenistic Religion: The Age of Syncretism*. New York: Bobbs-Merrill, 1953.

Gregory Thaumaturgus. *Epistula Canonica*. Edited by J.-P. Migne. Patrologia Cursus Completus, Series Graece. Paris: Garnier Fratres, 1878ff. Vol. 10, cols. 1044ff.

Hermas. *The Shepherd*. Translated by Kirsopp Lake. *The Apostolic Fathers*. Loeb Classical Library. London and Cambridge, MA: Heinemann, 1912–13.

———. *The Shepherd*. Edited and translated by Robert Joly. *Hermas: Le Pasteur*. 2d ed. Sources chrétiennes 58 (bis). Paris: Editions du Cerf, 1968.

Hippolytus. *The Apostolic Tradition*. Edited and translated by Gregory Dix. *The Treatise on the Apostolic Tradition of St. Hippolytus*. London: SPCK, 1953.

———. *The Apostolic Tradition*. Edited and translated by B. Botte. *Hippolyte de Rome: La Tradition Apostolique*. Second edition. Sources chrétiennes 11 (bis). Paris: Editions du Cerf, 1968.

———. *The Apostolic Tradition*. Edited by W. Till and J. Leipoldt. *Die koptische Text der Kirchenordnung Hippolyts*. Berlin: Akademie Verlag, 1954.

———. *Commentary on Daniel*. Edited and translated by G. Bardy and M. Lefèvre. *Hippolyte: Commentaire sur Daniel*. Sources chrétiennes 14. Paris: Editions du Cerf, 1947.

Ignatius of Antioch. *Epistles*. Edited by F. X. Funk and K. Bihlmeyer. *Die apostolischen Väter*. Sammlung ausgewählter kirchen- und dogmengeschichtlicher Quellenschriften, second series, I.l. Tübingen: Mohr (Siebeck), 1970.

———. *Epistles*. Translated by Kirsopp Lake. *The Apostolic Fathers*. Classical Library. 2 vols. London and Cambridge, MA: Heinemann, 1912–13.

Inscriptiones Italiae. Edited by A. Degrassi. Rome: Lib. dello Stato, 1934.

Inscriptions du port d'Ostie. Edited by Hilding Thylander. Skrifter Utgivna av Svenska Institutet im Rom. Lund: Gleerup, 1952.

Inscriptions grecques et latines de Syrie. Edited by P. Le Bas and H. Waddington. 3 vols. Paris: Didot, 1898.

Justin Martyr. *Apologia*. Edited by G. Krueger in A. W. F. Blunt. *The Apologies of Justin Martyr*. Cambridge: Cambridge University Press, 1911.

Lactantius, Lucius Caecilius Firmianus. *De mortibus persecutorum*. Edited by S. Brandt and G. Laubmann. Corpus Scriptorum Ecclesiasticorum Latinorum 27.2. Vienna: C. Geroldi filium Bibliopolem, 1897.

Lampridius. *Historia Augusta, Severus Alexander*. Edited by H. Peter in David Magie. *Scriptores Historiae Augustae*. Loeb Classical Library. 3 vols. London and Cambridge, MA: Heinemann, 1921–25.

Lewis, Naphtali, and Meyer Reinhold, eds. *Roman Civilization: A Sourcebook*. Vol. II: *The Empire*. New York: Harper, 1966.

Lipsius, R. A., and M. Bonnet, eds. *Acta Apostolicorum Apocrypha*. 3 vols. Leipzig: Herman Mendelssohn, 1891–1903.

Migne, J.-P. *Patrologia Cursus Completus,* Series Graece. 161 vols. Paris: Garnier Fratres, 1886ff.

———. *Patrologia Cursus Completus,* Series Latina. 222 vols. Paris: Garnier Fratres, 1878ff.

Michigan Papyri XIV. Edited by Vincent P. McCarren. American Studies in Papyrology 22. Chico: Scholars Press, 1980.

Minucius Felix. *Octavius*. Edited and translated by G. H. Rendall. Loeb Classical Library. London and Cambridge, MA: Heinemann, 1931.

———. *Octavius*. Edited by C. Halm. Corpus Scriptorum Ecclesiasticorum Latinorum II. Vienna: C. Geroldi filium Bibliopolem, 1867.

Musurillo, Herbert, ed. *The Acts of the Christian Martyrs*. Oxford Early Christian Texts. Oxford: Clarendon, 1972.

The Nag Hammadi Library in English. Translated by Members of the Coptic Gnostic Library Project of the Institute for Antiquity and Christianity. James M. Robinson, director. San Francisco: Harper & Row, 1977; Leiden: E. J. Brill, 1977.

Naldini, Mario. *Il Cristianesimo in Egitto: Lettere private nei papiri dei secoli II–IV*. Studi e Testi di papirologia 3. Florence: Le Monnier, 1968.

Optatus of Mileve. *De schismate Donatistarum*. Edited by C. Ziwasa. Corpus Scriptorum Ecclesiasticorum Latinorum 26. Vienna: C. Geroldi filium Bibliopolem, 1893.

Origen. *Contra Celsum*. Edited by P. Koetschau. Die griechischen christlichen Schriftsteller der ersten drei Jahrhunderte. 2 vols. Leipzig: J. C. Hinrichs, 1899.

———. *Contra Celsum*. Translated by Henry Chadwick. Cambridge: Cambridge University Press, 1953.

———. *De oratione*. Edited by P. Koetschau. Die griechischen christlichen Schriftsteller der ersten drei Jahrhunderte. Leipzig: J. C. Hinrichs, 1899.

The Oxyrhynchus Papyri. Edited by B. P. Grenfell, E. Hunt, et al. London: Egypt Exploration Society, 1898–1978.

Passio Pauli. Edited by R. A. Lipsius and M. Bonnet. *Acta Apostolicorum Apocrypha*. 3 vols. Leipzig: Herman Mendelssohn, 1891–1903.

Passiones sancti Justini et socii. Edited by Herbert Musurillo. *The Acts of the Christian Martyrs*. Oxford Early Christian Texts. Oxford: Clarendon, 1972.

Plinius Caecilius Secundus, Gaius. *Plinius Minor, Epistularum libri decem*. Edited by R. A. B. Mynors. Oxford Classical Texts. Oxford: Clarendon, 1963.

———. *Pliny the Younger, Letters and Panegyricus*. Translated by Betty Radice. 2 vols. LCL. Cambridge: Harvard University Press, 1969.

Porphyrius. *Adversus Christianos*. Edited by A. Harnack. *Porphyrius: Gegen die Christen*. Abhandlung der deutschen (preussischen) Akademie der Wissenschaft, phil.- historischen Klasse I. Berlin: Akademie Verlag, 1916.

Tacitus, Cornelius. *Annals of Imperial Rome*. Translated by J. Jackson. Loeb Classical Library. 3 vols. London and Cambridge, MA: Heinemann, 1924–37.

Tertullianus, Quintus Septimius Florens. *Adversus Marcionem*. Edited by A. Kroymann. Corpus Christianorum, Series Latina I. Turnholt: Typographi Brepols Editores Pontificii, 1954.

———. *Adversus Valentinianos*. Edited by A. Kroymann. Corpus Christianorum, Series Latina II. Turnholt: Typographi Brepols Editores Pontificii, 1954.

———. *Apologeticum*. Edited by E. Dekkers. Corpus Christianorum, Series Latina I. Turnholt: Typographi Brepols Editores Pontificii, 1954.

———. *Apology*. Translated by T. R. Glover. Loeb Classical Library. London and Cambridge, MA: Heinemann, 1931.

———. *De baptismo*. Edited and translated by Ernest Evans. *Tertullian's Homily on Baptism*. London: SPCK, 1964.

———. *De fuga in persecutione*. Edited by J. J. Thierry. Corpus Christianorum, Series Latina II. Turnholt: Typographi Brepols Editores Pontificii, 1954.

———. *De idololatria*. Edited by A. Reifferscheid and G. Wissowa. Corpus Christianorum, Series Latina II. Turnholt: Typographi Brepols Editores Pontificii, 1954.

———. *De poenitentia*. Edited by J. W. P. Borleffs. Corpus Christianorum, Series Latina I. Turnholt: Typographi Brepols Editores Pontificii, 1954.

———. *De pudicitia*. Edited by E. Dekkers. Corpus Christianorum, Series Latina II. Turnholt: Typographi Brepols Editores Pontificii, 1954.

Vermaseren, Maarten J., ed. *Corpus Inscriptionum et Monumentorum Religionis Mithriacae*. 2 vols. The Hague: Martinus Nijhoff, 1956–60.

Secondary Studies and Collections

Abrahamsen, Valerie. "Bishop Porphyrios and the City of Philippi in the Early Fourth Century," *VC* 43 (1989) 80–85.

Afanasieff, N. "L'assemblée eucharistique unique dans l'église ancienne." *Kleronomia* 6 (1974) 1–36.

Antier, Gilles. "La galerie du fanum gallo-romain." *Information d'histoire de l'Art* 20 (1975) 210–14.

Applebaum, Shimon. *Jews and Greeks in Ancient Cyrene*. Leiden: Brill, 1979.

———. "The Organization of Jewish Communities in the Diaspora." In S. Safrai and M. Stern, eds., *The Jewish People in the First Century,* 1.1. 464–503. CRINT. Philadelphia: Fortress, 1974.

Armstrong, Gregory T. "Imperial Church Building and Church–State Relations, A.D. 313–363." *CH* 37 (1967) 3–17.

———. "Imperial Church Building in the Holy Land in the Fourth Century." *BA* 30 (1967) 90–102.

———. "Constantine's Churches: Symbol and Structure," *Journal of the Society of Architectural Historians* 33 (1974) 5–16.

Attridge, Harold W. "The Philosophical Critique of Religion under the Early Empire." *ANRW* 2.16.1 (1979) 45–68.

Avi-Yonah, Michael. "Ancient Synagogues." *Ariel, A Quarterly Review of Arts and Letters in Israel* 32 (1973) 29–43. Reprinted in J. Gutmann, ed., *The Synagogue: Studies in Origins, Archaeology and Architecture*. New York: KTAV, 1975.

———. "Synagogue Architecture." *Encyclopedia Judaica*, 2d ed. (1971) 15. 595–600.

Bagatti, B. "Oggetti inediti de Cafarnao." *Liber Annuus de Studium Biblicum Franciscanum* 14 (1964) 261–72.

Bakirtzis, Charalambos. "*To Episkopeion ton Philippon*," in *Proceedings of the Second Symposium on Kavala and its Environs (1986)*, 149–57. Kavala: Center for Historical Studies, 1987.

Baldi, D. *Enchiridion Locorum Sanctorum*. Jerusalem: Studium Biblicum, 1935.

Banks, Robert. *Paul's Idea of Community: The Early House Churches in their Historical Setting*. Grand Rapids: Eerdmans, 1980.

Barley, M. W., and R. P. C. Hanson, eds. *Christianity in Britain 300–700*. Leicester: Leicester University Press, 1968.

Barnes, Timothy D. *Tertullian: A Historical and Literary Study*. Oxford: Clarendon, 1971.

Baslez, Marie-François. "Déliens et étrangers domiciliés à Délos (166–155)," *REG* 89 (1976) 343–60.

Bauer, Walter. *Rechtgläubigkeit und Ketzerei im ältesten Christentum*. Beiträge zur historischen Theologie 10. Tübingen: Mohr (Siebeck), 1934. Second edition by Georg Strecker. Tübingen: Mohr (Siebeck), 1963. Eng. trans.: *Orthodoxy and Heresy in Earliest Christianity*. Edited by R. A. Kraft and G. Krodel. Philadelphia: Fortress, 1971.

Baur, P. V. C. "The Christian Chapel at Dura-Europos." *AJA* 37 (1933) 377–80.

Beare, Francis W. *Commentary on the Epistle to the Philippians*. Harper's New Testatment Commentary. 2d ed. New York: Harper & Row, 1969.

Becatti, Giovanni. *I Mitrei*. Vol. II of *Scavi di Ostia*. Edited by Guido Calza. Rome: Lib. dello Stato, 1954.

———. *Edificio con opus sectile fuori Porta Marina*. Vol. VI of *Scavi di Ostia*. Edited by Guido Calza and G. Becatti. Rome: Lib. dello Stato, 1969.

Bedard, Walter M. *The Symbolism of the Baptismal Font in Early Christian Thought*. Washington: Catholic University of America Press, 1951.

Beilen, Heinz. "Συναγωγὴ τῶν Ἰουδαίων καὶ θεοσεβῶν, Die Aussage einer bosporanischen Freilassungsinschrift (CIRB 71) zum Problem der 'Gottfürchtigen'." *JAC* 8–9 (1965–66) 171–90.

Benko, Stephen, and John J. O'Rourke, eds. *The Catacombs and the Colosseum: The Roman Empire as the Setting for Early Christianity*. Valley Forge, PA: Judson, 1971.

Bernheimer, R. "An Ancient Oriental Source of Christian Sacred Architecture." *AJA* 43 (1939) 647–88.

Bertacchi, L. "Architettura e mosaico." In B. Forlati Tamaro, ed., *Da Aquileia a Venezia,* 95–332. 2d ed. Milan: Garzanti, 1986.

Betz, Hans Dieter. "The Mithras Inscriptions of Santa Prisca and the New Testament." *NT* 10 (1968) 62-80.

Bianchi, U., and M. Vermaseren. *Mysteria Mithrae: Attii del Seminario*

Internazionale su 'La specificita storico-religiosa die Misteri Mithra, con particolare riferimento alle fonti documentarie di Roma e Ostia' (Rome/Ostia, 1978). EPRO 80. Leiden: Brill, 1979.

———. *La Soteriologia dei Culti Orientali nell'Impero Romano: Atti del Colloquio Internazionale (Rome, 1979)*. EPRO 82. Leiden: Brill, 1982.

Blake, M. E. *Roman Construction in Italy from Tiberius through the Flavians*. Washington: CASVA, 1959.

———. *Roman Construction in Italy from Nerva to the Antonines*. Philadelphia: CASVA, 1973.

Blank, Horst. *Einführung in das Privatleben der Griechen und Römer*. Die Altertumswissenschaft. Darmstadt: Wissenschaftliche Buchgesellschaft, 1976.

Boersma, J. S. *Amoenissima civitas*. Leiden: Brill, 1987.

Bonz, Marianne P. "The Jewish Community of Ancient Sardis: A Reassessment of Its Rise to Prominence." *Harvard Studies in Classical Philology* 93 (1990) 343–59.

———. "Differing Approaches to Religious Benefaction: The Late Third Century Acquisition of the Sardis Synagogue." *HTR* 86 (1993) 139–54.

Bornkamm, Günther. "Der Philipperbrief als paulinische Briefsammlung." *Neotestamentica et Patristica, Freundesgabe O. Cullmann*. Supplements to Novum Testamentum 6. Leiden: E. J. Brill, 1962.

———. *Early Christian Experience*. Translated by P. L. Hammer. New York: Harper & Row, 1969.

Botermann, H. "Die Synagoge von Sardes: Eine Synagoge aus dem 4. Jahrhundert?" *ZNW* 81 (1990) 103–21.

Bovini, Giuseppe. *La proprietà ecclesiastica e la condizione giuridica della chiesa in età preconstantiniana*. Publicazioni dei Università di Roma dell'istituto di Diritto Romano 28. Milan: Università di Roma, 1948.

———. *Le Antichità cristiane di Aquileia*. Bologna: Patron, 1972.

Boyle, Leonard. *St. Clement's, Rome*. 2d ed. Rome: Collegio San Clemente, 1989.

Brady, Thomas A. "The Reception of the Egyptian Cults by the Greeks (330–30 B.C.)." *University of Missouri Studies* 10:1 (1935).

Bragantini, I. "Le decorazioni parietali dell'Edificio del Mitreo." In F. Guidobaldi, ed., *San Clemente: Gli Edifici Romani, La Basilica Paleocristiana, e Le Fasi Altomedievali,* 317–26. San Clemente Miscellany 4. Rome: Collegio San Clemente, 1992.

Brezzi, P. "La composizione sociale della communità cristiani." *Studi e materiale di storia della religioni* 22 (1949–50) 42–57.

Brooten, Bernadette. *Women Leaders in the Ancient Synagogue: Inscriptional Evidence and Background Issues* Brown Judaic Studies 36. Chico, CA: Scholars Press, 1982.

———. "Ιαηλ Προστάτης in the Jewish Donative Inscription from Aphrodisias." In B. Pearson, ed., *The Future of Early Christianity: Essays in Honor of Helmut Koester,* 149–62. Minneapolis: Fortress, 1991.

Bruneau, Philippe. *Recherches sur les cultes de Délos à l'époque hellénistique et à l'époque imperial.* Bibliothèque des Écoles françaises d'Athènes et de Rome 217. Paris: École Française, 1970.

———. "La synagogue juive de Délos." *BCH* 87 (1963) 873–88.

———. "'Les Israelites de Délos' et la Juiverie délienne." *BCH* 106 (1982) 465–504.

Bruneau, P., and R. Ducat. *Guide de Délos*. 2d ed. Paris: Boccard, 1964.

Brusin, Giovanni. *Gli scavi di Aquileia*. Udine: Edizione de "La Panarie," 1934.

Brusin, G., and P. L. Zovatto. *Monumenti paleocristiani di Aquileia e di Grado*. Udine: Edizione de "La Panerie," 1957.

Budge, E. A. Wallis. "The Martyrdom of Isaac of Tiphre." *Transactions of the Society of Biblical Archaeology* 9 (1893) 74–111.

Bujard, Walter. *Stilanalystische Untersuchungen zum Kolosserbrief als beitrag zur Methodik von Sprachvergleichen*. Studien zur Umwelt des Neuen Testament 11. Göttingen: Vandenhoeck & Ruprecht, 1973.

Bultmann, Rudolf. *Primitive Christianity in its Contemporary Setting*. Translated by R. H. Fuller. Cleveland, OH: Meridian Books, 1956.

Cabrol, Fernand, and Henri Leclercq, eds. *Dictionnaire d'Archéologie chrétienne et de liturgie*. 24 vols. Paris: Letouzey et Ané, 1907–51.

Cadbury, Henry J. *The Making of Luke-Acts*. 2d ed. London: SPCK, 1958.

Calder, W. M. "A Fourth Century Lycaonian Bishop." *The Expositor* (1908) 385–93.

———. "Studies in Early Christian Epigraphy." *Journal of Roman Studies* 10 (1920) 42–59.

———. "The Epigraphy of the Anatolian Heresies." In W. H. Buckler and W. M. Calder, eds., *Anatolian Studies Presented to Sir W. M. Ramsay*, 59–91. Manchester: University Press of Manchester, 1923.

Campbell, Leroy A. *Mithraic Iconography and Ideology*. EPRO. Leiden: E. J. Brill, 1968.

———. "Typology of Mithraic Tauroctones." *Berytus* 1 (1954) 1–34.

von Campenhausen, Hans Freiherr. *Kirchliche Amt und geistliche Vollmacht*. Tübingen: Mohr (Siebeck), 1953. Eng. trans.: *Ecclesiastical Authority and Spiritual Power in the Church of the First Three Centuries*. Translated by J. A. Baker. Stanford, CA: Stanford University Press, 1969.

Capelle, B. "L'introduction du catéchumenat à Rome." *Recherches de théologie ancienne et médiévale* 5 (1933) 120–54.

Carcopino, Jerome. *Daily Life in Ancient Rome*. Translated by E. O. Lorimer. New Haven: Yale University Press, 1959.

Case, Shirley Jackson. *The Social Origins of Christianity*. Chicago: University of Chicago Press, 1923.

di Cavalieri, Franchi. "Note agiografiche 6°." *Studi e Testi* 33 (1920) 10–14.

Cecchelli, Carlo. "Gli edifici e i mosaici paleocristiani nella zona della Basilica." In *La Basilica di Aquileia. Comitato per ceremonie celebrative del IX° centenario della Basilica*. Bologna: il Mulino, 1933.

———. "Il problema della basilica cristiana preconstantiniana." *Palladio* 7 (1943) 1–18.

Ceci, E. *I Monumenti cristiani di Salona*. 2 vols. Milan: Edizioni Pleion di Bietti, 1963.

Chastagnol, André. *La Préfecture urbaine à Rome sous le bas-Empire*. Paris: Université de France, 1960.

Clark, G. W. "Two Christians in the Familia Caesaris." *HTR* 64 (1971), 121–24.

Conzelmann, Hans. *Die Mitte der Zeit*. 2d ed. Tübingen: Mohr (Siebeck). 1957. Eng. trans.: *The Theology of St. Luke*. Translated by G. Bushwell. New York: Harper & Row, 1960.

———. *Der erste Brief an die Korinther*. Kritisch-exegetischer Kommentar über das Neue Testament, begründet von H. A. W. Meyer, 11. Göttingen: Vandenhoeck & Ruprecht, 1969. Eng. trans.: *1 Corinthians*. Translated by J. W. Leitch. Hermeneia. Philadelphia: Fortress, 1975.

———. *Geschichte des Urchristentums*. Göttingen: Vandenhoeck & Ruprecht, 1969. Eng. trans.: *History of Primitive Christianity*. Translated by J. E. Steely. Nashville, TN: Abingdon, 1973.

Corbett, G. U. S. "Investigations at 'Julianos' Church' at Umm-el-Jemal." *Papers of the British School at Rome* 25 (1957) 39–66.

———. "A Note on the Arrangement of the Early Christian Buildings at Aquileia." *RivAC* 32 (1956) 99ff.

Corbo, Virgilio. *The House of St. Peter at Capharnaum, a preliminary report of the first two campaigns of Excavations, 1968*. Translated by S. Saller. Studium Biblicum Franciscanum, Collectio minor 5. Jerusalem: Studium Biblicum Franciscanum, 1969.

———. *Cafarnao I: Gli edifici della citta*. Studium Biblicum Franciscanum 19. Jerusalem: Studium Biblicum Franciscanum, 1975.

Countryman, L. William. "Patrons and Officers in Club and Church." In Paul J. Achtemeier, ed., *Society of Biblical Literature Seminar Papers, 1977*. Missoula, MT: Scholars Press, 1977.

———. *The Rich Christian in the Church of the Early Empire: Contradictions and Accommodations*. Texts and Studies in Religion. New York: Edwin Mellen, 1980.

Crawford, M. "Money and Exchange in the Roman World." *JRS* 60 (1970) 40–48.

Cumont, Franz. "The Dura Mithraeum." Edited and translated by E. D. Francis. In J. Hinnels, ed., *Mithraic Studies: Papers of the First International Conference of Mithraic Studies (1971)*, 1. 151–214. Manchester: Manchester University Press, 1975.

———. "La grande inscription bachique du Metropolitan Museum, II—Commentaire religieuse de l'Inscription. Planches xxx–xxxiii." *AJA* 37 (1933) 232–70.

———. *Les Mystères de Mithra*. 3d ed. Brussels: H. Lamertin, 1913. Eng. trans.: (from second French edition) *The Mysteries of Mithra*. Translated by T. J. McCormack. Chicago: Open Court, 1903. Reprint, New York: Dover, 1956.

———. *Les religions orientales dans le paganisme romain*. 3d ed. Paris: Collège de France, 1924. Eng. trans. (from second French edition): *The Oriental Religions in Roman Paganism*. Translated by G. Showerman. London: Routledge & Kegan Paul, 1911. Reprint, New York: Dover, 1956.

———. *Textes et monuments figurés relatifs aux mystères de Mithra*. 2 vols. Brussels: H. Lamertin, 1896–98.

Cuscito, G. "*Hoc cubile sanctum:* contributo per un studio sulle origini cristiane in Istria," *Atti e memorie della Societa istr. di archeologia e storia patr.* ns. 19 (1971) 77–99.

———. *Cristianesimo antico ad Aquileia e in Istria*. Fonti e studi per la storia della Venezia giulia. Serie secondo, III. Trieste, 1977.

———. "I santi Mauro e Eleuterio di Parenzo l'identità, il culto, le reliquie," *Atti di centro di ricerche storiche Rovigno* 16 (1985–86) 31–46.

———. "Vescovo e cattedrali nella documentazione epigrafica in occidente," *Acta XI CIAC (1988)*. In *Studi di Antichità cristiana* 41 (1989) 741–49.

Dahl, Nils Alstrup. "Paul and the Church at Corinth." *Studies in Paul: Theology for Early Christian Mission*. Minneapolis, MN: Augsburg, 1977.

Daniels, C. M. "The Role of the Roman Army in the Spread and Practice of Mithraism." In J. Hinnels, ed., *Mithraic Studies*. 2 vols. Manchester: Manchester University Press, 1975.

———. *Mithras and His Temples on the Wall*. 2d ed. Newcastle on Tyne: Hill, 1967.

D'Arms, John H. *Commerce and Social Standing in Ancient Rome*. Cambridge, MA: Harvard University Press, 1981.

Davies, J. G. *The Architectural Setting of Baptism*. London: Barrie & Rockliff, 1962.

———. *The Early Christian Church*. New York: Anchor Books, 1967.

———. *The Origin and Development of Early Christian Church Architecture*. London: SCM, 1952.

———. *The Secular Use of Church Buildings*. New York: Seabury, 1968.

Davis-Weyer, C., and J. J. Emerick. "The Early Sixth-Century Frescoes at S. Martino ai Monte in Rome." *Römisches Jahrbuch für Kunstgeschichte* 21 (1984) 1–60.

Dehio, G. *Die Genesis der christlichen Basilika*. Sitzungsbericht der k. bayerischen Akademie der Wissenschaften, phil.- historische Klasse 12. Munich: Kaiser, 1882.

Deichmann, F. W. "Basilika." In Theodore Klauser, ed., *Reallexikon für Antike und Christentum*, 1. 1225–59. Leipzig and Stuttgart: J. C. Hinrichs, 1941ff.

———. "Zur Datierung der Unterkirche von S. Clemente in Rom." *Mitteilung des deutschen archäologischen Institut*. Römischen Abteilung 58 (1943) 153–60.

———. "Von Tempel zur Kirche." *Mullus: Festschrift Theodor Klauser*. JAC Erganzungsband 1. Münster: Aschendorff, 1964.

Deissmann, Adolf. *Licht vom Osten*. 4th ed. Tübingen: Mohr (Siebeck), 1923. Eng. trans.: *Light from the Ancient East*. Translated by L. Strachan. London: Hodder & Stoughton, 1928. Reprint, Grand Rapids: Baker Book House, 1978.

———. *Paulus*. 2d ed. Tübingen: Mohr (Siebeck), 1925. Eng. trans.: *Paul, A*

Study in Social and Religious History. Translated by W. E. Wilson. New York: Harper, 1957.

Delling, Gerhard. “Zur Taufe von ‘Häusern’ im Urchristentum.” *NT* 7 (1965) 285–311.

De Vries, Bert. “Research at Umm el-Jimal, Jordan, 1972–1977.” *BA* 42 (1979) 49–55.

Dickey, S. “Some Economic and Social Conditions of Asia Minor affecting the Expansion of Christianity.” In S. J. Case, ed., *Studies in Early Christianity presented to F. C. Porter and B. W. Bacon*. New York: Century, 1928.

Dinkler, Eric. “Dura-Europos III, Bedeutung für die christliche Kunst.” *RGG*[3] 2. 290–92.

Dix, Gregory. *The Shape of the Liturgy*. 2d ed. London: Dacre, 1945.

von Dobschutz, Ernst. *Die urchristlichen Gemeinde*. Leipzig: J. C. Hinrichs, 1902. Eng. trans.: *Christian Life in the Primitive Church*. Translated by G. Bemner. New York: Williams & Norgate, 1904.

Dolger, Franz Joseph. “Die Bedeutung des neuentdeckten Mithras Heiligtums von Dura-Europos für die handschriftliche Überlieferung der heidnischen Mysteriensprache bei Firmicus Maternus und Heironymus.” In *Antike und Christentum: Kultur- und religionsgeschichtliche Studien*, 5. 286–88. Münster-Westfalen: Aschendorff, 1929–50.

Donfried, Karl Paul. “False Presuppositions in the Study of Romans.” In K. P. Donfried, eds., *The Romans Debate*. Minneapolis, MN: Augsburg, 1977.

———. “A Short Note on Romans 16.” In K. P. Donfried, eds., *The Romans Debate*. Minneapolis, MN: Augsburg, 1977.

Donnay-Rocmans, C. “‘Basilique’ dans la litterature chrétienne d’Afrique au IVe s.” *Annuaire de l’Institut de Philologie et d’histoire orientales et slaves* 15 (1960) 153–62.

Downey, Glanville. *Ancient Antioch*. Princeton, NJ: Princeton University Press, 1963.

Duchesne, L. *Les Origines du culte chrétien*. 3d ed. Paris: A. Fontemoing, 1903. Eng. trans.: *Christian Worship: Its Origin and Evolution*. Translated by M. L. McClure. London: SPCK, 1903.

du Mesnil du Buisson, Comte R. “La nouvelle découvertes de la synagogue de Doura-Europos.” *RB* 43 (1934) 546–63.

———. *Le peintures de la synagogue de Doura-Europos, 244–256 après J.-C*. Paris: Collège de France, 1939.

———. "L'inscription de la niche centrale de la synagogue de Doura-Europos." *Syria* 40 (1963) 303–14.

Duncan, G. S. *St. Paul's Ephesian Ministry. A Reconstruction with Special Reference to the Ephesian Origin of the Imprisonment Epistles*. London: Hodder & Stoughton, 1929.

Duncan-Jones, Richard. "Costs, Outlays and Summae Honoriae from Roman Africa." *Papers of the British School at Rome* 30 (1962) 47–115.

———. *The Economy of the Roman Empire: Quantitative Studies*. 2d ed. Cambridge: Cambridge University Press, 1981.

———. "An Epigraphic Survey of Costs in Roman Italy." *Papers of the British School at Rome* 33 (1965) 189–306.

———. "The Finances of the Younger Pliny." *Papers of the British School at Rome* 33 (1965) 177–88.

Dungan, David. *The Sayings of Jesus in the Churches of Paul: The Use of the Synoptic Tradition in the Regulation of Early Church Life*. Philadelphia: Fortress, 1971.

Dyggve, E. *History of Salonitian Christianity*. Oslo: Van Gorcum, 1951.

Eck, Werner. "Das Eindringen der Christentums in den Senatorenstand bis zu Konstantin d. Gr." *Chiron* 1 (1971) 381–406.

Egger, Rudolf. *Forschungen in Salona*. Vol. II: *Die altchristliche Friedhof Manastirine*. Vienna: Beck'schen Universitäts-Buchhandlung, 1926.

Elliot, John H. *A Home for the Homeless: A Sociological Exegesis of 1 Peter, Its Situation and Strategy*. Philadelphia: Fortress, 1981.

Ellis, E. Earle. "Paul and His Co-workers." *NTS* 17 (1971) 437–52.

———. *Paul and His Recent Interpreters*. Grand Rapids: Eerdmans, 1961.

Emmett, A. M., and S. R. Pickering. "The Importance of P. Bodmer XX, *The Apology of Phileas*, and its Problems." *Prudentia* 7 (1975) 95–103.

Englemann, Helmut. *The Delian Aretalogy of Serapis*. EPRO. Leiden: E. J. Brill, 1975.

Eriksen, R. T. "Syncretistic Symbolism and the Christian Roman Mosaic at Hinton St. Mary: A Closer Reading." *Proceedings of the Dorset Natural History and Archaeology Society* 102 (1980) 43–48.

Faivre, A. "Les fonctions ecclésiales dans les Écrits Pseudo-Clementins, Proposition de Lecture." *Revue de Sciences Religieuses* 50 (1976) 97–111.

Fakhry, Ahmed. *The Oases of Egypt*. 2 vols. Cairo: Services des Antiquités de l'Égypte, 1973–74.

Feissel, D. *Recueil des inscriptions chrétiennes de Macédoine du IIIè au VIè siecle*. BCH Supplements 8. Paris: Boccard, 1983.

Feldman, L. H. "Jewish Sympathizers in Classical Literature and Inscriptions." *Transactions of the American Philological Association* 81 (1950) 200–208.

———. "The Omnipresence of Godfearers." *BAR* 12 (1986) 58–63, 64–69.

Filson, Floyd V. "Ancient Greek Synagogue Inscriptions." *BA* 32 (1969) 41–46.

———. "The Significance of Early Christian House Churches." *JBL* 58 (1939) 105–12.

Finkelstein, Louis. "The Origin of the Synagogue." *Proceedings of the American Academy for Jewish Research* 1 (1928–30) 49–59. Reprinted in J. Gutmann, ed., *The Synagogue: Studies in Origins, Archaeology and Architecture*. New York: KTAV, 1975.

Finley, M. I. *The Ancient Economy*. Slather Classical Lectures 43. Berkeley, CA: University of California Press, 1973.

Finn, Thomas M. "Social Mobility in the Roman Empire: A Perspective for Christian Expansion." Paper presented at the Annual Meeting of the Society of Biblical Literature, New Orleans, LA, 1978.

Finney, Paul Corby. "TOPOS HIEROS und christlicher Sakralbau in vorkonstantinischer Überlieferung." *BOREAS: Münstersche Beiträge zur Archäologie* 7 (1984) 193–225.

———. "Early Christian Architecture: The Beginnings (A Review Article)." *HTR* 81 (1988) 319–39.

Fiocchi Nicolai, V. "Notizario delle scoperte avvenute in Italia nel campo dell'archeologia cristiana degli anni 1981-1986," *Studi di Antichità cristiana* 61.3 (1989) 2221–44.

Flusser, David. "Theses on the Emergence of Christianity from Judaism." *Immanuel: A Bulletin of Religious Thought and Research in Israel* 5 (1975) 74–84.

Foerster, G. "Notes on Recent Excavations at Capernaum." *IEJ* 21 (1971) 207–11.

Forlati, F. "L'architettura della basilica." *La Basilica di Aquileia*. Comitato per ceremonie celebrative del IX. centenario della Basilica. Bologna: il Mulino, 1933.

———. "Gli ultimi restauri nella Basilica Eufrasiana di Parenzo." *Atti e memorie della Societa istr. di archeologia e storia patr*. 42 (1930) 43–57.

———. "Ricerche sull'aula Teodoriana nord e sui battisteri di Aquileia," *Aquileia Nostra* 34 (1963) 86–98.

———. *Da Aquileia a Venezia.* 2d ed. Milan: Garzanti, 1986.

Fougeres, G. "Inscriptions de Mantinée." *BCH* 20 (1896) 159–61.

Francis, E. David. "Mithraic Graffiti from Dura-Europos." In J. Hinnels, ed., *Mithraic Studies.* 2. 424–45. Manchester: Manchester University Press, 1975.

Frantz, Allison. "The Athenian Agora." *Hesperia* 40 (1971) 266–70; 42 (1973) 156–64.

Frend, W. H. C. *The Donatist Church: A Movement of Protest in Roman North Africa.* Oxford: Clarendon, 1952.

———. *Martyrdom and Persecution in the Early Church.* New York: New York University Press, 1967.

Funk, Robert W. "The Watershed of the American Biblical Tradition: The Chicago School, First Phase, 1892–1920." *JBL* 95 (1976) 4–22.

Gager, John G. "Christianity and Social Class in the Early Roman Empire." In S. Benko and J. J. O'Rourke, eds., *The Catacombs and the Colosseum: The Roman Empire as the Setting of Primitive Christianity.* Valley Forge, PA: Judson, 1971.

———. *Kingdom and Community: The Social World of Early Christianity.* Englewood Cliffs, NJ: Prentice-Hall, 1975.

———. "Shall we marry our enemies?: Sociology and the New Testament." *Interpretation* 36 (1982) 256–65.

Gamber, Klaus. *Domus Ecclesiae: Die ältesten Kirchenbauten Aquilejas sowie im Alpen- und Donaugebiet bis zum Beginn des 5. Jahrhunderts liturgiegeschichtliche Untersucht.* Regensburg: Pustet, 1968.

———. "Die frühchristliche Hauskirche nach *Didascalia apostolorum* II. 57.1–58.6." *Studia Patristica* 10 (1970) 337–44.

Gamble, Harry, Jr. *The Textual History of the Letter to the Romans: A Study in Textual and Literary Criticism.* Grand Rapids: Eerdmans, 1977.

Geanakoplos, Deno J. "Church Building and 'Caesaropapism,' A.D. 312–565." *GRBS* 7 (1966) 167–86.

Georgi, Dieter. *Die Gegner des Paulus in 2. Korintherbrief: Studien zur religiösen Propaganda in der Spätantike.* Wissenschaftliche Monographien zum Alten und Neuen Testament 11. Neukirchen-Vluyn: Neukirchener Verlag, 1964.

von Gerkan, A. "Zur Hauskirche von Dura-Europos." In *Mullus: Festschrift*

Theodore Klauser. RAC, Ergänzungsband I. Münster-Westfalen: Aschendorff, 1964.

Gilliard, Frank D. "The Social Origins of Bishops in the Fourth Century." Ph.D. Thesis, University of California at Berkeley, 1966.

Gilmore Eaves, Ffiona. "Annulling a Myth: A Reassessment of the Earlier Phases of the Eufrasian Basilica at Porec_, and the Evidence for *Domus Ecclesiae.*" Ph.D. diss., University of Nottingham, 1993.

Goguel, Maurice. *Jesus et les origines du Christianisme*. Pt. III: *L'Église primitive*. Paris: Payot, 1947. Eng. trans.: *The Primitive Church*. Translated by H. C. Snape. London: George Allen and Unwin, 1964.

Goldstein, Michael S. "The Nature and Setting of the Ritual Meal." Paper presented at the Annual Meeting of the Society of Biblical Literature, New York, NY, 1979.

Goodenough, Erwin R. *Jewish Symbols in the Graeco-Roman Period.* Bollingen Series 37. 13 vols. New York: Pantheon Books, 1952–65.

Goodenough, E. R., and A. T. Kraabel. "Paul and the Hellenization of Christianity." In J. Neusner, ed., *Religions in Antiquity: Studies in Memory of E. R. Goodenough*. Leiden: E. J. Brill, 1968.

Goppelt, Leonhard. *Die apostolische und nachapostolische Zeit*. Göttingen: Vandenhoeck & Ruprecht, 1962. Eng. trans.: *Apostolic and Post-Apostolic Times*. Translated by R. A. Guelich. London: A. & C. Black, 1970.

Gordon, R. L. "Franz Cumont and the Doctrines of Mithraism." In J. Hinnels, ed., *Mithraic Studies,* 1. 215–48. Manchester: Manchester University Press, 1975.

———. "Mithraism and Roman Society: Social Factors in the Explanation of Change in the Roman Empire." *Religion* 2 (1972) 92–121.

———. "The Sacred Geography of a Mithraeum: The Example of Sette Sfere." *Journal of Mithraic Studies* 1 (1976) 119–65.

———. "Mithraism since Franz Cumont." *ANRW* 2.17.2 (1979).

Gough, Michael. *The Early Christians*. Ancient Peoples and Places 19. New York: Frederick A. Praeger, 1961.

Gounaris, G. *To Balneio kai ta Boreia prosktismata tou Oktagonou ton Philippon*. Thessalonika: Society for Macedonian Studies, 1987.

Grabar, Andre. *Early Christian Art: A.D. 200–395, From the Rise of Christianity to the Death of Theodosius*. Translated by S. Gilbert and J. Emmons. New York: Odyssey, 1968.

Graham, J. W. "Notes on Houses and Housing-Districts at Abdera and Himera." *AJA* 76 (1972) 295–309.

Grant, Robert M. *Augustus to Constantine: The Thrust of the Christian Movement into the Roman World*. New York: Macmillan, 1970.

———. *Early Christianity and Society*. New York: Harper & Row, 1977.

———. "Eusebius H.E. VIII: Another Suggestion." *VC* 22 (1968) 16–18.

———. "The Social Setting of Second Century Christianity." In E. P. Sanders, ed., *Jewish and Christian Self-Definition*. Vol. 1: *The Shaping of Christianity in the Second and Third Centuries*. Philadelphia: Fortress, 1980.

———. "Temples, Churches and Endowments." In *Early Christianity and Society*. New York: Harper & Row, 1977.

Green, C. J. S. "The Significance of Plaster Burials for the Recognition of Christian Cemeteries." In R. Reece, ed., *Burial in the Roman World*, 46–57. London: CBA, 1977.

Green, Michael. *Evangelism in the Early Church*. Grand Rapids: Eerdmans, 1970.

Groh, David. "The Ostian Mithraeum." In *Mithraism in Ostia: Mystery Religion and Christianity in the Ancient Port of Rome*. Garrett Theological Studies 1. Evanston, IL: Northwestern University Press, 1967.

Gülzow, Hennecke. "Kallist von Rom: Ein Beitrag zur Soziologie der römischen Gemeinde." *ZNW* 58 (1967) 102–21.

Guidobaldi, Federico. *San Clemente: Gli Edifici Romani, La Basilica Paleocristiana, e le Fasi Altomedievali*. San Clemente Miscellany IV, 1. Rome: Collegio San Clemente, 1992.

———. "Il complesso archeologico di S. Clemente: Risultati degli scavi più recenti e riesame dei resti architettonici." In L. Boyle, E. Kane, and F. Guidobaldi, eds., *Art and Archaeology*, 215–309. San Clemente Miscellany 2. Rome: Collegio San Clemente, 1978.

Guterman, Simeon L. *Religious Toleration and Persecution in Ancient Rome*. London: Aiglon, 1951.

Gutmann, Joseph, ed. *Ancient Synagogues: The State of Research*. Brown Judaic Studies 23. Chico, CA: Scholars Press, 1981.

———, ed. *The Dura-Europos Synagogue: A Re-Evaluation, 1932–1972*. Religion and the Arts 1. Missoula, MT: Scholars Press, 1973.

———, ed. *The Synagogue: Studies in Origins, Archaeology and Architecture*. New York: KTAV, 1975.

Hahn, Ferdinand. *The Worship of the Early Church*. Translated by D. E. Green. Philadelphia: Fortress, 1973.

Hanfmann, G. M. A. "Excavations at Sardis, Lydia: Yearly Reports." BASOR 170 (1963) 38ff.; 174 (1964) 30ff.; 177 (1965) 17ff.; 182 (1966) 34ff.; 187 (1967) 9ff., 60ff.; 191 (1968) 26ff.; 199 (1970) 45ff.; 206 (1972) 20ff.

———. *Letters from Sardis*. Cambridge, MA: Harvard University Press, 1972.

Hanson, R. P. C. "Transformation of Pagan Temples into Churches in the Early Christian Centuries." *JSS* 23 (1978) 257–67.

Harnack, Adolf. *Die Mission und Ausbreitung des Christentums in den ersten drei Jahrhunderten*. 2d ed., Leipzig: J. C. Hinrichs, 1906. 4th ed., Leipzig: J. C. Hinrichs, 1924. Eng. trans. (from the second German edition): *The Mission and Expansion of Christianity in the First Three Centuries*. Translated by J. Moffatt. London: Williams & Norgate, 1908.

Harnack, Adolf. *Marcion: Das Evangelium vom Fremden Gott*. 2d ed. TU 45. Leipzig; J. C. Hinrichs, 1924.

Hengel, Martin. *Judaism and Hellenism: Studies in Their Encounter in Palestine during the Early Hellenistic Period*. Translated by J. Bowden. 2 vols. Philadelphia: Fortress, 1974.

———. *Property and Riches in the Early Church*. Translated by J. Bowden. Philadelphia: Fortress, 1974.

———. "Proseuche und Synagoge: Judische Gemeinde, Gotteshaus, und Gottesdienst in der Diaspora und in Palastina." In J. Gutmann, ed., *The Synagogue: Studies in Origins, Archaeology, and Architecture*. New York: KTAV, 1975.

———. "Die Synagogeninschrift von Stobi." *ZNW* 57 (1966) 145–83. Reprinted in J. Gutmann, ed., *The Synagogue: Studies in Origins, Archaeology, and Architecture*. New York: KTAV, 1975.

Henig, Martin. *Religion in Roman Britain*. London: Batsford, 1984.

Herbig, Rinehard. *Neue Beobachtungen am Fries der Mysterienvilla in Pompeji*. Deutschen Beiträge zur Altertumswissenschaft 9. Berlin: Akademie Verlag, 1958.

Hinnels, John R., ed. *Mithraic Studies: Papers Presented at the First International Conference for Mithraic Studies, 1971*. 2 vols. Manchester: Manchester University Press, 1975.

Hinson, E. Glenn. *The Evangelization of the Roman Empire: Identity and Adaptability*. Macon, GA: Mercer University Press, 1981.

Hock, Ronald F. "Paul's Tentmaking and the Problem of His Social Class." *JBL* 97 (1978) 555–64.
———. *The Social Context of Paul's Ministry: Tentmaking and Apostleship.* Philadelphia: Fortress, 1980.
Holladay, Carl R. *Theios Aner in Hellenistic Judaism.* SBLDS. Missoula, MT: Scholars Press, 1977.
Hopkins, Clark, and Comte R. du Mesnil du Buisson. "La Synagogue de Doura-Europos." *Comptes Rendus de l'Académie des Inscriptions et Belles-Lettres* (1933) 243–54.
Hopkins, Clark. *The Discovery of Dura-Europos.* New Haven: Yale University Press, 1984.
Horst, Pieter Willem van der. "The Jews of Ancient Crete." In *Essays on the Jewish World of Early Christianity,* 148–65. Göttingen: Vandenhoeck & Ruprecht, 1990.
———. "The Samaritan Diaspora in Antiquity." In *Essays on the Jewish World of Early Christianity*, 136–47.
———. *Ancient Jewish Epitaphs: An Introductory Survey.* Kampen: Kok-Pharos, 1991.
Hurd, John C. "Pauline Chronology and Pauline Theology." In W. R. Farmer, C. F. D. Moule, and R. R. Niebuhr, eds., *Christian History and Interpretation: Studies Presented to John Knox.* Cambridge: Cambridge University Press, 1967.
Huskinson, J. "Some Pagan Mythological Figures and their Significance in Early Christian Art," *PBSR* 42 (1974) 68–97.
Huttmann, Maude A. *The Establishment of Christianity and the Proscription of Paganism.* New York: Columbia University Press, 1914.
Jäggi, C. "Aspekte der städtebaulichen Entwicklung Aquileias in frühchristlicher Zeit," *JAC* 33 (1990) 158–96.
Jarry, J. "L'Ambon dans la liturgie primitive de l'église." *Syria* 40 (1963) 148–61.
Jeremias, Joachim. *The Eucharistic Words of Jesus.* 3d ed. Translated by N. Perrin. London: SCM, 1966.
———. *Jerusalem in the Time of Jesus: An Investigation into Economic and Social Conditions during the New Testament Period.* Translated by F. H. and C. H. Cave. Philadelphia: Fortress, 1975.
Johnson, Sherman E. "Asia Minor and Early Christianity." In J. Neusner, eds., *Christianity, Judaism, and other Greco-Roman Cults: Studies in Honor of Morton Smith at Sixty.* 3 vols. Leiden: E. J. Brill, 1975.

———. "Christianity in Sardis." In A. Wikgren, ed., *Early Christian Origins: Studies in Honor of H. R. Willoughby*. Chicago: University of Chicago Press, 1961.

Jones, Arnold Hugh Martin. *The Cities of the Eastern Roman Provinces*. 2d ed. Oxford: Clarendon, 1971.

———. *Constantine and the Conversion of Europe*. New York: Macmillan, 1948. Reprint, Toronto: Toronto University Press, 1978.

———. *The Later Roman Empire 284–602: A Social, Economic, and Administrative Survey*. 2 vols. Norman, OK: University of Oklahoma Press, 1964.

Judge, Edwin A. "The Early Christians as a Scholastic Community." *Journal of Religious History* 1 (1960–61) 4–15, 125–37.

———. *Social Patterns of Christian Groups in the First Century*. London: Tyndale, 1960.

Judge, E. A., and S. R. Pickering. "Papyrus Documentation of Church and Community in Egypt to the Mid-Fourth Century." *JAC* 20 (1977) 47–71.

Jungmann, Josef A. *The Early Liturgy to the Time of Gregory the Great*. Notre Dame, IN: Notre Dame University Press, 1959.

Junyent, Eduardo. "La maison romaine du titre de Sainte Anastasie." *RivAC* 7 (1930) 91–106.

———. "Nuove indagini sotto la basilica primitiva di S. Clemente." *RivAC* 15 (1938) 147–59.

———. "La primitiva basilica di S. Clemente e le costruzione antiche circostanti." *RivAC* 5 (1928) 231–78.

———. *Il titolo di S. Clemente in Roma*. Studi di antichità cristiana 6. Rome: Pontificio Istituto di archeologia cristiana, 1932.

Juster, J. *Les Juifs dans l'Empire romain: leur condition juridique, economique, et sociale*. 2 vols. Paris: Geuthner, 1914.

Kähler, Heinz. *Die spätantiken Bauten unter dem Dom von Aquileia und ihre Stellung innerhalb der Geschichte des frühchristlichen Kirchenbaues*. Saarbrücken: Universität des Saarlandes, 1957.

Kane, J. P. "The Mithraic Cult Meal in its Greek and Roman Environment." In J. Hinnels, ed., *Mithraic Studies*, 2. 313–51. Manchester: Manchester University Press, 1975.

Kastelic, Joze. "Lo Stile e il concetto dei Mosaici della bisilica Eufrasiana a Parenzo." *Atti VI CIAC (1962)*. Vatican City: Pontificio Istituto di archeologia cristiana, 1965.

Kautsky, Karl. *Foundations of Christianity, A Study in Christian Origins*. Translated from the 13th German ed. New York: Monthly Review, 1972.

Keck, Leander E. "On the Ethos of the Early Christians." *JAAR* 42 (1974) 435–52.

Kelly, J. N. D. *Jerome: His Life, Writings, and Controversies*. San Francisco: Harper & Row, 1975.

Kirsch, J. P. *Die römische Titelkirchen im Altertum*. Paderborn: Schöningh, 1918.

Kittel, Gerhard. "Der kleinasiatische Judentum in der hellenistisch-römische Zeit." *TLZ* 69 (1944) 16–30.

Kitzinger, Ernst. "A Survey of the Early Christian Town of Stobi." *DOP* 3 (1946) 83–161.

Klauck, Hans-Josef. *Hausgemeinde und Hauskirche im frühen Christentum*. Stuttgart: Katholisches Bibelwerk, 1981.

Klauser, Theodore. "Taufet in lebendigem Wasser! Zum religions- und kulturgeschichtlichen Verständnis von Didache 7.1–3." *Pisciculi, Festschrift für Franz Joseph Dölger*. Münster-Westfalen: Aschendorff, 1939.

Klein, S. "Das Fremdhaus der Synagoge." *Monatschrift für Geschichte und Wissenschaft des Judentums* 77 (1932–33) 545–57, 603–4.

Klijn, A. F. J. "An Ancient Syriac Baptismal Liturgy in the Syriac Acta of John." In *Charis kai Sophia, Festschrift für Karl Heinrich Rengstorf*. Leiden: E. J. Brill, 1964.

Koester, Helmut. "GNOMAI DIAPHORAI: The Origin and Nature of Diversification in the History of Early Christianity." In J. M. Robinson and H. Koester, eds. *Trajectories through Early Christianity*. Philadelphia: Fortress, 1971.

Kohl, H., and C. Watzinger. *Antike Synagogen in Galiläa*. Wissenschaftliche Veröffentlichung der deutschen Orientgesellschaft 29. Leipzig: J. C. Hinrichs, 1916.

Korschorke, Klaus. "Gnostic Instructions on the Organization of the Congregation: The Tractate Interpretation of Knowledge from CG XI." In B. Layton, ed., *The Re-Discovery of Gnosticism: Proceedings of the International Conference for the Study of Gnosticism at Yale University (1978)*, vol. 2. Leiden: E. J. Brill, 1981.

Kraabel, Alf Thomas. "The Diaspora Synagogue: Archaeological and Epigraphic Evidence since Sukenik." *ANRW* 2.19.1 (1979) 488–510.

———. "Judaism in Western Asia Minor under the Roman Empire with a preliminary study of the Jewish Community at Sardis, Lydia." Th.D. Thesis, Harvard University, 1968.

———. "Melito the Bishop and the Synagogue at Sardis: Text and Context." In D. G. Mitten et al., eds., *Studies Presented to G. M. A. Hanfmann*. Fogg Art Museum Monographs in Art and Archaeology 2. Cambridge, MA: Harvard University Press, 1971.

———. "The Social Systems of Six Diaspora Synagogues." In J. Gutmann, ed. *Ancient Synagogues: The State of Research*. Brown Judaic Studies 23. Chico, CA: Scholars Press, 1981.

———. "Synagogues, Ancient." *New Catholic Encyclopedia* (Suppl., 1974) 16. 436–39.

———. "*Hypsistos* and the Synagogue at Sardis." *GRBS* 10 (1969) 81–94.

———. "The Disappearance of the 'Godfearers.'" *Numen* 28 (1981) 113–26.

Kraabel, A. T., and R. W. MacKinnon. "The Godfearers — A Literary and Theological Invention." *BAR* 12 (1986) 46–53, 64.

Kraeling, Carl H. *The Synagogue.* The Excavations at Dura-Europos. Final Report 8.1. New Haven: Yale University Press, 1956.

———. *The Christian Building*. Excavations at Dura-Europos. Final Report 8.2. New Haven: Dura-Europos Publications, 1967.

Krauss, S. *Synagogale Altertümer*. Berlin: Akademie Verlag, 1922.

Krautheimer, Richard. "The Beginnings of Early Christian Architecture." *Review of Religion* 3 (1939) 144–59. Reprinted in *Studies in Early Christian, Medieval, and Renaissance Architecture*. Leiden: E. J. Brill, 1972.

———. "The Constantinian Basilica." *DOP* 21 (1967) 117–40.

———. *Corpus Basilicarum Christianarum Romae*. 5 vols. Vatican City: Pontifical Gregorian Institute, 1939–56.

———. *Early Christian and Byzantine Architecture*. 3d ed. Pelican History of Art. New York: Penguin, 1979.

Laeuchli, Samuel. *Mithraism in Ostia: Mystery Religion and Christianity in the Ancient Port of Rome*. Garrett Theological Studies 1. Evanston, IL: Northwestern University Press, 1967.

———. "Urban Mithraism." *BA* 31 (1968) 71–78.

Lake, Kirsopp, and Frederick John Foakes Jackson. *The Beginnings of Christianity*. 5 vols. London: Routledge & Kegan Paul, 1922–33.

Lampe, G. W. H. *The Seal of the Spirit*. 2d ed. London: SPCK, 1967.

Lang, S. "A Few Suggestions toward a new solution of the origin of the Early Christian Basilica." *RivAC* 30 (1954) 189–208.

von Lange, K. *Haus und Halle*. Leipzig: J. C. Hinrichs, 1885.

Lanzione, F. "I titoli presbiteriali di Roma antica nella storia e nella leggenda." *RivAC* 2 (1925) 195–257.

La Piana, George. "Foreign Groups in Rome during the First Centuries of the Empire." *HTR* 20 (1927) 183–403.

Lassus, Jean. "Les edifices du culte autour de la basilique." *Atti VI CIAC (1962)*. Vatican City: Pontificio Istituto di archeologia cristiana, 1965.

———. *Sanctuaires chrétiens de Syrie*. Paris: P. Geuthner, 1947.

Laum, B. *Stiftungen in der griechischen und römischen Antike*. 2 vols. Berlin: Akademie Verlag, 1914.

Lawlor, Hugh Jackson. *Eusebiana: Essays on the Ecclesiastical History of Eusebius Pamphilii, ca. 264–349, Bishop of Caesarea*. Oxford: Clarendon, 1912.

Lawlor, H. J., and J. E. L. Oulton. *Eusebius: The Ecclesiastical History and the Martyrs of Palestine*. 2 vols. London: SPCK, 1954.

Lebreton, Jules, and Jacques Zeiller. *L'Église Primitive*. Part 1 of *Histoire de l'Église*. Edited by A. Fliche and V. Martin. Paris: Bloud & Gay, 1934ff. Eng. trans.: *A History of the Early Church*. Translated by E. C. Messenger. New York: Collier Books, 1962. 4 vols.

Leclercq, Henri. "Basilique." In F. Cabrol and H. Leclercq, eds., *Dictionaire du archeologie chrétienne et la liturgie,* 2. cols. col. 525–602. Paris: Letouzey et Ané, 1907–51.

Lee, Clarency L. "Social Unrest and Primitive Christianity." In S. Benko and J. J. O'Rourke, eds., *The Catacombs and the Colosseum: The Roman World as the Setting for Early Christianity*. Valley Forge, PA: Judson, 1971.

Lemaire, R. *L'Origine de la basilique Latine*. Brussels: Lamertin, 1911.

Lentz, W. "Some Peculiarities not hitherto fully understood of 'Roman' - Mithraic Sanctuaries and Representations." In J. Hinnels, ed., *Mithraic Studies*, 2. 358–77. Manchester: Manchester University Press, 1975.

Leon, Harry Joshua. *The Jews of Ancient Rome*. Philadelphia: Jewish Publication Society, 1960.

Levick, Barbara. *Roman Colonies in Southern Asia Minor*. Oxford: Clarendon, 1967.

Lietzmann, Hans. *An die Römer*. 4th ed. HNT 8. Tübingen: Mohr (Siebeck), 1933.

———. *Messe und Herrenmahl*. Bonn: R. Habelt, 1926. Eng. trans.: *Mass and Lord's Supper*. Translated and revised by D. H. G. Reese. Leiden: E. J. Brill, 1953–72.

———. "Notizen: Ein Synagogen-Inschrift aus Jerusalem." *ZNW* 20 (1921) 171–73.

———. "Notizen: Die Synagogeninschrift in Stobi/Ausgrabungen in Doura-Europos." *ZNW* 32 (1933) 93–95.

Lifshitz, Baruch. *Donateurs et Fondateurs dans les Synagogues juives*. Cahiers de la Revue Biblique 7. Paris: J. Gabalda, 1967.

Liversidge, J. and M. Weatherhead. "The Christian Paintings." In G. W. Meates, eds., *The Roman Villa at Lullingstone,* 2.11–40. Chichester: Phillimore, 1987.

Lloyd, J. A., R. Reece, and J. M. Reynolds. *Excavations at Sidi Khrebish, Benghazi (Berenice)*. Supplements to Libya Antiqua 5. 2 vols. Tripoli: Libya Antiqua, 1977, 1979.

Lofreda, S. "The Late Chronology of the Synagogue at Capernaum." *IEJ* 23 (1973) 37–42.

Lohse, Eduard. *Colossians and Philemon*. Translated by W. R. Poehlmann and R. J. Karris. Hermeneia. Philadelphia: Fortress, 1971.

Lowrie, Walter. *Art in the Early Church*. Rev. ed. New York: Pantheon, 1947.

Lüderitz, G. *Corpus jüdischer Zeugnisse aus der Cyrenaika*. Wiesbaden: Reichert, 1983.

MacMullen, Ramsay. *Paganism in the Roman Empire*. New Haven: Yale University Press, 1981.

———. "The Power of Bishops Outside the Church." *The Role of the Christian Bishop in Ancient Socicty*. Center for Hermeneutical Studies, Thirty-fifth Colloquy, 1979. Berkeley, CA: Graduate Theological Union, 1980.

———. *Roman Social Relations, 50 B.C. to A.D. 284*. New Haven: Yale University Press, 1974.

———. *Christianizing the Roman Empire*. New Haven: Yale University Press, 1984.

McKay, A. G. *Houses, Villas, and Palaces in the Roman World*. London: Thames & Hudson, 1975.

Malherbe, Abraham J. "The Inhospitality of Diotrophes." In W. A. Meeks and J. Jervell, eds., *God's Christ and His People: Festschrift for Nils Alstrup Dahl*. Oslo: Universitetsforlaget, 1977. Reprinted as "Hospitality and Inhospitality in the Church" in *Social Aspects of Early Christianity*, 2d ed. Philadelphia: Fortress, 1983.

———. *Social Aspects of Early Christianity*. 2d ed. Philadelphia: Fortress, 1983.

Marcillet-Jaubert, Jean. *Les Inscriptions d'Altava*. Publications des Annales de la Faculté des lettres, Aix-en-Provence, n.s. 65. Gap: Éditions Ophrys, 1969.

Markus, R. A. "The Problem of Self-Definition: From Sect to Church." In E. P. Sanders, ed., *Jewish and Christian Self-Definition*, vol. 1: *The Shaping of Christiantity in the Second and Third Centuries*, 1–15. Philadelphia: Fortress, 1980.

Marrou, Henri Irenee. "La basilique chrétienne d'Hippone d'après le résultat des dernièrs fouilles." *Revue des Études Augustiniennes* 6 (1960) 109–54.

Marucchi, O. "La recente scoperte del Duomo di Parenzo." *NBAC* 2 (1896) 9–10.

———. "Scoperta (indagini) nella basilica dei SS. Giovani e Paolo." *NBAC* 7 (1901) 175–76, 226; 15 (1909) 144–49; 21 (1915) 62–63.

———. "Scoperta dell'antica basilica di S. Crisogono." *NBAC* 14 (1908) 149–59, 259–65.

———. "L'antica basilica di S. Crisogono." *NBAC* 17 (1911) 5–15.

Matthews, John B. "Hospitality and the New Testament Church: An Historical and Exegetical Study." Th.D. Thesis, Princeton Theological Seminary, 1965. Ann Arbor, MI: University Microfilms, 1966.

Mazur, Belle D. *Studies on Jewry in Greece*. Athens: Hestia Printing Office, 1935.

Meates, G. W. "Lullingstone Park, Yearly Field Reports." *Archaeologia Cantiana* 63 (1950), 1ff.; 64 (1951), 160; 65 (1952), xlvii, 26ff.; 66 (1953), xlii, 15ff.; 67 (1954), xliv, 206ff.; 69 (1955), xlv, 201ff.; 70 (1956), 249; 71 (1957), xlv; 72 (1958), xlviii seq.; 73 (1959), xlviii; 76 (1961), xlix seq.

———. *The Lullingstone Roman Villa*. London: William Heinemann, 1955.

———. "Lullingstone Roman Villa." In R. L. S. Bruce-Mitford, ed., *Recent Archaeological Excavations in Britain*. London: Routledge & Kegan Paul, 1956.

———. *Lullingstone Roman Villa*. Department of the Environment Guide. London: HMSO, 1963.

———. *The Roman Villa at Lullingstone*. 2 vols. Chichester: Phillimore, 1979, 1986.

Meeks, Wayne A. "The Image of the Androgyne: Some Uses of a Symbol in Earliest Christianity." *History of Religions* 13 (1974) 165–208.

———. “The Social Context of Pauline Theology.” *Interpretation* 36 (1982) 266–77.

———. *The First Urban Christians: The Social World of the Apostle Paul.* New Haven: Yale University Press, 1983.

Meiggs, Russell. *Roman Ostia.* 2d ed. Oxford: Clarendon, 1971.

Menis, G. C. *La Basilica Paleocristiana nelle diocesi settentrionali della metropoli d'Aquileia.* Studi di antichita cristiana 24. Rome: Pontificio Istituto di archeologia cristiana, 1958.

Mesnard, M. *La basilique de Saint Chrysogone à Rome.* Studi di antichita cristiana 9. Rome: Pontificio Istituto di archeologia cristiana, 1935.

Merkelbach, Reinhold. *Mithras.* Königstein/Ts: Verlag Anton Hain, 1984.

Meyers, Eric M. “Ancient Synagogues in Galilee: Their Religious and Cultural Setting.” *BA* 43 (1980) 97–108.

———. “Synagogue, Architecture.” In G. Buttrick et al., eds., *Interpreter's Dictionary of the Bible*, Supplement: 842–45. Nashville, TN: Abingdon, 1964, 1976.

———. “The Niche in the Synagogue at Dura-Europos.” *BA* 47 (1984) 174.

Meyers, E. M., and J. F. Strange. *Archaeology, the Rabbis, and Early Christianity.* Nashville, TN: Abingdon, 1981.

Meyers, E. M., A. T. Kraabel, and J. F. Strange. “Archaeology and Rabbinic Tradition at Khirbet Shema^c, 1970 and 1971 Campaigns.” *BA* 35 (1972) 2–31.

———. *Ancient Synagogue Excavations at Khirbet Shema^c, Israel (1970–72).* Durham, NC: Duke University Press, 1976.

Millar, Fergus. “Paul of Samosata, Zenobia, and Aurelian: The Church, Local Culture and Political Allegiance in the Third Century.” *JRS* 61 (1971) 126–34.

Mirabella Roberti, Mario. “Considerazione sulle aule teodoriane di Aquileia.” *Studi aquileiisi offerti à Giovanni Brusin, il 7 ottobre, 1953.* Padua: Tipographia Antoniana, 1953.

———. “Notizie di Parenzo.” *Atti e memorie della Società istr. di archeologia e storia patr.* 51–52 (1942) 289–93.

Moe, Dean L. “Cross and Menorah.” *Archaeology* 30 (1977) 148–57.

Molajoli, B. *La Basilica Eufrasiana di Parenzo.* 2d ed. Padua, 1943.

Morris, R. *Churches in the Landscape.* London: Dent, 1989.

Müller, V. “The Roman Basilica.” *AJA* 61 (1937) 250–61.

Munck, Johannes. *Paul and the Salvation of Mankind.* Translated by F. Clarke. London: SCM, 1959.

Muñoz, R. "Chiesa di S. Martino ai Monti." *NBAC* 17 (1911) 109–10.

Murray, Robert. "The Exhortation to Candidates for Ascetical Vows at Baptism in the Ancient Syriac Church." *NTS* 21 (1974) 59–80.

Musurillo, Herbert. "Early Christian Economy: A Reconsideration of P. Amherst 3(a) (Wilken, *Chrest.* 126)." *Chronique d'Égypte* 31 (1956) 124–34.

Nassivera, J. C. "Ancient Temples to Pagan Goddesses and Early Churches to the Virgin in the City of Rome." *Échos du monde classique* 20 (1976) 41–54.

Neuenzeit, Paul. *Das Herrenmahl: Studien zur paulinischen Eucharistie auffassung.* Studien zum Alten und Neuen Testament 1. Munich: Kösel, 1960.

Nilsson, Martin P. *Geschichte der griechischen Religion.* 3d ed. 2 vols. Munich: C. H. Beck, 1955–56.

Nock, Arthur Darby. *Conversion: The Old and the New in Religion from Alexander the Great to Augustine of Hippo.* London: Oxford University Press, 1933.

———. *Early Gentile Christianity in its Hellenistic Background.* New York: Harper, 1964.

———. *Essays on Religion in the Ancient World.* Edited by Z. Stewart. Oxford: Clarendon, 1972 (repr. 1986). 2 vols.

Obermann, Julian. "Inscribed Tiles from the Dura-Europos Synagogue." *Berytus* 7 (1942) 89–138.

Orfali, G. *Capharnaum et ses ruines.* Paris: Boccard, 1922.

Orr, D. G. "Roman Domestic Religion: The Evidence of Household Shrines." *ANRW* 2.16.2 (1978) 1559–91.

Packer, James E. "Housing and Population in Imperial Ostia and Rome." *JRS* 57 (1967) 80–95.

Painter, K. S. "Christianity in Roman Britain: Recent Finds, 1962–1969." *Atti VIII CIAC (1969)*, 373–75. Vatican City: Pontificio Istituto de archeologia cristiana, 1972.

———. "Villas and Christianity in Roman Britain." *British Museum Quarterly* 35 (1971) 156–75.

———. "The Roman Site of Hinton St. Mary, Dorset." *British Museum Quarterly* 32 (1968) 15–31.

de Palol, Pedro. "Los monumentos de Hispania en la arqueologia paleocristiana." *Atti VIII CIAC (1969).* Vatican City: Pontificio Istituto di archeologia cristiana, 1972.

de Palol, P., and M. Sotomayor. "Excavationes en la villa de Bruñel (Quesada) de la provincia de Jaen." *Atti VIII CIAC (1969)*. Vatican City: Pontificio Istituto di archeologia cristiana, 1972.

Pavolini, Carlo. "Ostia (Roma): Saggi lungo la via Severiana." *Notizie degli Scavi di Antichit*à (Atti della Accademica Nazionale de Lincei). series 8, 35 (1981) 115–43.

Pelekanidis, Stylianou. "Excavations in Philippi," *Balkan Studies* 8 (1967) 123–26.

———. "*Palaiochristianikos taphos en Philippois*." In *Meletes palaiochristianikes kai Byzantines archaiologias*. Thessaloniki: Institute for Balkan Studies, 1977.

———. "*Anaskaphe Oktagonou Philippon*." In *Praktika Archaiologikes Etaireias* (1978) 69–73

———. "Kultprobleme in Apostel Paulus-Oktagon von Philippi im Zusammenhang mit einem ältern Heroenkult," *Atti IX CIAC* (Rome, 1978) 2. 393–99.

———. *Hoi Philippoi kai ta christianika mnemeia tous, Aphieroma Tessarokontaeteridias Etaireias Makedonikon Spoudon*. Thessaloniki: Society for Macedonian Studies, 1980.

Penella, R. J. "Alexander Severus 43.6–7: Two Emperors and Christ." *VC* 31 (1977) 229–30.

Percival, John. *The Roman Villa: An Historical Introduction*. London: Batsford, 1976.

Perkins, Ann. *The Art of Dura-Europos*. Oxford: Clarendon, 1973.

Peterson, J. M. "House Churches in Rome." *VC* 23 (1969) 264–72.

Piccottini, Gernot. *Mithrastempel von Virunum*. Klagenfurt: Geschichtsvereins für Kärnten, 1994.

Poland, Franz. *Geschichte der griechischen Vereinswesen*. Leipzig: Teubner, 1909.

Prandi, Adriano. "Scoperte e restauri nella basilica delimontana dei SS. Giovanni e Paolo," *Atti I CIAC (1950)*. Rome: Pontificio Istituto di archeologia cristiana, 1952.

———. *Il complesso monumentale della basilica celimontana del SS. Giovanni e Paolo*. Vatican City: Pontificio Istituto di archeologia cristiana, 1953.

Quasten, Johannes. "The Blessing of the Baptismal Font in the Syrian Rite of the Fourth Century." *Theological Studies* 7 (1946) 309–13.

———. *Patrology*. 3 vols. Utrecht: Spectrum Publishers, 1950–62.

Raeder, Joachim. *Priene: Funde aus einer griechischen Stadt im Berliner Antikmuseum*. Berlin: Gebr. Mann Verlag, 1984.

Ramsay, W. M. *Cities and Bishoprics of Phrygia*. 2 vols. Oxford: B. Blackwell, 1895, 1897.

———. *The Cities of St. Paul: Their Influence on his Life and Thought*. London: Hodder & Stoughton, 1907.

———. "Deux jours in Phrygie." *Revue des Études anciennes* 3 (1901) 272.

———. "A Laodicean Bishop." *The Expositor* (1908) 409–17, 546–53.

———. *Luke the Physican*. London: Hodder & Stoughton, 1908.

———. "Nouvelles remarques sur les textes d'Acmonie." *Revue des Études anciennes* 6 (1902) 270.

Rea, J. R. "P. Oxy. XXXIII.2673.22: ΠΥΛΗΝ to ῾ΥΛΗΝ!" *ZPE* 35 (1979) 128.

Reece, R. "The Roman Coins." In G. W. Meates, ed., *The Roman Villa at Lullingstone,* 2. 48–51. Chichester: Phillimore, 1987.

Reinach, S. "Synagogue juive à Phocée." *BCH* 10 (1886) 327–35.

Reinach, Theodore. "L'inscription de Theodotos." *REJ* 70 (1920), 46–56.

Reitzenstein, Richard. *The Hellenistic Mystery Religions*. Translated by J. E. Steely. Pittsburgh: Pickwick, 1978.

Reynolds, Joyce M., and Robert Tannenbaum. *Jews and Godfearers at Aphrodisias: Greek Inscriptions with Commentary*. Cambridge: Cambridge Philological Society, 1987.

Richardson, Cyril C. *The Christianity of St. Ignatius of Antioch*. New York: Columbia University Press, 1935.

Richmond, I. A. "The Cult of Mithras and its Temple at Carrawburgh." In R. L. S. Bruce-Mitford, ed., *Recent Archeological Excavations in Britain*. 2d ed. London: Routledge & Kegan Paul, 1957.

Richmond, I. A., and J. P. Gilliam. *The Temple of Mithras at Carrawburgh*. Newcastle on Tyne: Newcastle, 1951.

Riddle, D. W. "Early Christian Hospitality: A Factor in the Gospel Transmission." *JBL* 57 (1938) 141–54.

Rivet, A. L. F., ed. *The Roman Villa in Britain*. London: Routledge, 1969.

Robert, J., and L. Robert. "Bulletin épigraphique." *Revue des Études grecques* (listed by year).

Robert, Louis. "Inscriptions grecques de Side." *Revue Philologique* 32 (1958) 15–53.

———. *Nouvelles Inscriptions de Sardes*. Paris: Librairie d'Amérique et d'Orient, 1964.

Robinson, John A. T. *The Body: A Study in Pauline Theology*. Studies in Biblical Theology 5. London: SCM, 1952.

Rodwell, W., ed. *Temples, Churches, and Religion*. British Archeological Reports 77. London: Oxford University Press, 1980.

Rordorf, Willy. "Was wissen wir über die christlichen Gottesdienstraum der vorkonstantinischen Zeit?" *ZNW* 55 (1964) 110–28.

Rostovtzeff, Mikhail I. *Dura-Europos and Its Art*. Oxford: Clarendon, 1943.

Rostovtzeff, M. I., C. B. Welles, F. E. Brown, H. F. Pearson, et al. *The Excavations at Dura-Europos, Preliminary Reports of the First through Ninth Seasons*. 11 vols. New Haven: Yale University Press, 1931–40.

Rostovtzeff, Mikhail I. "Das Mithraeum von Dura." *Mitteilungen des deutschen archäologischen Instituts*. Römische Abteilung 49 (1934) 180–207.

———. *The Social and Economic History of the Roman Empire*. 2d ed. by P. M. Fraser. 2 vols. Oxford: Clarendon, 1957.

———. "Die Synagoge von Dura." *RQ* 42 (1934) 203–18.

Roussel, P. *Les cultes égyptiens à Délos du IIIe au Ier siècle av. J.-C.* Annales de L'Est 3.6. Nancy: Berger-Levrault, 1916.

Rutgers, Leonard V. *The Jews in Late Ancient Rome: Evidence of Cultural Interaction in the Roman Diaspora*. Leiden: Brill, 1995.

de Ste. Croix, G. E. M. "Why were the Early Christians Persecuted?" *Past and Present* 26 (1963) 6–35.

Saller, Richard. *Personal Patronage under the Early Empire*. Cambridge: Cambridge University Press, 1982.

Salway, Peter. *Roman Britain*. Oxford: Clarendon, 1981.

Sampley, J. Paul. *Pauline Partnership in Christ: Christian Community and Committment in the Light of Roman Law*. Philadelphia: Fortress, 1980.

Sanders, E. P., ed. *Jewish and Christian Self-Definition*, vol. 1: *The Shaping of Christianity in the Second and Third Centuries*. Philadelphia: Fortress, 1980.

Sanders, E. P., A. Baumgarten, and A. Mendelson, eds. *Jewish and Christian Self-Definition*, vol. 2: *Aspects of Judaism in the Graeco-Roman Period*. Philadelphia: Fortress, 1981.

Sanders, E. P., and B. F. Meyer, eds. *Jewish and Christian Self-Definiton*, vol. 3: *Self-Definition in the Graeco-Roman World*. Philadelphia: Fortress, 1982.

Schede, Martin. *Die Ruinen von Priene*. 2d ed. Berlin: de Gruyter, 1964.

Schultze, M. V. *Archäologie der altchristlichen Kunst.* Munich: Kaiser, 1895.

Schürer, Emil. *Geschichte der jüdischen Volkes im Zeitalter Jesu Christi.* 3d/4th ed. 3 vols. Paris/Leipzig: J. C. Hinrichs, 1901–11. Eng. trans.: *A History of the Jewish People in the Age of Jesus Christ (175 B.C.–A.D. 135).* Edited and translated by M. Black, G. Vermes, and F. Millar. 2 vols. Edinburgh: T & T Clark, 1973.

Seager, Andrew R. "The Architecture of the Dura and Sardis Synagogues." In J. Gutmann, ed., *The Dura-Europos Synagogue: A Re-appraisal (1932–1972).* Religion and the Arts 1. Missoula, MT: Scholars Press, 1973.

———. "The Building History of the Sardis Synagogue." *AJA* 76 (1972) 425–35.

Seager, A. R., and A. T. Kraabel. "The Synagogue and the Jewish Community." In G. M. A. Hanfmann, ed., *Sardis: from Prehistoric to Roman Times.* Cambridge, MA: Harvard University Press, 1983.

Seager, A. R., A. T. Kraabel, and J. H. Kroll. *The Synagogue at Sardis.* Archaeological Explorations at Sardis 5. Cambridge, MA: Harvard University Press, forthcoming.

Selhorst, H. *Die Plätzanordnung im Gläubigenraum der altchristlichen Kirche.* Münster: Aschendorff, 1931.

Setton, K. M. *Christian Attitudes toward the Emperor in the Fourth Century.* New York: Columbia University Press, 1914.

Sève, Michael. "Chronique des Fouilles: rapports Phillipes," *BCH* 104 (1980) 699–716; 105 (1981) 918–23; 106 (1982) 651–53.

Sève, Michael and P. Weber. "Le Côte Nord du forum de Phillipes," *BCH* 110 (1986) 531–81.

Shanks, Hershel. *Judaism in Stone: The Archeology of Ancient Synagogues.* New York: Harper & Row, 1979.

Sheppard, A. R. R. "Pagan Cults of Angels in Roman Asia Minor," *Talanta* 12–13 (1980–81) 81–102.

Sherwin-White, A. N. *The Letters of Pliny: A Historical and Social Commentary.* Oxford: Clarendon, 1966.

———. "The Persecutions and Roman Law Again." *JTS* n.s. 3 (1952) 199–213. Reprinted with addendum in *The Letters of Pliny: A Historical and Social Commentary.* Oxford: Clarendon, 1966.

———. *The Roman Citizenship.* Oxford: Clarendon, 1939.

Silvagni, S. "Il titolo constantiniano di Equizio." *NBAC* 19 (1913) 167–74.

Smallwood, E. Mary. *The Jews under Roman Rule, from Pompey to Diocletian*. Leiden: Brill, 1976.

Smith, Dennis E. "The Egyptian Cults at Corinth." *HTR* 70 (1977) 201–31.

———. "Forms of Dining Rooms in Greek Sanctuaries." Paper presented at the Annual Meeting of the SBL, New Orleans, LA, 1978.

———. "Social Obligation in the Context of Communal Meals." Th.D. Thesis, Harvard University, 1980.

———. "Meals and Morality in Paul and his World." In K. Richards, ed., *Society of Biblical Literature Seminar Papers, 1981*. Chico, CA: Scholars Press, 1981.

Smith, Jonathan Z. "Fences and Neighbors: The Contours of Early Judaism." In W. S. Green, ed., *Approaches to Ancient Judaism,* vol. 2. BJS 9. Chico, CA: Scholars Press, 1980.

———. "The Social Description of Early Christianity." *RSR* 1 (1975) 19–25.

Snyder, Graydon F. *Ante Pacem: Archaeological Evidence of Church Life before Constantine*. Macon, GA: Mercer University Press, 1985.

Šonje, Ante. "Il complesso della prima basilica nella zona della basilica Eufrasiana a Parenzo." *Atti VI CIAC (1962)*. Vatican City: Pontificio Istituto di archeologia cristiana, 1965.

———. "Contributo alla soluzione della problematica del complesso della basilica Eufrasiana di Parenzo." *Felix Ravenna* 97 (1968) 27–65.

———. "Arheoloska istrazivanja na prodrucju Eufrazijeve bazilike u Poreču." *Jadranski Zbornik* 7 (1969) 249–51.

———. "Sarcofagi paleocristiani dell'Istria." *Atti VIII CIAC (1969)*. Vatican City: Pontificio Istituto di archeologia cristiana, 1972.

———. "I mosaici parietali del complesso architettonico della basilica Eufrasiana a Parenzo." *Atti del centro di ricerche storiche di Rovigno* 12 (1982–83) 65–138.

Sonne, I. "Synagogue." In G. Buttrick et al., eds., *Interpreter's Dictionary of the Bible*. 4. 476–91. Nashville, TN: Abingdon, 1964, 1976.

Sordi, Marta. *Il Cristianesimo e Roma*. Bologna: Licinio Capelli, 1965.

Sordi, M., and M. L. Cavigiolo. "Un'antica 'chiesa domestica' di Roma? (*Il Collegium quod est in domo Sergiae L. F. Paulinnae*)." *Rivista di storia della chiesa in Italia* 25 (1971) 369–74.

Squarciapino, Maria Floriani. "La sinagoga di Ostia." *Bolletino d'Arte* 46 (1961) 326–37.

———. "The Synagogue at Ostia." *Archaeology* 16 (1963) 193–203.

———. "La sinagoga di Ostia: Secondo campagna di scavo." *Atti VI CIAC (1962)*. Vatican City: Pontificio Istituto di archeologia cristiana, 1965.

Stambaugh, John E. "The Functions of Roman Temples." *ANRW* 2.16.1 (1978) 554–607.

———. *The Ancient Roman City*. Baltimore: Johns Hopkins University Press, 1988.

Standaert, Benoit. "L'Évangile de Verité: Critique et Lecture." *NTS* 22 (1975) 243–75.

Strobel, August. "Der Begriff des 'Hauses' in griechischen und römischen Privatrecht." *ZNW* 56 (1965) 91–100.

Sukenik, Eleazar Lipa. *Ancient Synagogues in Palestine and Greece*. London: Oxford University Press, 1934.

———. "The Present State of Ancient Synagogue Studies." *Bulletin of the Louis M. Rabinowitz Fund* 1 (1949) 1–23.

Swift, Emerson H. *Roman Sources of Christian Art*. New York: Columbia University Press, 1951.

Syme, Ronald. *Ammianus and the Historia Augusta*. Cambridge: Cambridge University Press, 1968.

Syria: Publications of an American Archaeological Expedition to Syria in 1899–1900. Edited by R. Garrett, H. C. Butler, W. K. Prentice, and E. Littmann. 4 vols. New York: Columbia University Press, 1903–30.

Syria: Publications of the Princeton University Archaeological Expeditions to Syria in 1904–1905 and 1909. Edited by H. C. Butler, F. A. Norris, E. Littmann, and W. K. Prentice. 8 vols. Leiden: E. J. Brill, 1907–49.

Tabbernee, William. "Montanist Regional Bishops: New Evidence from Ancient Inscriptions." *JECS* 1 (1993) 249–80.

———. *Montanist Inscriptions and Testimonia: Epigraphic Sources Illustrating the History of Montanism*. Macon, GA: Mercer University Press (forthcoming).

Tannenbaum, Robert. "Jews and Godfearers in the Holy City of Aphrodite." *BAR* 12 (1986) 54–57.

Tavano, Sergio. *Aquileia Cristiana*. Udine: Friulane, 1972.

Taylor, Charles. *Christianity in Roman Britain to A.D. 500*. London: Batsford, 1981.

Tchalenko, Georges. *Villages antiques de la Syrie du Nord*. Bibliothèque archeologique et historique de l'institut français d'archéologie de Beyrouth 50. 3 vols. Paris: J. Gabalda, 1953–58.

Terry, Ann. "The Architecture and Architectural Sculpture of the Sixth-Century Eufrasius Cathedral Complex at Porec." Ph.D. Thesis. Urbana-Champagne: University of Illinois, 1984.

———. "The Conservation History of the Mosaic Pavements at the Cathedral Site of Poreč," *Hortus Artium Medievalium* 1 (1995) 176–86.

———. "The *Opus Sectile* in the Eufrasius Cathedral at Poreč." *DOP* 40 (1986) 147–64.

———. "The Sculpture at the Cathedral of Eufrasius in Poreč." *DOP* 42 (1988) 13–64.

Testa, Emmanuele. *I graffiti della casa di S. Pietro*. Studium Biblicum Franciscanum 18. Jerusalem: Studium Biblicum, 1972.

Testini, P. *Archeologia Cristiana: Nozioni generali dalle origini alla fine del sec. VI*. Rome: Desclée e soc., 1958.

Theissen, Gerd. "Legitimation und Lebensunterhalt: Ein Beitrag zur Soziologie urchristlicher Missionäre." *NTS* 21 (1975) 192–221. Reprinted in *The Social Setting of Pauline Christianity: Essays on Corinth*. Translated by J. Schütz. Philadelphia: Fortress, 1982.

———. *Soziologie der Jesusbewegung*. Munich: Kaiser, 1977. Eng. trans.: *Sociology of Early Palestinian Christianity*. Translated by J. Bowden. Philadelphia: Fortress, 1978.

———. "Soziale Integration und sakramentales Handeln: Ein Analyse von 1 Kor. 11:17–34." NT 16 (1974) 179–206. Reprinted in *The Social Setting of Pauline Christianity*.

———. "Soziale Schichtung in der korinthischen Gemeinde: Ein Beitrag zur Soziologie des hellenistischen Urchristentums." *ZNW* 65 (1974) 232–72. Reprinted in *The Social Setting of Pauline Christianity*.

———. "Die Starken und Schwachen in Korinth: Soziologische Analyse eines theologischen Streits." *Evangelische Theologie* 35 (1975) 155–72. Reprinted in *The Social Setting of Pauline Christianity*.

———. "Theoretische Probleme religionssoziologischer Forschung und die Analyse des Urchristentums." *Neue Zeitschrift für Systematische Theologie und Religionsphilosophie* 16 (1974) 35–56.

———. "Wanderradikalismus: Literatursoziologische Aspekte der Überlieferung von Worten Jesu im Urchristentum." *ZTK* 70 (1973) 245–71.

Thomas, J. D. "Chronological Notes on Documentary Papyri." *ZPE* 6 (1970) 177–80.

Todd, M., ed. *Studies in the Romano-British Villa*. Leicester: Leicester University Press, 1978.

Torrey, C. C. "The Beginning of the Dura-Europos Synagogue Inscription." *JQR* 38 (1938) 295–99.

Toynbee, J. M. C. "The Christian Roman Mosaic, Hinton St. Mary, Dorset," *JRS* 54 (1964) 7–14.

———. "The Christian Roman Mosaic, Hinton St. Mary, Dorset." *Proceedings of the Dorset Natural History and Archaeology Society* 85 (1964) 116–21.

Tracey, R. "Jewish Renovation of an amphitheatre," *NDIEC* 4 (1987) 202–9.

Turner, Harold W. *From Temple to Meeting House: The Phenomenology and Theology of Places of Worship.* Religion and Society 16. The Hague: Mouton, 1979.

Urman, Dan and Paul V. M. Flesher, *Ancient Synagogues: Historical Analysis and Archaeological Discovery, 1.* Leiden: E. J. Brill, 1995.

Van der Meer, F., and C. Mohrmann. *Atlas of the Early Christian World.* Translated and edited by M. Hedlund and H. H. Rowley. London: Thomas Nelson, 1966.

Vermaseren, Maarten J. *Corpus inscriptionum et monumentorum Religionis Mithriacae.* 2 vols. The Hague: Martinus Nijhoff, 1956, 1960.

———. *Mithras the Secret God.* Translated by T. and V. Megaw. London: Chatto & Windus, 1963.

———. *Mithraica I: The Mithraeum at S. Maria Capua Vetere.* EPRO. Leiden: E. J. Brill, 1971.

Vermaseren, M. J., and C. C. Van Essen. "The Aventine Mithraeum adjoining the Church of Sta. Prisca." *Antiquity and Survival* 1 (1955) 3–36.

———. *The Excavations in the Mithraeum of the Church of Santa Prisca in Rome.* Leiden: E. J. Brill, 1965.

Vielliard, René. *Recherches sur le origines de la Rome chrétienne, les églises romaines et leur rôle dans l'histoire et la topographie de la ville depuis la fin du monde antique jusqu'à la formation de l'État pontifical.* Màcon: Protat frères, 1941.

———. *Les origines du titre de Saint Martin-aux-Monts à Rome.* Studia di antichita cristiana 4. Rome: Pontificio Istituto di archeologia cristiana, 1931.

Vilela, Albano. *La condition collegiale du prêtres au IIIe siècle.* Theologie historique 14. Paris: Beauchesne, 1971.

Vincent, H., and F. M. Abel. *Emmaus, sa basilique et son histoire.* Paris: E. Leroux, 1932.

Voelkl, Ludwig. "Die konstantinischen Kirchenbauten nach Eusebius." *RivAC* 29 (1953) 60–94.

———. "Die konstantinischen Kirchenbauten nach den literarischen Quellen des Okzidents." *RivAC* 30 (1954) 99–136.

Vogliano, Achille. "La grande Iscrizione Bacchia del Metropolitan Museum, I—Tavole xxvii–xxix." *AJA* 37 (1933) 215–31.

Vogt, Joseph. "Pagans and Christians in the Family of Constantine the Great." In A. Momigliano, ed., *The Conflict of Paganism with Christianity in the Fourth Century*. Oxford: Clarendon, 1963.

Vööbus, Arthur. *Celibacy, a Requirement for Admission to Baptism in the Early Syrian Church*. Stockholm: Estonian Theological Society in Exile, 1951.

———. "Regarding the Background of the Liturgical Relations in the Didache." *VC* 23 (1969) 81–87.

Walters, C. C. *Monastic Archaeology in Egypt*. Warminster: Aris & Phillips, 1974.

Walters, Vivienne J. *The Cult of Mithras in Roman Provinces of Gaul*. EPRO. Leiden: Brill, 1974.

Waltzing, Jean. *Études historique sur les corporations professionalles chez les Romains*. 4 vols. Louvain: Publications universitaires, 1895–1900.

Ward-Perkins, J. B. "Constantine and the Origins of the Christian Basilica." *PBSR* 22 (1954) 69–90.

———. "Memoria, Martyr's Tomb, and Martyr's Church." *JTS* 17 (1966) 20–38.

———. "Recent Work and Problems in Libya." *Atti VIII CIAC (1969)*. Vatican City: Pontificio Istituto di archeologia cristiana, 1972.

Ward-Perkins, J. B., and R. G. Goodchild. "The Christian Antiquities of Tripolitania." *Archaeologia* 95 (1953) 1–84.

Watts, D. *Christians and Pagans in Roman Britain*. London: Routledge, 1991.

Weaver, P. R. C. *Familia Caesaris: A Social Study of the Emperor's Freedmen and Slaves*. Cambridge: Cambridge University Press, 1972.

———. "Social Mobility in the Early Roman Empire: The Evidence of the Imperial Freedmen and Slaves." *Past and Present* 37 (1967) 3–20.

Weber, Winfried. "Antike Kirche im Bereich von Dom und Liebfrauen." In H. Cüppers, ed., *Die Römer in Rheinland-Pfalz*, 632–35. Stuttgart: A. Druckenmüller, 1990.

———. "Die Anfänge des Trierer Dom." *Trierer Theologische Zeitschrift* 2 (1989) 147–55.

Weill, R. "La cité de David, Campagne de 1913–1914." *REJ* 69 (1919) 30–34; 70 (1920) 186–90.

Weiss, Johannes. *Der erste Korintherbrief.* Kritisch-exegetischer Kommentar über das Neue Testament begründet von H. A. W. Meyer 5. 10th ed. Göttingen: Vandenhoeck & Ruprecht, 1925.

———. *Earliest Christianity: A History of the Period A.D. 30–150.* Translated by F. C. Grant. 2 vols. New York: Harper, 1959.

Welles, C. B., R. O. Fink, and J. F. Gilliam. *The Parchments and Papyri*: The Excavations at Dura-Europos. Final Report 5.1. New Haven: Yale University Press, 1959.

White, L. Michael. "Scholars and Patrons: Christianity and High Society in Alexandria." In W. E. Ferguson, ed., *Christian Teaching: Studies in Honor of LeMoine G. Lewis*. Abilene, TX: Abilene Christian University, 1981.

———. "Adolf Harnack and the 'Expansion' of Early Christianity: A Reappraisal of Social History," *TSC* 5 (1985–86) 97–127.

———. "The Delos Synagogue Revisited: Recent Fieldwork in the Graeco-Roman Diaspora." *HTR* 80 (1987) 133–66.

———. "Shifting Sectarian Boundaries in Early Christianity," *BJRL* 70 (1988) 7–24.

———. *Building God's House in the Roman World: Architectural Adaptation among Pagans, Jews, and Christians*. Baltimore: Johns Hopkins University Press, 1990.

———, ed. *Social Networks in the Early Christian Environment: Issues and Methods for Social History*. *Semeia* 56 (1991). Atlanta: Scholars, 1992.

———. "Finding the Ties that Bind: Issues from Social Description." In *Social Networks*, 3–22.

———. "Synagogue and Society in Imperial Ostia: Archaeological and Epigraphic Evidence." *HTR* (forthcoming).

Wiegand, T., and H. Schrader. *Priene: Ergebnisse der Ausgrabungen und Untersuchungen in den Jahren 1895–1898*. Berlin: Akademie Verlag, 1904.

Wilken, Robert L. "Collegia, Philosophical Schools and Theology." In S. Benko and J. J. O'Rourke, eds., *The Catacombs and the Colosseum: The Roman Empire as the Setting for Primitive Christianity*. Valley Forge, PA: Judson, 1971.

———. *The Christians as the Romans Saw Them*. New Haven: Yale University Press, 1985.

Williams, Margaret H. "The Jews and Godfearers Inscription from Aphrodisias — A Case of Patriarchal Interference in Early 3rd Century Caria?" *Historia* 41 (1992) 297–310.

Wischnitzer, Rachel. *The Architecture of the European Synagogue*. Philadelphia: Jewish Publication Society, 1974.

———. *The Messianic Themes in the Paintings of the Dura Synagogue*. Chicago: University of Chicago Press, 1948.

Wiseman, J., and Dj. Mano-Zissi. "Excavations at Stobi, 1970." *AJA* 75 (1971) 395–411.

———. "Excavations at Stobi, 1971." *AJA* 76 (1972) 407–18.

———. "Excavations at Stobi, 1972." *AJA* 77 (1973) 391–405.

———. "Excavations at Stobi, 1973–1974." *JFA* 1 (1974) 117–48.

———. "Stobi: A City of Ancient Macedonia." *JFA* 3 (1976) 269–302.

Wiseman, James, ed. *Studies in the Antiquities of Stobi I*. Belgrade: University of Belgrade, 1973.

———. "Stobi in Yugoslavian Macedonia: Archaeological Excavations and Research, 1977–1978." *JFA* 5 (1978) 391–429.

Witt, R. E. *Isis in the Graeco-Roman World*. Ithaca, NY: Cornell University Press, 1971.

Wuellner, Wilhelm H. "The Sociological Implications of 1 Corinthians 1.26–28 Reconsidered." *Studia Evangelica VI*, TU 112. Berlin: J. C. Hinrichs, 1973.

Youtie, H. C. "P. Gen. Inv. 108." *ZPE* 7 (1971) 170–71.

———. "Hypographeus: The Social Impact of Illiteracy in Graeco-Roman Egypt," *ZPE* 17 (1975) 201–21.

———. "'Because they do not know letters,'" *ZPE* 19 (1975) 101–8.

Zeitlin, S. "The Origins of the Synagogue." In J. Gutmann, ed., *The Synagogue: Studies In Orgins, Archaeology and Architecture*. New York: KTAV, 1975.

Zestermann, A. C. *Die antike und christlichen Basiliken*. Leipzig: J. C. Hinrichs, 1847.

Zink, Jochen. "Die Baugeschichte des Trierer Doms von Anfängen im 4. Jahrhundert bis zur letzten Restaurierung." In F. J. Ronig, ed., *Der Trierer Dom*, 17–111. Neuss, Rheinland-Pfalz: Vereins, 1980.

Index

▲ ▲ ▲

Inscriptions

Epigraphic collections are listed according to standard abbreviations in L-S-J. For other sources used below, see list of abbreviations and bibliography. All listings are by page number. Bracketed references in boldface indicate the item is an entry in the catalogue, giving the catalogue number followed by the page numbers; other citations follow.

Papyri

Papyrological collections are listed according to standard abbreviations in L-S-J. For other sources used below, see list of abbreviations and bibliography. All listings are by page number. Bracketed references in boldface indicate the item is an entry in the catalogue, giving the catalogue number.

Personal Names and Titles (Ancient)

This list includes only real persons identified in either literary or documentary texts included in the catalogue, or discussed in notes to these entries. Listing is according to a Latin alphabet, and Greek names are integrated by transliteration to the Latin. Notations will be made for variant Greek orthography and transliterations. Names found in both Greek and Latin form will be noted in the original. For Roman *dua-* and *trianomina* (whether Latin or Greek) order is according to the given (or putative) *cognomen*. Names of ancient authors are not be listed here unless they are also active in events under discussion.

Roman Emperors

Other Individuals

A

B

Greek Terms

Latin Terms

f. 152 house of St. Peter